American Paintings

in the

Detroit

Institute

of Arts

American Paintings

in the Detroit Institute of Arts

Volume II
Works by Artists
born 1816–1847

Hudson Hills Press • New York
In association with the Detroit Institute of Arts Founders Society

First Edition

Published in the United States by Hudson Hills Press, Inc., Suite 1308, 230 Fifth Avenue, New York, NY 10001-7704.

Distributed in the United States, its territories and possessions, and Canada by National Book Network.

Distributed in the United Kingdom, Eire, and Europe by Art Books International Ltd.

Distributed in Australia by Peribo PTY Limited.

Distributed in New Zealand by Nationwide Book Distributors Ltd.

Exclusive representation in China by Cassidy and Associates, Inc.

For Hudson Hills Press

Editor and Publisher: Paul Anbinder

Assistant Editor: Faye Chiu

Proofreader: Lydia Edwards

Indexer: Karla J. Knight

Designer: David Skolkin

Composition: Angela Taormina

Manufactured in Japan by Toppan Printing Company.

For the Detroit Institute of Arts Founders Society

Director of Publications: Julia P. Henshaw

Editor: Judith Ruskin

Copy Editor: Fronia W. Simpson

ISBN: 1-55595-142-2 (alk. paper)

The Library of Congress has catalogued Volume I as follows:

Library of Congress Cataloging-in-Publication Data

Detroit Institute of Arts
American paintings in the Detroit Institute of Arts / introduction by Nancy Rivard Shaw ; essays by Mary Black . . . [et al.] — 1st ed.
p. cm.—(The collections of the Detroit Institute of Arts)
"In association with the Founders Society Detroit Institute of Arts."
Includes bibliographical references and index.
Contents: v. 1. Works by artists born before 1816.
ISBN 1-55595-044-2 (alk. paper):
1. Painting, American—Catalogues. 2. Painting—Michigan—Detroit—Catalogues. 3. Detroit Institute of Arts—Catalogues. I. Shaw, Nancy Rivard, 1945– II. Black, Mary (Mary C.) III. Founders Society. IV. Title. V. Series: Detroit Institute of Arts. Collections of the Detroit Institute of Arts.
ND205.D298 1991
759.13′074′77434—dc20 90-85027
CIP

Contents

Color Plates

Foreword

WORKS BY AMERICAN ARTISTS have always been an integral part of the Detroit Institute of Arts's collection, beginning with the museum's first acquisition in 1883, Francis D. Millet's *Reading the Story of Oenone* (cat. no. 66), purchased before the new institution opened its doors on Jefferson Avenue in 1888. Throughout its history the museum has added to and refined the collection of paintings by American artists born before 1875. At first the formation of the collection was gradual and haphazard, its growth almost entirely dependent on gifts and bequests. Since the first decade of the twentieth century, however, acquisitions have been made in a more systematic fashion, with an eye to developing a collection of consistently high quality covering the entire spectrum of American painting and aesthetics from the eighteenth century through the early twentieth century. Today, the collection of American paintings in Detroit is one of the finest and most representative in the world. It is, therefore, imperative to continue the in-depth examination of the collection begun with volume one of *American Paintings in the Detroit Institute of Arts* with this book, the second in a projected three-volume series. The first volume, published in 1991, studied those artists born before 1816 and included works by this country's earliest painters such as Benjamin West, John Singleton Copley, and Thomas Cole. The third volume will explore works by artists born after 1847, including paintings by William Merritt Chase, John Singer Sargent, and John Sloan.

This handsome second volume deals with the work of artists born between 1816 and 1847 and includes such masterpieces as Frederic Edwin Church's *Cotapaxi* (cat. no. 13), James McNeill Whistler's *Nocturne in Black and Gold: The Falling Rocket* (cat. no. 87), landscapes by Albert Bierstadt and Martin Johnson Heade, portraits by Mary Cassatt and Thomas Eakins, and several works by Winslow Homer. Other artists represented include Sanford Gifford, Eastman Johnson, John F. Kensett, Albert Pinkham Ryder, Elihu Vedder, and Alexander Wyant, as well as lesser-known painters who have enriched our cultural history, such as John George Brown, Robert Duncanson, Thomas Hovenden, Homer Dodge Martin, Jervis McEntee, Louis Rémy Mignot, Thomas Moran, William Rimmer, and Thomas Waterman Wood.

The artist biographies and entries on the paintings were written by outstanding scholars in the field of American art history. We thank them for their hard work and dedication to the project. The three-volume series on American paintings has been organized and overseen by Nancy Rivard Shaw, curator of American art at the Detroit Institute of Arts since 1975. The fine works added to the collection in the last quarter of the century have been selected under her watchful eye. The present volume of this series was supported by a grant from the Luce Fund for Scholarship in American Art, as was volume one. Both books were published by Hudson Hills Press.

SAMUEL SACHS II
Director

Acknowledgments

No acknowledgments in a book of this kind can begin without paying tribute to the Henry Luce Foundation, which provided the financial support through its Fund for Scholarship in American Art to make publication of this volume possible. I am deeply grateful to Henry Luce III, chairman and chief executive officer, and to Robert E. Armstrong, John W. Cook, Mary Jane Crook, and Ellen Holtzman, for their assistance and encouragement over the ten years this catalogue has been in preparation.

My appreciation goes to the catalogue authors—Elizabeth Broun, Gerald Carr, Leigh Culver, Norman Geske, Patricia Hills, Joseph Ketner II, Ellen G. Miles, Angela Miller, William T. Oedel, Janice Simon, Susan M. Sivard, Tara Tappert, and Jeffrey Weidman—for their foresight and scholarship. Many thanks go also to Nicolai Cikovsky, Jr., Anthony Janson, Franklin Kelly, Marc Simpson, and H. Barbara Weinberg, who read portions of the manuscript and contributed valuable suggestions.

Several members of the museum staff have been particularly helpful, and I am indebted to them all. In the Department of American Art, James W. Tottis coordinated the photography and conservation of the paintings, wrote catalogue entries, and assisted with numerous administrative details. Anita Calvert, succeeded by Yvette L. Coneal, handled myriad clerical tasks with efficiency and grace.

The Publications Department shares much of the credit for the catalogue. Particular recognition is due Judith Ruskin, who supervised and coordinated all of the editorial details and guided the catalogue through production. Director of Publications Julia Henshaw offered good advice at crucial moments. Matthew Sikora organized the comprehensive bibliography. The project benefited greatly from freelance editor Fronia W. Simpson's careful attention to the manuscript.

Recognition is also due Barbara Heller of the museum's Conservation Services Laboratory and her staff, who performed such treatment of the collection as was necessary and provided the authors with detailed condition reports and technical analyses of questionable paintings. Dirk Bakker produced the superb photographs with the assistance of Robert Hensleigh and Marianne Letasi.

A number of scholars across the country aided this effort in various ways. The authors give acknowledgment to the following: Dita Amory, Carolyn Carr, Susan Danly, Brandon Fortune, Kathleen A. Foster, Ebenezer Gay, Abigail Booth Gerdts, Lucretia Giese, Wendy Greenhouse, Peter Hassrick, Martha Hoppin, Evlene King, William Lang, David Lewis, Amy Lyford, Katherine Manthorne, Andrew Marvick, Merl M. Moore, Jr., Kate Nearpass Ogden, Sally Pierce, Jan Seidler Ramirez, Darrel L. Sewell, Margaret Smith, E. Harrison Sohmer, Della Sperling, Marilyn Symmes, Lois Woodyatt, Paul Worman, the library staff at the National Museum of American Art, and the staff of the Smithsonian Inventory of American Paintings.

Finally, I would like to acknowledge the expertise of Paul Anbinder, president of Hudson Hills Press, and the skill of the catalogue designer David Skolkin for making this book a worthy successor to *American Paintings in the Detroit Institute of Arts,* volume one.

Nancy Rivard Shaw

Contributors to the Catalogue

Elizabeth Broun—E. B.
Gerald Carr—G. C.
Leigh Culver—L. C.
Norman Geske—N. G.
Patricia Hills—P. H.
Joseph Ketner II—J. K.
Ellen G. Miles—E. G. M.
Angela Miller—A. M.
William T. Oedel—W. T. O.
Nancy Rivard Shaw—N. R. S.
Janice Simon—J. S.
Susan M. Sivard—S. M. S.
James W. Tottis—J. W. T.
Tara Tappert—T. T.
Jeffrey Weidman—J. W.

A Note on the History of the Collection

No one individual can be credited with shaping the Detroit Institute of Arts's stellar collection of American paintings. Through the years many people have contributed to the building and refinement of the collection—museum directors, curators, and astute donors and private collectors.

The interest in the work of American artists predates the very existence of a Detroit art museum. Francis D. Millet's classically inspired *Reading the Story of Oenone* (cat. no. 66) was purchased with the proceeds of the Detroit Art Loan Exhibition of 1883 as the first acquisition of the Detroit Museum of Art, forerunner of the present Institute of Arts, five years before the new museum opened. In those early days, the decided emphasis was on contemporary (that is, late-nineteenth- and early-twentieth-century) American art, which constituted the subject of the first consistent series of temporary exhibitions. Acquisitions during the last quarter of the nineteenth century were consistent with this philosophy and included Ellen Kendall Baker's *Young Artist* (cat. no. 1) and J. G. Brown's *A Surprise Party* (cat. no. 7).

The attention paid to contemporary artists was pursued into the early twentieth century under the guidance of Clyde H. Burroughs, a Monroe County, Michigan, schoolteacher who came to the museum in 1901 as assistant to Director Armand H. Griffith. Burroughs, who served as museum director from 1917 to 1924, was primarily interested in those artists who formed the progressive movement in American art at that time, such as Robert Henri and Maurice Prendergast. A number of the museum's American impressionist and tonalist paintings were acquired during this period.

While these painters will be the focus of volume three of the series, on artists born after 1847, many of the paintings included in volume two were also acquired during the first thirty years of this century. An important impetus to the acquisition of works in contemporary styles was the establishment of the Picture Fund, which existed from 1906 until 1916. The fund enabled the museum to purchase one painting per year by an American artist and served to encourage private collectors to give other works. Notable among such patrons was Edward Chandler Walker, president of the Detroit Museum from 1907 to 1909, who presented Mary Cassatt's *Women Admiring a Child* (cat. no. 11) in 1908. The Picture Fund attracted the attention of other important patrons and collectors, among them Isabella Stewart Gardner of Boston who, in 1907, gave the museum eight American paintings, the most significant of which is *The Ball Players* (cat. no. 46) by William Morris Hunt.

A few years later, with plans in the air for a new and expanded museum building, staff members proposed a variety of new acquisition programs. One of them called for a gallery of self-portraits by American artists similar to the one devoted to European artists in the Galleria degli Uffizi in Florence. Although the gallery of self-portraits as such was never formally created, the collection is especially rich in the self-images of esteemed American artists, including Rembrandt Peale, William Page, and James McNeill Whistler (cat. no. 86).

The excitement generated by the new building being raised on Woodward Avenue in the early 1920s stimulated many Detroit families to respond with gifts. The strength of the current collection owes much to the donors and trustees who helped the Institute both in their own time and through permanent funds established specifically for the purchase of American works of art. These funds have continued to support the American art department's purchases long after the donors' deaths. One of the first and most devoted patrons was the Detroit seed merchant Dexter M. Ferry, Jr., president of the museum from 1913 to 1917 and of its supporting group the Founders Society from 1920 to 1948. Working with Clyde Burroughs during the 1920s, he laid the foundation of the collection of early American portraiture. Donor by direct gift, fund, or bequest of nearly a quarter of the American paintings in the collection, Ferry remains the department's largest single benefactor.

Except for owning a few late-nineteenth-century canvases—by George deForest Brush, Ralph Blakelock, and the Detroit artist Myron Barlowe—Ferry was not himself a collector. His involvement with historic American art was limited to his museum interests, which began to take form in the early 1920s following the appointment of William R. Valentiner as adviser to the museum. Under Valentiner's leadership as director from 1924 to 1945, the museum initiated an acquisitions program designed to make the collection a comprehensive survey of the history of art; America's cultural heritage was a major component of this scheme. In 1922 Ferry set up an endowment fund for the purchase of American paintings and in 1927, the year the new museum opened to the public, presented the collection with four eighteenth-century portraits. These gifts signaled the beginning of a plan to develop the collection of American art in a serious, complete, and systematic way. Portraits by John Neagle and Chester Harding followed in 1929, and in the early 1930s Ferry presented Thomas Eakins's portrait of Robert M. Lindsay (cat. no. 25), and an oil sketch of the same subject (cat. no. 26).

Other significant acquisitions made during the first thirty years of this century include Frederic Edwin Church's *Syria by the Sea* (cat. no. 14), given by Mrs. James F. Joy in 1910; Charles Caryl Coleman's *Garden of the Villa Castello, Capri* (cat. no. 15), the gift of a group of Detroiters who befriended that artist during his visit to Detroit in 1911; and Mary Cassatt's

In the Garden (cat. no. 12), one of twenty-four works by the artist belonging to James Stillman, an art collector and close friend of Cassatt, and given to the museum by Dr. Ernest G. Stillman in 1922. In 1923 the museum acquired two paintings by George Inness, *Hudson River Valley* (cat. no. 48), given by the Founders Society, and *Apple Orchard* (cat. no. 49), presented in memory of Henry Brockholst Ledyard by his children. John Frederick Kensett's *Cascade in the Forest* (cat. no. 58), given by Guy P. Turnbull, joined the collection in 1927, and in 1930 the Institute purchased a portrait of Eakins's friend Dr. Horatio C Wood (cat. no. 24) from Mrs. Eakins.

In 1930, with the appointment of Edgar P. Richardson as educational secretary, the development of the collection took a somewhat different turn. Richardson, then twenty-eight years old, had studied painting at the University of Pennsylvania (1920–21) before attending Williams College, from which he was graduated summa cum laude in 1925 (later receiving the school's honorary degree of Doctor of Letters in 1947). With the intention of pursuing a career as an artist, Richardson entered the Pennsylvania Academy of the Fine Arts, where he remained until 1928. Realizing a short time later that he had "more of a scholar's mind" (Richardson papers, DIA archives), Richardson turned his attention to museum work—a timely decision for Detroit.

Richardson belonged to the generation that rediscovered the Hudson River school, the early genre painters, and the mid-nineteenth-century portraitists. During his lengthy tenure as an assistant director in charge of curatorial and exhibition activities from 1934 to 1945 and as director from 1945 to 1962, he expanded the collection from one chiefly concerned with turn-of-the-century examples to one that illustrates the development of American painting from the close of the seventeenth century to the early twentieth.

Richardson began to acquire major nineteenth-century landscape and genre paintings in the late 1930s while continuing to expand the eighteenth-century portraiture collection, buying at bargain prices works that are invaluable today. In 1938, through Ferry's beneficence, Eastman Johnson's *In the Fields* (cat. no. 55) joined the collection. Winslow Homer's *Girl and Laurel* (cat. no. 43), *The Dinner Horn* (cat. no. 41), and *Defiance: Inviting a Shot before Petersburg* (cat. no. 40) were Ferry gifts in the 1940s.

Other important acquisitions made during Richardson's tenure through Ferry's remarkable munificence include Bierstadt's *Wolf River, Kansas* (cat. no. 2); Whistler's *Nocturne in Black and Gold: The Falling Rocket* (cat. no. 87); Albert Pinkham Ryder's *Tempest* (cat. no. 76); Richard Caton Woodville's *Card Players* (cat. no. 93); Worthington Whittredge's *Landscape in the Harz Mountains* (cat. no. 90); Alexander Wyant's *Sunset in the Hills, New York* (cat. no. 94); and *Sunset* (cat. no. 35), *Hummingbirds and Orchids* (cat. no. 36), and *Cherokee Roses* (cat. no. 37), all by Martin Johnson Heade. Ralph Blakelock's *Landscape* (cat. no. 4) was a Ferry bequest in 1960. There are many other distinguished works that testify to this unique collaboration.

Although not directly advised by Richardson, other collectors filled gaps in the museum's holdings. Outstanding was Robert H. Tannahill, who served the museum as trustee (1931–69), commissioner (1932–62), and honorary curator of American art (1927–69), and contributed significantly in many other ways.

Because of his generosity to the museum, the galleries housing the American collections were named the Robert Hudson Tannahill Wing of American Art in 1969. Homer's *Four-Leaf Clover* (cat. no. 42) was included in the Tannahill bequest to the museum in 1970. The Tannahill Foundation Fund has since provided the monies for several important American works, including Cassatt's *Alexander J. Cassatt* (cat. no. 10), Heade's *Seascape: Sunset* (cat. no. 34), and most of the funding for Church's monumental *Cotopaxi* (cat. no. 13).

In the decade following Richardson's departure from Detroit to accept the directorship of the Winterthur Museum in Delaware in 1962, subsequent curators—Charles Elam, Graham Hood, and Larry Curry—under the guidance of two directors—Willis F. Woods and then Frederick J. Cummings—significantly strengthened the collection. William Rimmer's *Victory* (cat. no. 73) came to the museum during this period, as did the first example by Jasper Cropsey, *Sunset after a Storm in the Catskill Mountains* (cat. no. 16). Two other events also served to enrich the collection. In 1967 Beatrice Rogers made the museum the major beneficiary of her estate, with the stipulation that the money be used for the acquisition of traditional American art. The same year, under Hood's leadership, an important auxiliary of the Founders Society—called the Associates of the American Wing—was formed to ensure continuing interest in America's cultural heritage. Notable among individual members' contributions to the collection are Homer Dodge Martin's *In the Adirondacks* (cat. no. 64), George Fuller's *Tomato Patch* (cat. no. 30), and Fuller's *Self-Portrait* (cat. no. 29), all presented by Raymond C. Smith; Thomas Waterman Wood's *Sherry Sir?* (cat. no. 92), given by Mr. and Mrs. James O. Keene; William Rimmer's *Civil War Scene* (cat. no. 72), the gift of Dr. and Mrs. Sheldon Stern; and Thomas Hovenden's *Hoc Signo Vinces* (cat. no. 45) from Mr. and Mrs. Harold O. Love. Homer Dodge Martin's *Autumn* (cat. no. 62) was given by the Associates in memory of former member James A. Beresford in 1977. Mr. and Mrs. Richard A. Manoogian have made generous contributions to several recent acquisitions and have placed important examples from their collection on long-term loan to the museum. They have also provided the funding for several beautiful period frames, including the one recently selected for Eakins's portrait of Dr. Horatio C Wood.

Although the art market has changed dramatically during the curatorship of this author (1975 to the present), efforts to combat deficiencies in the collection have resulted in some outstanding successes. Luck played a major role in the acquisition in 1976 of *Cotopaxi* (cat. no. 13), one of Church's finest achievements, purchased through a New York dealer from the heirs of James Lenox, who commissioned the work in 1862. Cassatt's 1880 portrait of her brother Alexander J. Cassatt, one of the artist's rare depictions of an adult male and, to modern eyes, perhaps the most successful, was acquired in 1986. Maria Oakey Dewing's lovely still life, *Irises and Calla Lilies* (cat. no. 18) joined the collection in 1991, and Frederick Bridgman's orientalist fantasy, *Moorish Interior* (cat. no. 5), was acquired in 1993.

In 1990, as the first volume of this series went to press, the author pointed out regrettable gaps in the collection, including the lack of a classic luminist work. Given the dwindling art market, and the increasingly high prices commanded by such works, it was feared these gaps might well remain permanent in the Detroit collection. One year later, in 1991, one of our most glaring deficiencies was corrected with the acquisition of Martin Johnson Heade's powerful *Seascape: Sunset* (cat. no. 34). The painting, purchased with funds from the Robert H. Tannahill Foundation Fund, would undoubtedly have pleased the donor who, on a visit to a New York dealer in 1946, fell in love with two paintings by Heade. Unable to decide on which of the two to suggest to Richardson, a landscape of marshland or a flower painting, Tannahill had both canvases sent to Detroit for presentation to the Acquisitions Committee. The landscape, *Sunset* (cat. no. 35), was subsequently purchased for the museum by Dexter M. Ferry, Jr. The flower painting was returned to the dealer.

It is hoped, as this volume goes to press, that the future will be as kind as the past.

Nancy Rivard Shaw
Curator of American Art
1997

American Paintings

in the

Detroit

Institute

of Arts

Ellen Kendall Baker

1839 Fairfield, New York–
Chalfont St. Giles, Buckinghamshire, England 1913

Ellen Kendall Baker was born in Fairfield, New York, on June 30, 1839, and "spent her girlhood in Buffalo" (*American Art Annual* 1914, 389). From 1870 she exhibited crayon portraits, studies of flowers, and landscapes at the Buffalo Fine Arts Academy. She moved to Paris by the end of the decade, becoming a student of the French genre painter and printmaker Paul Soyer. She was also a student of Charles Müller, a French genre, history, and portrait painter, and of Harry Thompson, an English genre and landscape painter, whom she married in 1896.

Baker, a painter of portraits and genre scenes, was known for her images of children. Her work was exhibited at the Paris Salon from 1879, when she showed *Portrait de Mme XXX,* through 1900. She is said to have also exhibited in Munich, Berlin, and St. Petersburg. In the United States she exhibited at the National Academy of Design, New York, in 1881–84, 1892–93, and 1902; at the Pennsylvania Academy of the Fine Arts in 1881–85, 1887–91, 1895, and 1898; and at the Brooklyn Art Association in 1882 and 1883. Her work was included in the Chicago Inter-State Industrial Exposition in 1881, 1883–85, and 1887–90, and in the Art Institute of Chicago's annual exhibitions in 1888, 1891, 1894–99, and 1904. When *Sans Souci* (unlocated) was exhibited at the World's Columbian Exposition in Chicago in 1893, a reviewer alluded to her international reputation: "Miss Ellen K. Baker... has sent a painting to the exposition in Chicago. She has had a studio in Paris over fifteen years. She has sent over many pictures which were first exhibited in the Paris Salon and sold readily in this country" (*Detroit Tribune,* March 19, 1893). Baker lived at Puteaux, near Paris, from 1883 to at least 1907 and also had an address in Buffalo, New York, where her brother William J. Baker lived and where her work was occasionally exhibited at Hoddick and Company. In 1901 at the Pan-American Exposition in Buffalo she received an honorable mention for *Two Little Friends* (unlocated). After about 1907 she moved from Paris to Chalfont St. Giles, Buckinghamshire, England, where she died. Her work, not well known today, can be found in the collections of the Albright-Knox Art Gallery in Buffalo and the Henry Morrison Flagler Museum in Palm Beach, Florida. She usually used her maiden name when signing her work.
E. M.

Bibliography Inventory of American Painting. Passport Applications, no. 34029 (July 17, 1873). Sheldon 1890, 134. Buffalo 1891(?). *Detroit Tribune,* March 19, 1893, 9. Buffalo, Pan-American Exposition, 1901, 9, no. 187. *American Art Annual* 1907–8, 424. Pattison 1911, 72. *American Art Annual* 1914, 389. Earle 1924, 29. Marlor 1970, 111–112. Naylor 1973, 1:22. Falk 1985, 28. Petteys 1985, 696. Yarnall and Gerdts 1986, 160–161. Falk 1989, 75. *NYPL* 1989. Falk 1990, 79, 887. Fink 1990, 317–318.

1

The Young Artist, 1885

Oil on canvas
71.1 × 58.4 cm (28 × 23 in.)
Gift of the Friends of the Museum (88.2)

A blond, pigtailed girl holds a slate board on which a stick figure has been drawn in chalk. She shows the drawing to a baby, who is seen in profile, seated in a wooden chair. The baby reaches a chubby hand toward the picture. The girl wears a reddish brown dress trimmed with white at the collar. The baby is in a long white gown and cap. A beige sack hangs on the post of the chair.

Ellen Baker exhibited *The Young Artist* as *Le Premier Essai* at the Paris Salon in the spring of 1885 and at the Inter-State Industrial Exposition in Chicago that fall. The label for the Inter-State Exposition is still attached to the stretcher. The painting was exhibited again in January and February 1886 at the Boston Art Club as *The First Attempt* (a literal translation of its French title). A reviewer described the work: "'The First Attempt,' by Miss E. K. Baker, is particularly good. The character of the two children is unusually intimate and refined. The child who holds the artistic effort up for admiration of the small baby is a genuine child. This is most excellent work" (*Boston Daily Evening Transcript,* January 19, 1886, 4). The painting was renamed with its present title by the time of the opening exhibition of the Detroit Museum of Art in 1888, although a brief mention of the artist in the *Detroit Tribune* on March 19, 1893, referred to the painting as "The Lesson."

Baker was well known for such genre scenes. *Two Little Friends* depicts a young girl holding a rabbit (unlocated; Chicago 1881, no. 313). *Le Tricot* represents two girls doing crochet (unlocated; *Art Amateur* 1883). Titles of other works, such as *Mussel Gatherer* (unlocated; Fink 1990, 318) and *First Communion* (unlocated; Naylor 1973, 1:22), suggest that Baker's themes of French peasant life were the same ones that were popular with many French and American artists in the late nineteenth century. *Tranquillity* (unlocated), for example, depicted "an old peasant woman, clad in simple costume... seated beside a window... in one hand she holds her half finished knitting, while the other is around her little grandson" (Buffalo n.d.). According to a contemporary writer, the painting "deals with types of Picardy, where the artist is accustomed to spend her summers, and it tells its simple story with naturalness, ease, and grace" (Sheldon 1890, 134, ill. 127).
E. G. M.

Inscription At lower left, *E. K. Baker*

Provenance Purchased by subscription through the efforts of Mrs. E. C. Skinner and Mrs. H. P. Jenkins and presented to the museum.

Exhibitions Paris, Salon, 1885, no. 122. Chicago, Inter-State Industrial Exposition, 1885, no. 352. Boston 1886. Detroit 1888, no. 5.

References *Boston Daily Evening Transcript,* January 19, 1886, 4. *Detroit Tribune,* March 19, 1893, 9. Scripps 1895, 39, no. 75. Detroit 1907a, 7, no. 75. Detroit 1910, 7–8, no. 91, ill. Pattison 1911, frontispiece, 72. Earle 1924, 29. Fink 1990, 318. Chadbourne, Gabosh, and Vogel 1991, 62.

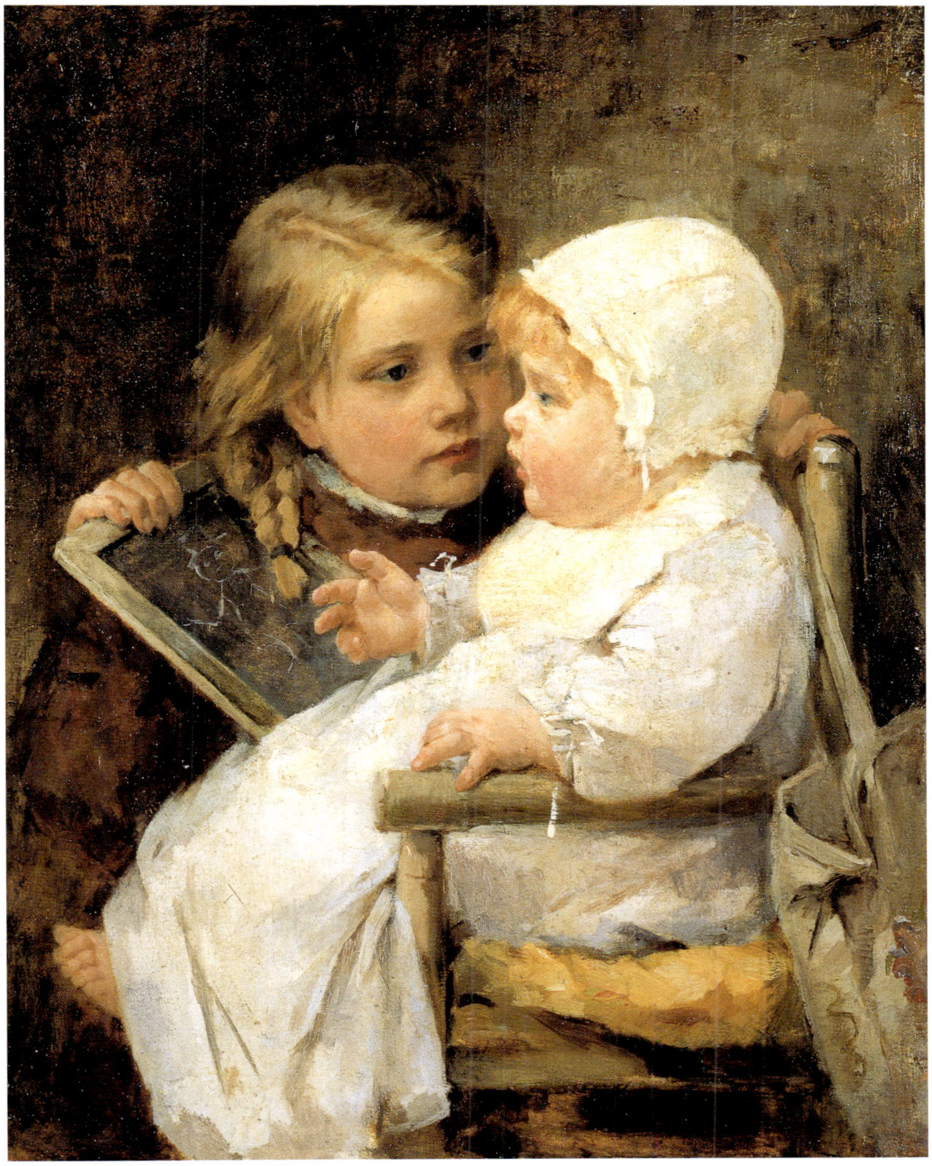

The Young Artist

Albert Bierstadt

1830 Solingen, Prussia–New York 1902

"Between the primitive past of American art and the bright future, Albert Bierstadt, with a few more men of his age and bent, holds a large and honorable place. He stands, like one of the grand old pines he has so often painted, erect and vigorous" (Ishmael 1891, 245). So began a sketch of the Düsseldorf-trained artist who was as much a maestro of the art marketplace as of grand scenery. In America and Europe alike Bierstadt courted the affluent and the influential. He painted big pictures of big places that commanded big prices. As his chief rival, Frederic Edwin Church, located Eden in Niagara and the Andes, so Bierstadt discovered Paradise in Yosemite and the Rockies.

Unlike Church, Bierstadt braved the obstacles of humble origins, and this self-made man fascinated Americans. The sixth child of Henry and Christina, Albert was only two when his family immigrated to New Bedford, Massachusetts. His father and brothers worked in various trades, and Bierstadt briefly followed suit as a frame maker; by 1851 he offered lessons in monochromatic painting. Crucial to Bierstadt's artistic development was his three-year study in Düsseldorf and subsequent travels to the Alps and Italy (1853–57). In addition to mastering the technical skills of his new profession and viewing majestic scenery, Bierstadt connected with such American artists as Worthington Whittredge (q.v.) and Sanford R. Gifford (q.v.). Bierstadt debuted at the National Academy of Design in New York in 1858 with *Lake Lucerne (Switzerland)* (1858; National Gallery of Art, Washington, D.C.), which was so well received that he was elected an honorary member.

His first of many travels to the Far West in 1859 with Colonel Frederick William Lander's survey party, however, altered Bierstadt's career forever. Even though other artists had profited from their journeys across the Mississippi, none matched Bierstadt in technical proficiency, artistic bravura, nationalistic mind-set, and entrepreneurial genius. "Bierstadt" quickly became synonymous with spectacles of the American West. As he established himself in the Tenth Street Studio Building in New York, he arranged his studio into a showplace of Rocky Mountain memorabilia with Indian artifacts, animal skins, photographs, and sketches surrounding the gigantic showpieces he crafted for touring exhibitions. The *Rocky Mountains, Lander's Peak* (1863; Metropolitan Museum of Art, New York) was the first of such western panoramas to catapult Bierstadt into Church's league as a painter of America's manifest destiny. Bierstadt's second trip west, an expedition to the West Coast in 1863 with the literatus Fitz Hugh Ludlow, and the resulting monumental canvases of Yosemite, Oregon, the Sierra Nevada, and the Rockies, guaranteed his reputation as a painter of the American sublime. The trip had personal ramifications as well—in 1866 Bierstadt married Rosalie Ludlow, Fitz's ex-wife.

On Bierstadt's working honeymoon to London and Paris (1867–69), he regained the acclaim that had dwindled in America. But Bierstadt was not spared the adversity of shifts in aesthetic taste. After the Exposition Universelle of 1889 in Paris rejected his work, Bierstadt, the showman now shaken, avoided exhibiting at the World's Columbian Exposition four years later in Chicago.

J. S.

Bibliography Hendricks 1973. Brooklyn et al. 1991.

2

The Wolf River, Kansas, ca. 1859

Oil on canvas

122.6 × 97.2 cm (48¼ × 38¼ in.)

Founders Society Purchase, Dexter M. Ferry, Jr., Fund (61.28)

Albert Bierstadt first arrived at the Wolf River, located west of Troy, Kansas, in the northeast corner of the state, on May 10, 1859. As part of Colonel Frederick William Lander's government survey expedition to the Rocky Mountains (and beyond to California), Bierstadt and the Boston artist Francis Shedd Frost traveled along the Platte River through the heart of the Nebraska and Wyoming territories. Bierstadt and Frost left the Lander expedition just west of the Rockies, journeying back through the Wind River Mountains and returning to the Wolf River for a two-week stay at the beginning of September. Bierstadt created *The Wolf River, Kansas* from oil studies and stereographs he produced on this trip.

Detroit's painting of deep green foliage near the river's edge resembles the scenery in Bierstadt's stereograph of the Wolf River Ford (Wilfred Thompson collection), though minus the wild trailing vines he made special note of in his letter of September 3. As is true of all Bierstadt's exhibition canvases, however, *The Wolf River, Kansas* is not a realistic portrait of a particular place but a concoction based as much on pictorial conventions and western types as on observation. He used virtually the same trees and sky in *Indian Encampment, Shoshone Village* (1860; New-York Historical Society) but altered the location and possibly the tribe by placing the snow-covered Wind River Mountains of Wyoming Territory in the background. It is as if every perceived detail of his trip was fodder for his painted fabrications. In the process of representing his experiences of the Plains and the Rockies in works such as *The Wolf River, Kansas,* Bierstadt participated in the nineteenth-century invention of the American West.

The Wolf River, Kansas presents two trappers with a loaded packhorse traversing the ford and in effect serving as the viewer's scouts into Indian territory. In the foreground, half on shore and half in the water, rests a large, weathered log.

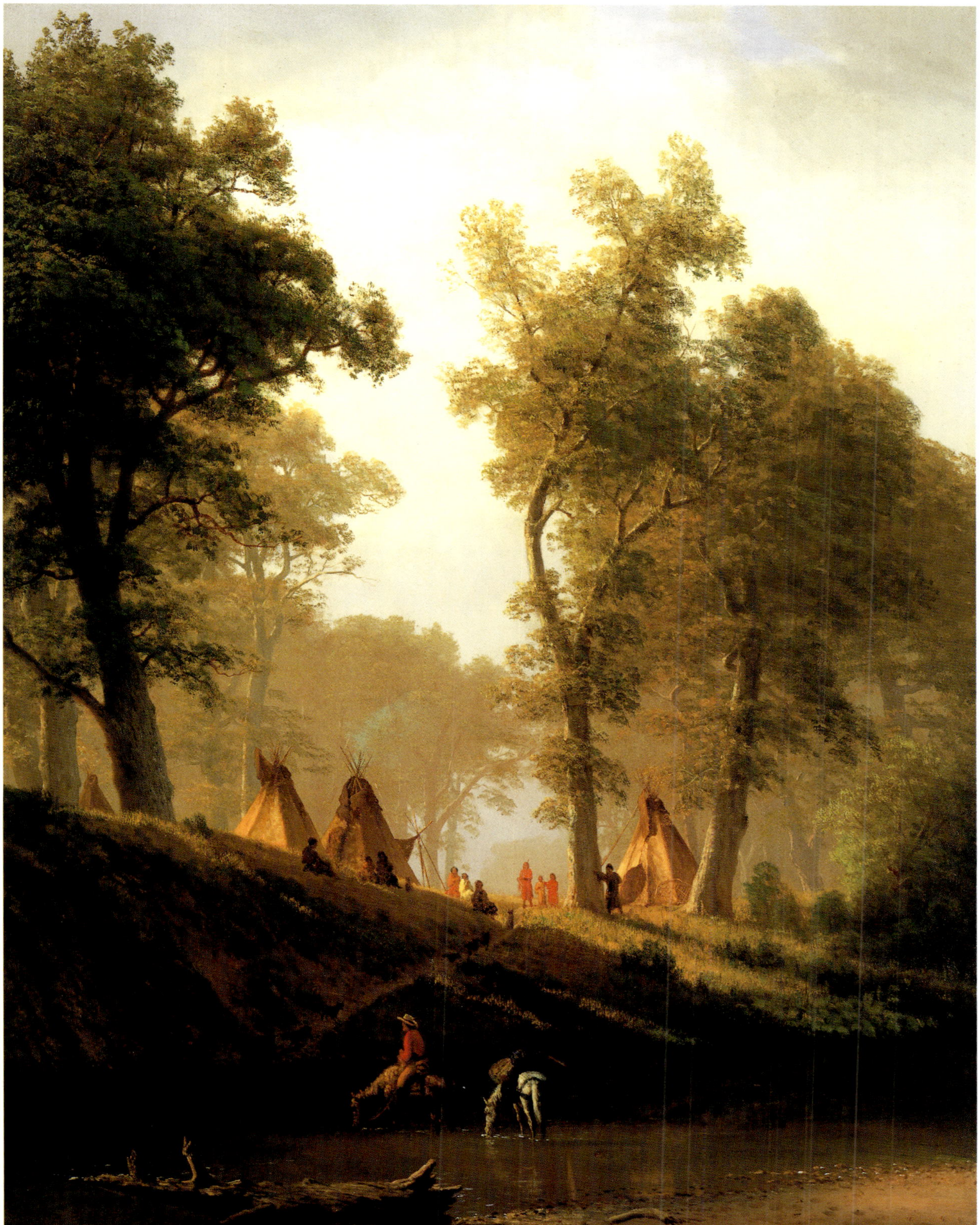

The Wolf River, Kansas

Bierstadt repeatedly employed this pictorial sign of decay as a spatial and symbolic device in his western wilderness scenes. Here, the log functions like a prop in a stage set: its expressive openings and gestural limbs announce that the viewer has entered an alien realm fraught with danger. Compositionally, its extremities point to the two trappers as it follows their lateral movement. And, like the foreground debris in Bierstadt's stereograph of Wolf River Ford, this large and apparently foreshortened log simulates an experience of deep space, especially in its contrast to the smaller, less detailed figures in the background. The spotlights on the right shore, log projections, water, packhorse, and red-shirted trapper work with the shadowed middle ground to enhance the picture's drama: one seems to pass from the light of familiarity through the darkness of mystery to the brilliance of discovery.

Above the trappers, on the river's edge, an Indian encampment appears in bright sunlight. A small nomadic band of Native Americans responds without agitation to the trappers' arrival. As Roger Stein has pointed out, Bierstadt's use of a zigzag movement—from right-hand shore to trappers to diagonal path to left-hand slope—provides a gradual passage for the trappers (and the Caucasian viewer) into Native American habitat. Symmetry governs the arrangement of the Indians and four tepees: on each side of the composition two trees frame a single tepee; in the center, two more dwellings follow the ridge's tree line. Sunlight falling across the grassy slope creates a crisscross pattern of light and shade; five natives are illuminated and five are silhouetted. So too are the trappers lit alternately light and dark. A dog sits like a sentinel, marking the threshold between shadow and sunshine, wilderness and camp, Caucasian and Indian.

Although Bierstadt omitted details of clothing and ornamentation, thus making precise identification of the tribe impossible, he did include enough cultural specifics to indicate that we are entering the world of the Plains Indians. In particular, the sturdy, many-poled tepees and the attacking dogs rushing toward the river were characteristic of the Plains tribes. Dogs were plentiful, frequently used as sentries, transportation, and, for the Arapaho and Dakota, as ceremonial food. Women erected and maintained the tepees and were considered their owners. Significantly, Bierstadt depicted primarily women and children assembled before the nomadic settlement. The netted hoop resting against the right tepee, however, refers to an exclusively masculine sport of the Plains tribes—the popular hoop-and-pole game. Indeed, the most prominent figure pictured among the Native Americans appears to be a male standing in red garb with a single feather rising from his hair. His position below the arched trees, behind the sentinel dog, and in line with the red-shirted trapper designates him as a chief or elder figure prepared to greet the whites. By placing the natives in a bucolic landscape removed from immediate access, thereby diminishing their size in relation to the trappers', Bierstadt assured an amiable meeting between the two cultures.

The Wolf River, Kansas combines the fact and the type, the real and the ideal, in a manner characteristic of Bierstadt's dualistic approach to painting his western travels. During his first trip west Bierstadt made stereographs of the features and dwellings of the Plains Indians; in addition, he painted their portraits as intimate oil studies, writing their names below each image. This regard for individual identity, however, is absent in *The Wolf River, Kansas.* Unlike Bierstadt's celebrated *Rocky Mountains, Lander's Peak* (1863; Metropolitan Museum of Art, New York), *The Wolf River, Kansas* distances the natives, reducing anthropological realities to picturesque ornaments. In a letter addressed to the New York art periodical *The Crayon,* recounting his travels to the Rocky Mountains, Bierstadt revealed a similar contradictory attitude toward painting the Native American:

> We do not venture a great distance from the camp alone, although tempted to do so by distant objects, which, of course, appear more charming than those near by; also by the figures of the Indians so enticing, travelling about with their long poles trailing along on the ground, and their picturesque dress, that renders them such appropriate adjuncts to the scenery. For the figure painter, there is an abundance of fine subjects. The manners and customs of the Indians are still as they were hundreds of years ago, and now is the time to paint them, for they are rapidly passing away; and soon will be known only in history. I think that the artist ought to tell his portion of their history as well as the writer; a combination of both will assuredly render it more complete. (July 10, 1859; quoted in Hendricks 1964, 337)

In short, Bierstadt sought both aesthetic pleasure and historical truth; in *The Wolf River, Kansas* he intertwined them into a construct that western-bound easterners found most appealing. Tragically, whether regarded for its picturesque allure or anthropological significance, the Indian was a curiosity bound for extinction.

J. S.

Inscription At lower right, *ABierstadt* (AB in monogram)

Provenance Vose Galleries, Boston. Kennedy Galleries, New York. Acquired in 1961.

Exhibitions Lawrence 1961, no. 17. Detroit 1964. Fort Worth 1972. Topeka 1985, 10. Brooklyn et al. 1991, 153, ill. Rome 1993.

References *BDIA* 1960–61a, 52–53. Hendricks 1964, 338, 365, fig. 7. Lindquist-Cock 1970, 365–367, ill. Hendricks 1973, 82, no. CL-135, fig. 63. Rivard 1978, 1040. Stein 1985, 12, 14, ill.

3

Vernal Fall, ca. 1863

(traditionally known as *Yosemite Falls*)

Oil on paper, mounted on canvas
48.3 × 35.6 cm (19 × 14 in.)
Gift of Carl F. Clarke (53.126)

In *The Heart of the Continent: A Record of Travel across the Plains and in Oregon,* Fitz Hugh Ludlow recounted how the artists who accompanied him in 1863 went about beholding Yosemite—"a new heaven and a new earth into which the creative spirit had just been breathed" (Ludlow 1870, 426):

> Sitting in their divine workshop, by a little after sunrise our artists began labor in that only method which can ever make a true painter or a living landscape,—*color-studies on the spot;* and though I can not here speak of their results, I will assert that during their seven weeks' camp in the Valley they learned more and gained greater material for future triumphs than they had gotten in all their lives before at the feet of the greatest masters. (Ludlow 1870, 434)

Albert Bierstadt produced his oil sketch of Vernal Fall as well as numerous others while on this very expedition. Mistitled *Yosemite Falls,* Detroit's color study, like Bierstadt's other western oil sketches, combines specificity and spontaneity, transcription and emotion. Broad and rather dry strokes of brown and green suggest the sheer, roughly carved wall; quick curved blots of forest green convince the viewer that fir trees surround the fall. Energetic, scumbled strokes of white, green, and ocher convey the power of the almost four-hundred-foot descent of water nearly sixty feet in width. One seemingly experiences the misty spray. Remarkably, Bierstadt's study resembles the National Parkways' photographic view of Vernal Fall in its 1989 guide to Yosemite. The artist did not merely document the sights of his western tour, however, but in addition displayed his artistic process.

Bierstadt initially set foot in Yosemite Valley sometime between August 2 and 21, 1863, accompanied by Fitz Hugh Ludlow, the popular author of *The Hasheesh Eater* (1857), and the artists Enoch Wood Perry and Virgil Williams, who were painting in California at the time. He was not the first artist to do so. Thomas Ayres, who arrived in 1855 with the entrepreneur James Mason Hutchings, preceded the many painters and photographers who would follow; his renderings of Yosemite were published as subscription lithographs and as engravings in *Hutchings' California Magazine* (July 1856). The photographer Carleton Watkins created a sensation with his large wet-plate photographs of the Sequoia forest and Yosemite (1858 and 1861, respectively), which were distributed throughout the East. Not only did these images inspire artists, writers, and tourists to venture out west to see Yosemite firsthand, but they also led to the establishment of Yosemite Valley and Mariposa Big Trees as a California state park in 1864. Bierstadt and Ludlow studied Watkins's dramatic views while in San Francisco before their departure for Yosemite. Such photographic records prepared Bierstadt for the natural monuments he would see. They not only provided examples of how compositional conventions applied to eastern scenery could be imposed on western landscapes but offered a visual challenge to the enterprising painter. Although Bierstadt took cues from Watkins's stereographs and mammoth-plate prints, he was freer to manipulate and reconstruct the scene. Bierstadt's modest oil sketches, unlike Watkins's photographic plates, were necessary preliminaries to the grand canvases that represented the spiritual as well as the visual experience of Yosemite. Memory and invention mediated to a higher degree in the painter's finished works than in the photographer's. Indeed, in his large exhibition pieces, Bierstadt masterfully transformed view into vision, site into spectacle.

Yosemite offered Bierstadt scenery even more startling and sublime than that of the Rockies. Located in the Sierra Nevada, this extraordinary valley of towering granite and thundering waterfalls was named by Lafayette Houghton Bunnell of the Mariposa Battalion in March 1851 for its Native American inhabitants, "the full grown grizzly bear tribe." Ludlow's effusive descriptions of Yosemite Valley as the "Promised Land" and "a sweep of emerald grass turned to chrysoprase by the slant-beamed sun,—chrysoprase beautiful enough to have been the tenth foundation-stone of John's apocalyptic heaven" (Ludlow 1870, 431, 432) were typical of the period and found appropriate visual expression in Bierstadt's finished paintings.

Nineteenth-century viewers identified moments of grandeur in Bierstadt's simple oil sketches. Placed on view in San Francisco after the expedition's return from Yosemite, the color studies sparked admiration for their emotional depth: "Any skillful copyist might do this, but Mr. Bierstadt with the instinct of genius has gone further. He has made us feel something of his own awe in the presence of sublimity. . . . Bierstadt has given us what the photograph lacks" *(Golden Era,* September 27, 1863, quoted in San Diego 1986, n.p.). The *San Francisco Alta,* reporting on Bierstadt and Ludlow's departure for Oregon, was equally effusive though recognizing the practical purpose of the oil sketch:

> Mr. Bierstadt has been very industrious, and has taken a multitude of sketches which, though made in six or eight hours each, have an excellence that would entitle them to rank with finished pictures. Indeed, several of them are great works of art. In sketching, it is admitted that Bierstadt has no equal in America. His sketches, however, are merely made as guides for pictures, which will require months, perhaps years, to complete, but when completed they will be masterpieces, valuable and enduring contributions to the artistic wealth of the world. (September 29, 1863; quoted in Hendricks 1964, 346)

Unlike Bierstadt's studies of Yosemite Falls (Cho-looke), the most celebrated waterfall of the valley, this study of Vernal Fall did not result in any large canvas. The Detroit picture seems to be, in fact, the only record extant of Bierstadt's looking at the waterfall. This is curious in that the site was already accessible to the traveler and highly acclaimed for its beauty. Vernal Fall and Nevada Fall, located in the upper valley along Mist Trail near Liberty Cap and Mount Broderick, could be reached by a horse trail and stairs completed in 1857 that allowed a close ascent alongside the steep Vernal Fall. Ludlow remarked that the two successive waterfalls "in apparent breadth and volume, far surpass Cho-looke" and Nevada is nearly as high as Bridal Veil Fall, which Bierstadt repeatedly featured in his panoramas of the valley (Ludlow 1870, 441). Visitors before and after Ludlow also marveled at how multiple rainbows, some forming complete circles, arose from the misty cauldron of Vernal Fall and entranced the viewer for an extended time. Watkins produced a stereoview of the celebrated foot of Vernal Fall, though his image of 1861 necessarily captures the blur of white water rather than circles of color. Surprisingly, Bierstadt's color study does not indicate the rainbow arcs or even much of the brilliant color associated with this waterfall. Instead, the painter focused on the water's fierce rush off the ledge and the irregular boulders below. Watkins, concerned with creating a sense of depth, photographed the waterfall for a mammoth-plate print from a position farther away from the sheet of water so that the cataract rushing over a labyrinth of boulders commands the foreground and the photograph as a whole. Bierstadt dispensed with the compositional conventions governing Watkins's photograph and his own exhibition paintings by orienting the spectator close to the waterfall, cutting off from view much of the sky, trees, and mountain. His color study invites one simply to experience the momentum of falling water.

Neither as identifiable nor as redolent with national and religious associations as was Yosemite Falls, Vernal Fall granted Bierstadt the opportunity to study, record, and respond to a waterfall of extraordinary power. Bierstadt's sole product of this experience permits the viewer, in turn, to examine the "labor in that only method which can ever make a true painter or a living landscape"—the color study.

J. S.

Inscription At lower right, *ABierstadt* (AB in monogram)

Provenance Carl F. Clarke. Acquired in 1953.

Exhibitions Northampton 1964. Peoria 1968, no. 9, ill.

Reference Hendricks 1973, no. CL-136, ill.

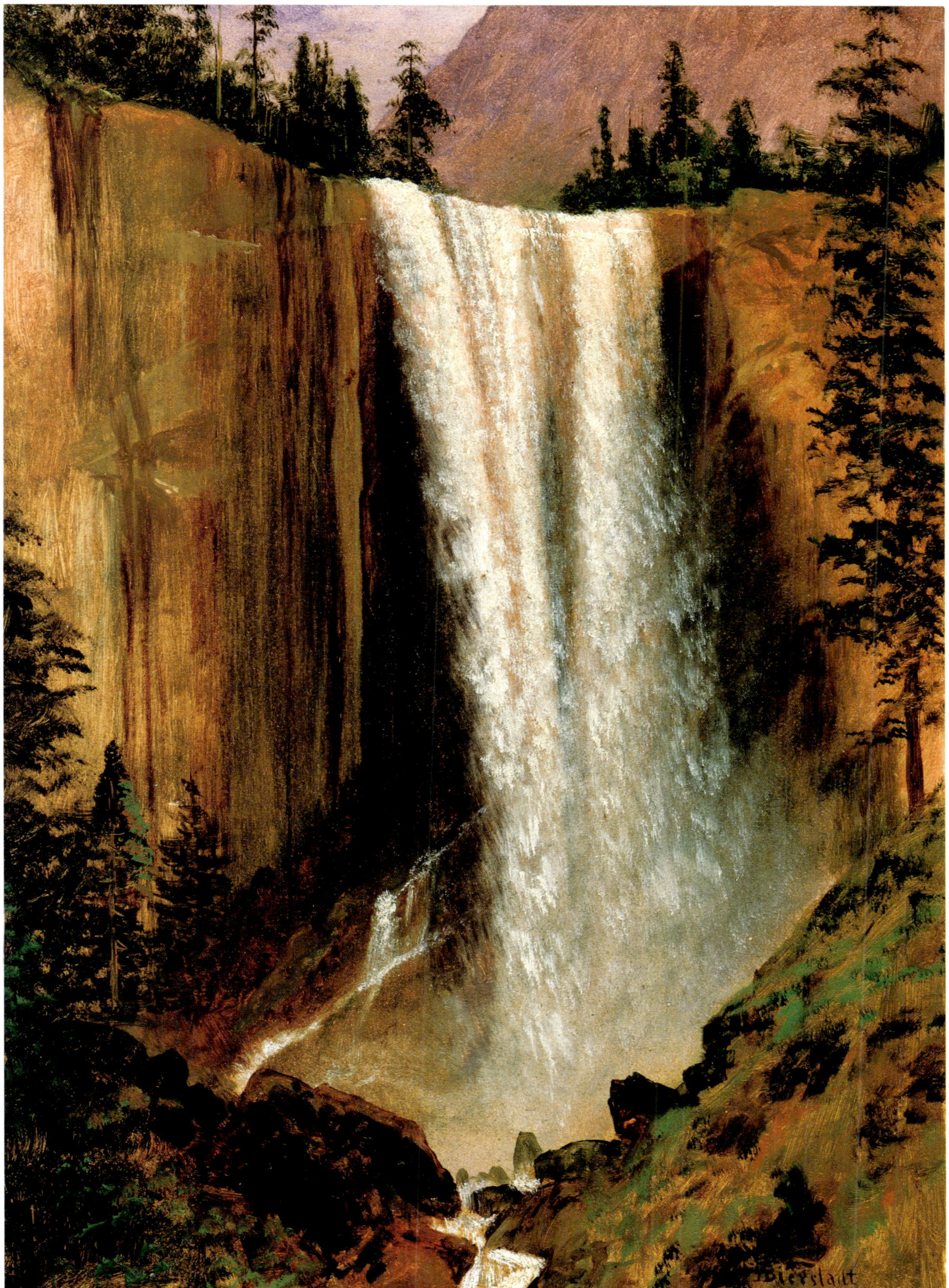

Vernal Fall

Ralph Albert Blakelock

1847 NEW YORK–ELIZABETHTOWN, NEW YORK 1919

RALPH BLAKELOCK's primary artistic concern, like that of many of his contemporaries in the second half of the nineteenth century, was with the opportunities offered by landscape painting. Yet within that framework his contribution was of a distinctly personal kind. He perceived the American landscape with a romanticism marked by a deeply personal note, introspective, poetic, and, at the end, expressionist, which sets him apart as an artist whose vision was both genuinely innovative and prophetic of developments to come.

Born in New York City, the son of a recently immigrated English physician, Blakelock was expected to continue in his father's profession. He nonetheless entered the Free Academy of New York (later City College) in 1864 but left after two years without graduating to follow his developing interest in art. He received encouragement and some instruction from James A. Johnson, a friend of the family who was a musician and avocational painter. Otherwise self-taught, by 1867 Blakelock had progressed to the point where one of his paintings was accepted by the National Academy of Design for its annual exhibition.

In 1869 he took a trip, traveling alone, which was to be the major event of his life. Extending over several years, this trip was an exploration of the area of present-day Colorado, the Dakotas, Wyoming, Utah, and California. The great number of extant drawings are, for the most part, records of the landscape and, to a lesser degree, the life of the Indians he saw. He returned to the East by way of Mexico, Panama, and Jamaica.

He married Cora Rebecca Bailey in 1875, and the first of their nine children was born the following year. The rest of Blakelock's life is poorly documented, but the picture that can be established is marked by the many difficulties he encountered in establishing a professional practice, in spite of the fact that his work was recognized and included in the important exhibitions of the day. The responsibilities of his increasing family eventually caused a nervous breakdown and, in 1891, the first of several commitments to a hospital. Although there were brief periods of return to normal activity, he was eventually admitted to the state hospital at Middletown, New York, in 1901, where he remained intermittently until his death.

During this time Blakelock was the object of considerable public attention through the efforts of his friends to return him to an active artistic life. Unfortunately, this very effort created the prejudicial conception of the mad genius. This image and the fact that one of his finest works, *Brook by Moonlight* (ca. 1891; Toledo Museum of Art), was purchased by the museum for twenty thousand dollars (at that time the highest price ever paid at auction for the work of a living American artist) contributed to the beginning of the forgery of his work.

During his hospitalization he remained active on a very limited scale and produced a body of small paintings of exceptional quality and importance that demonstrate conclusively that his creative abilities remained alive.

N. G.

Bibliography New York 1947a. Santa Barbara et al. 1969. Lincoln and Trenton 1975. Geske 1976. Davidson 1987. New York 1987b.

4

Landscape, ca. 1880–90

Oil on canvas

40.6 × 61 cm (16 × 24 in.)

Bequest of Dexter M. Ferry, Jr. (60.67)

KNOWN MOST PARTICULARLY as the painter of scenes of Indian encampments and moonlight landscapes, Ralph Blakelock actually produced a wide range of paintings that explore the landscape theme through a number of differing types. Most notable among them are the paintings that can be called open-sky landscapes. They do not have the exoticism of the Indian motif nor the rhapsodic poetry of the moonlit views. Instead, they develop the subtler beauty of sunrise and sunset; at heart they are paintings of space. There is often a flat ground plane illuminated by bodies of reflective water. Shrubs, groves, or single trees stand against the lighted sky, whose color can range from an almost lurid red and gold to the milky whiteness of an early morning fog or the creeping darkness of twilight.

The Detroit painting is exceptional even among comparable examples in having a remarkably cool palette of brown, gray, and white, enlivened with touches of yellow. The tall trees that dominate the composition are definitive examples of Blakelock's interest in the organic outline of trees against the sky. One of the most personal traits of his technique, the way he paints the color of the sky into the darkness of the foliage, is seen here at its best. One can almost visualize the twist

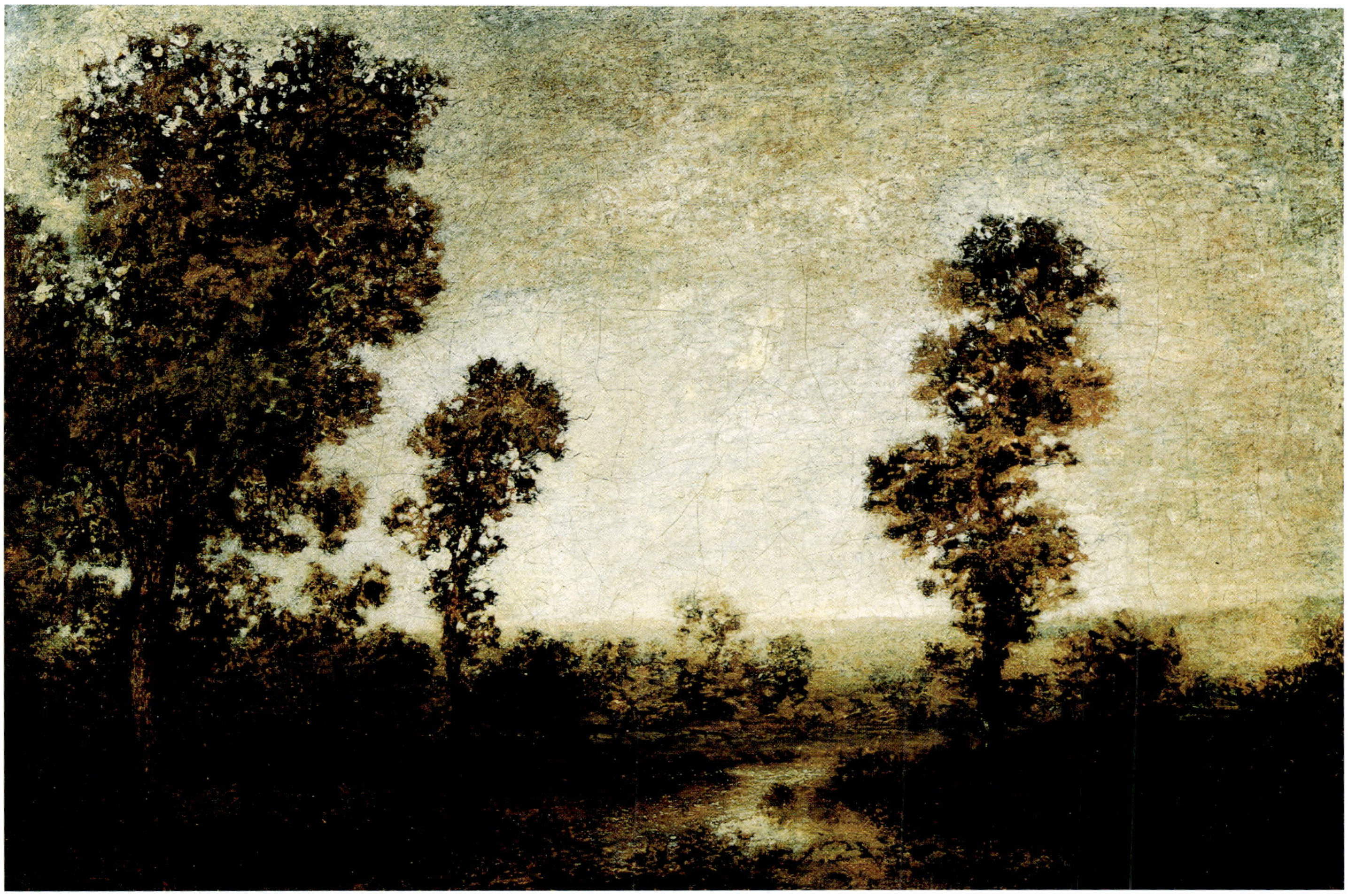

and flip of the brush. If there is one single habit to identify Blakelock's hand, it is his almost obsessive love of the textural and coloristic intricacies of growing plants and trees, especially as seen in forests or in open, uncultivated fields. At times line and color interweave in a purely abstract way.

Blakelock's open-sky landscapes stand apart from his trademark subjects and are perhaps more personal and genuinely felt than the better-known themes. With their exalted appreciation of the nuances of light and air, they are surely among his finest achievements. They forecast, in a way, the impassioned intensity of the paintings he did in the last decade of his life as examples of a sensory experience of phenomena that is distinctly in advance of the conventional practice of his day.

N. G.

Inscription At lower left, *R. A. Blakelock*

Provenance Dexter M. Ferry, Jr., Grosse Pointe, Mich. Acquired by bequest in 1960.

Exhibitions East Lansing 1966, no. 33. Santa Barbara et al. 1969, no. 60.

References Nebraska Blakelock Inv. no. NB1–222-II. *BDIA* 1960–61, 16–17.

Frederick Arthur Bridgman

1847 TUSKEGEE, ALABAMA–ROUEN, FRANCE 1928

FREDERICK ARTHUR BRIDGMAN, a late-nineteenth-century expatriate American artist, achieved an international reputation with his orientalist paintings of harems, Arab life, and archaeological reconstructions. Acknowledged for his peasant scenes, idealized figure paintings, history paintings, landscapes, and portraits, Bridgman was also recognized as an accomplished engraver, photographer, author, composer, and musician. Born in Tuskegee, Alabama, Bridgman moved to New York City in 1863 for a two-year apprenticeship in the engraving department of the American Bank-Note Company. At the same time he studied at the Brooklyn Art School and the National Academy of Design. In 1866 Bridgman went to Paris, where he was admitted to the École des Beaux-Arts in February 1867; he also joined the studio of the academician Jean-Léon Gérôme.

Bridgman summered for five years in the Brittany village of Pont-Aven, using his experiences there in paintings of peasant life. Seeking more far-flung locales, Bridgman traveled in northern Africa three times. The first was in 1872, when he visited Morocco, Algeria, and Tunisia. The following year he went to Egypt with the Philadelphia artist Charles Sprague Pearce, seeing Cairo and sailing to the second cataract of the Nile. At the end of the decade, in 1879, he explored the oasis communities bordering the Sahara and eastern Tunisia.

Typical of many artists traveling in the Near East in the late nineteenth century—and as he had done in Brittany—Bridgman collected local costumes, accessories, and bric-a-brac items. He also made some three hundred sketches that included everything from studies of ruins, landscape scenes, and details of the local flora, to faithful depictions of costumes, ethnic physiognomy, and distinctive customs. Bridgman's experiences in Africa influenced the themes of his major exhibition pieces shown at the annuals in France, England, and America during the 1870s, where his paintings of reconstructions of ancient Egypt and Assyria met with great success.

His marriage in July 1877 to the wealthy Bostonian Florence Mott Baker freed him from the necessity of selling his work and allowed him to indulge such other interests as musical composition and performance, writing, and sports. Yet Bridgman continued to paint, and his subject matter expanded to include contemporary orientalist genre imagery. Throughout the 1880s and 1890s he exhibited regularly at the major venues in Paris and London. After the first major exhibition of Bridgman's work in the United States, at the American Art Gallery in New York in 1881, he was elected academician of the National Academy of Design. (He had been elected associate in 1874.)

In 1914, during World War I, Bridgman moved to Lyons-la-Forêt, in Normandy, where he painted from memory Algerian scenes that became progressively sugary and unreal. He died in Rouen.

T. T.

Bibliography *NCAB* 2:110. *DAB* 3:36–37. Dayton et al. 1976, 88–89 and passim. Jacobs 1985, 46, 49, 52. Fort 1990.

5

Moorish Interior, ca. 1875–79

Oil on canvas

27 × 40.6 cm (10⅝ × 16 in.)

Founders Society Purchase, Eleanor and Edsel Ford Exhibition and Acquisition Fund (1993.20)

FREDERICK ARTHUR BRIDGMAN was first introduced to images of women in the Orient in the 1860s at the Paris Salon, where he saw such paintings as *Dance of the Almeh* (1863; Dayton Art Institute) and *Slave Market* (1866; Sterling and Francine Clark Art Institute, Williamstown, Mass.), both created by his teacher at the École des Beaux-Arts, Jean-Léon Gérôme. By the 1870s, when Bridgman began his own travels in the Near East, his fascination with exotic and mysterious dark-eyed beauties heightened and eventually found artistic expression in numerous depictions of the harem.

Bridgman completed this elaborately staged picture just a few years after he finished his academic training with Gérôme, and it reflects the style and subject matter of his master. Similar to analogous works by Gérôme, *Moorish Interior* is a diagonally structured figurative composition painted in a realistic style and imbued with narrative content. Yet unlike that of Gérôme, who often presented erotically titillating harem fantasies, Bridgman's interpretation is closer to the less provocative and more genteel approach of the English artist John Lewis, rendered with the clearly defined patterns and minute detail favored by many Victorian artists.

Moorish Interior is set in an Ottoman Empire reception room typical of the period. The room contains a wooden doorway with stairs leading to an outside balcony, an entry area with a fountain sunk in a tessellated pavement, a lofty wood-bracketed ceiling, and a raised alcove with a high bay window covered with a *mashrabiyyah* (a latticed openwork wooden screen). Hanging from the ceiling of the alcove is a ceramic orb, and on the right wall are a mirror, a frieze of blue-and-white Islamic tiles, and a painted mother-of-pearl inlaid wooden panel, with niches designed for the display of ceramics, which here exhibit a tureen, a ewer, several small vessels, and a vase of flowers. A luxurious maize-colored divan runs along the walls of the alcove, while a salmon-colored cushion and tasseled bolster are fitted to the seat in the bay window. In front of the divan, on the round metal serving tray balanced on a carved base, is a simple copper coffee urn and two coffee cups. Carpets cushion the floor of the alcove and the edge of the entry by the pool, on which is pre-

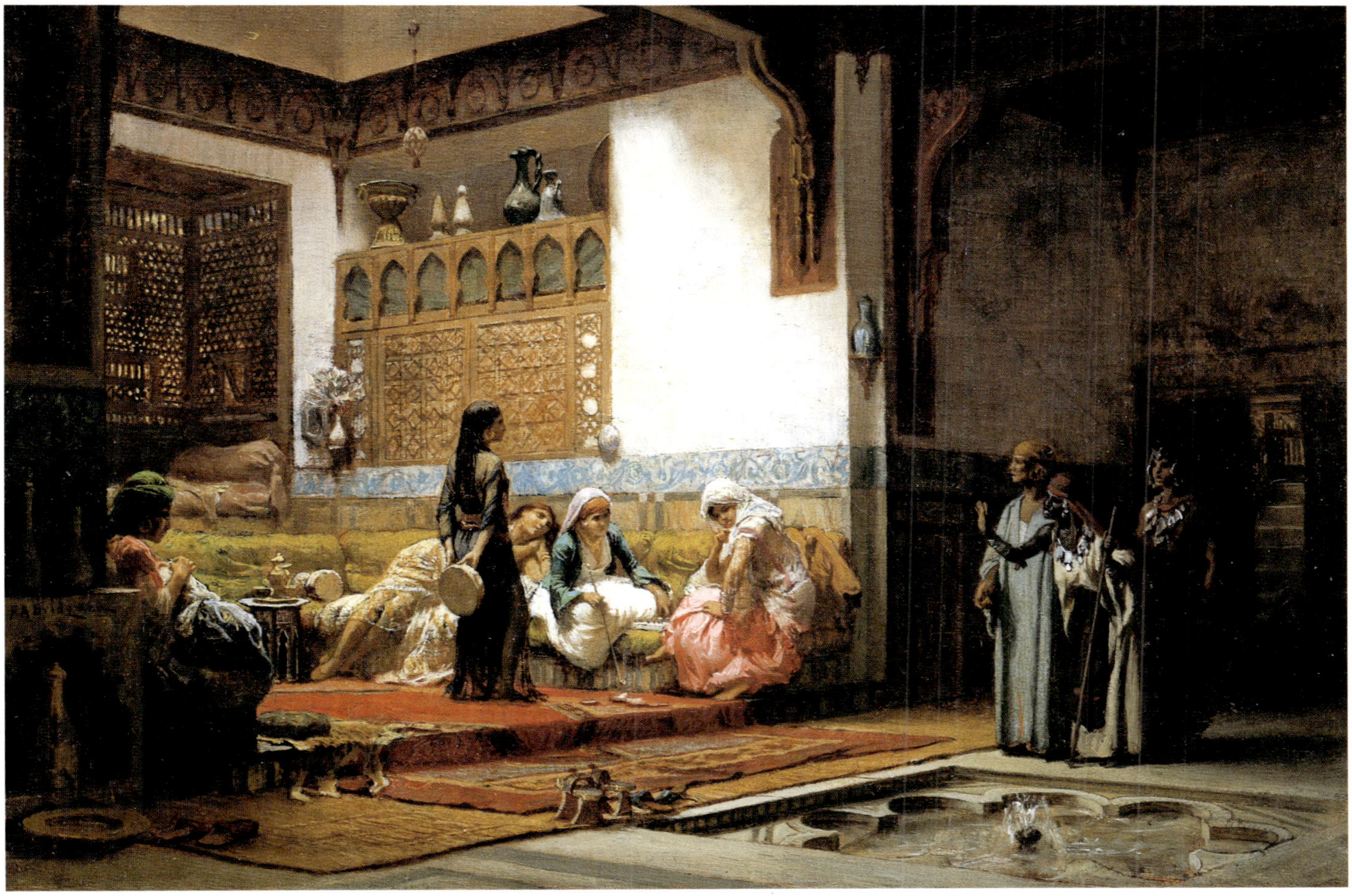

Moorish Interior

sented a further array of objects—a carved table with three faience vases, a wooden bowl, an animal skin, a foot cushion, two sets of slippers, and a pair of high-platform wooden pattens.

Nine women are portrayed in the reception room pursuing a variety of activities. One woman, dressed in a demure caftan and wearing large hooped earrings and a turban, is seated alone on the left side of the room quietly embroidering. Three more women are seated across from her. The first pauses in her play of the ancient board game *mankal'ah*, the second holds a long-stemmed *shibuk* pipe, and the third stares into space as she reclines on the divan. Individually costumed, the first woman wears a pink tunic and white-hooded burnous; the second a white tunic, blue jacket, gold turban, and white scarf; and the third a diaphanous garb that leaves her legs and slippered feet exposed. Standing in the alcove and facing the three women on the right is a bare-headed young beauty outfitted in a sheer gossamer costume typically worn by Egyptian dancing girls. Captured during a momentary lull in her performance, the young *almeh* (female entertainer) calmly holds a *tar* (tambourine) behind her back, while her *taabla* drum rests on the divan. In the entryway are three Nubian women: one is a story- or fortuneteller bending forward in spellbinding conversation with the women in the alcove, and the other two are her attendants. Except for their ornate jewelry and the headdress of the youngest one, these visiting women are simply clothed in dark-colored utilitarian tunics, robes, and head scarves. Finally, a shrouded figure is crouched in the doorway guarding the entrance to the harem, a sentry posted there to protect the women from the outside world.

Bridgman's picturesque narrative, filled with imaginative notions regarding the character and life-style of the oriental woman, reveals the artist's obsession with these beauties but also suggests the myths and fantasies bred in the nineteenth century as a result of the inaccessibility of Eastern females to Western males. Virtually barred from entry to the harem quarters in Muslim houses, Western artists interpreted the Eastern reality of the harem—a closely guarded and lavish sanctuary that women willingly consented to enter—as a fantasy of restricted lives devoted to sensuous leisure (Fort 1990, 217, 225–228; Thornton 1983, 15). Bridgman included some of the delectable pleasures thought to be the mainstay of the harem woman's life. Because coffee represented to the West one of the many consumable sweets of the Orient, it symbolized the harem itself. Thus, the ubiquitous coffee ceremony is indicated by the small serving tray and utensils. As Ilene Fort has pointed out, "the beautiful harem women involved in the coffee ceremony became for the Westerner the sublimation of what he believed to be the aromatic soul of the Orient: she not only represented languor and reverie but the 'metaphysics of refreshment and odiferous absorption'" (Fort 1990, 229–230).

Bridgman's perspective also reveals a transformation of the harem from a place of forbidden pleasure to a domestic and social institution populated by well-bred and genteel women pursuing interests acceptable in either the East or the West. Such an approach was first popularized in the mid–nineteenth century by English Victorian artists responding to cultural attitudes toward the harem as a distasteful place of female seclusion, polygamy, and slavery. Artists such as John Lewis preferred to downplay the harem's sensual elements in favor of an interpretation of the harem as a respectable home (Fort 1990, 227–240 passim). Even though the harem women and their visitors in *Moorish Interior* are seen engaged in what were considered classic harem activities—smoking, game playing, lounging, embroidering, playing music, and story- or fortune-telling—Bridgman's wholesome treatment of them deflates whatever erotic associations the subject might have and substitutes the idea of the harem as a home devoted to beauty and taste. This approach brought Bridgman professional recognition and financial success. Scenes like *Moorish Interior* were highly salable because they validated an idealized way of life that reflected what his Western patrons professed to follow (Fort 1990, 239–241, 245).

T. T.

Inscription At left edge below table top, *F A Bridgman*

Provenance Arlington Art Galleries, Brooklyn. Mack Pratt, Hamilton, Ohio. Private collection, Hamilton, Ohio. Jordan-Volpe Gallery, New York. Acquired in 1993.

References Thornton 1983, 15. Fort 1990, 213, 217, 225–245.

John George Brown

1831 Durham, England–New York 1913

The successful genre painter of urban urchins and country girls John George Brown discussed with the art critic George Sheldon his realist-idealist approach to recording American life:

> Art should express contemporaneous truth, which will be of interest to posterity. I want people a hundred years from now to know how the children that I paint looked, just as we know how people of Wilkie's and Hogarth's times looked. I paint what I see, and in my own way.... I put J. G. Brown into them. And a good reporter in like manner would have put himself into them. (Sheldon 1879, 141)

A consummate professional, Brown approached his art like a businessman or newspaperman—create a product that the middle class as well as the affluent find appealing and reproduce it in quantity. Present characters typical of the age, but not uncomfortably close to the real thing. Brown unapologetically whitewashed the crudity and ugliness of urban existence. His street urchins, invariably clean and cheery, upheld the Protestant work ethic that Brown himself stringently followed. As several contemporary art critics recognized, Brown filtered his reportorial vision through an idealistic artistic imagination and conservative social agenda. Brown's diligent, traditional approach to artistic production earned him great wealth and popular acclaim during his lifetime.

Brown credited his success to his humble working-class origins in England. His parents redirected his early artistic interests toward trade work, apprenticing him at the age of fourteen to a glassworker in Newcastle upon Tyne. In 1852 Brown moved to Edinburgh for a year, where he worked at the Holyrood Glass Works and took evening art classes in antique-cast drawing at the Trustees Academy. After a brief summer stay in London, Brown immigrated to the United States in 1853 and found work at the Brooklyn Flint Glass Factory. From 1855 to 1860 Brown secured his domestic life and professional direction: he married the boss's daughter, Mary Owen, and supported the family during the great financial panic of 1857 with portraits and genre pictures of children. From 1861 to 1883 he solidified his artistic reputation as the painter of bootblacks while fathering seven children: two daughters were borne by his wife, Mary, who died in 1867; three sons and two more daughters were born after he married his sister-in-law Emma Owen in 1871.

Brown systematically pursued his career. He enrolled in drawing classes at the National Academy of Design, exhibiting there from 1858 until his death. Elected associate member in 1861 and full member in 1863, Brown served in various academy positions, including vice president (1899–1903). In 1859 he became a founding member of the Brooklyn Art Social and two years later of its successor, the Brooklyn Art Association. In 1860 he moved into the prestigious Tenth Street Studio Building, where he would occupy a studio for fifty-three years. Brown rarely lacked patrons and often marketed his paintings through such popular mediums as Prang's chromolithographs and periodical illustration. Brown's affinity for Victorian sentimentalism and Pre-Raphaelite art, however, marked him as increasingly reactionary, especially as the French painting he detested preempted American art. While other painters enthusiastically embraced Continental techniques, Brown berated their "aping all those Gallic tricks, and seeing their own life through French glasses" (Ishmael 1891a, 622).

J. S.

Bibliography Springfield et al. 1989.

6

Claiming the Shot: After the Hunt in the Adirondacks, 1865

Oil on canvas
81.3 × 127 cm (32 × 50 in.)
Robert H. Tannahill Foundation Fund
(73.226)

The second of two pictures John George Brown painted for the wealthy members of sporting clubs, *Claiming the Shot: After the Hunt in the Adirondacks* demonstrates the artist's mastery of group portraiture and his reliance on the conventions of the English sporting picture, wilderness scenes, and history painting. This seven-figure ensemble followed the success of Brown's *Curling;—a Scottish Game at Central Park* (1863; Lady Eden Gordon; Springfield et al. 1989, 8, fig. 4), which contributed to his election as a full member of the National Academy of Design. Exhibited at the academy in 1865 under the title *Claiming the Shot: A Group of Portraits after the Hunt in the Adirondacks,* it was commissioned by William Brand, who was a founding member with Robert Gordon of the St. Andrew's Curling Club. Gordon's commission of the artist's first sporting-group portrait, *Curling,* most likely inspired Brand to follow suit. Indeed, according to the Brown scholar Martha Hoppin, Brand is the portly gentleman with sideburns, jeweled pin, and light tan suit prominently featured in each painting. Portrait studies made for *Claiming the Shot* include this exact figure in a full-length pose with gun in hand and displaying the same expression as in the final work. Although dealers have identified this gentleman as John Jacob Astor III of real-estate fame, the fact that William Brand owned the large group portrait, possessed an uncanny resemblance to the prominent figures in *Curling* and *Claiming the Shot,* and was socially acquainted with Gordon, secures his identification in both pictures.

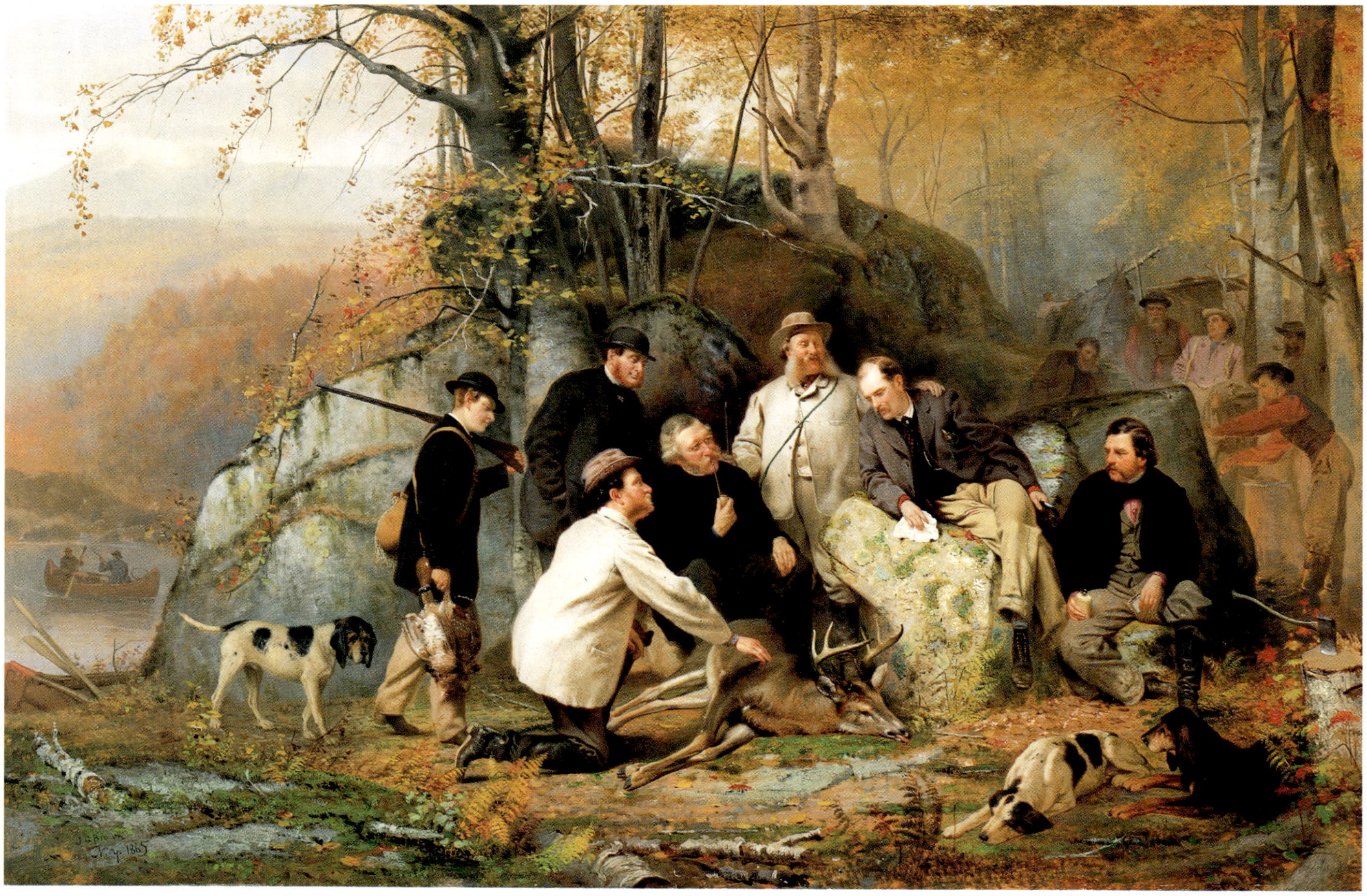

Additional portrait studies featuring two of the seated gentlemen exist, but they are known only as types—the hunter and the sage. The figure on the far right with his open flask and cup in hand, hunting boots, rather dapper pink shirt, and focused gaze appears in a study entitled *The Hunter* (1865; private collection, Cleveland). He is the hunter at rest, imbibing refreshment after the kill. *Contemplation* (1865; Bernard & S. Dean Levy, New York) presents the affable, graying, pipe-smoking gentleman seated in the center of Brown's ensemble on a stoop before an open door. Except for the location, the addition of visible shoes, and greater exposure of his shirt cuffs, the figure appears exactly as he does in *Claiming the Shot.* He and "the hunter" mirror one another with their seated pose, relaxed right hands, and absorption in the event before them. The former, however, is light-haired, restrained in his dress, and actively indulges in his smoking pleasure. Noticeably older, he supplies an image of lifelong experience to the scene.

Significantly, this pipe-smoking sage occupies the center of *Claiming the Shot,* flanked by parties of three. Rising behind him in a form of natural architecture is an arched outcropping with autumnal trees. He crouches directly over the hunter's prize—the dead stag whose lifeless eye staring out at the viewer is matched by the droopy gaze of the hound joining the group on the left. As the eldest gentleman, he appears to act as judge of the claim, with the apparent victor the man seated on the large thronelike rock to the right. Brand congratulates the victor with a pat on the shoulder; the hunter confirming the shot's entry looks up to him, literally and figuratively. The victor glances down as his hand grasps a white handkerchief, responding in effect to the kneeling hunter's about-to-be bloodied fingers. To the left, a hefty man and a strolling youth look on with interest. The adolescent is fully outfitted for the hunt, including accompaniment by a faithful hound. With grouse in hand, he represents the ideal boy whose youthful successes at shooting fowl will ably prepare

Claiming the Shot

him for the adult hunt for game. He adds an appropriate coda to this hunting fraternity, for Brown's tableau is a celebration of lifelong masculine camaraderie and accomplishment.

Masculinity emerged as a significant theme in American art and culture with the advent of the Civil War, and as social challenges to male dominance increased through the remainder of the century, the image of the rugged, adventurous male became prevalent. The sportsman, in particular, epitomized the skill, patience, endurance, and courage regarded as desirable in the American male. Hunting clubs, exclusively male in their membership, expanded among the middle class as tourism intruded into wilderness areas. *Claiming the Shot* features members of such a club, though it conveys a more aristocratic aura than characterized the typical American hunting and camping scene. In this manner it is indebted to the English sporting picture. Of Scottish birth, William Brand undoubtedly knew the pictorial type and believed the English-born Brown would most likely be familiar with its conventions. Indeed, Brown, a great admirer of British art, turned not only to the precedent of eighteenth-century hunting scenes but also to the famed art of the Victorian painter Sir Edwin Landseer, whose pictures of heroic stags and sentimental pets were widely engraved. Landseer's *Death of the Stag in Green Tilt* (1824–30; Duke of Atholl collection) and other pictures of royal figures gathered around their dead game provided an excellent model for Brown's adoption. Brown grafted this civilized image onto the frontier genre that John Mix Stanley, among others, depicted, specifically the theme shown in *The Disputed Shot* (1858; Corcoran Gallery of Art, Washington, D.C.). Unlike Stanley's rough-hewn trappers, however, Brown's congenial gentlemen never threaten to erupt in violent contention for the stag. They respond to the felled animal as a trophy in a sporting match. Only the Adirondack woods and camping guides in the background allude to the difficulties of wilderness life that artists such as Stanley sought to recapture on canvas. In fact, the shot stag and the ax-imbedded tree trunk each connote that the powers of patriarchy can subdue the environment.

Claiming the Shot not only presents symbols of civilization amid wilderness but also makes use of a genre long regarded as representative of the height of culture. Brown imbued his meticulously rendered figures with a decorum and grandeur characteristic of history painting, a genre that sporting art had in the past emulated. As in Benjamin West's famous *Death of General Wolfe* of 1770 (National Gallery of Canada, Ottawa), a ritualistic tone pervades the hunters' composed gathering around the dead carcass. Representative of several generations from adolescence to old age, the protagonists of *Claiming the Shot* perform as individuals and universal types. Also characteristic of history painting is the inclusion of a young witness, here the adolescent hunter, signaling the importance of the event to posterity. For, in fact, they are all participants in and witnesses to a "historic" event—one with direct implications for the group and the individual, if not the nation.

American artists were all too aware of the intersection of private and public histories at this time: by 1865 many an individual life had been irrevocably altered by the national event of the century—the Civil War. Popular periodicals featured articles and illustrations alluding to the relationship between hunting and war. Many of the war's volunteers were experienced hunters; one Pennsylvania regiment was even dubbed "the Bucktails" for its renowned deer hunters. During the Civil War there was little sport hunting owing to the fact that many of the best shots were engaged in battle. When the war ended, rifle matches and shooting manuals proliferated, but so did analogies between the hunted animal and the wounded soldier. Sportsmen took more care than ever before to follow hunting etiquette and play the game fairly. Shooting at vulnerable targets or using cruel methods were judged unseemly for the true hunter. *Claiming the Shot: After the Hunt in the Adirondacks,* painted the year the war ended, portrays individuals whose actions in the hunting field epitomized justice and virtue. Although many of their identities may now be lost to us, the painting's significance for the Civil War generation is not.

J. S.

Inscription At lower left, *J. G. Brown / N. Y. 1865*

Provenance William Brand, 1865. Sotheby and Company, London, 1971. Meredith Long and Company, Houston, Texas, 1972 Acquired in 1973.

Exhibitions Houston 1976. Leningrad et al. 1976, 11, no. 47, ill. Paris 1976, no. 34, ill. Springfield et al. 1989, 8–9, 47, no. 9.

Reference *BDIA* 1977, 93–94, ill.

7
A Surprise Party, 1888

Oil on canvas
63.5 × 50.8 cm (25 × 20 in.)
Detroit Museum of Art Purchase (88.1)

John George Brown was at the height of his popularity when J. T. Cowles of the Detroit Club invited him to send a picture for an upcoming exhibition to be held in Detroit in February 1888. Brown wrote in reply on January 12, 1888: "I assure you if I have one at the time I will take great pleasure in sending it, as I have a great many friends in your city." A week later, on January 19, Brown wrote again to Cowles to report that he was then working on a painting—"one of my best subjects"—expressly for the Detroit show. Brown must have been eager for the opportunity to show his work in Detroit, for the same day he also wrote Charles L.

Freer, the vice president and treasurer of the Peninsular Car Company, who was then chairman of the Art Committee of the Detroit Club and who was to become a leading art collector. Brown reassured Freer: "I am painting a picture expressly for your club which I hope to have finished in time" (correspondence, curatorial files, DIA).

Correspondence on file at the Detroit Institute of Arts charts the progress of *A Surprise Party* from this first exchange of letters to its sale. Brown apparently heard from neither Cowles nor Freer, because on February 9 he wrote a letter addressed to the Art Committee itself: "I have not heard a word from you in some time, and as your exhibition was to be on the 15th of this month I take the liberty of writing." The painting, he declared, was ready to go. A second letter, addressed to the "Comm. of the Detroit Club," spells out packing instructions for the return trip to Brown's studio and titles the painting "A Surprize Party" *[sic]* with a price of $800. The painting made it to the exhibition, and the patrons in the Detroit Club must have been pleased. Freer sent a telegram on February 23 asking if $800 was the lowest sale price; Brown replied the next day that he would take off 10 percent (correspondence, curatorial files, DIA). Eight hundred dollars, less 10 percent, was a handsome sum in 1888; comparison might be made to the average annual wage of a minister, which was $794 in 1890, or to the $439 earned by an average worker in manufacturing (U.S. Department of Commerce 1975, 168). Brown's painting was purchased for the Detroit Museum of Art, forerunner of the Detroit Institute of Arts; it was the museum's first acquisition in 1888, the year the museum opened on Jefferson Avenue.

Brown's fame rested on such pictures as *A Surprise Party*, a depiction of a young bootblack holding up a jack-in-the-box while another boy clutches a small dog and looks on with great curiosity. Brown here uses his typical, smoothly finished style and exercises fidelity to local color and texture and to the details of dress and individual physiognomy. To Brown, the exhibition-going public, and critics in the late 1870s and 1880s, these pictures were "truthful" to the times, since bootblacks had become a common sight on the streets of New York. The critic Samuel G. W. Benjamin praised Brown in 1882 for shrewdly seizing on subjects that were quickly becoming a part of the picturesque, contemporary American urban scene:

> The immigration from Europe had now been going on for so many years that it had begun to modify the types of human nature in the streets, while the increasing number of poor foreigners accustomed to out-of-door occupations introduced new effects. Street vendors and booths, groups of strolling musicians, and other characters common to European cities, also began to show themselves in the cities of America, and nowhere more than in New York, modified in its turn by the condition of things in the United States. Mr. Brown was quick to perceive the artistic possibilities of these effects, and to reap profit from his observations. (Benjamin 1882, 266)

Art "should express contemporaneous truth, which will be of interest to posterity," Brown told a critic and added: "I want people a hundred years from now to know how the children that I painted looked. . . . I paint what I see, and in my own way" (Sheldon 1881, 141). His own way necessitated bringing in models off the streets, "getting them to act the part allotted to them" *(Harper's Weekly* 1880), and faithfully rendering the details.

Brown further believed, like others of his generation who had imbibed the aesthetic theories of John Ruskin, that art should have a moral purpose. "There is a moral in everything—in the way a man looks and talks, and his paintings ought to have this in them," he told the critic George Sheldon, who responded with admiration for "the roughly-clad, adventuresome, happy, poverty-compassed boyhood of the American metropolis" represented in Brown's pictures (Sheldon 1882, 149–150). To both Brown and Sheldon the specific but tacit moral and the unquestioned "contemporaneous truth" were visualized by such adventuresome gamins learning entrepreneurial skills that would catapult them out of poverty.

Brown was not the first artist to mine such a subject. His slightly older contemporary, Eastman Johnson (q.v.), had painted urban children as street musicians, chimney sweeps, or feather-duster sellers from the early 1860s. And in 1867 Horatio Alger published *Ragged Dick,* the first of his popular books about young "street arabs" who achieve social status and material wealth through pluck and luck. While the rags-to-riches mythology that lay behind such images guaranteed the success of Brown's pictures and Alger's stories among patrons and readers who themselves had been, or yearned to be, part of the American success story, such images of well-scrubbed, bright-eyed children also mollified fears that homeless youth would become the hardened criminals described by Charles Loring Brace in his influential book *The Dangerous Classes and Twenty Years' Work among Them* (1872). To Brace, the filth and poverty of the slums would inevitably convert young innocents into a life of crime, unless they had a vision of alternative options. Thus, Brace organized excursions to the countryside through his organization, the Children's Aid Society; fresh air and nature would mitigate criminal ambitions (Burns 1989, 311). As the Brown scholar Martha Hoppin points out, Brace's generally positive attitude toward the spirit of individualism exemplified in the young street children was shared by Brown (Springfield et al. 1989, 22).

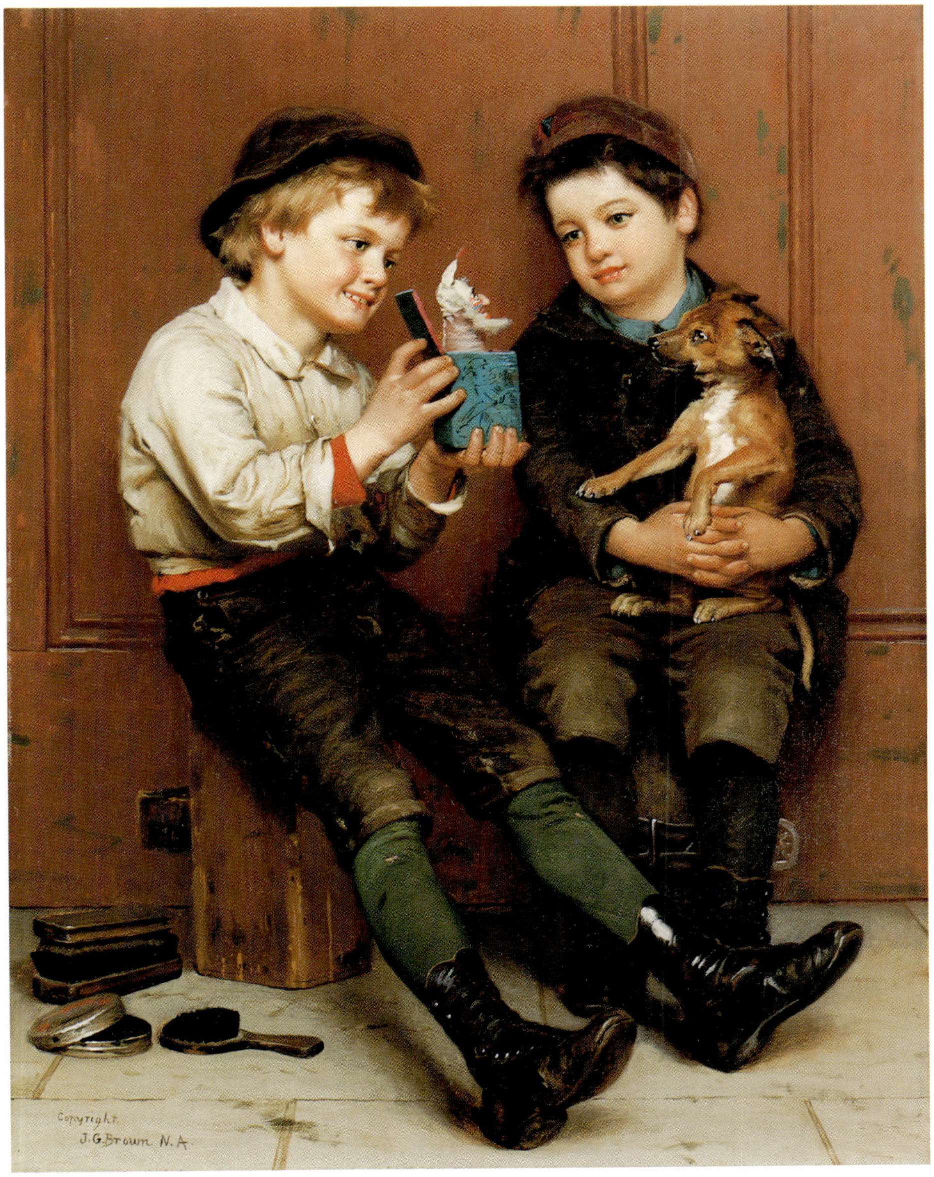

The moral of *A Surprise Party* resides in the joy that comes from the control of spontaneity. Punch might seem to jump out unexpectedly at his audience, but his motions are controlled and he can be shut up in his box when work needs to be done.

P. H.

Inscription At lower right, *Copyright / J. G. Brown, N.A.*

Provenance Acquired in 1888.

Exhibitions Detroit 1888, no. 24. Detroit 1889, p. 8, no. 11.

References *Harper's Weekly* 1880. Sheldon 1881, 141–144. Sheldon 1882, 148–152. Benjamin 1882, 265–270. McClinton 1979, 247, fig. 9. Springfield et al. 1989, 22. Burns 1989, 310–311.

To Brown, style reinforced the moral message. He took care to remove his well-scrubbed bootblacks from the debris and filth of ghetto gutters and to portray them with the smooth, orderly, craftsmanlike brushwork that Renaissance masters used to depict the Holy Family. In this stylistic tradition, Brown's children would be above the temptations of real crime. Their innocent dramas take place upon neat sidewalks abutting either stone facades or wooden doors of the "better" neighborhoods, as they sit on the boxes that hold their polish and brushes and enjoy a moment of mild mischief, bantering, or relaxed camaraderie removed from the company of their customers. Their lives were ones of purpose, unlike the children portrayed in the slapdash, painterly—and to Brown, amoral—style of the Munich painters then moving into prominence in the art world.

A Surprise Party

Thomas Mickell Burnham

1818 Boston 1866

Thomas Burnham, a genre, landscape, and portrait painter, was born in Boston. Nothing is known of his training. He went to Detroit in the mid-1830s at about the same time as his brother George, who founded the *Detroit Evening Spectator and Literary Gazette* with his brother-in-law Benjamin Kingsbury, Jr., in October 1836. By 1838 Burnham was painting genre scenes and portraits. A letter published in the May 26 *Detroit Morning Post,* from "A FRIEND," commented: "Although he has been but a short time engaged in his profession he has succeeded in obtaining several very accurate, and excellently executed portraits. His *forte* is in depicting scenes in low life, and many of his sketches have been pronounced equal in truth to any extant save Hogarth's." Burnham exhibited a painting entitled *The Burning of the Steam Boat "Great Western"* (unlocated) in November 1839, placing a notice in the *Detroit Daily Advertiser* on November 30: "The subscriber having painted a representation of the burning of the Steam Boat 'Great Western,' respectfully invites the *firemen* of Detroit and the citizens generally to call at his room, (Cole's building, 3 doors above Wayne Street, up stairs,) where it may be seen for a few days. THOS. M. BURNHAM."

Returning to Boston, Burnham exhibited several paintings in 1840–44 at the Boston Athenaeum and the Boston Art Association, and in New York at the Apollo Association and the National Academy of Design. They included *The Young Artist* (Indianapolis Museum of Art) and *Preparing for Market, Dead Game, The Early Inkling,* and *Boys Playing "Paw Paw"* (also called *Stable Scene—Boys Playing Paws* or *Boys Playing at Paw),* all unlocated today. When *The Young Artist* was exhibited at the Athenaeum in 1840, verses in the catalogue asked the viewer not to scorn the artist:

Fair lady, turn not by in scorn
At talent to the pencil born.
Genius knows naught of age or clime;
'Tis God's own mind—'tis all divine.

The poem continued with a comment on the figure of the African American in the painting:

Fair lady turn not up the lip
Because our sitter is black scrip;
'Tis not the color of the skin,
That makes us good or prone to sin.

The heart is often black as night,
Encased in flesh of purest white;
If that be pure in black or fair
God makes his holy temple there.

The commentary added: "This picture being the first effort of a very young painter deserves great praise for accuracy of drawing, color and expression" (quoted in Perkins and Gavin 1980, 284). The painting was purchased by the Athenaeum and exhibited there frequently over the next thirty years. *Boys Playing at Paw* also included the figure of an African American. When it was exhibited at the National Academy in 1842, it was reviewed as "a composition of much comic merit.... The expression of disappointment and mortification in the face and attitude of the black boy, who leans against the wall, is extremely well given, as well as the air and gesture of insolent triumph in his successful antagonist" *(New York Evening Post,* July 9, 1842).

Very little is known about Burnham. In his correspondence with J. P. Ridner of the Apollo Association in 1841 (Wallace 1953), he mentioned the encouragement of Washington Allston. His genre scenes have an affinity with the work of David Claypoole Johnston (see cat. no. 9). He lived in the Boston area until the late 1840s, when he may have gone to New York and then back to Detroit. His paintings *The Burning of the Steam Boat "Great Western,"* then owned by the LaFayette Fire Company No. 4, and *First State Election in Detroit, Michigan, 1837* (cat. no. 9) were exhibited in Detroit's first public exhibition at the Firemen's Hall in 1852. Burnham soon returned to Boston, where he was one of the painters of a large panorama of the American West that was based on daguerreotypes taken by J. Wesley Jones (1853). Among his few works located or identified today are *One Too Many* (Addison Gallery of American Art, Phillips Academy, Andover, Mass.) and *View of the Housatonic* (private collection).

E. G. M.

Bibliography Robinson 1953. Inventory of American Painting. *Detroit Morning Post,* May 26, 1838. *Detroit Daily Advertiser,* November 30, 1839. *New York Evening Post,* July 9, 1842. Farmer 1890, 673. Burton 1922, 2:1194. Cowdrey 1943, 1:60. Cowdrey 1953, 51. Groce and Wallace 1957, 97. Gibson 1975, 63. Perkins and Gavin 1980, 29, 284. Janson and Fraser 1981, n.p. Yarnall and Gerdts 1986, 521.

8

Stevens Thomson Mason, ca. 1837
(formerly *C. C. Trowbridge*)
Oil on canvas
30.5 × 25.4 cm (12 × 10 in.)
Gift of Mrs. Samuel T. Carson (57.268)

This small waist-length portrait shows a handsome young man with dark hair and brown eyes, dressed in a brown coat, a dark vest, a white shirt and collar, and a black tie. Behind him is a red curtain. The portrait is painted in a precise, controlled technique. The flesh colors are warm, the lips almost red. When the painting came to the museum as a loan in 1905, it was identified as a portrait of Stevens Thomson Mason (1812–1843), the first governor of the state of Michigan. The sitter's identification was later changed to Charles Christopher Trowbridge (1800–1883), Mason's opponent in the 1837 election. Burnham depicted their election supporters in his painting *First State Election in Detroit,*

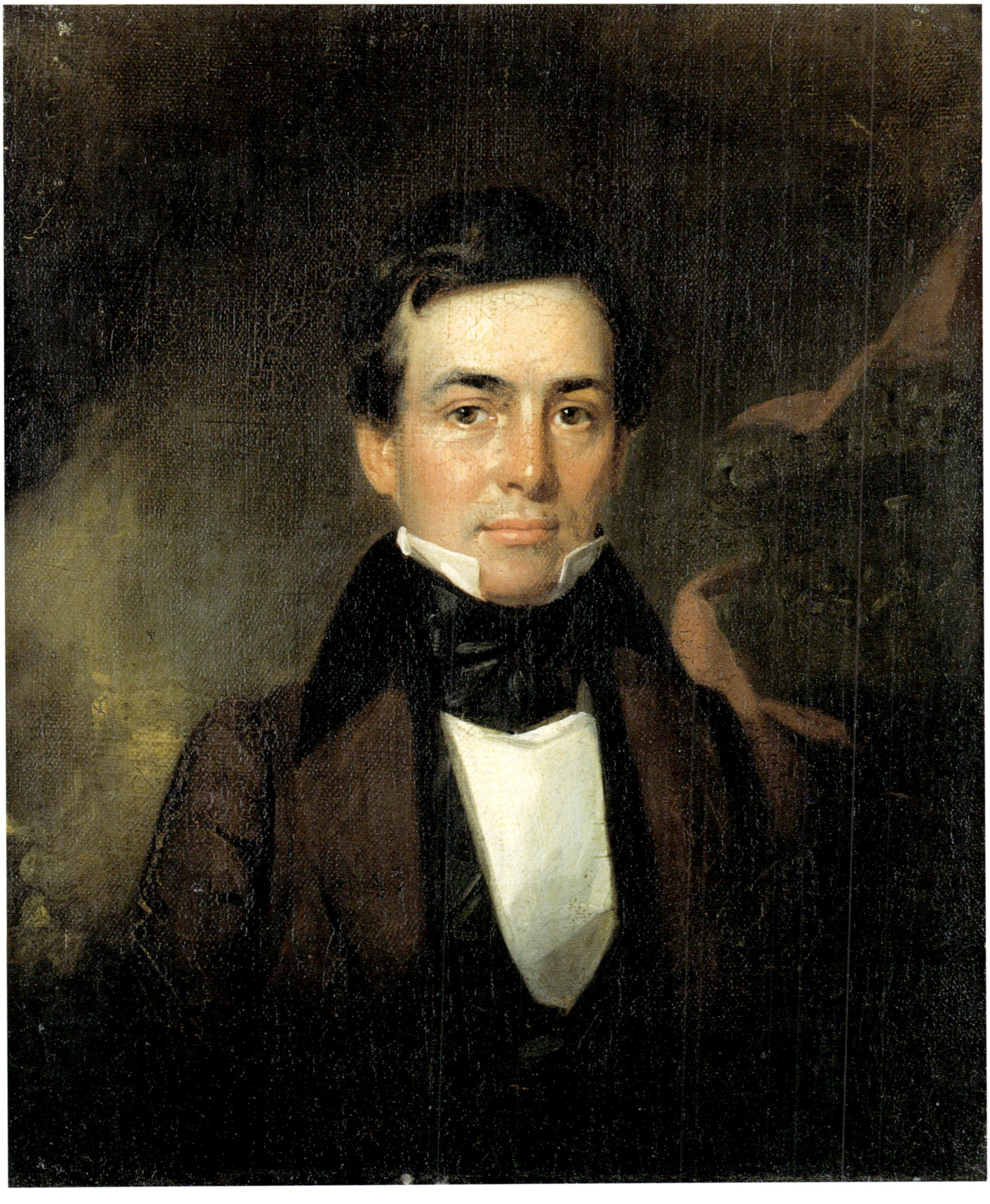

Stevens Thomson Mason

Michigan, 1837 (cat. no. 9); Mason is in the left foreground.

The original identification appears to be correct. The man in the painting looks like Mason as depicted by the early Michigan artist Allen Smith, Jr., whose full-length portrait of the governor was the gift of several citizens to the state of Michigan in 1837; the portrait is still owned by the state. Smith painted a similarly posed three-quarter-length at about the same time (University of Michigan, Ann Arbor) and also did a smaller head-and-shoulder portrait that is signed on the reverse, *A. Smith Jr. Pinxt / Detroit Augst 1838 / Gov. Mason of Michigan* (private collection, recorded by the Catalog of American Portraits, National Portrait Gallery). These portraits all depict a dark-haired, fine-featured man with a boyish appearance. By contrast, portraits of Trowbridge by Lewis T. Ives (oil on canvas, 1877; Detroit Historical Museum) and Samuel Conkey (relief sculpture, 1878; Detroit Historical Museum) show that Trowbridge had a larger head and larger features.

This portrait was published as an image of Mason in 1907, with the artist not identified (Heineman 1907, 243). The attribution to Burnham may have come about because the painting was owned by the owner of Burnham's painting *First State Election in Detroit.* Although Burnham was described by contemporaries as a portrait painter, no other examples of his portraits can be located. He is not known to have painted a portrait of Mason other than the small image in his election scene. However, the attribution of this portrait to Burnham seems reasonable. His documented work is in this same small scale, indicating his comfort and experience in painting less-than-life-size figures.

E. G. M.

Provenance Louise Tillman (Mrs. Samuel T.) Carson, who placed the painting on loan at the museum on January 31, 1905.

Exhibitions Detroit 1934. Detroit 1938. Detroit 1949.

References Heineman 1907, 243. Hemans 1920, ill. opp. 64. *BDIA* 1934, 12, 13. *BDIA* 1938, 55.

9
First State Election in Detroit, Michigan, 1837, ca. 1837

Oil on canvas
62.2 × 78.1 cm (24½ × 30¾ in.)
Gift of Mrs. Samuel T. Carson (57.267)

MICHIGAN WAS GRANTED STATEHOOD in January 1837. Its first state election was held the following November. Burnham's painting shows the electioneering that took place on the day of the voting and is in a comic style that is almost more typical of a caricature than of a genre scene.

The candidates for governor were Charles Christopher Trowbridge (1800–1883), a Whig, and Stevens Thomson Mason (1812–1843), a Democratic-Republican, acting governor of the state. The *Detroit Daily Advertiser* for February 4, 1852, described the painting when it was exhibited in Detroit's first public art exhibition at the Firemen's Hall:

> No picture in the whole collection at Fireman's Hall [*sic*] excites more genuine fun than that of the view of the Polls of the election at the City Hall, when Tom Mason was elected Governor. It was the work of Burnham, then a mere boy. Its execution is rough and inartistic, but the spirit of the art is there. There is "Tom" Mason, with his easy, affable smile, in the act of giving that very *dollar* to little John Weisse, the butcher; there is old Major McKinstry, natural as life, and poor Frank Sawyer, (rest his soul) with his time-honored cap, in full and sharp argument with that prince of blackguards, Kingsbury of the *Post,* and there is George C. Bates, backing up Sawyer, while Major Harris does the same thing for Kingsbury: stop and admire the logical angles of Sawyer's face, which tell as plainly as words can that every inch of the ground is to be fought for that is gained of him and there is the redoutable Stilson upon his everlasting horse, with his chapeau blazing with political mottoes, the admiration of boundless crowds of ragged boys, *roaring* through the streets at the top of his lungs the virtues of his friend "Tom," the candidate for Governor.
>
> What changes the fifteen years bring about! In that time the grave has closed over many of the busy actors in this mimic scene of strife and has changed the circumstances of the living. This rough sketch is, after all, a deep moral lesson if rightly studied.

The painting represents the large public meeting space in front of the first city hall in Detroit, called the Campus Martius, on election day, 1837. Stevens Thomson ("Tom") Mason is seen in the left foreground, giving the man next to him a piece of paper with the slogan "FOR GOVERNOR STEVENS T. MASON." The recipient is John Weese (or Weisse), a local butcher. Mason was accused of vote buying in the August 1837 congressional election because he was seen giving a banknote to Weese. This event is alluded to by the newspaper in the left corner of the picture, which is printed with the words "ROCHESTER DEMOCRAT JOHN WEESE GOV. MA." The Rochester newspaper was the first to carry the story of the bribery. Other acts of bribery are apparently taking place. To the left,

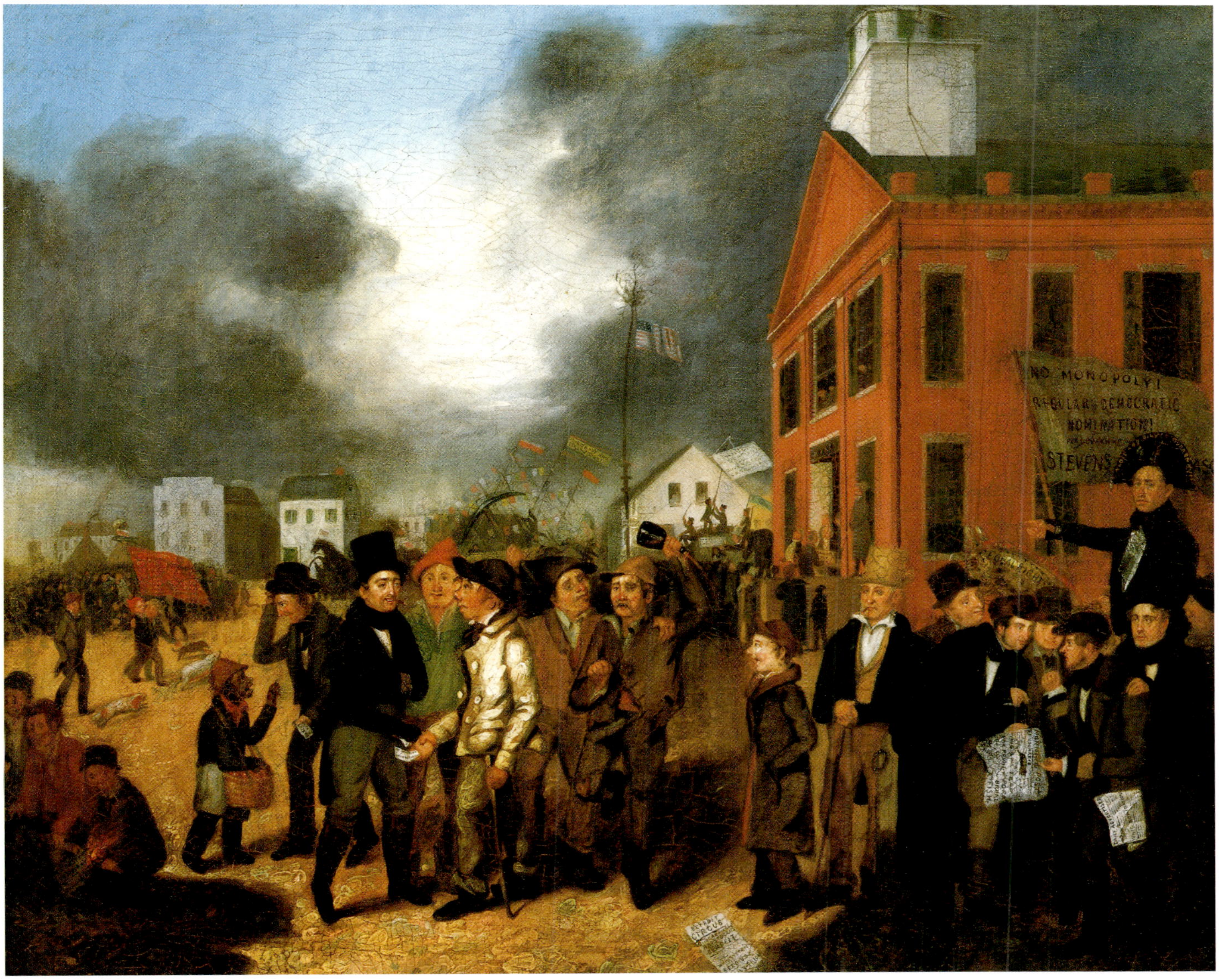

First State Election in Detroit

behind Mason, a man hands a paper that seems to be inscribed "BANK OF LAPEER" to an African-American boy who holds a large basket.

In the right foreground are two men, arguing and surrounded by their supporters. On the left is Benjamin Kingsbury, founder and publisher of the *Detroit Morning Post,* the Democratic paper. (It was the second paper founded by Kingsbury and George P. Burnham, the artist's brother.) Kingsbury holds a newspaper and gestures to the headline: "MORNING POST DEMOCRATIC NOMINATION WHIG COL. [?] TRAP ONE POUND OF PORK do do [ditto] BREAD do do [ditto] FISH." Facing him is Franklin Sawyer, editor of the *Detroit Daily Advertiser,* the Whig newspaper. His right fist is clenched, and with his left he gestures toward the paper. In his pocket is another newspaper, whose headline reads, "DAILY ADVERTISER WHIG NOMINATIONS."

To the left of these two men, facing the viewer, is Major David C. McKinstry, chairman of the state Democratic-Republican party, wearing a top hat and leaning on his walking stick. He was proprietor of a Detroit theater and a museum. Near his feet is a piece of paper inscribed, "DETROIT CIRCUS Great Attraction! ARISTOCRATS BENEFIT WHIG SYSTEM SEED BOX TORY TRICK KICK OF THE DYING ASS!" Next to McKinstry, in a black top hat, is F. (or S.) H. Harris. On the right is George C. Bates. Behind the group, on horseback, is James Stilson, a well-known Detroit auctioneer and ardent supporter of Mason. He holds a banner that reads, "NO MONOPOLY! REGULAR DEMOCRATIC NOMINATION! FOR GOVERNOR STEVENS T. MASON." (The letters *T* and *M* are blocked by his hat.) On the mane of his horse, which is draped with a cloth of gold, is written: "EQUAL RIGHTS," and on his hat is the slogan "A GOLD AND SILVER CURRENCY," a reference to Mason's stand that banks in the state be granted charters only if the banknotes were convertible to gold and silver. Stilson was the organizer and grand marshal of the election-day parade in support of Mason, a parade that included "some two hundred newly made citizens from the Emerald Isle; they were employed on city work, and . . . formed the 'balance of power' that carried the day for Mason" (Farmer 1890, 113). Brought to Michigan by the territorial government to work on a canal and other public projects, these Irish workmen, who surround Mason, voted Democratic, providing the votes that won the election for him. One holds up a bottle, its alcoholic contents spilling to the ground. A young man in the right foreground, next to McKinstry, laughs in amusement, probably because one charge against Mason at the time of the election was intemperance.

A procession of Whig supporters of Trowbridge comes into view in the left background, carrying a banner. Pigs run in the street nearby. A ship, on wheels, seen in the center background, was part of the procession; it represented the Ship of State, with a banner flying from its mast that reads, "FREE TRADE AND SAILORS RIGHTS." The ship was manned by Whig supporters, carpenters from Oliver Newberry's shipyard. When the two processions met, the Democrats tried to capture the ship, and a rout resulted. People can be seen jumping from the ship, whose masts, set at an angle, indicate that it is in distress. On the flagpole to the right of the ship, in front of a small white building, are an American flag and a small sign reading, "EQUAL RIGHTS." To its right a group of men riding in a coach carry a banner that reads, "WHIG NOMINATION FOR GOVERNOR C. C. TROWBRIDGE." Finally, several people climb the steps to city hall, where a box labeled "BALLOT BOX" is placed. Mason won the election by a vote of 15,314 to 14,800.

This painting is the first election scene painted in frontier America, and one of the earliest images of an American election. It could be one of the paintings alluded to by the writer of the letter in the May 26, 1838, *Detroit Morning Post* (see biography), who commented that Burnham's "*forte* is in depicting scenes in low life, and many of his sketches have been pronounced equal in truth to any extant save Hogarth's." Although it is first documented in 1852, when it was lent by the Detroit merchant James W. Tillman to the city's first public art exhibition at Firemen's Hall, with the title "Election Scene," the commentary in the *Detroit Daily Advertiser* makes it clear that it was painted at the time of the election. Of the other well-known paintings that represent early-nineteenth-century American elections, only John Lewis Krimmel's views, including *Election Day at Philadelphia* of 1815 (Henry Francis du Pont Winterthur Museum, Winterthur, Del.), predate Burnham's work. The genre scenes by the Missouri artist George Caleb Bingham, for example, were done in the late 1840s and early 1850s, including *Country Election* (Saint Louis Art Museum) of 1851–52.

The painting has been described as a "youthful effort, akin in its obvious satire to the graphic work of David Claypoole Johnston" (Williams 1973, 103). Johnston, a Boston artist, was known for his humorous paintings and book illustrations. He is said to have been "the first American comic artist to have a sustained and popular career" (Tatham 1970, 1). Born in Philadelphia, he moved to Boston in 1825 and by the 1830s was known for political satire and illustration. Johnston's figures are very similar in proportion, stance, and gesture to those in Burnham's painting. No connection between the two men is known, however. Unlike the work of Krimmel or Bingham, the painting has strong similarities to cartoons and caricatures, notably in the frequent use of words on signs and as newspaper headlines to make the messages clear.

E. G. M.

Provenance James W. Tillman (d. 1866). His widow, Martha Conant Tillman (later Mrs. Alpheus S. Williams, d. 1903). Her daughter Louise Tillman (Mrs. Samuel T.) Carson, who placed the painting on loan at the museum on January 31, 1905.

Exhibitions Detroit 1852, no. 21. Detroit 1853, no. 245. Detroit 1883, 74, no. 829. Detroit 1944a, no. 22. Detroit 1949. Washington 1950, no. 137. Detroit 1962. Dearborn 1964. St. Louis 1977, no. 15. Lansing 1985. East Lansing et al. 1986, no. 4.

References *Detroit Daily Advertiser*, February 4, 1852. Roberts 1884, 106–107. Farmer 1884, 112–113. Ross 1894. Palmer 1906, 452, 719–720. Hemans 1920, 306–312. C. Burroughs 1936a, 396–397. Michigan Writers' Program 1941, 137. Drepperd 1942, 52. Kenny 1965, 19, 20, 187. *Antiques* 1965, 305. Woodford and Woodford 1969, 82, 380, no. 17. Williams 1973, 103. Gibson 1975, 64. Yarnall and Gerdts 1986, 52[illegible]. Gerdts 1990, 2:232.

Mary Cassatt

1844 Pittsburgh–Mesnil-Théribus, France 1926

Cassatt was born in Allegheny City, today a part of Pittsburgh, to Katharine Kelso Johnston and Robert Simpson Cassatt, the first mayor of Allegheny City. When her family moved to Philadelphia, her father became a partner in a brokerage house. The five Cassatt children were Lydia, seven years older than Mary; Alexander, five years older, who later became president of the Pennsylvania Railroad; Mary; Robert, who died young; and finally Joseph Gardner, who pursued a career in banking.

In 1850 the family went to Europe to seek medical help for Robert and to educate Alexander. After long periods spent in Paris and Germany, they returned to Philadelphia. In 1860 Cassatt began four years of art training at the Pennsylvania Academy of the Fine Arts and in late 1865 or 1866 went to Europe for advanced study, with the financial support of her brother Alexander. In Paris she studied with Charles Chaplin and Jean-Léon Gérôme and, typical of art students of the day, painted copies after the old masters in the Louvre. She also traveled to Italy and the popular art colonies outside Paris. She studied genre painting with Pierre-Edouard Frère at Ecouen, with Paul Soyer at Villiers-le-Bel, and with Thomas Couture (Mathews 1987, 14–16). During the Franco-Prussian War and siege of Paris (1870–71), she went home to Philadelphia.

Returning to Europe in 1872 with Emily Sartain, an artist friend from Philadelphia, she lived for eight months in Parma and traveled for the next few years to Seville, Antwerp, Paris, and Rome. After a return visit to Philadelphia, she finally settled in Paris in 1875.

At first using the name Mary Stevenson (her maternal grandmother's maiden name) and declaring herself a pupil of Charles Chaplin and Paul Soyer, she showed *A Mandolin Player* (private collection) at the Paris Salon in 1868. Exhibiting in the 1870 Salon, she named Soyer and C. Bellay as her teachers, as she did when showing again in 1872 through 1876 (Fink 1990, 327–338, 392). Degas took note of her work at the 1874 Salon and, in 1877, he and the painter Léon Tourny visited Cassatt and invited her to join the Independents (the impressionists) in their next exhibition. To that fourth exhibition, held in 1879, she sent eleven pictures. She never again sent a picture to the Salon.

Cassatt and Degas developed a warm, professional friendship, which included visiting each other's studios almost daily and attending museums and the opera together. She admired his art, and with his encouragement her art blossomed into a distinct style. In 1880 and 1881 she exhibited in the fifth and sixth Independents' exhibitions. When Degas boycotted the seventh exhibition, she sided with him, but both showed again at the eighth, and last, exhibition in 1886, which she helped organize.

Painting alone did not occupy her, for when her mother, father, and sister Lydia moved in with her in 1877, she became more involved in family affairs and increasingly used her family as models. She also developed a close friendship with the wealthy Louisine Elder (later Mrs. H. O. Havemeyer), whom she advised to collect impressionist paintings.

In America her work became known through exhibitions held at the Pennsylvania Academy of the Fine Arts and the Durand-Ruel galleries in New York. She also received a commission to paint a major mural, *Modern Women,* to decorate the Women's Building at the 1893 World's Columbian Exposition held in Chicago. In 1895 she had a major solo exhibition at the Durand-Ruel galleries in New York. In 1915 she was included in a fund-raising exhibition held at M. Knoedler in New York in support of the suffragist movement.

In 1894 she bought the Château de Beaufresne in Mesnil-Théribus, about fifty miles from Paris, and continued to paint and care for her mother. One by one her family died, and for the last ten years of her life, although she painted little, she was still active in art benefits and in advising collectors and young students.
P. H.

Bibliography Sweet 1966. Breeskin 1970. Pollock 1980. Mathews 1984. Philadelphia 1985. Mathews 1987. Mathews 1994.

10

Alexander J. Cassatt, ca. 1880

Oil on canvas
65.4 × 92.4 cm (25¾ × 36⅜ in.)
Founders Society Purchase, Robert H. Tannahill Foundation Fund (1986.60)

Supported by family money, Mary Cassatt had no need to accept portrait commissions. She did, however, paint many portraits of her family and their domestic help. These are almost always women and children. One of the exceptions is the striking portrait she painted of her brother Alexander Johnston Cassatt, five years her senior, at the family's country house at Marly-le-Roi in 1880.

Alexander Cassatt (1839–1906) studied engineering at European schools and at Rensselaer Polytechnic Institute in New York State. In 1861 he began working at the Pennsylvania Railroad, and when the Pennsylvania expanded in the post–Civil War years, he rose to greater positions of responsibility. In 1882 he retired from the daily operations of the railroad, although he continued to serve as a director. He lived in semiretirement until 1899, when the railroad called him back to be president because of his engineering, organizational, and financial skills. His achievement was to secure a solid financial base for the Pennsylvania Railroad and to build Pennsylvania Station in New York (*DAB* 1929, 564–567).

Cassatt painted two portraits in oil of her brother (this one and one in a

Alexander J. Cassatt

private collection) and a double oil portrait of Alexander and his son Robert (Philadelphia Museum of Art); she also drew a pastel portrait (private collection). Based on a reading of Cassatt's letters, Adelyn Breeskin dated the private collection oil portrait to 1880 and the Detroit version to 1882–83 (Breeskin 1970, no. 79). However, for the 1985 exhibition *Mary Cassatt and Philadelphia,* held at the Philadelphia Museum of Art, Suzanne Lindsay reexamined Cassatt's letters and took into account the destination of each painting—the private collection version went to the Cassatt home in Philadelphia, whereas the Detroit version stayed in France—and concluded that the Detroit version was the first, 1880, image. Cassatt's letter in which she discusses the portrait was to her niece, Minnie, dated February 26, 1907, two months after Alexander's death: "I have a picture I think Rob may like to have, a portrait of his father done at Marly and very like what he was in those days. The picture was never finished but the hair and shoulders are. Last summer a dealer came out and rummaged in the garret at Beaufresne carrying off a lot of canvases, and I burned the rest but kept this portrait, too good to destroy" (Sweet 1966, 173). Other letters seem to confirm that the portrait done at Marly was the 1880 version.

A modern, informal portrait is always a collaboration between artist and sitter. While the artist brings talent, skill, and preferences for some poses over others, the sitter, particularly when a mature person, brings a physiognomy and a body language that have been shaped by the experiences of years. It is tempting to interpret the Detroit portrait of Alexander Cassatt in terms of his situation at the time. In the summer of 1880 Alexander was forty-one and had achieved the position of first vice president in the corporate structure of the Pennsylvania Railroad. He had amassed considerable wealth and was socially prominent. Married with four children, he yet found time to pay many extended visits to his mother, father, and sisters living abroad.

This unfinished painting seems to catch him unawares as he leans back in his chair, his coat tightly buttoned and his head pulled into a restricted opening allowed by a short and slightly flaring collar and the knot of a tie. His sensuous mouth is masked by the trim but drooping mustache, and his eyes retreat into the fortress of his head. It must have been a time of intense introspection for him as he contemplated staying with the railroad at a high-level management position or choosing a life of semiretirement that would afford time to pursue his many interests, such as horse racing and breeding, coaching, yachting, and art collecting. The only extension to his compact body is his outstretched left arm; the unfinished hand further suggests an indecisiveness or cessation in the handling of his own affairs. His sister Mary, of course, was the painter constructing the picture, but her empathetic response to her brother would have colluded with his own thoughts.

In contrast, the later 1882–83 oil portrait (private collection; Philadelphia 1985, ill. 57) projects a self-assured individual in the tradition of state portraiture. Alexander sits in a chintz-covered armchair placed before a well-ordered bookcase; his expression is thoughtful as he looks off to his left. He had, by that time, left the full-time employ of the Pennsylvania Railroad and could afford the time—twenty-eight sittings—that Cassatt took to paint his picture. His right hand is placed on his crossed leg, while the left arm stretches outside the canvas. This portrait thus renders the public side of Alexander Cassatt—a businessman with a firm grasp of issues but one who could reach into the unknown. Cassatt, however, in a letter to Alexander of October 14, 1883, confessed that she much preferred the earlier Detroit version and explained her delay in sending the second: "I like much better the head I painted of you at Marly, & I could not bear to send you a poor thing" (Philadelphia 1985, 58).

Two years later Cassatt painted the double portrait *Alexander Cassatt and His Son Robert* (1884–85; Philadelphia Museum of Art; Philadelphia 1985, ill. 59). Alexander had now settled into a role of greater domesticity, and he had the freedom to make a short visit to Paris with his eleven-year-old son for the express purpose of visiting his mother. Robert presses his face against that of his father and wraps his arm around the father's neck. Both Robert's hands are directed toward his father's hands, which hold a newspaper. Both focus their eyes off the canvas. The intimacy between father and son—with the son echoing the demeanor of the father—suggests the bonds that come when a scion is groomed to assume the mantle of his father's business acumen. The three oil portraits together form an image of Alexander as a complex man—an introspective, a public, and a family man.

P. H.

Provenance Robert Cassatt. Cassatt family. Acquired in 1986.

Exhibitions Philadelphia 1931, no. 4. New York 1966, no. 18.

References Breeskin 1970, 74, no. 126. Philadelphia 1985, 57–58, fig. 15a. *BDIA* 1988.

11

Women Admiring a Child, 1897

(Femmes et enfant)

Pastel

66 × 81.3 cm (26 × 32 in.)

Gift of Edward Chandler Walker (08.8)

The mid-1890s marked a turning point for Mary Cassatt; it was a high point in terms of her public reputation, and her domestic arrangements changed. Following the exhibition of her mural

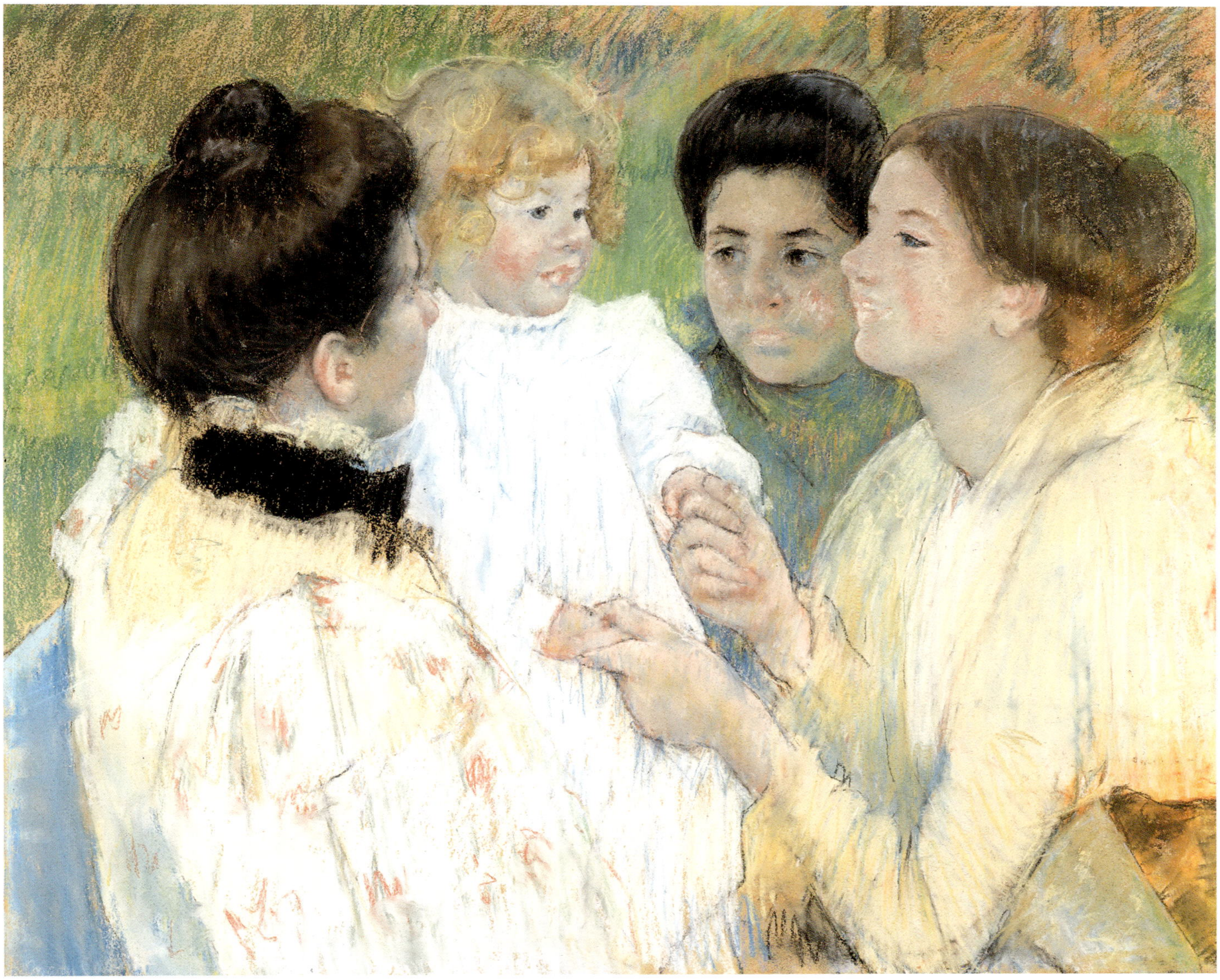

Wo-nen Admiring a Child

Modern Women at the World's Columbian Exposition in Chicago in 1893, the Paris dealer Durand-Ruel mounted a major exhibition of her work. Two years later Durand-Ruel arranged a second major exhibition at his gallery in New York.

Between these two events, in 1894, she purchased a seventeenth-century manor house, the Château de Beaufresne at Mesnil-Théribus in Oise, some fifty miles northwest of Paris. The effort to remodel it to a standard that would bring comfort to herself and her elderly mother brought her vexations she had not anticipated. She despaired of the workmen and at one point contemplated selling the house, to be rid of the problems.

It is not surprising that following the urgency to complete paintings for the two shows and her settling into new summer quarters, she might take up the intimate and rewarding medium of pastel, which could easily accommodate outdoor sittings. There, at Beaufresne, surrounded by young country women and their children, she turned her attention with increasing frequency to the theme she had begun in the early 1880s, that of the interaction of mothers and children. The pastels she did during the 1890s are among her best.

Nancy Mowll Mathews has noted that the child in *Women Admiring a Child* appears in several compositions at this time, including the aquatint *Under the Horse Chestnut Tree* (ca. 1896; Metropolitan Museum of Art, New York; Mathews 1987, 113). Held by one young woman, presumably her mother, the child in Detroit's picture looks at another young woman holding her hands while a third looks on. The blond child in her white dress contrasts with the darker-haired women and their tinted dresses. It is a touching image of the nurturing of a child with love, play, and attention.

Cassatt uses the pastel medium to advantage to give an impression of a daily, seemingly incidental happening. She deploys the crayon in a number of ways. For the background, she places light and dark strokes of different colors to form a mosaic of color; for flat areas of color, for instance, the pale yellow bib of the woman's dress on the left, she applies the pastel with an up-and-down scrubbing stroke. The impressionist touch, however, has been modified when she uses a darker color to outline the hands and features of the figures. A firm structure, articulated by such outlining, always forms the basis of Cassatt's compositions.

As an enthusiast of pastel, she studied older examples in the museums in Paris. She also found time to visit the museum at Saint-Quentin to study the pastels of the eighteenth-century artist Maurice Quentin de La Tour, of whose work she was particularly fond. Before a day trip to Saint-Quentin in February 1896, she wrote to Eugénie Heller that "he was an artist, most simple most sincere, no 'brio,' no facility of execution, but his portraits are living & full of character" (Mathews 1984, 263). Later, when she was named honorary president of the Paris Art League, an organization that ran a hostel for American girl students, she offered two scholarships with the condition that the recipients spend a year in Saint-Quentin studying the seventeenth- and eighteenth-century French pastelists (Hale 1975, 198).

P. H.

Inscription At lower left, *Mary Cassatt*

Provenance Edward Chandler Walker. Acquired in 1908.

Exhibitions West Palm Beach 1953. Buffalo et al. 1976.

References *BDMA* 1909. Detroit 1930, no. 275. Breeskin 1970, no. 272. Rivard 1978, 1052. Detroit 1985, 206–207. Shaw 1986, 527, pl. XVI.

12

In the Garden, 1903 or 1904

Oil on canvas
68 × 82.6 cm (26¾ × 32½ in.)
Gift of Dr. Ernest G. Stillman (22.6)

After the turn of the century, Mary Cassatt became known as the painter of mothers and children; in fact the first full-length biography of Mary Cassatt, written by Achille Segard and published in Paris in 1913, was called *Mary Cassatt, un peintre des enfants et des mères.* Women and children from the village near her country home, Château de Beaufresne, were ready models. Moreover, the pond and parklike setting of the Beaufresne grounds provided a pleasing site for light-filled studies of domestic intimacy.

The child Simone was a particular favorite, and Cassatt often dressed her in hats, such as this one of yellow straw with a black ribbon. According to the Cassatt scholar Adelyn Breeskin, a pastel version of this oil painting was in a Paris collection in the 1960s, and another pastel of the two models, with Simone sporting the same hat, belonged in 1980 to a private collector in Rochester, New York (correspondence, 1980, curatorial files, DIA). In this painting Simone holds a dark red rose, while a woman, presumably her mother, dressed in a white dress with splashes of yellow flowers, appears to be tugging on the shoulder of the child's deep pink dress. Behind Simone the bright spots of color from the foliage of a bush beyond the path form a halo over her hat. The blue-green bench appears in a number of the Beaufresne garden scenes.

Adelyn Breeskin suggests that *In the Garden* (alternative title, *Simone and Her Mother in the Garden)* was exhibited in the famous *International Exhibition of Modern Art,* held at the 69th Regiment Armory in New York in 1913. The work was then

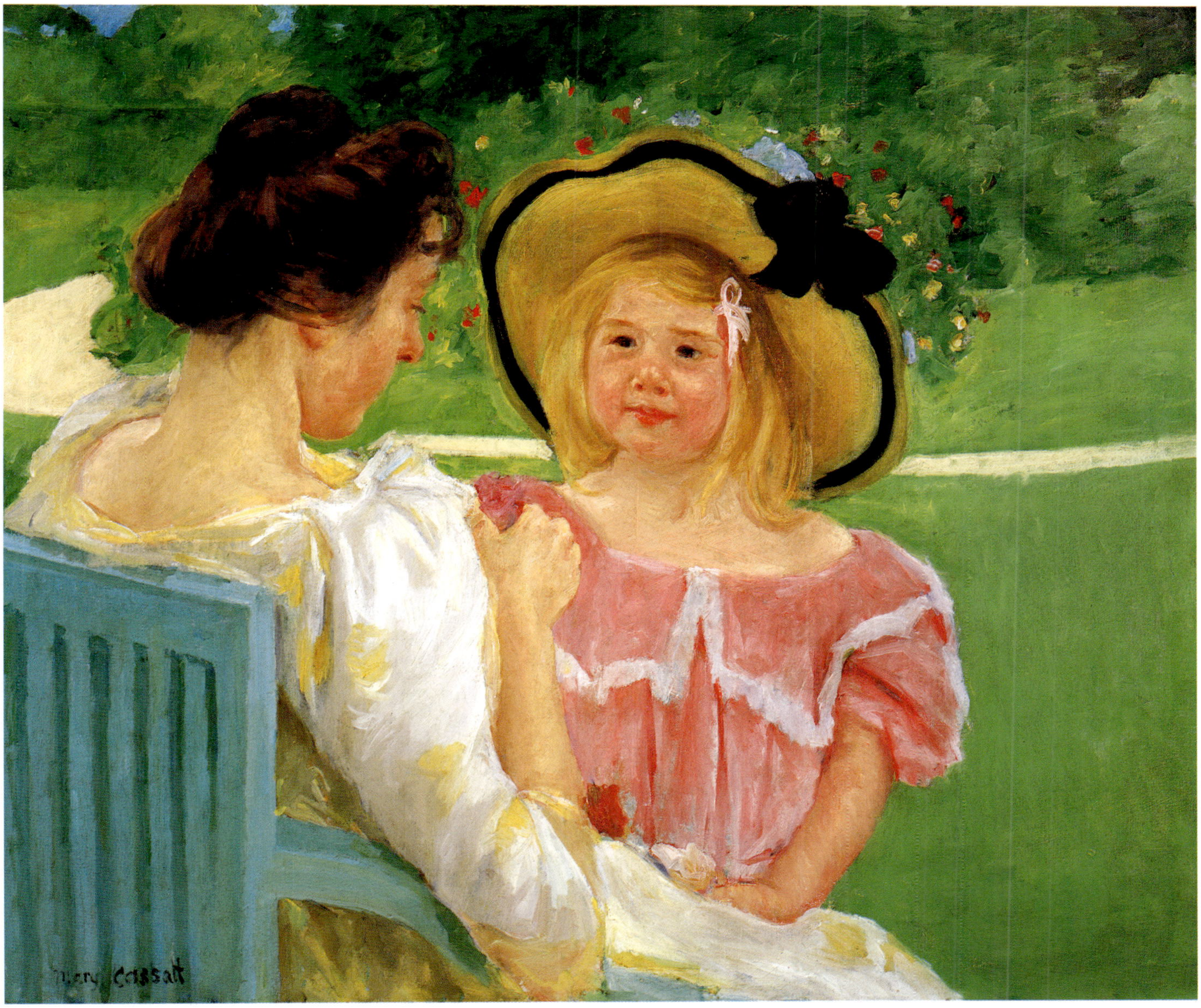

In the Garden

called *Mère et enfant* and dated 1903 (M. Brown 1988, no. 493). While Breeskin assigned a date of 1903 in her catalogue raisonné of Cassatt's work (Breeskin 1970, no. 452), in a letter to Frederick J. Cummings, dated March 18, 1980 (curatorial files, DIA), she concedes that it could well have been done in 1904.

P. H.

Inscription At lower left, *Mary Cassatt*

Provenance Durand-Ruel. Cyrus J. Lawrence; his sale, American Art Galleries, New York, 1910. James Stillman. Acquired from an anonymous donor [Dr. Ernest G. Stillman] in 1922.

Exhibitions Detroit 1922, no. 25. Grand Rapids 1955. Flint 1961. Albuquerque 1965, no. 4. Grand Rapids 1974, no. 3. Nagoya 1983, no. 55. Tokyo 1989, no. 67.

References C. Burroughs 1922. Detroit 1930, no. 276. Breeskin 1970, no. 452. M. Brown 1988, no. 493.

Frederic Edwin Church

1826 Hartford, Connecticut–New York 1900

Frederic Edwin Church was the foremost painter of the second generation of the Hudson River school. Born in Hartford, Connecticut, the young Church studied with two local artists, Benjamin H. Coe and Alexander H. Emmons, before moving to Catskill, New York, to become the first pupil of Thomas Cole. Following that period of tutelage, which lasted from mid-1844 to mid-1846, Church returned briefly to Hartford before moving to New York City, where he established himself during the winter of 1846–47.

He was soon numbered among the nation's rising artists. Over the next few years his sketching tours took him across northeastern and central southern states, from western Massachusetts (1847), southern Vermont (1848, 1849), and western New York (1848), to coastal Maine (1850), inland Virginia and Kentucky, and maritime Canada (all 1851). A sojourn during mid-1852 in the Mount Katahdin area of Maine substituted for a planned voyage to South America that year. Church did, however, reschedule the equatorial journey to 1853, accompanied by the future Atlantic telegraph entrepreneur Cyrus W. Field. In their five-month trek across Colombia and Ecuador, both men followed the footsteps of the Prussian naturalist Baron Alexander von Humboldt, who had toured Latin America a half-century earlier but whose writings remained a vital force in Western thought into the 1860s. Throughout the 1850s to the early 1860s Church revisited coastal Maine several times, and maritime Canada and inland Maine at least once. After going twice to Niagara Falls in 1856, he returned to Ecuador in 1857, this time accompanied by Louis Rémy Mignot (q.v.), then in mid-1859 he went with Louis L. Noble, Cole's biographer and former pastor, to the Labrador coast in search of icebergs.

Church used the diverse sketches from his Catskill sojourn and his subsequent journeys as ingredients for quantities of studio paintings, many but not all of which he showed at the National Academy of Design, the American Art-Union, the Pennsylvania Academy of the Fine Arts, and the Boston Athenaeum. He was already identified with South American scenery when he decided, no later than the winter of 1856–57, to exhibit his next masterwork and most ambitious canvas to date, *Niagara Falls* (1857; Corcoran Gallery of Art, Washington, D.C.), at a commercial gallery as a one-picture attraction, or "Great Picture," rather than at one of the group shows with which he had been associated. In so doing, he was following the examples of his mentor, Cole, and numerous American and European artists going back to the time of Benjamin West, John Singleton Copley, and John Trumbull. Thenceforth, Church allocated most of his major paintings, such as *The Heart of the Andes* (1859; Metropolitan Museum of Art, New York), *Twilight in the Wilderness* (1860; Cleveland Museum of Art), *The Icebergs* (1861; Dallas Museum of Art), and *Cotopaxi* (1862; cat. no. 13), as well as numbers of lesser works, to the ambiences of the "Great Picture" and the commercial gallery, while curtailing his contributions to group displays.

His marriage in 1860 to Isabel Mortimer Carnes of Dayton, Ohio, settled Church down. Thereafter he endeavored to convert a functioning farm he purchased near Hudson, New York, located not coincidentally across the Hudson River from the town of Catskill, into a family homestead. Now and then, however, he managed to undertake extended trips, notably to the island of Jamaica (1865) after the sudden deaths of the couple's first two children, and to Europe and the Near East (1867–69). Accompanied by colleagues and at least once by Mrs. Church, he revisited the Mount Katahdin region five times during the late 1870s and early 1880s. Meanwhile, during the early and mid-1870s, while painting a sequence of Near Eastern and Mediterranean subjects such as *Syria by the Sea* (1873; cat. no. 14) and tropical scenes, he designed and helped supervise the construction of a sizable Near Eastern–style house, which he and his wife eventually christened Olana, on a hilltop site above his farm; he had the building considerably enlarged, again to his own specifications, between 1888 and 1891. Taken over by New York State in 1966, the property, including the house and its contents, now comprises a public park and museum.

Over the last two decades of his life, although increasingly debilitated by rheumatism that sharply reduced his artistic output, Church was able to travel to Mexico fourteen times, largely for reasons of health and often in the company of family, friends, and colleagues. Although comparatively few in number, the best of his Mexican sketches rival his earlier ones in terms of dexterity and vigor. While in Mexico during November 1899, he reportedly pondered a resumption of work at his easel, but his final datable paintings and drawings are from two years earlier, the winter of 1897–98.

Church's reputation reached its zenith around 1860, the year of his marriage. Contemporaries called him "America's greatest artist" and exulted in his successes and in his exacting yet facile and adaptable technical ability, which, under favorable circumstances, could have gained him prominence as a painter of animals and perhaps of figural subjects, as well as of landscapes. His sketches made in the Mediterranean, the studio paintings he developed from them, and his work with Olana demonstrate his proficiency with architectural rendering and composition. In this last regard he was belatedly returning to the example of his master, Cole, while also filtering that sensibility through his (Church's) personal predispositions toward the natural sciences and surface realism, and his newfound respect for the old masters.

Although he was revered in Mexico during the 1890s, Church's reputation was largely eclipsed among his compatriots by the time he died in New York City on April 7, 1900. The modern rehabilitation of that standing was accomplished by the late David C. Huntington, who spearheaded efforts to preserve Olana and whose 1966 monograph on the artist revolutionized study of the Hudson River school.

G. C.

Bibliography Huntington 1960. Huntington 1966. Carr 1980. Washington 1985. Kelly and Carr 1987. Kelly 1988. Washington 1989. Carr 1994.

13
Cotopaxi, 1862

Oil on canvas
121.9 × 215.9 cm (48 × 85 in.)
Founders Society Purchase, Robert H. Tannahill Foundation Fund, Gibbs-Williams Fund, Dexter M. Ferry, Jr., Fund, Merrill Fund, Beatrice W. Rogers Fund, and Richard A. Manoogian Fund (76.89)

A SELF-SUFFICIENT WORK sometimes regarded as Frederic Edwin Church's masterpiece, the museum's painting of the Ecuadorian volcano Cotopaxi (elev. 19,347 ft.) occupies two broader contexts in the artist's oeuvre. On the one hand it culminated a sequence of studio compositions of the subject commenced while he was traveling in South America in 1853, and on the other hand it was conceived as part of an ambitious trilogy of South America, also comprising *The Heart of the Andes* and *Chimborazo* (1864; The Huntington Library, San Marino, Calif.), produced after his second trip to Ecuador in 1857. Commissioned in 1861 by the New York philanthropist and bibliophile James A. Lenox (1800–1880) and completed by December 1862, *Cotopaxi* augmented Lenox's considerable art collection already noteworthy for Thomas Cole's *Expulsion from the Garden of Eden* (1828; Museum of Fine Arts, Boston) and for two major works by J. M. W. Turner, *Staffa, Fingal's Cave* (1832; Yale Center for British Art, New Haven, Conn.) and *Fort Vimieux* (1831; private collection, England). Between March and April 1863 John McClure, Church's agent and publisher of Scottish descent, had *Cotopaxi* exhibited in New York; three years later, McClure sent the painting to London, where it was shown during the summer of 1865 and where work leading to an engraving (never finished; see below) was begun. When Lenox's art holdings were opened to view at the Lenox Library (later the New York Public Library) in January 1877, *Cotopaxi* resurfaced for regular public viewing. Since the mid-1960s the painting has appeared frequently in displays of American art in general and of Church's work in particular, and in 1985 (see Washington 1985) it was the centerpiece of an exhibition devoted to the artist's drawings and paintings of Cotopaxi.

Nearing the end of his first trip to South America, in August 1853, as his few extant sketches (Cooper-Hewitt National Design Museum, New York) of the subject demonstrate, Church had viewed the snow-crested Cotopaxi at differing distances and times of day and under varied meteorological conditions. Notwithstanding that Baron Alexander von Humboldt had endorsed it as one of the world's most active and most perfectly shaped volcanoes, the mountain managed only modest discharges of steam while Church observed it. After the artist departed its vicinity but while he was still in Ecuador, however, it commenced a prolonged sequence of escalated eruptions, of which he was not fully aware until he returned four years later. Then, as his newer sketches (Cooper-Hewitt National Design Museum and Olana State Historic Site, Hudson, N.Y.) show, the whitened cone was still venting turgid columns of dark smoke mixed with steam that drifted slowly toward the right (south) from his vantage point.

The sketches of 1857 became the raw materials for the present painting, the third canvas of medium-to-large size by Church of equatorial themes, after *Cayambe* (1858; New-York Historical Society) and *The Heart of the Andes,* developed from his second journey to South America. The distant peak, its surface faintly glistening with snow, is depicted in the finished canvas much as he saw it, though the slope of the cone and volume of smoky discharge are amplified. The foreground of the completed *Cotopaxi* is a contrivance, however: a pair of preparatory drawings on recto and verso of one sheet (ca. 1861; private collection) and an oil study dated 1861 (Nelson H. White collection) indicate that Church composed the features of that area intuitively, referring to several of his previous paintings, including *The Heart of the Andes,* for the placement and configuration of the waterfall at lower middle.

The rising, reddened sun burning through the smoke and brightly reflected on the lake surface at the right is—considering Lenox's existing holdings—deliberately suggestive both of Turner's art and of the hue and internal illumination of molten lava. Looking more closely, much of the middle of the scene appears to have been pressed downward by an immense force, while the section at the right immediately beneath the sun almost begins to melt and glow like lava, although no lava is depicted anywhere. Much of the far distance, middle distance, and parts of the foreground are barren, but the misty waterfall suggests fertility, the plain at the far left is flecked with low green vegetation, and there are green trees at the lower left and atop the ridges at middle right. At the lower left, a single figure wearing colorful Hispanic clothing and accompanied by a llama adds the lone human touch to the scene, while the flight of birds at the lower right plunges the viewer's eye into space. The

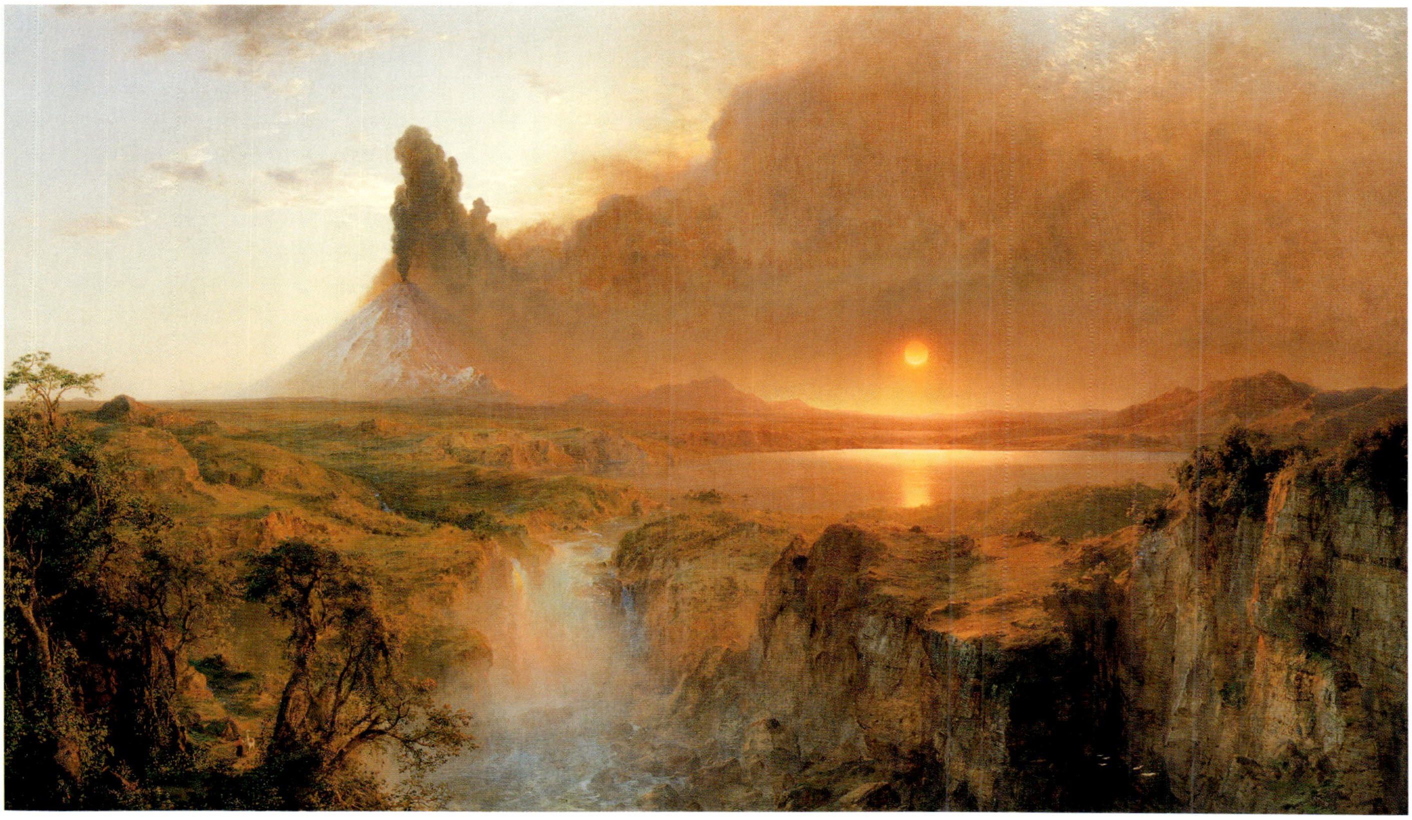

Cotopaxi

effect of aerial perspective in the sky above is among the artist's best.

The first clear mention of the Detroit *Cotopaxi* occurs in a letter from John McClure sent to Church from 100 Buchanan St., Glasgow (Scotland), and dated September 10, 1861 (David C. Huntington Archives, Olana State Historic Site): "I suppose you have either begun or are about to begin the picture for Mr Lennox [*sic*], I hope that it will do for a companion plate to the [Heart of the] Andes—and that you will have it ready for exhibition either in N.Y. or London in the Spring." The earliest published report evidently is that in the *New York Evening Post* of September 21, 1861: "Mr. Lenox, who has one of the finest private galleries in the country, has given Church a commission for a $5000 picture. We have not heard the subject stated." The next mention of the work likewise appeared in the *Evening Post* (January 30, 1862): "Church has on his easel another South American scene, if not so large, corresponding in its general character with his 'Heart of the Andes,'—one of those views which combine[s] so many elements of beauty and power, and so fitted in their amplitude to his genius." A few weeks later, the *New York Daily Tribune* (March 3, 1862) offered some details:

> Mr. Church is now engaged on a large landscape for Mr. Lennox [*sic*] of Fifth Avenue, which offers a very striking contrast to his last work, the Icebergs. It is a view of a volcanic mountain near Quito, in South America. The subject is full of grandeur, and the picture promises, in its present state even, to be one of his greatest achievements.

Further notices of the in-progress painting appeared in the *Boston Daily Evening Transcript* (July 17, 1862; December 2, 1862). In the earlier article, the Boston paper's well-informed New York correspondent (perhaps Henry Theodore Tuckerman) characterized the picture as "perhaps more startling and original than any previous work by this distinguished painter" and described "sullen, sombre clouds of smoke [that] roll off to the right, through which shines the setting [*sic*] sun like the great eye of some Cyclopean monster." The same writer began his later report by stating that the painting, "a masterpiece [that] would have delighted Humboldt from its scientific accuracy and detail," was finished.

Under McClure's auspices, the completed canvas was exhibited the following spring at Goupil's (later Knoedler's) Gallery, New York, as a single-picture attraction, or "Great Picture," to use the parlance of the day. Visitors to the display, which took place at the height of the Civil War, were handed a one-sheet broadside (copies at Olana State Historic Site and New York Public Library), which emphasized the volcano itself and its history of explosive activity, and which remarked of the painting merely that it resulted from "studies made in the summer of 1857." The handout concluded with McClure's "Proposals for Publication," an engraving "in the highest manner of line by William Forrest, [to] correspond with his masterly engraving of 'THE HEART OF THE ANDES.'" A fuller discussion of the painting by the Reverend Louis Legrand Noble, Thomas Cole's former pastor and biographer who had authored a pamphlet (1859) for the inaugural exhibitions of *The Heart of the Andes,* and who wrote an eyewitness book-length narrative, *After Icebergs with a Painter* (1861), to commemorate Church's voyage to Labrador in mid-1859, was set aside in favor of the shorter explanation. Noble's text, which survives in a handwritten copy (Olana State Historic Site; reprinted in Washington 1985, 60–64), championed *Cotopaxi* from artistic as well as geographic standpoints.

The Goupil's showing was a mixed success. Most metropolitan and out-of-town journalists praised the artist extravagantly, while Church informed his father, Joseph Church, that McClure was "doing finely with the Cotopaxi—better than he has done with any picture" (Church to Joseph Church, New York, March 1863; David C. Huntington Archives, Olana State Historic Site). Yet three New York writers ("Fine Arts. Mr. Church's 'Cotopaxi,'" *New York Herald,* March 16, 1863; "Art. Mr. Church and His Painting of the Volcano of Cotopaxi," *New York Commercial Advertiser,* March 21, 1863; "Art Feuilleton. By Atticus. Church's 'Cotopaxi,'" *New York Leader,* March 28, 1863), in long paragraphs unlike all but a few to which he had been subjected in his adoptive city since his ascendancy to "Great Picture" heights, sharply criticized both the painting and the artist. An important contemporaneous canvas by Church of smaller dimensions, *Coast Scene, Mount Desert* (1863; Wadsworth Atheneum, Hartford, Conn.), which focuses on a bright sun thinly veiled by clouds à la Turner and which he submitted concurrently to the National Academy of Design after several years' virtual absence from its annual exhibitions, generated but few favorable responses in the press.

Hence, Church's and McClure's hopes probably were riding high two years later, when *Cotopaxi* opened at Thomas McLean's Gallery in London, alongside Church's *Chimborazo* and *Aurora Borealis* (1865; National Museum of American Art, Washington, D.C.), and works by two compatriots, *The Bison Bull at Bay* (1865; Glenbow Institute, Calgary), a large canvas by Church's New York colleague and friend, William Jacob Hays, and five plaster statuette groups of Civil War subjects by John Rogers. Advertisements for the exhibition gave Church's paintings top billing and described *Cotopaxi* and *Chimborazo* as "pendants" to *The Heart of the Andes.* Altogether the McLean's exhibit generated more than twenty reviews in the local press, some very favorable, at least three of which *(London Times,* June 28, 1865; *Reader,* 1865; *Art Journal,* 1865) were reprinted in the United States. One of the most perceptive British notices was that in the *London Illustrated Times* (July 22, 1865), whose art writer referred to *Cotopaxi* as "a masterpiece on which Church might well rest his reputation":

> It is impossible to look at this picture without feeling an almost insurmountable desire to see with our own eyes so awful a revelation of the grandeur of creation as this seemingly boundless plain, with its distant chain of mountains, which are all of stupendous height, but which yet shrink to dwarfs beside the Titanic proportions of Cotopaxi, whose flaming head seems almost to touch the sky.

But in general the London critics took notice more slowly than they had during four prior exhibits of Church's work in the British capital between 1857 and 1863; there, too, his star was beginning to fade.

Thomas McLean, an eminent art publisher-dealer and proprietor of the London gallery that bore his name, was well positioned to assist Church's and McClure's cause. Beginning a decade earlier, McLean had commissioned John Martin's monumental *Last Judgment* triptych (1853f.; Tate Gallery, London), had organized a multicity British and American tour of Martin's three paintings, and had successfully overseen the manufacture of large, high-quality engravings of the whole series. Still, none of the printed reproductions of Church's three canvases shown in 1865 came to fruition. William Forrest, Scotland's premier reproductive engraver of the day, whose folio-size engraving of *The Heart of the Andes* was well received in Britain and the United States in 1862 and 1863, labored for years on the plate of *Cotopaxi* before abandoning it; the other prints may not have been begun.

The painting itself, meanwhile, retained its reputation in the United States through the 1860s, judging by a writer of late 1868 *(Galaxy* 1868) who distinctly favored Church's six-year-old masterpiece over Albert Bierstadt's recent *Mount Vesuvius at Midnight* (1868; unlocated), then on display at Putnam's Gallery, New York. Church, the critic recalled,

> gave us a vast expanse of plain, across which the eye glanced with the quickness of light to the great cone of the volcano rising majestically above the far horizon, and dominating every object in the scene. From its summit shot upward a vast column of flame [*sic*] and smoke and ashes, rising to its utmost height, and falling backward and spreading out over the land. The effect was majestic, and there was in the picture no disturbing element. The reflection in the lake, repeating the magnificent spectacle in the distance, adds to its grandeur and impressiveness.

But by the late 1870s, when James Lenox's entire collection was opened to public view, *Cotopaxi* had suffered widespread devaluation; those local commentators who referred to it at that juncture (e.g., *New York Daily Tribune,* January 20, 1877) did so only in passing. Following the artist's death, the canvas, not included in his memorial exhibition held at the Metropolitan Museum of Art, was scorned by a contemporary writer *(Art Interchange* 1900), who cited it as an example of the era's "thin manner and scenic style, the same absence of true quality and lasting beauty." Even so, eleven years later, after Lenox's holdings were moved to the new New York Public Library, one local journalist (Walton 1911, 638) cited the "big" painting as "an imposing and most original conception carried out with great skill and infinite care." The modern reassessment of *Cotopaxi* was accomplished by David C. Huntington during the 1960s.

Besides the compositional oil study already mentioned (Nelson H. White collection), several other paintings of Cotopaxi by or partially by Church dating from the 1860s, and at least one copy not by Church of the Detroit *Cotopaxi,* are extant. In mid-1863, at McClure's behest and using Church's studio in New York, De Witt Clinton Boutelle, a landscapist from eastern Pennsylvania, made an authorized replica of Lenox's painting, with which Church was dissatisfied and which, as a result, he subsequently retouched before it was sent to Edinburgh. That work, presumably the unsigned canvas now in the Reading (Pennsylvania) Museum, enabled the engraver, William Forrest, to proceed with the plate in Edinburgh; eventually the Boutelle-Church version was returned to the United States. Toward the end of 1864 Church himself painted a South American scene with a smoking Cotopaxi in the distance for an album (Century Association, New York; see Washington 1985, 56, 75) presented in November 1864 to William Cullen Bryant on his seventieth birthday; Church's contribution was publicly recognized in the *New York Evening Post* (January 16, 1865). Around 1865 Church produced three or more small variants (private collections; see Washington 1985, 49, 55, 75–76) of the Detroit composition, at least one of which remained in his possession; and in 1867 he painted another small, quieter reprise of the subject (Yale University Art Gallery, New Haven, Conn.; see Washington 1985, 77), which was shown without fanfare at Goupil's Gallery during the spring of 1867. A small, unfinished canvas by Church (ca. late 1860s; Olana State Historic Site; see Carr 1992, 30–32; Carr 1994, 1:346–348), in which a strongly erupting, snowcapped volcano is stationed in the upper right corner, derives from both the last-named work and the more active *Cotopaxi* of 1862, and perhaps from a sighting by Church in 1869 of Mount Vesuvius. The sizable replica of the

1862 *Cotopaxi* formerly at the Chrysler Museum, Norfolk, Virginia, has an uncertain provenance and in any event cannot be Church's handiwork.

G. C.

Inscription At lower right, *F.E. CHURCH / 1862*

Provenance James Lenox, New York, 1862–80. Lenox Library (later New York Public Library), New York, 1877–1945. M. Knoedler and Co., New York, 1945. John Astor, New York, 1945–76. Hirschl & Adler Galleries, New York, 1976. Acquired in 1976.

Exhibitions Goupil & Co. (M. Knoedler & Co.), New York, March–April 1863. Thomas McLean and Company Gallery, London, June–September 1865. Lenox Library (later New York Public Library), New York, January 1877f. New York 1943, no. 49. Memphis 1945, no. 23. Oberlin 1946, no. 10. Washington et al. 1966, no. 82. New York 1970, no. 107. Dallas 1971, no. 24. New York 1976, no. 29. Boston et al. 1978, 24–25. Boston et al. 1983, 248–249, no. 45. Washington 1985, 7, 25–27, 73–74, no. 10. New York 1987, 254–257. Washington 1989, 61, 112, no. 36.

References Goupil's Gallery, New York, "Cotopaxi: Painted by Frederic E. Church[,] From Studies Made in the Summer of 1857," broadside, March 1863, 4. "Cotopaxi Exhibition a/c / Sundry expenses," MS, ca. 1863, Olana State Historic Site. *New York Herald,* March 16, 1863, 4. *Journal of Commerce,* March 17, 1863, 2. *New York Leader,* March 21, 1863, 1. *Harper's Weekly,* April 4, 1863, 210. *London Observer,* June 18, 1865, 6. *London Weekly Times,* June 18, 1865, 5. *London Daily News,* June 19, 1865, 7. *London Review* 1865, 662. *London Morning Star,* June 26, 1865, 5. *London Evening Star,* June 26, 1865, 4. *London Daily Telegraph,* June 28, 1865, 3. Tom Taylor, in *London Times,* June 28, 1865, 6. *Bell's Weekly Messenger* (London), July 1, 1865, 3 (a reprise of the *Times*'s notice). *Art Journal* 1865. *Illustrated London News,* July 8, 1865, 18. *Reader* 1865. *London Sunday Times,* July 9, 1865, 2. *Court Journal* (London), July 15, 1865, 712. *London Morning Post,* July 21, 1865, 6. *London Standard,* August 1, 1865, 3. [Palgrave] 1865. *Art Journal* 1865a. Bayley 1865. *Art Interchange* 1900, 12. Walton 1911, 638. Richardson 1944, 29. Huntington 1960, 111–114. Huntington 1966, 10–20, 47–49. Wallach 1976, 30, 35. Rivard 1978, 1049. Rivard 1978a. Heslip 1978. Carr 1980, 62, 66. Talbot 1980, 153, 156. Detroit 1985, 198–199. Shaw 1986, 69, 72–73. Minks 1989, 100–101. Carr 1994, 1:239–241. Davis 1996, 174–175.

14
Syria by the Sea, 1873

Oil on canvas

142.2 × 215.9 cm (56 × 85 in.)

Gift of Mrs. James F. Joy, 1910 (10.11)

Purchased at an early date and possibly commissioned by James Frederick Joy (1810–1896) of Detroit, *Syria by the Sea* was Church's fourth work of large size of a Mediterranean subject, following *Damascus* (1869; destroyed), *Jerusalem* (1870; Nelson-Atkins Museum, Kansas City, Mo.), and *The Parthenon* (1871; Metropolitan Museum of Art, New York). In each of these paintings and the one of comparable size that succeeded *Syria by the Sea, El Khasné Petra* (1874; Olana State Historic Site, Hudson, N.Y.), the artist portrayed a site of venerable human habitation which he had observed during his recent tour of the Near East and Europe. With the Detroit work, however, he revived a generalized approach to architectural themes—the capriccio—developed by European artists during the Renaissance and further defined by their successors (Claude Lorrain, Giovanni Paolo Panini, J. M. W. Turner, and Church's teacher, Thomas Cole, among many others) from the seventeenth through the mid–nineteenth centuries. In so doing, Church also reverted to the methodology he himself had used in some of his earliest paintings of Near Eastern themes, notably that now called *Ruins at Baalbek* (1868; private collection), the first sizable work reflecting his Mediterranean travels, and another canvas that bore two titles in Church's day, *The Valley of the Lebanon* (alternatively, *Anti-Lebanon;* 1869; private collection), which was exhibited several times in New York and Chicago between 1869 and the mid-1870s.

The present title of the Detroit painting, the principal one of two alternates it bore at its maiden showing in December 1873 (see below) and probably Church's verbal invention, indicates what he had in mind: the scene is evocative of the locale without being a portrait of a particular place. Moreover, neither the ruins in the foreground nor the Crusader castle in the left distance apparently depict actual objects. Instead, they and the composition as a whole are meant to re-create the development, dissolution, and varied essences of centuries-old human civilizations from ancient Rome onward in the southern Mediterranean.

The scene is set in a bay or arm of the sea ringed by distant low mountains. In the central middle distance toward the left, a promontory descends abruptly to a steep hill toward the right, while uneven eminences of smaller dimensions extend across the right middle ground and foreground. As a whole the geography is rocky, forbidding, and desolate, yet the surfaces are also eroded, with few sharp edges; vegetation is limited to sparsely scattered trees and sprigs of growth clinging to the artificial ruins.

The last are clustered toward the near right. With two conspicuous exceptions they comprise a detritus of cyclopean

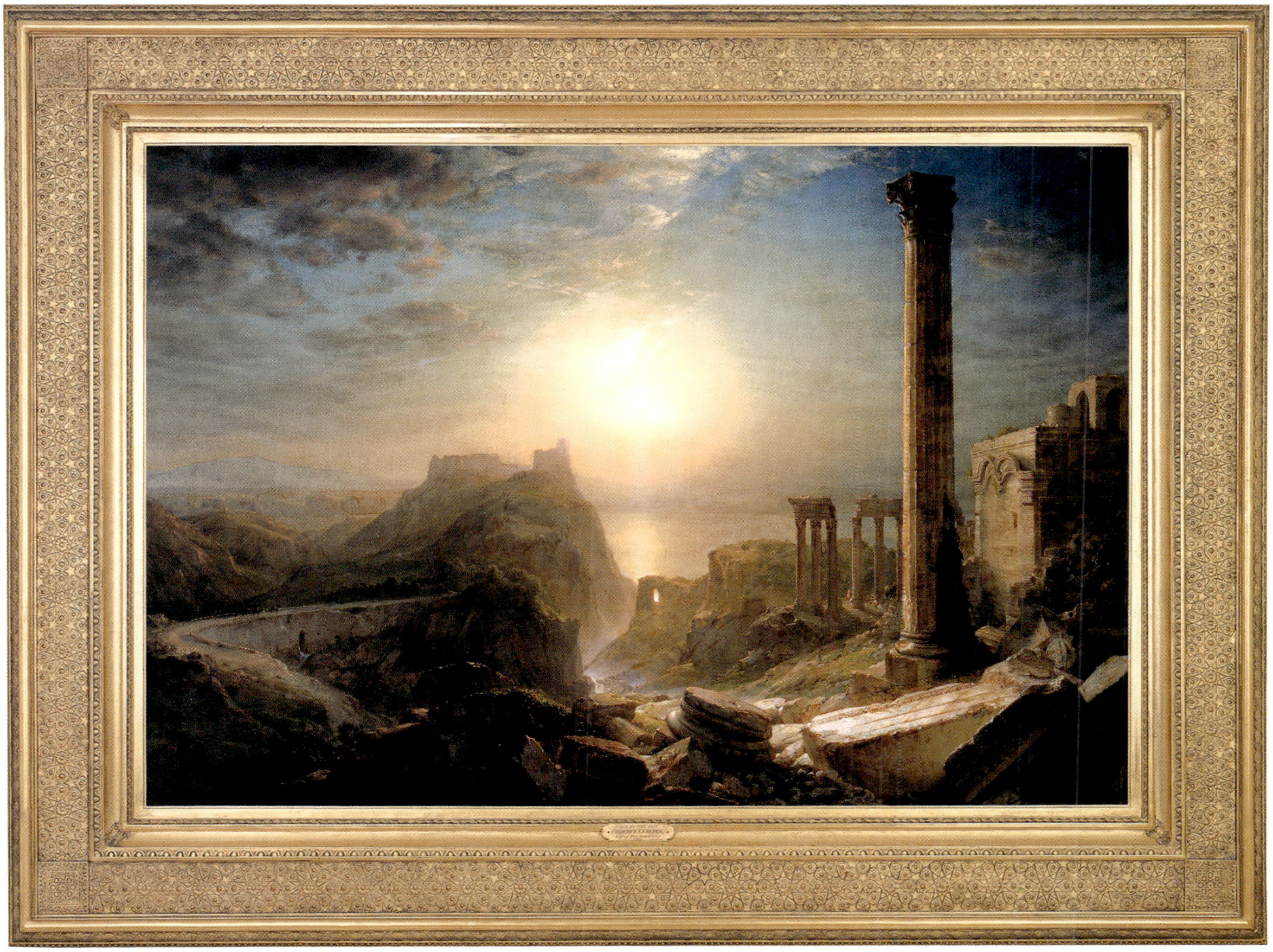

Syria by the Sea

walls and fragmentary columns and entablatures, most or all of the latter of imperial Roman character. Conceivably, the large column base at middle right (the column itself evidently unfluted) and the fallen fluted column fragment toward the right could be construed as Greek, but they, too, are logically Roman. Somewhat paradoxically, the single most prominent object, the tall, elegant fluted Corinthian column at middle right reaching nearly to the top of the canvas, brings to mind the northern rather than the southern Mediterranean, specifically the column of Phocas on the Forum Romanum, of which Church owned at least two photographs (Olana State Historic Site) and of which he painted an oil study (Cooper-Hewitt National Design Museum, New York). Farther away and oriented at right angles to one another, groups of three and six (two of them hidden) unfluted Corinthian columns supporting entablatures resemble the colossal remnants of Baalbek in Lebanon, to which Church and his wife paid a visit during May 1868, and of which he made a number of drawings and oil studies (Cooper-Hewitt National Design Museum and Olana State Historic Site) and purchased a number of photographs (Olana State Historic Site). To a lesser extent the same fragments also are reminiscent of those at Palmyra, which Church planned to visit in 1868 although for unknown reasons did not, but of which he managed to acquire about two dozen photographs (Olana State Historic Site). Preceding the column groups spatially but not chronologically is the compact walled structure at the far right. Hemmed in by rubble but in better repair and obviously newer than its antique surroundings, it exhibits a blend of blind round arches (on the left wall) and full pointed arches (in the turret) characteristic of Islamic architecture of the southern Mediterranean.

At a lower elevation in the middle distance, a single-arch structure suggests a crumbled gateway or aqueduct, although an analogy to a natural arch—such as that which Church first observed in Virginia in 1851 and painted one year later (Bayly Art Museum, University of Virginia, Charlottesville)—is doubtless intentional. The reflected light streaming through the opening recalls features in some compositions by Church's mentor, Cole, and, in turn, selected specimens of Church's own prior oeuvre, in particular *The After Glow* (1867; Olana State Historic Site). Separated by a chasm of time and dispensation as well as of geology, the Crusader castle perched atop the promontory toward the left, though evidently decayed, is nevertheless accessible via a sturdy, curving thoroughfare—the only artificial artery in the scene—at the left, traversed by a modest camel caravan. The overall theme, a meditation on the architectural past, and through it, Old World human history in general, brings to mind Cole's *Architect's Dream* (1840; Toledo Museum of Art), and especially *Desolation* from Cole's series *The Course of Empire* (1836; New-York Historical Society), which Church later declared he admired above all paintings in the world.

The foremost natural feature of the Detroit picture is the bright sun hovering in a hazy, seemingly motionless sky crested by fleecy clouds; in turn, the sun is strongly reflected by the glassy water surface below. Bathing the entire scene in an amber light at once suggestive of late afternoon, of paintings by Claude and Turner, of discolored varnish on old-master paintings, and of archival parchment, the radiance eradicates colors while almost obliging the spectator to shield his or her eyes. From the outset of his career and especially since the mid-1850s with *The Cordilleras: Sunrise* (1854; Hirschl & Adler Galleries, New York) and *The Andes of Ecuador* (1855; Reynolda House, Winston-Salem, N.C.), Church occasionally had contrived daringly bright illumination effects in his studio paintings similar to those in Turner's works. By 1861 Church had become acquainted with the two Turner canvases owned by James Lenox (see cat. no. 13), and while passing through London in late 1867 he reportedly sought out works by Turner. With *Syria by the Sea* the affinity to Turner may well have been reinforced by the British master's *Slave Ship* (R.A. 1840; Museum of Fine Arts, Boston), formerly owned by John Ruskin, which arrived in New York in 1872. A controversial painting for years thereafter among art critics in the United States, *The Slave Ship* nevertheless elicited a favorable response from Church (Sherwood 1900), whose precise style generally contrasts to Turner's legendary looseness. One may wonder if Church intended *Syria by the Sea* as a correction of sorts to Turner's *Slave Ship*.

Church explored the thematic implications of *Syria by the Sea* in smaller studio paintings of approximately concurrent date. In one such work, recently (erroneously) called *Landscape in Greece* (1873; Sotheby Parke-Bernet, New York, April 25, 1980, lot 26), columnar and walled ruins are grouped at the near left, while at the right the scene opens to a calm sea and a late afternoon sun warm in tone and blinding in its brightness. Another painting, now entitled *Mediterranean Castle* (1873; private collection), also tinted yellow-orange throughout, evokes while it transforms Cole's scenes of Italian Roman ruins. A third kindred work, currently entitled *Syrian Landscape* (1868 or ca. 1872/73–75; Reading [Pa.] Museum), mixes Roman ruins derived from those of the southern Mediterranean (including Baalbek and Petra) and from Urbs Roma (the Temple of Venus and Roma) with a Crusader fortress and modern Arab inhabitants, all distributed around a rugged inlet illuminated by both a setting sun—this time positioned behind the spectator—and a full moon rising over the water.

Little is now known about either Church's relationship with James F. Joy or the latter's propensities as an art collector, or exactly when or under what circumstances Joy acquired *Syria by the Sea*. On the one hand, it is perhaps conceivable that Joy, an important figure in Detroit politics and society during the late nineteenth century, and during the mid-1870s the leading advocate of a proposed bridge or tunnel between Detroit and Windsor, Ontario, was not the first owner of the painting, although in that case *Syria by the Sea* would stand as the only major work by Church for which the initial purchaser has not been identified. On the other hand, two pieces of presumably reliable evidence specify Joy's ownership of the painting at an early date. First, Henry Willard French, who consulted Church while compiling his (French's) book *Art and Artists in Connecticut*, published in 1879, states (p. 130) that "Syria by the Sea" was painted "for James F. Joy, Detroit." Second, in a letter of late 1885 to John Denison Champlin, who was then compiling a dictionary of American art, Church himself noted that "Syria by the Sea" was owned by "James F. Joy–Detroit—," although the painter was uncertain about the date of the work (Church to John D. Champlin, 32 Park Ave., New York, November 6, 1885; copy, Olana State Historic Site). Proceeding on the assumption that French's and Church's data are essentially correct, linkages between Joy and Church and a context for Joy's interest in Mediterranean antiquities can be reasonably inferred.

The root conjecture concerns Joy's profession. A remarkably energetic railway pioneer and executive, he was closely involved with (among others) the Chicago, Burlington, and Quincy, the Burlington and Missouri, the Illinois Central, and the Michigan Central roads. As it happened, one of Church's closest friends and his principal patron for many years, William Henry Osborn, was also director of the Illinois Central railroad from 1854 to 1876; Osborn brokered useful contacts for Church at home and abroad and helped smooth his path in various ways. Hence, Church and Joy may well have become acquainted through Osborn; at minimum, Osborn probably helped further the two men's relationship. Moreover, as were Church and Osborn, Joy was an ardent Unionist during the Civil War, and Joy's second wife was born in Hartford, Connecticut, Church's hometown.

In addition, Joy traveled in Europe, as did Church and Osborn, and over the years Joy amassed a large library comprising "the best editions of the French, English, Latin, and Greek classics" *(Detroit Evening News,* September 24, 1896). His contemporaries testified that he had reading fluency in multiple languages including Latin. One of his obituary writers described him as "a scholar" who "loved a good book" *(Detroit Evening News,* September 24, 1896), while another summarized him as "a man of large ability, a great reader, well informed, a thorough Calvinist and a stanch Puritan" *(New York Daily Tribune,* September 25, 1896). As already noted, Joy's interests in the visual arts are difficult to assess today, in part due to his public reticence about his private life, but he and his second wife were both instrumental in organizing the "Detroit Art Loan" exhibition of September to November 1883, an event that led directly to the founding of the Detroit Museum of Art, afterward the Detroit Institute of Arts. On balance, Joy looks to have been an archetypal Church patron. Joy's widow donated *Syria by the Sea* to the Detroit Museum of Art in mid-1910, near the end of a successful fund-raising campaign that led to the relocation of the museum on its present site. One of their sons, Henry B. Joy, contributed five thousand dollars to the effort at that time *(Detroit Free Press,* June 18, 1910).

On November 29, 1873, Church wrote from Olana to Martin Johnson Heade (q.v.), cotenant of Church's studio in the Tenth Street Studio Building in New York, saying that he (Church) had "ordered Knoedlers [his dealer and primary source for artists' supplies] to send the frame (a big one) of my last picture to the Studio on Wednesday and also directed them to see that the frame was screwed to that stout pair of legs of yours ~~wh~~ if you can spare them—dont be alarmed—I dont mean your own natural legs—but your artificial ones which run on castors" (AAA, roll D5, frames 664–665). At the bottom of the letter, Church sketched a cartoonish, knock-kneed man on roller skates holding a large framed painting; the image within the picture area is recognizably *Syria by the Sea*. The frame to which he referred, recently rediscovered in a Detroit Institute of Arts storeroom and now reunited with the painting, is elaborately decorated with the Mamluk star motif he previously had used in the frame for *Jerusalem* and also employed for *El Khasné Petra* and *The Aegean Sea* (1878; Metropolitan Museum of Art, New York), the last his final large work on an Old World theme.

One week later, at the December 6, 1873, monthly meeting of the Century Association in New York, of which he was a member and which on that occasion he attended with several colleagues, Church unveiled *Syria by the Sea*. At least three journalists who also were present or in touch with the display discussed the painting, listed in the catalogue under its current title but without an owner's name (Yarnall and Gerdts 1986, 1:717), in subsequent reviews. Two of the reporters, writing for the *New York Evening Post* (December 8, 1873) and *New York Daily Tribune* (December 9, 1873), respectively, one or both of whom could have spoken with the artist, were enthusiastic. The former was fairly specific:

Mr. Church sent the largest picture in the collection, evidently a reminiscence of his travels in the Orient. It is entitled "Syria by the Sea," and illustrates a rugged landscape covered with ruined temples overlooking the water. The effect is that of afternoon. In the foreground are broken sections of massive colonnades, some with the columns yet standing and supporting the entablatures, while others have been thrown down, and the ruined capitals and other fragments yet retain enough of their original beauty of form to tell of former grandeur. The subject gives a masterly conception of the splendor of these famous ruins of the East.

The latter, comparatively succinct and disinterested, was equally accurate:

Mr. Church has a large and important picture which he calls "A Syrian Sea-Coast." It represents no scene in nature, but shows how men of genius would group their hills and their ruins if history would give them the chance. It is a noble and imposing composition—one of the most imaginative and elevated works which Mr. Church has produced.

The critic employed by *Appleton's Journal* (December 27, 1873, 827), however, characterizing the 1870s as a "realistic age," decried the artist's contrivance in "plac[ing] imaginary ruins on a coast where we know there are no real ones, like those depicted. . . . Even Baalbecs and Palmyras do not satisfy us when obviously fictitious."

In common with other paintings by Church of the 1870s, portions of the outer paint surface latterly have become transparent, allowing the outlines of his underpainting to show through.

G. C.

Inscription At lower right, *F. E. CHURCH. / 1873*

Provenance James Frederick Joy, Detroit, ca. 1873–74 until 1896. Mrs. James F. Joy, Detroit, 1896 until 1910. Acquired in 1910.

Exhibitions New York 1873, no. 16. Detroit 1944a, no. 74. East Lansing 1966, no. 28. Washington 1989, no. 47.

References BDMA 1910a. Detroit 1910, 11–12; Huntington 1960, 203. Huntington 1966, 96. Davis 1987, 90–91. Davis 1991, 263–268. Carr 1992, 33–34. Carr 1994, 1:369, 391, 398. Davis 1996, 197–201.

Charles Caryl Coleman

1840 Buffalo, New York–Capri, Italy 1928

In 1859, at the age of nineteen, Charles Caryl Coleman traveled to France from his hometown of Buffalo and studied painting with Thomas Couture. On arriving in Italy in 1861, he became enthralled, it is said, by the Italian revolutionary Giuseppe Garibaldi and wanted to enlist under his command (Cerio 1957, 111). He returned to America in 1862, however, to join the Union Army and fight in the Civil War.

In 1866 Coleman joined his friend the artist Elihu Vedder (q.v.) in France and Rome. By the 1870s, while keeping a studio in Rome and working often in Venice, Coleman began spending time in Capri, like a number of other American and British expatriates. Ironically, for he was a notorious philanderer, Coleman purchased what had been the guesthouse of a convent. There he created an extraordinary dwelling, which he named the Villa Narcissus. Its extravagant decoration combined baroque, Moorish, Gothic, and Greco-Roman elements. Coleman designed the doors, grillwork, tiles, mosaics, and stained glass (De Kay 1902; Marguerite Tarjan, MS, curatorial files, DIA). He filled the villa and his Roman studio with "soft, rich-hued satins, rare old brocades, tapestry, faïence and bric-à-brac" (*Art Amateur* 1880, 45). The result was described as a "little museum" and was visited annually by the students of the American School of Archaeology in Rome.

Coleman himself was an added attraction, as he often dressed in costume to complement the decoration of his villa—as a Venetian senator, a monk, an Arab, or in a white suit with a wide-brimmed hat or beret. While collecting antiques and decorative arts for his own use, he also worked as a dealer, buying in Italy and selling in America (Soria 1970, 207–208).

Coleman's paintings and pastels, which have often been compared to the work of the British artist Sir Lawrence Alma-Tadema, focus on the beauty of Italy. Their subjects include imaginary scenes of Capri during antiquity, Capri women dancing, Capri gardens and villas, other Italian landscapes (such as a series of views of Vesuvius seen from his Capri studio), and some religious paintings. One contemporary writer noted that, "Having met the artist, one would naturally look for only the cheerful, the beautiful and the refined in his work,—and this is exactly what one finds" (*BDMA* 1907, 14:4). The bulk of his work was exported to the United States, purchased by Americans who were captivated by Italy. He also exhibited at the Paris Salon, the Royal Academy, and the Art Club in London.

S. M. S.

Bibliography Dayton et al. 1976, 91, 148–149. Money 1986, 35–36.

15

Garden of the Villa Castello, Capri, 1906

(or *A Moonrise Effect in the Garden of Villa Castello, Capri*)
Oil on canvas
94 × 61 cm (37 × 24 in.)
Presented by friends of the artist (11.3)

A few doors away from Coleman's Villa Narcissus on Capri was the Villa Castello. In 1900 Thomas Spencer Jerome and Charles Lang Freer bought the villa, and in 1906, the year Coleman painted *Garden of the Villa Castello, Capri,* Jerome bought out Freer's share. A former lawyer, Jerome was the United States consular agent at Capri beginning in 1901 (Money 1986, 63).

Coleman painted the Villa Castello and its garden many times, including before 1900, as in *The Villa Castello, Capri* (1895; Mr. Graham Williford; see Boston et al. 1992, 376–377, no. 100), when it was owned by the British artists Sophie and Walter Anderson. Sophie Anderson specialized in painting nudes "that had no carnal savour" (Cerio 1929, 114). The villa's garden had been the site of a notorious incident during one of Mrs. Anderson's annual garden parties for the "right people" on Capri, held to exhibit her latest paintings. One year, a British resident, reportedly Lord Grantley, arrived uninvited—and naked. After the maid and a number of guests fainted, the visitor was ushered out, and Walter Anderson had four holes drilled in the garden door so that the maid could view callers before opening it (Money 1986, 40–41).

Any reference to that incident is excluded from this serene painting, a misty scene in which a figure works in the garden under the pergola, constructed of a trellis resting on Doric columns. In an article on the villa and garden published in *House and Garden* in 1902, Jerome described the profusion of flowers and vines around the pergola, which he said was "a great feature of all Capri gardens." "Along the sides, low down, grow wall-flowers, ivy geraniums, nasturtiums and other low-growing flowers, and, higher up, between the columns, solid masses of many varieties of roses. Overhead, the ten foot width is spanned by the branches of the grape vines, and in the summer there is a dense roof of green, from which hang, as the time of vintage approaches, the bunches of many kinds of grapes" (Jerome 1902, 350). In the background of the painting the pines and cypresses that dominate the garden loom below a full moon.

In 1907 the painting was included in an exhibition of Coleman's work at the Detroit Museum of Art, in which it was titled *A Moonrise Effect in the Garden of Villa Castello, Capri.* Four of the twelve oil paintings in the exhibition had the words *Moonlight* or *Moonrise* in their titles. At the close of the exhibition, Coleman donated to the museum one of the pastels, *Vesuvius from Pompeii,* from his series *Songs of Vesuvius* depicting Vesuvius in eruption (*BDMA* 1907). That gesture, along with Coleman's "genial agreeable manner" that "made him many fast

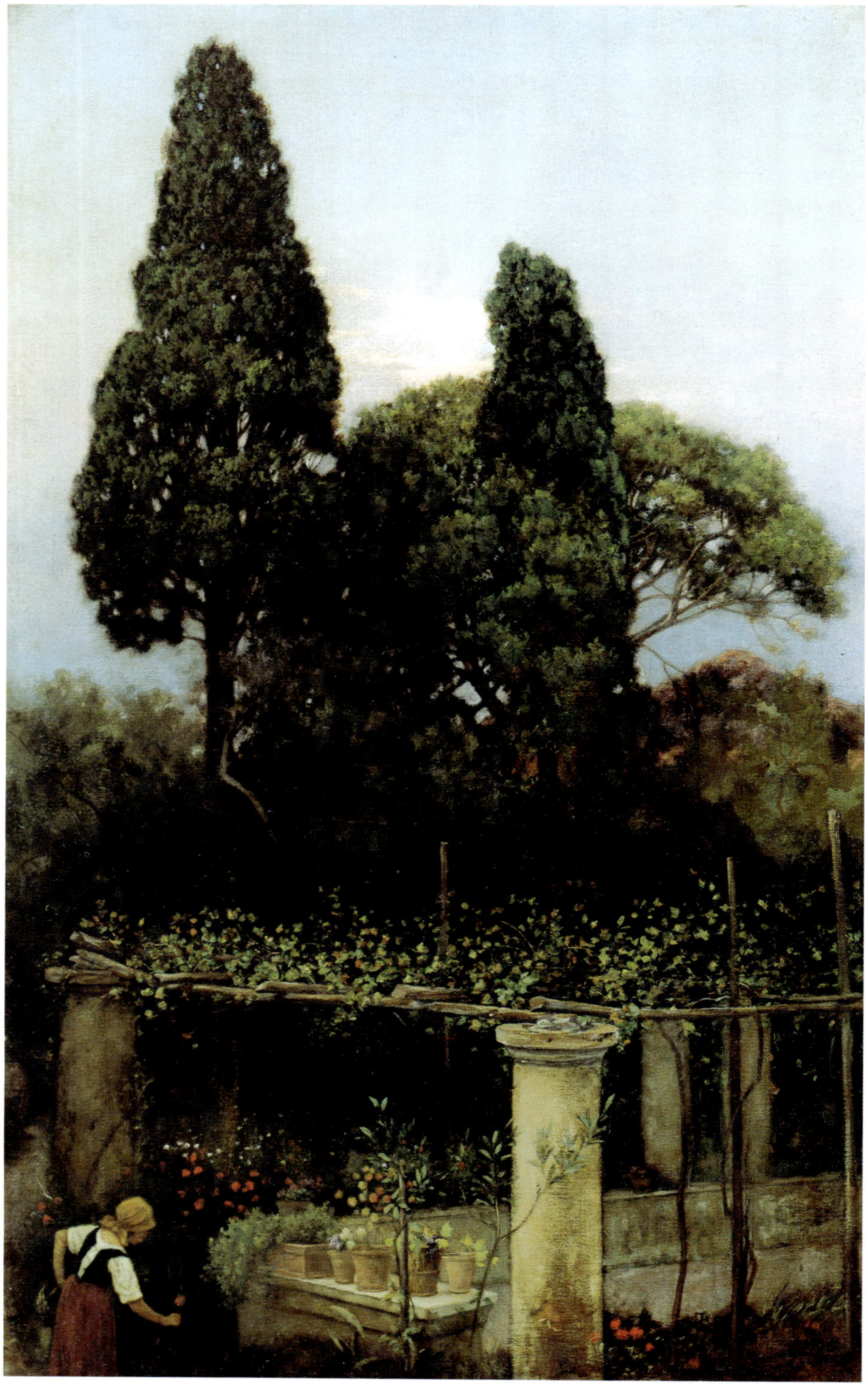

friends among the people with whom he came in contact" during his visit to the exhibition (*BDMA* 1911), encouraged the museum to add one of his paintings to the collection. This painting elicited the most favorable comments of any in the exhibition, and the museum left it hanging with the hope that it would be purchased through popular subscription. In 1911 a group of men, including George H. Russel, Walter S. Russel, John R. Russel, and J. L. Hudson of Detroit, and William A. Rogers of Buffalo, purchased the painting from the artist and donated it to the museum.

S. M. S.

Inscription At lower right, *C. C., Capri, 1906*

Provenance Acquired in 1911 from the artist.

Exhibition Detroit 1907, no. 41, as *A Moonrise Effect in the Garden of Villa Castello, Capri.*

References *BDMA* 1907. *BDMA* 1911. Detroit 1944, 149. Soria 1982, 92. Boston et al. 1992, 377.

Garden of the Villa Castello

Jasper Francis Cropsey

1823 Rossville, Staten Island, New York–
Hastings-on-Hudson, New York 1900

Jasper F. Cropsey, above all other members of the Hudson River school, "spared an incredulous Europe not one jot of the blazing vermilion of the autumn foliage" (Isham 1905, 235). Indeed, his *Autumn—On the Hudson River* of 1860 (National Gallery of Art, Washington, D.C.) garnered rave reviews from the English press. Some critics believed it surpassed the majesty of Frederic Edwin Church's *Niagara Falls* (1857; Corcoran Gallery of Art, Washington, D.C.) and *Heart of the Andes* (1859; Metropolitan Museum of Art, New York). When his painting was selected for inclusion in the London International Exhibition of 1862, awarded a medal by Queen Victoria, and then later that year purchased for two thousand dollars, Cropsey's reputation as one of America's most celebrated landscape painters was secured. Cropsey, however, created works of art that were as varied in subject as they were in quality. This preeminent painter of America's autumn produced Cole-like allegories, medieval fantasies, Civil War scenes, Italian views, and architectural designs throughout his long career.

Cropsey's humble beginnings hardly presaged his future success as an artist. Of Dutch-French parentage and the eldest of eight children, Cropsey grew up on a large farm that barely sustained the family. Early on Cropsey displayed artistic talent, especially in architectural design, and became an apprentice to the New York architect Joseph Trench for five years (1837–42). While producing architectural compositions, Cropsey experimented with oil studies and ventured into New York's burgeoning artistic community. By 1844 the young artist was elected an associate member of the National Academy of Design with his landscape of Greenwood Lake, New Jersey, receiving special notice. It was a subject he would paint for over forty years, partially for its sentimental value, because it was there he met his future wife, Maria Cooley.

After his wedding in May 1847, Cropsey and his bride departed for a two-year tour of Europe, with an extended stay in Italy. Thomas Cole's old studio in Rome served as Cropsey's home base; he traveled and sketched throughout the Campagna and the southern coast. He established friendships with a number of American artists studying in Italy at that time, including William Wetmore Story and Christopher Pearse Cranch. Although this Italian tour contributed much to the formation of Cropsey's landscape style, his extended stay in England a decade later (1856–63) resulted in great artistic success and significant professional contact with the likes of John Ruskin. If Cole's influence permeated Cropsey's art before England, then Turner and the Pre-Raphaelites certainly affected his use of color and detail afterward.

Reestablished in New York during the Civil War, Cropsey participated in the Sanitary Fairs, received substantial remuneration for his Hudson River landscapes, and in 1867 became a founder of the American Watercolor Society. He continued to make sketching trips in New England and to exhibit regularly until he suffered a severe stroke in 1893. It is most fitting that this painter of the American pastoral would spend the last fifteen years of his life overlooking the Hudson River from a house he named Ever Rest.

J. S.

Bibliography College Park 1968. Washington et al. 1970.

16

Sunset after a Storm in the Catskill Mountains, 1860

Oil on canvas

30.5 × 50.8 cm (12 × 20 in.)

Founders Society Purchase, Dexter M. Ferry, Jr., Fund (70.617)

"Of all the gifts of the Creator, few are more beautiful, and less heeded, than the sky." With those words Jasper Cropsey began his essay "Up among the Clouds" for the art periodical *The Crayon,* and in effect became the American version of John Constable, the English artist who in paint and print declared that the sky is "the chief organ of sentiment" in the landscape. Cropsey's oil paintings and watercolor sketches repeatedly prove that he did heed his self-designated "lessons" of the sky, fulfilling the artist's mission "to give the delicate and evanescent beauty that every hour in the day presents itself in the sky, and thus make man happier by the purity and beauty he breathes on his canvas" (Cropsey 1855, 79). The oil sketch *Sunset after a Storm in the Catskill Mountains* illustrates the expressive truths of the sky that Cropsey perceived, remembered, and recorded in his nature outings and studio productions.

Cropsey painted this oil study during his residence in London. Its spontaneity and freshness are all the more remarkable because it is a recollected effect rather than a transcribed observation. Although clearly scenery of the northeastern United States, the exact location is uncertain; as Kenneth Meyers has noted, the topography resembles the White Mountains more than it does the Catskills. Cropsey did frequent both areas in the year before his departure for England in 1856. Cropsey successfully captured the vivid sunsets and autumnal shades typical to northern climates, whether New Hampshire or New York. This oil study is one of many Cropsey produced during his career; its equal in vigorous brushwork and color is his *Storm with Sunburst over Catskills* of 1876 (Newington-Cropsey Foundation, Hastings-on-Hudson, N.Y.). Such works rival the oil sketches of Frederic Edwin Church, whose highly lauded sunsets must have inspired Cropsey to apply his own brush to the subject.

Painterly touches and shifting illumination throughout *Sunset after a Storm*

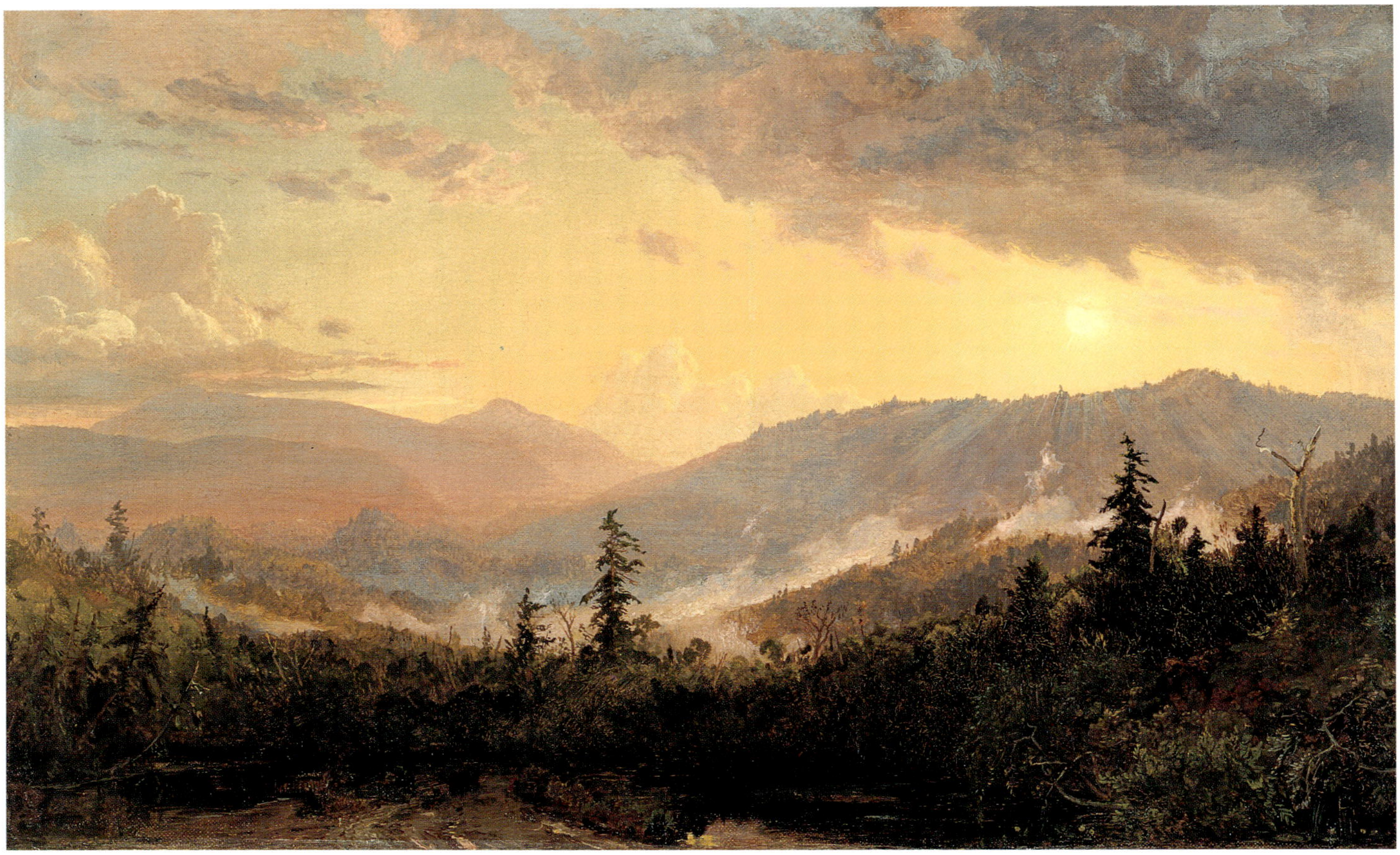

enhance its dramatic power. The energetic sky, so mutable in its configuration and coloring, announces that we are viewing a giant weather factory: threatening rain clouds suddenly invade the blue sky and then depart, leaving cumulus formations to enchant the viewer. The pervasive glow of twilight and the sudden burst of sun rays further transform sky, mountains, and water into a pictorial event. As the fiery orange-brown clouds that drape heavily above the foreground sweep away to reveal a more tranquil scene, Cropsey seems to have created the perfect visual corollary to his written description of the sky's emotive effects: "If the cirrus and cumulus regions awaken soothing and poetical thoughts of serenest beauty, the rain region can certainly stir the heart as much, even though it appeal to the coarser elements of our nature" (Cropsey 1855, 80).

Indeed, this simple study demonstrates an essentially romantic sensibility, one in which Cropsey perceived natural oppositions as equivalent to contrasting emotions. *Sunset after a Storm* juxtaposes darkness and light, conflict and calm. The sun with its enlivening rays intervenes between shrouded sky and shadowed ridge. Evergreens confidently reach upward to the clearing sky; the dead tree on the right imploringly gestures its bare limbs to the glowing disk. While heavy orange clouds still threaten above, a soothing white mist meanders below. A solitary bear sniffs along the foreground path oblivious to the wilderness altering behind him.

The Detroit picture served as a study for a larger view, done in 1861 (Newington-Cropsey Foundation), which is strikingly different in tone. The sky, mountains, and evergreens are virtually the same, but Cropsey has transformed his isolated wilderness into an inhabited family settlement. Following the tradition of Thomas Cole's *Home in the Woods* (1845; Reynolda House, Winston-Salem, N.C.), Cropsey has domesticated the landscape: a log cabin complete with a smoke-spewing chimney, young children with a dog, and a garden behind a prominent autumnal tree fill the left foreground. The bear has disappeared. Nature's transformations now serve as a symbolic backdrop for an image of the American frontier steeped in myth and Civil War politics.

J. S.

Inscription At lower right, *J. F. Cropsey / 1860;* frame has sticker of O'Brien Gallery, Chicago.

Sunset after a Storm

Provenance Art market, Chicago. Raymond L. McKanny, Douglas, Mich. Acquired in 1970.

Exhibition New York 1969, 20, no. 15.

Reference *BDIA* 1977, 87–88, fig. 10a.

17

Indian Summer, 1866

Oil on canvas

134.6 × 241.3 cm (53 × 95 in.)

Founders Society Purchase, Robert H. Tannahill Foundation Fund, James and Florence Beresford Fund, Gibbs-Williams Fund, and Beatrice W. Rogers Fund (78.38)

Second in size only to Cropsey's tour de force, *Autumn—On the Hudson River* (60 × 108 in.; 1860; National Gallery of Art, Washington, D.C.), *Indian Summer* is a pendant of sorts to this earlier image of fall. Cropsey produced his grandest and most celebrated autumnal scene on the eve of the Civil War and completed its more restrained successor as the nation sought to heal its social, political, and economic war wounds. Although *Indian Summer* did not receive the prolix praise of the larger autumn picture, a writer for the *New York Sunday Herald* (November 11, 1966) recognized its importance to Cropsey's career, describing it as "that glorious summary of his life long studies of scenery on the Hudson and in autumn. Few if any of our painters have equalled Cropsey in depicting 'that beautiful season' so exquisitely sung by Longfellow." Cropsey's focus on a season Americans regarded as uniquely their own, and which Northerners believed they could experience in a superior way, conferred a nationalistic appeal on *Indian Summer.* By invoking Henry Wadsworth Longfellow, the *Sunday Herald* bestowed on Cropsey's art an exceptional poetic status, for Longfellow was America's "Chief Singer," her most popular and internationally renowned bard.

Cropsey courted a poetic sensibility in his choice of color and subject. Autumn as well as twilight encouraged the use of varied, brilliant hues that could compete with the expressive language of poetry—an art form to which many a nineteenth-century painter aspired. Both subjects ceaselessly appeared in the poetry featured in nineteenth-century American periodicals and, in turn, in the American paintings produced during the second half of the century. Cropsey, like his fellow landscape painters Thomas Cole and Asher B. Durand, chose poetic excerpts to accompany his exhibited pictures. He wisely selected a line from Longfellow to add poetic resonance to his first painting exhibited in the Royal Academy in London, *Indian Summer Morning in the White Mountains* (1857; Currier Gallery of Art, Manchester, N.H.): "Filled was the air with a dreamy and magical light" (quoted in College Park 1968, 24). *The Crayon,* New York's art journal, quoting a British paper, featured several stanzas of Longfellow's early poem "Autumn" in its description of Cropsey's highly lauded *Autumn—On the Hudson River (Crayon* 7 [1860]: 142). The poem served as a lyrical annotation to the painting. Hailed in Britain as well as in America, Longfellow was the ideal choice for Cropsey's poetic doppelgänger.

Indian Summer especially shares the festive spirit of Longfellow's ode to the season. The lines "There is a beautiful spirit breathing now / Its mellow richness on the clustered trees / And, from a beaker full of richest dyes, / Pouring new glory on the autumn woods, / And dipping in warm light the pillared clouds" capture in words the vitality and hope Cropsey conveys in paint. The mood of *Indian Summer* is true to the connotations of its name—a period of tranquillity occurring near the end of something. Yet it does not completely deny autumn's "solemn hymn that Death / Has lifted up for all." The autumnal scenes Cropsey produced in London, however, possess the melancholic tinge and theatricality of effect characteristic of other poems by Longfellow. Certainly this difference in expression between *Autumn—On the Hudson River* of 1860 and *Indian Summer* of 1866 could be attributed to a shift in style, from a Turneresque expression to a more Ruskinian deliberateness. But *Indian Summer's* calm tenor and meaningful details appealed to a nation that had just ended its bloodiest and most divisive war. A close study of its details suggests how eloquently *Indian Summer* voiced the national spirit.

As in Cropsey's *Autumn—On the Hudson River, Indian Summer* begins its view down the Hudson from a forested mountaintop. The point of origin, however, is farther north in the Hudson Highlands than Cornwall and West Point, renowned sites of the earlier picture, looking south from the environs of Newburgh. At this more northern point in the river lie the famous Gates of the Hudson—Breakneck and Storm King mountains and Pollepel Island (now known as Bannerman's Island)—that compose the entranceway to what were the most strategic sites of the Revolutionary War. For example, Plum Point Battery was across from Pollepel Island. Beyond the Gates stand Constitution Island and West Point, known as America's Gibraltar and the site of the United States Military Academy. Cropsey makes this historic locale the focus of the viewer's panoramic gaze. Closer to the ridge, in the left middle ground, is a prominent white Georgian house with an American flag situated on the riverbank; this may be the Hasbrouck House in Newburgh, which served as George Washington's headquarters in 1782–83. By 1850 all of these sites in the Hudson Highlands attracted a million tourists annually. Americans and Europeans fascinated equally with heroic tales of the Revolution, Dutch folklore, and wilderness scenery took the fashionable northern tour up the Hudson by steamboat. In Cropsey's *Indian Summer,* one of these "floating palaces," as the tourist steamboats carrying several thousand patrons were known, can be seen making its way up the river toward Newburgh.

Cropsey bathes these historic islands and mountains in soft pinks, purples, and yellows. The clouds are undramatic. Purple-rose wisps float in the upper sky; cumulus clouds mount in the distance. Twilight has only just begun. Two successful hunters have placed their rifles at ease and engage in relaxed conversation by a log in the right foreground. They seem oblivious to the panoramic scene before them. Their dog sniffs the well-trodden ground. Boulders and logs litter the foreground but do not barricade the viewer from joining the hunters as they do in Cropsey's *Autumn*. A felled tree on the right indicates that human hands have cleared away some of the vegetation on the ridge. To the left wilderness still flourishes: a green-yellow elm rises upward as a leafless, uprooted tree leans leftward behind it. Golden yellows, bright orange-reds, and somber mauves color the foliage shading a vigorous brook. Below this wild foregound, just over the ridge, one sees cows grazing, a pond and houses nestled among bright autumn foliage, and sailboats at port. In the distance, white sails catch the light, and the mountains and islands create mirrorlike reflections in the river. Although a tourist steamer speeds along, puffing black smoke, repose pervades the scene. All is clear, still, and quiet.

Indian Summer is a pastoral vision of a historic site. It shares the Claudean composition, panoramic viewpoint, and contemplative spirit of paintings such as *The Valley of Wyoming* (Metropolitan Museum of Art, New York) and *Starrucca Viaduct, Pennsylvania* (Toledo Museum of Art) produced the previous year. All three paintings evoke the harmonic middle landscape in which nature and man, wilderness and technology, past and present are seemingly forever balanced. Like *The Valley of Wyoming, Indian Summer* presents a view of the national landscape associated with the legends of the Revolutionary War and the history of American democracy. Both images appealed to a public supremely fascinated with national identity and destiny.

The end of the Civil War inspired many landscape painters to profess the successful restoration of America's democratic union and to celebrate her providential fortune. Cropsey did so repeatedly, and perhaps with the greatest assurance in *Indian Summer*. The Hudson Highlands, suffused with the bright colors of autumn —the American season, crowned with an elm, the American tree, and decorated with the Star-Spangled Banner, the American flag—convey a patriotic spirit. Appropriately, in the same year that Cropsey completed *Indian Summer* he exhibited *Gettysburg* (unlocated) at the National Academy of Design. If *Gettysburg* presented the sight of a nation torn asunder, then *Indian Summer* offered the vision of a country recovering auspiciously. The nineteenth-century viewer could look upon the Hudson Highlands of *Indian Summer* and indeed believe in the truth of Longfellow's "Autumn": "O what a glory doth this world put on / For him who, with a fervent heart, goes forth / Under the bright and glorious sky, and looks / On duties well performed, and days well spent!"

J. S.

Inscription At lower right, *J. F. Cropsey / 1866*

Provenance H. H. Leeds and Miner, and H. W. Derby, 1867. Frank Johnston Jones. University of Cincinnati, Ohio, 1928–77. Hirschl & Adler, New York. Acquired in 1978.

Exhibitions Washington et al. 1970, 94, 95, no. 50, fig. 94. New York 1977, no. 24.

References *New York Sunday Herald,* November 11, 1866. Tuckerman 1867, 536. Talbot 1972, 1:183–184, 188; 2:433, no. 147; 3:639, fig. 128. Talbot 1980.

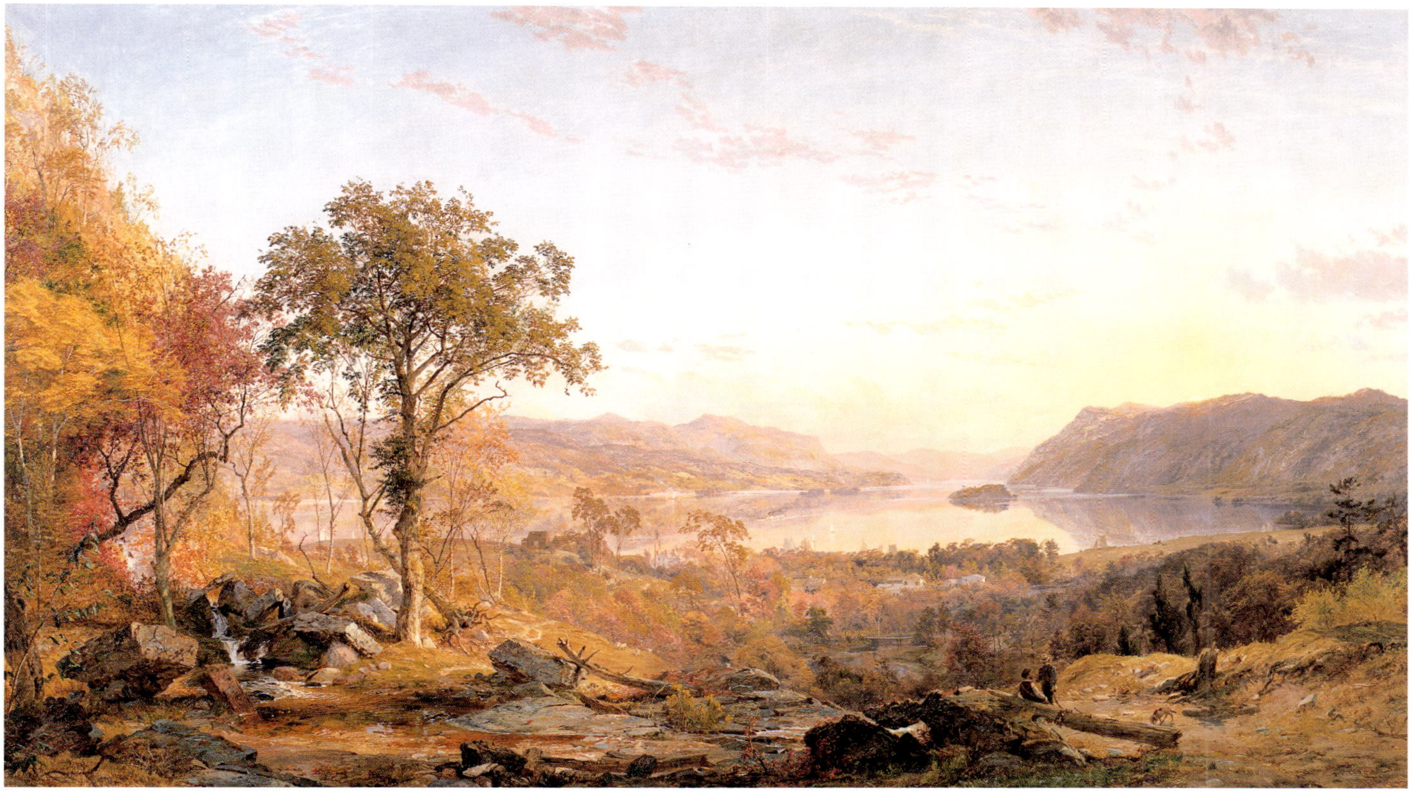

Indian Summer

Maria Richards Oakey Dewing

1845 New York 1927

In 1915, in an article on flower painters written for the periodical *Art and Progress,* Maria Oakey Dewing stated: "The flower offers a removed beauty that exists only for beauty, more abstract than it can be in the human being, even more exquisite.... In painting the flower one must... begin at the exquisite and distinguished. Let not the student think that flower painting is the business of the amateur" (Dewing 1915, 255). Dewing's accomplishments in the late nineteenth and early twentieth centuries were both artistic and literary, but her reputation rested on her flower paintings. During her lifetime she was celebrated by her contemporaries as the successor to the still-life painter John La Farge and as the American counterpart to the French flower painters Henri Fantin-Latour and Antoine Vollon (J. Martin 1977, 48, 116).

Dewing, the fifth of ten children, was raised in a genteel but frugal environment. Her mother wrote articles for *Scribner's Monthly Magazine* on her youth, which was spent in the fashionable circles of London, New York, Philadelphia, and Boston. She also wrote pieces on home management and home etiquette. Dewing took up related topics in her own books, *Beauty in Dress* (1881) and *Beauty in the Household* (1882), but couched the discussion in terms of aesthetics.

Dewing began her art training in 1866, studying at the Cooper Union School of Design for Women, under William Rimmer (q.v.), George Butler, Edwin Forbes, and Robert Swain Gifford. By 1871 she was enrolled at the National Academy of Design in the Antique School, staying there until 1875. During this period she also studied with John La Farge, undoubtedly her most important mentor. It was probably La Farge who suggested that she continue her studies with his own teachers, William Morris Hunt (q.v.) in Boston and Thomas Couture in Paris, which she did.

Even before she went to Europe in 1876, Dewing had made something of a name for herself. In 1875 she helped found the Art Students League and showed flower paintings at the National Academy of Design and at Cottier and Company, a New York gallery. On her return she began to exhibit regularly at the Society of American Artists, Boston's Copley Society, and in London.

In 1881 she married the Boston painter Thomas Wilmer Dewing, and in 1885 they established Doveridge, a summer residence in Cornish, New Hampshire. There Thomas, an amateur horticulturist, cultivated a garden, and Maria began to develop expertise as a botanist.

Although Thomas and Maria collaborated on some projects—he illustrated one of her poems for the *Century Magazine* in 1883 and she added the foliage to his painting *Hymen* in 1886 (Cincinnati Art Museum), signing the work jointly with him—she seems not to have competed with him for prominence in the art world. Nonetheless, she continued to paint, winning bronze medals at both the World's Columbian Exposition in Chicago in 1893 and the Pan-American Exposition in Buffalo in 1901, and her work was displayed in solo exhibitions in Philadelphia (1907) and New York (1914). Despite these successes, she seems to have been unsatisfied with her career. Shortly before she died she wrote: "I have hardly touched any achievement, it was a handsome talent the Lord gave me and though [Royal] Cortissoz calls my flowers & still lifes 'consummate'... this seems only a mockery, I dreamed of groups & figures in big landscapes & still I *see* them" (J. Martin 1976, 25; J. Martin 1977, 116).

T. T.

Bibliography Dewing 1915. J. Martin 1976. J. Martin 1977. Foshay 1979, 280–281. Hoppin 1981, 44.

18

Irises and Calla Lilies, ca. 1890/1905

Oil and silver leaf on panel

41.9 × 34.3 cm (16½ × 13½ in.)

Founders Society, Dexter M. Ferry, Jr., Fund (1991.112)

Maria Oakey Dewing was not only an accomplished flower painter but also an enthusiastic gardener, participating in a horticultural craze popular in the late nineteenth century, actively cultivating informal and old-fashioned gardens in both Cornish and Green Hill, New Hampshire. Transferring her botanical expertise to canvas, Dewing became known for both her vigorous out-of-door flower paintings and her animated studio flower pictures. The ambiguous *Irises and Calla Lilies* suggests both settings—the edge of an out-of-doors flower box or a studio tabletop. Looking at the motif from the vantage point of a working gardener, Dewing created a picture with a shallow, tightly controlled downward perspective, balancing the vertical composition of the botanically accurate and richly textured irises and calla lilies with the diagonally grounded flower box or table. Placed against a gold-washed silver-leaf background, the decorative and delicately colored irises and calla lilies, rimmed in hues of violet, display harmonious and subtle shades of yellow, cream, amber, green, violet, red, and blue. The composition is so closely cropped that petals and leaves extend beyond the edges of the canvas. This poetic and atmospheric painting—remarkable for its fusion of the intensely observed with the decorative—suggests the organic vitality of the flower while also validating Dewing's belief that gardening was necessary if one wished to understand flowers fully enough to paint them well (Dewing 1915, 262; Clayton 1990, 894–895; M. Hill 1992, 732–734).

Irises and Calla Lilies highlights the cultural and artistic influences on Maria Oakey Dewing's art. Echoing the work

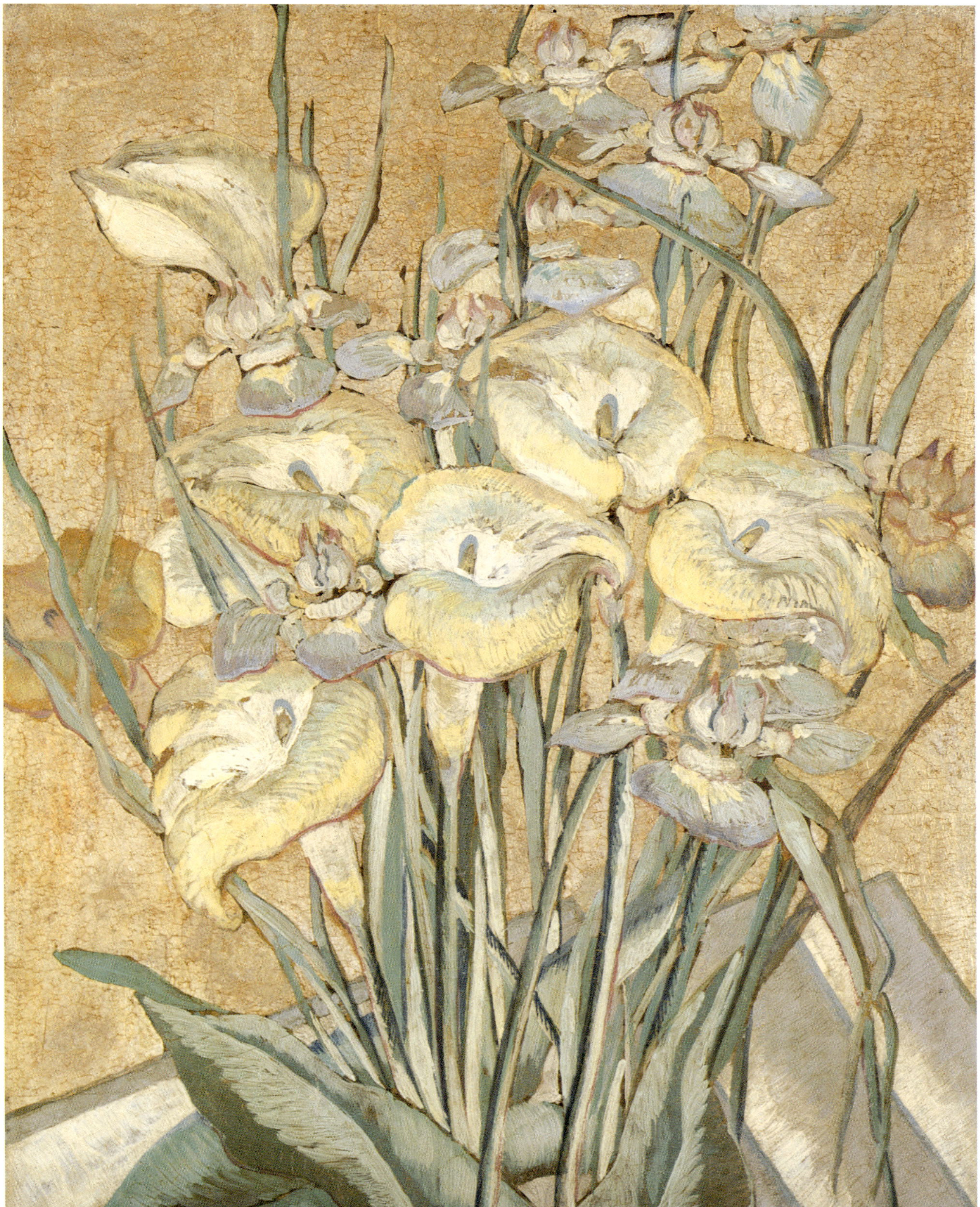

Irises and Calla Lillies

of her teacher, John La Farge, who made her aware of Ruskin's and the Pre-Raphaelites' call for botanic and geographic accuracy in the observation of nature, Dewing produced a tour-de-force image of two flowers that normally blossom at different times in the spring. The picture suggests that she planned the composition, carefully cultivating lilies, not easily raised in New Hampshire, to bloom at the same time as the irises, so that she could create a painting of two aesthetically compatible flowers.

While on one level the picture contradicts her general dismissal of Dutch old-master painters who frequently grouped together flowers with no botanical relationship, on another level it gives evidence of Dewing's awareness of the late-nineteenth-century conception of "truth to nature" found in the survival theories of the naturalist Charles Darwin. The composition depicts two flowers in their proper environment, painted directly from nature and reflecting a new perception of nature as a dynamic cosmos defined by the interaction of living organisms. Dewing captured the growth process and development of these two plants on canvas, reflecting a fascination with the physiology of plant life that may very well have been nurtured by Darwin's exploration of this subject in his botanical publications following *Origin of Species* (Foshay 1979, 284–289; New York 1984, 60–67; Foshay 1990, 15–20; Tulsa et al. 1981, 139–147).

Such an organic approach to nature is also evident in the work of Dewing's teacher, John La Farge, who also provided her with her first exposure to Asian art when she studied with him in the 1870s. Although La Farge owned numerous books as well as prints and paintings on the subject, Dewing probably gained greater familiarity in the 1890s when she visited the significant Asian art collection amassed by her husband's patron, the Detroit industrialist Charles Lang Freer, who also purchased her painting *Poppies and Mignonette* (n.d.; unlocated).

Irises and Calla Lilies—which was first owned by the fashionable late-nineteenth-century architect Stanford White—has calligraphic and lyrical qualities (Hobbs 1985, 14). Like *Poppies and Mignonette,* the picture suggests the decorative seventeenth-century Japanese screen paintings of Sotatsu and Koetsu, with whom the art historian Arthur Edwin Bye compared Dewing's out-of-doors work. Dewing herself admired Sotatsu's screen of red field lilies owned by Freer. The asymmetrical arrangement, the diagonal composition, and the abrupt cropping appealed to her, as did the drawing, which was "miraculously close to nature . . . [with] the red lily stretching far away into a landscape that is not represented . . . exceedingly perfect in its silhouette, diminishing in size in the distance, subtly fainter in color, telling like a repeated note of music" (Dewing 1915, 258). Dewing similarly evokes a vigorous, harmonic chorus filled with shimmering blue grace notes in her painting *Irises and Calla Lilies.*

Lilies were a favored subject for Dewing in the early 1890s, and two such paintings, *Lilies* (1882 or 1893) and *Lilies and Delphinium* (1894), were purchased by Smith College in 1894. She also painted a picture of an iris (1899; private collection) that bears a close similarity to this painting (J. Martin 1977, 117–118; Clayton 1990, 898). The exact date of *Irises and Calla Lilies* is not known, but comparisons with other known work, the time period in which she had concentrated exposure to Asian art, as well as the painting's provenance make it possible to suggest when it was painted.
T. T.

Inscription At lower right on verso, *Maria Oakey Dewing*

Provenance Stanford White. Associate of Stanford White. Descendant of August Belmont. George Guerry, 1962. Mr. and Mrs. George J. Arden, New York, 1968–87. Berry-Hill Galleries, New York, 1987. Acquired in 1991.

Exhibitions New York 1978, no. 26, as *Iris.* New York 1988, 102–103.

Reference Foshay 1979, 287 n. 50.

Robert S. Duncanson

1821 Fayette, New York–Detroit 1872

Growing up in the Lake Erie town of Monroe, Michigan, Robert Duncanson learned house painting and glazing from his family, a clan of free mulatto tradesmen. In 1838 he entered the painting trade with a partner, John Gamblin, for about a year *(Monroe Gazette,* April 17, 1838–April 9, 1839), before moving around 1840 to Cincinnati, Ohio, where he tried to establish himself as an artist. For ten years Duncanson worked as an itinerant artist, moving among Cincinnati, Monroe, and Detroit, copying prints, painting portraits and "fancy pieces," or genre subjects. While working in Detroit in the summer of 1848 Duncanson received his first important landscape commission for *Cliff Mine Lake Superior* in 1848 (private collection, Calif.). This commission sparked his interest in nature and initiated his career as a landscape painter. A contemporary of the East Coast artists John F. Kensett (q.v.), Frederic Edwin Church (q.v.), and Albert Bierstadt (q.v.), Duncanson worked in a regional variation of the Hudson River school tradition. He earned international acclaim for his painting, the first African-American artist to do so.

In 1849 Duncanson returned to Cincinnati, where he moved into a studio adjoining that of William Louis Sonntag (q.v.). In Cincinnati during this period a group of Ohio River valley painters in the Hudson River school style had formed around Worthington Whittredge (q.v.) and Sonntag. After Whittredge left for Europe in 1849, Sonntag and Duncanson carried on this tradition. Duncanson's early accomplishments in landscape painting, such as *Blue Hole* (1851; Cincinnati Art Museum) and the Belmont murals (ca. 1850–52; Taft Museum, Cincinnati), earned him sponsorship for his first grand tour of Europe in 1853 with Sonntag. On their return in 1854, Sonntag remained in New York, while Duncanson returned to Cincinnati, where he established a reputation as the foremost landscape painter living in the Ohio River valley.

By 1860 Duncanson's artistic ambitions had swollen beyond the Ohio River valley region. He was determined to create a masterpiece and with it make a triumphal tour of Europe. The resulting work was the artist's largest easel painting, *Land of the Lotus Eaters* (1861; King of Sweden, Stockholm). The painting was emphatically praised by the regional press, which declared him "the best landscape painter living in the West" *(Cincinnati Daily Gazette,* May 30, 1861). The outbreak of the Civil War interrupted Duncanson's plans of touring the painting. As a "free man of color" living on the border of the South, he was forced north to Canada in 1863, before continuing on to England in 1865. In Toronto, Montreal, Dublin, Glasgow, and London Duncanson's series of landscapes was greeted with acclaim from the art world. He returned to Cincinnati in 1867 to enjoy the laurels of international critical and popular success for his style, which synthesized landscape aesthetics with elevated literary sentiments.

J. K.

Bibliography Ketner 1993.

19

The Drunkard's Plight, 1845

Oil on canvas
38.7 × 50.2 cm (15¼ × 19¾ in.)
Gift of Miss Sarah M. Sheridan (44.277)

This painting is an early attempt by Robert Duncanson at an imaginary genre subject inspired by common American life, with moralizing overtones. The main figure stands in tattered clothes outside an inn with a broken jug at his feet. A woman and boy confront the man who, ashamed, looks down his bulbous, red nose at the ground. In the background another woman and child watch from the doorway of a cabin. Although the title of this painting, *The Drunkard's Plight,* was assigned by Francis W. Robinson (former director of the Detroit Institute of Arts) one hundred years after it was painted, it aptly describes the narrative of the picture. Temperance subjects were very popular in Protestant America during the 1840s and 1850s, and this painting certainly reflects the vogue for such pictures.

At this point in his burgeoning career Duncanson was working as an itinerant artist, seeking commissions while moving between Cincinnati and Detroit. He arrived in Detroit in the fall of 1845 and announced in the local press that he intended "to employ his time in the art of Portrait and Historical painting" *(Detroit Free Press,* December 16, 1845). Shortly after his arrival in Detroit, the local press announced: "We have intended for some time to call the attention of our citizens to the paintings of Mr. Duncanson, a young artist who has been some weeks here.... Mr. Duncanson has already taken the portraits of a number of our citizens and has designed and finished several historical and fancy pieces of great merit.... Mr. Duncanson deserves, and we trust will receive the patronage of all lovers of the fine arts" *(Detroit Daily Advertiser,* February 2, 1846).

Duncanson was first recorded as being in Detroit only in December 1845. *The Drunkard's Plight* is dated *1845* and has been in Detroit since its creation. This suggests that Duncanson may have painted the work in December 1845 and that it may be one of the "fancy pieces of great merit" referred to in the press notice of February 1846. The *Liberator,* William Lloyd Garrison's Boston-based abolitionist newspaper, noted a similar subject in Duncanson's studio in Cincinnati the following summer. The reviewer remarked on visiting the home of a Negro artist who had no professional training but who had been working as a house painter. He proclaimed that the works by the artist "are really beautiful" and that he was particularly struck by a humorous picture of a man carrying

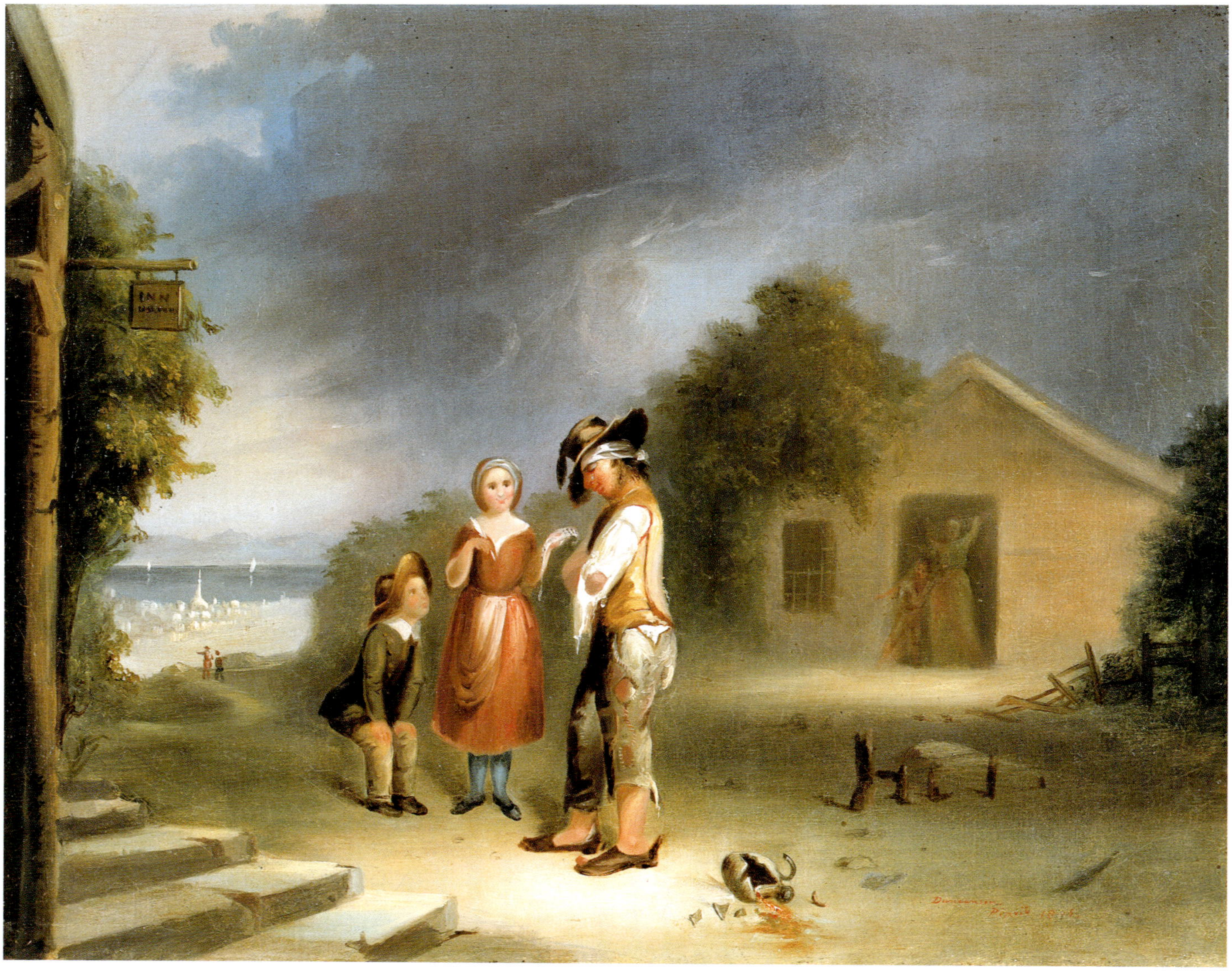

a basket of fruit and vegetables that had split open and spilled its contents (*Liberator,* August 21, 1846).

In a manner typical among early American limners, *The Drunkard's Plight* is immature in its rendering. These shortcomings should be expected in an early work by a self-taught artist. The figures are awkwardly proportioned and stiff in their gestures, while the cabin and the distant town are simply conceived.

Duncanson's interest in narrative subjects from common life was certainly inspired by the popularity of English anecdotal prints after works by William Hogarth, Thomas Rowlandson, and George Cruikshank. These prints were widely circulated in America and Duncanson would have been familiar with them. Equally influential was the work of Duncanson's contemporary in Cincinnati, James H. Beard. From the time of Duncanson's arrival in that city, Beard was one of the most successful artists working in the area. He gained popularity for his genre subjects, such as *The Long Bill* (1840; Cincinnati Art Museum), which offered humorous and moralizing anecdotes on contemporary life. Beard's style, and *The Long Bill* in particular, would have been well known to Duncanson, who could have seen Beard's work at the local exhibitions of the Society for the Promotion of Useful Knowledge in 1840 and 1841. Duncanson's *Drunkard's Plight* is not a direct copy of any painting by Beard or a particular British print. Rather, any stylistic similarities to these works demonstrate Duncanson's aware-

The Drunkard's Plight

ness of them and his ability to absorb the lessons of these sources in order to compose a unique composition.

In the 1840s genre paintings of everyday American life were very popular, as evidenced by the successful careers of Francis William Edmonds, William Sidney Mount, and George C. Bingham. Despite its weaknesses, Duncanson's painting did have an impact on the arts at this early stage in Detroit cultural history. *The Drunkard's Plight* seems to have influenced the development of another young Detroit artist, Frederick E. Cohen. Within months after Duncanson began to advertise his trade in the Detroit newspapers, Cohen placed a remarkably similar ad for his work. Although Cohen had been living and working in Detroit since 1837, there is no record that he had advertised his work to the public before he announced that he "intends following Portrait, Miniature, Historical and Scriptural Painting" *(Detroit Free Press,* April 29, 1846) in a studio just down the street from Duncanson. Cohen's early *Near Old Post Office, Detroit* (ca. 1846; private collection; see Ketner 1987, pl. 10) is a humorous, anecdotal picture that illustrates his stylistic similarity to the American tradition of genre painting and Duncanson's *Drunkard's Plight.* Particularly, Cohen's fruit vendor, whose basket has split open, spilling its contents, recalls Duncanson's painting cited in *The Liberator* at this time.

By 1852 and 1853, when Detroit hosted its first art exhibitions, the Firemen's Fair expositions, Duncanson had become recognized for his artistic contributions, founded on works such as *The Drunkard's Plight.*

J. K.

Inscription At lower right, *Duncanson Pinxit 1845*

Provenance James A. Roys, Detroit, ca. 1845–1904. Ella Grace Roys, Detroit, 1904–44. Acquired in 1944.

Exhibitions Detroit 1949. Detroit 1952. Washington 1967, 14. Boston 1972. Cincinnati 1972, no. 1. New York 1976a. Battle Creek et al. 1977. Detroit 1980.

References Cavallo 1950–51, 24. J. Porter 1951, 108–109. Dover 1960, 25, pl. 18. *Boston Sunday Globe,* January 9, 1972. *Peabody* (Mass.) *Times,* January 19, 1972. *Phoenix,* January 26, 1972, 29. Gibson 1975, 94. Parks 1980, 37. Ketner 1993, 19, 22, fig. 7, 191–192, no. 10.

20

William Berthelet, 1846

Oil on canvas

76.2 × 63.5 cm (30 × 25 in.)

Gift of William T. Berthelet (52.207)

THIS PAINTING portrays William Berthelet (1841–1846), the grandson of Henri Berthelet (1776–1846), a businessman and patriach of a prominent Detroit family. According to the oral history of the Berthelet family, this is one of five portraits commissioned from Duncanson during his stay in Detroit in early 1846. However, a stylistic analysis of the five portraits does not support the family recollection. Among this group of paintings just the portrait of William—the only one in the group that is signed and dated—and that of his grandfather Henri (Detroit Historical Museum) resemble Duncanson's portrait style. Apparently the Berthelets only commissioned the portraits of William and Henri from Duncanson, motivated by the desire to have memorial portraits of two family members whose demise was imminent.

After becoming an itinerant portrait and genre painter Duncanson rented a studio in Detroit by December 1845 *(Detroit Free Press,* December 16, 1845). In February 1846 he was reported to be painting the portraits of several local citizens, which may have been a reference to the Berthelet portraits *(Detroit Daily Advertiser,* February 2, 1846). Duncanson advertised his trade in Detroit until April 26, 1846, and was recorded as being in Cincinnati again by July 29. As William Berthelet died and was buried on July 19, 1846, Duncanson must have painted the work before then.

William is depicted wearing a fashionable two-piece checkered suit while seated in a chair in front of a drapery backdrop. This was a stock portrait composition for Duncanson, who placed the figure at a one-quarter turn with the eyes staring back at the spectator. The rigid pose and blank stare from the ovoid face of the young sitter recall Duncanson's earlier portrait of William Baker as a child (1844; Baker-Hunt Foundation, Covington, Ky.). Although it is two years earlier, a close examination of the facial features of the Baker portrait reveals a similar treatment of the almond eyes, oval face, and hairline. Furthermore, the poses of the two children are almost exactly the same, if in reverse, with one hand on the knee and the other pulled back. The earlier painting, however, is more dynamic owing to

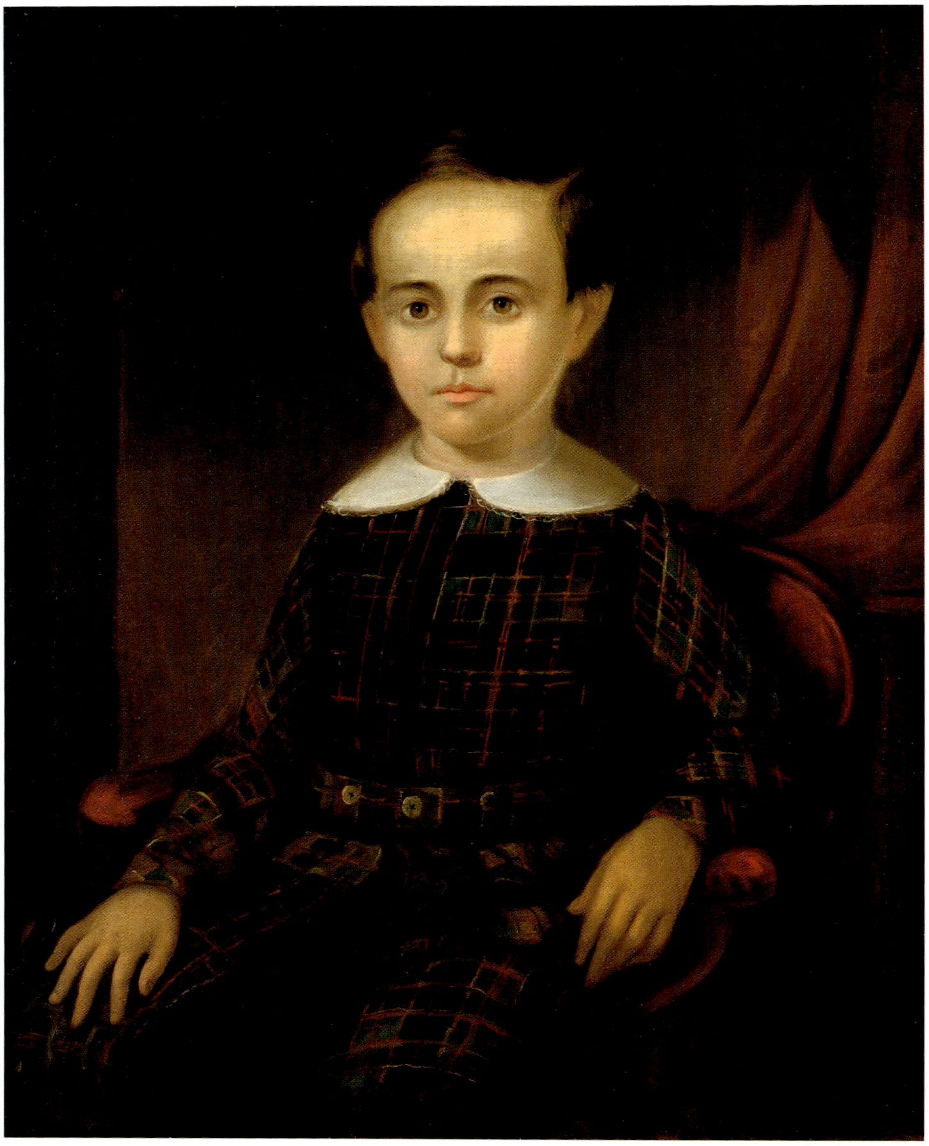

its landscape background and playful, barking dog, which the boy is petting. The stylized treatment of the human figure in these two works was typical of Duncanson's portraits and marked his figure painting throughout his career. In *William Berthelet* the stiff drawing and decorative patterns lend to the design a folklike charm.

J. K.

Inscription On verso, *R. S. Duncanson 1846*

Provenance Joseph Berthelet, Detroit, 1846–83. Berthelet family. William Thomas Berthelet, d. 1952. Acquired in 1952.

Exhibitions Washington 1967. Boston 1972. Cincinnati 1972, 7, no. 3. New York 1976a. Durham 1984, 14, 17, no. 8. Sandwich 1985.

References J. Porter 1951, 122–125, 148. Fine 1973, 49. Gibson 1975, 95. Parks 1980, 11, ill. 13. Ketner 1993, 19, fig. 5, 192, no. 11.

21

Fruit Piece, 1849

Oil on canvas
35.7 × 50.8 cm (14 × 20 in.)
Gift of the Estates of Miss Elizabeth Gray Walker and Mr. Henry Lyster Walker (57.84)

Fruit Piece is a fine representative example of American still-life painting in the mid–nineteenth century. Duncanson has arranged fruits and nuts on a draped table and enframed the ensemble in a proscenium-crested niche. The random assortment of berries and nuts at the base of the still life is built up with leafage and fruit that rise to form a pyramid, with a pineapple at the top. The compositional formula and realistic rendering derive from the early American still-life tradition established by James and Raphaelle Peale in Philadelphia. Whereas the Peales' paintings are generally restrained and austere, Duncanson demonstrates a greater freedom in using a more random arrangement, which became typical of the mid-nineteenth-century still-life paintings of Severin Roesen, for example. The proscenium format for the niche in *Fruit Piece* is a device rarely seen in other American still lifes of this period but is common in Duncanson's work in this genre.

In 1849 Duncanson was working out of rooms in Detroit, where he was producing "fruit and fancy pieces" on commission. He earned a considerable reputation in this field, winning a premium at the Michigan State Agricultural Fair in October 1849, and with his only entry to the American Art-Union in 1850 (*Michigan Farmer,* October 1, 1849, 299; *American Art-Union,* December 1850, no. 313). When Duncanson moved back

William Berthelet

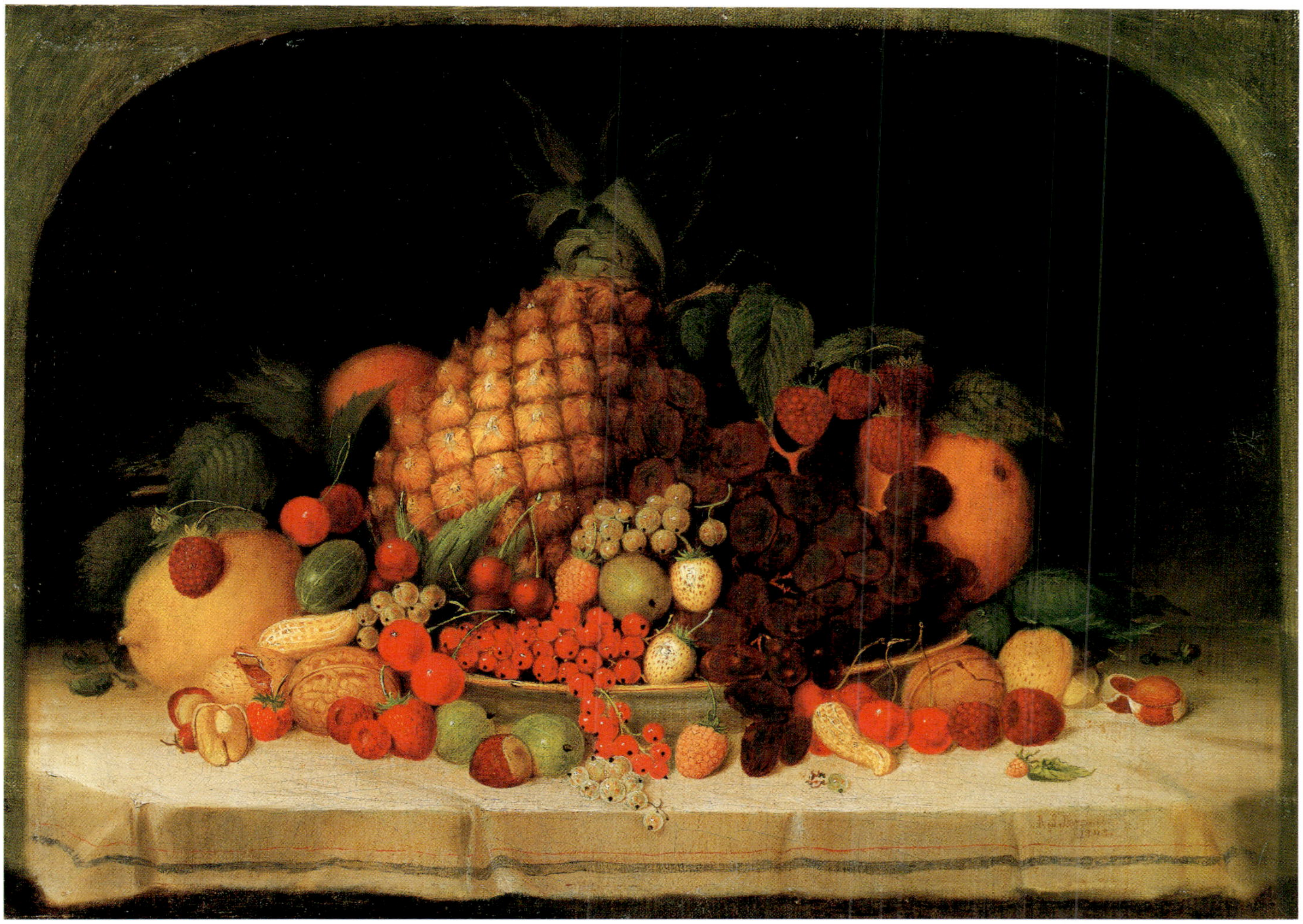

Fruit Piece

to Cincinnati in the fall of 1849 to take a studio next to William Sonntag (q.v.), he made his debut at the Western Art Union in October with a "Fruit" painting as well as a landscape. The Cincinnati press announced to the public that he was "favorably known as a fruit painter" *(Daily Cincinnati Gazette,* January 30, 1850).

Duncanson's years as an itinerant painter, from 1845 to 1850, were difficult ones for the young artist. During this time he regularly moved among Cincinnati, Monroe, Michigan, and Detroit. Commissions were often hard to secure and at times he became destitute. However, Duncanson endured with the support of a few benefactors. One such benefactor was Henry N. Walker, whose descendants related the history behind *Fruit Piece* in their 1957 bequest to the Detroit Institute of Arts. Walker was a successful Detroit attorney who served in the state government from 1843 to 1846. He became interested in Duncanson's work in the mid-1840s and provided him with financial support. When Duncanson's career was more established in 1849, after he won the state-fair premium, Duncanson returned Walker's generosity by giving him this painting.

Duncanson's *Fruit Piece* is one of the finest of his seven extant still-life paintings. Five of these date to about 1849; the other two works are extremely early examples *(Roses Still Life,* ca. 1841; *Fancy Still Life,* ca. 1843; both National Museum of American Art, Washington, D.C.). The Detroit painting is very closely related to Duncanson's *Still Life* in the Los Angeles County Museum of Art. The two paintings share the same format of a tabletop arrangement of fruits and nuts crowned by a pineapple and set into a proscenium niche. The Detroit painting is considerably "fancier," with a more sumptuous arrangement on a nicely draped table. A third still-life painting from 1849 *(Fruit—Fancy Still Life;* National Afro-American Museum and Cultural Center, Wilberforce, Ohio) has a lush setting of fruits and flowers, including the pineapple motif, surrounding a robin's nest. But the *Fruit—Fancy Still Life* is set before a natural backdrop of foliage, not a proscenium niche. On stylistic grounds, it appears that the Detroit *Fruit Piece* and the *Fruit Still Life* in the Corcoran Gallery of Art (Washington, D.C.) are the most accomplished of Duncanson's still lifes. These two paintings must have been painted later in 1849, while the other three works, *Watermelons and Peaches* (private collection, Seattle), *Fruit—Fancy Still Life* (National Afro-American Museum and Cultural Center), and *Still Life* (Los Angeles County Museum of Art), which are far less developed in composition and rendering, were probably painted earlier in the year.

Another group of Duncanson's works have been closely related to the still-life paintings: the Belmont murals in the Taft Museum, Cincinnati. This large mural scheme is the most accomplished domestic mural decoration in antebellum America. Commissioned by the homeowner Nicholas Longworth from Duncanson around 1850, the murals consist of eight large landscape views and three overdoor floral vignettes in the entrance hall of the mansion. Each of the scenes is bordered with neorococo trompe-l'oeil frames to give the illusion of enframed paintings hanging on the walls. The vignettes of flowers in vases are entirely different from Duncanson's easel still lifes, in that they are formally and stylistically related to interior decoration and wallpaper fashions. Although the landscape murals were painted by Duncanson, studies of the Belmont mural decorations have suggested that, on a commission of this scale, the overdoor vignettes were probably executed by assistants (Ketner 1988). In this comparison, the design for the floral murals was adapted from the tradition of interior decoration that was most appropriate to the function of the painting. In the easel painting of *Fruit Piece,* Duncanson skillfully enhanced the Peale family still-life style with a bountiful cornucopia of fruit. J. K.

Inscription At lower right, *R. S. Duncanson 1849*

Provenance Henry N. Walker, Detroit, from ca. 1849. Walker family, Detroit, to 1957. Acquired in 1957.

Exhibitions Detroit 1883, no. 799. Cincinnati 1955, no. 26. Washington 1967. Boston 1972. Cincinnati 1972, 27, no. 17. New York 1976a. Pittsburgh 1976. Tulsa et al. 1981, fig. 5.23.

References J. Porter 1951, 117, 119, 152. Dwight 1953. Bearden and Henderson 1972, 28–29. Gibson 1975, 94. Ketner 1993, 101, fig. 66, 193, no. 24.

22

Uncle Tom and Little Eva, 1853

Oil on canvas
69.2 × 97.2 cm (27¼ × 38¼ in.)
Gift of Mrs. Jefferson Butler and Miss Grace R. Conover (49.498)

Robert Duncanson's painting *Uncle Tom and Little Eva* derives from Harriet Beecher Stowe's *Uncle Tom's Cabin,* the most popular novel in the United States at the time. Stowe's dramatic narrative of a Southern family and its slaves took the country by storm, bringing the plight of enslaved blacks to public attention. The Reverend Francis Conover, the benefactor who commissioned the painting, and Duncanson, a mulatto artist, were certainly attuned to the social significance of the subject matter; their abolitionist and religious beliefs are reflected in Duncanson's sensitive interpretation of the subject.

Harriet Beecher Stowe was the daughter of the noted Calvinist minister and theologian Lyman Beecher. While living with her domineering father in Cincinnati, Beecher acquired the

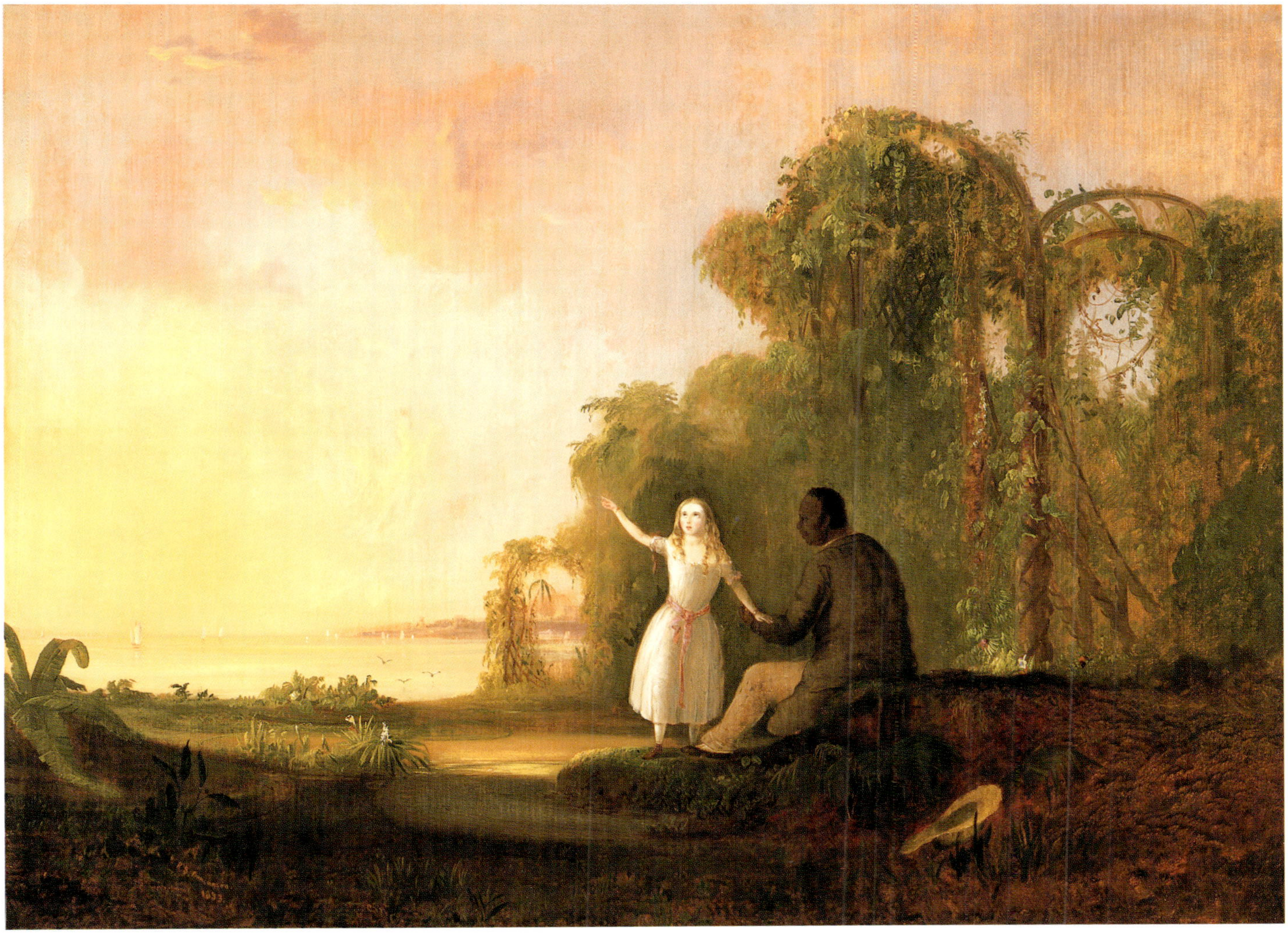

Protestant theological beliefs that mark her literary works. *Uncle Tom's Cabin* established her place in literary and social history. After the story was published in novel form in 1852, it quickly became a best seller. By 1853 stage productions of the book were sweeping the country.

From around 1840 Duncanson lived in Cincinnati and would have known of the Beecher family. Although Stowe wrote *Uncle Tom's Cabin* shortly after she left the city, Duncanson was aware of her work. The Reverend Conover was also a transplanted Cincinnatian, moving to Detroit in 1853 to practice law; he eventually became the editor of the *Detroit Advertiser and Tribune.* Formerly an Episcopalian rector, Conover was known to hold strong abolitionist beliefs. Having just moved from Cincinnati, Conover may have been familiar with Duncanson's growing reputation as an artist there. Duncanson's racial background may have led to his receiving the commission for *Uncle Tom and Little Eva,* his only treatment of an African-American subject from literature.

Seated on a mossy bank, Uncle Tom is portrayed holding little Eva's outstretched hand. They are enshrouded by thick, semitropical trees draped with Spanish moss and exotic flowers. Bamboo arbors create a repeated arched pattern against the richly colored sunset. The scene is derived from chapter 22 of *Uncle Tom's Cabin,* where Eva is teaching Tom to read the Bible. Eva has dropped her Bible and is gazing up at the sky, where she sees the heavens open before her. Pointing to her vision she proclaims to her faithful slave, "'I'm going there,' she said, 'to the spirits bright, Tom. I'm going before long.'"

The patron probably chose the moment portrayed. The Reverend Conover could have selected a more dramatic

Uncle Tom and Little Eva

passage, such as the freeing of the slaves or the flogging death of Tom, but he decided on a crucial passage with profound religious significance that is central to the theme of the story. While she is teaching her slave to read the words of God, Eva's death is foreshadowed. The sickly child's death symbolized the Calvinist-Christian ethic of love and sacrifice for salvation. Salvation could be interpreted here as both spiritual salvation, for Eva, and physical emancipation, for slaves.

The scene is set in a lush landscape that conveys the religious solemnity appropriate to the narrative. Duncanson's imagery for this setting came from Stowe's description of the view from the villa on Lake Pontchartrain, near New Orleans, where Eva beheld the vision, "[s]urrounded by light verandas of bamboo-work.... The common sitting room opened on to a large garden, fragrant with every picturesque plant and flower of the tropics, where winding paths ran down to the very shores of the lake, whose silvery sheet of water lay there, rising and falling in the sunbeams.... It is now one of those intensely golden sunsets which kindles the whole sky into one blaze of glory, and makes the water another sky." Duncanson deviated from the description only slightly, re-creating the many details of Stowe's novel with great assiduity.

The compositional source for this painting was the engraving of this scene in the original edition of *Uncle Tom's Cabin* (Stowe 1852, 2:63). The illustration portrays the slave sitting in the arbor holding Eva's hand as she experiences her heavenly vision. In the left distance is a view of Lake Pontchartrain dotted with sailboats. Duncanson drew directly on the motifs and their vignette arrangement in this illustration for his own work. The painter has merely expanded the landscape setting and endowed Eva with a more dramatic gesture. There are few other paintings of this popular literary scene, with the exception of a folk-art painting by a Canadian, Ira Barton, from the mid-1850s (Upper Canada Village, Morrisburg, Ontario), that replicates the illustration exactly.

Duncanson's painting received considerable attention from the press when it was created. A series of reviews in Cincinnati and Detroit newspapers shed light on the contemporary reception of the painting and help establish the sequence of events in the commission. In February 1853 Duncanson was exhibiting three landscapes, a still life, and a portrait at Detroit's second art exhibition, the Firemen's Fair. He had also exhibited at the fair the year before and had an established reputation in Michigan by this time. Conover may have seen Duncanson's work at the Firemen's Fair in February and commissioned *Uncle Tom and Little Eva* then. After Duncanson returned to his Cincinnati studio in March 1853, the press ran a special "Personal and Artistical" notice on this painting before it was completed: "Duncanson is putting finishing touches to another fine picture —called 'Uncle Tom'" *(Daily Cincinnati Gazette,* March 17, 1853). The painting was in Detroit by April 21, when it was reviewed by the local press. Duncanson departed for Europe on April 26 from New York and probably had delivered the painting early in April. After it arrived, the *Detroit Free Press,* Conover's rival newspaper, reprinted a severely critical article from the *Cincinnati Daily Commercial,* "AN UNCLE TOMITUDE.—Uncle Tom, according to the artist, is a very stupid looking creature, and Eva, instead of being a fragile and fading floweret, is a rosy-complexioned, healthy-seeming child, not a bit ethereal" (April 21, 1853).

This reviewer perceptively noted the principal weakness in *Uncle Tom and Little Eva:* the figures are poorly drawn and unconvincing. In his thirty-year career Duncanson was never able to master figure painting. The clumsy, ill-proportioned characters of Tom and Eva betray this weakness and are sufficient cause for the harsh criticism by the *Daily Commercial* reviewer. It is the landscape that sensitively responds to the sentiment of the literary source. The richly glowing sunset and exotic land convey Duncanson's, and his patron's, hope for a resolution to the slavery question through the religious application of love and sacrifice.

J. K.

Inscription At lower left, *R. S. Duncanson 1853*

Provenance Rev. James F. Conover, Detroit, 1853–1902. Conover family, Detroit, 1902–49. Acquired in 1949.

Exhibitions Michigan State Fair, 1865. Detroit 1949. Detroit 1952. Detroit 1952b, no. 140. Denver 1953. Cincinnati 1955, 206, no. 29. Indianapolis 1961, no. 13. Flint 1963, no. 7. Brunswick 1964. Washington 1967. Philadelphia 1969, no. 74. San Diego 1970. Boston 1972. Cincinnati 1972, 11, 12, no. 8. Los Angeles et al. 1976, no. 25. Salt Lake City 1976. Durham 1984, 6, no. 12. Muskegon and Detroit 1987, 63, 211. Los Angeles 1987, 16, fig. 11. Washington and Brooklyn 1990, 46. New York et al. 1993, 20, fig. 10.

References *Daily Cincinnati Gazette,* March 17, 1853, 2. *Detroit Free Press,* April 21, 1853, 21. J. Porter 1943, 43–46. J. Porter 1951, 128–129, 147. Cavallo 1950–51, 21–25. Detroit 1952, 47, no. 140. *Detroit News Pictorial Magazine,* November 23, 1958. Dover 1960, 25, 84. Kenny 1965, 23. *Apollo* 1972. Fine 1973, 50–51. Gibson 1975, 95. Parks 1980, 1–14. Washington 1985a, 54–55, fig. 13. Ketner 1993, 105, pl. 7, 195, no. 45.

23

Ellen's Isle, Loch Katrine, 1871

Oil on canvas

72.4 × 124.5 cm (28½ × 49 in.)

Gift of the Estate of Ralzemond D. Parker (F80.215)

AFTER FOUR YEARS as an expatriate artist living in Canada and England to escape the Civil War, Duncanson returned to Cincinnati in 1867, having been recognized by the London *Art Journal* as a "master" landscape painter. On his return, he commenced a series of landscapes inspired by romantic literature that expressed his fascination with the land and lore of Scotland. One of his final paintings, *Ellen's Isle, Loch Katrine,* culminates Duncanson's career. Inspired by Sir Walter Scott's epic poem *Lady of the Lake* (1810), Duncanson created a "Great Picture" that resonates with meaning for both Euro- and African Americans.

Among the most popular authors in mid-nineteenth-century America, Scott was memorialized with a statue in New York's Central Park in 1872. At its dedication the poet William Cullen Bryant anointed Scott "a genius of a new order" (Ketner 1993, 158). In *Lady of the Lake* Scott intertwines Scottish legends of Highland and Lowland wars with the theme of three men embattled over the love of a woman, Ellen Douglas. Although Duncanson did not portray a particular passage from the poem, nineteenth-century spectators would have associated the location with Scott's literature. Scott introduced the poem by describing the pastoral effect of the golden light shining on the lake: "gleaming with the setting sun, / One burnish'd sheet of living gold, / Loch Katrine beneath him roll'd." The author continues, referring to the sublime and picturesque qualities of the rugged Highland scenery: "High on the South huge Ben-venue / Down on the lake in masses threw / Crags, knolls, and mounds, confus'dly hurl'd, / The fragments of an earlier world. / A wilderning forest feathered o'er / His ruined sides and summit hoar / While on the north, Through middle air, / Ben-an heaved high his forehead bare" (Scott 1851, 24–25).

With a steady iambic pentameter Scott extols the picturesque wonders of this scenic vale. Duncanson captured the landmarks mentioned in Scott's text with Ellen's island home hidden by the domineering mountains of Ben-venue. Two boats with figures pass over the smooth sheet of the lake, but they are merely anecdotal elements and do not refer to a specific passage in Scott's text. Duncanson was able to convey the pastoral mood and picturesque setting of the literary subject through the aesthetic qualities of his painting. The pastel-tinted mountains dissolve in the golden light on the horizon. The glow of the sunset imbues *Ellen's Isle* with a serene mood, reflected in the shimmering surface of the loch. With a transparent touch, Duncanson delicately brushed onto the canvas the rays of light and the mirror-smooth lake. Breaking through the clouds and shining across the landscape, the light in this picture is one of Duncanson's most accomplished passages. The tranquil beauty of the light, the sublime presence of the mountains, and the picturesque vitality of the surrounding forests demonstrate Duncanson's sensitive interpretation of Scott's subject with his command of landscape aesthetics.

Duncanson painted *Ellen's Isle* as a pendant to *Paradise and the Peri* (1871; unlocated) with the intention of touring the two paintings across the United States. These paintings constituted a major statement of his ambitions as a landscape painter of elevated literary subjects. *Paradise and the Peri* was the last of four paintings inspired by Thomas Moore's orientalist poem "Lalla Rookh" (1817) and has remained unlocated since it was vandalized in the Detroit sheriff's office in 1876. Duncanson spent the winter of 1870–71 working on these paintings. A small sketch dated 1870 was the preliminary source for *Ellen's Isle* (Mr. and Mrs. Meyer Potamkin, Philadelphia), but the Detroit painting was not finished until late June 1871. At that time the *Cincinnati Daily Enquirer* mentioned that Duncanson "has about completed a Scotch scene, 'Ellen's Isle'" (June 25, 1871). After it was placed on exhibition with *Paradise and the Peri* in August the critic declared: "In '*Ellen's Isle*' the artist has probably produced the chef d'oeuvre of his life" (*Cincinnati Daily Enquirer,* August 20, 1871). The two paintings were received with ecstatic praise by the local press for their elevated literary aspirations and beautiful landscape scenery. After a month on exhibition at Wiswell's Gallery in Cincinnati, Duncanson prepared his paintings for a national tour to begin in Detroit and conclude in Boston. At this time Duncanson's brother, John Dean, died, and Robert returned to his family home in Monroe, Michigan, in September, where he exhibited his paintings for two weeks. He then displayed his paintings at the Western Art Association, where they attracted considerable attention in the cultural circles of Detroit. The Detroit public was universal in its praise for the paintings, and *Paradise and the Peri* was acquired for the City of Detroit.

Not only were Duncanson's paintings and Scott's poem popular with the Euro-American public, but they also held special significance for the African-American community of the time. As Frederick Douglass related in the narrative of his life, on successfully escaping from slavery he abandoned his slave name and adopted his surname from that of the Douglas clan in Scott's poem. Furthermore, W. E. B. Du Bois spoke fondly of Scott's poem as a memorable literary work from his youthful education and described the Highland scenery around Loch Katrine as the "sort of world we want to create for ourselves and for all in America" (Lubin 1994, 146).

From its inception, Duncanson planned to culminate the tour of his paintings with the presentation of his chef d'oeuvre to Senator Charles Sumner, as an expression of gratitude for the abolitionist politician's efforts in securing emancipation for African-American slaves. Following the Detroit exhibition, Duncanson took *Ellen's Isle* to Boston for the public presentation of his painting that depicted the world that African Americans aspired to create in America. As a public figure Sumner was reluctant to accept gifts and accepted the painting only after repeated urgings by Duncanson *(Pacific Appeal,* November 14, 1874). Before being placed in Sumner's home, the painting was publicly exhibited in Washington, D.C. Sumner retained the painting until his death in 1874, when it was given with the rest of his collection to the Museum of Fine Arts, Boston. There it was exhibited with the Sumner bequest before it was returned to the Duncanson family as Sumner had stipulated in his will (Ralzemond D. Parker papers, Burton Historical Collection, Detroit Public Library).

During the time Duncanson created *Ellen's Isle,* he was troubled by deep psychological problems. He was reported to have become a "spiritualist" and to be possessed by a master, a woman, who assisted him in creating his paintings. In posthumous articles several Cincinnati newspapers mentioned that Duncanson received "superhuman aid" in the creation of *Ellen's Isle* and *Paradise and the Peri.* The press concluded by noting that "evidences of mental derangement were painfully abundant to Mr. Duncanson's admirers at the time these pictures were on view and subsequently" *(Cincinnati Daily Enquirer,* December 28, 1872). Duncanson's psychotic behavior became increasingly pronounced throughout 1871 and 1872. He produced no known works during the last year of his life: however, he had enough material to hang an exhibition in Detroit in October 1872. While hanging his exhibition he collapsed and was hospitalized until his death three months later.

J. K.

Inscription At lower right, *R. S. Duncanson Cinti. O. 1871*

Provenance Charles Sumner, 1871–74. Museum of Fine Arts, Boston, 1874–84. Mrs. Phoebe Duncanson, 1884–88. Ralzemond Parker, Detroit, from 1888. Ralzemond D. Parker, Washington, D.C., to 1980. Acquired in 1980.

Exhibitions Wiswell's Gallery, Cincinnati, August–September 1871. Monroe, Mich., September 1871. Western Art Association, Detroit, 1871. Boston 1874, no. 29. Washington 1967. Cincinnati 1972, 15, no. 32.

References *Cincinnati Daily Enquirer,* June 25, 1871, 4; July 30, 1871, 8; August 12, 1871, 8; August 20, 1871, 8; August 27, 1871; September 24, 1871, 4; November 26, 1871, 5. *Monroe Commercial,* September 14, 1871, 3. *Detroit Free Press,* September 15 and 16, 1871, 1. *Detroit Daily Union,* September 16, 1871, 4. *Detroit Daily Post,* September 16, 1871, 4. *Daily Cincinnati Commercial,* December 27, 1872, 8. *Pacific Appeal* (San Francisco), November 14, 1874, 1. *The Aldine* (Virginia), February 1875, 277. J. Porter 1951, 140, 151. Elleine Stones to James Porter, February 11, 1953 (Burton Historical Collection, Detroit). Parks 1980, 24, 42. Ketner 1983, 45–46. Washington 1985a, 63. Pringle 1985, 48. Muskegon and Detroit 1987, 66–67. Ketner 1993, 169, 174–176, pl. 20, 204, no. 143.

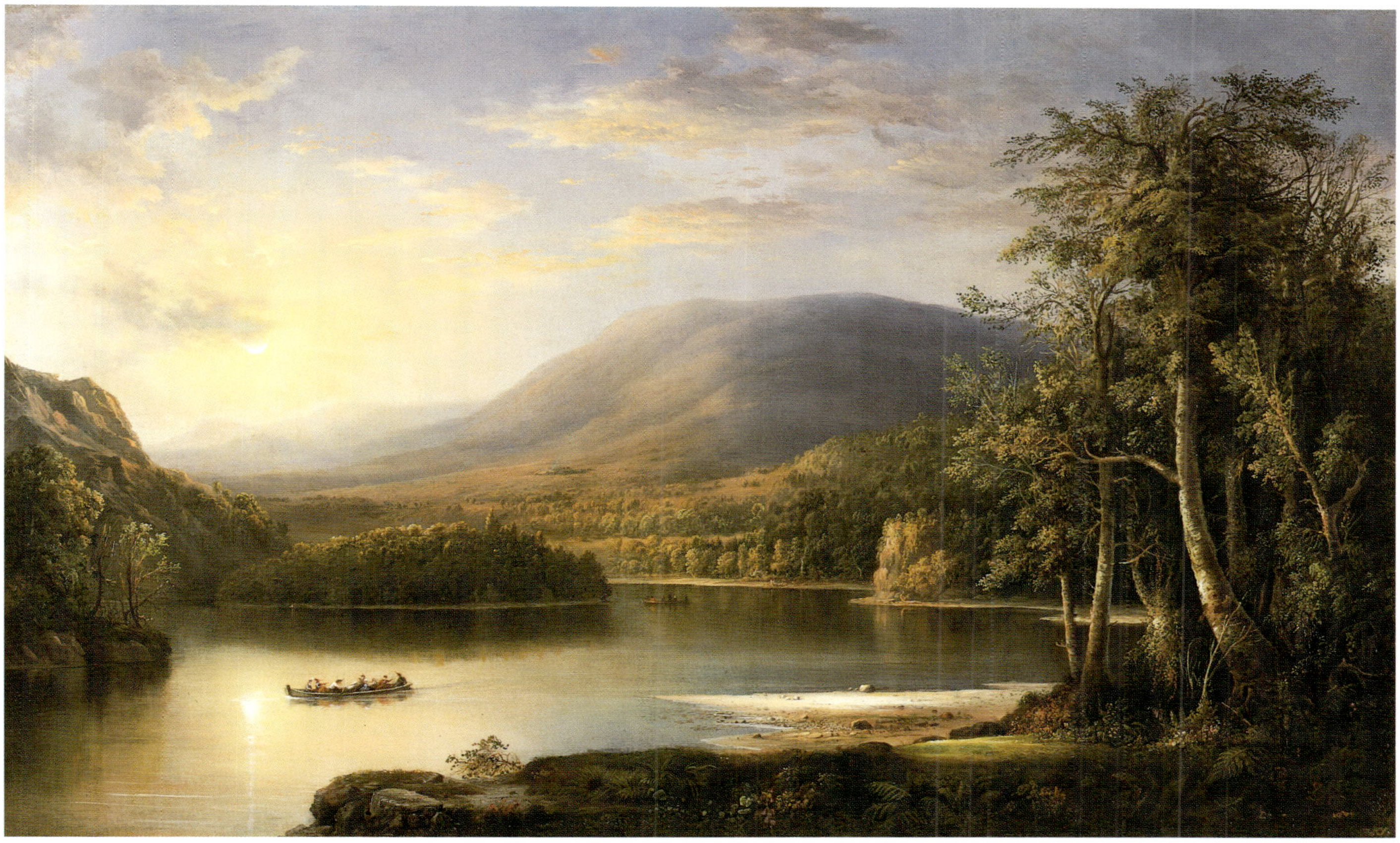

Ellen's Isle

Thomas Cowperthwait Eakins

1844 Philadelphia 1916

Eakins's unique gifts and independent personality have made him one of the most admired of American nineteenth-century artists. He was closely associated with the city of his birth, Philadelphia, its traditions, its intellectuals, and its life in the arts. Except for four years in Europe, he grew up, married, taught, and painted in this city. In the fall of 1862, a year after his graduation from Central High School, he began his professional training at the Pennsylvania Academy of the Fine Arts. His early drawings of nude models reveal his extraordinary talent. He also studied anatomy at Jefferson Medical College. After four years he continued his education in Europe, as the student of Jean-Léon Gérôme in Paris and with travel to Italy, Germany, Belgium, and Spain. He returned to Philadelphia in the summer of 1870.

Almost immediately Eakins began to paint his now familiar subjects, including rowing pictures like *Max Schmitt in a Single Scull* (1871; Metropolitan Museum of Art, New York) and portraits, such as *Professor Benjamin Howard Rand* (1874; Medical College of Thomas Jefferson University, Philadelphia). As his perspective drawings, watercolors, and oil studies show, his concern was with the mechanics of painting and the intellectual and emotional lives of his subjects. His work combined the closely observed detail of the visible world with subjects of intense personal energy. The startling realism of his heroic image *The Gross Clinic* (1875; Medical College of Thomas Jefferson University, Philadelphia) led to his first rejection, by the art selection committee of the Centennial Exposition, which opened in Fairmount Park, Philadelphia, in May 1876. The painting was shown instead with the medical exhibits.

Eakins taught at the Philadelphia Sketch Club in 1874 and 1875 and continued these drawing classes when the new building of the Pennsylvania Academy opened in 1876, serving from 1878 as assistant professor and then professor of painting. Around him gathered a number of young students who spent time with him in his classes and on painting trips. In the early 1880s he became fascinated with photography, using photographs to record figures in academic poses as well as in motion. He was appointed director of the academy schools in 1882 and married his student Susan Macdowell in 1884.

His use of nude male models in the academy's female life-drawing classes led to his dismissal in 1886. He then turned almost exclusively to portrait painting, both large canvases and head-and-shoulder portraits, among them *Miss Amelia C. Van Buren* (ca. 1890; Phillips Collection, Washington, D.C.) and *The Agnew Clinic* (1889; University of Pennsylvania School of Medicine, Philadelphia). Most of his portraits were uncommissioned studies of people who interested him. Although he was widely recognized as a gifted teacher, appreciation of his work grew only gradually. He was awarded a bronze medal at the World's Columbian Exposition of 1893 in Chicago. *The Gross Clinic* was awarded a gold medal at the Universal Exposition in St. Louis in 1904. After his death his wife made it possible for his work to become better known through exhibitions and sales to public collections. He is now recognized as one of the United States' most influential and creative painters.

E. G. M.

Bibliography Hendricks 1974. Goodrich 1982. Johns 1983. Foster and Leibold 1989.

24
Dr. Horatio C Wood, 1886

Oil on canvas
162.6 × 127 cm (64 × 50 in.)
City of Detroit Purchase (30.296)

When Eakins painted this portrait of the Philadelphia physician Horatio C Wood (he used the *C* without a period for his middle initial), the artist was at a critical turning point in his life, having recently been forced to resign from his position as director of the Pennsylvania Academy Schools. Wood (1841–1920), who received his medical degree from the University of Pennsylvania in 1862, held a clinical professorship in nervous diseases at the University of Pennsylvania and was on the neurological staff of the Pennsylvania Hospital. An energetic man, he worked in four fields: natural science; experimental pharmacology, physiology, and pathology; medical jurisprudence; and nervous diseases. His publications included *A Treatise on Therapeutics* (1874) and *Nervous Diseases and Their Diagnosis,* which was published the year after the portrait was painted (*DAB,* 459–460). Wood, who knew Eakins's father, admired the artist's work and in 1878 had purchased *The Courtship* (Fine Arts Museums of San Francisco; Anderson 1980, 35, no. 2; Goodrich 1933, 171–172, no. 119). In November 1886, after the portrait was painted, he bought Eakins's watercolor *Mending the Net* (1882; Goodrich 1933, 175, no. 158; Goodrich 1982, 2:166).

Eakins painted Wood's portrait in the spring of 1886, recording two payments in his journal, the first on April 23, "to Dr. Wood's portrait 100"—and then on April 29, "to Dr. Wood's portrait 50"—(Eakins 1883–88, 96). Wood described the circumstances of the painting many years later, in 1917, when, after the artist's death, he and Mrs. Eakins disputed the ownership of the portrait (they apparently had forgotten the payments; Bregler 1989, fiche II 1/D/8–1/E/10, and Foster and Leibold 1989, 32, 274, 411). The College of Physicians of Philadelphia asked Wood if there was a portrait of him that could be hung at the college, and he remembered the sittings for Eakins and contacted the artist's widow. On March 22 Wood asked Samuel Murray, who was acting on behalf of Mrs. Eakins, to ask the artist's widow to "allow me to present

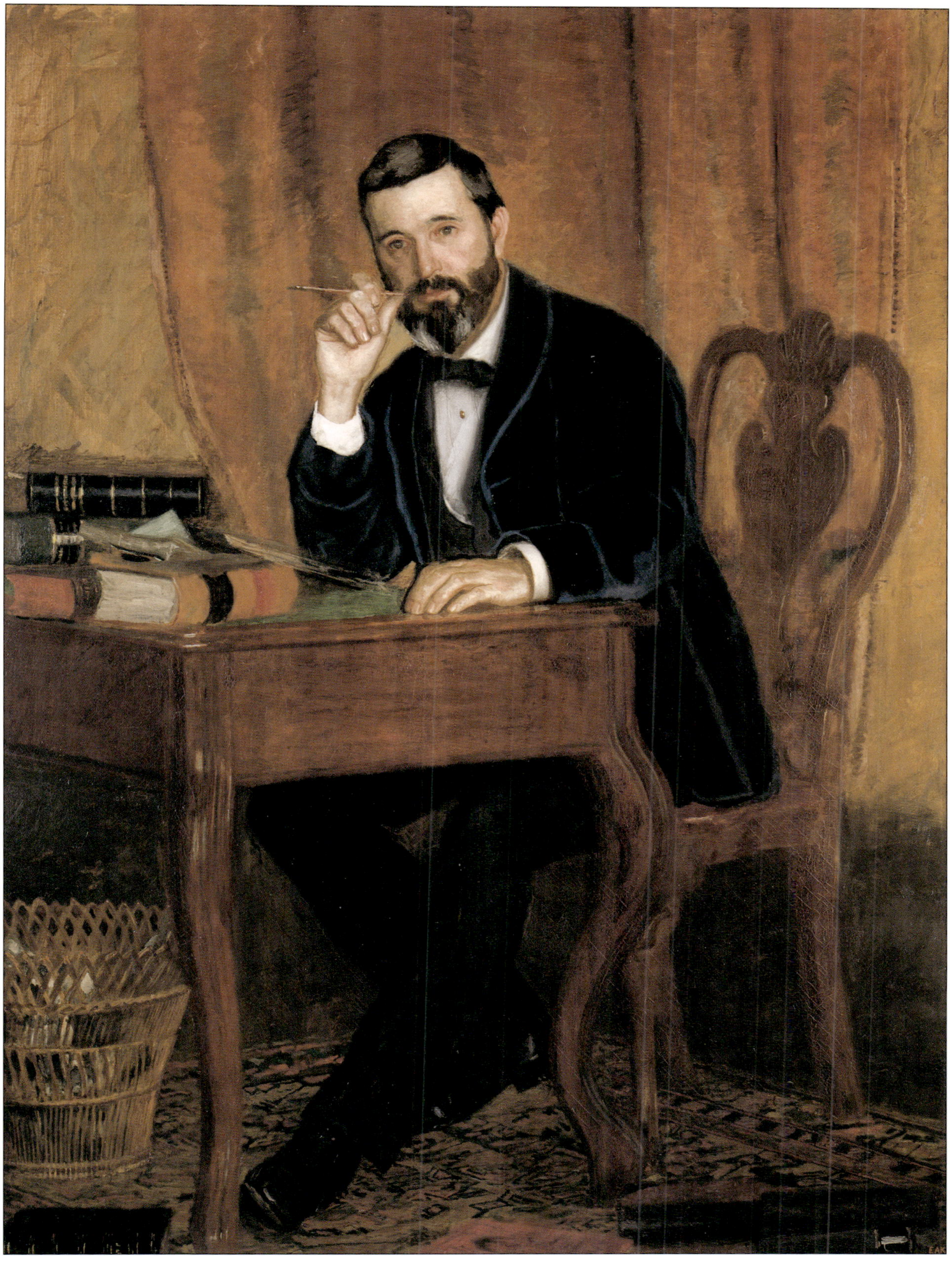

Dr. Horatio C Wood

the picture in her name to be put in the Hall of the Presidents of the College of Physicians. I will of course have it appropriately framed." Susan Eakins responded on March 26 with the assumption that he wanted to buy the portrait. Wood then recalled the circumstances of the sitting, writing on March 29: "I sat for the portrait, not by my own desire but at the request of your husband to allow him to make a picture of me; and the time I gave him was worth to me more money than was the time he spent in the working out of his desire." Mrs. Eakins answered on April 2 that "Mr. Eakins painted many remarkable men and always said, such men should be painted without regard to the future market value. The portrait of you, which is a good likeness, representing you in your younger days, not smiling with a bunch of flowers in your hand, but after the manner of Mr. Eakins portraits, engaged at your noble work, as in the case of the portraits of Dr. Henry Beates, Dr. Forbes, Dr. Gross, Dr. Agnew, Prof. Roland and others all serious and showing them interested in their lifework." She suggested an exchange, *The Courtship* and *Mending the Net* for the portrait. Wood replied on April 3 that he had bought those two pictures because "I wanted some of his work, and because I admired them very much." He thought the "tacit understanding" was that he was also to own the portrait, although "I did not ask Mr. Eakins to paint it, he asked me to sit for him. . . . I have none of that vanity which makes a man desire to have his own portrait, but I was approached by the College of Physicians . . . and then remembered once going for a number of engagements to Mr. Eakins' studio, and his remarking that my punctuality and general behavior was so different towards him from some other doctors."

Wood then asked his sons James and George about the portrait. Wood recounted to Susan Eakins on April 7 that one of his sons remembered his taking the portrait home, where "it was received with so much disfavor that Mr. Eakins, hearing the criticism, asked me to bring it back to him, and he would try if he could make it more of a likeness. I suppose I got tired of sitting, or my sons did not think the likeness improved, and I was so busy myself that finally I forgot all about it." He ended: "The father of your husband was for many years my teacher in penmanship, and was much respected by me. Your husband was my friend. Your husband was never strong in portraiture, though he did wonderful work in picture-making, and I want to say that the two pictures which I own I consider gems." Ultimately Mrs. Eakins kept the painting, believing that she had title to it.

The portrait is a sympathetic one. Wood, dark-haired and with a black beard touched with white, is seated at a mahogany writing table. He holds a pen, its upper end in his mouth, and looks up, apparently in the midst of taking notes in one of the notebooks on the table. Several large bound volumes are piled on the table or scattered on the floor at his feet. Warm brown tones dominate the painting, with accents in brighter details. The blue of Wood's velvet jacket and the red, brown, blue, and green leather book bindings enliven the darker colors of the sitter's black trousers and vest, the brown furniture, and the reddish brown curtain. The patterned rug on the floor is a mixture of green, red, black, and brown.

Wood played a major role in Eakins's recovery from the traumatic events of 1886. He arranged for the artist to spend several months in the summer of 1887 at the B-T Ranch in the Dakota Territory, near Dickinson (North Dakota) (Schendler 1967, xi; Hendricks 1974, 172; Anderson 1980, 21–23, 35; Johns 1983, 136; Leibold 1988; and Foster and Leibold 1989, 90–93). Wood, part owner of the ranch, held that "modern life . . . tends to produce nervous exhaustion" (quoted in Johns 1983, 160). He was a proponent of the "Camp Cure," in which a "return to the wilder areas of the country was essential . . . the first step in a therapeutic treatment which sought to reverse . . . the routine of the patient's city life" (Anderson 1980, 21). He wrote Albert Tripp, the manager, in June 1887: "Mr. Eakins is an especial friend of mine who proposes to spend some time with you studying cowboy life in order to paint pictures of it" (Goodrich 1982, 2:16; Leibold 1988, 3; Bregler 1989). Eakins left Philadelphia in late July 1887 for the ranch; Tripp arranged to meet him in Dickinson on July 26 (Tripp to Eakins, July 4, 1887; Bregler 1989, fiche I 6/D/10). Eakins wrote his friend J. Laurie Wallace that he would be at the ranch until October 10 (Eakins to Wallace, October 9, 1887; Bregler 1989, fiche I 4/E/14). Wood's fifteen-year-old son, George, was there at the same time. William G. Macdowell, Eakins's brother-in-law, sent him some money on August 29, writing: "Hope you are having a good time & getting into first class physical condition" (Bregler 1989, fiche I 7/B/7).

When Eakins returned, Walt Whitman commented that the artist had been "sick, rundown, out of sorts: he went right among the cowboys: herded: built up miraculously . . . it [the trip] must have done much toward giving him or confirming his theory of painting: he has a sort of cowboy broncho method: he could not have got that wholly or even mainly in the studios of Paris—he needed the converting, confirming, uncompromising touch of the plains" (quoted by Leibold 1988, 3, from Traubel 1953, 135).

E. G. M.

Inscription At lower right, *EAKINS*

Provenance Purchased from Susan Macdowell Eakins, the artist's widow, through Clarence W. Cranmer, Philadelphia, in 1930.

Exhibitions The New Students League, Philadelphia, date unknown. New York 1917, no. 25. Philadelphia 1917, no. 81. New York 1923, no. 19. Detroit 1937, no. 13. Washington et al. 1961, no. 56.

Philadelphia 1965, no. 52. New York 1970a, no. 52. London 1993, no. 25.

References Eakins 1883–88, 96. A. Burroughs 1924, 332. C. Burroughs 1930. Detroit 1930, no. 297. Detroit 1930a, 72. Marceau 1930, 23, no. 114. Goodrich 1933, 181, no. 239. F. Porter 1959, pl. 41. Schendler 1967, xi, 116, 118. Cummings and Elam 1971, 147. Hendricks 1974, 172, 329, no. 144. Goodrich 1982, 2:16, 53, 166, 167. Johns 1983, 78n, 136, 160–161. Bregler 1989, fiche II 1/D/8–1/E/10. Foster and Leibold 1989, 32, 92, 176, 269, 274, 383, 411.

25

Robert M. Lindsay, 1900

Oil on academy board
29.9 × 27 cm (11¾ × 10⅝ in.)
Gift of Dexter M. Ferry, Jr. (35.14)

THIS SMALL OIL on buff-gray academy board, the study for the portrait of Robert M. Lindsay (cat. no. 26), focuses on the sitter's figure. The artist blocked out the pose and the patterns of light and shadow, setting Lindsay against a deep red-brown background, the color that he used for the wall in the final painting. In the sketch, Eakins depicts Lindsay with a small number of strokes, using a heavily loaded brush. His face is loosely painted also, but with more details than his body and with strong highlighting, especially on his forehead. Lindsay's gray beard becomes a notable feature of the image. The figure seems more stout than in the final portrait and also holds the print at more of an angle than in the final image.
E. G. M.

Provenance Purchased from the artist's widow, Susan Macdowell Eakins, by Ernest Lee Parker, Philadelphia. Purchased through Clarence W. Cranmer, Philadelphia, with funds donated by Dexter M. Ferry, Jr., in 1935.

Exhibitions Philadelphia 1917, no. 13. New York 1929, no. 4. Detroit 1937, no. 18. East Lansing 1966, no. 39.

References A. Burroughs 1924, 332. Marceau 1930, 28, no. 212. Goodrich 1933, 191, no. 336. C. Burroughs 1935. F. Porter 1959, pl. 63. Hendricks 1974, 329, no. 145.

26

Robert M. Lindsay, 1900

Oil on canvas
61 × 50.8 cm (24 × 20 in.)
Gift of Dexter M. Ferry, Jr. (35.13)

ROBERT M. LINDSAY (ca. 1837–1912) was a Philadelphia book and print publisher and seller. He was the son of Jeremiah M. and Catherine M. Lindsay (*Philadelphia Public Ledger,* April 27, 1912). He is listed in *Gopsill's Philadelphia City Directory for 1886* as a bookseller at 1028 Walnut Street and in *Boyd's Co-Partnership and Residence Business Directory of Philadelphia City* for 1901 at the same address as a picture dealer. By 1910 he had moved to 926 Walnut Street according to *Boyd's Directory* for 1910. The Philadelphia auctioneer Stan. V. Henkels held the sale *Artists' Proof Etchings, Choice Line Engravings, Elegant Watercolors* "from the noted gallery of Mr. Robert M. Lindsay" at Thomas Birch's Sons on November 11–12, 1892, and the sale of his estate, including prints and art reference books, at Samuel T. Freeman and Company on June 7–8, 1912. According to Ernest Lee Parker, owner of the portrait before it came to the Detroit Institute of Arts, Lindsay was "very friendly with Mr. Eakins—his scholarly attainments proved an attraction to the artist; which led to the painting, you now have. The Lindsay Galleries had a great attraction for the artists and collectors of that time, due to the fine knowledge and character of its owner" (correspondence, curatorial files, DIA).

This small portrait, with its dark, rich colors and serene mood, shows Lindsay, wearing a black suit with a small red boutonniere in the lapel, seated in a Chippendale-style chair. He looks closely at a print that may have come from the portfolio on the stand to the left, peering at the paper through dark-framed glasses. The room, with its oak-paneled print cabinets and oriental carpet, may depict his gallery. Along the top of the cabinets, against the dark red wall, are two paintings in gilt frames, some books, and, on the far right, a bronze bust of a man. The larger painting is a portrait in black and white of a man in seventeenth-century Dutch clothing—a dark coat, a large white neck ruff, and a broad-brimmed hat. Hendricks (1974, 330) has suggested that the sculpture is Samuel Murray's bust of Benjamin Eakins, the artist's father, who had recently died, but this is difficult to judge from the small size of the image.

The painting has been called *The Print-Collector* and *The Book-Collector.* The Detroit Institute also owns Eakins's sketch for it (cat. no. 25).
E. G. M.

Inscription At right center, *EAKINS 1900*

Provenance Purchased from the sitter's sister and heir, Matilda Lindsay, by Ernest Lee Parker, Philadelphia. Purchased, through Clarence W. Cranmer, Philadelphia, with funds donated by Dexter M. Ferry, Jr., in 1935.

Exhibitions New York 1929, no. 3, as *The Book-Collector, Mr. Lindsay.* Detroit 1937, no. 19. Pittsburgh 1945, no. 28. Vancouver 1955, no. 25. East Lansing 1966, no. 40. New York 1970a, no. 78.

References A. Burroughs 1924, 332. Goodrich 1929, 77, as *The Book-Collector.* Marceau 1930, 28, no. 213. Mather 1930, ill. 48, as *Lindsay, Book-Collector.* Goodrich 1933, 191, no. 335. C. Burroughs 1935. F. Porter 1959, pl. 62. Gowans 1966, repro. 133. Hendricks 1974, 330, no. 146.

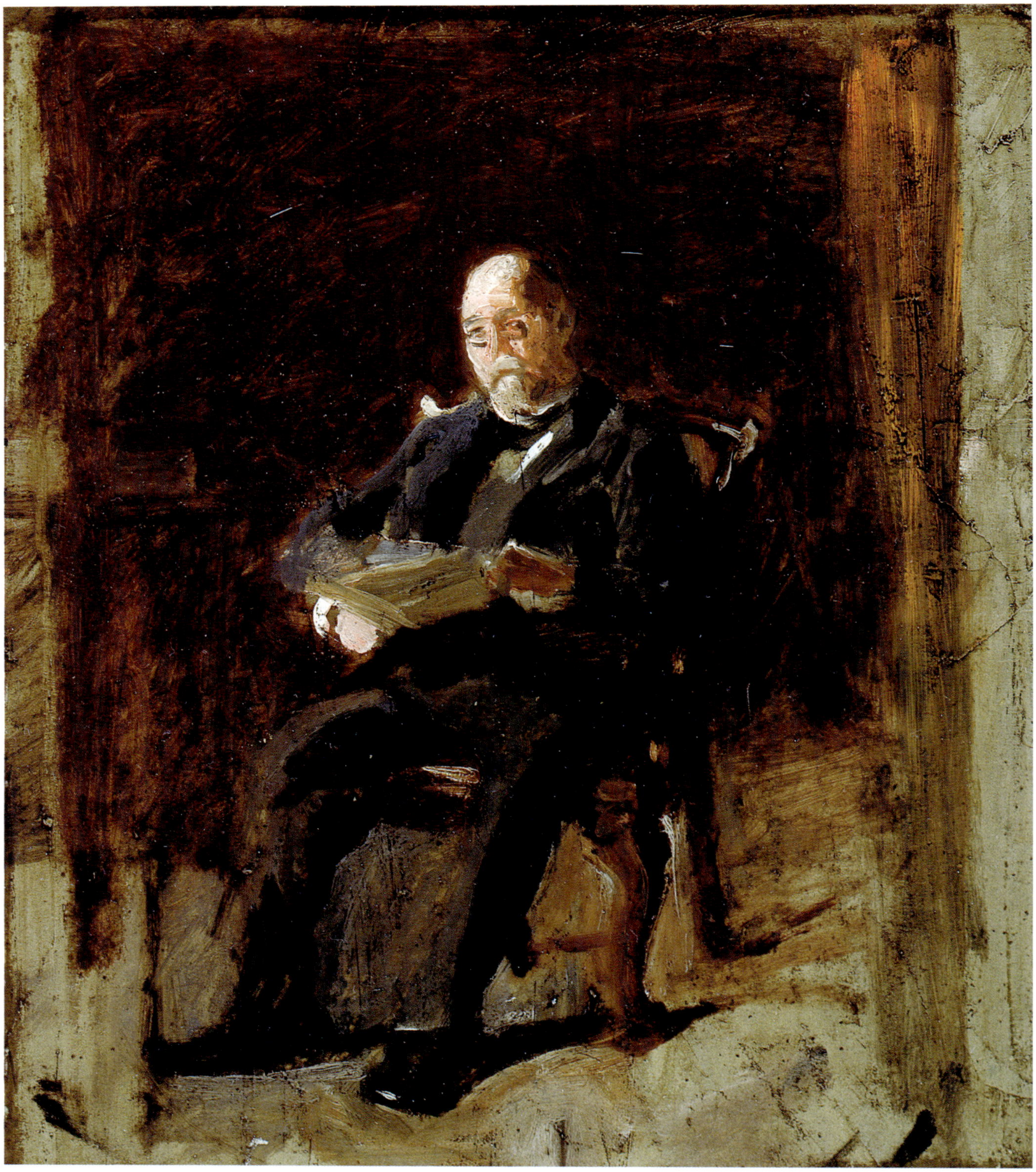

Robert M. Lindsay (sketch)

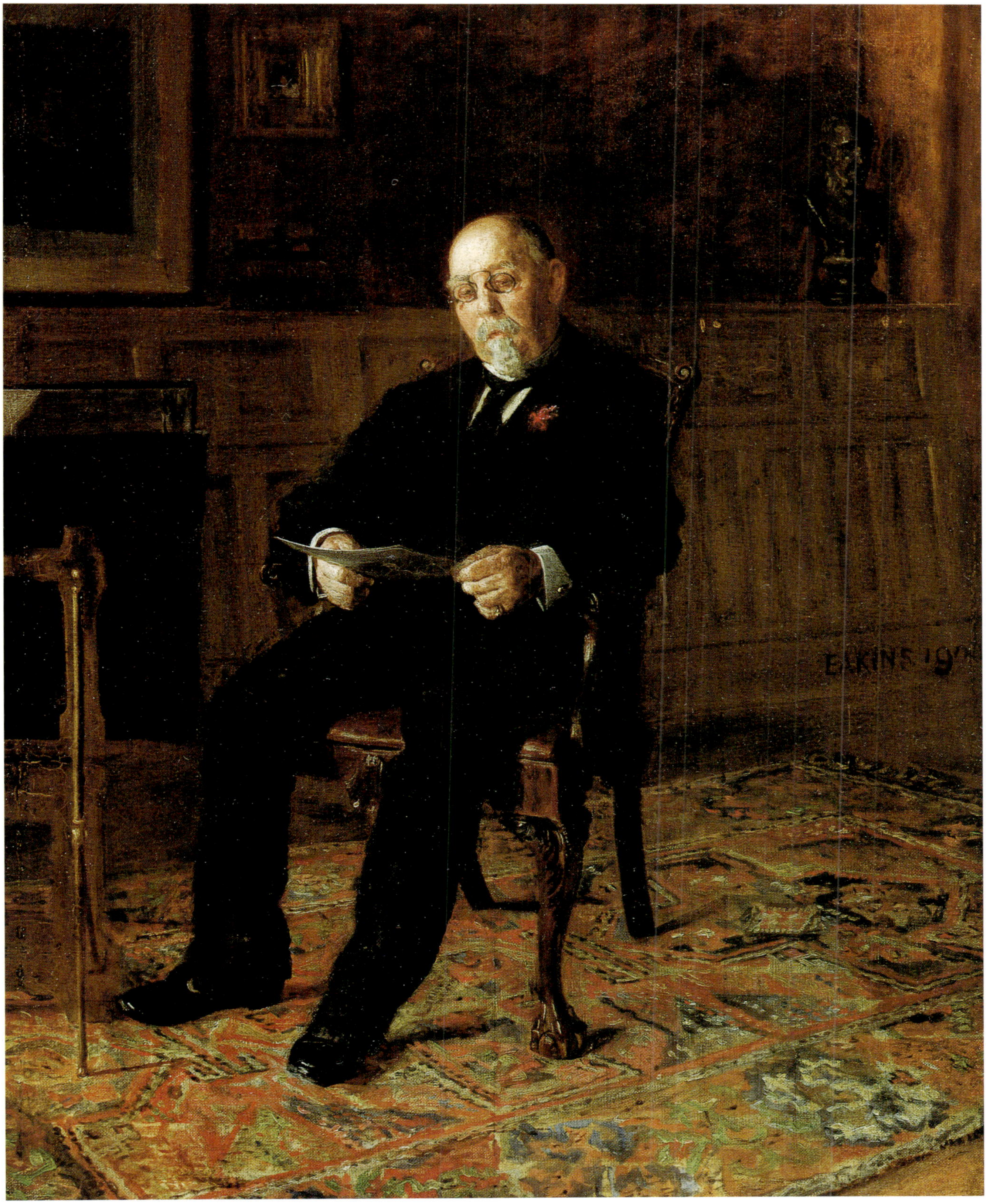

Robert M. Lindsay

Martin Edgar Ferrill

1836 or 1837 Lansingburgh, New York 1897

The few paintings by Martin Edgar Ferrill that have been discovered so far depict the leisure activities of Lansingburgh, his hometown in upstate New York. Biographical information about the artist has been compiled by Frances D. Broderick, a local historian in Lansingburgh (see correspondence, curatorial files, DIA). The artist's birth date has not been firmly established; the cemetery records and death certificate differ on his age at his death as sixty or sixty-one. His parents, Matthew and Eliza Farrell, Ferrell, or Ferrill (different spellings appear in local records), were born in Ireland and about 1835 settled in Lansingburgh, now incorporated into Troy, New York. In 1857 Ferrill married Delia Adams, with whom he had two children, who died in early childhood. The Ferrills may have lived in New York City for a time, as their daughter died there in 1865. In various Lansingburgh street directories Ferrill is listed as a brushmaker, like his father; during this period there were thirty-five brush factories in Lansingburgh, making this one of the largest industries in the town. Later he is listed as an "agent" (Broderick believes this may indicate he was making a living selling his own or other artists' paintings), and his death certificate lists his occupation as artist.

S. M. S.

Bibliography Julie Aronson in Chotner 1992, 109.

27

Sleighing Scene, 1873

Oil on canvas

46 × 61.6 cm (18⅛ × 24¼ in.)

Gift of Mrs. Lillian Henkel Haass (43.28)

Although the sleighs depicted in the foreground of *Sleighing Scene* are driving in different directions, Frances D. Broderick speculates that they may be taking part in a cutter race on Whipple Avenue (now called Fifth Avenue) in Lansingburgh, the first incorporated village in New York State (correspondence, curatorial files, DIA). Cutter or sleigh racing was a popular pastime in Lansingburgh, especially on evenings and weekends, and the races were covered in the local newspapers. The races often ended at Harlow's Hotel, where a prize of a bottle of liquor was awarded. Agnes Halsey Jones noted that during the nineteenth century, paintings of activity on public roads, especially of famous horses and drivers, were in great demand (Cooperstown et al. 1958, 40).

The brick house at right is still standing in Lansingburgh, on the west side of Fifth Avenue, between 104th and 105th streets (correspondence, curatorial files, DIA). The train seen at the foot of the hills and the telegraph poles that line the street attest to the modernity of the village. The hills in the background border the village on the east while the Hudson River borders it on the west.

The sizable Irish community of Lansingburgh is signaled by a fragment of a name, *P. O'B',* painted on the sleigh at the far right. Below the name is inscribed "MEAT AN," and the back of the sleigh holds slabs of meat, suggesting that this belongs to the local butcher. The figure on the sleigh, who winks at the viewer, is represented in caricature. Other men and women in the painting are individually characterized by a variety of hats and comical facial types. As Julie Aronson notes in describing another painting by Ferrill, *The Country Dance* (1883; National Gallery of Art, Washington, D.C.; see Aronson in Chotner 1992, 109–111), the figures in Ferrill's paintings are often caricatured.

The composition of *Sleighing Scene* is similar to the work of other "plain painters," such as Edward Hicks's *Cornell Farm* (1848; National Gallery of Art, Washington, D.C.). In both, animals and vehicles are depicted in profile in the foreground, while fields and trees diminish in the background to form a clear recession to the horizon. An overall dense pattern of forms on the surface contributes to the liveliness of the composition.

Jones and Aronson both remark on the parallel between Ferrill's paintings and lithographs published by Currier and Ives, several of which are of winter and sleighing subjects. Another sleighing scene by Ferrill is known: *Sleighing Scene in the Moonlight* or *Winter Scene, Moonlight* (1880; Frances D. Broderick, Lansingburgh, N.Y.).

S. M. S.

Inscription At lower right, *M. E. Ferrill. / NOV 1873 / Lansingburgh*

Provenance Downtown Gallery, New York. Mrs. Lillian Henkel Haass, 1932. Acquired in 1943.

Exhibitions Detroit 1932, no. 23. Chicago 1943, no. 37. Cooperstown et al. 1958, 40–41, no. 35. Mason City 1966, no. 9. Detroit 1976, 172, no. 214, ill.

References Detroit 1944, 46, no. 527. Holbrook 1955, 18. Chotner 1992, 109.

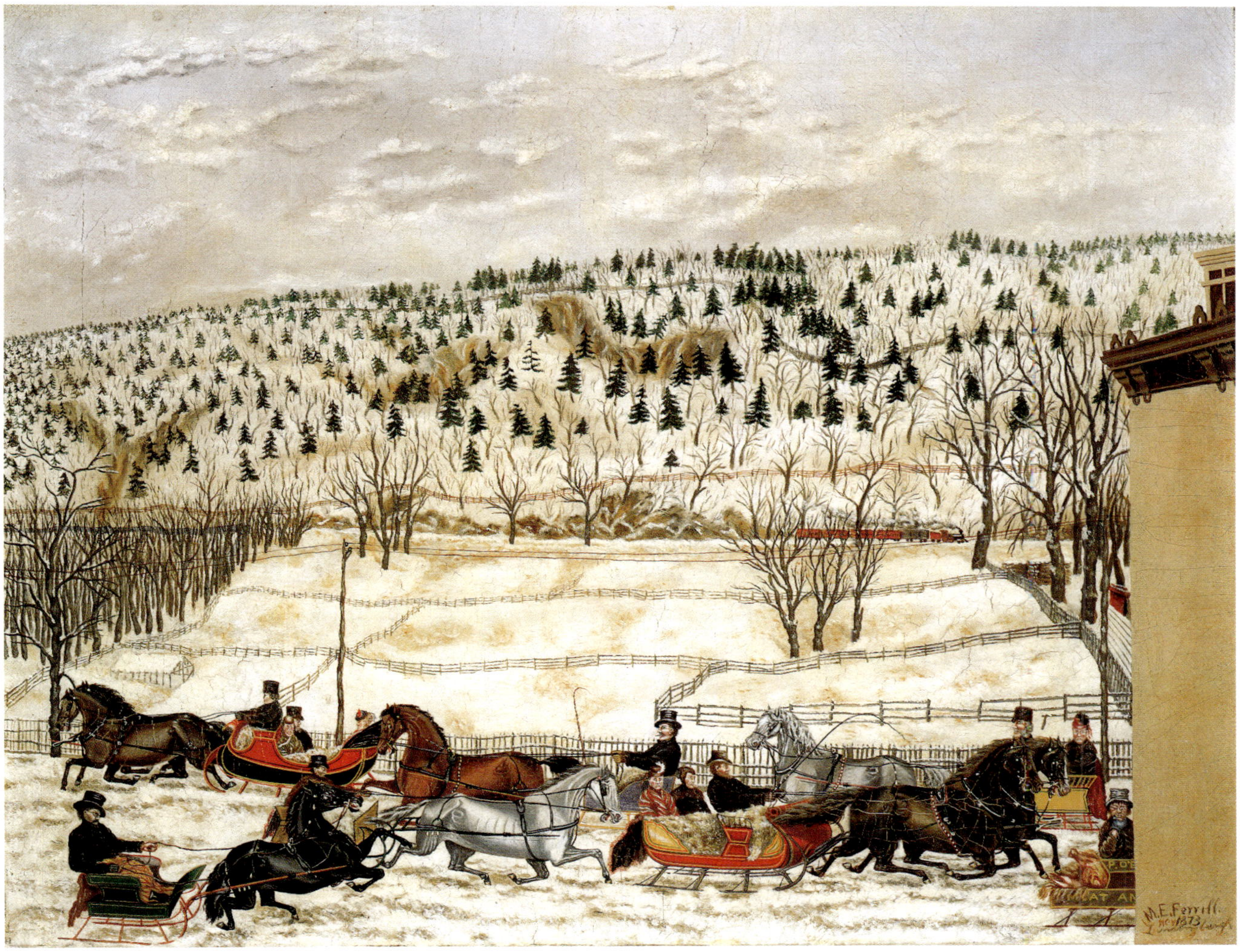

Sleighing Scene

[William] Mark Fisher

1841 Boston–London 1923

Mark Fisher spent his early life in Boston, where he was apprenticed to his cousin William Lawless, a house and sign painter. He received his first formal training at the Lowell Institute, where the landscape artist George Cass suggested that he move to Medfield to be near George Inness (q.v.). About 1861 Inness suggested that Fisher move in with his family, and through that close association he learned of the work of Camille Corot and the Barbizon painters. Inness's influence may also have steered Fisher away from studying in Düsseldorf in favor of France and Italy.

In 1863 he traveled to France and entered the École des Beaux-Arts, where he studied with Charles Gleyre. It was here that he met Claude Monet, Pierre-Auguste Renoir, Alfred Sisley, and Frédéric Bazille. He returned to the United States in 1868, prior to the Franco-Prussian War. That year at the Boston Athenaeum he exhibited *The Housewife* (unlocated). He spent the majority of the next few years in Boston; by 1871 he had returned to Europe. Although France was in the middle of political upheaval, he found Normandy to be relatively stable. He established a studio there and concentrated on painting landscapes.

A year later, Fisher moved to England, which would become his permanent home. His first few years were in London, after which he settled in the English countryside, occasionally traveling to France, Italy, and North Africa. By 1879 he was a member of the Royal Institute and in 1892 joined the New English Art Club. George Moore, the early champion of the impressionists, referred to Fisher in 1898 as the "greatest living painter in England" (quoted in Quimby 1967). In 1911 Fisher became an associate of the Royal Academy and achieved full status in 1919.

Fisher exhibited widely in both Europe and the United States, winning medals at the Paris Exposition Universelle, 1889; the World's Columbian Exposition, Chicago, 1893; the Pan-American Exposition, Buffalo, 1901; and the St. Louis Exposition, 1904. He showed continuously from 1897 to 1913 at the Carnegie Institute in Pittsburgh as well as the Royal Academy, London. His last exhibition was in London at the Leicester Galleries in 1920.

J. W. T.

Bibliography Boston 1963. Quimby 1967.

28

Land and Sea, 1871

Oil on canvas

50.8 × 71.1 cm (20 × 28 in.)

Gift of Mrs. John L. Gardner (07.11)

Land and Sea was one of seven paintings Isabella Stewart Gardner gave to the museum in 1907, having learned through its *Bulletin* that the institution wanted to collect American art. Compelled by what she read, Gardner offered an unsolicited gift consisting of works by Dennis Bunker, J. Foxcroft Cole, W. Allen Gay, William Morris Hunt (q.v.), Dodge MacKnight, and Fisher. All the artists had worked in Boston and were well represented in Gardner's own collection, with the exception of Fisher, who had only this painting among her holdings. It is probable that Gardner came in contact with Fisher during his brief return to Boston (1868–71); however, there is no record of their meeting.

How and when the painting entered her collection is something of a mystery. In 1880 Gardner lent several works to the Museum of Fine Arts, Boston, while her home was being renovated, and the Fisher was among them. It was painted in Normandy after the artist's return to France in 1871, but whether Gardner purchased it in Europe or Boston is not known, and there are no receipts pertaining to this painting in the Gardner archives. Although Gardner traveled to Europe often in the 1870s, there is no record of her meeting Fisher in either France or England, where he spent most of the decade.

Fisher is a bit of a conundrum: although he exhibited extensively and received numerous awards, there is little contemporaneous commentary. His patrons are not known, although he achieved relative success once he settled in England. Shortly after his death, however, his reputation fell into near obscurity.

Land and Sea was painted during his brief return to France, prior to his move to England. The coastal scene clearly demonstrates that he was still under the influence of the Barbizon painters. He has provided an idyllic Norman seashore complete with the figures necessary to convey the leisurely life-style of a humble village. This quality is reinforced by the warm gold-toned atmospheric effects and reemphasized by the subdued golden sails on the boats. Fisher continued to paint in this manner until the 1880s, when he began to embrace more closely the style and techniques of his former classmates, Monet, Sisley, and Renoir.

J. W. T.

Inscription At lower left, *W. M. Fisher 71*

Provenance Isabella Stewart (Mrs. John L.) Gardner, as early as 1880. Acquired in 1907.

Exhibitions Exhibited along with twenty other works from the Gardner collection at the Museum of Fine Arts, Boston, April 1880–June 1881. East Lansing 1966.

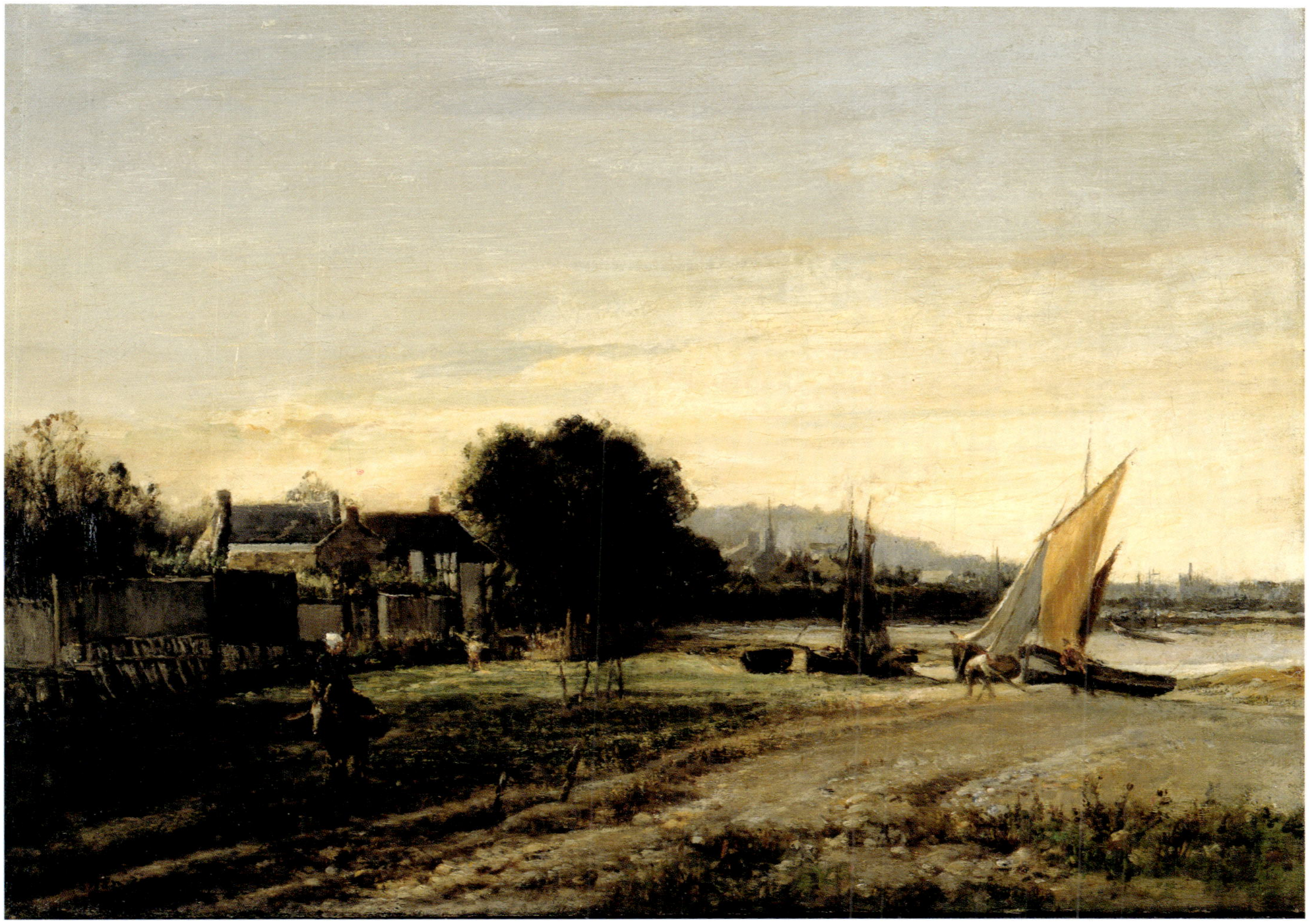

Land and Sea

George Fuller

1822 Deerfield, Massachusetts 1884

Born on his family's tobacco farm in Deerfield, Massachusetts, George Fuller first planned to become a daguerreotypist and bought a camera but soon abandoned that occupation. Instead, in 1841 he joined his half-brother, Augustus, as an itinerant portrait painter in upstate New York, beginning the first phase of his career as an artist. After studying drawing with Henry Kirke Brown in Albany, Fuller moved to Boston, where, like many other young artists during this period, he was impressed by the romantic paintings of Washington Allston. In 1847 he moved to New York City and attended drawing classes at the National Academy of Design. While he built his reputation as a portrait painter, he also tried his hand at landscape and history painting, and increasingly at scenes of daily life. On trips to the South in 1849, 1856, and 1858, he made sketches of slaves working in the fields and in domestic environments. In 1858 he attended an exhibition of French paintings at the National Academy of Design and was especially affected by the paintings of, as he wrote his family, "lowly or everyday life" by the Barbizon artist Edouard Frère (quoted in Burns 1981, 17). He had little time to respond to this interest in his own work, however, for the following year his father died, and Fuller had to assume management of the family farm.

Before returning to Deerfield, he traveled to Europe to visit museums, and he absorbed the work of other Barbizon artists such as Camille Corot and Jean-François Millet, as well as that of Velázquez, Titian, and Rembrandt. The next fifteen years were spent primarily as a farmer, but he continued to paint privately. In 1876, on the suggestion of his students, William Morris Hunt (q.v.) visited Fuller in Deerfield and encouraged the Doll & Richards Gallery in Boston to look at his work. The resulting exhibition drew considerable acclaim. Fuller reentered the art world with a higher profile than when he had left it.

Fuller's new paintings were strikingly different from his earlier, relatively tight and realistic work. Figures and background are enveloped in an overall atmosphere, a style that was influential in the development of tonalism. He used his materials freely, sometimes applying paint with a palette knife, scraping or rubbing the picture with his finger, and then painting over with thin color or glaze (Howells in Millet 1886, 46–47). Unfortunately, his use of bitumen has darkened his paintings over time and caused extensive crackle.

During these few years before his death, he specialized in several subjects: ideal female figures, such as *Psyche* (1882; Art Institute of Chicago); genre paintings of blacks, like *Negro Funeral, Alabama* (ca. 1881–84; Museum of Fine Arts, Boston); and, still under the influence of Allston, poetic landscapes. While many of the landscapes are similar to the Barbizon agricultural subjects by Millet he had long admired, Fuller's figures are less heroicized and more unified with the landscape.

S. M. S.

Bibliography Millet 1886. Burns 1979. Burns 1981.

29

Self-Portrait, ca. 1840–51

Oil on canvas

55.9 × 44.8 cm (22 × 17⅝ in.)

Gift of Raymond C. Smith (55.295)

There is no clear provenance for this painting before 1893, when it was owned by Thomas B. Clarke, the celebrated collector and dealer of contemporary American art in New York during the last quarter of the nineteenth century (see correspondence from Weinberg, curatorial files, DIA; Weinberg 1976, 74). Clarke also owned two other paintings by Fuller. Clarke exhibited this painting in 1893 at his gallery, Art House, as a self-portrait by Fuller and gave its date as 1840, when Fuller would have been eighteen. The first known portraits by Fuller date from 1841. Although William Howe Downes, in an article on George Fuller in 1922, identified this painting as a self-portrait at age twenty-nine (Downes 1922, 265), making the date of the painting about 1851, it may well have been painted earlier.

The catalogue for the auction of Clarke's collection in 1899 does not give a date for the painting but includes a description: "The virility, the charm, and the sentiment of this painter are all fully in evidence in this canvas, which represents his art at its best period. The portrait is simply conceived, with the face in contrast to a rich, mellow background. Modelled with appreciation of mass and form, there is a sumptuous quality of color rarely obtained. The work is distinctly personal and is a fine example of the individual style of the artist" (Clarke sale, no. 178; see Provenance).

Early in his career, Fuller admired portraits by Washington Allston and Gilbert Stuart. Sarah Burns finds elements of both artists in this painting, "in its dark-toned background and broadly rendered head" (Burns 1981, 14). Two other self-portraits by Fuller are known. One was given by the artist to the National Academy of Design in 1853, when he was elected an associate. Shown at the annual exhibition of the academy in 1855 (no. 207), it is undated and is larger (75.9 × 63.5 cm) than the Detroit painting. The second was given in 1954 by the artist's daughter, Mrs. Augustus Vincent Tack, to the National Gallery of Art, from where it was transferred to the National Portrait Gallery in 1965. When exhibited at the memorial exhibition of Fuller's works at the Museum of Fine Arts, Boston (Boston 1884, no. 68), it was dated 1849. Comparing photographs of all three portraits reveals that they are probably, but not definitively, portraits of the same person and by the same artist. The National Academy of

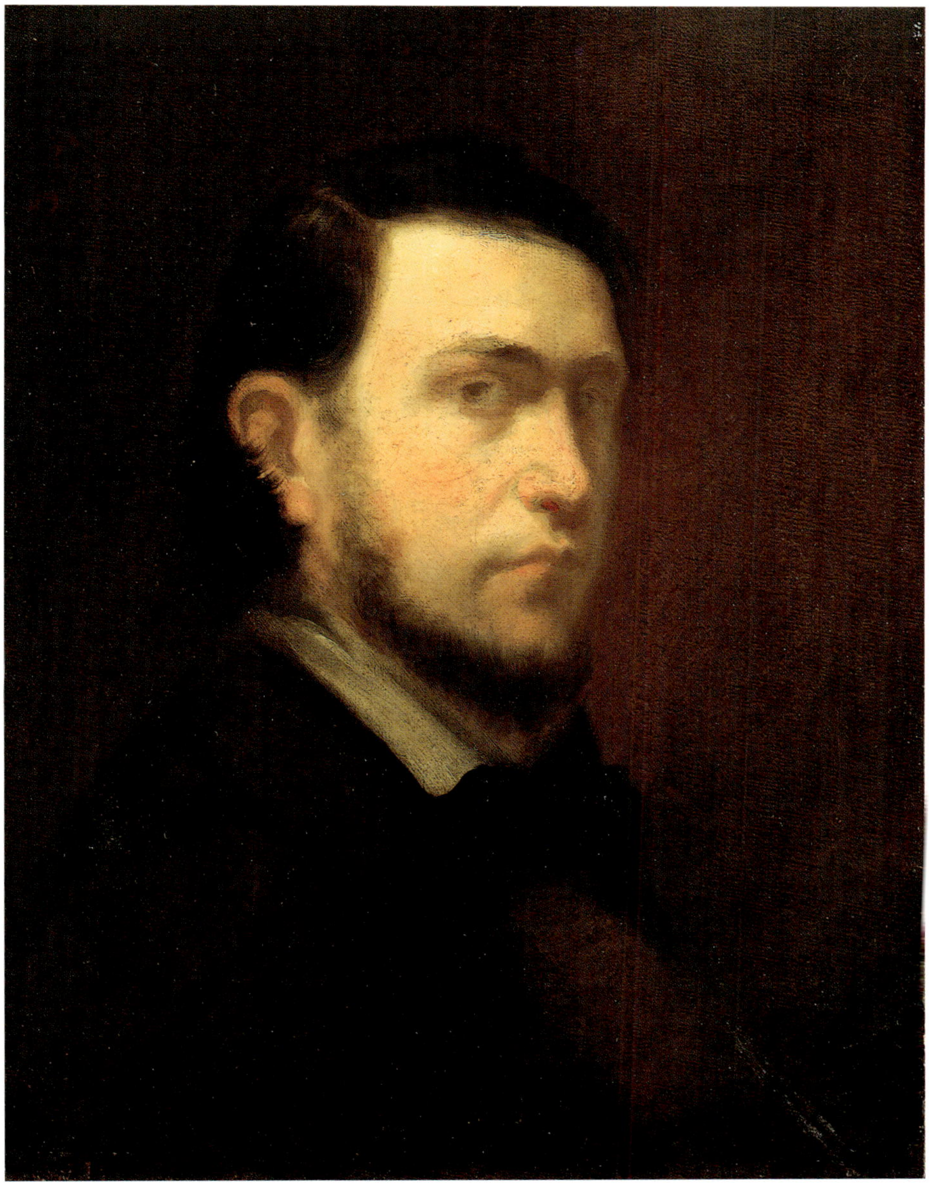

Design and the National Portrait Gallery portraits are similar in style, which is more precise than the Detroit painting, and both appear to depict a slightly older man with a mustache who has shorter hair and a fuller beard than the man in the Detroit portrait. All three are three-quarter profile views against a dark background. The artist did not include tools of his trade in any of the paintings.

S. M. S.

Provenance Thomas B. Clarke, New York, by 1893. Fifth Avenue Art Galleries sale, January 27, 1896, no. 20, according to H. Barbara Weinberg (correspondence, curatorial files, DIA), probably brought in by Clarke. Thomas B. Clarke sale, American Art Association, New York, February 15, 1899, no. 178, as *Early Portrait of the Artist.* Colonel E. D. Page. Milch Galleries, New York. Purchased by Conrad H. Smith, Grosse Pointe Farms, Mich., in 1927. By descent to Raymond C. Smith, Grosse Pointe Farms, Mich. Acquired in 1955.

Exhibitions New York 1893, no. 42, as *Portrait of the Artist,* 1840. New York 1898, no. 10. Detroit 1934.

References Downes 1922, 265. *BDIA* 1934, 14, as *Portrait of a Man.* Homer and Robb 1961, 288, 290. Weinberg 1976, 74. Burns 1979, 376. Burns 1981, 11, 14.

30

The Tomato Patch, ca. 1878

Oil on canvas

51.4 × 76.2 cm (20¼ × 30 in.)

Gift of Raymond C. Smith (53.471)

AFTER 1876 Fuller painted a number of works on the subject of farming, which, as Sarah Burns describes them, are "quiet ruminations on American agricultural rituals" (Burns 1981, 30). In style and subject, they show the influence of the French Barbizon artists Jean-François Millet and Constant Troyon. These paintings, which depict harvesting, berry picking, and the gathering of faggots, are a kind of self-portrait, since Fuller spent the years from 1860 to 1876 running his family's farm in Deerfield and, after his art career gathered momentum, continued to supervise it, spending summers in Deerfield and winters in Boston. Although Fuller depicted the everyday chores of his farm, he seldom painted out-of-doors, instead building up his paintings with layers of pigment and glazes in his studio (Howells in Millet 1886, 48).

In *The Tomato Patch,* a woman and a man work in a field; a plow and a basket are in the foreground. Little attempt was made to distinguish the figures from the landscape. Fuller's son described his father's theories on painting: "He preferred to remove the object of interest in his picture a degree into its atmosphere,

Self-Portrait

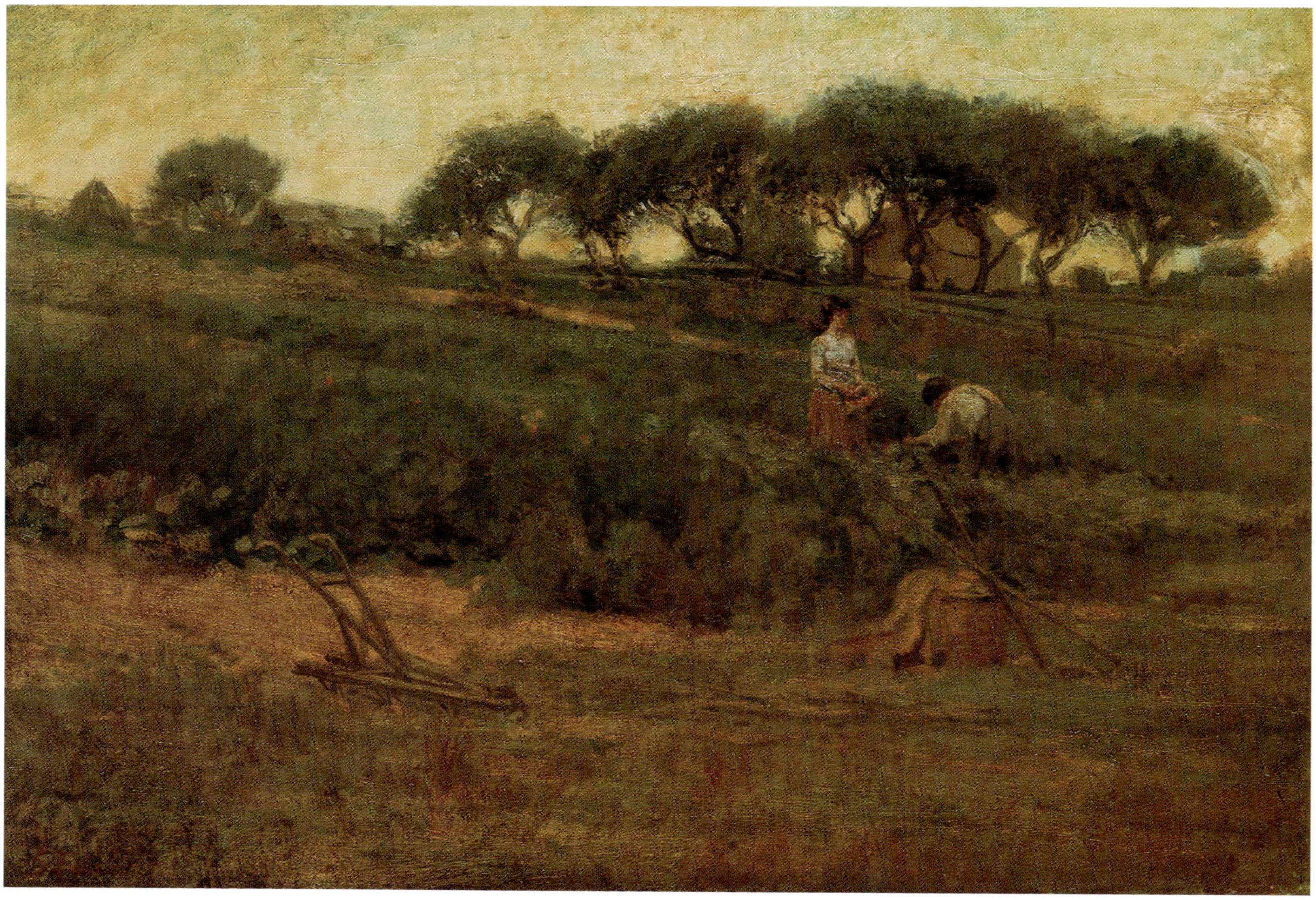

believing that this gave a greater chance for expression. When painting a figure with a landscape background he would nearly always, as he termed it, beat the figure back into the landscape" (quoted by Howells in Millet 1886, 46). John J. Enneking also discussed Fuller's devotion to atmospheric haze: "He liked nature best when the lines of objects were softened a little by a haze, and consequently chose those conditions for subjects in his paintings. He thought that a warm atmosphere pervading everything is not only agreeable to enjoy... but is the best suited condition to give a poetical impression, and help one to simplicity and breadth, mystery and tone" (Enneking in Millet 1886, 78). The haze erases bright color, creating a subdued tonality in which the red in the basket and the blue at the woman's waist stand out.

The painting is not found under this title in the list of Fuller's paintings published by Millet in 1886, suggesting that it originally had a different title. The similarity of *The Tomato Patch* in subject and composition to *Turkey Pasture in Kentucky* (1878; Chrysler Museum, Norfolk, Va.) led Carmine Dalesio, of Babcock Galleries, New York, to propose a similar date for the Detroit painting (correspondence, curatorial files, DIA).

S. M. S.

Inscription At lower left, *G. Fuller*

Provenance Levy Galleries. Conrad H. Smith, Grosse Pointe Farms, Mich. By descent to Raymond C. Smith, Grosse Pointe Farms, Mich. Acquired in 1953.

Exhibition Washington 1975, 81, 140, no. 36.

References Richardson 1956, 246, fig. 113. Homer and Robb 1961, 290, 291. Burns 1979, 110, 116, 120, 128, 129, 381. Burns 1981, 25, 30.

Tomato Patch

George B. Gardner

1835 Grossegarten, Germany–
Hillsdale, Michigan 1904

At an early age, George Gardner exhibited an interest in drawing and by the age of eight had begun to use watercolors. He immigrated to the United States in 1852, settling in Pittsburgh, where he established a studio. Three years later he married Henrietta Ares of Great Bend, Ohio. He traveled to Europe in 1863 for a year of study, visiting the great collections in England, France, Germany, and Holland.

Gardner returned to America in 1864, spending a brief time in New York City and Buffalo before settling in Detroit. Over the next two years he held teaching positions in Port Huron, Michigan, and at Adrian College, Adrian, Michigan. In 1866 he joined the faculty of Hillsdale College, Hillsdale, Michigan, and became head of the art department two years later, a position he held until his resignation in 1900.

Over his long career his oeuvre encompassed many subjects, including, but not limited to, biblical and allegorical subjects, landscapes, and portraiture. He was very fond of portraiture and concentrated a great portion of his career on the genre.

J. W. T.

Bibliography Gibson 1975, 110.

31

West Street from the Campus of Hillsdale College, 1873

Oil on canvas

23.2 × 43.5 cm (9⅛ × 17⅛ in.)

Gift of Mrs. H. C. Miller (46.224)

Hillsdale College was founded in 1844 as Michigan Central College at Spring Arbor. As with many of central Michigan's small colleges, it was rooted in one of the various Protestant sects. The college moved in 1853 when Hillsdale County provided $21,000 and the necessary land for a campus. The name was changed and the new buildings opened in 1855. This scene, which looks over West Street in Hillsdale, provides a record of typical midcentury midwestern homes with their wooden facades and fences, while beyond lie the vast farmlands for which central Michigan was so well known.

The street still serves as the western boundary of the college, but it has become a major thoroughfare. The farms are gone, now replaced by residential structures necessary to sustain college life. However, some of the houses depicted still stand. Originally built by faculty members, the houses continue to serve as single-family homes.

The elevated point of view strongly suggests that the painting was done in one of the campus buildings, quite possibly the one housing artists' studios and classrooms Throughout Gardner's career he documented various aspects of the Michigan landscape. His daughter's correspondence describes trips during summer vacations to locations across the state, where he recorded images of farming communities and lakefront activities.

Gardner was not attempting to capture the majesty of the landscape but rather to convey a story of contemporary life. In this canvas, as in others of his weekend paintings, he has meticulously recorded a variety of architectural styles and the activity of the people on campus. Instead of an interest in idealization, Gardner was fascinated with the mundane. He has clearly drawn attention to the drying laundry and the young man working on his front porch. His interest in such recurring genre motifs appears to have developed relatively early in his career. These were works he did during his leisure hours, for private consumption and thus tended to remain with his family.

J. W. T.

Provenance The artist's daughter, Ellen E. Gardner (Mrs. H. C.) Miller, until 1904. Acquired in 1946.

Exhibition East Lansing et al. 1986, no. 6.

Reference Gibson 1975, 109, ill.

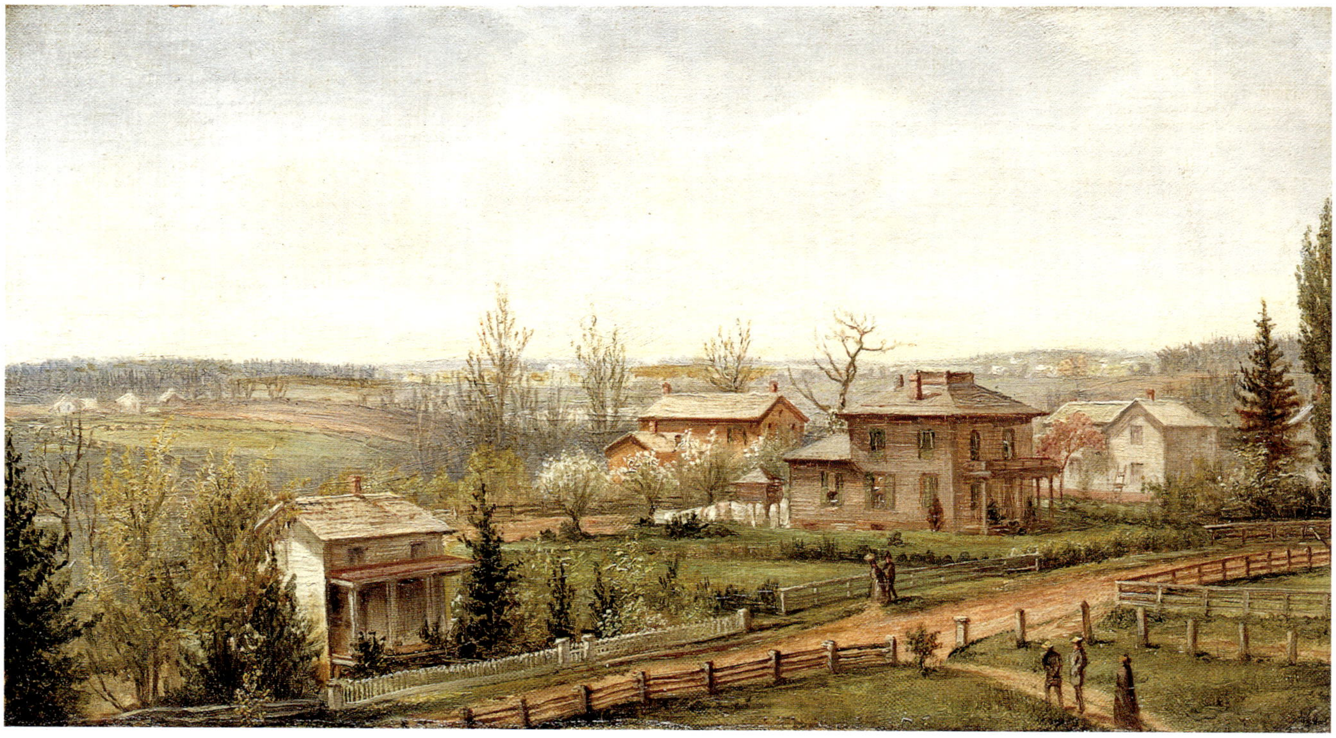

West Street

Sanford Robinson Gifford

1823 Greenfield, New York–New York 1880

Sanford R. Gifford held a position of high esteem in the New York art community in the third quarter of the nineteenth century. Projecting dignity and reserve, Gifford was "even toned, fixed in spirit, and . . . above all irregular impulses" *(New York Evening Post,* March 20, 1866). He grew up in comfortable surroundings facing the Hudson River and Catskill Mountains at Hudson, New York, where his father was co-owner of a successful iron foundry. Money in the family raised expectations that Gifford would become a learned professional, so in 1842 he entered Brown University; in 1844 he left to study art. In New York in 1845 he worked with John R. Smith, a figure draftsman of some note, but within a year Gifford turned from portraiture to landscape. He enjoyed the freedom of it, not being constrained to the rendering of human likeness. The atmospheric, poetic, and spiritual were central to his interests, as was the achievement of his inspirational role model, Thomas Cole.

Gifford's wealth, zeal, refined sensibility, and gentlemanly manners served him well. In 1851 he was named associate of the National Academy of Design and in 1854 academician. Thus secure, he traveled in 1855 to Europe, where, during the next two years, he toured England, Belgium, Holland, Switzerland, Austria, and Italy, and resided in Paris and Rome. In England he met John Ruskin and made a point of looking at paintings by J. M. W. Turner and John Constable; in France, Barbizon school landscapes impressed him powerfully, and he met Jean-François Millet at Barbizon. Returning to New York in 1857, Gifford established his studio at 51 West Tenth Street, the hive of the Hudson River school; he stayed there throughout his career.

Gifford continued to travel. In 1861 he joined the Seventh New York Regiment in defense of Washington, D.C., and he served with the regiment again in 1862 and 1863 in an affirmation of his commitment to Unionism. Soon after the war, in 1868–69, Gifford spent another year abroad, this time in Italy, Greece, Turkey, Syria, Lebanon, Jerusalem, and Egypt. In 1870 he traveled to the Rocky Mountains with John F. Kensett (q.v.) and Worthington Whittredge (q.v.), and he joined Colonel Ferdinand V. Hayden's survey expedition to Wyoming. On a second trip west in 1874 he journeyed up the coast from California to Oregon, British Columbia, and Alaska. Gifford was an avid angler and routinely made seasonal sketching and fishing excursions in upstate New York, New England, and Canada. When his health declined in the summer of 1880 he sought relief on a fishing trip to Lake Superior, but he did not revive and died in New York of malarial fever and pneumonia.

Gifford was especially recognized for his treatment of light and air. One critic called him "that rare and genuine son of Helios" (quoted in Yonkers et al. 1988, 135); another observed that "with Mr. Gifford landscape-painting is air-painting; and his endeavor is to imitate the colour of the air" (Sheldon 1877, 284); the artist John F. Weir stressed that "Gifford loved the light" (New York 1881, 9). Jervis McEntee (q.v.), like many commentators, associated this reverence for "aerial luminism" with Gifford's poetic sensibility: "The poetic soul revels in the sunshine and the air, seeking everywhere the expression of its serene joy" (quoted in Weiss 1977, 359). None of these remarks addressed how light, air, and paint functioned metaphorically for Gifford, who reportedly stated that "the really important matter is not the natural object itself, but the veil or medium through which we see it" (Sheldon 1877, 285). William Hazlitt had expressed the same idea in 1816 in assessing Turner's paintings as "too much abstractions of aerial perspective, and representations not properly of the objects of nature as of the medium through which they were seen" (quoted in New York 1966a, 13). "Medium" in these instances was a loaded word—connoting at once paint and varnish, the artist's intercession, atmosphere, and light—but its thrust was spiritual. Just as to Turner "light is God," to Gifford the large purpose of landscape painting was the revelation of spiritual principles and the divine design of nature. For Gifford and other so-called luminists, including Kensett and Martin Johnson Heade (q.v.), the imperative was to associate that revelation with the distinctively American environment so forcibly that the land's inhabitants would be seen to pursue their interests and assert their moral convictions under special favor from God. Further, as these artists congregated in the Northeast, were pro-Union, and painted recognizably Northern subjects, their landscapes located the "true," divinely inspired America in the North during the era of the Civil War and Reconstruction.

W. T. O.

Bibliography Weiss 1977. Weiss 1987.

32

Kaaterskill Falls, 1871

Oil on canvas

37.5 × 31.8 cm (14¾ × 12½ in.)

Gift of Katherine French Rockwell (56.185)

"As an artist," Whittredge wrote of his friend Gifford, "he was born in the Catskill Mountains. He loved them as he loved his mother, and he could not long stay away from either" (Whittredge 1942, 59). The earliest known landscape by Gifford is a view of the upper drop of Kaaterskill Falls, which he painted in 1846 (Yonkers et al. 1988, 69, 133). It sprang from a vision that he had had two years earlier when he was wrestling "betwixt his desire to please his father and at the same time to please himself." As he hiked Mount Merino, he looked out on the Catskills and down on the studio of Thomas Cole, "around which we may well believe there was a halo of light that morning which lighted up the path [Gifford] was to follow" (Whittredge 1942, 56). Gifford opted for the artist's life rather than the family business, and he returned again and again to the region of his epiphany. He worked there for prolonged periods in 1848–50, 1860–62, probably 1863, and 1865–67. When he returned from England in 1869, he went straight to Scribner's Boarding House near the top of Kaaterskill Falls; he also stayed at nearby Laurel House with his friends, Jervis McEntee and his wife. After returning from Wyoming in September 1870 he built his own studio in Hudson, and throughout the decade (except 1877, when he secretly married the widow Mary Canfield) he was a regular seasonal visitor. In sum, "no autumn came that he did not visit [the Catskill Mountains], and for a long period of his artist life he went in summer to . . . the Catskills as a boy goes to school" (Whittredge 1942, 59).

What did Gifford learn in this school? Whittredge put it this way: "He said in general terms that no historical or legendary interest attached to landscape could help the landscape painter, that he must go behind all this to nature as it had been formed by the Creator and find something there which was superior to man's work, and to this he must learn to give intelligible expression. These ideas were not new or wonderful, but he impressed me as a man earnestly looking into a problem, as in truth he was" (Whittredge 1942, 56). Kaaterskill Falls, however, did have historical and autobiographical associations of enormous consequence for Gifford, not only because his family was identified with the region and dependent on its natural resources, or because it was the object of his own earliest memories, but also because the falls themselves, Lake Creek, and the gorge were the very seeds of the Hudson River school. Cole's seminal paintings in 1825 were compositions based on Kaaterskill Falls and Clove, and the site remained the wellspring of landscape imagery at midcentury. Its significance was memorialized in particular by Asher B. Durand in *Kindred Spirits* (1849; New York Public Library), but virtually every American landscape painter at the time paid homage. So closely identified was the Hudson River school with the site that when the school passed from favor so did the subject matter.

Gifford produced more paintings of the falls and Clove than of any other subject. Even though he was well known in the 1870s for his Italian scenes (Sheldon 1880, 19), he kept returning to the Kaaterskill landmarks. The paintings were his signature pieces, as he repeatedly quoted himself in refining the varied expressive potential of the motifs, and characteristically they were subjective interpretations of the recognizable topography. As Weir remarked, "Gifford's art was poetic and reminiscent. It was not realistic in the formal sense. It was nature passed through the alembic of a finely-organized sensibility" (New York 1881, 8).

The Detroit painting well represents the type. It is organized in a conventional way, as the ravine and overarching limbs of the trees form a tunneling perspective that leads from the pool and small cascade to the increasingly mist-veiled falls and the opening of sky; secondary arches within the primary arch frame each of the falls. The color is similarly orchestrated, lightening from the structural foreground siennas to ochers, gold, and the pale, barely roseate blue of the sky. (Gifford's palette organization is described in Sheldon 1880, 17.) Gifford has fashioned the creek bed, trees, falls, and sky into a natural Gothic cathedral, replete with ribbed vaults, pointed arches, buttresses, long nave, clerestory, and effulgent stained-glass windows in the apse. In some of Durand's woodland interiors, notably *In the Woods* (1855; Metropolitan Museum of Art, New York), he had worked with this kind of cathedral imagery, but Gifford's construction of nature's church is considerably more obvious and elegant, despite the broken, choppy brushwork. The small figure of a man descending on the right bank establishes scale and recession, as well as draws the viewer into the scene serving as surrogate in a votive, worshipful affirmation of the rite of nostalgia and the realization of the divine design of nature.

Gifford probably made the Detroit painting, small and sketchy as it is, as a readily salable parlor ornament rather than as a study for a slightly larger, unlocated view of the falls from the same year (see Weiss 1977, 334; Weiss 1987, 292). Since he dated other views of the Catskills in 1871 (New York 1881, 39), he likely painted in the region that autumn, as he had the autumn before. The paintings—all relatively small—include *An October Afternoon,* two versions of *Autumn in the Catskills,* and two versions of *Kauterskill Falls.* The Detroit painting is arguably the *Kauterskill Falls* listed in the *Memorial Catalogue* (New York 1881, 39, no. 577) as owned by Augustus E. Bachelder of Boston and as measuring 13 by 15 inches (in that case the compiler of the catalogue erred in citing width before height). The only other painting identified from the group is the 20-by-16-inch *Autumn in the Catskills* (The Parthenon, Metropolitan Board of Parks and Recreation, Centennial Park, Nashville, Tennessee).

W. T. O.

Inscriptions On the back, *S R Gifford 1871 / Hudson, N. Y.;* stenciled on the back, *Prepared by Edwd Dechaux, New York*

Provenance Possibly Augustus S. Bachelder, Boston. Katherine French Rockwell, Shrewsbury, Mass. Acquired in 1956.

Exhibitions Indianapolis 1961, no. 16. Austin et al. 1970, 29, 70, no. 49. Coral Gables 1974.

References Weiss 1977, 334–335. Weiss 1987, 292. Simon 1993.

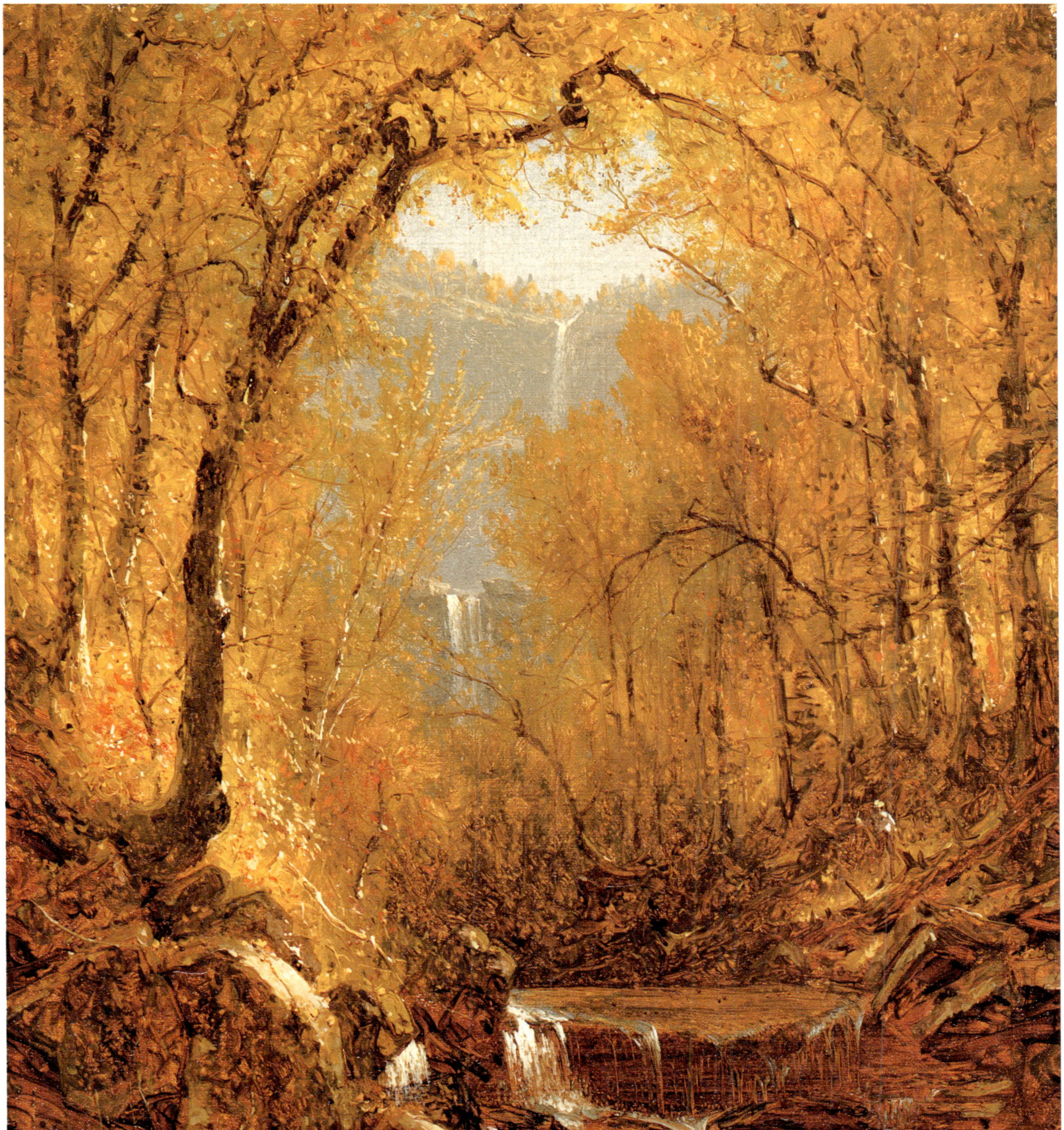

Kaaterskill Falls

William Stanley Haseltine

1835 Philadelphia–Rome 1900

After graduating from Harvard University in 1854, William Stanley Haseltine returned to Philadelphia to work with the landscape painter Paul Weber, who also taught William Trost Richards (q.v.). Haseltine accompanied Weber to Düsseldorf for additional study in 1855. There Haseltine followed the meticulous rendering and clear structure taught by Andreas Achenbach. He spent summers sketching in Germany, Switzerland, and Italy with other Americans studying in Düsseldorf: Worthington Whittredge (q.v.), Emanuel Leutze, and Albert Bierstadt (q.v.). On his return to the United States in 1858, Haseltine set up a studio in New York. He exhibited views of European scenery and of the East Coast at the annual exhibitions of the National Academy of Design.

In 1866 he returned to Europe, settling in Paris, where he opened a studio and painted plein-air landscapes. Although he became friendly with such academic artists as William Bouguereau and Jean-Léon Gérôme, he particularly admired the work of Claude Monet, which influenced his representation of reflected light and the movement of water.

In 1867 Haseltine opened a studio in Rome, where he lived for the next thirty years until his death. He continued to exhibit in the United States and became part of the European art establishment. He was elected a member of the Kunst Verein in Munich and of the Società degli Amatori e Cultori delle Belle Arti in Rome. He traveled extensively in Europe, especially in Italy, to find subjects for his paintings. He brought his pencil sketches and watercolors back to his studio in Rome to make into finished paintings.

In 1867 Henry Tuckerman wrote, "Few of our artists have been more conscientious in the delineation of rocks" than Haseltine (Tuckerman 1867, 556). A related interest was the depiction of the texture of old, often crumbling, buildings; Haseltine was especially drawn to ancient architecture in striking scenic landscapes or in water settings, such as *Ruins of the Roman Theatre at Taormina, Sicily* (1889; Fine Arts Museums of San Francisco). Appropriately, in 1894 he was one of the founders of the American School of Architecture in Rome, which became the American Academy in Rome.
S. M. S.

Bibliography Plowden 1947. New York 1983. San Francisco and Chadds Ford 1992.

33
Venice I, ca. 1875

Oil on canvas
59.7 × 123.2 cm (23½ × 48½ in.)
Gift of Mrs. Roger H. Plowden, the artist's daughter (51.253)

Haseltine probably first visited Venice in 1856, while a student in Düsseldorf. In 1859 the *Crayon* reported that his studio in New York was hung with sketches of such picturesque sites in Italy as Venice (San Francisco and Cleveland 1984, 43). After he moved back to Europe in 1866, he usually spent a few weeks each summer and autumn in Venice (Plowden 1947, 150). Three sketchbooks of pencil drawings and watercolors of Venetian subjects from the 1860s and 1875 are in the Karolik Collection, Museum of Fine Arts, Boston. Margaretta M. Lovell concludes that Haseltine painted this view of Venice around 1875 (Lovell 1989, 53).

Haseltine's daughter described his way of working in Venice. He was always out before sunrise, before the fishing boats had left: "[O]ne of his sketches . . . was painted on the Riva degli Schiavoni when the morning had not yet dawned; on finding all the fishing-boats with red and yellow sails set and ready to start, he whipped out his painting materials and succeeded in getting his sketch finished as they were moving out to sea, twenty minutes later" (Plowden 1947, 150). On some days he searched for subjects in a gondola, meandering through the narrow canals. On others he went to one of the islands in the late afternoon to paint the larger lagoons.

In *Venice I,* Haseltine worked from a spot in front of the Public Gardens identical to the one used by Robert Salmon in his *View of Venice* (1845; Thyssen-Bornemisza Collection), the first painting by an American in Venice (see San Francisco and Cleveland 1984, no. 51). Haseltine did not include the parapet of the gardens seen in the foreground of Salmon's *View of Venice,* so we seem to be hovering over the water of the lagoon. In the Detroit painting, the fishing boats hide part of the villa visible on the right in Salmon's work.

The pink reflections and the deep shadows cast on the villa and on the sails of the boats suggest that it is dawn, when the fishermen are readying their boats for the day. Just as the precisely drawn boats, buildings, and small figures in the foreground contrast with the pale and insubstantial vision of the Campanile, Doge's Palace, and domes of the Salute in the background, so too "the modest picturesqueness of these poor but colorful peasant folk contrasts markedly with the pale heroic scene portrayed on the horizon" (Lovell 1989, 53).
S. M. S.

Provenance Artist's estate, 1900. His daughter, Helen Haseltine (Mrs. Roger H.) Plowden. Acquired in 1951.

Exhibitions San Francisco and Cleveland 1984, 44–45, no. 19. San Francisco and Chadds Ford 1992, no. 54.

Reference Lovell 1989, 53.

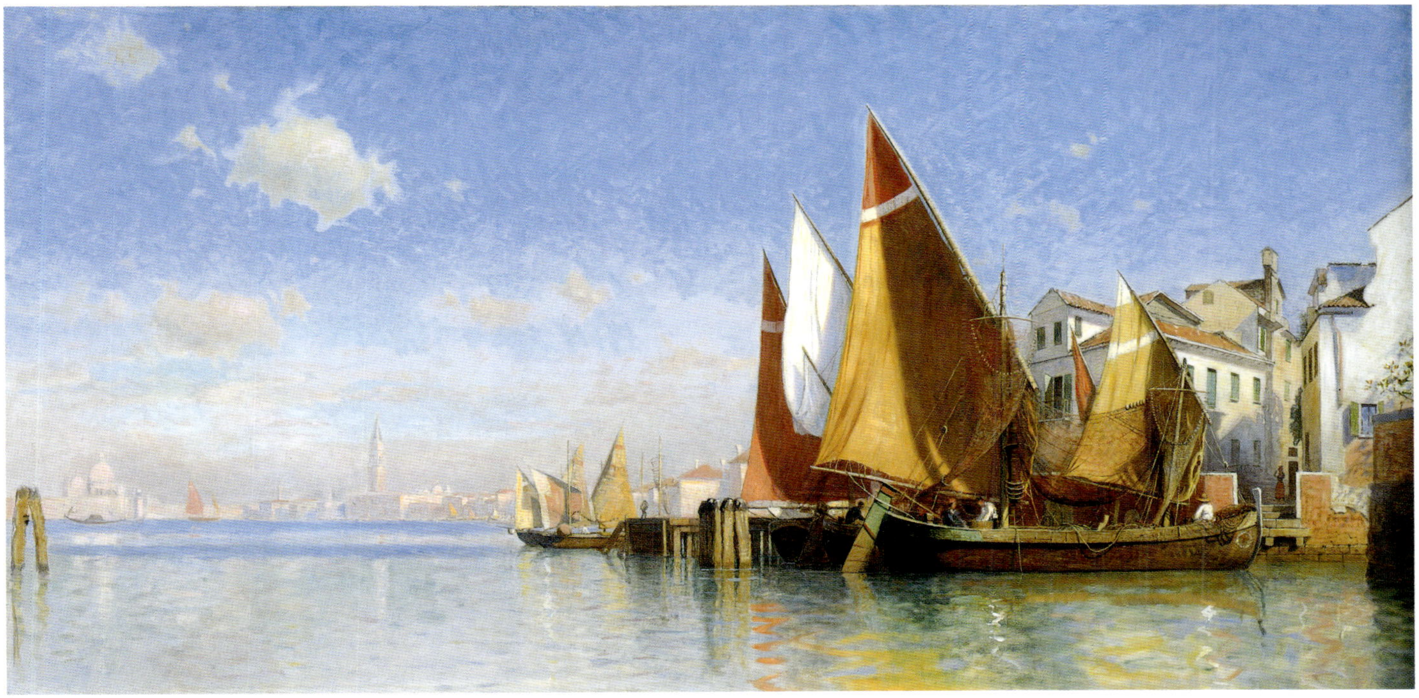

Venice I

Martin Johnson Heade

1819 Lumberville, Pennsylvania–
St. Augustine, Florida 1904

An adventurer and naturalist, sportsman and conservationist, Victorian and iconoclast, Martin Johnson Heade reenvisioned the pictorial traditions of American landscape and still-life painting. Duality distinguished the man and his art. Indeed, Heade explicitly identified with this aspect of his nature: his pen name, whether on his earliest poem of 1845 or his last article on hummingbirds of 1904, was always the same—"Didymus." As a variation of "didymous" from the Greek *didumos,* meaning "double," "twin," or "testicles," Heade's pseudonym conveyed the artist's twofold, and often contrary, disposition. Although a close friend of the highly lauded Frederic Edwin Church (q.v.), Heade was essentially a loner barely acknowledged among his contemporary landscape painters. Heade gained some notoriety at the end of his life, but he was often regarded as eccentric in both artistic style and personality. By changing his name from his father's *Heed,* Johnson, as he was called, could in a small but significant manner reinvent himself as an individual apart from his large family. Heade resembled the transcendentalist writer Henry David Thoreau (who was born David Henry) in yet another notable way: his original visions of nature incarnated a doubled self who was at once realist and idealist, scientist and artist, ascetic and sensualist. By tenuously wedding such polarities as hard and soft, loud and silent, detail and abstraction, tension and repose within highly ordered compositions, Heade demonstrated his true Victorian nature.

The eldest son of a farmer and lumber-mill proprietor, Heade decided at the age of twenty-one to pursue a painting career under the guidance of his Quaker neighbor, Edward Hicks, and his nephew Thomas. Like many fledgling artists, Heade began as a portraitist, graduated to genre pictures, and then by 1860 committed his artistic energies to landscape scenes and still-life compositions. He traveled frequently. His first European tour took place in the early forties and he returned to Rome in 1848 and London in 1865. Nine cities in the United States served as his home: New York; Brooklyn; St. Louis; Chicago; Trenton, New Jersey; Providence, Rhode Island; Boston; Washington, D.C.; and St. Augustine, Florida. Although Heade's stay in Boston from 1861 to 1863 resulted in his most productive period, his continuing residence in New York's Tenth Street Studio Building from the fifties through the eighties placed him literally in the center of American art activity. Paradoxically, Heade's nearly annual exhibition at the National Academy of Design never resulted in even an associate membership.

Crucial to Heade's artistic development were his journeys to Latin America. In Brazil (1863–64) Heade first formulated his distinctive hummingbird images. Subsequent trips to Nicaragua and Colombia (1866–67), and to Colombia, Jamaica, and Panama (1870), transformed Heade's conception from ornithological study into evocative landscape. He refined his South American scenes until his death, as well as pursuing with equal fascination haystack-filled marshes, seacoast imagery, and thunderstorm effects.

Heade married at the age of sixty-four and settled with his forty-year-old wife, Elizabeth Smith, in St. Augustine. As senior painter in an expanding artistic community under the patronage of the oil magnate Henry Morrison Flagler, Heade turned his attentions to the distinctive Florida marshes. There, in domestic bliss, Heade created his most sensuous of inventions—the reclining giant magnolia.
J. S.

Bibliography Stebbins 1975. Manthorne 1989.

34
Seascape: Sunset, 1861

Oil on canvas
66 × 111.8 cm (26 × 44 in.)
Founders Society Purchase, Robert H. Tannahill Foundation Fund (1995.26)

Painted after Heade's initiation into the New York art scene at the Tenth Street Studios (1859–60), *Seascape: Sunset* reveals an artist of new maturity. In this picture Heade refined the subject of waves colliding against lichen-covered rocks that first intrigued him in *Storm Clouds on the Coast* of 1859 (Farnsworth Library and Museum, Rockland, Maine) and continued to do so through, and intermittently after, 1863. Heade's confident handling of detail, color, composition, and imagery marks every inch. His use of inventive combinations of reds, yellows, and greens enriches its intense palette. *Seascape: Sunset*'s illuminated sky, eerily tranquil over thunderous waves, establishes a tension between peace and violence peculiar to Heade's oeuvre. Both its style and subject acknowledge the artistic success and metaphoric significance of Frederic Edwin Church's *Twilight in the Wilderness* (1860; Cleveland Museum of Art). Indeed, with this reposeful sunset over an untamable sea, Heade created "a twilight in the wilderness" of his own kind.

When exhibited at the National Academy of Design in March 1861 under the title *Marine Sunset,* however, Heade's painting provoked censure rather than the acclaim granted to *Twilight in the Wilderness.* Unlike his friend Church, Heade rarely received extended commentary on his art, and seldom commendation. The *Boston Transcript* alone praised *Seascape: Sunset*'s exceptional "truthfulness and spirit" that invited the viewer to "listen in imagination to the roar of the breakers, and inhale the odor of salt that

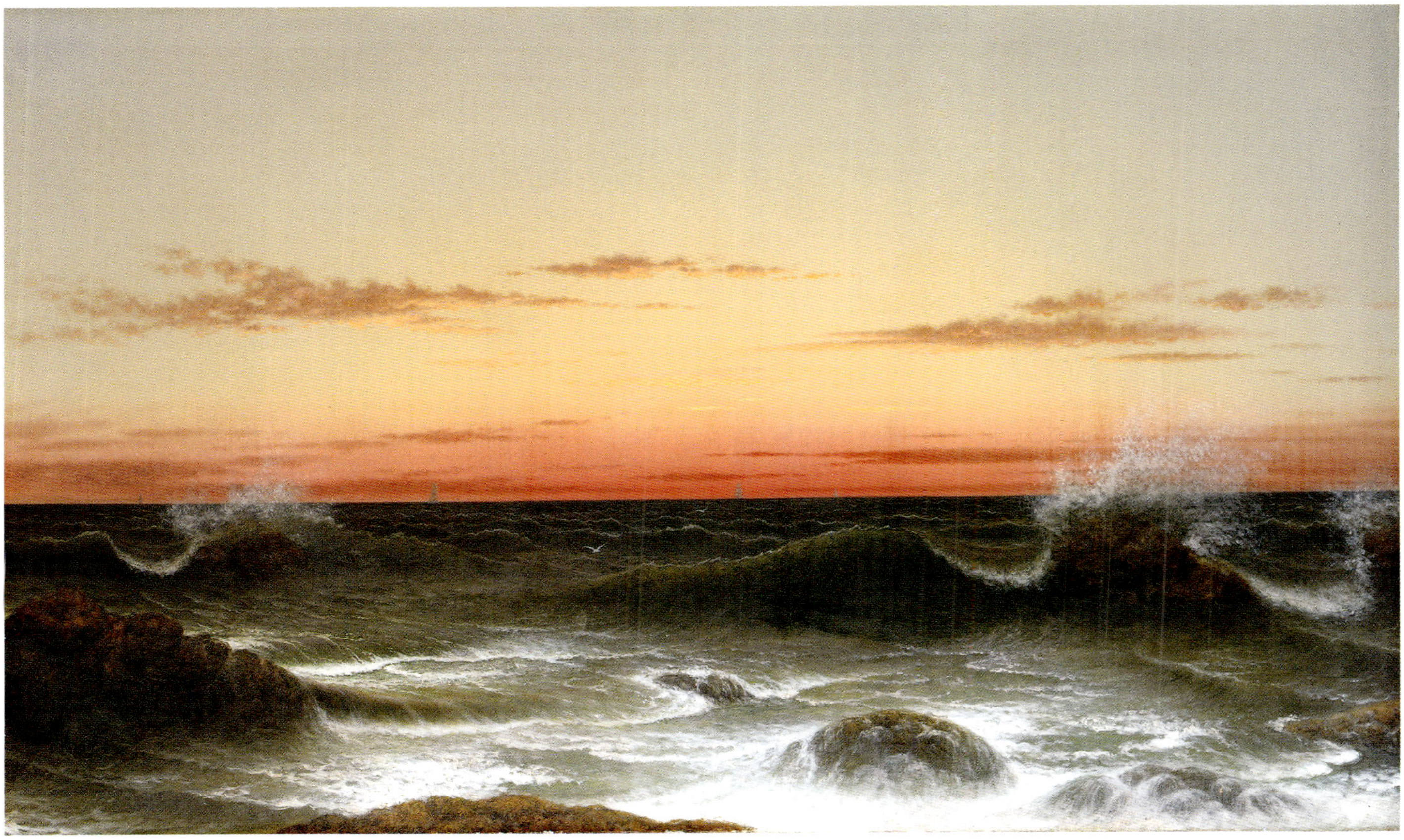

Seascape: Sunset

impregnates the atmosphere" *(Boston Transcript*, February 27, 1861). The *New York Daily Tribune* (March 27, 1861) raised the specter of falsity that critics would later echo in their derision of Heade's "peculiar" seascapes:

> Do all our marine painters paint from recollection of scenes which they study only occasionally or imperfectly? The rich hue of the sky in this Sunset of Mr. Heade is a picture by itself, and only needed a foreground that do it no harm. Now, it may be possible for the eye to look upon such a western sky over an expanse of heaving waters and catch no sight of any crimson reflection in the thin crests of the tossing waves; but we doubt. Whoever had the good fortune to see the western horizon on Sunday evening last, saw the repetition of this glowing color of Mr. Heade's picture; and whoever saw it, as we happened to do, over a sheet of water not even very roughly moved by the March "nor'–wester" of that evening, may have marked how the crimson light was caught and tossed from wavelet to wavelet, and how it settled in a deeper glow upon the wet rocks and illumined any old ivy or rough hillock that lay in its way. And whoever lingered in the lovely ruddy light of such a scene will be unable to understand how those dark green waves of Mr. Heade's can toss without one lingering kiss from the blushing skies beyond. Perhaps we are wrong in supposing the artist is not true here to nature; but if he is, it is only in some exceptional mood of hers, or, more properly, to some peculiar relative position he may have stood in, at some time, to the landscape before him. But, in that case, the effect he has reproduced can only be exceptional, and therefore, in the main, untrue. It is a pity that this should be so in a work in which there is really so much beauty and so much that is true.

Seemingly divorced from the laws of natural experience, the "exceptional" effects of the foreground waters "harmed" the picture's essential integrity. Heade violated the tenuous balance between authenticity and invention, realism and idealism, that American landscape painters were required to maintain in light of John Ruskin's "truth to nature" directive. The *New York World* concurred with the *Tribune* that Heade, by omitting tinges of purple light on the crests, failed to capture the reflective transparency of water. Unlike other twilight scenes, Heade's marine, though the best in the exhibition, lacked an entirely unifying sunset glow. Heade, however, was not interested in creating a reposeful harmony. On the contrary, *Seascape: Sunset*'s power resides in the stark contrast between angry sea and elegiac sky.

Although over half of *Seascape: Sunset* is composed of a serene sky, the viewer's gaze focuses on the visually active sea. Swirling patterns of foaming water among protruding, lichen-covered rocks are in stark contrast to the insistent line of the horizon repeated in the parallel wisps of clouds. Eight rough, knobby rocks of varying sizes punctuate the foreground and middle ground. As if participating in a rhythmic dance, three breakers spew white water upward, interrupting the harsh green and red horizon. A seagull glides toward the viewer at the juncture of the two breaking waves; its wings serve as pointers to the two large ships on the horizon. Another seagull follows, leading one's eye diagonally back to the ship slightly right of center. Two smaller, less distinct ships denote both distant points on the horizon and changes in the foreground wave: one floats above the wave curving downward on the left; the other, barely visible in the distance, marks the wave's upward rise on the right. With such details Heade creates a cadence of rise and fall above and below the horizon.

Mathematical relationships tie the picture together. Ships and waves form equal divisions along the horizon. For example, the distance between the three prominent ships, beginning with the smaller left-hand one, is the same. Heade continued the proportional sequence with the rising foam of the right-hand waves: the largest wave repeats this identical distance whether between its left side and the central ship or with the rising foam of its right-hand companion. This spatial pattern even governs the placement of the principal seagull between the two breaking waves. Such harmonies lend a restraining order to the turbulent water surface.

With simple polarities *Seascape: Sunset* pictures the natural drama of change and opposition. The crimson-colored sky complements the forest green sea. An ever-steady horizon line balances the constantly breaking waves. Horizontal stretches of clouds ease the vertiginous swirls of water. Over and over one seemingly insignificant element answers another: nearby waves by distant sails; flying birds by stationary rocks; lichen-covered earth by foam-topped sea; man-made sails by nature-made wings. Instances of swift and deliberate transformation, safety and danger, are present simultaneously. Corporeal rocks are eroded by the mutable force of water. Anchored into the ocean floor, these thick and gravity-bound rocks counter the thin, gravity-defying clouds floating across the sky. The coarse, bulky rock on the left is an image of endurance against the sensuous, serpentine wave disintegrating into foam on the right. Ships, each safe within its own perimeters, avoid the potent contact of sea and shore. But their security is fleeting. *Seascape: Sunset* lacks the quiet certainty of Heade's pictures of low tide. After witnessing his friend Church create *Twilight in the Wilderness* in New York, Heade, who moved to Providence late in 1860 and resided there and in Boston through 1863, painted his own version. *Wilderness Sunset* of 1861 (Stebbins 1975, 35, no. 40, 219) with its deserted marsh could be regarded as Heade's only true attempt, but it lacks the apocalyptic drama and study in antithesis that Church's incendiary sky and still waters provide. *Seascape: Sunset* offers a similar contrast but reverses the elements engaged in the drama: ocean, not sky, creates swirls of deep, rich colors; sky affords a calm mirror for reflection. Like Church's trees, Heade's rocks have a distinct character and seem silent witnesses to nature's power. Church's painting lacks any sign of human presence; Heade's merely hints at it with tiny, ghost gray sails. The sea, like the forest-covered mountains, was long associated with the concept of wilderness—the powerful, untamable, and mysterious forces of nature. In *Seascape: Sunset* nineteenth-century American viewers encountered, as they did in Church's wilderness view, primeval beginnings and apocalyptic endings.

Heade's seascape borrows from an iconographic tradition favored by ministers, politicians, poets, and artists during the Civil War era to express political and social unrest: tumultuous seas, searing skies, thundering clouds, and ships of state. Such imagery filled the many sermons and eulogies delivered by the likes of Henry Ward Beecher and Noah Hunt Schenck, patrons of Heade. In 1861 Schenck compared the war's ruinous bloodshed to waves slamming against a rocky shore, of the never-ending "on-rolling tide of war" (quoted in Fort Worth 1994, 41–46). Shipwrecks and thunderstorms appeared as well in the art of the period, including Heade's *Coastal Scene with Sinking Ship* of 1863 (Shelburne Museum, Shelburne, Vt.) which, like Detroit's picture, presents waves crashing against rocks. In *Seascape: Sunset,* however, the ship of state has not yet wrecked. Two seagulls cut between the ships on the central horizon and the treacherous waves in the foreground. These white birds may portend that conflict will be resolved before its full eruption. Completed in advance of the war's outbreak, *Seascape: Sunset,* like Church's *Twilight in the Wilderness,* can be understood as an allusion to the nation's changing fortunes as the new decade unfolded.

J. S.

Inscriptions On rocks at lower left, *M. J. Heade 1861;* verso bears original colorman stencil: *Vose & Jenckes / dealers in artist materials, / frames, engravers & co. / Prov. RI*

Provenance Maxim Karolik collection, Newport, R.I., 1959. Mr. J. Watson Webb. His wife, Electra Havemeyer Webb. Shelburne Museum, Shelburne, Vt. Altman/Burke, New York. Acquired in 1991.

Exhibitions Boston, Williams & Everett 1861 (possibly this picture). New York, National Academy of Design, 1861, no. 227, as *Marine Sunset.* New York 1987a, no. 11, ill.

References *Boston Transcript,* February 27, 1861, 4 (possibly this picture). *New York Daily Tribune,* March 27, 1861, 8. *New York World,* April 6, 1861, 3. Stebbins 1975, 68–69, ill., 220, no. 43, ill. Muller 1976, 74, no. 158, ill.

35
Sunset, ca. 1880

Oil on canvas

43.8 × 92.4 cm (17¼ × 36⅜ in.)

Founders Society Purchase, Dexter M. Ferry, Jr., Fund (46.135)

SALT MARSHES, whether in New England, New Jersey, or Florida, fascinated Heade. This farmer's son painted salt hay stacked amid placid marshes from the beginning of his mature landscape style in the early sixties through the year of his death, 1904, when he produced a "reminiscence" of Newburyport, Massachusetts, meadows. Although contemporary critics most identified Heade with the tropical world of his South American travels, they often noted with higher approval the "quieter and more familiar scenes" of his marshlands punctuated by cows and haystacks (*Forest and Stream* 1904). Unlike his novel renditions of the tropics, Heade's salt-marsh landscapes were appealing to the art-buying public; his many versions sold with relative ease.

Sunset has the intensity of color, generalization of form, thick application of paint, cigar-shaped clouds, and absence of figures or winding rivers typical of Heade's late marsh landscapes. It is decidedly different in composition and tone from his first decade of marshes (1863–76) inspired by travels to Newburyport and Rhode Island. In such pictures, Heade contrasted an ever-changing sky to the constancy of work on the marshes. *Sunset* lacks the dramatic moment of these earlier paintings, in which storms threaten at any moment as dark clouds hover in the distance or intrude into the foreground, or in which skies suddenly burst with morning light or cloudy haze lifts to reveal blue. Instead, *Sunset,* like many of Heade's late marsh scenes, displays the quiet, though brilliant, transfiguration of the sky from day to night.

Although painted late in Heade's career, *Sunset* retains those qualities that distinguish his marshlands from other nineteenth-century landscapes. Emphatically horizontal in format, twice as long as high, *Sunset* presents an expansive view of a rather homely topography. Sky constitutes a little over half the composition. The low meadow extends from the high cattails of the foreground, across ponds and puddles amid the valuable "black grass," to the distant low mountains that characteristically frame the marshland of New Jersey. After the sixties Heade virtually abandoned his decade-long attraction to Newburyport meadows and their distinctive winding rivers for the rougher marshes of Hoboken, New Jersey; Long Island; and Connecticut. *Sunset* has the wetter, more pitted surface of those marshes. Five haystacks of diminishing size lead the eye across the middle ground of *Sunset* and back to the amphitheater-like mountain range. Directly in the center of the painting sits a hay wagon, its horizontality countering the plump vertical rise above the horizon of the large haystack to its left. Both forms cast gray shadows in the pond spread out before them. To the right of these symbols of man's presence, four cows graze; placed alongside the hay wagon, they present an ensemble equal to that of the haystacks. The cows seem as static as the hay arranged on staddles. Their blocky shapes, like the wagon's, produce a welcome contrast to the round haystacks and bumpy mountains. Overall, *Sunset*'s rhythmic patterns of haystacks and cows, cigar-shaped clouds and mirroring pond strips, *repoussoir* cattails and skirting mountains denote the relentless presence of the artistic eye. *Sunset* repeatedly affirms that even in irregular terrain order can be imposed, that the actual and the ideal can be made one.

A stationary blue heron in the foreground pond enhances the timeless repose of *Sunset*'s rather ordinary scene. Until Heade's residency in Florida, herons rarely populate his marsh landscapes, though he probably saw many herons on his trip of 1880 to the Maryland shore. A heron does appear in a painting of similar dimensions and components, *Gathering Hay in the Salt Marshes* (ca. 1875–85; Montclair Art Museum, N.J.; see Stebbins 1975, 259, no. 243), as well as in the smaller, sparer *Sunset on Long Beach* (ca. 1875–85; Museum of Fine Arts, Boston; see Stebbins 1975, 261, no. 252). However, those herons have less compositional importance or symbolic presence. In *Sunset* the heron, alone in the foreground, demarcates the apex of two triangles formed by the haystack patterns. As in many of Heade's marsh scenes, seemingly random arrangements exhibit an underlying calculated order; the heron marks one of those instances. Frozen in a moment of transfixed sight, the heron looks back to the towering haystack, central hay wagon, and extraordinary orange-yellow clouds, the most viscid elements in the picture. It acts as if mesmerized by the sunset. Indeed, the heron functions much as the isolated, immobile figure does in romantic landscapes—as a surrogate for the viewer and an emblem of transcendent vision.

Like Heade's marsh and coast scenes in general, *Sunset* partakes of the stylistic and expressive features associated with the landscape mode art historians define as luminism. Beginning with the art periodical *The Crayon* (1855–61) and continuing through the turn of the century, contemporary aesthetic discourse, as well as nature descriptions and poetry, emphasized, particularly in landscape portrayals, those characteristics now identified with luminism: attention to detail combined with breadth of form, highly ordered compositions repeated with infinite modifications, intimacy of size and effect, and expressions of solitude and tranquillity. Above all, critics promoted "the ideal of the actual"—perception that embodies the highest thought and deepest emotion—and a reposeful spirit as antidotes to the era's economic and social discord. Extravagant narratives or allegories were rejected in favor of the "miraculous of the commonplace" and "a holiness of the present hour" derived from the writings of William Cullen Bryant, Ralph Waldo Emerson, and William Wordsworth.

Heade's art, especially his marsh scenes, conveys this reverence for the ordinary, though frequently an impassioned tension ruffles the seeming tranquillity. In *Sunset,* quiet itself disturbs. The immobile heron and strident clouds intimate that something unexpected may occur. Indeed, an ordinary marsh, a place of work, suffused with extraordinary colors, metamorphoses into a space for the imagination. Color transforms the marsh into an unearthly realm. Much of the sky appears as a smooth, blue-green atmosphere that progressively turns into lurid pinks and purples. Dark green mountains on the left convert into purple mounds as they proceed to the right; the large haystack marks the point of transformation. At that juncture, thickly painted clouds of deep purple, searing orange, and bright yellow crowd over the marsh. Wisps of purple and pink fill the edges above the horizon. The land, which began green and yellow in the foreground, takes on the orange-yellow glow of the sunset sky. Distant puddles shine as intense glimmers of orange. *Sunset*'s vivid colors and highly ordered composition render the marsh at once tangible and wondrous.

With such simple means, Heade informs *Sunset* with a contradictory nature equivalent to that of the marsh landscape in late-nineteenth-century America. Salt marshes linked the domesticated to the wild. They were not cultivated like farmlands but instead harvested for fodder and straw. Farmers waited for the tide to recede, then gathered hay to be stacked on staddles above the water plain. *Sunset* pictures work completed; the farmers have returned home and the hay, best stored out-of-doors, now functions as a monument to human labor in nature. Cows, haystacks, and hay wagon testify to the temporary mastery of the salt marsh for human use. Marshes, however, maintained a full range of wildlife, something that Heade the hunter undoubtedly appreciated. The heron wading in the foreground pond reminds the viewer of the marsh's dual nature and its ecological importance. As his many letters to *Forest and Stream* attest, Heade joined others in promoting a conservationist agenda while industrialization, land development, and tourism undermined coast and forest habitats. Heade's marsh scenes, especially those in the sixties and early seventies with their ubiquitous wagons and farmhands, appealed to the many Americans who elevated the yeoman farmer to the status of cultural hero.

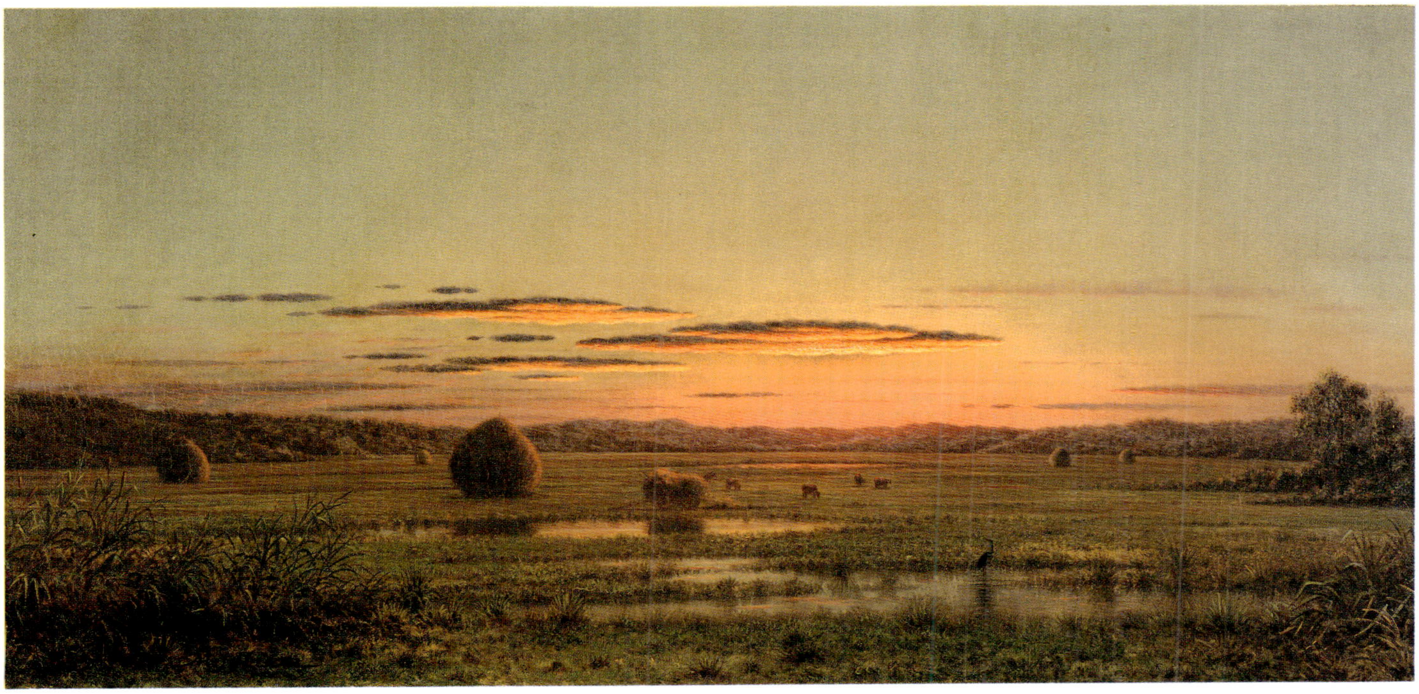

Sunset

Yet *Sunset* seems more of a lamentation than a celebration, for by the eighties, the western prairies and California valleys attracted those most disposed to farming, making the marshes obsolete as agrarian spaces. As debates raged regarding land speculation versus nature conservation, the salt marsh became a threatened property.

Sunset's evocation of loss is more tranquil, however, than that of *Seascape: Sunset* (cat. no. 34). As previously discussed, in his coast scenes produced during the Civil War, Heade incorporated the sunset imagery popularly identified with apocalypse, death, and resurrection. His marshland sunset, less strident in its coloring, evokes "the gathering twilight holy," a frequent refrain in late-nineteenth-century American poetry. "Touched by the twilight's silent spell," the viewer welcomes *Sunset*'s message of inevitability—whether the ending of a day, a life, or an era (Thompson 1889, 199–200). Heade, an Episcopalian and in his sixties, must have found the elegiac associations of sunset especially appropriate for his late marsh landscapes; he never painted hummingbirds and orchids in twilight. Nor did Heade paint autumnal scenes resonant with similar meaning as did Frederic Edwin Church and Jasper Cropsey. Instead, Heade's marshes drenched in the colors of sunset served as ruminations on the cycles of life. In *Sunset* the stilled water, iconic haystacks, and effulgent sky create an atmosphere of silence, solitude, and remembrance. The heron, in some ways a surrogate for Heade himself, seems to be looking with reverie on a landscape, now drenched in twilight, that for twenty years preoccupied the artist and with which he was most identified.

J. S.

Inscription At lower left, *M. J. Heade*

Provenance A. F. Mondschein. Acquired in 1946.

Exhibitions Detroit 1883. Kalamazoo 1964. Boston et al. 1969, no. 39.

References Grigaut 1947, 18, ill. Stebbins 1975, 259, no. 242.

36
Hummingbirds and Orchids, 1880s

Oil on canvas
36.2 × 56.5 cm (14¼ × 22¼ in.)
Founders Society Purchase, Dexter M. Ferry, Jr., Fund (47.36)

"FROM EARLY BOYHOOD I have been almost a monomaniac on hummingbirds, and there is probably very little regarding their habits that I do not know" (Didymus 1892). With those retrospective words Heade expressed his complex, forty-year artistic engagement with a bird native only to the Americas. It was a marriage of passion and observation, poetry and objectivity, anthropomorphism and empiricism. Inspired to follow the footsteps of the German naturalist Alexander von Humboldt and the explorations of the American painter Frederic Edwin Church (q.v.), Heade traveled to South America, specifically Brazil, in 1863. There, greeted warmly by Emperor Dom Pedro II, Heade studied hummingbirds and their tropical environment firsthand and produced at least twelve small oil paintings in preparation for his proposed but never completed volume of twenty chromolithographs, *The Gems of Brazil.* Subsequent trips to Central and South America, especially Jamaica (1870), further invigorated his lifelong immersion in "the all-absorbing hummingbird craze" (Didymus 1904).

Detroit's *Hummingbirds and Orchids* follows the formula Heade conceived after his Jamaica trip and continued to his death: hummingbirds dramatically share the stage with the equally exotic and celebrated orchid. With his many pictures featuring this combination of flora and fowl, Heade reinvented American painting, creating a genre that transcended the neat appellations of floral still life, ornithological study, or landscape view.

Hummingbirds and Orchids features a large *Cattleya labiata* orchid in the left foreground of a misty tropical landscape. Alighted on the orchid's leaf, forming the picture's compositional center, a Cora's shear-tail hummingbird flaunts its distinctive plumage upward, but it is not yet fully displayed for courtship. His bill points to the right as wings spread out in a seeming tightrope-balancing act. Most likely, he has just descended on the leaf. In direct opposition to the Cora's implied movement, another hummingbird, with wings contracted downward, perches on a thin, moss-covered branch. Though similarly colored at the throat, this hummingbird is a male of another species, a Brazilian amethyst, of which Heade was quite fond. In the contemporaneous *Orchids and Spray Orchids with Hummingbirds* (Museum of Fine Arts, Boston; Stebbins 1975, 266, no. 279), Heade furnished his performing Cora's shear-tail with a female mate in subdued green and white; both balance above a sensuous *Cattleya labiata.* Although Heade's earliest hummingbird depictions paired male and female near their nest in the spirit of an ornithological study, a decade later he virtually abandoned the domestic nest for the passionate orchid.

Until the end of his life, in pictures akin to Detroit's, Heade portrayed two species of male hummingbirds as rivals for the viewer's enraptured attention and the orchid's luscious nectar. Indeed, in *Hummingbirds and Orchids* the two birds, perched opposite and facing bill to bill, lean toward each other in anticipated combat. Such contests fascinated Heade. Writing as Didymus for *Forest and Stream,* Heade noted the antagonistic nature of hummingbirds: "They are the most inveterate little warriors, two seldom coming together without a conflict, and when one has found a field that is worth protecting he stations himself on the nearest dead twig and holds possession until

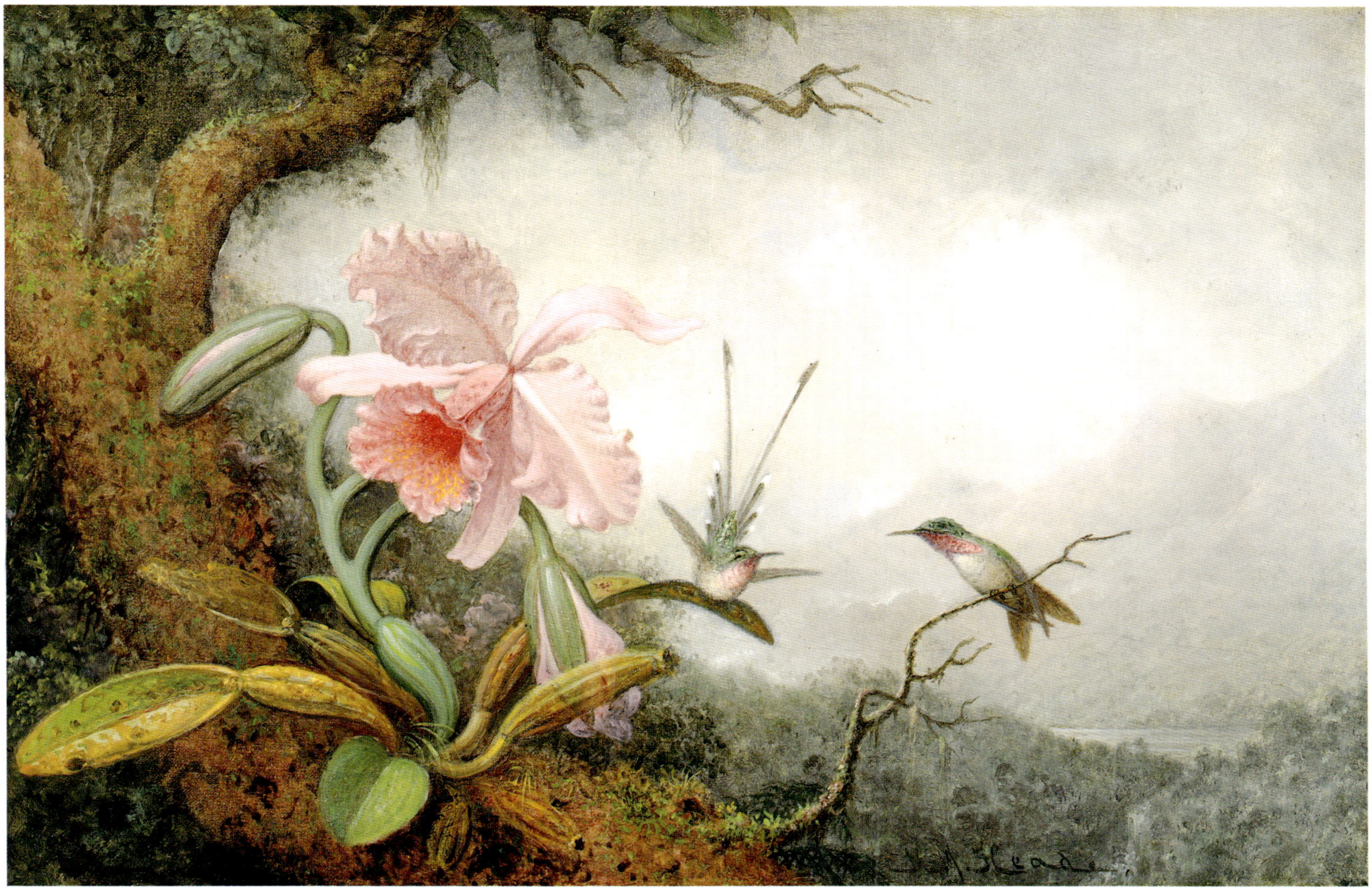

Hummingbirds and Orchids

driven off by a stronger bird" (1892). Hummingbirds rarely travel in pairs: "the only time when one will tolerate the presence of another is at the mating season, and even then they are seldom seen together except at the nest" (Didymus 1892a). Yet Heade regularly depicted twosomes.

When Heade first set out to produce his hummingbird study, *The Gems of Brazil,* the natural-history precedents of John James Audubon and John Gould remained firmly in his memory. But Heade, already an established landscape artist, departed from the truths of natural history to create tropical scenes animated by intimate dramas and narrative tension. Heade's natural tendency to anthropomorphize colored his writings as much as his paintings. He could not resist characterizing the hummingbirds as having domestic squabbles, writing that one "had a mate who was bossing him and dragged him northward" (Didymus 1891). Another "left like a well-trained husband, in the wake of his lordly little wife" (Didymus 1892). Such assertions of dominance among the species, further accented by the luscious orchid, underlie Detroit's hummingbird picture.

As the most complex and colorful element in the painting, the orchid visually overwhelms the smaller hummingbirds as well as the summarily described landscape. Painted life-size but seeming bigger than life, the orchid twists and turns its sepals, stems, buds, and leaves directly before the viewer. The elaborate furls of the orchid petals easily capture the beholder's attention. And the trumpet-like labellum with traces of yellow pollen coating its inner edges invites an even more probing gaze. On each side of the orchid a bud droops with the weight of an emerging blossom; one barely reveals the pink orchid within its green tube, while the other's soft masses pop out, mimicking the coloring of the hummingbird beside it. Together, luxurious blossom, flowers-in-waiting, decayed leaves, and alighted hummingbirds denote the cyclical processes and vitalistic nature of life.

Indeed, the hummingbirds' proximity to and parroting of the orchid's colorful display reiterate the crucial role hummingbirds play in the pollination, and therefore survival, of the species. After publishing *Origin of Species* in 1859, Darwin turned to the orchid and the process of cross-fertilization to further substantiate his theory of natural selection. Published a year before Heade's trip to Brazil, Darwin's *On the Various Contrivances by Which Orchids Are Fertilized by Insects* (1862) analyzed the plant's unique and diverse structures that have been adapted and thus preserved through time. Darwin singled out the labellum as the most important external element of the orchid's success as a species: attractive in form and color, its channeled and often tubular shape invites insects to land on its surface and hummingbirds to penetrate its opening. Heade preferred to paint variations of the Cattleya orchid that have an especially prominent labellum, as seen in *Hummingbirds and Orchids.* Dominant in size, color, and foreground placement, such labella aggressively seduce the viewer's attention as much as they would that of any bird or insect. Perhaps more than any other flower, the orchid conveys a sexual aura that even Victorian America could not ignore, especially folklore extolling the orchid's powers as an aphrodisiac and herbal restorer of virility. Heade's orchids with their vaginalike labella and phallus-like pods, so evident in Detroit's painting, reiterate their gynandrous character (i.e., female pistils and male stamens in a single column) and the process of cross-fertilization necessary to their survival. Interestingly, Heade's pen name, Didymus, and *orchis* share the same meaning—testicle.

Heade's visual mimicry in *Hummingbirds and Orchids,* with flower petals and bird feathers echoing one another, corresponds to the clever adaptations of form that Darwin himself noted as essential to the endurance of the orchid. It was this quality of mimicry, in which orchids took on the appearance of insects, animals, and anthropomorphic forms, that most entranced the public in the nineteenth century. From the sixties on, an orchid craze stimulated the market for hothouse flowers, horticultural articles, and later in the century, decorative orchid patterns. In the *American Naturalist* of 1868 C. M. Tracy marveled at how the bizarre shapes of orchids "tempted [him] sometimes to believe they are animated creatures under some strange disguise of enchantment" (Tracy 1868). *Harper's Monthly* devoted considerable space in its illustrated article of 1879, "The Mimicry of Nature," to the extraordinary and humorous visual transformations of the orchid into strange insects and dancing puppets. Heade, of course, never departed from an essentially accurate transcription of his natural specimen; rather, it was through juxtaposition and emphasis that he attained an expressive representation of the tropics.

Hummingbirds and Orchids conveys a union of the natural and the magical appropriate to the tropics that travel books called the "Gardens of Paradise." Heade captured the mysterious, life-renewing powers of this environment, not by painting the volcanoes, rivers, and snow-covered mountains that so intrigued his friend Church, but instead by focusing on the orchids and hummingbirds that ancient Americans worshiped for their erotic and medicinal potency. Tiny hummingbirds (in actuality some measure only 2¼ inches long) and small flowers disconcertingly loom before gigantic mountain ranges, lakes, and moss-covered trees. With its summary definition of tropical surroundings, *Hummingbirds and Orchids* effects an even greater disparity between foreground specimen and background habitat. The mossy, curtainlike tree that Heade frequently included in his tropical compositions is merely sketched in here (and its top branches possibly reconstructed). Still, *Hummingbirds and Orchids* displays the horizontal format, composition, and pink tonality Heade favored in his hummingbird scenes from the 1880s until his death.

As the art historians Katherine Manthorne and Ella Foshay have stressed, Heade progressively adopted a dynamic rather than a static conception of the natural world, one that paralleled Darwin's controversial theories on the interdependence of environment, species, and competitive instincts. Indeed, in *Hummingbirds and Orchids*, Heade disarmingly juxtaposes hummingbird study and landscape painting, microcosm and macrocosm, romanticism and Darwinism. No wonder contemporary critics regarded works like this as "clever" and "novel."
J. S.

Inscription At lower right, *M. J. Heade*

Provenance Mrs. R. O'Hair, Detroit. Acquired in 1947.

Exhibitions Tucson 1964, no. 122. Montreal 1967, no. 312. New York 1970, no. 141, ill. Jacksonville and Palm Beach 1981, 26, no. 12.

References Grigaut 1947, 16–17, ill. Richardson 1965, 227, fig. 94. Canaday 1969, color ill. 343. Stebbins 1975, 151–152, 267, no. 283.

37
Cherokee Roses, ca. 1890

Oil on canvas
25.4 × 41.3 cm (10 × 16¼ in.)
Founders Society Purchase, Dexter M. Ferry, Jr., Fund (57.248)

THIS SPARSE YET ENGAGING image is one of numerous floral still lifes Heade painted while living in St. Augustine, Florida. No longer a bachelor, Heade renewed his post–Civil War interest in flowers, the only still-life subject to which he devoted his talents. His earlier images (1865–75) incorporated the theatrical predilections and symbolic conventions that the ascending middle class craved in their Victorian floral arrangements. In the late eighties, however, Heade forsook his elaborate combinations of mixed flowers and Victorian objects for sparer designs of native plants reclining on velvet. By doing so, he exchanged a strained Victorian abundance for a serenely vibrant sensuousness. Even in old age Heade continued to reinvigorate the traditions of American painting.

A prickly, climbing evergreen rose common to the southeastern United States, the Cherokee rose *(Rosa laevigata)* provided Heade with an opportunity to combine the wildness of nature with the artifices of the still life. Unlike the full-bodied red roses, lotus flowers, magnolias, and orchids that concurrently attracted Heade's eye, the Cherokee rose conveyed for him a fragile simplicity rather than a voluptuous exoticism. As in his painted marshes and seascapes, Heade effected drama in this ordinary subject through the juxtaposition of bold color contrasts and the subtle play of natural forms within a repeated format.

In this version, one of nine studies of the Cherokee rose, three fully opened blossoms rest along and even over the table's edge on a lush, red velvet cloth. The table's low placement in relation to the neutral brown backdrop accentuates the picture's horizontal orientation and re-creates the proportions of Heade's landscapes. The red cloth, at once a bright receding plane and a deep maroon band in the foreground, provides a rich bed of color for the complementary green leaves and the stark white petals with yellow centers. Although aligned across the picture plane as if set in a shallow relief, the roses twist and turn, displaying a variety of surfaces and light effects. Indeed, Heade's mastery of light endows the clipped branch with renewed life. Leaves, stems, buds, and blossoms, like performers on a stage, gesture laterally, vertically, and even outwardly, toward the viewer's space. Four buds, in progressive stages of opening, extend in different directions from the four stationary blooms, including the one almost entirely hidden behind the central flower. These buds, with their thorny bases, spiky scales, and shiny pointing leaves, create stiff yet energetic rhythms that dramatically accentuate the soft, droopy stillness of the white blossoms. The three flowers orient their faces slightly from left to center to right as shadow increasingly darkens their petals. Two sets of leaves rise above the table in opposition: the central group openly reveals its smooth surfaces to the viewer; the other dramatically turns to the right, displaying its coarse underside. The floral ballet climaxes in two stems protruding into the viewer's space: the just-opening bud and freshly pruned branch splay out in counterpoint offers of softness and sharpness, of life commencing and life cut short. As with much of Heade's art, in *Cherokee Roses* the seemingly simple becomes the disarmingly complex.

Like its eight companion paintings, *Cherokee Roses* is a highly calculated composition that evolved out of several informal oil sketches Heade produced from life. In preparation for his orchid, rose, magnolia, and hummingbird pictures, Heade painted unfinished naturalistic studies of various birds, blooms, buds, and leaves from different points of view, which served as a catalogue of observations for his high-art compositions. Two studies of Cherokee rose branches survive as part of the twenty-four oil sketches Heade gave to the young art student Wilma E. Davis in 1910 and are now owned by the St. Augustine Historical Society; they are the only sketches of their kind still extant. The studies possess a freshness and exuberance that Heade later embellished with elaborate details and refined arrangements. None of the Cherokee blossoms in the nine still lifes reappears exactly as Heade recorded them in his studies. The four-leaved stem that pops up to the right revealing its underside in the Detroit picture is taken from his most involved study, but the leaves are now fuller and more assertive.

Heade employed this same stem in his *White Wild Roses* (ca. 1880s; private collection; Stebbins 1975, no. 306), but there its more delicate form is overshadowed by the large blossom opening behind it. Although Heade composed the two pictures similarly (in fact six in the series have Cherokee roses prone on a velvet cloth), the Detroit flowers are less robust, more shadowed, and surrounded by fewer and less mature buds. The dark red velvet cloth, however, confers a sensuous intensity not present in *White Wild Roses* with its staid greenish gray drapery. Heade differentiated the other pictures of Cherokee roses resting on red velvet by reducing or increasing the number of their blossoms and buds, arranging the branches farther back on the cloth, or making the buds project in the same direction. Distinctive to the Detroit picture is the assertive and individualistic quality of each of the flower parts, including the extent to which they threaten to protrude into the viewer's space. Heade painted a few compositions of Cherokee roses arranged in a glass of water or resting on a shiny table: their greater contrast of textures and surfaces distracts the viewer from the fragile and luxurious presence of blossoms reclining on velvet. The defining aspect of the Cherokee rose series is Heade's ingenious use of the reclining flower format without repeating configurations or mood. Every element has been manipulated to create arrangements that mesmerize the viewer with their singular character.

Heade's Cherokee roses and their concomitant invention, the reclining magnolias on velvet, appear all the more extraordinary when considered within the context of American still-life painting at the end of the century. They avoid the Japanese, symbolist, or impressionist aesthetics that elevated painterly technique and poetic mood over observation. Nor do they truly partake of the popular trompe-l'oeil mode even though Heade's obituary credited him with such effects: the magazine *Forest and Stream* praised him for "putting on canvas the Florida magnolia and the Cherokee rose with a vraisemblance so perfect as sometimes to be astonishing in the illusion" *(Forest and Stream* 1904, 233). For as Theodore Stebbins has noted, no still-life image from the period compares. Heade's reclining flowers combine careful observation with a design artfully constructed to communicate emotion, not deception. Their presentation on velvet cloth makes them more than flowers—they evoke the power of human gesture and desire. Heade's *Cherokee Roses* and his magnolia series prompt the viewer to see, touch, and smell blossoms recumbent on a seductive red cloth in such a way that, in effect, they become the nudes of still-life painting. Or as John I. H. Baur once remarked, they resemble "odalisques on a couch" (quoted in Stebbins 1975, 176).

Heade's orchid and hummingbird pictures embodied for nineteenth-century Americans sexual associations appropriate to the tropical wilderness; his reclining floral still lifes, however, introduced sexuality and sensuality into Victorian America's more temperate domestic sphere. Certainly Heade's marriage to Elizabeth Smith inspired their creation. Although contemporary images frequently depicted the female within the context of floral decoration—whether in the garden, home, or as part of an overall architectural design—in Heade's art, flower and woman are metaphorically one. Contributing to such a conception were the popular midcentury floral dictionaries, which ascribed moral qualities and affections to specific flowers in various stages of development. With *Flora's Dictionary* of 1855 Americans could decode the buds, blossoms, and colors of floral arrangements like *Cherokee Roses* into a narrative of passion that progressed from innocence to admiration, love, and marriage (Wirt 1855, 106–114). Books like Samuel B. Parsons's *Rose: Its History, Poetry, Culture, and Classification* (1856) offered a combination of scientific knowledge including medicinal properties, practical advice on cultivation, history of the rose in ancient and medieval ceremonies, and a collection of poetic associations. Repeatedly in such texts the rose was equated with various stages of love, death, and mourning. Regarded as the queen of flowers and the emblem of beauty and fragility, the rose found its type in the "gentle maiden," or, as Leigh Hunt wrote, its only rival flower was "joy-abundant woman" (Parsons 1856, 74, 78, 98). Indeed, it is in this dualistic approach to nature as natural specimen and emotional emblem that one can best understand the significance of the reclining flower on velvet as a "passionate type" for Heade. As he revealed in a now-lost notebook, "Every man who possesses a soul has loved once, if not a dozen times, for passion was created with man, and is a part of his nature" (quoted in Stebbins 1975, 142).

J. S.

Inscription At lower right, *M. J. Heade*

Provenance Paul Magriel, New York. Acquired in 1957.

Exhibitions Washington 1955, no. 18. Northfield 1967. Jacksonville and Palm Beach 1981, 27, no. 14. Mansfield 1991, no. 11, ill.

References McCausland 1955, 326, ill. 327. Baur 1957–58, 18, ill. *BDIA* 1957–58, 31, ill. Stebbins 1975, 170, 272, no. 309.

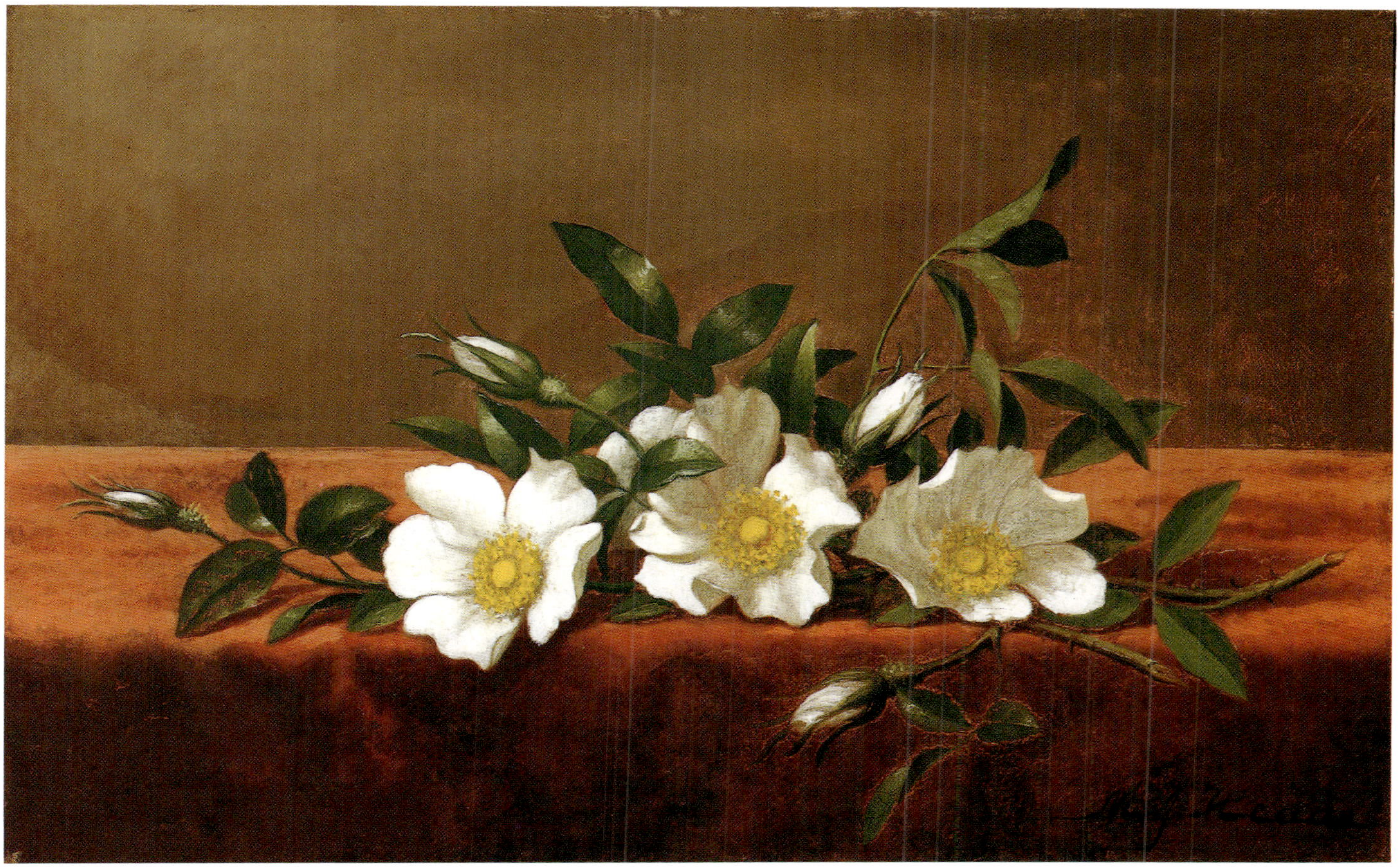

Cherokee Roses

Edward Lamson Henry

1841 Charleston, South Carolina–
Cragsmoor, New York 1919

Little is known of Henry's early childhood other than that he was the son of Frederick and Elizabeth Fairbanks Henry and went to New York as a seven-year-old orphan to live with cousins. When he was about fourteen years old he briefly took lessons with the genre painter Walter M. Oddie in lower Manhattan, but by 1858 he had moved to Philadelphia, where he studied at the Pennsylvania Academy of the Fine Arts and with Paul Weber. His earliest works were landscapes and farmyard scenes, one of which received commendation in a newspaper review in 1859 when exhibited at the National Academy of Design, New York.

In September 1860 Henry sailed for London, where he stayed briefly before going on to Paris in late October. Family records maintain that he studied with both Charles Gleyre and Gustave Courbet and traveled to Rome, Florence, Naples, Venice, up through Germany, and back to England and Ireland. Henry returned to America in June 1862. By 1863 he had a studio in New York's popular Studio Building at 51 West Tenth Street. At that time he was one of its youngest occupants, along with John Ferguson Weir. Although Henry still used his Italian sketches as the basis of paintings executed in 1863 and 1864, he began to turn to American scenes.

The Civil War had begun in April 1861, and Henry, like many other artists, found new subjects. In the fall of 1864 he served as a clerk to a captain on a Union transport ship. He kept a small sketchbook that he filled with sketches of African-American soldiers and scenes of the Union camps along the James, Appomatox, and Potomac rivers. He eventually worked up these river views into larger oils, such as *City Point, Virginia, Headquarters of General Grant* (1865–72; Addison Gallery of American Art, Phillips Academy, Andover, Mass.), first owned by the Union League Club. Henry also received a five-hundred-dollar commission from the Union League Club to paint *A Presentation of Colors in the First Colored Regiment of New York by the Ladies of the City in Front of the Old Union League Club, Union Square, New York City, in 1864* (1868). Successes with such paintings assured his election in 1869 as a full academician in the National Academy of Design.

After the war Henry's popularity grew among collectors. He began to specialize in scenes that included railroad cars and/or horse-drawn carriages, conversation pieces of couples seated in well-appointed libraries, and historical genre. Such pictures have an allover, bright surface coloration and random focus that accentuate the anecdotal and animated mood of the works. He also joined several men's clubs that provided a milieu for meeting important patrons, such as John Taylor Johnston, president of the New Jersey Central Railroad and later president of the Metropolitan Museum of Art, who along with Henry joined the Century Club in 1866. The following year Johnston ordered *The 9:45 Accommodation* (1867; Metropolitan Museum of Art, New York) and paid Henry $500. Another influential patron was Samuel P. Avery, a dealer in American art with an international reputation.

Henry revisited Europe in 1871, and in 1875 he stayed abroad for about a year with his bride, Frances Livingston Wells, an amateur flower painter. He made yet another trip in 1881–82. By 1885 he had moved to 3 North Washington Square, which provided him with a more commodious studio. Beginning in 1883 he spent summers at Cragsmoor, near Ellenville, New York, where he built a house. His presence attracted other painters to this Catskill community, and an artists' colony developed. Although he usually spent part of the winter in New York, he kept his major collection of costumes and antique carriages at Cragsmoor. The art critic Clarence Cook called the house "a museum of antiquarian curiosities in the field of relics of colonial life." Cook compared Henry with the French painter Ernest Meissonier, who also painted costume pieces with attention to the details of furniture, architecture, and costume, and declared that "if he have not Meissonier's skill, he has far more invention and variety" (Cook 1888, 3:267). Henry's penchant for reconstructions of colonial scenes and his own collection of early Americana helped spur the colonial revival, earlier initiated by the 1876 Centennial Exposition in Philadelphia.

Well into the twentieth century, Henry continued to paint horses and carriages moving along the muddy roads of Catskill villages with colonial buildings and churches in the backgrounds. He used photographs to help him maintain a faithfulness to details. Like many of his contemporaries, he found humor in the depiction of old geezers, nervous spinsters, and African-American children, but the latter group are rarely caricatures. To his admirers Henry was painting the rustic life of plain ways and simple desires that was quickly disappearing during a period of rapid industrialization.

His last winter he spent in Daytona, Florida, where he attempted to recuperate from a long illness; he died in Cragsmoor shortly after returning in the spring of 1919. In 1940 relatives of Henry's widow gave a collection of sketchbooks, paintings, sketches, photographs, letters, and other memorabilia, including an unpublished memoir by the widow, to the New York State Museum in Albany.

P. H.

Bibliography Cook 1888, 3:266–267. McCausland 1945. Cragsmoor et al. 1981. Spassky 1985, 558–562.

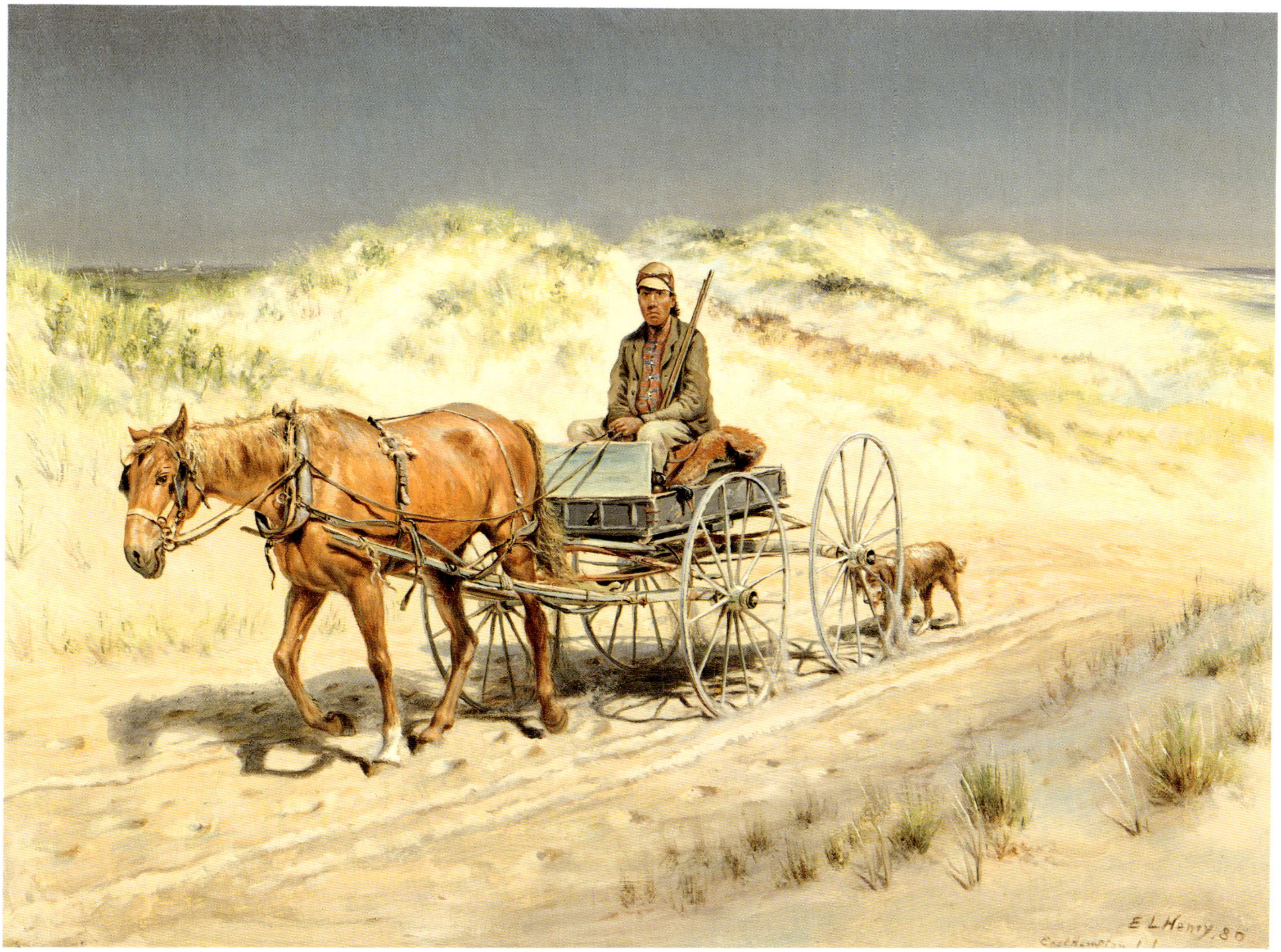

38

The King of the Montauks, 1880

Oil on canvas

29.2 × 40.6 cm (11½ × 16 in.)

Gift of Dexter M. Ferry, Jr. (47.37)

Elizabeth McCausland, who assembled Henry materials in the early 1940s for a book and who sketched in his life and oeuvre from disparate sources, had words of praise for the paintings that Henry did during his visit to East Hampton, Long Island. McCausland writes:

> A few pictures suggest that Henry had a potential lyric gift. Sketches and paintings made at East Hampton, Long Island, from 1879 to 1881, are well executed and poetic, implying that Henry had a sensitivity to form not always evident in his work. Did he perhaps consult a good model like Boudin? These paintings . . . express light and air, to judge from photographs in the Henry Collection.

To McCausland such paintings "seem to have genuine esthetic appeal" (McCausland 1945, 89).

The King of the Montauks represents one of the last of the surviving Montauk Indians as he sits in his carriage holding the reins of his horse with one hand while cradling a rifle in the crook of his elbow. His dog walks along behind. The horse pulls the wagon slowly through a trail in the dunes, and the wagon wheels throw off sand as they turn. In this picture, Henry concentrates all the details in the center of the picture, with his usual fastidious attention to the exact placement of harnesses and belly straps, axles and wheels. Without background archi-

King of the Montauks

tectural elements, the picture projects the freedom and lightness that McCausland admired. The dunes with their tufts of beach grass reflect a bright, sunny light; a wedge of ocean in the upper right background hints at the seaside locale; the distant windmill and the lighthouse were features of the local geography. The sky above the high horizon expands into a cloudless band of light blue color. *The King of the Montauks* contrasts sharply with the busyness of Henry's other anecdotal scenes filled with wagons, carriages, barnyard animals, and people.

McCausland speculates that a picture titled *Prince of the Mohawk,* with the same measurements and listed as number 50 in a sixteen-page catalogue of Henry's work by Christian Klackner (1906), may be the same painting as *The King of the Montauks.* The New York State Museum, Albany, owns *Beach Wagon,* a smaller (7⅜ × 9⅝ in.) oil-on-paper work by Henry that has an almost identical image and composition.

The Montauk Indians lived on the southern fork of Long Island from East Hampton to Montauk Point. According to Gaynell Stone Levine, they were "one of the thirteen extended family groups of Algonquian culture and language," each of which settled various geographical locales of the island. Ethnohistories of the Montauk rightly begin with the account written in 1761 by the internationally known educator Reverend Samson Occum, which was published by the Massachusetts Historical Society in 1804. Occum was born a Mohegan and adopted into the Montauk family when he married Mary Fowler, one of the Montauks (Suffolk County 1979, 2).

The legal concept of property rights, as practiced by white settlers, and the flexible custom of common land use (usufruct), as understood by the Montauk, were always in contention. During the 1870s, when real-estate speculators were eyeing eastern Long Island for its potential as summer-resort property, these issues came to a head. An article in the September 18, 1871, issue of *Harper's New Monthly Magazine* estimated that the Montauk had by then "dwindled to about a dozen persons"—the descendants of the Montauk who in 1660 had conveyed land to the white freeholders of East Hampton, in exchange for land-use fees or rents. The article shamelessly noted that the "two hundred descendants of the original purchasers are waiting for the time when the tribe will be extinct, and there shall be no lien upon the land" (see Suffolk County 1979, 153). However, in a July 1878 court case the Montauk families of David Pharaoh, Stephen Pharaoh, and William Fowler were recognized as the rightful tenants in common with the white proprietors, and hence the Montauk could retain rights to the use of their land (Suffolk County 1979, 155). However, white interests advocating partition succeeded, and a partition sale was held on October 22, 1879, when Arthur Benson bought Montauk for $151,000.

At this point, we cannot be absolutely certain whom Henry has portrayed in his painting. At the time of the July 1878 court case, David Pharaoh (1838–1878; a variant spelling is "Faro") was known as the "King of the Montauks," but he died within the next couple of months of tuberculosis. He was succeeded by his cousin, Stephen Pharaoh (1819–1879), also known as Steve Talkhouse, since David's own son Wyandank Pharaoh (1863–1895) was still a minor. Stephen Pharaoh was a well-known walker and looked so much like a white man's image of an Indian—"gaunt cheeks, long face and long hair and long sad eyes"—that P. T. Barnum had signed him up for his touring show and had billed him as "King of the Montauks" (Suffolk County 1979, 115). Yet, in spite of his reputed good health, Stephen Pharaoh was found dead in the dunes in August 1879. Funeral notices called him "King of the Montauks." His death was obviously convenient to Arthur Benson's land interests; Pharaoh's demise seems to have eliminated any resistance to the imminent partition sale. This left Wyandank Pharaoh, still a minor, next in line for the title.

John H. Morice, a local historian who wrote about the Montauk in 1944, identified the subject of Henry's picture as David Pharaoh. (Winslow Homer [q.v.] also did a pencil-and-watercolor drawing of a figure, inscribed and dated *East Hampton / July 21, 1874,* that has been identified as "David Pharaoh, the Last of the Montauks"; see Hendricks 1979, fig. 169. Indeed, Homer's figure looks like the image from an ambrotype in the collection of the East Hampton Free Library.) But according to McCausland, Henry did not come to East Hampton until 1879, after David Pharaoh had died and during the interregnum when Stephen Pharaoh acted as "king." However, the youthful face of Henry's subject would suggest that the subject was meant to be the seventeen-year-old Wyandank, described in the November 1878 issue of *Lippincott's Magazine* as a lad who "occasionally visits the few houses on the peninsula and the nearest villages, selling berries" (Young 1878, 537).

P. H.

Inscription At lower right, *E. L. Henry, 80 / East Hampton L I*

Provenance Baruch Feldman, Philadelphia. Thompson Galleries, Detroit. Acquired in 1947.

Exhibitions New York 1942, no. 22. Indianapolis 1961, no. 23.

References Klackner 1906, no. 50. McCausland 1945, 89.

Thomas Hill

1829 Birmingham, England–Raymond, California 1908

With his mother and brother, Thomas Hill followed his father, a tailor, from his birthplace in England to America in 1844. They settled in Taunton, Massachusetts, where Hill began working for a carriage painter. He later moved to Boston and then to Philadelphia, where he enrolled in the life class at the Pennsylvania Academy of the Fine Arts directed by Peter Frederick Rothermel, a portrait and history painter. Hill first specialized in portraits and still lifes and also painted landscapes, such as scenes in the White Mountains of New Hampshire, which show the influence of the Hudson River school. In 1861, owing to poor health, he moved to California and opened a portrait studio in San Francisco. The following year he made his first trip to Yosemite Valley and began to form a portfolio of sketches of California scenery from which he made many paintings. In 1866 he exhibited his *View of the Yosemite Valley* (1865; New-York Historical Society) at the National Academy of Design. The same year, he traveled to Paris, where he studied with the German artist Paul Friedrich Meyerheim, who encouraged him to specialize in landscape.

After Hill had settled in Boston, he received much acclaim for his landscapes featuring Yosemite Valley. In 1871 he returned to San Francisco and, with William Keith, became California's leading landscape painter, concentrating on paintings of Yosemite. He sold some of his large canvases to the wealthiest residents of California for as much as ten thousand dollars. During the 1870s, Hill's yearly sales averaged twenty thousand dollars. After an economic depression struck California in 1879, prices for his paintings rapidly declined.

In 1877 the politician and railroad official Leland Stanford commissioned Hill to depict the meeting of the Union Pacific and Central Pacific railroads, which had taken place on May 10, 1869, and created a transcontinental railroad. Stanford, however, ultimately refused the monumental finished painting, *The Driving of the Last Spike* (1881; State of California, Sacramento), a major disappointment for the artist. It remained unsold until after Hill's death, when it was purchased by David Hewes, a collector of the artist's work.

Hill spent much of the year at the Yosemite studio he built in 1883 and painted an estimated five thousand canvases for the tourist trade. He also visited other celebrated North American landscape sites such as Muir Glacier in Alaska and Yellowstone National Park, in order to broaden his subject matter. He suffered a stroke in 1898 and died ten years later. S. M. S.

Bibliography Oakland 1980.

39

The Grand Canyon of the Yellowstone, ca. 1884

Oil on canvas

167.6 × 243.8 cm (66 × 92 in.)

Gift of Mrs. George O. Robinson (17.19)

Although Thomas Hill is best known for his paintings of Yosemite, he also painted other major American landscape sites, including several that had already been depicted by the artist Thomas Moran (q.v.). With *The Grand Canyon of the Yellowstone,* Hill was probably inspired by Moran's even larger painting of the same subject done in 1872 (96 × 144 in.; National Museum of American Art, Washington, D.C., on loan from the Department of the Interior, Office of the Secretary). Moran's painting had been purchased by Congress for ten thousand dollars to hang in the Capitol to commemorate the declaration of Yellowstone as the first national park (Kinsey 1992, 43).

Hill visited Yellowstone National Park in August 1884 (Oakland 1980, 31). This painting is probably the same *Grand Canyon of the Yellowstone* that he exhibited at the World's Industrial and Cotton Centennial Exposition in New Orleans during the winter of 1884–85. In all, he sent five paintings to the fair, including *The Driving of the Last Spike.* They were discussed in the *San Francisco Evening Bulletin* of March 24, 1885: "Mr. Hill is seen to better advantage in his large picture of the Yellowstone and the Yosemite Valleys and the 'Heart of the Sierras'. These vast panoramic canvases give an idea of these wonderful regions, the one of the Yellowstone being particularly fortunate in its point of view" (quoted in *California Art Research* 1937, 88; microfiche frame 0268).

From a viewpoint similar to that in Moran's painting, we see the Lower Falls and the canyon walls of the Yellowstone River. The painting is described in the catalogue for the sale in 1916 and 1917 of the collection of paintings by Hill owned by David Hewes, a millionaire San Francisco collector:

> Nature in her grandiloquent moods made a potent appeal to Tom Hill. Into this canvas he has painted the very soul of the canyon, with its impenetrable gorges, its frightful precipices, its solemn grandeur and its awful beauty. Over the brink of the yawning gorge the Yellowstone plunges to its bed in the age worn canyon. The stormy green of the water as it winds a snake-like course through the canyon is in sharp contrast to the reddish yellow walls which tower on both sides to hem it in. Slim trees claim a precarious rooting in the shelter of the barren slopes and in the foreground a brooding eagle has perched her aerie on the topmost point of a rocky pinnacle. Topping the cliffs, as far as eye can see, an undulating country clad in soft summer green, sweeps away to the distant horizon. Overhead rests a sky of intense blue, coldly clear. Here again Mr. Hill has portrayed the greatness and sublimity of nature.

Hill did not include the rocky ledge with the small figures found in the foreground of Moran's paintings, so the viewer seems to be hovering over the deep canyon. In place of a human presence, large birds that Peter H. Hassrick identifes as ospreys are prominent (correspondence, curatorial files, DIA). Hill's loose, almost impressionistic handling of paint is closer in technique to Moran's second representation of the site, *Grand Cañon of the Yellowstone* (1893–1903; National Museum of American Art, Washington, D.C.).

According to the Hewes sale catalogue, this painting was part of Hill's estate, much of which was acquired by Hewes. At Hewes's death he owned more than two hundred paintings by Hill. Besides this painting Hewes's collection included two small views of the Grand Canyon of the Yellowstone (San Francisco 1916 and Pasadena 1917, nos. A-9 and A-45) and five paintings of the Old Faithful geyser (San Francisco 1916 and Pasadena 1917, nos. A-27, A-39, A-44, B-96, and B-110). (Two smaller paintings of the same subject, *Yellowstone Falls*, are now in private collections [see Oakland 1980, 32, fig. 19; and Cody 1990, 26, pl. 23].)

During his lifetime, Hill had been unable to sell some of his most monumental canvases, such as *The Grand Canyon of the Colorado* (57 × 78 in.), *The Muir Glacier* (61 × 94 in.), two views of Yosemite Valley from Inspiration Point that were about six by eight feet in size, and this painting, all of which were acquired by Hewes. However, according to an article on the purchase of *The Canyon of the Yellowstone* from the Hewes estate sale, Hill once refused $7,500 for this canvas (unidentified clipping, curatorial files, DIA).

In the catalogues for the Hewes sale, this painting was mistakenly listed as having won the gold medal at the 1893 World's Columbian Exposition in Chicago (it was not exhibited there). It may have been confused with Moran's second *Grand Cañon of the Yellowstone,* which was included in the Wyoming exhibition of that exposition. In a 1917 article on the acquisition of Hill's *Grand Canyon of the Yellowstone* by the Detroit Museum of Art (unidentified clipping, curatorial files, DIA), the painting was incorrectly dated 1891, probably as a result of the information given in the Hewes sale catalogue.
S. M. S.

Inscription At lower right, *T. Hill*

Provenance Artist's estate, 1908. San Francisco 1916, no. A-4. Pasadena 1917, no. A-4. Mrs. George O. Robinson. Acquired in 1917.

Exhibition New Orleans 1884, no. 128 (probably this work).

References *California Art Research* 1937, 87–88; microfiche frames 0267–0268. Detroit 1944, 150.

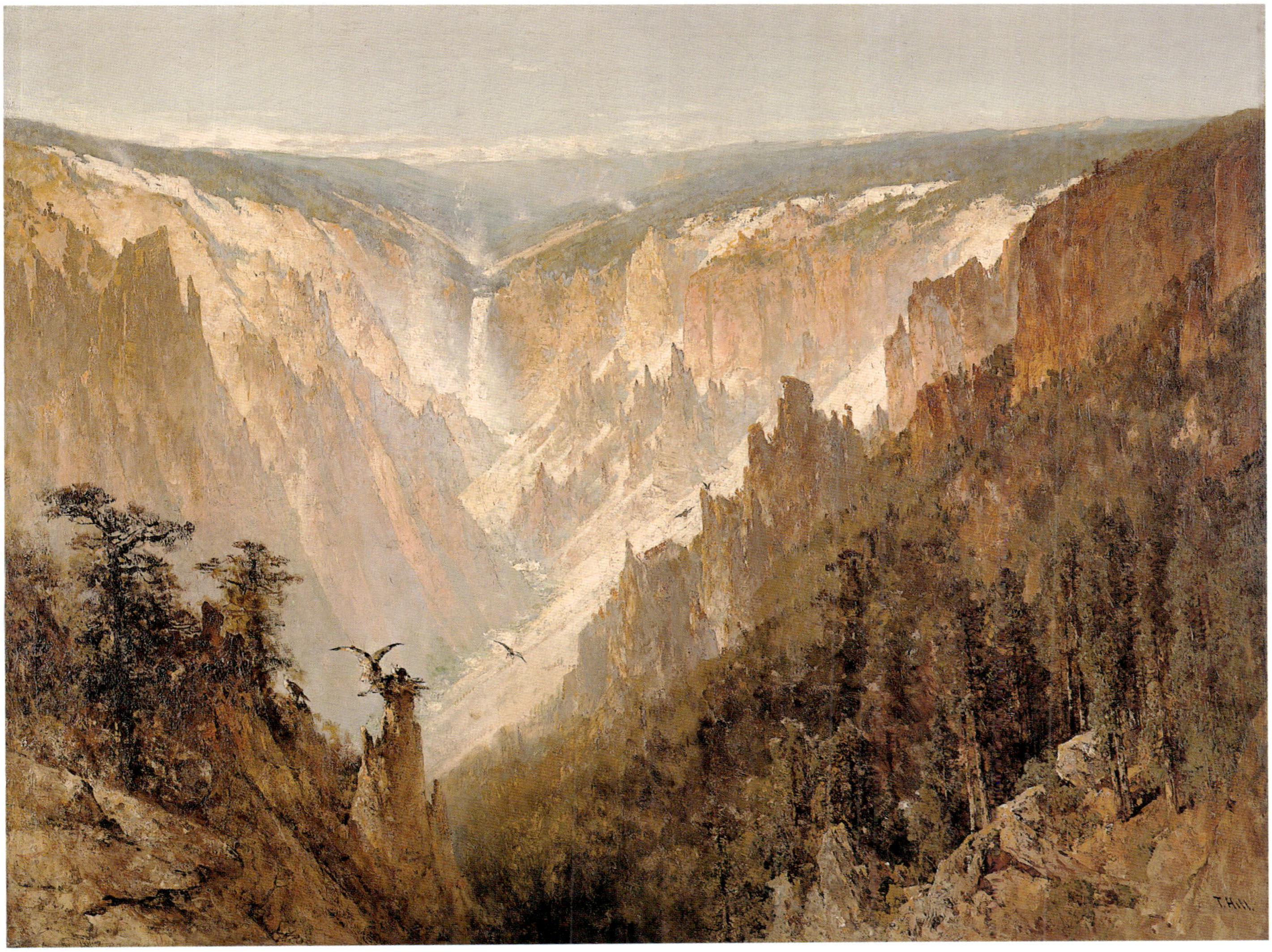

Grand Canyon of the Yellowstone

Winslow Homer

1836 Boston–Prout's Neck, Maine 1910

Born in Boston on February 24, 1836, Winslow Homer was raised in Cambridge, Massachusetts. His precocious artistic talents were encouraged by both his parents, particularly his mother, Henrietta Maria Benson Homer, a skilled amateur watercolorist. In 1854 Homer entered the lithographic firm of J. H. Bufford, in Boston, and served as an apprentice for more than two years, during which time he designed sheet-music covers. By 1857 he had become a freelance illustrator who specialized in genre scenes. His assignments continued to come from Bufford as well as from *Ballou's Pictorial Drawing-Room Companion*, a Boston weekly, and *Harper's Weekly*, a new publication from New York. In 1859 Homer moved to New York, where he continued his career as an illustrator, but he also took classes at the National Academy of Design and studied briefly with the French painter Frédéric Rondel.

Homer became one of *Harper's* Civil War illustrators, along with Alfred R. Waud and Theodore R. Davis. Homer made several trips to the front with the Union troops and sent back sketches that were engraved by members of the *Harper's* staff. Unlike Waud and Davis, however, Homer also pursued a career as a painter during the war years. Hence, during the periods at home in New York, he began painting Civil War scenes of soldiers enjoying moments of rest and leisure, using the sketches he had made at the front, and sent them to the National Academy of Design beginning in 1863. Elected an associate of the academy in 1864, he became a full academician in 1865. *Prisoners from the Front* (1865; Metropolitan Museum of Art, New York), exhibited at the academy's annual exhibition in 1866 and at the Paris Exposition Universelle in 1867, secured his reputation.

In late 1866 Homer sailed for France and stayed several months in order to see the Paris exposition and try his hand at peasant subjects. On his return to New York in the fall of 1867 he took up residence again in the University Building, where Eastman Johnson (q.v.) had a studio, but moved into the Studio Building at 51 West Tenth Street in 1872. He continued to support himself as a magazine and book illustrator until 1875, while regularly sending paintings of genre subjects to the National Academy of Design annual exhibitions. He made frequent trips to visit his family in the Boston area and to resorts and vacation areas in Saratoga, the Adirondacks, New England, Long Island, and the Jersey shore. In the mid-1870s he also traveled to Virginia and painted several pictures of the life of rural African Americans.

In March 1881 he traveled to England; after a brief stay in London, he traveled to the fishing village of Cullercoats, near Tynemouth. He sent back pictures to America but did not sail home until November 1882 (Washington et al. 1995, 396). This long sojourn in Cullercoats initiated his paintings of heroic men and women engaged in commercial fishing in the North Atlantic. A stay in Atlantic City, New Jersey, and Prout's Neck, Maine, during the summer of 1883 gave him further material for the broad theme of men and women struggling against the elements of nature, such as *The Life Line* (1884; Philadelphia Museum of Art) and *Undertow* (1886; Sterling and Francine Clark Art Institute, Williamstown, Mass.).

From 1884 until his death, he based himself in Prout's Neck, just south of Portland, where he built a studio near the ocean. But during this time he also made frequent trips to the Bahamas, Cuba, Florida, the Adirondacks, and Quebec. The results were stunning plein-air watercolors and broadly brushed oil paintings completed in his Prout's Neck studio. In the summer of 1906 he had a long illness, and in 1908 he suffered a stroke. He died in Prout's Neck on September 29, 1910.

P. H.

Bibliography Downes 1911. Goodrich 1944. Hendricks 1979. Houston et al. 1988. San Francisco et al. 1988. Washington et al. 1995.

40

Defiance: Inviting a Shot before Petersburg, 1864

Oil on panel

30.5 × 45.7 cm (12 × 18 in.)

Gift of Dexter M. Ferry, Jr. (51.66)

Homer's small painting, representing a moment in the long siege of Petersburg, Virginia, by the Army of the Potomac under the leadership of General Ulysses S. Grant against General Robert E. Lee's Army of Northern Virginia, has been extensively discussed, debated, and interpreted in recent scholarship.

As a "special artist" for *Harper's Weekly*, earning thirty dollars a week, Homer made his first brief visit to the war front in October 1861, with a pass signed by an adjutant to General George B. McClellan. He apparently was at Fort Lyon, near Alexandria (San Francisco et al. 1988, 18). By April and early May 1862, he was with McClellan's army on the Peninsular campaign; at Yorktown, Virginia, he was attached to the staff of Lieutenant Colonel Francis Channing Barlow, his cousin and a Harvard classmate of Homer's brother, Charles, and then commander of the Sixty-first Regiment of New York Volunteers (Grossman 1974, 61). No hard evidence indicates Homer's presence at the front in 1863, a year when he busied himself with painting his first oils of the conflict and worked with Louis Prang of Boston on a portfolio of lithographs, published as *Campaign Sketches*.

In 1864, however, Homer returned to the front. He apparently witnessed the Battle of the Wilderness of May 5–7, a conflict that engaged the division led by his cousin Barlow, by now a general, and

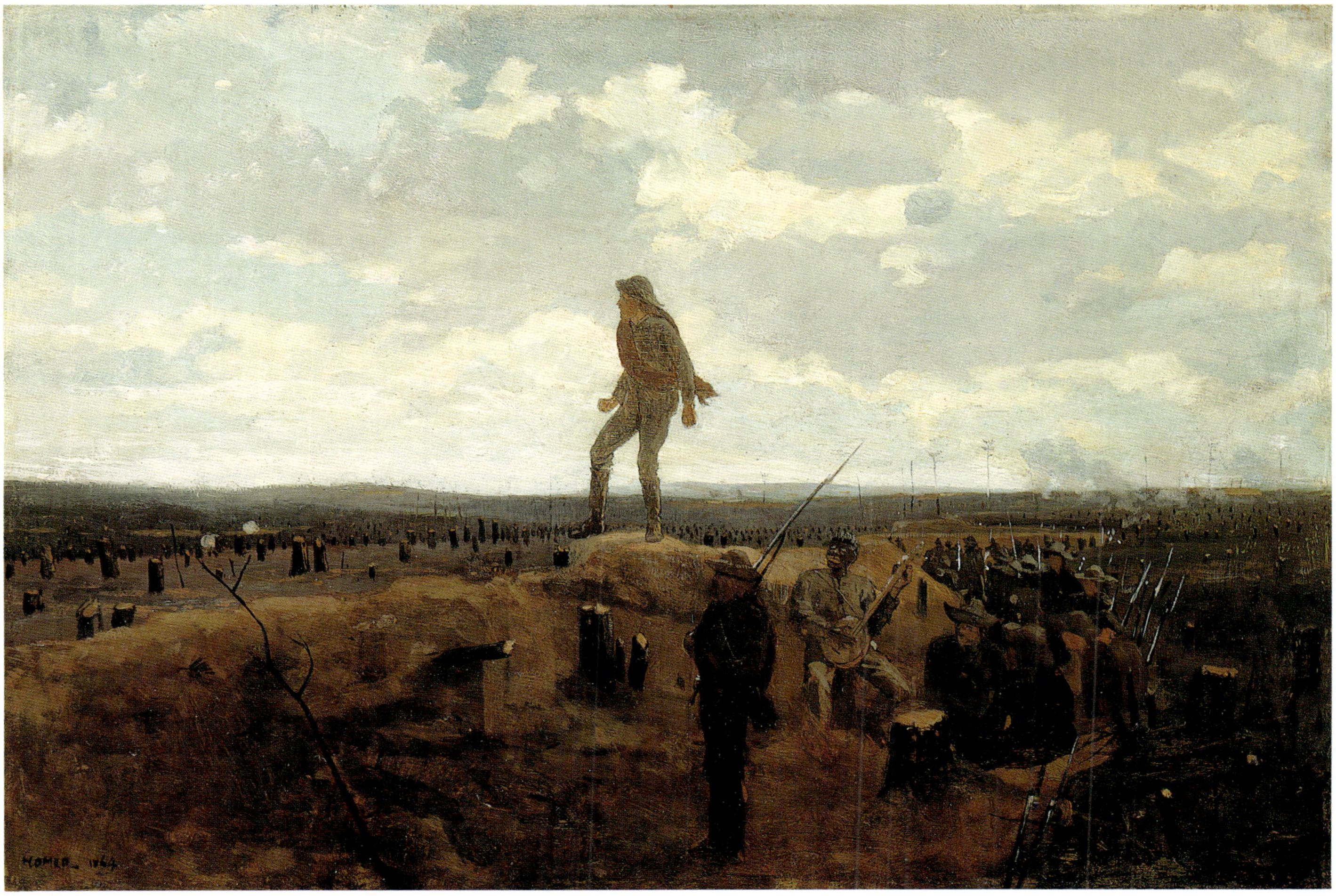

Defiance: Inviting a Shot

made the sketches that formed the composition and details of *Skirmish in the Wilderness* (1864; New Britain Museum of American Art, New Britain, Conn.).

After the Battle of the Wilderness, Grant and his generals, including Barlow, moved south toward Spotsylvania (May 8–20), North Anna (May 22–27) and Cold Harbor (June 1–12), and then headed for Petersburg, Virginia, to mount an assault on the considerable defenses that Lee's Confederate Army had erected on the outskirts of the city (McPherson 1988, 718–743). Petersburg was crucial to Lee because major supply routes went through the area, and Lee's generals managed to resist the Army of the Potomac for more than nine months. But Grant made some advances, and during June 15–17 the Army of the Potomac pushed the Confederate line back a mile, where it remained until Lee's final retreat on the night of April 2, 1865.

Scholars have long acknowledged that Homer's picture depicts the Confederate side of the siege at Petersburg; the setting of the picture was based on his pencil sketch, *Landscape with Tree Stumps (Petersburg, Virginia)* (Cooper-Hewitt National Design Museum, New York), showing the terrain of tree stumps, trenches, and breastworks erected by the Confederates (San Francisco et al. 1988, 183, fig. 10a). But the question remained: how did Homer get to that side? Gordon Hendricks doubts Homer's presence in Petersburg altogether (Hendricks 1979, 55). Nicolai Cikovsky, Jr., in his early Homer scholarship, speculated that "Homer may actually have visited the Confederate side" (Cikovsky 1978, 164). In actual fact, the Confederates abandoned their original line of defenses and moved west during the night of June 17 to within one mile of Petersburg. Hence, Homer could have safely visited the site and made his sketch sometime after June 18, but certainly before July 4, the date when he was back with his family in Belmont, Massachusetts (where he sketched and dated *July 4* a portrait of a cousin; see Hendricks 1979, fig. 97). Moreover, the fact that a pencil sketch of the head of General Barlow graces the verso of the drawing of the terrain would suggest that the sketch was done sometime in late June 1864 and certainly before Barlow went on sick leave in mid-August (Warner 1959, 18–19). Although Homer dated *Inviting the Shot* in 1864, he returned in March 1865 to the Petersburg area, where he was again sketching Union scouts (Houston et al. 1988, 117).

Homer probably saw something like the incident he depicts—the defiance of a rebel soldier with his havelock slung across his chest, poised on the breastwork and dodging the volleys of the Union sharpshooters (Cikovsky 1990, 24)—perhaps even witnessed it at Yorktown (Washington et al. 1995, 4). Marc Simpson has researched the eyewitness accounts of such daredevil figures and discovered this recklessness was common enough among soldiers on both sides frustrated by the constant waiting for the action to begin (San Francisco et al. 1988, 181–191). For example, John Gardner Perry, a Union soldier, recalled such an event on June 20, 1864:

> Toward noon yesterday, weary, I suppose, of the inaction, a Confederate sharpshooter mounted his earthwork and challenged any one of our sharpshooters to single combat. Lieutenant G—, a fine fellow, standing at least six feet two in his stockings, accepted the challenge, and they commenced what to them was sport. Life is cheap in this campaign! Both fired, and the Confederate dropped. (quoted in Botkin 1960, 384–385)

Edwin Forbes, a special artist for *Leslie's Illustrated Magazine,* also did a drawing of a Union cavalryman standing on similar breastworks (Forbes 1894, 1:3).

The figure of the black man playing the banjo has struck many Homer scholars as something of an embarrassment. How does one interpret what seems to be a stereotypical minstrel-like figure anomalously placed in the midst of an impending battle? Peter H. Wood and Karen C. C. Dalton discuss the figure in the historical context of the Battle of the Crater, a bold and unsuccessful attempt by Union soldiers to storm the Confederate defenses by tunneling under the line and laying in explosives. The explosion, which occurred on July 30, 1864, blasted open a thirty-foot-deep crater, but in the debacle that ensued, advancing Union forces—many of whom were African-American soldiers—tumbled into the crater, where the rebels easily massacred them. Even before the explosion the Confederates had become suspicious and had sunk listening shafts to determine if tunneling was underway. Wood and Dalton speculate that viewers of Homer's picture would make the connection to that historical situation and would envision the Confederate daredevil as standing above some 320 kegs of explosives. In such circumstances, "Idle shouts and banjo music provided a respite from agonized stretches of attentive stillness." They then interpret the African American as symbolic of the racist preconceptions held by Northern generals who "still regarded blacks as banjo-playing minstrels and failed to utilize their proven strength as determined soldiers" (Houston et al. 1988, 51). While Wood and Dalton have touched on one, among many, of the fatal consequences of persisting racist stereotypes, their interpretation minimizes Homer's agency as the producer of content. The Homer scholar Lucretia Giese focuses her interpretations on Homer himself but readily admits that "Homer's position on racial issues is not known." She continues:

> There is, however, an unmistakable difference in the consideration Homer as a painter gave blacks after the start of the war. He can be said to have used the black as 'color' in at least one painting—

> *Defiance: Inviting a Shot before Petersburg, Virginia,* of 1864. The banjo-playing black man assumes the conventional role of witless entertainer, although it can be argued that he serves to cement the painting's topicality rather than its slander. (Giese 1990, 23)

It seems likely that the banjo-playing minstrel on the battlefield comes from Homer's recollections of such figures, decidedly unexaggerated, entertaining at the camps or on the troop ships. A similar figure, photographed on board the *Hunchback* (National Archives; Davis 1983, ill. 383), strums while his fellow seamen look at the camera. However, one might well ask what audience Homer had in mind when he painted such an odd, ineffectual trio of Confederates: the featureless, youthful defiant soldier without a rifle on the crest of the breastworks; the barely articulated sentry in the foreground, stiff as a doll, with bayonet in place although the situation would preclude the opportunity for man-to-man combat; and the exaggeratedly black-faced minstrel strumming on his banjo (not unlike a white man smeared with burnt cork characteristic of contemporary, popular entertainment; see Lott 1993). It is as if Homer were playing up the folly—poignant perhaps, but nonetheless folly—of the Southern side in 1864, as an ill-prepared lot not up to the military comportment of the Army of the Potomac.

The painting does not seem to have been exhibited during the 1860s or 1870s (Yarnall and Gerdts 1986, 1776–1783), nor commented on by contemporary critics. Its first public notice came in 1899 at the exhibition of the collection of the prominent Republican politician and government reformer Frederick Seymour Gibbs. Indeed, Gibbs might be the clue to a picture that is neither heroic nor sentimental, but poignantly comic. He joined Company A of the 148th New York Volunteers in 1862 and served until the end of the war, by which time he had risen to the rank of first lieutenant. He was wounded by a bullet to his face on June 3, 1864, during the campaign against Cold Harbor, the site of the last battle before Grant arrived at Petersburg. He was also at Petersburg during the final push against General Robert E. Lee's troops and wounded in the leg on April 2, 1865. Yet he stayed in the field and witnessed the final surrender at Appomattox. He was later successful in business and prominent in the Republican Party of New York *(NCAB* 1904, 12:533–534). We can only speculate about whether or not Homer met Gibbs at the front, or in what ways *Inviting the Shot* appealed to Gibbs. But nonetheless Gibbs must have been drawn to the painting because he himself had been shot in the face, perhaps because of recklessness. If Homer was not at Petersburg, Gibbs was. In any event, Gibbs and many like him survived the war, and their memories of the events and of the mood on the battlefield may have found a parallel in this small souvenir of the siege of Petersburg.

P. H.

Inscription At lower left, *Homer 1864*

Provenance Frederick S. Gibbs; his sale, American Art Galleries, New York, February 25, 1904, lot 157. Thomas R. Ball; his sale, American Art Galleries, New York, March 14, 1919, lot 96. M. Knoedler & Co., New York. American Art Association, New York, January 6, 1927, lot 132. Edward Ward McMahon, New York; his sale, American Art Association, New York, January 24, 1929, lot 79. Pascal M. Gatterdam, New York, 1931. Macbeth Gallery, New York, 1931. Whitney Museum of American Art, New York, 1950. M. Knoedler & Co., New York, 1951. Acquired in 1951.

Exhibitions New York 1936, no. 1. Pittsburgh 1936, no. 44. Columbus 1937, no. 1. Detroit 1944a, no. 25. Washington 1944. Richmond 1947, no. 27. Washington et al. 1958, no. 3. Washington and Boston 1961, no. 61. Tucson 1963, no. 43. Buffalo et al. 1976. San José 1978, no. 5. San Francisco et al. 1988, no. 10. Washington et al. 1995, no. 5.

References Gibbs 1899, no. 36. Henry 1901, ill. 218. Downes 1911, 48. Bolton 1932. Mangravite 1935. Watson 1942, 56. Goodrich 1944, 44 and 230. Richardson 1944, pl. 210. Richardson 1951–52. *Life History* 1963, 23. Wilmerding 1972, 22. Grossman 1974, 176–177. Cikovsky 1978. Hendricks 1979, 50, fig. 69. Shaw 1986, 530, fig. 5. Houston et al. 1988, 48–51, figs. 21, 22. Cikovsky 1990, 24 and 19, ill. Giese 1990, 23, fig. 9.

41
The Dinner Horn, 1873

Oil on canvas
30.2 × 36.2 cm (11⅞ × 14¼ in.)
Gift of Dexter M. Ferry, Jr. (47.81)

After Homer's return from his 1867 trip to Europe, he turned his attention to rural scenes, some of which were made into wood engravings for *Harper's Weekly,* and others that were independent oil and watercolor paintings, which he sold and exhibited in New York. There are five known versions of a young woman holding a dinner horn to her mouth, facing away from the viewer, with arm akimbo. First, there is a small sketch of the upper portion of her body (Cooper-Hewitt National Design Museum, New York). Second, a small oil sketch of 5 by 9 inches (Museum of Fine Arts, Boston; Washington et al. 1995, ill. 109) represents a woman just beyond the edge of a vine-covered building and pointing her horn toward a field, where farmers seem to be haying. Third, *The Dinner Horn* (1870; National Gallery of Art, Washington, D.C.; Washington et al. 1995, ill. 108), a vertical oil painting measuring 19¼ by 13¾ inches, eliminates most of the landscape. The fourth, *The*

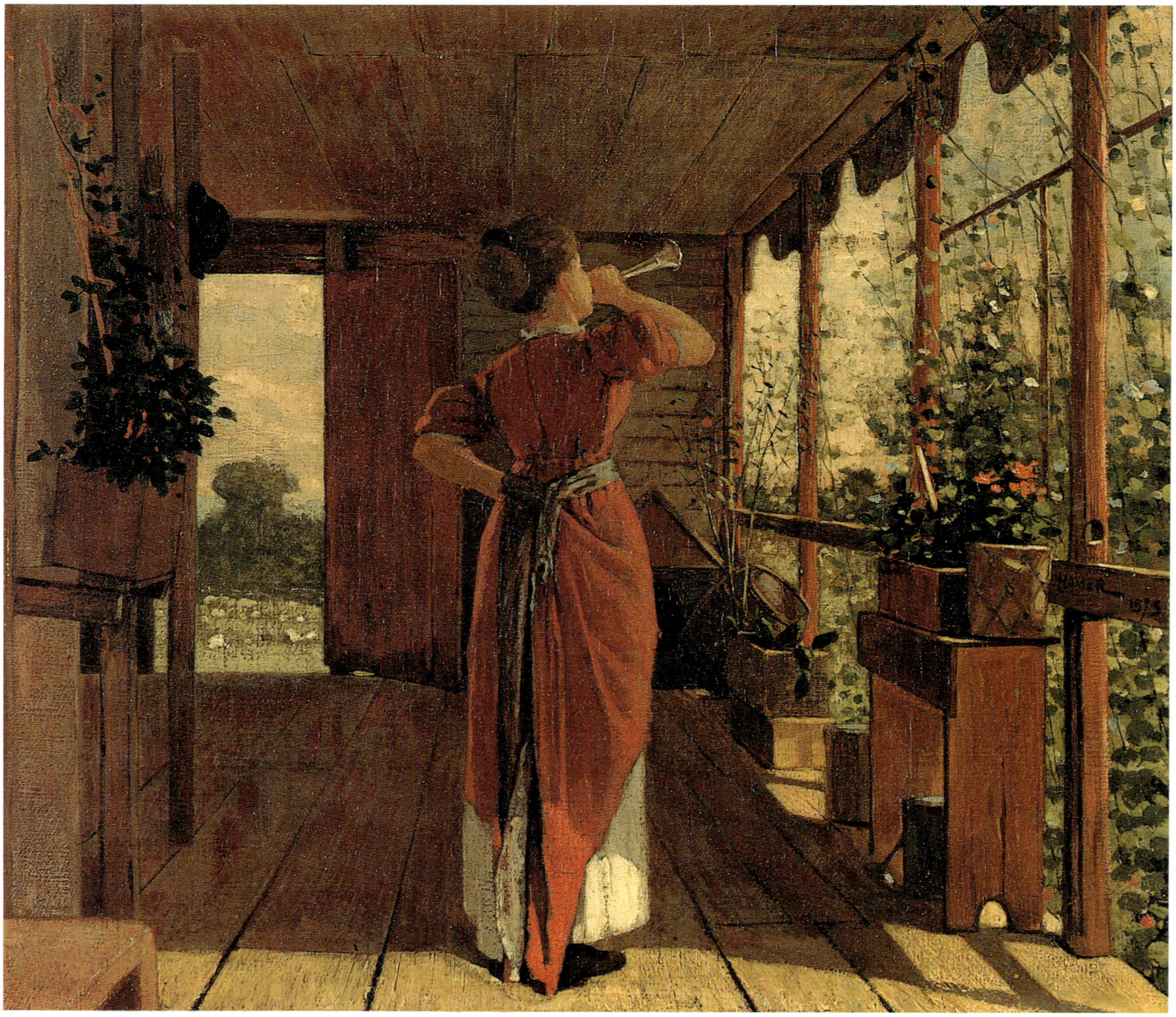

The Dinner Horn

Dinner Horn, reproduced as a wood engraving for the June 11, 1870, issue of *Harper's Weekly,* includes the details of a cat rubbing its back against the door frame of a clapboard house with an interior view of a pot boiling on the hearth and a table set with plates (Washington et al. 1995, ill. 108). A shore scene (with small figures of bathers and a jetty protruding into the ocean) has replaced the setting of the other versions. A picture entitled *Blowing the Horn at the Sea Side,* exhibited at the Century Association in January 1871 (Yarnall and Gerdts 1986, 1776), may be the oil version of the woodcut.

A final, fifth version is Detroit's *Dinner Horn,* dated three years after the original conception, which substitutes an enclosed porch for the out-of-doors setting. This porch is the ambience for a small oil genre sketch, titled *Shelling Peas* (Cooper-Hewett National Design Museum, New York; Richardson 1948, 154). Hence, in the final version Homer has mixed and matched and altered and refined. Here the woman, now in a red dress with a white petticoat no longer ruffled by the wind, raises her horn toward the open side of the porch. Edgar P. Richardson, director of the Detroit Institute of Arts when the painting was acquired, observed of *The Dinner Horn:*

> The image which finally satisfied him seems artlessly unstudied, a single and straightforward observation of the hot sunlight pouring through the vines into the porch of a farm house, reflecting upward into the rafters, and touching the red dress of the young girl blowing the dinner horn to summon the men home from the fields for dinner. But the matchless freshness and naturalness of feeling, which gives the observer a sense of being there in person and feeling the warmth of the sun and hearing for himself the hum of summer, is not the result of a simple snapshot by a photographic mind. It is the product of careful study, followed by the simplifying and intensifying power of memory, reflection and artistic style, that result eventually in an image whose art totally conceals the art by which it was created. (Richardson 1948, 154)

Indeed, it was Homer's stylistic "artlessness" that made his art seem so American to subsequent generations.
P. H.

Inscription At middle right on rail, *HOMER 1873*

Provenance James Carr, New York. Inherited by granddaughter, Mrs. Clarence Crocker, East Orange, N.J. On consignment with Ferargil Galleries, New York. On consignment with Kleemann Galleries, New York, 1936. Stephen C. Clark, 1937. On consignment with Macbeth Gallery, New York. Acquired in 1947.

Exhibitions New York 1936. Northampton 1951, no. 11. Washington et al. 1958, no. 26. Indianapolis 1961, no. 25. Big Rapids 1964. New York et al. 1973, no. 23.

References Richardson 1948, 153–157. Wilmerding 1972, 71 and pl. 22.

42
The Four-Leaf Clover, 1873

Oil on canvas
36.2 × 51.8 cm (14¼ × 20⅜ in.)
Bequest of Robert H. Tannahill (70.150)

During the summers of the 1870s Winslow Homer would leave his Tenth Street studio in New York and return to New England to visit with family and to seek out subjects for his *Harper's Weekly* commissions. To Homer scholars, 1873 is notable because that summer in Gloucester Homer began in earnest to produce series of watercolors in vivid colors (Washington et al. 1986, 20–51). From June through August he roamed the thriving fishing town and resort on Cape Ann, looking for boys and girls playing on the rocky shore, sitting in boats, hunting for swallow eggs, or picking berries. The local newspaper, the *Gloucester Telegraph,* noted his activity in its August 20, 1873, issue: "Winslow Homer, the artist, has been spending the summer at the Atlantic House, and the pages of 'Harper's Weekly' have been heightened by his seaside sketches" (Chicago 1990, 10). Many of the scenes eventually also became oil paintings, most likely done in his New York studio in the winter.

Like *The Four-Leaf Clover,* not all the summertime scenes dated 1873 are of the shore, nor do we have any certainty as to the exact site in the New England or New York area. Homer was not offering his audience a geography lesson; instead, he was constructing imaginative pictures from sketches, from visual memories of places, events, and people, and with an appreciation of what would make a good composition. For example, his earlier *Snap the Whip* (1872; Metropolitan Museum of Art, New York) might have been inspired by boys either in Hurley, New York, or in East Hampton on Long Island (see Spassky 1985, 457). The setting for *Snap the Whip* gives no hard evidence of the locale, since when he painted an identical picture (Butler Institute of Art, Youngstown, Ohio), he included a background range of blue mountains.

More to the point when considering Homer's pictures of the 1870s was the representation of energetic boys and comely girls offered up to an audience still in the process of healing the psychic wounds inflicted by the Civil War. Images of such healthy children, many on the verge of adulthood, were urged on the gallery-going and literate middle class by the critic Henry T. Tuckerman, who wrote a long panegyric, "Children," for the *Galaxy* in 1867:

> [W]hether holding a shell to the ear, chasing a butterfly, companioned by a deer or lamb, wor-

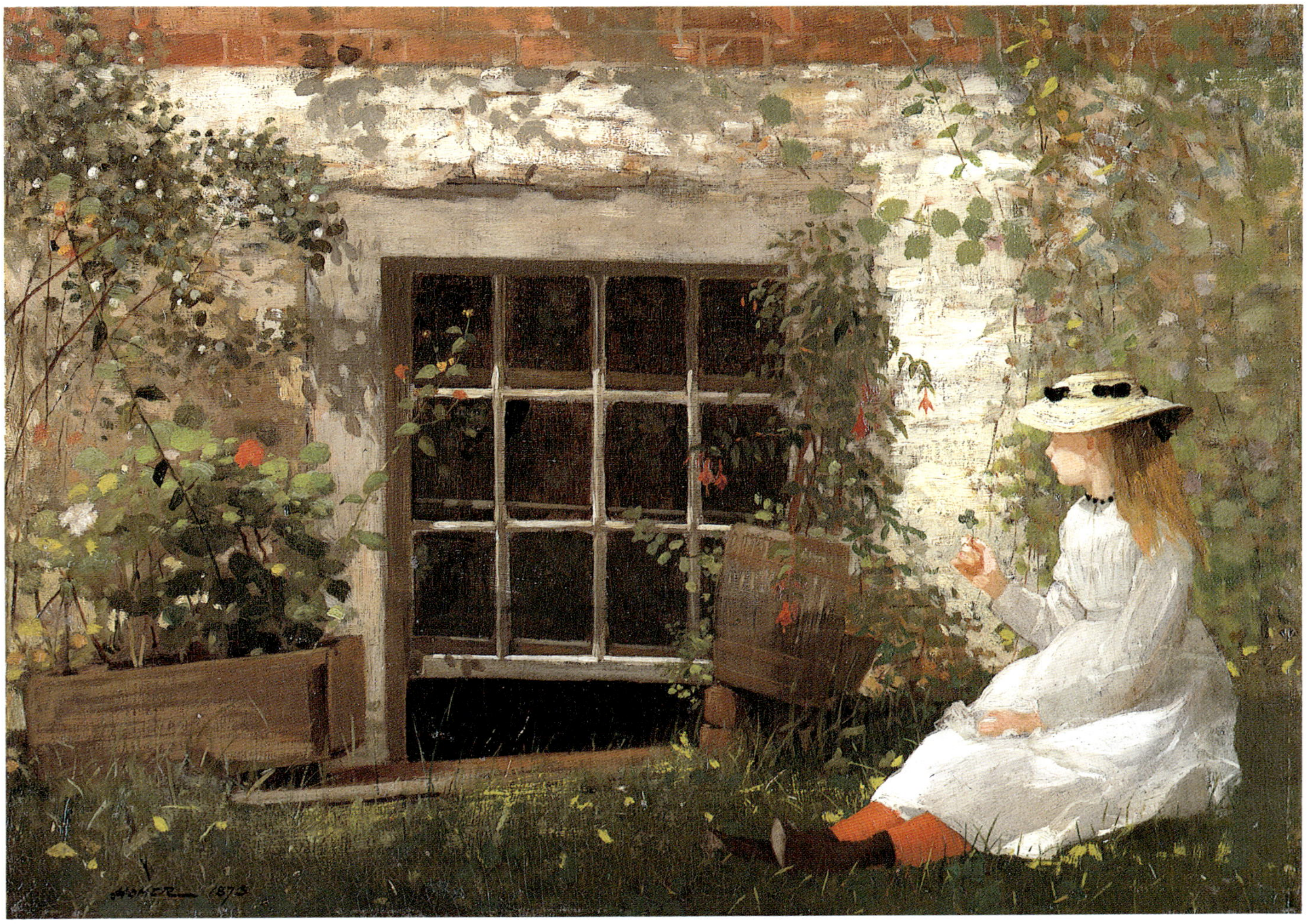

The Four -Leaf Clover

> shipped by Magi as incarnate love and truth, sportive, tranquil, awed, elated, fond or wayward—always and everywhere the image of childhood to poet and painter, to the landscape, the household, the shrine, the temple and the grave—is a redeeming presence, a harmonizing and hopeful element, the token of what we were, and prophecy of what we may be.
> (Hills 1977, 95)

Another major critic, Eugene Benson, echoed Tuckerman when he wrote "Childhood in Modern Literature," for the April 24, 1869, issue of *Appleton's Journal:* "The child—the sanctity, freshness, and mystery of child-life—in literature, owes its advancement beyond the idea of a healthy little animal to the worship of the infant Jesus. In contemporary literature childhood is a special and individual presence, not an accidental and accessory one" (Hills 1977, 97). To our modern sensibilities such paeans to childhood verge on saccharine effusions, but we must remember that in that era "sentiment" ranked high as a description of quality paintings. It is to the credit of Louisa May Alcott, Mark Twain, and Winslow Homer that the image of childhood developed elements of spunk and adventurousness.

However, in its setting, *The Four-Leaf Clover* relates to other images painted by Homer during 1873 and 1874. The backdrop of a many-paned window, set into a stuccoed basement story, against which vines and planters of flowers grow, also figures in Homer's watercolor *Rustic Courtship* (1874; Mr. and Mrs. Paul Mellon collection, Upperville, Va.) and his oil *The Rustics* (1874; private collection; Washington et al. 1995, ill. 113). And the motif of sitting on the grass with a farmhouse in the distance occurs in Homer's *"The Nooning,"* a woodcut depicting three boys on the grass published in the August 16, 1873, issue of *Harper's Weekly*. For his oil painting, also titled *The Nooning* (Wadsworth Atheneum, Hartford, Conn.), Homer lifted the left boy of the woodcut and moved him into a solitary center. What marks Detroit's painting as special in Homer's oeuvre is that it initiated for him the theme of the solitary and idle girl posed in a flower-filled outdoor setting, a theme also developed in the popular paintings of young women and girls done in the early 1870s by Eastman Johnson (q.v.), George Lambdin (q.v.), and John George Brown (q.v.). The four-leaf clover—that portent of good luck—held in the hand of Homer's girl is a fitting symbol of the "hopeful element . . . and prophecy of what we may be" that Tuckerman saw in "the image of childhood."

In its style, *The Four-Leaf Clover* might be compared to the impressionism of the French artists Claude Monet, Camille Pissarro, and Alfred Sisley during the 1870s. Like them, Homer studied M.-E. Chevreul's color theory, placed his figures in the outdoors, and steered clear of developing an a priori "method" that might stifle the artist's vision and imagination. As Lloyd Goodrich observed, "Without any recipes for outdoor color, he put down his visual sensations of it, and the results were true and alive. From the beginning his color was fresher and more living than that of almost any American of the time. . . . [H]e had the simple sensuous feeling for color itself, the pure pleasure of the eye, that marks the born colorist" (Goodrich 1944, 32). In *The Four-Leaf Clover* Homer uses short strokes of bright, dappled color (not color broken down into the primary hues as the impressionists were to do) to catch the effects of sunshine and shadow on grass, leaves, and flower petals, that in tandem rustle up an impression of a carefree summer's day.

P. H.

Inscription At lower left, *Homer 1873*

Provenance O. Lagrange LaDue. Oliver Ladew, Baltimore. Pascal Gatterdam, New York, 1904. Macbeth Galleries, New York. Robert H. Tannahill, 1944. Acquired in 1970.

Exhibition Grosse Pointe 1978.

References Goodrich 1944, 32. Rivard 1978, 1049.

43
Girl and Laurel, 1879

Oil on canvas
57.5 × 40 cm (22⅝ × 15¾ in.)
Gift of Dexter M. Ferry, Jr. (40.56)

During part of the summer of 1878 Homer went to Houghton Farm in Mountainville, New York, the summer retreat and experimental farm of his patron Lawson Valentine, a manufacturer of varnishes and the employer of Homer's brother Charles. Homer had first gone to Houghton Farm in 1876, when Valentine purchased it. The rural area provided subjects for Homer's sketchbooks, watercolors, and oil paintings, which he completed in his New York studio during the winter months. Most of the subjects of shepherdesses have been assigned to his Houghton Farm sojourns (Hendricks 1979, 133). But the following summer, in 1879, Homer went to West Townsend, Massachusetts, where he stayed at the family home of his sister-in-law, Martha French Homer, and he also stayed in Winchester, Massachusetts, the town bordering Belmont. Hence, we might assume that many of the pictures of the late 1870s were fashioned from his various summer sketches, with some of the sites and models from Houghton Farm and others from Massachusetts. Although the subject of *Girl and Laurel* is not a shepherdess, the figure—standing frontally and looking off to the side, bathed in light, with shrubs and dappled clouds in the background—is close in style and feeling to such pictures as *Peach Blossoms* (1879; Mr. R. Philip Hanes, Jr.; Washington et al. 1995, 168).

Anecdotal information from the Homer family gives another spin to the picture. Hazel Lewis, on the staff of the William Macbeth Gallery in New York, wrote to Clyde H. Burroughs of the Detroit Institute of Arts on August 2, 1940. Regarding *Girl and Laurel,* which the gallery sold to the museum in 1940, Lewis followed up with information from her employer, the recently deceased Robert Macbeth:

> Two interesting bits of information I remember hearing Mr. Macbeth tell about the picture are that the "girl" was in reality a local boy named Sanders, who posed for Homer; and the second was that the farmer, on whose property the laurel grew, was very much interested in the painting of the picture and asked Homer to paint his portrait. Homer replied that he was not a portrait painter and therefore could not comply. The next morning when Homer went to the spot to continue the painting of "Girl with Laurel," all the laurel bushes had been cut down to the ground, for spite. (correspondence, curatorial files, DIA)

Gordon Hendricks, who assigned the origin of such a rumor to Homer's sister-in-law, Mrs. Charles Savage Homer, Jr., decided to track down this information and reported: "Local historians in West Townsend, where this work evidently had its beginnings, believe that the model was a local girl, Fanny Sanders. Mrs. Sanders's age in 1879 was correct for the picture" (Hendricks 1979, 302).

However, a remark regarding Homer's use of a boy model for his pictures of girls appears in Philip Beam's *Winslow Homer at Prout's Neck.* About an unfinished sketch of a shepherdess that Homer was trying to finish in the summer of 1879, Beam states: "The original model was Sergeant Joseph Keenan of the Belmont, Massachusetts, police, who posed as a boy in shepherdess costume for the girl-shy Homer when the artist was doing his shepherdess series in the Belmont area during the late '70s" (Beam 1966, 154). Since Beam's biography drew on the letters and papers of Homer's nephew, Charles L. Homer, who wrote a foreword to the book, we may assume that the assertion of Joseph Keenan as model came from the papers in Charles Homer's possession. More recently, in 1990, Henry Adams published his investigations into Joseph Keenan as a model and found an article in the *Belmont Citizen,* dated September 25, 1936, that referred to Keenan as one of Homer's shepherdesses who posed in 1876 along with another boy from Belmont, John Carney (Adams 1990, 249–250). Since Keenan was born in 1864, in 1879 he would have been about fifteen—the approximate age for the model of *Girl and Laurel.* Whatever the gender of the model, it is beside the point, since Homer was constructing fictions, not documentaries—in this case an image of a youthful farm girl bathed in the light of an early summer day.

During the years when the younger, European-trained painters, such as William Merritt Chase, Will S. Low, and John Singer Sargent, were bringing European subjects along with the new European styles to America and organizing exhibitions for the Society of American Artists, Homer not only persisted in representing rural American girls (whether or not the actual models were boys) but also seems to have disassociated himself from the younger artists. (He did not participate in the exhibitions of the society.) What the younger cosmopolitan artists thought of Homer is unclear. However, Henry James, in an extended exhibition review for the July 1875 issue of the *Galaxy,* found Homer's work "very honest, and vivid, and manly" but "damnably ugly."

> We frankly confess that we detest his subjects—his barren plank fences, his glaring, bald, blue skies, his big, dreary, vacant lots of meadows, his freckled, straight-haired Yankee urchins, his flat-breasted maidens, suggestive of a dish of rural doughnuts and pie, his calico sun-bonnets, his flannel shirts, his cowhide boots. He has chosen the least pictorial features of the least pictorial range of scenery and civilization; he has resolutely treated them as if they *were* pictorial, as if they were every inch as good as Capri or Tangiers; and, to reward his audacity, he has incontestably succeeded. (James 1875, 93–94)

We note in the above passage that James yet respects Homer's efforts, even if he does not care for them. And he does admire Homer's ability to see "everything at one with its envelope of light and air."

James would, no doubt, consider *Girl and Laurel* to be one of Homer's pictures of "flat-breasted maidens." But had James known more about Homer's methods, he would have known that Homer was not "doggedly literal" but imaginatively constructing his scenes much like the most European-trained artists. And his paintings of the late 1870s were becoming richer in the handling of paint. Indeed, the most striking characteristic of Homer's *Girl and Laurel* is its beautiful and sensuous surface of creamy whites and tints of pinks and lavender. The viewer feels the brisk early summer air and the bright warmth of the sunshine that highlights the model's nose and smock. And yet the solidity of the figure portends the heroic women whom Homer would come to paint in Cullercoats and Tynemouth, during his twenty months spent on the English coast during 1881–82.

P. H.

Inscription At lower left, *HOMER / 1879*

Provenance Mr. and Mrs. Charles Savage Homer, Jr. Mr. Arthur Homer. Macbeth Galleries, New York. Acquired in 1940.

Exhibitions New York 1936, no. 18. Washington et al. 1958, no. 39. New York 1961. Tokyo 1989, no. 68.

References C. Burroughs 1940, 2–3, ill. Hendricks 1979, 138, plates 20, 21.

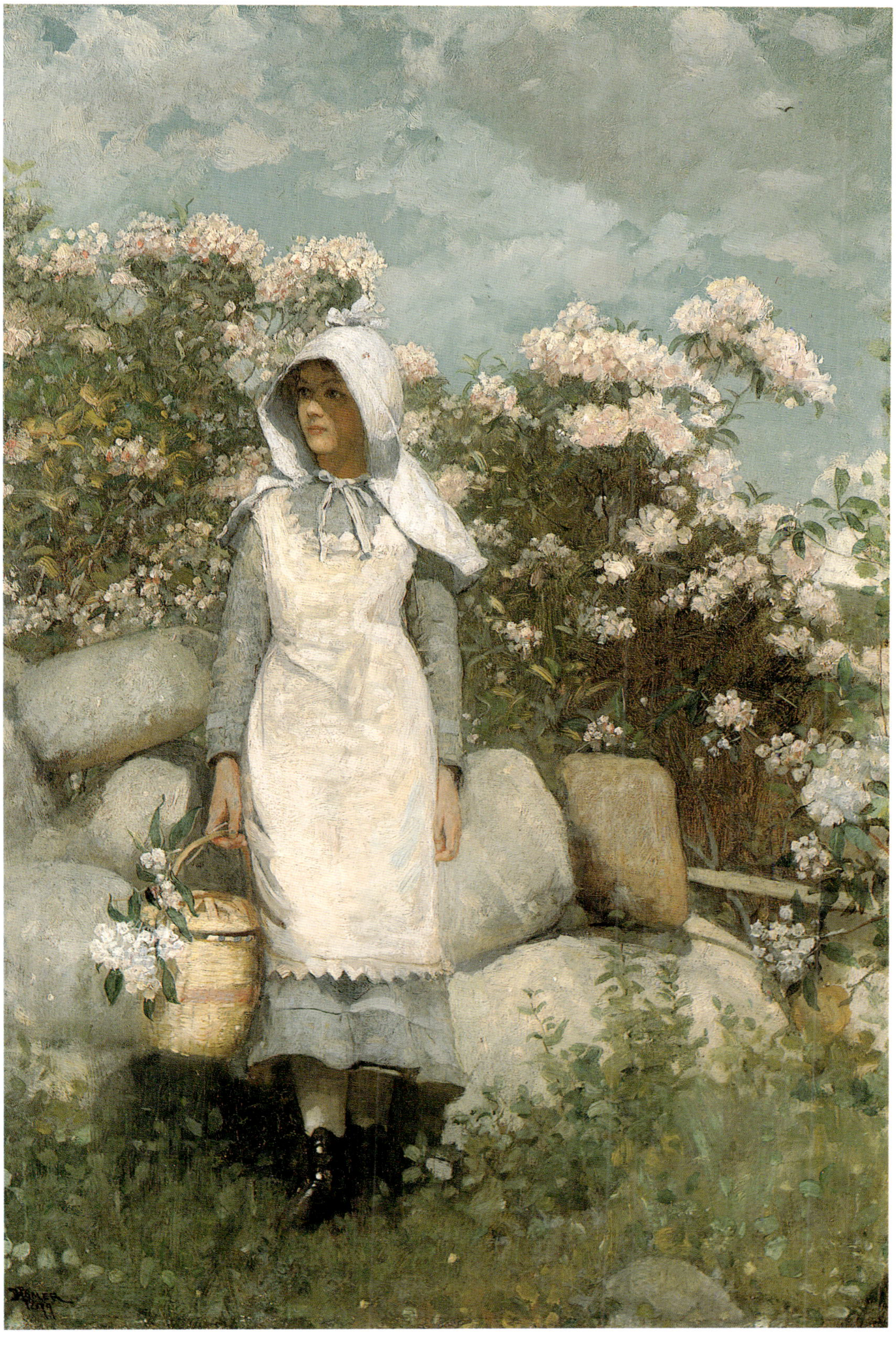

Girl and Laurel

Robert Hopkin

1832 Glasgow, Scotland–Detroit 1909

Heralded as the dean of Detroit artists and adored by his fellow citizens, Robert Hopkin had a well-established and successful career in Detroit as a decorator and a painter during the second half of the nineteenth century. Among the young artists who studied with him were Percy Ives, Joseph Gies, and Gari Melchers.

Born in 1832 in Glasgow, Scotland, Hopkin was encouraged at an early age by his father, a print and book dealer, to use those sources as inspirations for his drawings. The family immigrated in 1843 to Detroit, where Hopkin was enrolled in the public schools. At fourteen he was apprenticed to Tuttle and Patton, carriage painters. His first documented painting, *Seascape and Lighthouse* (1846; Dossin Great Lakes Museum, Detroit), was painted that same year. He received his only artistic training from Frederick E. Cohen, an itinerant Detroit artist, who taught him how to mix colors. Sprague and Teal's, a local grocery, provided Hopkin with his first opportunity to display his work. He married Evaline A. Godfrey on New Year's Eve, 1851; this occasion gave rise to the family's parties that were famous for the next half century.

From 1853 through 1869 Hopkin was involved with various firms that painted signs, steamboat interiors, and interior decorations for commercial and residential buildings, in addition to murals and theatrical scenery. Some of the more prominent commissions were for St. Anne's Cathedral, Detroit; the Detroit Opera House; the Houses of Parliament, Ottawa; and the Cotton Exchange, New Orleans. He was particularly proud of the silk Civil War banners he painted for the Detroit and Michigan regiments.

Hopkin left Detroit for a brief period, moving to Chicago in 1870. However, he remained only one year because his studio was destroyed in the Chicago fire. On his return to Detroit he established the firm of Hopkin and Sons, which remained in operation painting signs and doing architectural work until 1884 when he decided to devote all his energies to easel painting. This made it possible for him to travel and paint the seascapes, waterfronts, and wharves he admired. Working in both watercolors and oils, he began to exhibit widely. He participated in many of the Michigan State Fair exhibitions, receiving an honorable mention in 1868 and a silver medal in 1878. He also submitted a painting to the Centennial Exposition in Philadelphia. The 1880s and 1890s mark an immense rise in his production. He was represented in the Detroit Artists Association of 1886, 1887, and 1893; the Society of Western Artists in 1896, 1897, and 1898; the Detroit Museum of Art in 1890, 1897, 1901, 1903, 1907, and 1908, in addition to numerous other local exhibitions.

Hopkin achieved great fame in Detroit; his works hung in many homes, clubs, hotels, and art associations. Detroit's Scarab Club, an organization for artists founded in 1907, began its life as the Hopkin Society. In 1909 after a brief illness Hopkin died at the age of seventy-seven.

J. W. T.

Bibliography Gibson 1962.

44

Graveyard by the Sea, ca. 1875

Oil on canvas

114.3 × 137.2 cm (45 × 54 in.)

Gift of Charles Willis Ward (09.4)

Robert Hopkin received a commission from the Detroit Museum of Art, through a donation by Charles Willis Ward, to execute a painting suitable for the museum's collection, but he died before completing it. Ward instructed the then director of the museum, Armond Griffith, and John Donaldson, a trustee, to visit the William O'Leary Gallery in Detroit and select one of two works by Hopkin that were on deposit with the dealer. Griffith wrote Ward that he and Donaldson had chosen *Graveyard by the Sea* and would select a new frame for the painting, which he described at great length. It cannot be assumed that the painting was not framed; Griffith often would select a new frame for an incoming painting to be more sympathetic to his gallery installation. Griffith would later write, "the universal verdict being that it was one of Mr. Hopkin's greatest works, and makes a splendid showing in the new frame" (curatorial files, DIA). Hopkin had commented earlier that he had hoped that the painting might become part of the museum's collection, because it was one of his favorites.

The painting dates from the mid-1870s and was exhibited as early as 1877 at Angell's Art Gallery in Detroit. It was listed in the catalogue as *Churchyard by the Sea* and was accompanied by the following anonymous poem, which was later credited as the inspiration for the painting.

> Where ocean breezes sweep across the restless deep,
> It stands with headstones quaint, with Sculpture rude,
> Its green turf thickly sown with dust of lives unknown
> Like withered leaves on Autumn's pathway strewed.

In the 1870s Hopkin turned to seafaring poems for the basis of several canvases. These poems range from works by anonymous writers to those by Lord Tennyson. The idea of the sea- or landscape derived from a literary source may have been inspired by the work of Robert Duncanson (q.v.). Duncanson participated in several exhibitions in Detroit just before his death in 1872. His work, which included some of his literary landscapes such as *Ellen's Isle* (cat. no. 23), was highly praised in the local press. Hopkin was most assuredly aware of these paintings. As a relatively young artist who had just returned from an unsuccessful venture in Chicago, such an idea would be attractive.

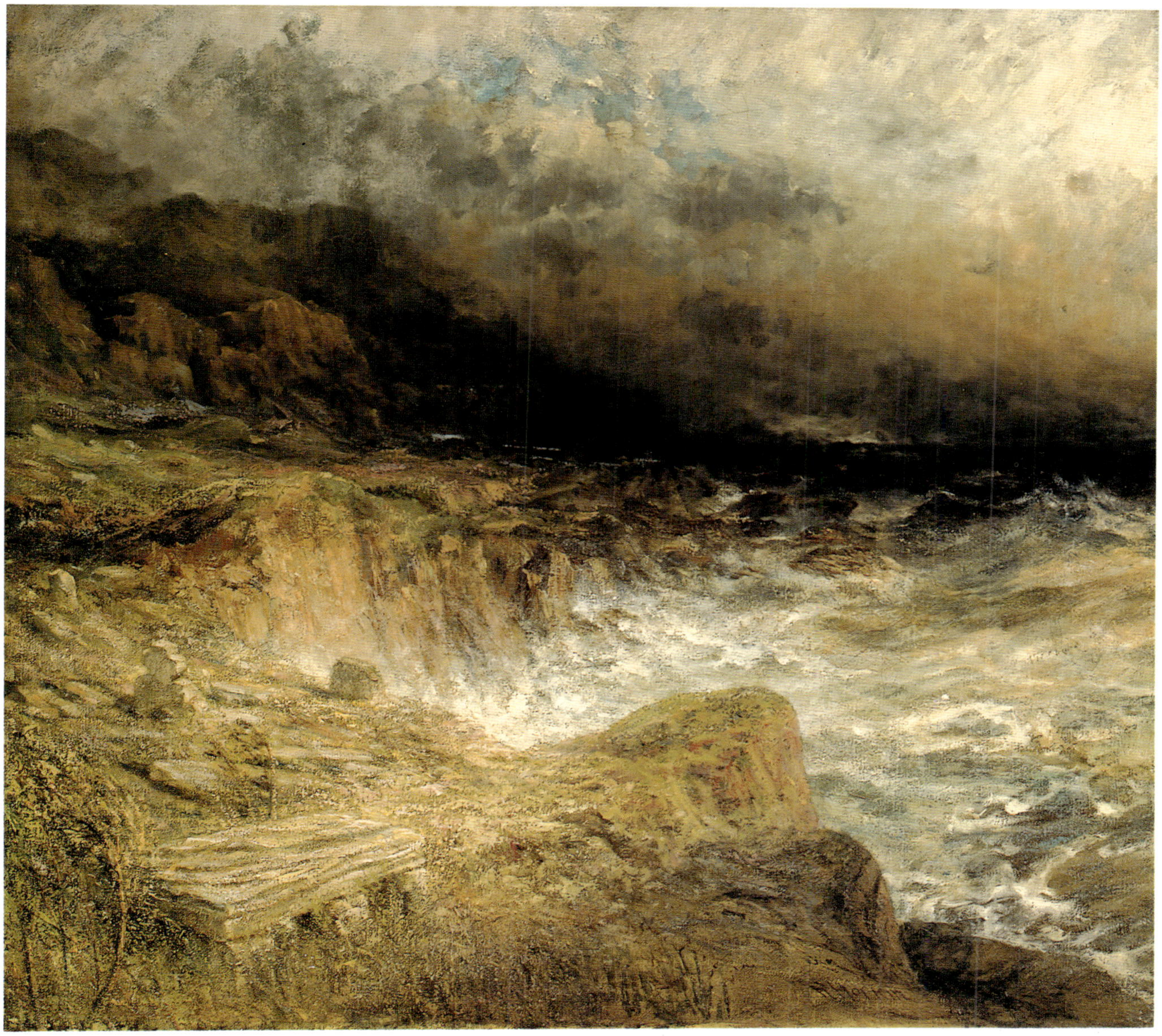

His oeuvre was dominated by romantic seascapes, and although he spent most of his life in an inland state surrounded by lakes, many of his marine scenes were ocean subjects or those reminiscent of his native Scotland. Such is the case with *Graveyard by the Sea*. The painting is a typical canvas, consisting of brooding, turbulent clouds, rocky seas, and a murky atmosphere. While there is no doubt that Hopkin was well aware of the Hudson River school painters, he was never able to capture their luminist, atmospheric qualities. Even though he enjoyed great success during his life and was represented in almost every collection in the Detroit area, his paintings do not go much beyond a genre statement.
J. W. T.

Inscription At lower right, *R. Hopkin*

Provenance The artist, until at least 1903. William O'Leary Gallery, Detroit. Acquired in 1909.

Exhibitions Detroit 1877, no. 26. Detroit 1901, no. 73. Detroit 1903, cat. no. 27. Detroit 1969.

References *BDMA* 1909a, 14. Detroit 1910, 21, no. 132. Detroit 1920, 131, no. 196. Valentiner and C. Burroughs 1927, 74. Detroit 1930, no. 314. Gibson 1962, 93, 199. *Detroit News*, May 27, 1971.

Graveyard by the Sea

Thomas Hovenden

1840 Dummanway, County Cork, Ireland–
Plymouth Meeting, Pennsylvania 1895

Thomas Hovenden's paintings are today recognized for their remarkable ability to penetrate the surface of everyday life, expressing the mixture of nostalgia and hope that accompanied the passage of the old and the coming of the new in the lives of ordinary people in the late nineteenth century. Hovenden's sentimental and anecdotal scenes include interpretations of Breton history and Breton peasants, humane renderings of African Americans, and American history paintings and genre scenes.

Hovenden's parents died when he was six, and he was placed in the Cork county orphanage, where he stayed until 1854, when he began a seven-year apprenticeship with a Cork county carver and gilder. Completing his apprenticeship in 1861, Hovenden immigrated to America two years later, working in New York City as a frame dealer for a year before continuing his art training in evening classes at the National Academy of Design.

While sharing a studio with the landscape painter Hugh Bolton Jones, Hovenden hand-colored photographs and worked as an illustrator for *Harper's Magazine.* In 1867 he began exhibiting at the National Academy of Design, with a portrait. By 1868 Hovenden had moved to Baltimore, where he occupied a studio in the Bolton Jones's family home. Four years later Hovenden's domestic scene *The Old Nurse's Visit* (1872; unlocated) came to the attention of the Baltimore art collector William T. Walters, who soon became the artist's patron. Walters financed Hovenden's move in 1874 to France, where he trained for a year in the Paris studio of Alexandre Cabanel. Hovenden spent another five years in Pont-Aven, a fledgling art colony in Brittany, where he met the American genre and history painter Robert Wylie. Following Wylie's example, Hovenden began to paint pictures of the Breton peasants, exhibiting two of them at the Paris Salon of 1876.

Hovenden returned to America in 1880. The following June Hovenden married Helen Corson, a Philadelphia artist whom he had met in Pont-Aven. The couple settled on the Corson family's ancestral farm in Plymouth Meeting, Pennsylvania, some ten miles outside Philadelphia.

His success with *Elaine* (1882; Westmoreland Museum of Art, Greensburg, Pa.), inspired by Tennyson's *Idylls of the King,* contributed to Hovenden's election as an academician of the National Academy of Design in 1882 (he had been made an associate the previous year). It may also have brought him the commission for *The Last Moments of John Brown* (1884; Metropolitan Museum of Art, New York).

Hovenden was active in the art world of his time. He was elected to membership in the American Water-Color Society and the Society of American Artists in 1882, to the Philadelphia Society of Artists in 1883, and the New York Etching Club in 1885. He also joined the faculty of the Pennsylvania Academy of the Fine Arts, succeeding Thomas Eakins (q.v.) as the head of instruction in 1886 and serving as director for a short time. Hovenden continued to paint and exhibit his work, producing both Civil War subjects and domestic and work scenes of African Americans.

In 1891 the Hovenden family left Plymouth Meeting to live in England in the village of Cranbrook in Kent, a colony of Victorian genre painters noted for their anecdotal domestic interior scenes. While there, Hovenden completed *When Hope Was Darkest* (1892; unlocated) and sent it, as well as *Breaking Home Ties* (1890; Philadelphia Museum of Art) and *Bringing Home the Bride* (1893; Gregory Shepard collection), to the World's Columbian Exposition in Chicago in 1893. *Breaking Home Ties* became the exposition's uncontested popularity winner.

Hovenden died in August 1895, attempting to save a five-year-old girl who had run out in front of a train. Eakins, who served as one of the pallbearers at Hovenden's funeral, described Hovenden as a man who "bore his honors very quietly and his success did not seem to affect him as it does many" (Edwards 1987, 36).
T. T.

Bibliography Philadelphia et al. 1982, 33–34. Terhune 1983. Jacobs 1985, 56–58. Edwards 1987. Philadelphia et al. 1989, 170–172. Washington 1993, 152, 178, 264–265.

45
Hoc Signo Vinces, 1880
(In This Sign Shalt Thou Conquer)
Oil on canvas
99.1 × 137.2 cm (39 × 54 in.)
Gift of Mr. and Mrs. Harold O. Love
(72.249)

The five years Thomas Hovenden spent in Pont-Aven, on France's Brittany coast, influenced not only his artistic technique but also his subject matter. Hovenden arrived in Pont-Aven in the summer of 1875, after studying for a year with the history painter and portraitist Alexandre Cabanel. There he had been trained to paint tightly constructed history pictures with polished enamel-like surfaces. In Pont-Aven, under the influence of Robert Wylie, Hovenden began to paint thematic pictures of Breton peasants, using a looser style of painting that incorporated flashes of brightly colored and thickly applied paint that highlighted certain elements of the composition.

While Hovenden's earliest paintings of Breton peasants were conventional genre images, by 1878 he had become fascinated by the history of the people. Not French at all, the independent-minded Breton peasants were Celts who had gone to France from England to escape the Anglo-Saxon invasions before the

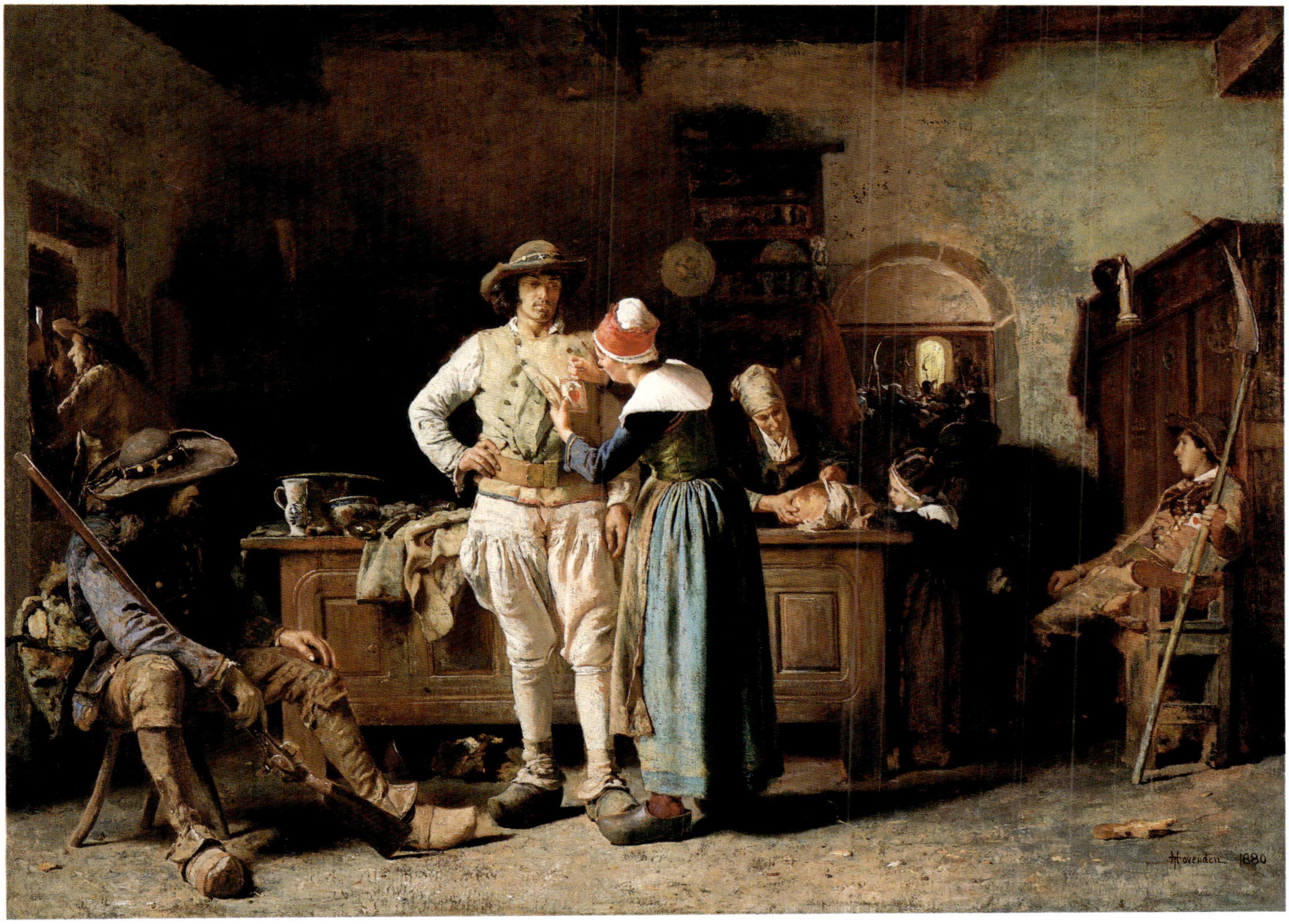

Hoc Signo Vinces

Norman Conquest. Later, in the 1790s, at the height of the Reign of Terror, the Bretons' intense Catholicism and strong national identity kept them loyal to clergy and king. Opposed to the Paris government, they rebelled against military conscription and conducted guerrilla campaigns against the troops of the Republic. Valiantly fighting in the Vendéan wars, they even formed their own bloody royalist uprising under the rebel-hero Jean Chouan. Not seeking separation from the rest of France, the Bretons instead were disputing the reign of an inflexible dictatorship. When the Revolution ended, the Breton people were severely punished for their royalist and clerical fealty (Jacobs 1985, 42; Boston et al. 1983, 298).

As a small oppressed race fighting to keep its national identity, the Bretons held great romantic appeal for the many artists who began going to the area in the 1860s. By the mid-1870s interest in the Bretons' heroic exploits during the Vendéan wars was given fresh impetus when a skeleton, still clutching a musket, was discovered in the hollow trunk of an old apple tree. Robert Wylie led the way in painting scenes of the Vendéan conflict, portraying the courage of the independent Bretons in his *Dying Chouan* (1877; unlocated), which was well underway when he suddenly died in February 1877 (Jacobs 1985, 42, 55; Edwards 1987, 12).

Soon thereafter Thomas Hovenden also took up the Vendéan war theme, painting *The Vendéan Volunteer* (1878; Dr. and Mrs. Robert M. Carroll collection) and exhibiting it in Paris in the

Exposition Universelle in 1878. This *tableau vivant,* set in a cottage interior, shows a young peasant husband, dressed in uniform, about to receive a newly sharpened sword from his father. To the side and in the background are the women and children of the family. The young man's mother and child are making gunshot over a charcoal fire, while his young wife tends a baby in a cradle. The painting suggests that domestic concerns must be set aside for the higher cause of duty.

This same message of patriotic obligation was even more poignantly portrayed two years later in Hovenden's companion painting, *Hoc Signo Vinces* ("In This Sign Shalt Thou Conquer"; originally titled *Le Dernier Préparatif).* Here, in a carefully detailed interior set in La Vendée in 1793, a wife pins a "sacred heart," the symbol of allegiance to church and crown, to her husband's shirt just before he departs for battle. This *tableau vivant,* peopled with peasant models and filled with Revolution-era furniture and costumes Hovenden purchased from various Breton families, emphasizes the wrenching emotional conflict inherent in civil strife (Edwards 1987, 13; Hood et al. 1977, 103–104).

In addition to the couple, who form the focus of the composition, a comrade with a gun lying against his knee is seated to the left, another man is peering through the slit in the window on the far left, and to the right, a young boy wearing a "sacred heart" on his jacket sits patiently waiting with his scythe mounted on a pole. In the background is a table covered with clothes, pistols, and crockery, and at the far end the young man's mother stuffs a loaf of bread into a cloth bag, while his little daughter looks on. Beyond the mother and child is a corridor jammed with peasant soldiers, a scene that suggests the final moment the young man has with his family.

Even though multifigured historical pictures, complete with narrative episodes and theatrical display, were routinely shown in the Paris Salon by nineteenth-century French academic artists, the subject matter of Hovenden's painting brought it a cool reception when it was exhibited at the 1880 Salon, the tenth year of the Third Republic. The painting challenged prevailing political anticlerical and antiroyalist sentiments, attitudes that were the result of shifts in power in the National Assembly among the Republicans, the Catholics, and the monarchists. Yet despite the unpopularity of Hovenden's subject, the critics considered it "the finest figure-piece in the exhibition" and regarded it as "a serious and noble performance." Goupil & Company even made a photogravure reproduction of it (Edwards 1987, 13; Boston et al. 1983, 298; Hood et al. 1977, 103; Hovenden papers, AAA).

The following year Hovenden sent the painting to New York's National Academy of Design exhibition, where it occupied "the place of honor in the east room" and was celebrated for its "excellent drawing and coloring" (Edwards 1987, 13; Hood et al. 1977, 104). The unanimous praise *Hoc Signo Vinces* was given in America brought Hovenden to the attention of the art-loving public and also brought him artistic recognition. One critic described his work as "heroic art, and when the public gaze upon it they will know full well that a star has risen in Israel. His greatness is accepted as a fact by all artists, who admit cheerfully that no figure-painter in America can come near to him" (Edwards 1987, 13). Hovenden was elected an associate member of the National Academy of Design on the strength of this painting. For the rest of his career he regularly produced carefully crafted historical-subject pictures filled with personal drama.

Seven preparatory drawings for *Hoc Signo Vinces* survive. Both single-figure studies and complete scenes, they are housed in the Detroit Institute of Arts's Department of Graphic Arts.

T. T.

Inscription At lower right, *T Hovenden 1880* (TH in monogram)

Provenance Robert Charles Hall. Gift of his daughter, Elizabeth Hall, and her sister to the Peabody Institute, Baltimore, 1924. Kennedy Galleries, New York, 1964. Mr. and Mrs. Harold O. Love, 1964–72. Acquired in 1972.

Exhibitions Paris, Salon, 1880, no. 1877, as *Le Dernier Préparatif.* New York, National Academy of Design Annual, 1881, no. 300, as *Hoc Signo Vinces (La Vendée, 1793).* Baltimore 1882, no. 43. Boston et al. 1983, no. 80. La Roche sur Von 1993, no. 266.

References Baltimore 1949, 12. Hood et al. 1977, 102–104. Boston et al. 1983, 297–298. Terhune 1983. Jacobs 1985, 56–57. Edwards 1987, 12–13.

William Morris Hunt

1824 Brattleboro, Vermont–
Appledore, Isles of Shoals, New Hampshire 1879

William Morris Hunt moved with his family to New Haven, Connecticut, after his father, a member of Congress, died in 1832. His mother hired an Italian portraitist, Spiridione Gambardella (or Gambadella), to teach drawing to her children. In 1843, after Hunt was suspended from Harvard, the family traveled to Europe and settled in Rome. There Hunt worked with the American sculptor Henry Kirke Brown and soon decided to become an artist. He studied at the Düsseldorf Academy in 1845 and 1846 but disliked the structure of the training and the precise style favored by the instructors. In 1846 he rejoined his mother in Paris, where he was inspired to concentrate on painting rather than sculpture after seeing the work of Thomas Couture, with whom he studied for five years. He was also moved by the paintings of Jean-François Millet and began to paint similar peasant subjects. He became a close friend of the Barbizon artist and a collector of his work.

In 1855 Hunt returned to America, where he lived first in Newport, Rhode Island, before moving to a studio in Boston in 1862. He became a major influence on Boston art and taste through the stylistic innovations of his own work and as an artist, teacher, and champion of contemporary French and American art. He devoted the 1850s to painting Barbizon-inspired genre subjects, such as *La Marguerite I* (1851; Musée du Louvre, Paris). In the 1860s, after painting *Judge Lemuel Shaw* (1859; Essex County Bar Association, Salem, Mass.), he became Boston's foremost portrait painter. The following decade he began to sketch out-of-doors and turned more and more to landscape painting.

He first taught informally such notable students as William and Henry James and John La Farge, and later he was active as a teacher of women art students in Boston, one of whom, Helen Mary Knowlton, recorded and published his comments on art in *Talks on Art* (1875 and 1883). In his teaching, he stressed that "'values' were the all in all; that everything existed by its relative value of light and shade" (Knowlton 1899, 84).

Through his teaching, as an adviser to private collectors, and as a founder of the Allston Club, he promoted modern art in Boston. He was influential in introducing both Barbizon paintings and the work of the American artists Elihu Vedder (q.v.), Frank Duveneck, and George Fuller (q.v.) to the Boston audience. Shortly before his death, he worked in a new medium when he was commissioned to paint two murals for the Assembly Chamber of the Albany State Capitol. His proposal for additional decoration was vetoed, however. This disappointment, combined with others of the previous decade such as a devastating fire in his Boston studio, the loss of his mother, and the estrangement from his family, lowered his spirits at the end of his life. He drowned while visiting friends on the Isles of Shoals, off the New Hampshire coast.

S. M. S.

Bibliography College Park and Albany 1976. Webster 1991.

46
The Ball Players, ca. 1877

Oil on canvas
40.6 × 61 cm (16 × 24 in.)
Gift of Mrs. John L. Gardner (07.12)

On a summer sketching trip in 1876, Hunt's students discovered the fishing village of Kettle Cove (later called Magnolia) on Cape Anne, Massachusetts. Hunt spent the summer and fall of 1877 there. He converted a barn and a carpenter's shop into a dormitory and studio, where he was joined by students and assistants (Webster 1991, 134).

The Ball Players, based on the charcoal sketch *Baseball* (1877; Museum of Fine Arts, Boston), was probably finished during the months in Magnolia. Hunt went on a sketching expedition almost daily, using a trailer as a mobile studio and taking along an assistant, John G. Carter, and a driver. Hunt often did a charcoal drawing before beginning work on a landscape painting. His student Helen Knowlton described his working method while in Magnolia:

> Arrived at the spot selected, Hunt would leap from the van, take a camp-stool and a block of charcoal paper, and, with a stick of soft charcoal, seize the salient points of the subject to be rendered. While thus engaged the assistant would arrange an easel and select necessary paints and brushes. Sometimes he was told to "lay-in" the first painting,—reproducing the effect of the charcoal-sketch, while Hunt would watch intently for the right moment to come, when he would seize palette and brushes, and perhaps complete the picture in one sitting. (Knowlton 1899, 118–119)

While some of his paintings were finished on the spot, he worked on others from memory, Knowlton reported: "He received at once a strong impression of his subject, fastened it in his memory, and endeavored to hold fast to that as his guide, omitting any details that might weaken its strength" (Knowlton 1899, 137).

As is evident in his other landscapes done in the 1870s, Hunt was inspired by the flat forms, indistinct contours, and simplified compositions of Barbizon paintings. In this painting, Hunt eliminated two figures that appear in the outfield in the charcoal sketch, distilling the baseball game to three figures: pitcher, batter, and either catcher or umpire (or both). Dark silhouettes with white details, the figures form a diagonal against the light ground. The softness and sketchiness of their contours reflect the forms in the charcoal drawing. The houses and trees lining the edge of the playing field give weight to the top of the composition.

Sally Webster complains that the painting seems "strangely empty" and that the three figures are "frozen in a dull wasteland of light brown space" (Webster 1991, 134–135). She finds the charcoal drawing less static than the oil painting. Only the stance of the batter incorporates movement; the other two figures, whose positions with hands on hips are similar, stand firmly on the triangle formed by their legs.

A year earlier, Hunt had painted views of agricultural work such as *Plowing* (1876; Chrysler Museum, Norfolk, Va.) that were close in subject to Barbizon paintings. In 1877 he turned to the subject of young men at leisure out-of-doors, such as in the two versions of *The Bathers* (Worcester Art Museum, Worcester, Mass., and Metropolitan Museum of Art, New York), which depict a nude boy balancing on the shoulders of another at a swimming hole, and in *Ball Players*. Games of organized baseball were first played in the early 1840s, and by the end of the 1860s baseball could be called the national game (Goldstein 1989, 4). These players seem to be in an amateur rather than a professional game. The batter and catcher or umpire are formally attired in a hat, jacket, and long pants, while the pitcher is in shirtsleeves. No crowd of supporters is included; instead, the players are presented alone on a field surrounded by the houses of the village.
S. M. S.

Provenance William Morris Hunt studio sale, Horticultural Hall, Tremont Street, Boston, February 3–4, 1880, no. 27, as *Ball Players, Magnolia,* 1877. Isabella Stewart (Mrs. John L.) Gardner. Acquired in 1907.

Exhibitions William Morris Hunt studio exhibition, Park Square, Boston 1877. Boston Art Club, 1878, as *Sketch of Ball Players*. Boston 1880, no. 27. Toledo 1912, 18, no. 45. Buffalo 1924, no. 44. New York 1935, no. 56. Pittsburgh 1936. Cambridge 1939, 36–37, no. 14. New York 1943, no. 110. Columbus 1948. New York 1952. New York 1962. New York 1968a. Boston 1979, 72, 84, no. 36. Brooklyn 1987, no. 49. Indianapolis et al. 1991, 50–51, no. 16.

References *BDMA* 1910, 15. Detroit 1930, no. 319. Detroit 1944, 65, no. 319. *Columbus Gallery of Fine Arts Bulletin* 1948, 5, no. 24. Richardson 1956, 260. Novak 1969, 247. Hoppin 1974, 190, 192–194, no. 225. College Park and Albany 1976, 34, 104. M. Brown 1977, 546. Burns 1979, 116. Webster 1991, 134–136.

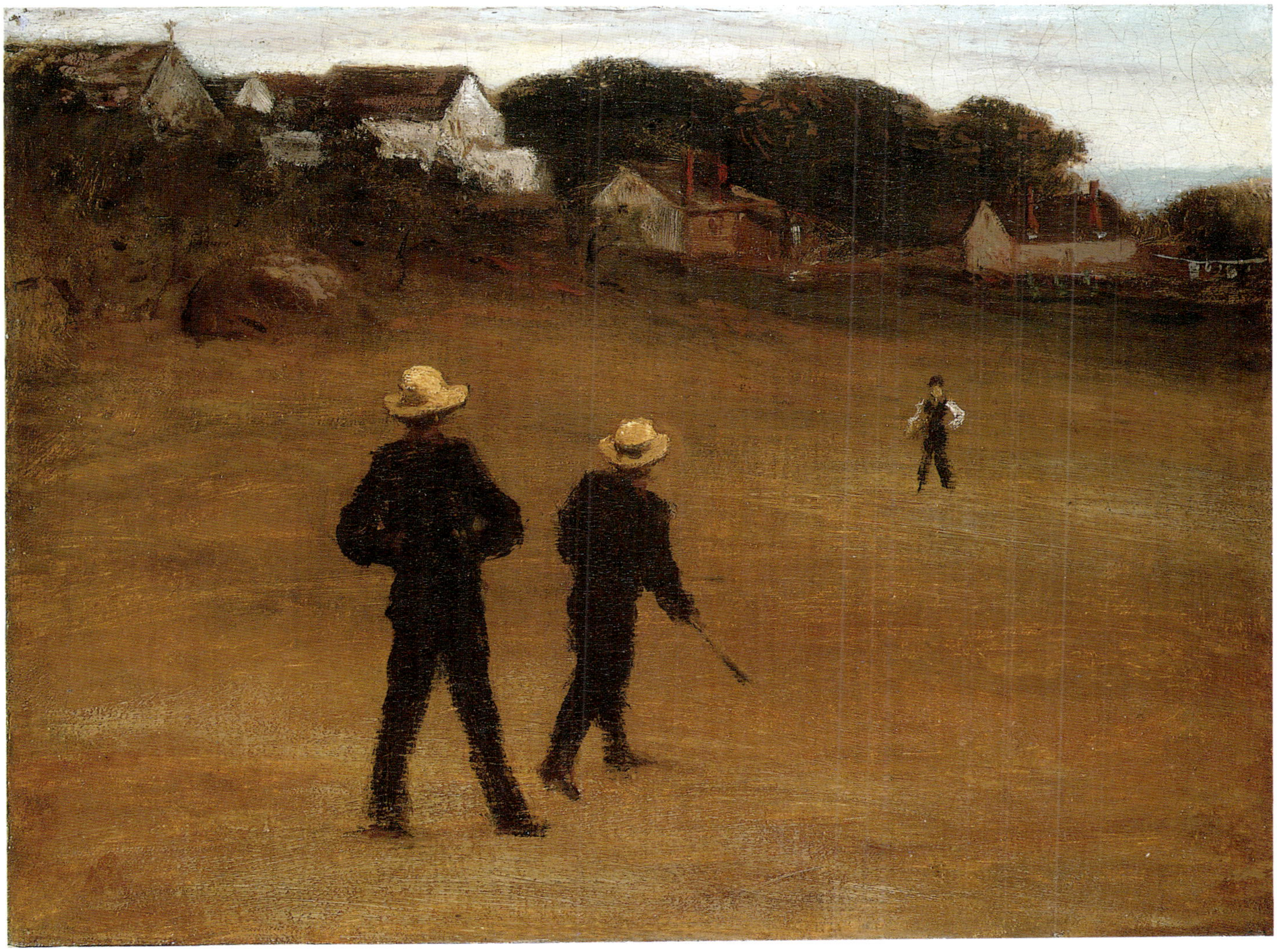

The Ball Players

Daniel Huntington

1816 New York 1906

Despite his reputation as one of the foremost portraitists of New York society, Daniel Huntington believed his paintings that conveyed a moral message were his most valuable contribution. Art, he asserted, "has a powerful influence for good or for ill on the minds of men" (Huntington, "Lecture on Christian Art," 1851, AAA, roll D316). The son of a New York stockbroker, Huntington studied for a semester at Yale University before transferring to Hamilton College. There he met the portrait painter Charles Loring Elliott, who encouraged him to pursue a career in art. In 1835 Huntington returned to New York City, where he was one of the students of Samuel F. B. Morse. By 1840, when he was elected an academician of the National Academy of Design at the age of twenty-three, his career as a portrait painter had taken off. For the next half century he was a leader of the artistic establishment of New York, a founding member of the Century Association in 1847 (and its president from 1879 to 1895), president of the National Academy of Design from 1862 to 1870 and again from 1877 to 1891, and a trustee of the Metropolitan Museum of Art and of the Lenox Library (later the New York Public Library). Beginning in 1839, he traveled and lived often in Europe, where he copied works by Italian Renaissance artists and exhibited at the Royal Academy in London. In 1850, when he was only thirty-three years old, a major retrospective of his work was shown at the American Art-Union in New York.

Although portraits, estimated to number more than one thousand, were probably the most lucrative part of his output, he also painted many other subjects, all of which he believed could be considered "Christian art" (AAA, roll D316). His landscapes were compared to those of Frederic Edwin Church (q.v.), John F. Kensett (q.v.), and Albert Bierstadt (q.v.; see New York 1980, 42). Subjects from British and American history, such as *Lady Washington's Reception or The Republican Court* (1861; Brooklyn Museum), and literary, religious, and allegorical themes, such as *Mercy's Dream* (1841; Pennsylvania Academy of the Fine Arts, Philadelphia), satisfied his interest in didactic art.

Huntington was an academic artist who espoused traditional methods of preparation and development of his paintings. His many drawings, primarily at the Cooper-Hewitt National Design Museum and the National Academy of Design (both in New York), attest to his practice of making numerous studies for each canvas. The compositions of his allegorical and religious paintings, in particular, are often homages to his favorite artists, among them Raphael, Titian, and the German Nazarene Johann Friedrich Overbeck.

S. M. S.

Bibliography Gerdts 1979. Spassky 1985, 56–58. Greenhouse 1989.

47

Justice and Peace, ca. 1886–91

Oil on canvas

203.2 × 162.6 cm (80 × 64 in.)

Gift of Mr. and Mrs. Harvey R. Hansen (59.453)

Although Daniel Huntington delivered a "Lecture on Christian Art" at the National Academy of Design in 1851, supporting the teaching of morality through art (AAA, roll D316), he actually painted relatively few works directly related to the Bible. One of those is *Justice and Peace,* an allegorical presentation of a psalm. The two figures—Justice on the left and Peace on the right—are seated on an elaborately carved throne, on the base of which is a Latin inscription taken from the second half of Psalm 84:11 in the Vulgate (Catholic) version of the Bible: "Misericordia et veritas obviaverunt sibi; justitia et pax osculatae sunt." An old label on the back of the painting, probably also written by Huntington, gives an English translation of the second half of Psalm 85:10, "Mercy and truth are met together; righteousness and peace have kissed each other," from the King James (Protestant) version of the Bible. (The numeration of psalms in the Catholic Bible differs from that in the Protestant version.)

The figure of Justice is depicted as one of the four cardinal virtues. Although Justice is traditionally female, in this painting she appears to be almost androgynous. She holds a sword, the emblem of her power, in her right hand, and her left hand is at the waist of Peace. Seated in a frontal, hieratic pose, she wears a headdress covering her hair, a breastplate, and a crimson robe over an olive green tunic. Peace, with long, flowing hair, a diaphanous white gown and blue sash, turns her torso to lean toward Justice, encircling her with both arms and touching her right arm gently. Her fragile, sensuous beauty and supplicating gesture contrast with the stern, unyielding demeanor of Justice.

The carved figures on either side of the throne represent the Old and New Testaments, suggesting that the more rigid Justice corresponds to the Old Testament and the more pliant Peace to the New. On the left Moses holds the tablets; his bearded visage appears to be repeated in low relief on Justice's breastplate. On the right, John the Evangelist, next to his attribute, the eagle, gestures toward the manuscript he holds. In the background, smoke from an erupting volcano or a fire on the left drifts toward the clear sky tinged with the colors of dawn on the right.

The painting is an amalgam of references to the Old and New Testaments, Judaism, Roman Catholicism, and Protestantism, depicted in a guise often taken by mythological figures, as in Jean-Auguste-Dominique Ingres's *Jupiter and Thetis* (1811; Musée Granet, Aix-en-

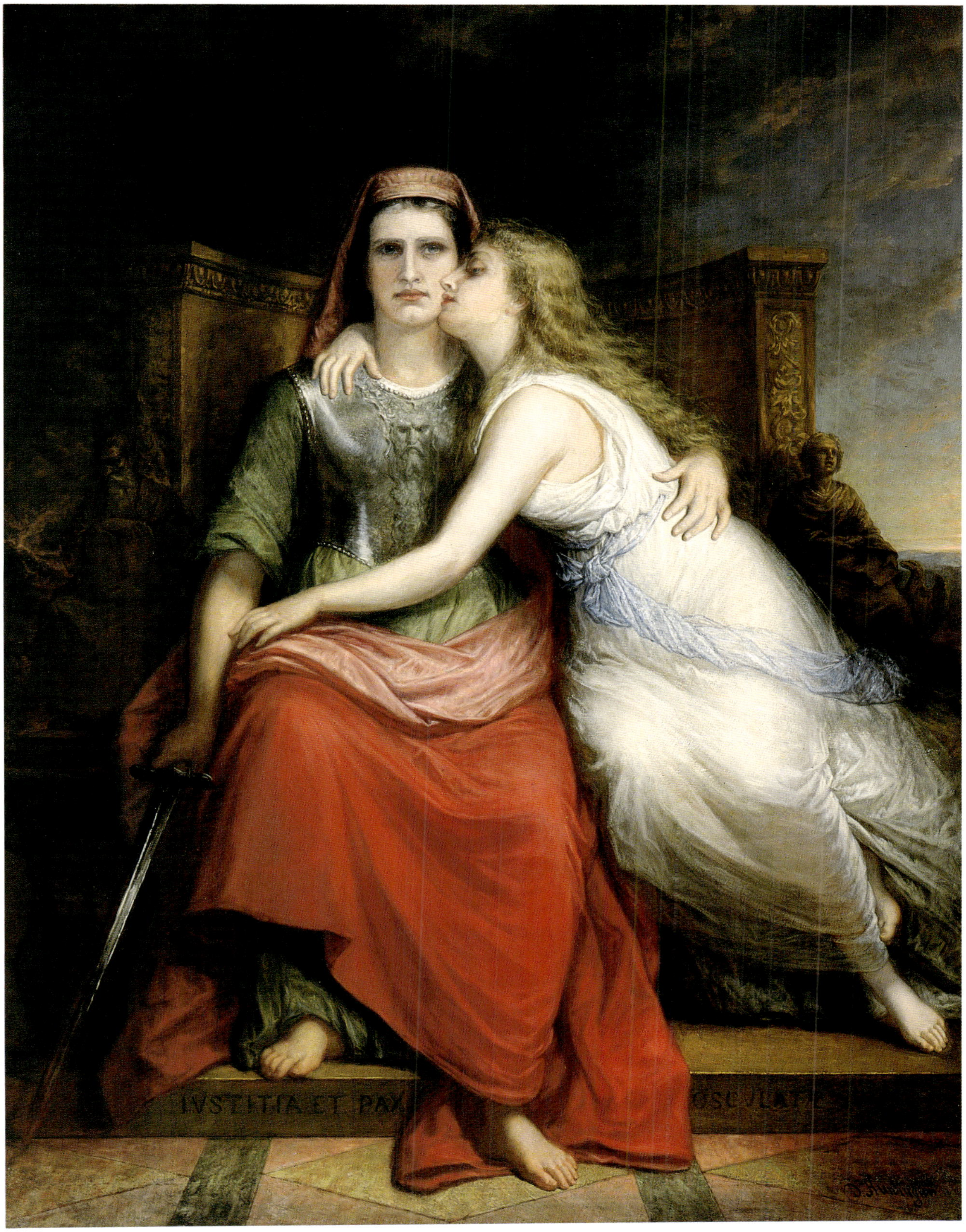

Justice and Peace

Provence). Wendy Greenhouse has investigated how Huntington's critical view of Roman Catholicism is reflected in his paintings of English history done in the 1840s. In 1851 he referred to the "tawdry puerilities of modern Romanism" (AAA, roll D316). According to Huntington's essay in the catalogue of his solo exhibition at the National Academy of Design in 1850, in his painting *Henry VIII and Catherine Parr* (1846; unlocated), Catherine pleads for the translation of the Scriptures from Latin into English, as she holds an English Bible. Greenhouse believes that in *Henry VIII and Catherine Parr* the artist may have been responding to an objection voiced by his brother, Jedidiah, a minister, to the use of Latin in Roman Catholicism. In 1849, however, Jedidiah converted to Roman Catholicism, and Huntington himself gradually grew more tolerant. In fact, unsubstantiated family legend maintains he also converted to Roman Catholicism during a trip to Europe in 1882 while working on this painting (Greenhouse 1989, 129 n. 147). *Justice and Peace,* then, may give a clue to Huntington's transformed conception of the religion. The use of the Latin version of Psalm 85 on the throne base may reflect the possible conversion.

For his allegorical and history paintings, Huntington's practice was to make many studies, which document his changing conception. At least twenty-seven preliminary drawings for the painting, dated from 1878 to 1886, are found at the Cooper-Hewitt National Design Museum and one or two more at the National Academy of Design. Some are compositional studies and others are for details such as feet and hands.

On each of three drawings at the Cooper-Hewitt—studies for the head of Peace—Huntington inscribed the name of a different model: (1) *Mrs. Levicz as 'Peace'/July 1878* (1942–50–40); (2) *Mrs. B. / for "Peace"* (1942–50–41); and (3) *Miss Fridleff for Peace / 1886* (1942–50–60). All are idealized rather than individualized, and all look close to the final painting. On a fourth, similar, study, he inscribed, *for Misericordia / Nov 1885* (1942–50–559), suggesting he may have planned a companion painting to illustrate the first half of the psalm.

In several of the compositional studies, the two figures are placed differently than in the final version. Huntington experimented with placing the heads farther apart and with the sword across Justice's lap and Peace's hand on Justice's right hand rather than touching her arm. In some of the studies, the two figures are seminude.

Justice and Peace is not dated and does not appear to have been exhibited during Huntington's lifetime or in the memorial exhibition of his work at the Century Association in 1908, nor was it included in his estate sales of 1912 and 1916 (correspondence, curatorial files, DIA). Greenhouse speculates that it was probably completed after 1891 because Huntington did not include it in his "Inventory of Effects and List of Paintings" (MS at National Academy of Design), which ends at this date (Greenhouse 1987, notes to 1986.15.59). However, the list mainly includes commissions, and Huntington may have painted this work on speculation. The large size of the canvas suggests he intended it as a major statement. In his "Lecture on Christian Art," Huntington encouraged his fellow members of the National Academy of Design to "cultivate high & pure aims. Let us strive not only to please *men* but God. Let us aim to elevate & spiritualize our artistic studies" (AAA, roll D316). In this painting from late in his career, Huntington attempted to meet those goals.

S. M. S.

Inscriptions At lower right, *D. Huntington;* on base of throne, *JUSTITIA ET PAX. . . . OSCVLATAE SUNT /VULVyLXXXIV.PS 85 / AV;* on old label on back of stretcher, *Righteousness and Peace have kissed each other. Psalm 85 / Painted by Daniel Huntington / 49 East 20th St. / New York City*

Provenance Mr. and Mrs. Harvey R. Hanson. Acquired in 1959.

References Greenhouse 1987, n.p. Greenhouse 1989, 114–115, as *The Kiss of Righteousness and Peace.*

George Inness

1825 NEWBURGH, NEW YORK–
BRIDGE-OF-ALLAN, SCOTLAND 1894

IN THE LAST TEN YEARS of his life, and up to twenty years after his death, George Inness was acclaimed as the greatest American landscape painter and one of the great modern masters. Art critics and patrons appreciated the qualities of Americanness, spirituality, and modernity in his landscapes: Inness dispelled characterizations of the national culture as imitative, soulless, and immature. An early exponent of French Barbizon landscape, he wrestled with convention more effectually than his contemporaries, finally arriving at a mode of painting—call it tonalist or intimist (from the French *paysage intime*)—with adherents much younger than he. He offered an antidote to materialism in an avidly materialistic age, and he stressed individual psychic response in tune with fin-de-siècle sensibility and anxiety.

Inness projected the persona of the anguished genius in pursuit of his inner light, unconcerned with the world of affairs. The posture was only partly affected. Apparently his wife did keep the purse and straighten his tie, he was rude to clients, and he rambled on for hours in metaphysical mazes. While most artists appeared as savvy professionals and dressed the part, the words applied to Inness were nervous, intense, ragged, eccentric, ardent, and sensitive: he, like his long black hair and goatee, seemed "always in disorder" (*Harper's Weekly* 1867, 433). Commentators described his work habits in the same terms ("he was painting like one mad" [Cobb 1963, 237]) but marveled that he was in the studio fifteen hours a day and kept several canvases in progress, moving from one to another as his mood changed. His subject matter was of a type, but variability and unpredictability characterized the development of his style and the quality of his paintings.

If part of Inness's appeal was his quickening, incorruptible genius, another was his reputation as a self-taught artist, an advantage in a society of self-made men and women. His family was well-to-do, but Inness flourished in neither school nor business because he preferred drawing and because he endured precarious health associated with epilepsy. "My whole early life and much of the whole," he confessed, "was bourn under the distress of a fearful nervous disease" (Inness 1884). The condition curtailed his training. He worked briefly with the itinerant painter John Jesse Barker and with the engraving firm of Sherman and Smith in New York, and then, unable to sustain the curriculum at the National Academy of Design, studied for a month with the émigré Régis-François Gignoux.

Aided by the New York auctioneer Ogden Haggerty, Inness visited Italy in 1851–52. On a second trip abroad in 1853–54 he worked in France, where the rural landscapes of Camille Corot, Théodore Rousseau, and Charles-François Daubigny impressed him so profoundly that even late in his career his indebtedness to the Barbizon school was patent: "had he been a Frenchman he would have been recognized as a member of it" (Sheldon 1895, 533). After residing in Brooklyn, in 1860, suffering from poor health, poor reviews, and poverty, Inness settled in Medfield, a distant suburb of Boston, the kind of country environment prescribed for nervous disorders. In 1863 or 1864 he moved to Eagleswood, Perth Amboy, New Jersey, where he forged an electric, volatile relationship with the artist William Page. Page ushered Inness into the New Church of the Swedish mystic Emanuel Swedenborg, whose liberalism and doctrine of correspondences among the natural, spiritual, and celestial orders inspired Inness for the rest of his life.

In the 1870s Inness was more restless than ever. On contract to his Boston dealers, he spent four years abroad between 1870 and 1875, staying most of the time in Rome and Paris. He resided for two years in Medfield and two in New York before establishing himself in 1878 at Montclair, New Jersey, a suburban town like Medfield. He had never succeeded financially, but in the 1870s the New York businessman and art dealer Thomas B. Clarke bought fourteen paintings (and subsequently many more), setting a trend among wealthy collectors and setting loose Inness's imagination. After a solo show in New York in 1884, Inness enjoyed unprecedented prosperity, commanding higher prices than any other living landscape artist and nearly unanimous praise. Ill health and attendant depression dogged him, however, and he died suddenly while on a curative sojourn in Scotland.

W. T. O.

Bibliography Inness 1917. Ireland 1965. Cikovsky 1971. Cikovsky 1977. Los Angeles et al. 1985.

48

Hudson River Valley, 1867

Oil on canvas
61 × 87.6 cm (24 × 34½ in.)
Founders Society Purchase (23.145)

THE LATE 1850s and 1860s—the era of the Civil War—changed Inness. In search of spiritual moorings, he undertook a prolonged theological inquiry, and his art—which was "very closely connected" to his theology (Inness 1917, 176)—became more experimental and less associable with the prevailing landscape aesthetic of what would be termed the Hudson River school. The move to Medfield in 1860 put him close to the former transcendentalist circle, the Barbizon-inspired artist William Morris Hunt (q.v.), Boston patrons who favored Barbizon art, and Boston dealers who specialized in it, so that Inness found sympathy for his radical style. Partly in response to the Reverend Henry Ward Beecher from Brooklyn, who was his principal patron in the early 1860s, Inness increasingly interpreted spiritual qualities in the rural landscape of such locales as Medfield, the Berkshires, and the Hudson valley: "he that reads Nature," Beecher claimed, "reads God's language" (Beecher 1862, 35). Inness also found in Beecher an abolitionist and Unionist as dedicated as himself (Inness even tried to enlist). He moved to Eagleswood at the invitation of Marcus Spring, another outspoken abolitionist and a founder of the religious utopia Raritan Bay Union. There Inness discovered much in common with William Page, who had also resided in Boston and Italy, revered Titian, and had a reputation for radical idealism, having been involved with Brook Farm and the transcendentalists. The effect on Inness of Page's insistent, often incoherent reasoning was common knowledge by 1867: "He is a disciple of Swedenborg, and believes that all material objects in form and color have a spiritual significance and correspondence" *(Harper's Weekly* 1867, 433). From that time on, the person who "stood closer to him than any other man" was John C. Ager, pastor of the New Jerusalem Church in Brooklyn and translator of Swedenborg (Inness 1917, 217).

The year 1867, when he painted *Hudson River Valley*, was especially consequential for Inness. Two of his paintings were shown in the American section at the Exposition Universelle in Paris, and the critic James Jackson Jarves praised them as original (Jarves 1869, 298–299). Henry T. Tuckerman devoted several pages to analysis of Inness's work in his *Book of the Artists*, published in 1867, and in July Inness received front-page notice in *Harper's Weekly* in the first profile of his character as an artist. Shortly thereafter, Inness moved from Eagleswood to Brooklyn, keeping a studio in New York (as he did throughout most of his life). His major work from the year was *The Triumph of the Cross*, three large canvases interpreting John Bunyan's *Pilgrim's Progress*. The paintings allegorized a spiritual odyssey that held both personal and national meaning. Inness had found regeneration through Swedenborg: Northern capital and moral purpose had redeemed the nation, renewing the promise of an American paradise. Northern victory justified the exertion of Northern values. "We must work our way to Paradise," Inness wrote, "the end of true culture" (Inness 1884).

Like virtually all landscape painters in New York and New England, Inness celebrated more than a generalized notion of nationalism in his art before, during, and for years after the Civil War; he celebrated the North and Northern experience. He painted not so much about Northern industrial prowess as about bedrock agrarian culture and the virtues of rural life. Inness's medium for "communicating human sentiment" was what he called the "civilized landscape." "Every act of man," he maintained, "every thing of labor, effort, suffering, want, anxiety, necessity, love, marks itself wherever it has been" (Inness 1878, 461). Instead of "savage and untamed" reaches (Sheldon 1895, 532), his subjects were family farms, free cultivators and harvesters, hayricks, cows, streams meandering through provident pastures, stone walls and split-rail fences, distant white church steeples and wood-framed houses, stately oaks and elms, wooded hillsides, autumn colors—the common environment of triumphant Northern values that he had memorialized in a group of high-profile paintings headed by *Peace and Plenty* (1865; Metropolitan Museum of Art, New York). His laterally expansive landscapes express freedom and mobility, as well as plenitude; his lone figures express individuality and independence, as well as the dignity of labor in a society of farmers who work their own land.

Such are the signs and values in *Hudson River Valley*. The central motif is a stand of large oaks and elms that divide an ample pasture and offer shade to the cows; along the base of the trees runs a rail fence. Contrasting bands of color of light gold and blue both delimit and draw interest to this middle zone. At the left the white buildings of the farm are brightly spotlighted at the upper edge of the zone where the plain adjoins the hill. The buildings thus project significance far greater than their smallness relative to the grand, harboring hillside; they govern the foreground domain of productive labor and self-sufficiency that extends to the cows by the stream. The viewer's raised vantage scans the tops of the central trees, with the effect that the upper half of the painting—the big abstracted shapes of hill and sky—constitutes an elevated zone rather than simply background. It is a domain of abstract, even spiritual activity at once distinct from and linked to the cultivated domain of labor and material productivity below. In this way Inness images the Northern arcadia as site of a special union of divine, natural, and human resources.

Perhaps those critics between the Civil War and the Centennial who praised Inness as an American artist based their judgment on his ability to convey such a union. The pro-North *Harper's* called him "thoroughly American, but of the highest aesthetical type of the American. . . . [H]e has a deep religious nature and an extraordinarily analytical philosophical mind" *(Harper's Weekly* 1867, 433). At the same time, Tuckerman rightly stressed Inness's allegiance "to his French ideal in landscape": that is, to the Barbizon mode. Inness did depart from mainstream landscape art, as Tuckerman concluded, to the degree that "his foreign proclivities and his suggestive method . . . contrast to . . . merely imitative skill and local fidelity" (Tuckerman 1867, 527, 532)—characteristics of the increasingly censured Pre-Raphaelite movement and Düsseldorf school, as well as the Hudson River school with which Inness briefly had identified. So compelling had this position become, particularly after successful exhibitions of French Barbizon

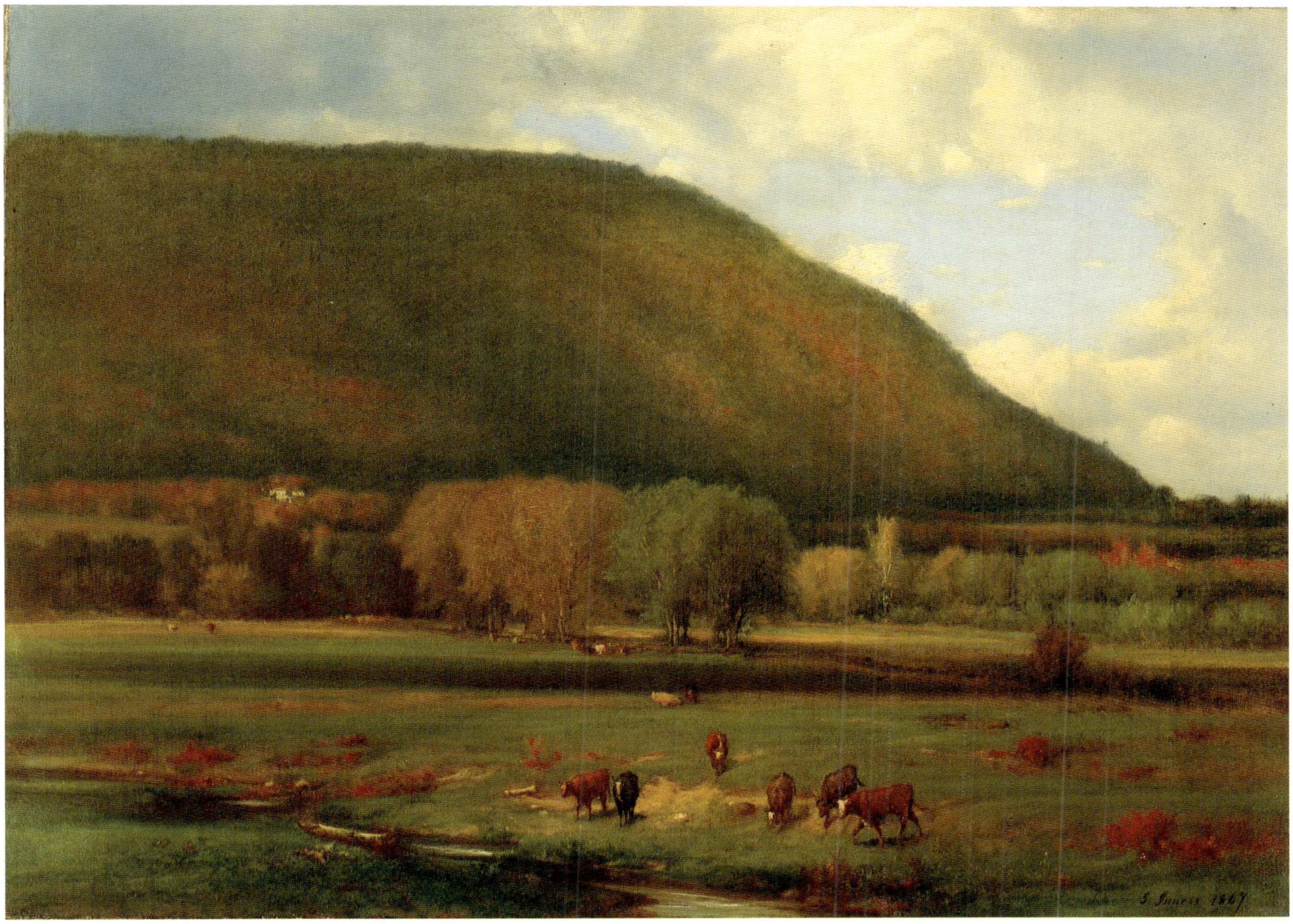

Hudson River Valley

paintings in Boston and New York in 1866, that the National Academy of Design finally awarded Inness full membership in 1868 and three years later named his friend Page president. Inness had developed what one critic called "a war style, which we may consider the result of the agitation produced by the four years of tumult and national anguish, and which shows itself in fluidity of outlines, a breaking-up of the old rigidity, a new grasp of what is magnificent in landscape breadth, a throwing overboard of the pettiness of the former style" (De Kay 1882, 62).

Hudson River Valley is typical of that departure. The handling is loose, forms are generalized, and colors are expressive. Likely the season is Indian summer—"that most heavenly of all seasons in any land" (Coxe 1908, 510) and a favorite of Inness—but depiction of a specific site is less at issue. While Inness worked a good deal in the Hudson valley in the 1860s and many landscapes pertained to the region, he was not bound to topographical description. His wife usually entitled his paintings (A. Hill 1922, 115), and when a buyer asked "what part of the country" a painting represented, the artist responded: "Nowhere in particular; do you suppose I illustrate guide-books? That's a picture" (Coxe 1908, 511). Certain configurations sustained aesthetic interest over the years: the same hillside, diminished in scale, recurs in a harvesting scene from 1875 entitled *Hudson Valley* (Ireland 1965, 186, no. 752). As Inness eliminates traditional picturesque framing and directional devices, such as foreground trees at the margins and emphatic diagonal recessions, his approach to composing is nonhierarchical and nonprocessional, just as his subject matter is commonplace rather than sensationalist or privileged in some way. He envisions both Northern agrarian values and his personal theology in an accessible, egalitarian manner.

Who, if anyone, bought *Hudson River Valley* in 1867 is unknown, but its owner of record, Jacob Henry Schiff, was influential in the formation of postwar culture. Schiff emigrated from Frankfurt, Germany, to New York in 1865, established himself in banking, and became head of Kuhn, Loeb & Co. He was director of railroads, banks, and corporations, chairman of the Semitic committee at Harvard, founder of Jewish charitable institutions in New York, and patron of New York museums and arts organizations. He was a member of the honorary committee of Inness's friends and patrons who were invited to the memorial exhibition at the American Fine Arts Society in December 1894, four months after the artist's death.

W. T. O.

Inscription At lower right, *G. Inness 1867*

Provenance Jacob H. Schiff, New York. On consignment, Anderson Galleries, New York, 1922. Acquired in 1923.

Exhibitions Frankfurt, n.d. (from Ireland 1965). Buffalo 1925, no. 19. Springfield et al. 1946, 30, 77, no. 18. Oshkosh 1962, no. 11. Stockholm and Gothenburg 1986.

References *BDIA* 1924. Ireland 1965, 102, no. 405.

49
Apple Orchard, 1892

Oil on canvas

76.2 × 114.6 cm (30 × 45⅛ in.)

Gift of Baroness Von Ketteler, Henry Ledyard, and Hugh Ledyard, in memory of Henry Brockholst Ledyard (23.100)

The apple orchard was a favorite motif of Inness's toward the end of his career. In the summers in the later 1870s and early 1880s he worked in "one of the humblest studios on the Hudson, a certain old barn in an apple-orchard at Milton [New York].... This old orchard has been a mine of artistic wealth" (Champney 1885, 846). The orchard by his house at Montclair, where he moved in 1878, also inspired many paintings, including *Apple Orchard.* In most of the orchard paintings Inness delighted in the gnarled silhouettes of the sometimes ancient trees and the effect of shaded, sheltering enclosure they provided at midsummer. Less often he painted fruit trees in blossom; in several instances he included walking or recumbent figures in the scene, but apparently only once did he paint a conventional sort of apple-picking event that brought couples together in vague reference to the Garden of Eden (1885; Dallas Museum of Art).

In its composition *Apple Orchard* is sufficiently like other paintings—none of them, however, depicting an orchard—to suggest that Inness had developed a structure that pleased him. One of the paintings, *The Passing Storm,* is markedly similar and also dates from 1892 (private collection; Ireland 1965, 362, no. 1405). As he often did, Inness placed the horizon line nearly at the center of the canvas, positioned the viewer on the ground, and conjured up a site that was as flat as a pond. The strategy produced a surface design of two large bands. Inness emphasized the resultant sense of flatness with nearly uniform strokes and texture over the entire surface. In contrast, he stressed spatial illusionism by parting the screen of trees to create a tunneling perspective focused on a distant group of buildings left of center. Further, he established the "three great planes" of space that he held to distinguish the ideal composition:

> the first two shall be foreground, the third... shall contain all the distance. The subject matter must not be within the first plane, but behind it, and whatever reaches above the horizon line, by its size and proportion becomes subject matter—therefore trees that find their plane within the first great section are too near... a figure, wherever placed, must not reach

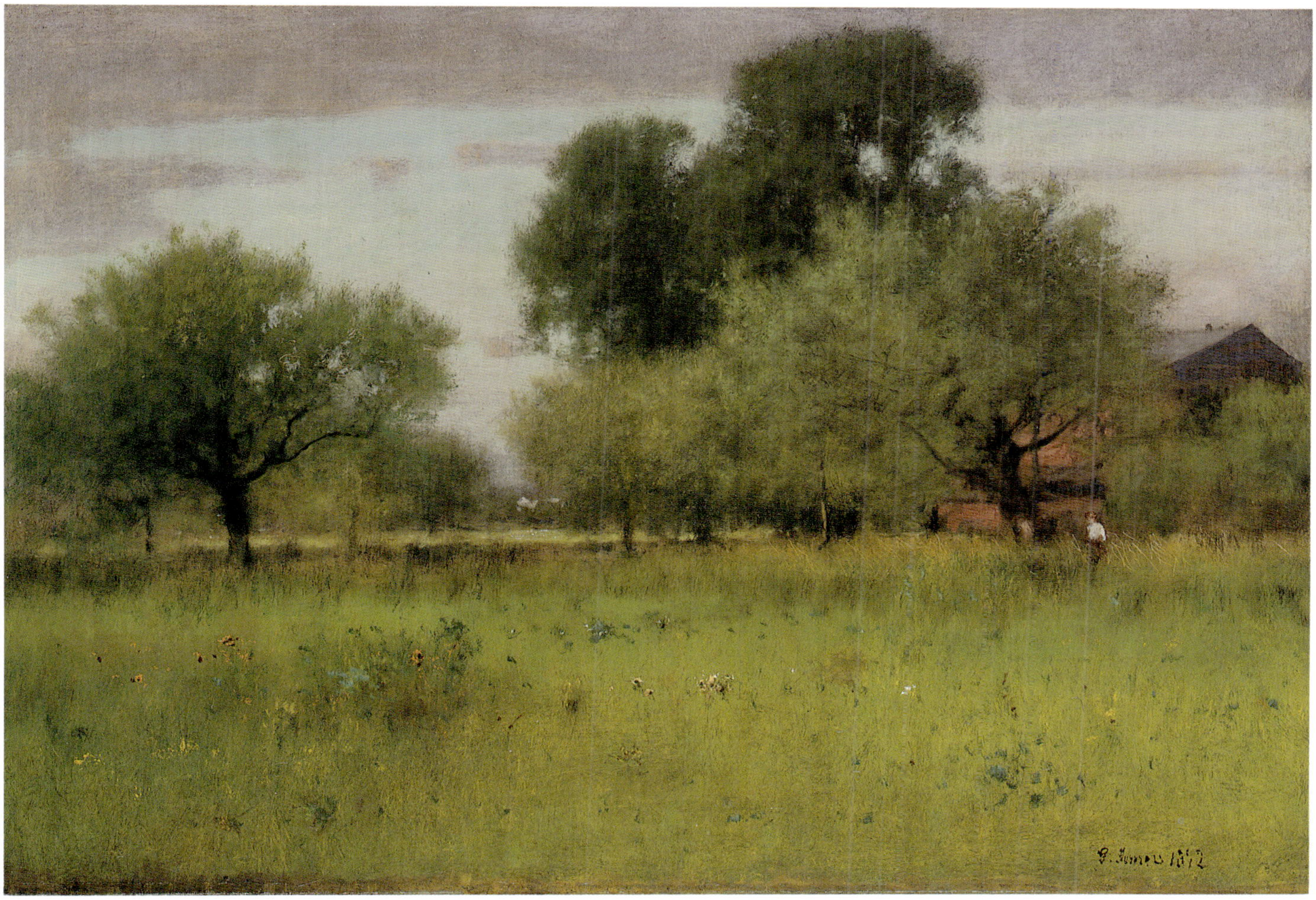

Apple Orchard

above the horizon. (Daingerfield 1911, 26)

The statement applies to *Apple Orchard* as consistently as it does to many of Inness's paintings. The composition, projecting harmony and balance, is contrived and formulaic: the grouping of trees mimics the form of the barn at the right, for instance, and the tree trunks are spaced with exquisite proportion and foresight. Detail is reduced. The buildings, like the orchard, signify a domestic landscape, but their features are masked, and even the figure at right is featureless. Inness denoted a few individual stalks of grass with the butt end of the brush and little impatient slashes. Pokes and taps of color in the foreground read as clusters of wildflowers that give pleasure in their discovery.

Inness's original and much vaunted use of color is evident in the myriad variations on green that bring tonal unity to the work. Benjamin Constant, a much-acclaimed French portraitist and history painter who met Inness in 1890, judged that "no eye was ever more sensitive than Inness's to the richness of the green tones brought about by the summer light" (Inness 1917, 183). The artist Elliott Daingerfield concurred: "No man before him . . . had the problem of the luxurious green of mid-summer, in a verdure as opulent, almost, as the tropics. Inness gave us a type of picture quite unknown before. Courageously he strove to render this powerful color, which artists know to be almost impossible when it, in itself, is the theme" (Daingerfield 1911, 26–27).

As the linear structure, spatial ambiguities, and measured rhythms in the painting imply, Inness embedded abstract philosophy within landscape. There was nothing new in that, but commentators placed Inness apart for the concertedness of his efforts to meld systems of vision, feeling, and theology. The critic Charles De Kay perceived what Inness was about: "Back of the landscapes, in whose confection rules founded on logic that can be expressed in the mathematical terms have been strictly followed, lies the whole world of immaterial spirits, of whom Swedenborg was the latest prophet. . . . You may learn from [Inness] how the symbolization of the Divine Trinity is reflected in the mathematical relations of perspective and aerial distance" (De Kay 1882, 63). Inness also had "a theory . . . of color entwined in a most ingenious way with Swedenborgianism" (Armstrong 1920, 199).

Swedenborgianism appealed to high-strung intellectuals throughout the century, from Ralph Waldo Emerson to William James. Disdaining tradition, it offered freedom from established denominations and dogmas: it supported individual freedom, social reform, and radicalism. The visual, material world was but an illusory metaphor for the fundamental truth or reality of the spiritual world that existed behind it, in a kind of parallel dimension. Inness, in true Swedenborgian parlance, asserted that "what is seen is not reality" (Sheldon 1882, 246) and seemed to envision that other dimension or reality in his landscapes. He rejected Darwinism, dabbled in homeopathic medicine and spiritualism ("the spiritist mediums . . . were forever telling him that Titian stood at his elbow" [Daingerfield 1917, 73]), and embraced numerology as a "science" of correspondences. Art critics and historians, however, have not been able to parse Inness's designs and color schemes in accord with Swedenborg's doctrine of correspondences, whereby an apple tree or green corresponds to a particular principle of the divine, and no evidence yet attests that patrons bought landscapes from Inness because they belonged to the New Church. According to his son, Inness regarded Swedenborgianism as a springboard "to other metaphysical research" and "did not adhere strictly to its tenets"; he was, as his son remembered him, a Christian, who believed in "the Lord Jesus Christ" and in the Bible as "the word of God" (Inness 1917, 61, 201). If for Inness landscape was "an expression . . . of the Godhead," and if in his art "religion, landscape, and human nature mingle so thoroughly that there is no separating the several ideas," still his paintings were not demonstrably religious. As De Kay concluded, "let us . . . say of his religion that he does not express, but hides it, in his art" (De Kay 1882, 63).

In 1892 Inness won a medal at the Sixth International Exposition in Munich, Germany, and he sustained his productivity of fifty paintings per year. He was at last wealthy and in a position to reflect, travel, and work in comfort; but he was also desperately ill and depressed, often unable to concentrate on painting. He and the doctors described his ailments as dyspepsia, rheumatism, indigestion, neuralgia of the spleen, and nervous exhaustion. He traveled a good deal in 1889–93, as much for his health as to paint, visiting Chicago, Nantucket, New Brunswick, Tarpon Springs, Florida, where he kept a house and studio, and San Francisco, where he visited with the Swedenborgian landscape artist William Keith. At times he was reinvigorated: "I tell you my boy," he confided to his patron-agent Thomas B. Clarke, "unless I am very much mistaken and have lost my cud, you are going to see something that will make people believe that there is a God in Israel." At other times he was despondent: "I am inclined to think that my days of impetuous painting are ended and that I shall be obliged to consider longer and do less" (Cikovsky 1977, 90). At still other times he was desperate: one day at Montclair in 1892 a friend found him "in his studio, slowly bleeding to death from an artery he had opened in his arm . . . when life seemed too dark to endure." It was noted, "How odd it seems that he has been ready to end his life for discouragement—he who stands the peer of any living landscape painter!" (Cikovsky 1977, 89). If *Apple Orchard* is reaffirmative,

other canvases from 1892, such as *Home at Montclair* (Sterling and Francine Clark Art Institute, Williamstown, Mass.), intimate soulful reckoning and contact with the spirit world.
W. T. O.

Inscription At lower right, *G. Inness 1892*

Provenance Henry Brockholst Ledyard. To his children, Baroness Von Ketteler, Henry Ledyard, and Hugh Ledyard. Acquired in 1923.

Exhibitions Buffalo 1925, 11, no. 18. Oxford 1959. Hamilton 1961, no. 32. Kalamazoo 1964. Montclair 1964, no. 47. Oakland and Santa Barbara 1978, 59. Tokyo 1989, no. 67.

References *BDIA* 1923. *BDIA* 1924. *American Art News* (March 1, 1924): 6 (from Ireland 1965). Ireland 1965, 368, no. 1427.

50
The Lonely Pine, 1893

Oil on canvas
76.2 × 114.3 cm (30 × 45 in.)
Gift of B. E. Ford (51.331)

THE ORDEALS OF ILL HEALTH and depression that plagued Inness in 1891 and 1892 did not abate in 1893 and 1894. In retrospect, one reads continuous struggle and auguries of death in the paintings of his last years. Perhaps because of his disabling disease, Inness's late career has a poignancy similar to Goya's and Van Gogh's and draws sympathetic interest from historians, just as it did from commentators at the time. "There appears to be a constitutional change going on in my system," Inness confessed in 1893 (Cikovsky 1977, 90), but in his art he sustained considerable consistency from about 1880 until his death.

The Lonely Pine, as the painting was entitled in the 1894 memorial exhibition, offers a slight exception to that rule. Only one other painting, *The Lonely Farm, Nantucket* (1892; Art Institute of Chicago; also in the 1894 show), is similarly entitled, and only a few landscapes are so minimal in aspect. Yet the mood is familiar from many late paintings, as are the pairing of broad bands of sky and foreground marsh and meadow, the brilliant sunset (a trademark of Inness's), the siting of the principal motif at an oblique rise off-center from the vertical axis, and punctuating the horizon with diminishing "echoes" of that motif. In characteristically evocative fashion, Inness equates sky and earth and compresses spatial planes by repeating the wedge shape of the clouds in the foreground marsh and creating a uniformly textured surface. Within the biographical context, the pine tree seems to be a metaphor for the vigil of the individual facing infinity at a moment of epiphany. There are parallels of feeling in the story "The Country of the Pointed Firs" (1896) by the Swedenborgian Sarah Orne Jewett, who wrote of "a sudden sense of space [when] nothing stopped the eye or hedged one in,—that sense of liberty in space and time which great prospects always give," and whose protagonist remarked that "every... tree has got its own livin' spring; there's folks made to match 'em" (Jewett 1896, 46, 84).

The Lonely Pine is typical of Inness's most effective late conjurings, manufactured in the studio from the artist's inner eye and energy. Although he studied from nature diligently, "very few of his pictures were finished from nature, and in the later days of his life, none. His pictures were expressions of himself, not imitations of what he saw"; "imitation is worthless," he maintained (Inness 1917, 250–251, 124). Intent on visualizing Swedenborg's spirit world and internalizing the divine impulses within nature, Inness became a medium, working in the studio from memory and imagination "without any reference to any particular nature; for he himself was nature" (Daingerfield 1917, 71). "Why," he asked, "should we undertake to say that states do not exist of which we have no physical perception, and can have none? Why could not we exist in a subtle condition imperceptible to sense?" (Sheldon 1882a, 246).

Much has been made of Inness's modernism, the ways in which the technical and formal properties of his art pertained to advanced trends abroad, especially in France, but also in England, where the American expatriate James McNeill Whistler (q.v.) was enormously influential. Inness developed his style in step with the progressive work of younger artists identified as tonalists or intimists, and critical acclaim for his late manner centered on qualities that also characterized the modernist trend, such as patchy brushstrokes, unifying color, expressive light, abstracted designs, and apparent interest in the integrity of the surface plane (see Los Angeles et al. 1985, 45–67). To a large degree, however, the similarities are superficial and misleading. If critics, historians, and dealers have touted Inness's avant-garde status, Inness himself labored to resolve a style that would evoke what hardly anyone understood: Swedenborg's New Jerusalem. Inness continued to paint "windows" that offered views into a three-dimensional reality; even if that reality was, to him, insubstantial, to others it was mundane matter rendered poetic by genius. Talk of his "impressionism"—applicable to *The Lonely Pine,* for example—must also be assiduously qualified. "Every artist must... depend on his feeling," he wrote, "and what I have devoted myself to is to try to find out the law of... impression." French impressionism, however (what he called "The Art of the Future"), was to him "a mere passing fad" and one of many "shams" in art. "It appears as though the Impressionists were imbued with the idea to divest painting of all mental attributes... [by] overleaping the traveled road which art has created by hard labor, by plastering over and presenting us with the original pancake of visual imbecility, the childlike naïveté of unexpressed vision" (Inness 1917, 173–175). He deemed impressionism an "error" (Inness 1884) for positing that "the material is the real" and refusing to recognize "the reality of the unseen" (Inness 1879, 377). Thus it was that in 1893 the critic George P. Lathrop could say that Inness was "modern among the moderns" (Lathrop 1893), while in 1917 (four years after the Armory Show) his friend Elliott Daingerfield stated flatly that "in his mind there was no particle of that quality which we have come to know as modern art" (Daingerfield 1917, 70).

Inness supported the doctrine of art for art's sake, but one should not construe from that that he was unconcerned with moral issues in his art. When asked to define "what... the painter tries to do," he responded: "Simply to reproduce in other minds the impression which a scene has made upon him. A work of art does not appeal to the intellect. It does not appeal to the moral sense. Its aim is not to instruct, not to edify, but to awaken an emotion." Excerpted from an interview, this passage, which is the most frequently quoted of his views on art, suggests that Inness had no moral purpose in painting. When asked, "What is the true use of art," however, he went on to say that "the moral element underlies all... only when the moral powers have been cultivated do the conditions exist necessary to the transmission of the artistic inspiration which is from truth and goodness itself" (Inness 1878, 458, 461).

By late in his career, Inness's views on a number of issues were widely known. His parting from the socially conservative Henry Ward Beecher to embrace Swedenborgianism placed him among radical idealists. In his professional life he was consistently rebellious, espousing the inherent socialism of Barbizon art, helping to found the Society of American Artists in 1877 in opposition to the National Academy of Design, and attacking the academy (although he was a member) as undemocratic and errant in assuming that "the pomaded culture of royal prerogative should represent our national art" (Inness 1879a). He became a fervent supporter of the social prophet and economic reformer Henry George, who wrote the explosive book *Progress and Poverty* (1879) and was a two-time New York mayoral candidate. Inness relentlessly advocated George's platform of a single tax that would confiscate all land rents for community use; the tax was based on the communistic convictions that land was a gift of nature, every person had a natural right to labor on the land, and private property of land as capital was the source of egregious social and economic problems.

Inness's "cultivated landscapes" speak to these issues, embodying what we know not only of his religious understanding but also of his social and economic views. *The Lonely Pine*, while not so clearly a cultivated landscape as Detroit's two other paintings by Inness, propounds an accessibility, an unusual spaciousness and openness, and a metaphor for individual will and worth that signify his larger system of belief. If Swedenborgianism is among the sources for the much-admired "synthetic style" of Inness's last years (De Kay 1882, 62), to which *The Lonely Pine* belongs, so, too, is the communistic Christian social conscience awakened by Henry George at the same time. One of many questions left unresolved in Inness scholarship is the degree to which critics and patrons understood, endorsed, or subsumed the radical ideological implications of his style and subject matter. Opposition to his early Barbizon style in New York was ideologically motivated, but acceptance of his late style ostensibly was not. His newly rich capitalist patrons adopted Barbizon art to distinguish themselves as the new class of power brokers and the new social elite. Only a few collectors of his paintings—notably George I. Seney and Edward B. Butler—were identified closely with philanthropy, while others—notably Potter Palmer and the McCormicks of Chicago—were giant figures in land speculation and development. Not one, so far as is known, advocated Swedenborgianism, attacked elitist institutions, or joined the egalitarian crusade of Henry George.
W. T. O.

Inscription At lower right, *G. Inness 1893*

Provenance Inness executor's sale, Fifth Avenue Art Galleries, New York, February 12–14, 1895, no. 158. Cyrus J. McCormick, Chicago. His wife. Her nephew, B. E. Ford, Dearborn, Mich. Acquired in 1951.

Exhibitions New York 1894, 31, no. 30, as dating from 1894. Art Institute of Chicago 1898, no. 221 (from Ireland 1965).

References *Masters in Art* 1908, 41. Ireland 1965, 393, no. 1498.

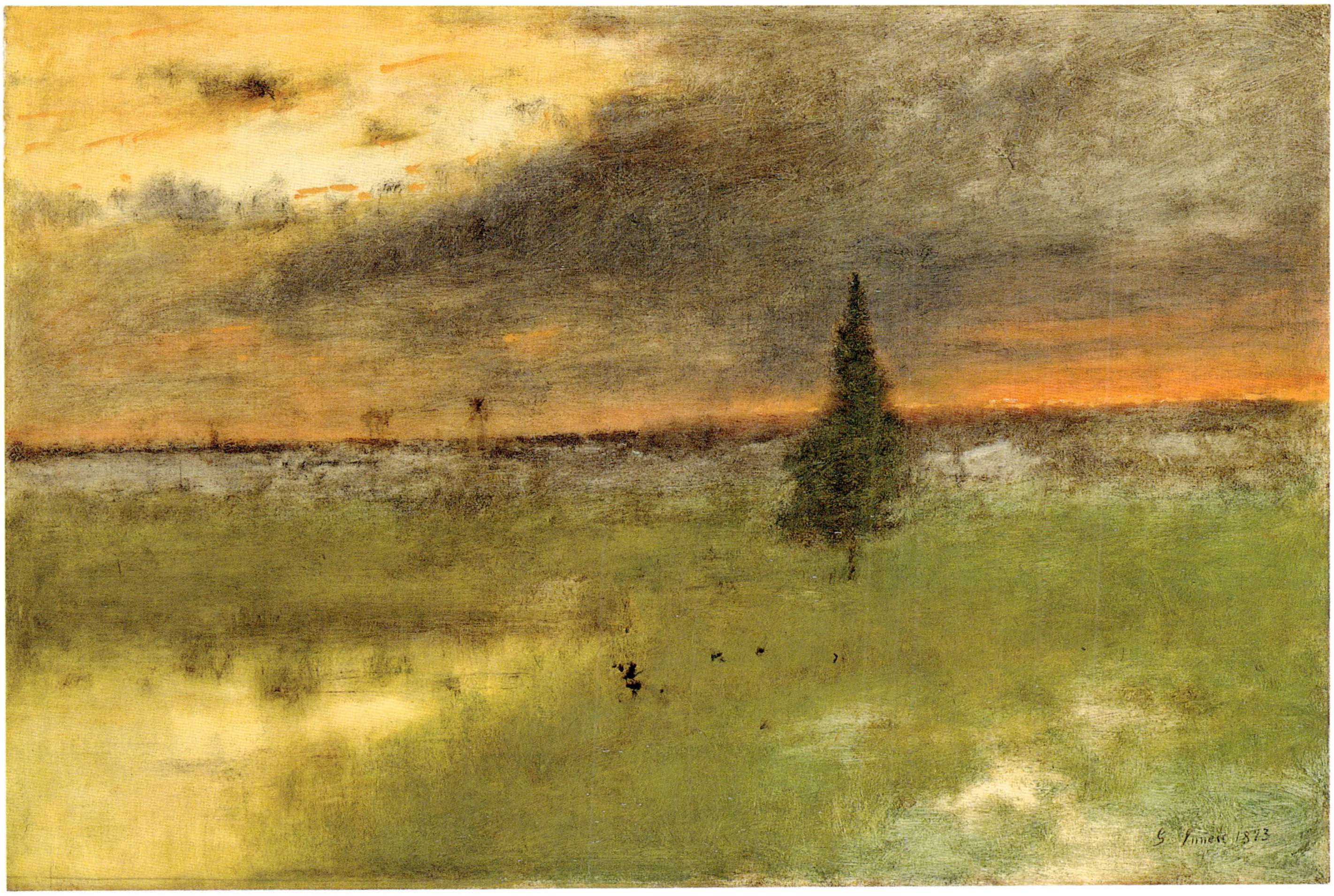

The Lonely Pine

Lewis Thomas Ives

1833 ROCHESTER, NEW YORK–DETROIT 1894

LEWIS IVES was a Detroit painter well known for his portraits of public officials. He was the son of Eardly and Ann (Wood) Ives, who moved when he was young to an eighty-acre farm on the shores of Three Mile Lake, near Pontiac, Michigan. When the farm failed, the family moved to Detroit, where Eardly Ives later worked as a bookkeeper. Lewis Ives studied with the local portrait painter Frederick Cohen and exhibited at the Michigan State Fair in 1851 and 1854. In 1852 he shared a studio with the landscape painter Charles Lum and exhibited five works, including *The Countess, Family Portrait,* and *Innocence,* in Detroit's first public art exhibition at the Firemen's Hall. He exhibited *Head of Rubens, Sibyl, after Huntington,* and several portraits in the second Firemen's Hall exhibition the following year. At about this time Lewis and his brother James went to Europe to study painting. In Rome their teacher was the American artist William Page, whose influence on Lewis Ives's early work, especially in his delicate use of glazings, was described in the *Detroit Sunday News-Tribune* review of the memorial exhibition of his work held in 1896 at the Detroit Museum of Art.

After the brothers returned to Detroit, they both turned to law as a career. Ives was admitted to the bar in about 1859. He married Margaret Leggatt in 1860. While working as a lawyer for the Detroit and Milwaukee Railroad and the Grand Trunk Railway, he continued his interest in painting. He studied with John Mix Stanley in 1867 and was a member of the Prismatic Club, a social arts organization in Detroit. Soon, however, failing eyesight and poor health led Ives to abandon his legal career.

After a second trip to Europe in 1872, Ives devoted more time to painting. In 1875–76 he exhibited with the Detroit Art Association, of which he was a founding member. His works included crayon and oil portraits, among them portraits of the painter John Mix Stanley (1872; Kennedy Galleries, New York, as of 1971) and Ralph Waldo Emerson. According to the 1896 review of his work in the *Sunday News-Tribune,* a change in his technique was noticeable in the early 1880s, as he broke free of the influence of Page.

Ives was one of the original incorporators of the Detroit Museum of Art and served as a trustee. The memorial exhibition of his work held at the museum two years after his death included numerous portraits as well as studies done in England, Scotland, Italy, and the American West. Among the drawings was a *Life Study, Gigi Academy, Rome,* probably done when he was a student there in the 1850s. His son Percy Ives was also a painter.

E. G. M.

Bibliography Passport Applications, no. 24035, August 5, 1872. Detroit 1896. *Detroit Sunday News-Tribune,* February 2, 1896, 12. Burton 1922, 2:1195. C. Burroughs 1936a, 403. C. Burroughs 1937, 44. Gibson 1975, 143. Yarnall and Gerdts 1986, 1904–1905. Gerdts 1990, 2:235, 238–240.

51
Frances Elizabeth Newbury (Mrs. John J.) Bagley, 1872–82

Oil on canvas

137.2 × 92.1 cm (54 × 36¼ in.)

Gift of James K. Watkins, Jr., George H. Watkins, John B. Watkins and Margaret H. Watkins in memory of Mrs. James K. Watkins (F77.113)

FRANCES ELIZABETH NEWBURY (1833–1898) was born in Rutland, Ohio, the daughter of the Presbyterian minister Samuel Newbury and his wife, Mary Ann Sargeant Newbury. In 1855 she married John Judson Bagley, who became a successful Detroit businessman and served as governor of Michigan from 1873 to 1877. Mrs. Bagley served as president of the board of trustees of the Woman's Hospital and Foundlings' Home and of the board of trustees of the Young Woman's Home. She was a member of the Archaeological Institute of America, organizer and president of the first Women's Club of Detroit, and a member of the Board of Lady Managers of the 1893 Columbian Exposition.

Mrs. Bagley, her hair parted in the center and pulled tightly back, wears a black dress with white ruching at the neck and sleeves and a black mantilla and, in dramatic contrast, a diamond crucifix. She stands next to a marble-topped table, turning the pages of a small book. Nearby is a silver vase with a fully opened rose and a rosebud. The interior setting of a wall, column, and curtain opens to a distant landscape.

E. G. M.

Inscription At lower right, *L. T. Ives 1872–82.*

Provenance The sitter's son John Newbury Bagley. His daughter Frances Bagley Wallace. Mrs. James K. Watkins. Acquired in 1977.

References Shaw 1936, 88–91. *BDIA* 1978, 269, 302, ill. Gerdts 1990, 2:240.

52
Portrait of Mr. William H. Brearley, 1884

Oil on preprimed canvas

71.1 × 58.4 cm (28 × 23 in.)

Gift of Mrs. William H. Brearley (96.1)

WILLIAM HENRY BREARLEY (1846–1909) served as manager of the advertising department of the *Detroit Evening News* from 1873, the year it was founded, to 1887, when he purchased the *Detroit Journal,* its rival. Brearley was the chairman of the executive committee for the Detroit Art Loan Exhibition of 1883 and led the fund-raising efforts for the Detroit Museum of Art. He later served as a trustee of the museum. Brearley was author of *Recollections of the East Tennessee*

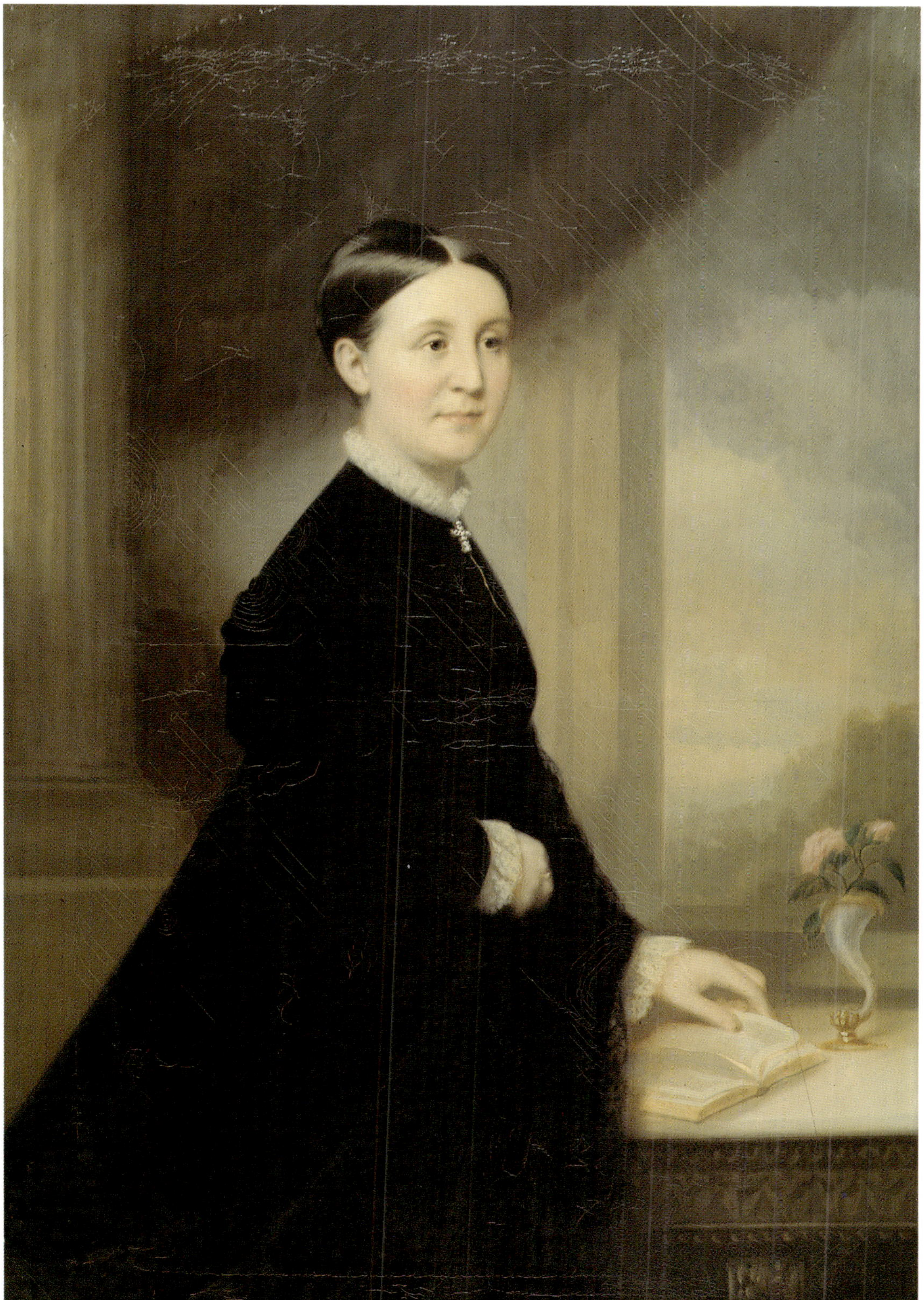

Mrs. John J. Bagley

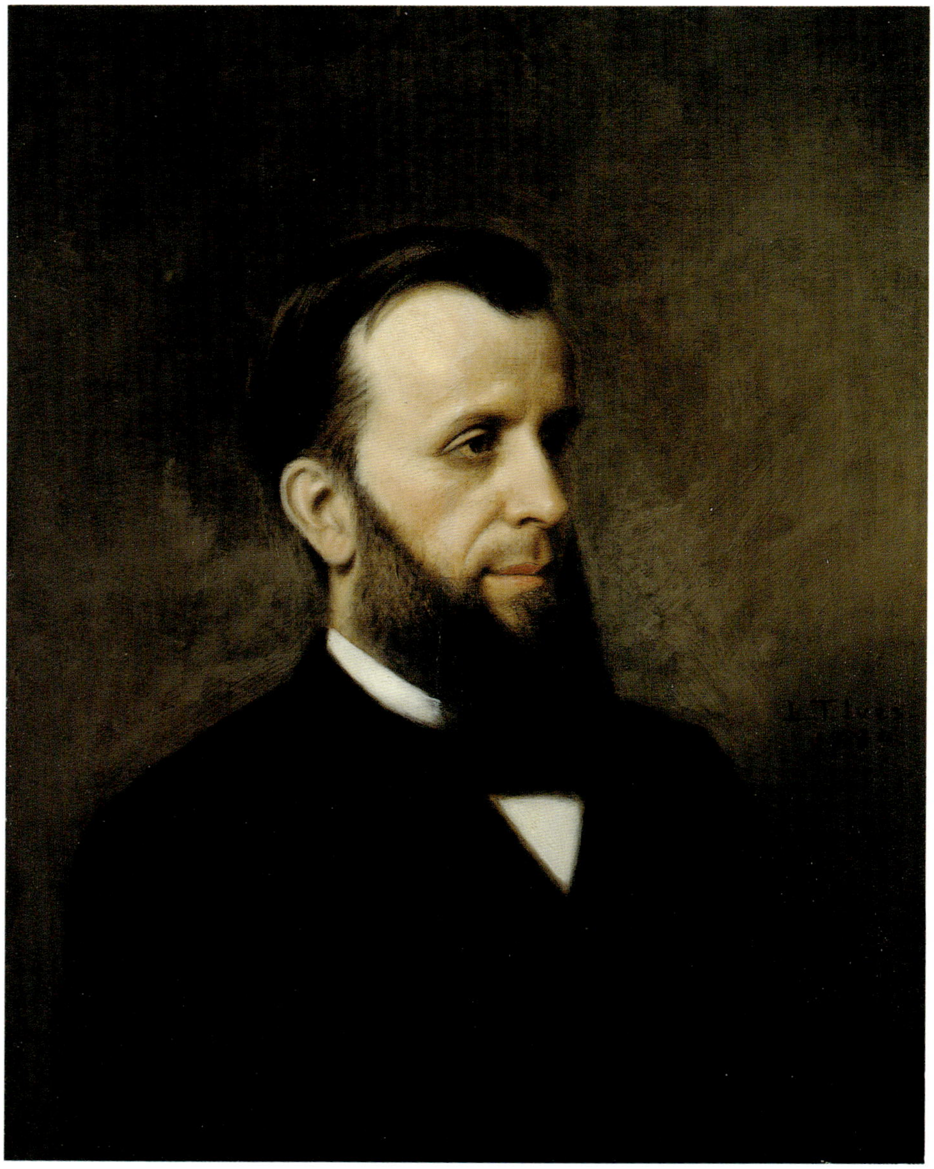

Campaign (1871), *Wanted, a Copyist* (1894), and *Leading Events of the American Revolution* (1895). He moved to New York in 1899 to serve as the corresponding secretary of the New York City Baptist Mission Society.

Ives painted Brearley's portrait at the height of the fund-raising efforts for the new museum. The head-and-shoulders portrait shows Brearley in a black coat and tie, with dark brown hair and a dark brown beard, seated in front of a dark green background and turned to the right. The portrait was probably based on a photograph: very precisely drawn lines can be seen under the paint along the lower edge of the left eye, along the top of the upper lip, along the outline of the nose, and along the line of the beard next to his cheek.

E. G. M.

Inscription At center right edge, *L. T. Ives. 1884*

Provenance By descent to the sitter's wife. Acquired in 1896.

Exhibition Detroit 1938.

References Detroit 1907a, 15, no. 92. Detroit 1910, 24, no. 136. Pattison 1911, 68–69. C. Burroughs 1937, 39–44. *BDIA* 1938, 55. *Who Was Who in America* 1966, 133.

William H. Brearley

[Jonathan] Eastman Johnson

1824 Lovell, Maine–New York 1906

Born the third of eight children to Philip C. Johnson and Mary Chandler Johnson, Eastman Johnson and his family lived in Fryeburg, Maine, and then Augusta, where his father held positions in the state government. In his late teens (1839–44), Johnson worked in an Augusta dry-goods store and a Boston lithography shop and began sketching portraits. When Johnson's father moved to Washington, D.C., young Johnson joined the family and established himself drawing notable Americans, such as John Quincy Adams and Dolley Madison. In 1846 he returned to the Boston area, where he drew portraits of Henry Wadsworth Longfellow and his circle.

Eager to advance in oil painting, Johnson sailed for Europe in 1849 for further training. He spent two years in Düsseldorf, then a leading art center, where he studied with Emanuel Leutze. In the late summer of 1851 Johnson moved to The Hague and became a professional portrait painter. However, he felt the need for additional training in figure and genre painting and, in August 1855, moved to Paris to study with Thomas Couture. This sojourn was cut short by news of Johnson's mother's death, and in October 1855 he returned to the States.

For the next three years (1855–58) he painted in the Washington, D.C., area; in Superior, Wisconsin, where he sketched the local Ojibwa; and in Cincinnati, where he executed portrait commissions. In April 1858 he settled into a studio in the University Building in New York. Although he had submitted paintings to the American Art-Union as early as 1849 and to the National Academy of Design beginning in 1856, his first real success came when his *Negro Life at the South* (1859; New-York Historical Society) received rave reviews at the academy's 1859 annual exhibition. Elected an associate of the academy that year, Johnson became a full academician the following year.

During the 1860s and 1870s Johnson was the leading genre painter in New York and consistently received praise both for his subjects of American life and for his skillful style of painting. During the Civil War he followed the Union troops in search of interesting subjects and painted several pictures sympathetic to the newly freed slaves, such as *The Freedom Ride* (1863; Brooklyn Museum). During the 1860s he was active in the National Academy of Design and the Artists' Fund Society and also participated in organizations that brought together artists and their patrons, such as the Century Club and the Union League Club; he was a founding trustee of the Metropolitan Museum of Art.

Johnson married Elizabeth Buckley in 1869, and, beginning in 1870, the couple with their daughter, Ethel, began summering in Nantucket, off the Massachusetts coast. On Nantucket Johnson painted typically "American" rural subjects, such as cornhusking bees and cranberry harvests.

By 1881 Johnson was painting fewer genre scenes, as he turned his energies to portrait commissions. For the next twenty years he painted business and political men such as John D. Rockefeller, Jay Gould, William H. Vanderbilt, and presidents Grover Cleveland and Benjamin Harrison. When Johnson died in his New York home in 1906, he was mourned by both the older artists and the younger men who felt he held views sympathetic to their generation.

P. H.

Bibliography Walton 1906. Brooklyn 1940. Hills 1972. Hills 1977. San Diego et al. 1990.

53
Worthington Whittredge, 1854

Oil on canvas
94 × 66.7 cm (37 × 26¼ in.)
Founders Society Purchase, Dexter M. Ferry, Jr., Fund (60.83)

Eastman Johnson and the artist Worthington Whittredge (q.v.) both arrived in Düsseldorf in 1849 and became fast friends. The magnetic personality of the German-American artist Emanuel Leutze inspired them, and they worked together in Leutze's Düsseldorf studio. Whittredge posed as Washington and as the steersman in Leutze's famous *George Washington Crossing the Delaware* (1851; Metropolitan Museum of Art, New York), while Johnson made a small oil copy of the painting for the engraver.

Whittredge stayed in Düsseldorf to study landscape painting until 1857, when he moved to Rome. Johnson, however, became less than satisfied with the dry method of the Düsseldorf style. After a trip to Holland and to London in the summer of 1851 to see the International Exposition, Johnson decided to move to The Hague, where he remained until mid-1855. During this time he made copies after Rembrandt and Van Dyck, painted genre pictures of cardplayers and Savoyard boys, and took on portrait commissions. Through the American ambassador, August Belmont, Johnson acquired a clientele of distinguished Americans and Europeans. According to the biography that William Walton wrote shortly after the artist's death, Johnson was offered the position of court painter, but by then he had decided to leave The Hague for Paris (Walton 1906, 268).

Johnson must have painted Whittredge on a return visit to Düsseldorf in 1854. The handsome oil portrait exhibits Johnson's mastery of the medium. The figure of the bearded Whittredge emerges from a dark brown background, and the strong chiaroscuro dramatizes the intelligent visage of a self-assured professional artist.

Other notable portraits of Whittredge exist. Johnson also made a smaller painting (oil on board, 11 × 8 in.; unlocated) that represents the head and shoulders of Whittredge looking to the right. While the smaller painting is not dated, it was

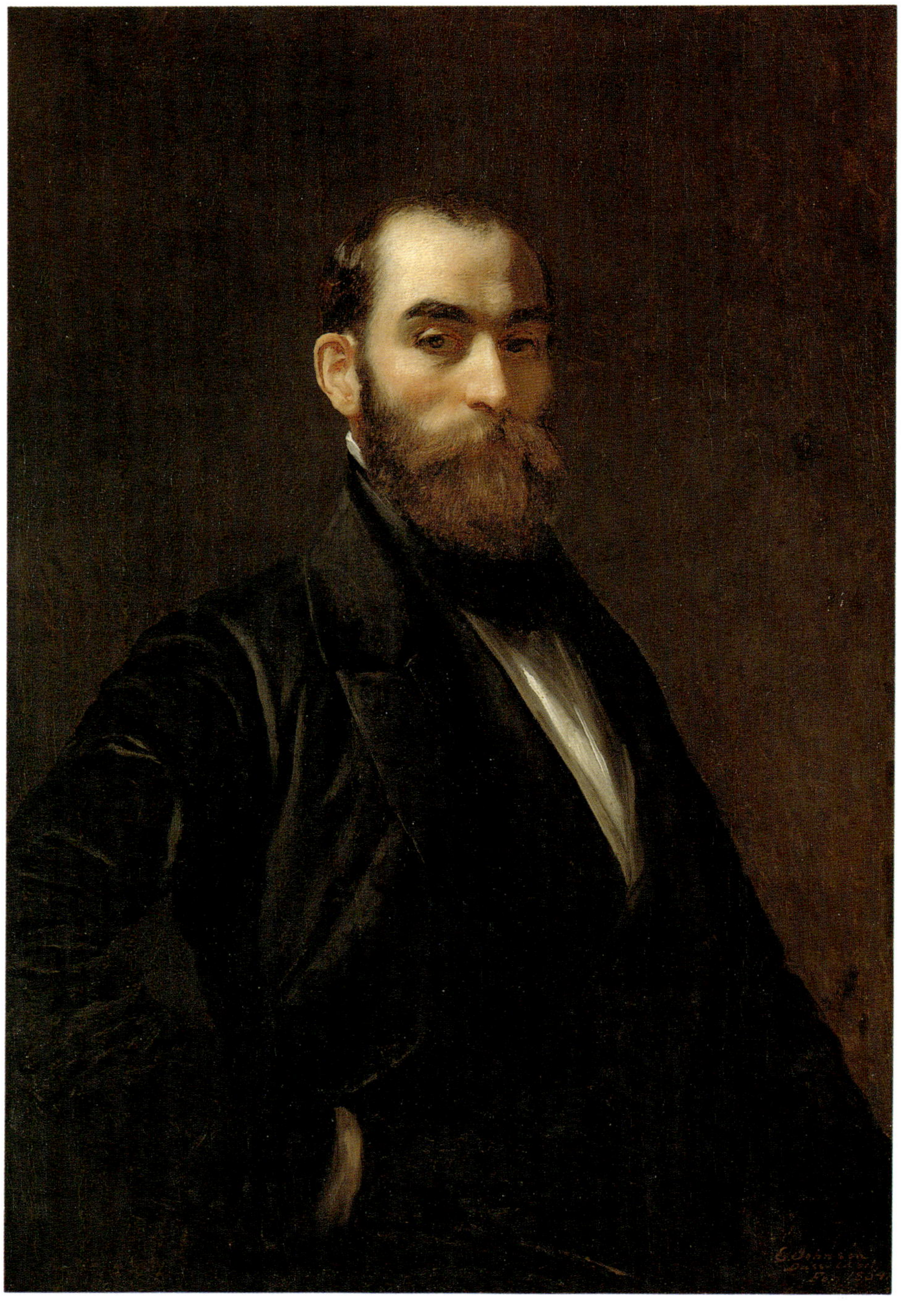

Worthington Whittredge

probably done at the same time as Detroit's larger version, since Johnson often made smaller, more sketchy oil studies in preparation for larger portraits. Two years later, in Düsseldorf in 1856, Leutze painted a three-quarter view of Whittredge dramatically dressed as a Spanish cavalier (Metropolitan Museum of Art, New York), and he made two more portraits in the 1860s (National Academy of Design, New York; and private collection).

P. H.

Inscription At lower right, *E. Johnson / Dusseldorf / 1854*

Provenance The sitter. His daughter. Wildenstein & Co., New York, 1959. Acquired in 1960.

Exhibitions New York et al. 1972, no. 13. Grand Rapids 1977, no. 57.

References Hills 1972, 17, ill. 20. Hills 1977, 43, fig. 27, 203.

54

Self-Portrait, ca. 1860–63

Oil on canvas

46.4 × 31.1 cm (18¼ × 12¼ in.)

Gift of Dexter M. Ferry, Jr. (40.34)

Eastman Johnson painted about two dozen self-portraits during his long career. Some, like the Detroit study, are small in scale, while others are life-size full-figure renderings. Some of them show Johnson costumed and holding props, and others focus on the head alone.

Johnson probably did this self-portrait with gloves sometime between 1860 and 1863. The face in the painting most clearly resembles in age the self-portrait that he presented to the National Academy of Design when he was elected to membership in 1859 and the self-portrait, dated 1863, belonging to the Art Institute of Chicago. Like the portrait of his friend Worthington Whittredge (cat. no. 53), the painting is dramatically

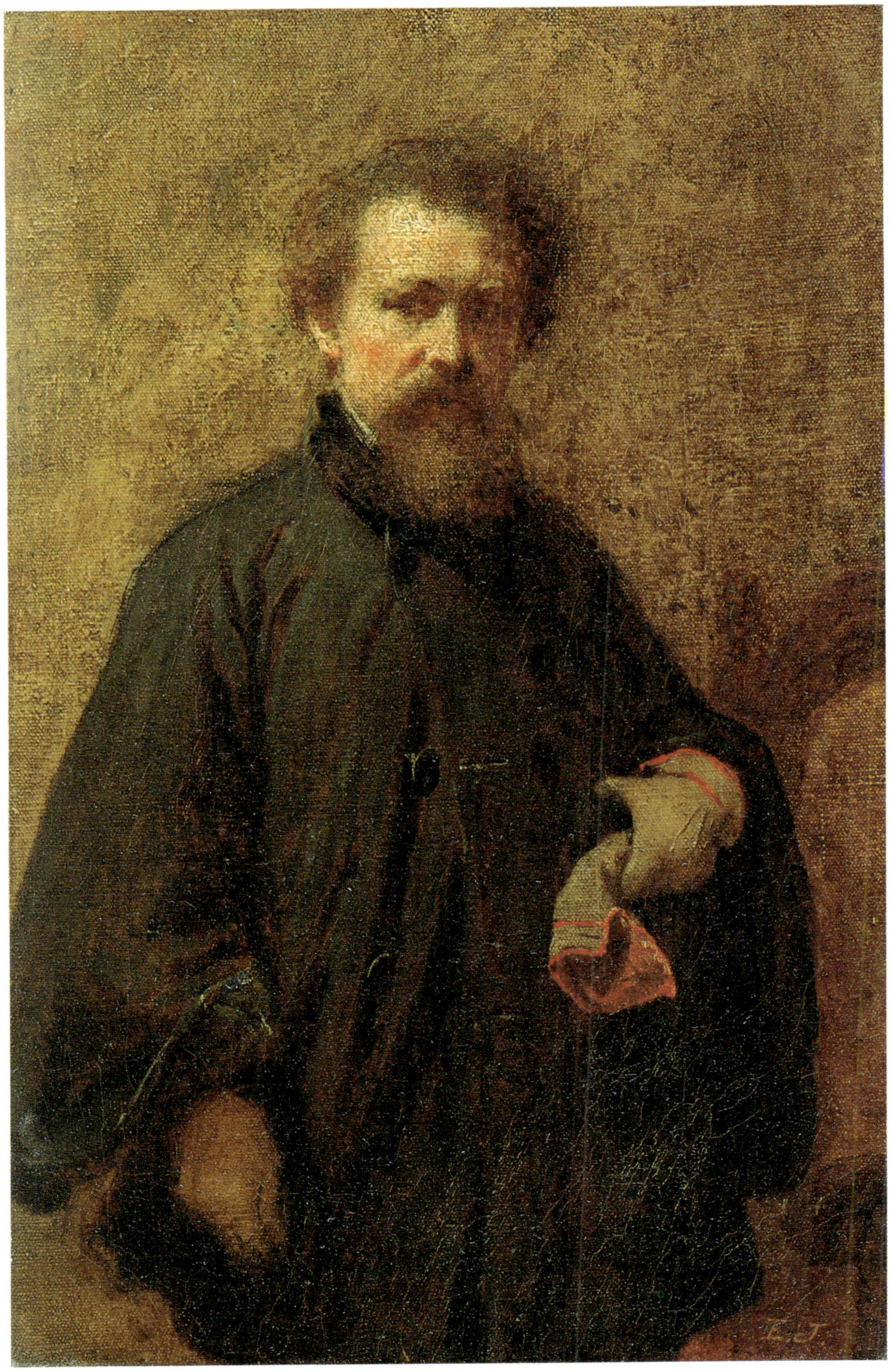

lit with the face looming out of dark shadows. The Chicago self-portrait shows Johnson as an artist, in his studio with his palette hanging on the wall, and as a bon vivant, dressed in a smoking jacket, slowly uncorking a bottle of champagne.

Johnson applies the paint to the surface of the canvas in the Detroit self-portrait with deft touches. Characteristic of many of Johnson's paintings, particularly the ones not shown at the major exhibitions, the background is painted somewhat thinly with the red-brown ground serving as the middle tone for the parts of the forms situated midway between the highlights and the deepest shadows. The result, much like the effects of Thomas Couture, was to merge the face and figure with the surface of the painting. Thus the face seems to emerge from the fabric of the canvas itself, and from a distance it seems almost Rembrandtesque. The gray-green leather gloves with red trim give a dash of color to this concentrated and exquisite study of the artist.

P. H.

Inscription At lower right, *E. J.*

Provenance Purchased from John Hanna, Inc., Detroit. Acquired in 1940.

Reference C. Burroughs 1940, 3–5, ill.

Self-Portrait

55

In the Fields, ca. 1878–80

Oil on board

45.1 × 69.9 cm (17¾ × 27½ in.)

Founders Society Purchase, Dexter M. Ferry, Jr., Fund (38.1)

FROM THE MID- TO THE LATE 1870S Eastman Johnson made pencil sketches and oil studies of cranberry pickers on Nantucket. It was a typically American and rural subject that appealed both to Johnson and to those patrons who preferred subjects that would take them away from the industrial and urban realities of the post–Civil War years. His biographer William Walton understood the subject's appeal only too well when he praised Johnson's ability to represent the pleasing aspects of rural life:

> His conception of the rendering of "the life of the poor," of "the tillers of the soil"... preaches no ugly gospel of discontent, as does so much of the contemporary French and Flemish art of this genre; his Nantucket neighbors know nothing of the "protestation douloureuse de la race asservie à la glèbe"; there is no "cri de la terre" arising from his cranberry marshes or his hay-stuffed barns. The happy combination of right feeling and sound technique is manifest in all the details. (Walton 1906, 270–271)

Although Johnson did sketches of pickers bent over cranberry bogs as early as 1875, most of the studies were probably done in 1878 and 1879. That year Johnson arrived in Nantucket late in the summer, and he wrote to his friend Jervis McEntee on October 26, 1879: "I have been industrious enough since here. I was taken with my cranberry fit as soon as I arrived... and I have done nothing else" (San Diego et al. 1990, 39). That year he stayed in Nantucket until mid-December to "get through with things begun," but he enjoyed the quiet and experienced "something very peaceful and satisfactory in our life here" (San Diego et al. 1990, 66).

The majority of the studies fall into two groups: those associated with the most finished version, *The Cranberry Harvest* (1880; Timken Art Gallery, San Diego), and those with the unfinished version, *Cranberry Pickers* (ca. 1878–79; Yale University Art Gallery, New Haven, Conn.). The Detroit painting relates to the Timken group, for it contains a woman standing taller than the surrounding pickers. This motif characterizes at least three other studies (Arizona State University, Tempe; Manoogian Collection, Detroit; private collection). That same motif of the standing woman looking into the distance over the heads and bent backs of her companions had earlier defined the composition of Jules Breton's popular painting *The Weeders (Les Sarcleuses)* (1860; Joslyn Art Museum, Omaha), exhibited at the Paris Exposition Universelle in 1867. Another version was owned by the Cincinnati collector Henry Probasco in 1868. We have no firm evidence that Johnson knew either of these works, but he was familiar with the popular French painter, since earlier, about 1865, he had made a copy (Santa Barbara Museum of Art) after Breton's *Village Perambulator.*

The Detroit painting shares with many of Johnson's other studies of the 1870s its bright sunlit highlights flashing off the edges of the figures. While some scholars have identified such a focus on lighted contours as proto-impressionist, it is a technique that can be seen to have come from Thomas Couture, whose book *Méthode et entretiens d'atelier* (Methods and conversations of the studio) was published in 1867. Albert Boime has discussed the influence of Couture in France, but Couture's impact on America was equally strong. Couture advised painters to make a sketch of their initial impression, laying in the places of the lightest lights and the darkest darks:

> You must establish what I call "dominants" for light and shade effects. Look carefully at your model, decide which is its brightest light, and situate the light in your drawing at the place it occupies in real life. Having made this your dominant, you will of course make sure that all other lights are subordinate to it. The same applies to shadow: find your strongest and deepest black and use it as a guide or tuning-fork to establish the values of your other shadows and half-tones. (quoted in Boime 1971, 28–29)

Couture was not the only established painter, however, who attempted through the placement of light and dark values to represent a lifelike realism. John Singer Sargent, a student of the fashionable French painter Carolus-Duran, also emphasized the strong lights skipping along the edges of forms in his smaller version of *The Oyster Gatherers at Cancale* (1878; Museum of Fine Arts, Boston), shown at the inaugural 1878 exhibition of the Society of American Artists, which Johnson would have seen.

But Johnson's *In the Fields* is sketchier than Sargent's painting, and he would never exhibit his studies as finished works. They were intended as preliminary aids to the final version. The sketch/finish debates raged through most of the nineteenth century, but as Boime observed: "Until deep into the nineteenth century... this [sketch/finish] conflict was controlled by confining original and spontaneous works to the privacy of the atelier, and placing only the polished painting on exhibition" (Boime 1971, 88). Johnson kept his sketches in his studio until his death, and, as one obituary noted, "he liked to keep his sketches, and knew they were better" (Hills 1977, 133). In fact, *In the Fields* was one such study that hung on his studio wall, documented in a photograph reproduced in Edgar French's tribute to Johnson, published in *World's Work* in 1906.

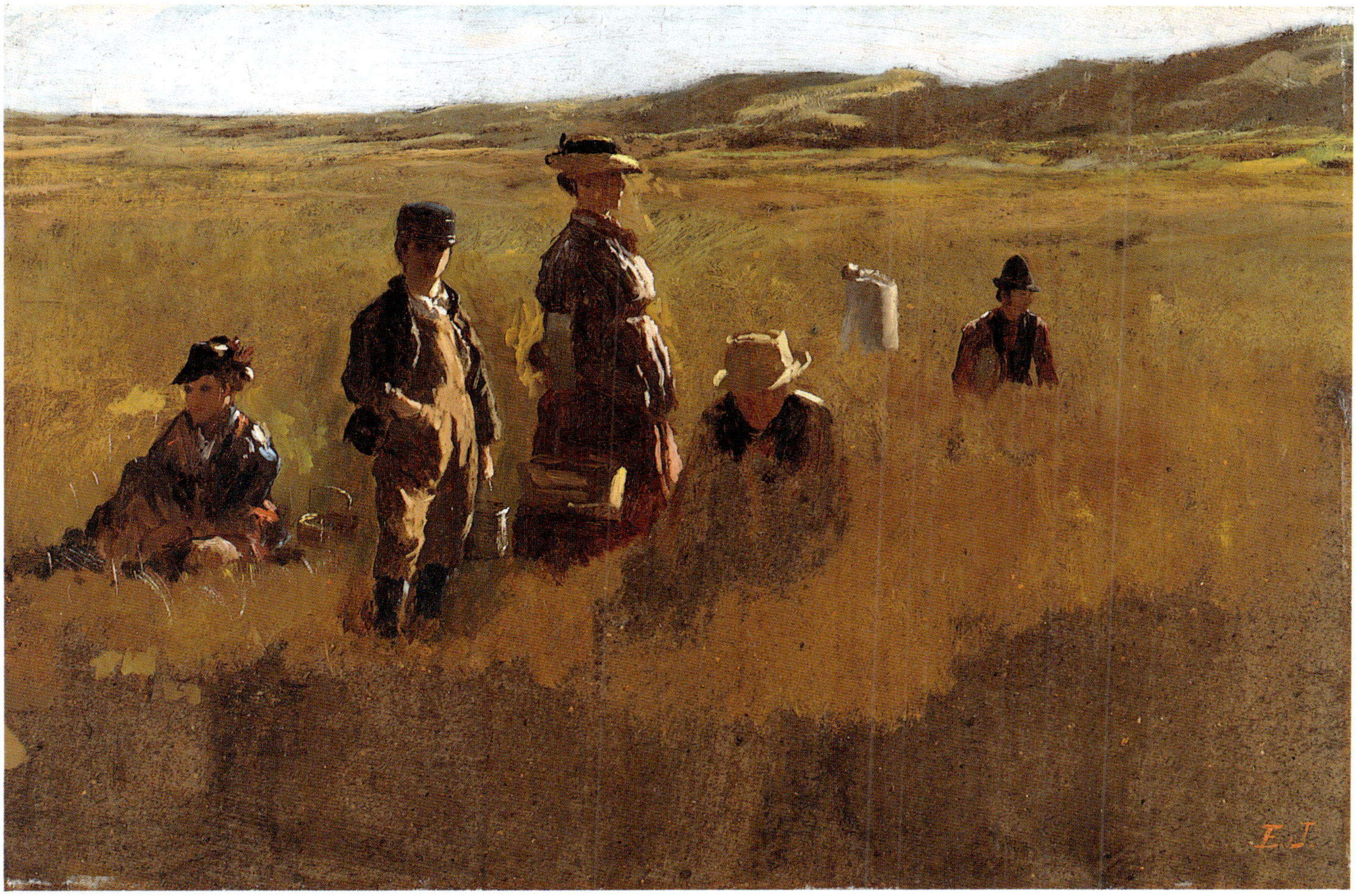

In the Fields

The initials at the lower left may have been done by another hand. The conservator Sheldon Keck, at the time of the Eastman Johnson retrospective at the Brooklyn Museum in 1940, subjected the *E. J.* initials on another cranberry-subject painting *(Woman on the Hill,* Brooklyn Museum) to a technical examination. He also examined other Johnson paintings with similar initials. He concluded that although the paintings were genuine, many of the initials were added at a later date, perhaps by Johnson's widow (Keck 1942, 79).

P. H.

Inscription At lower right, *E. J.*

Provenance Purchased from Frederic Frazier, Inc., New York. Acquired in 1938.

Exhibitions Brooklyn 1940, no. 64. Milwaukee 1960, no. 10. Hamilton 1961, no. 34. New York 1964, no. 18. New York 1970, no. 145. New York et al. 1972, no. 87. Buffalo et al. 1976. Moscow et al. 1987. San Diego et al. 1990, no. 13.

References *BDIA* 1938, 2. Crosby 1944, no. 6. Hills 1972, 99. Williams 1973, 149, fig. 133. Hills 1977, 241, fig. 105.

56
Catherine Butler Dusenberry (Mrs. Allan) Shelden, 1885

Oil on canvas

92.4 × 78.1 cm (36⅜ × 30¾ in.)

Bequest of Mrs. Allan Shelden III (1985.27)

By the mid-1880s Eastman Johnson was almost exclusively engaged in painting portraits. And while he was considered a painter of men, he also did handsome portraits of women, such as Mrs. Allan Shelden.

Mrs. Shelden, née Catherine Butler Dusenberry, married Allan Shelden in 1859 in New York State. Her son, Henry D. Shelden, was governor of Michigan (1885–1887) when she sat for her portrait. It is not clear where Johnson painted her. He is not known to have traveled to other cities to execute his commissions, although he sometimes brought unfinished portraits with him to Nantucket to complete. Hence, it was probably completed in his New York home and studio at 65 West 55th Street. Another version, almost identical in size and pose but sketchier in execution and not dated, is owned by the Philadelphia Museum of Art. The Philadelphia picture was included in the first large retrospective of Johnson's work held at the Brooklyn Museum in 1940.

Johnson frequently did two versions of portraits. One would be a study with a delicate but sketchy treatment of the features and clothing, and with the barest indication of setting. The background would often consist of a thin layer of red-brown (perhaps burnt sienna) color. These rarely receive Johnson's full signature, although often the initials *E. J.* are inscribed at the lower edge (see cat. no. 55 regarding the question of authenticity of the initials). Many such sketches remained in Johnson's possession. For the finished portraits—and a good example is Detroit's portrait of Catherine Dusenberry Shelden—Johnson was careful to exercise a delicate chiaroscuro on the face and to delineate the features and hands. Typically, such finished versions are signed *E. Johnson* followed by the date.

Detroit's version of *Catherine Butler Dusenberry (Mrs. Allan) Shelden* shows Johnson at his best as a portrait painter. He paints with a dry brush and scumbles the paint to give an effect of richness; it was a technique practiced as well by the French painter Thomas Couture. Johnson declined to introduce wet-into-wet painting, the *a la prima,* bravura style of such celebrity portraitists as John Singer Sargent. Johnson and his patrons seemed to prefer his more sober and conservative renderings, which are not without liveliness. The highlights on the tacks of the green upholstered armrests give additional sparkle to the painting and bracket the figure within a three-dimensional space. Mrs. Shelden's brown velvet dress with the ecru lace collar introduces an element of femininity that sets off her face, yet the calm composure of her intertwined fingers and her eyes looking off to her right express a woman of intelligence. It is a mark of the family's satisfaction with the portrait that it remained in the Shelden family until given to the museum in 1985.

P. H.

Inscription At lower left, *E. Johnson / 1885*

Provenance Henry D. Shelden, Sr. Allan Shelden III. Mrs. Allan Shelden III, Detroit. Acquired by bequest in 1985.

Reference Brooklyn 1940, 72, no. 261.

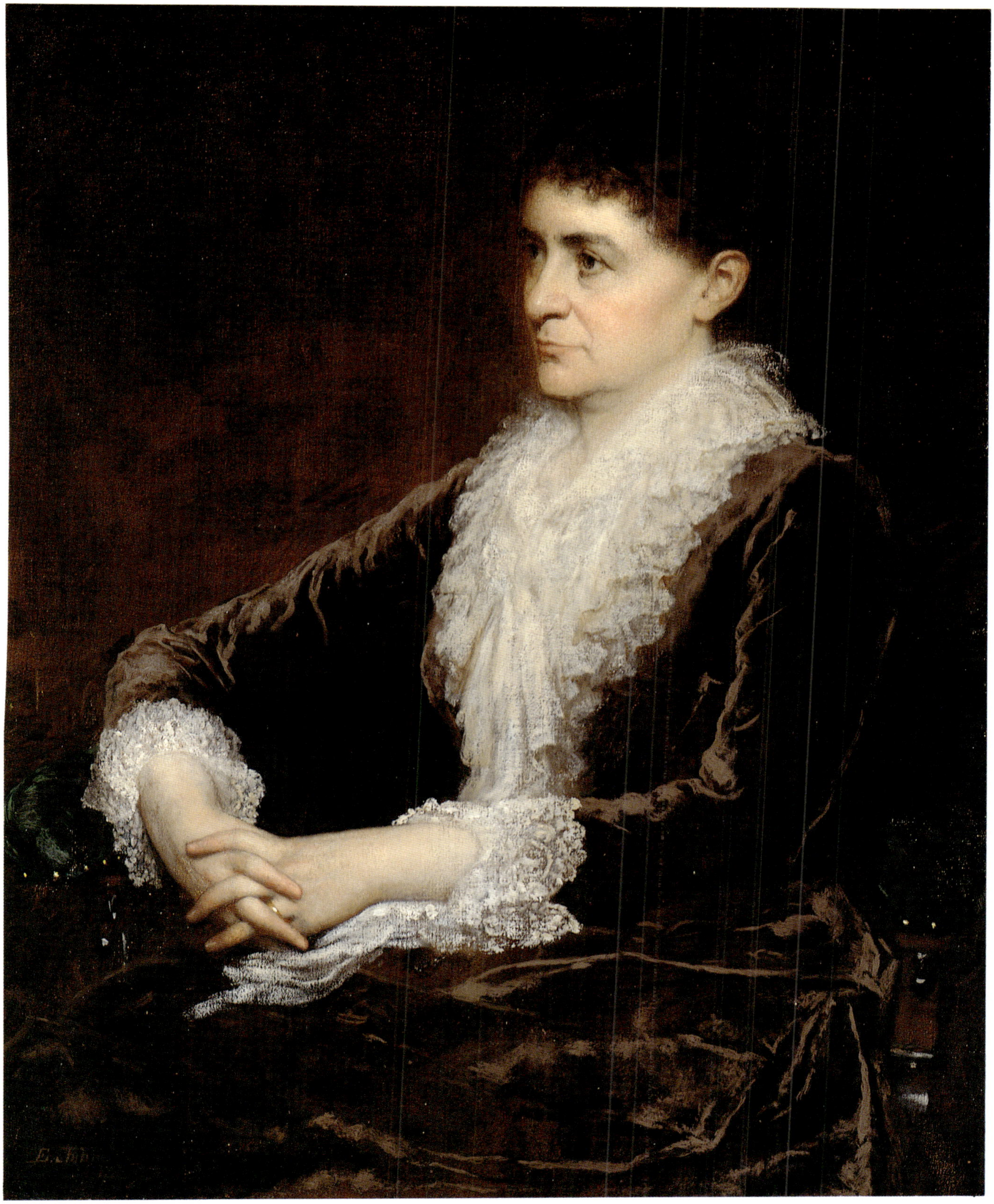

Mrs. Allan Shelden

John Frederick Kensett

1816 Cheshire, Connecticut–New York 1872

The historical record seems to document the incredible fact that during his lifetime John F. Kensett had no enemies or serious detractors. The art critic Henry T. Tuckerman could not bring himself to be critical: "Of all our artists, he has the most thoroughly amiable disposition, is wholly superior to envy, and pursues his vocation in . . . a spirit of love and kindliness." What is more, the artist managed to instill such saintliness into his art: "The calm sweetness of Kensett's best efforts, the conscientiousness with which he preserves local diversities—the evenness of manner, the patience in detail, the harmonious tone—all are traceable to the artist's feeling and innate disposition, as well as to his skill" (Tuckerman 1867, 510). Kensett was as prolific and rich as he was popular, widely recognized as one of the leading American artists at midcentury, and he turned his repute to good account, devoting considerable resources to charitable art causes. To contemporaries he represented all that was laudable in the highly moralistic native mode of landscape painting that grew from the stock of Thomas Cole. He even died the perfect gentleman, having contracted pneumonia while trying to retrieve the body of Mrs. Vincent Colyer, the wife of an artist friend, who had fallen from her carriage and drowned in Long Island Sound. After Kensett's untimely death, however, critical voices sounded out that earlier had been more respectful; only then was Kensett identified as a central figure in the movement that was pejoratively tagged in the later 1870s the "Hudson River school."

Kensett trained as an engraver with his father, Thomas, an emigrant from Hampton Court near London, and his uncle, Alfred Daggett, grandson of the president of Yale College. He worked professionally in New Haven, New York, and Albany before turning to landscape painting. In 1840 he traveled to Europe with the artists John W. Casilear, Asher B. Durand, and Thomas P. Rossiter on a tour that lasted, for him, seven years. He was much involved with the American art community in Europe, sharing a studio in Paris with Benjamin Champney and in Rome with Thomas Hicks, but by his own admission his formative experience came in 1843–45 while on his own in England, where he went to settle his grandmother's estate. He was impressed by English landscape painting, especially the work of Henry J. Boddington, and by the scenery around Windsor and Burnham (Tuckerman 1867, 510). Travels in Germany and Switzerland and extensive sojourns in Italy completed his education.

When Kensett returned to New York in 1847 he was already well known by the landscapes he had sent from abroad to the American Art-Union, so he entered readily into art society. He was named associate of the National Academy of Design in 1848 and academician the following year; before long he was a powerful figure in the academy, serving on both the Governing Council and the Committee on Arrangements, as well as spearheading the fund-raising drive for the new building, which opened in 1865. The rest of his résumé was equally impressive, as he moved lithely through the thickets of art politics. He was a member of the exclusive Century Association (elected 1849) and Sketch Club (1850), a founder in 1857 of the charitable Artists' Fund Society and its president from the later 1860s to his death, and one of the three members of the United States Capitol Art Commission appointed by President James Buchanan in 1859 to advise about the ornamentation program of the Capitol. In 1864 he was chairman of the Art Committee of the Metropolitan Fair, which raised money for the United States Sanitary Commission, forerunner of the Red Cross. He was a founding trustee of the Metropolitan Museum of Art in 1870 and served on the Executive Committee until his death.

Kensett devoted the same kind of energy to making his art. His seasonal sketching tours took him again to Europe (in 1856, 1861, possibly 1865, and 1867) and several times to the midwestern and western United States (in 1851, 1854, 1857, 1868, and 1870), but he was identified largely with the Northeast, with the Berkshires, the Adirondacks, the Green and White mountains, and the coast, especially Beverly, Massachusetts, and Newport, Rhode Island. Kensett understood how to be successful and painted sites popular among tourists or meaningful to the rising class of urban entrepreneurs who owned vacation properties in the mountains or on the coast. His landscapes, if often intense in their way, are not energetic but soothing—consummate palliatives for an anxious clientele. At the core of Kensett's experience was an undergirding quietude and sanctity that both critics and patrons were eager to contemplate as beyond their grasp. "When you see his pictures you see him," wrote one commentator. "And they are of such noble and permanent character and charm because they are so wholly sincere" (*Harper's Weekly* 1867, 433).
W. T. O.

Bibliography New York 1968. Worcester et al. 1985.

57
The Walking Tour, ca. 1847–51

Oil on canvas
35.6 × 50.8 cm (14 × 20 in.)
Gift of Miss Euphemia Holden in memory of her mother, Mrs. E. G. Holden (35.47)

The Walking Tour came to Detroit as the work of an unknown artist, but in 1942 the Institute director, E. P. Richardson, attributed it to Kensett. The attribution has held on all accounts. Kensett worked with the long horizontal format, the spare composition of a few large elements, and the subject matter of stream, falls, and unremarkable distant

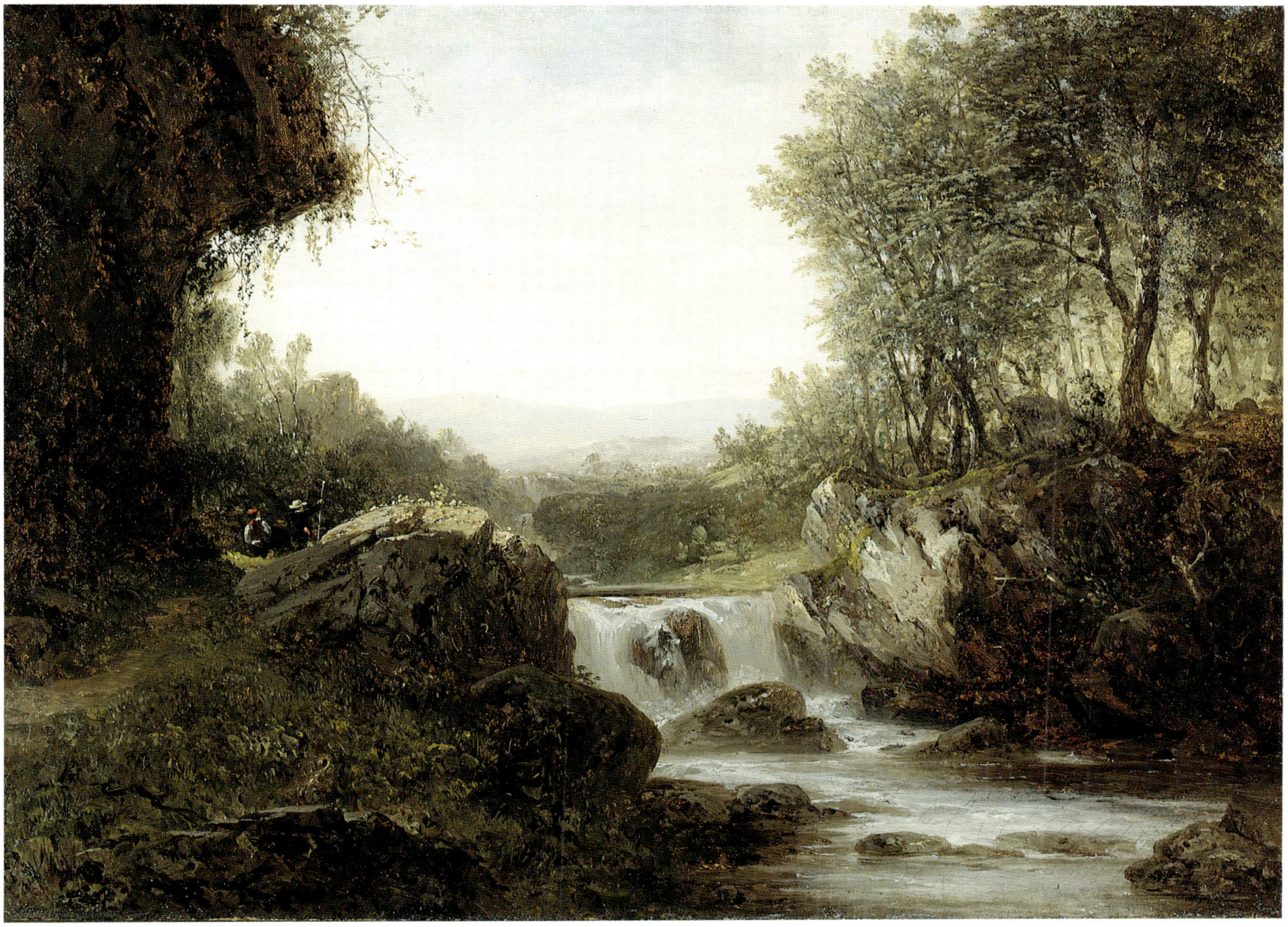

The Walking Tour

hills. He used walking figures of this type, some paired, backs toward the viewer, wearing clothes of yellow, white, and particularly red that enliven the color scheme. The palette is wholly characteristic of his work, low-keyed, harmonious, and both subtle and verging on monotony in its tonal variations. In many enclosed scenes such as this, Kensett controlled the lighting in bands, leaving the foreground dark, illuminating elements of interest in the middle ground (the figures, falls, flank of rock, foliage) with a raking streak of light set off by a darkened band beyond, and casting the upper register of hills and sky in a warm, atmospheric glow. His handling of paint ranged within individual canvases from broad and seemingly sketchy—even gestural—to layered and scumbled, to excessively tight in the rendering of details under focus, such as certain leaves and surfaces of rocks. The resulting paint film is richly and variously textured.

If there is no question that Kensett painted *The Walking Tour*, there is question as to when he painted it, and there is no evidence of how he entitled it. While certain principles of style and technique prevailed throughout his career, Kensett experimented considerably in the 1840s and 1850s before resolving a consistent, mature mode of expression in the 1860s, and he shifted again in the astonishing series of paintings from the three months before his death, the "Last Summer's Work" that his brother gave to the Metropolitan Museum of Art in 1874. Following his second trip to Europe and the example of Durand, in the later 1850s Kensett developed more expansive lighting and atmospheric effects and more open, geometric, or abstracted compositions in an apparent effort to clarify the harmony and equilibrium of nature, its divine design. The expression of such harmony, however, had consistently been his primary purpose; as early as 1844 he had avowed his conviction in "that beautiful harmony in which God has created the universe" (Worcester et al. 1985, 63). *The Walking Tour* pertains to that earlier context.

As it relates to the classical landscape tradition and the British picturesque aesthetic, the Detroit painting dates from early in Kensett's career, when he aimed to establish a reputation within the bounds of convention. It compares closely with the *View from Richmond Hill* (private collection), a landscape in the mode of Constable that Kensett completed while in England between 1843 and 1845 (Worcester et al. 1985, 52–53, pl. 1). The two paintings are almost exactly the same size (the size, about 14 by 20 inches, is distinctive), are similarly composed, depict similar distant topography, depend on similar figures to carry the narrative, and evince similar handling. The general aspect of the painting recalls the British sources of Kensett's vision: the tour literature of the Reverend William Gilpin from the late eighteenth and early nineteenth centuries; the early work of Turner and Constable; and other expressions of the picturesque, which associated touring the countryside with excitement, discovery, and nationalism through the visual properties of asymmetry, variety, and contrast. Yet, underlying the painting's composition is Kensett's understanding of the classical manner of Claude Lorrain, whose works he studied closely on his first European tour and whose influence found immediate expression in *The Shrine—A Scene in Italy* (1847; Worcester et al. 1985, 60, pl. 2).

The Detroit painting is not from Kensett's first European stay, but from the early years of his highly acclaimed career in New York. It is so like the 1851 landscape *A Holiday in the Country* (Worcester et al. 1985, ill. 64) as to be contemporaneous. Perhaps most telling among the many intersections between the two paintings are the subject matter, the location and attitudes of the figures, the illumination of the open grove of trees at the right, and the element at the left of the overhanging rock formation and its pendent vegetation silhouetted against the sky. There are parallels as well between the directional procession in *A Holiday in the Country* and the lively juxtaposition in *The Walking Tour* of the advancing waterfall and the receding figures, who descend the rise at the left to cross the log over the stream and ascend into the woods at the right and then to the village at the precise center of the canvas. The vitality of handling, relative wildness of the scene, and celebratory mood of the Detroit painting further suggest that Kensett created the landscape in the Northeast after his return from Europe in 1847 and before he abandoned the dependence on large framing devices in the horizontal format in the early 1850s.

Although Kensett's much-discussed late style differed from his early mode of expression, his personality informed both, so that what critics had to say about his mature works finds parallels in the praise of his first landscapes exhibited in New York. In 1848 Kensett was described as surpassing even Durand for the curious reason that his pictures savor less of mannerism and the conventionalities of art, and more of the unstudied freedom and largeness of nature (Worcester et al. 1985, 61). Similarly, in 1880 the critic Samuel G. W. Benjamin wrote that "we find very little evidence of foreign art in the style of Kensett.... His methods of rendering a bit of landscape were tender and harmonious, and entirely free from any attempt at sensationalism.... Mr. Kensett's art consisted in a certain inimitably winning tenderness of tone—a subtle poetic suggestiveness" (Benjamin 1880, 63–69). Tuckerman's estimate rings especially true: "Not great or extended in his range, not a colorist in the absolute sense of the term, but with an unfailing feeling for harmony, and of a judicious and liberal mind, noticeable for taste, Mr. Kensett has painted some of the most exquisite pictures that illustrate our art" (Tuckerman 1867, 512).

W. T. O.

Provenance Miss Euphemia Holden. Acquired in 1935.

Exhibition Oxford 1959.

Reference C. Burroughs 1936, 86–88, as by unknown artist.

58
Cascade in the Forest, 1852

Oil on canvas
74.9 × 66 cm (29½ × 26 in.)
Gift of Guy P. Turnbull (27.598)

In the 1840s and 1850s Kensett produced a large body of work based on the woodland interior. The paintings are medium size in a vertical format, and they characteristically represent a waterfall and pool hemmed in by highly figural rocks and dense, inward-leaning trees; a ravine carries the eye up to steep hillsides and finally release from the compressed space through a "window" to the sky. The formula provided one standard alternative to the horizontally formatted, laterally expansive or panoramic view and likely appealed to viewers through its intimacy, comfort of enclosure, and refreshing sense of coolness. Kensett painted a profitable series in this mode depicting Bash Bish Falls in South Egremont, Massachusetts. *Cascade in the Forest* belongs to the genre but was probably based on sketches made in the White Mountains of New Hampshire.

Kensett discovered for himself the White Mountains in 1849, while on a sketching tour with John W. Casilear. The next year he joined Casilear and Benjamin Champney for the summer at North Conway. They stayed at Thompson's Tavern (later known as the Kearsarge House), a gathering place for artists and one of the ever-increasing number of inns catering to the tourist trade that expanded along with the railroad and the publication of guidebooks (Durham et al. 1980, 44). Kensett's *White Mountains—Mt. Washington*, painted in 1851 (Wellesley College Museum, Wellesley, Mass.), was hugely successful as a testimonial to the region: it was steeped in Indian lore, and, with its cultivated fields against a backdrop of towering peaks, it documented the abrupt juncture between civilizable nature and its unredeemable, unusable counterpart, whose primary function was to be observed. Many more views issued from this and subsequent excursions in the White Mountains in 1851, 1852, 1855, and 1857, including, probably, *Cascade in the Forest*.

Apparently Kensett concocted this scene, as it does not represent one of the widely illustrated attractions, such as Crystal Falls or Glen Ellis Falls in Pinkham Notch. In its ruggedness and scale, however, the scene clearly pertains to the kind of cascade for which the White Mountains region was known, typified by the Lower Cascade in Crawford Notch. A favorite site for Kensett and Champney was such a place, Artist's Brook, a "beautiful little rocky stream" that "fascinated us with its sparkle, its amber color, and its gray rocks broken with patches of green moss." Another favorite was Thompson's Falls, a "wild" and "mysterious place," where the stream flowed through "dense woods . . . [and] chaotic masses of broken, ledgy rocks" (Champney 1900, 103–105). Although it does not depict Thompson's Falls, *Cascade in the Forest* pictures the same wildness, mystery, denseness, and chaos of broken masses, just as it piques the viewer's sense of discovery in happening upon a tranquil, uncharted gorge inhabited only by trout and deer. Kensett used similar devices—rugged topography, striking contrasts of light, careful description of selected trees and rocks, deer by the stream—in another composite painting based on summer sketches: *White Mountain Scene* (1853; The Huntington Library, San Marino, Calif.).

The 1850 summer tour resulted in exceptional work, as one reviewer noted after a visit to Kensett's New York studio the following winter. "If we may judge from the number and freshness of numerous studies from nature which meet the eye at every turn in his room, we venture to say that he has surpassed his brethren of the brush in quantity, variety and beauty, during the last sketching season": one painting finished from these sources was "a beautiful landscape in his usual felicitous style" (*Home Journal*, January 4, 1851). The following year, however, Kensett's entries at the annual exhibition of the National Academy evoked a mild rebuke: "The landscapes of this Exhibition . . . are not of the promising sort. They evince a sorrowful disrespect in the profession for the interests and beauties so peculiar to American scenery. It is evident that the greater part are composed without any reference to an existing object. . . . Even Mr. Kensett has fallen below his usual unerring aim" (*Home Journal*, May 15, 1852). His submissions included *Mountain Torrent, The Flume, Franconia Notch, a Study, Reminiscence of the White Mountains*, and *Early Autumn in the Franconia Mountains*. It was the last in particular that drew critical fire: one commentator singled out the painting as "excellent in its distance and careful in detail, but the foreground is weak and unnatural. There is no decision or distinction of parts: grass, and earth, and stones are melted and blended together with little regard to particular character" (*Knickerbocker* 1852).

The same may be said of *Cascade in the Forest,* which very well may have been the *Mountain Torrent* exhibited in 1852 and owned by the wife of Kensett's close friend Thomas P. Rossiter. A lack of distinction among various elements in the foreground and middle ground generates spatial incoherence, particularly evident along the lower right bank of the stream, and detail is sacrificed in the shaded areas. Kensett probably sought in these ways and through abrupt contrasts to impart a degree of mystery, sublimity, and visual difficulty appropriate to the wilderness scene he invites the viewer cautiously to enter, but such devices departed from what critics expected of him. His acclaimed virtues were clarity, simplicity, harmony, accessibility, and a study of the material facts of nature that was so intense as to become reverential or transcendental—revelatory, that is, of his understanding of the divine plan or inspiration of nature. The same virtues characterized the work of most second-generation artists of the Hudson River school, who, like Kensett, were followers of Durand. Perhaps in the case of his White Mountain paintings of the early 1850s Kensett was swayed by his relationship with Champney, whose indebtedness to French Barbizon artists resulted in broad handling and general effects.

If Kensett slipped in 1852, he was back in favor by 1854, when an observer noted that he "copies nature like a daguerreotype" (Clark 1854). Tuckerman, in 1867, emphasized "careful observation" as "the source of Kensett's eminent success.... It is rarely that, to use a common phrase, we can *locate* a landscape so confidently as Kensett's; the vein of rock, perhaps, identifies the scene." He concluded that "it is on this account that Kensett enjoyed an exceptional reputation among the extreme advocates of the Pre-Raphaelite school" (Tuckerman 1867, 511, 513–514). Yet Kensett's real accomplishment, according to the artist Daniel Huntington (q.v.), was to chart a middle course between "the certain wearisome detail of the antique school... [and] the dreamy indefiniteness of the new sentimentalism" (Huntington 1872, 5). *Cascade in the Forest,* which indeed is characterized by both a high degree of detail in many areas and suggestive, seemingly subjective handling in others, is an early example of the accommodation in technique that distinguished Kensett's mature work.
W. T. O.

Inscription At lower right, *JFK. 1852* (JF in monogram)

Provenance Guy P. Turnbull. Acquired in 1927.

Exhibitions Kalamazoo 1964. New York 1968, no. 17. Shreveport 1973, 45.

Reference *BDIA* 1928.

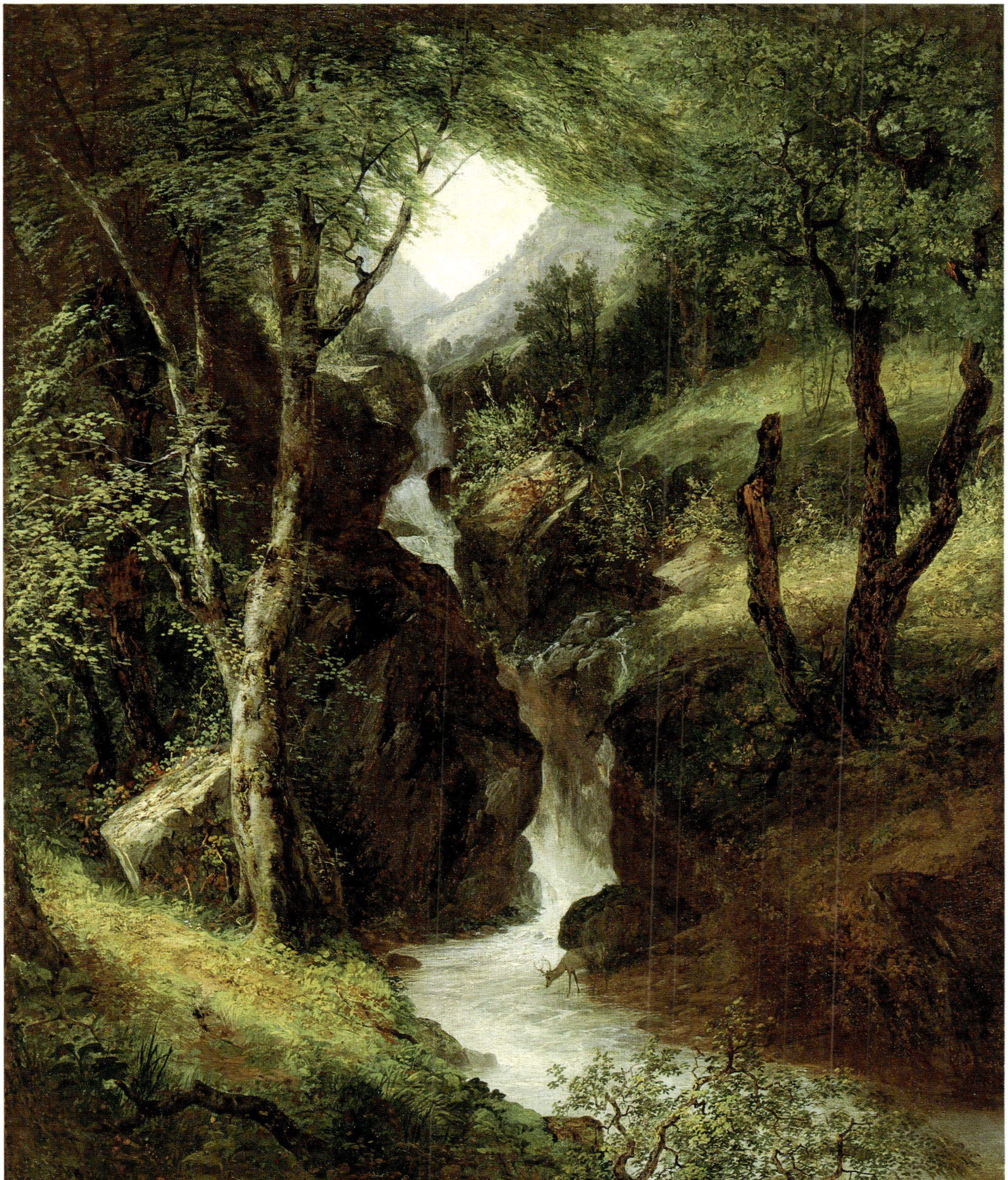

Cascade in the Forest

Daniel Ridgway Knight

1839 PHILADELPHIA–PARIS 1924

AN UPDATING OF THE DATA pertaining to the life and work of Daniel Ridgway Knight was recently attempted by Pamela Beecher, guest curator of an exhibition devoted to the paintings of Knight and his son Louis Aston Knight for the Herbert F. Johnson Museum of Art of Cornell University in 1989 (Ithaca 1989). Drawing on family scrapbooks and letters, the artist's descendant, Ridgway B. Knight, wrote an essay correcting some of the earlier errors of fact. Until then, information was still being pieced together from nineteenth- and early-twentieth-century sources, which was reliable in some details while contradictory in others.

Born in Philadelphia, Knight studied at the Pennsylvania Academy of the Fine Arts (1858–61) and exhibited two drawings in their annual exhibition of 1858 (Ithaca 1989, n.p.; Falk 1988, 115). In 1861 he left for Paris, where he studied in the studio of Charles Gleyre beginning in October 1861 and shortly thereafter was accepted into the prestigious École des Beaux-Arts (Ithaca 1989, n.p.; Weinberg 1991, 63). He later traveled to Italy and spent eight months at the Academy of St. Luke in Rome (Detroit 1983, 234), from where he sent back a portrait to be sold at the Pennsylvania Academy. In 1863, in response to his concerns about the Civil War, he returned to Philadelphia (Philadelphia et al. 1982, 115) and enlisted in a Pennsylvania regiment located in Chambersburg (Ithaca 1989, n.p.).

Even during the war, Knight attended to his artistic career. To the Great Central Fair held in Philadelphia in June 1864 to aid the Sanitary Commission, he sent *Time Raising Truth from the Well; On the Grand Canal, Venice;* and *Roman Peasant Boy* (locations unknown). Following the war, he attempted to earn a living from his art by sketching railroad passengers (Ithaca 1989, n.p.) and teaching art in his Philadelphia studio. He also involved himself with the Philadelphia Sketch Club, of which he had been a founder in 1861 and which held exhibitions in the 1860s (Ithaca 1989, n.p.). In 1867 he painted *The Burning of Chambersburg, Pennsylvania* (Washington County Museum of Fine Arts, Hagerstown, Md.), an infamous incident of the Civil War and one of his first ambitious American subjects. Until the early 1870s, when he returned to Paris, Knight developed a local clientele for his portraits, genre, and literary scenes, which included the Union League Club of Philadelphia, Asa Whitney, James L. Claghorn, J. B. Lippincott, and others (Child 1885, 104), and he exhibited at the National Academy of Design as well as at the Pennsylvania Academy.

Yearning for the stimulation of Paris, he returned to the city shortly after his marriage to Rebecca Morris Webster in September 1871. He plunged back into the Parisian art world and submitted *Les Fugitifs* to the Salon of 1873. Following the birth of their first son in August 1873, the family moved to Poissy, Seine-et-Oise, outside Paris, for the remainder of the season. The French painter Ernest Meissonier, a brother-in-law of his Paris neighbor and who lived in Poissy, agreed to offer Knight criticism and steered him in the direction of peasant subjects. During the summer of 1874, Knight, Will R. Low, and Henry Bacon painted in Barbizon, where all three attempted plein-air painting and came under the influence of Jean-François Millet (Ithaca 1989, n.p.).

About 1878 the Knights bought a large château in Poissy next to the Meissonier family and lived there permanently, although Knight also made several sketching trips to Normandy in subsequent years. Writing in 1885, the art critic Theodore Child called the château "a perfect museum of the cabinetmaker's art," which included a dining-room set of Louis XV furniture and an "ever growing collection of old furniture and bibelots, splendidly carved Dutch and French cupboards and cabinets, marquetry, brasswork, tapestry and other riches" (Child 1885, 105). In the mid-1890s, Knight also bought a house at Rolleboise, farther out from Paris by twenty-five miles, where he spent the summers painting.

Between 1875 and 1899 Knight exhibited regularly at the annual Salon showings in Paris, missing only 1878 (when he made a return trip to America), 1884, and 1890. Routinely he listed himself as a student of both Gleyre and Meissonier; in 1882 he received honorable mention at the Salon and in 1888, a third-class medal (Fink 1990, 254–255).

His reputation quickly became international. In 1889 he received a silver medal at the Paris Exposition Universelle and received the cross of the Legion of Honor of France (Ithaca 1989, n.p.). At the big Munich exhibition of 1888 he received a gold medal, and another medal at the Antwerp international exposition of 1894. He also continued to send paintings to both the Pennsylvania Academy and the National Academy of Design in America, although he seems never to have submitted work to the Society of American Artists, a group of younger European-trained American artists who organized in 1878 as a protest against the conservative National Academy. In 1893 Knight won a medal from the Columbian Exposition for his painting *Hailing the Ferry* (1888) and in 1896 received the Grand Medal of Honor from the Pennsylvania Academy, which had purchased *Hailing the Ferry.*

During World War I, Knight worked on behalf of France; reproductions of *Bas de laine* were distributed as propaganda for the drive for a third major war loan in 1917. He also served on the committee of the American Relief Clearing House. Knight never returned to live in the United States but had many American visitors to both Rolleboise and Poissy. He was known as a man of good taste; one of his two sons became an architect, the other a painter. Knight died in his flat at 53, rue de Clichy on March 9, 1924 (Ithaca 1989, n.p.).

P. H.

Bibliography Child 1885. Ithaca 1989.

59

The Water Carriers, 1892

Oil on canvas mounted on board

99.1 × 133.3 cm (39 × 52½ in.)

Gift of the C. J. Glascow Company (F68.111)

ALTHOUGH ENCOURAGED by Ernest Meissonier, his neighbor at Poissy, Knight was no doubt inspired by the plein-air effects of the peasant paintings of Jules Bastien-Lepage and Jules Breton, prominent French painters then in vogue. Knight spent his days sketching peasants in and around Poissy, Seine-et-Oise, carefully noting the changing effects of natural light on the river and landscape. He went so far as to have a glass house built in his garden so that he could paint his models in winter without the need for artificial illumination (Bacon 1883, 211). The soft light, grayed tones, and smooth application of paint combined with figures disengaged from vigorous activity impart a calming stillness to his compositions. In this way he created a distinctive storytelling art that appealed to patrons weary of the tensions of modern city life.

Theodore Child, writing one of the earliest articles on Knight, praised the artist's figural style and close attention to detail in his sketches. Comparing him with French painters of peasants, Child remarked:

> Mr. Knight does not paint the labors of the field with the austerity of Millet, showing us the human being in his function of perpetual struggle with the earth and the elements; nor, on the other hand, has he yielded too much to that urban sentimentalism by means of which Jules Breton has stolen the heart of the public. He has a natural tendency to see nature under an amiable and smiling aspect, and he certainly finds in the fields of Poissy, peasant girls far more goodly to look upon than the coarse and heavy peasants whom Millet has painted. (Child 1885, 105)

Throughout the 1880s and 1890s the artist continually returned to the theme of young women loitering on a riverbank and looking or gesturing toward the opposite bank. Knight's chef d'oeuvre of this genre is *Hailing the Ferry* (1888; Pennsylvania Academy of the Fine Arts, Philadelphia), which won him the silver medal at the Paris Exposition Universelle of 1889. Reviewing the American section for *Harper's New Monthly Magazine,* Theodore Child described the subject matter and the formal appeal of the painting:

> The pearliness of the atmosphere in this picture, the delicately studied gradations of luminous air penetrating in between the trees on the left, the exquisitely fine tones of the landscape, the vivid attitudes of the figures, are points which the eye remarks with always new pleasure. (Child 1889, 512)

The Water Carriers is close in size to *Hailing the Ferry,* as is the "pearliness of the atmosphere." The artist never repeated the exact subjects; instead, his compositions can be seen as variations on a theme as he altered the composition, the vantage point, the poses, and the expressions of the figures. In *The Water Carriers,* one young woman turns to walk toward us on the path while another pauses to wave to a young man astride a white horse on the opposite bank. Soft greens, browns, and grays permeate the painting; the gray, cloudless sky reinforces the calm, soothing composition with its diffuse light.

Knight and his younger contemporaries—Charles Sprague Pearce, George Hitchcock, Elizabeth Nourse, and his own son Louis Aston Knight, to name a few of the Americans—created peasant themes with smoothly painted, idealized female figure types and naturalistic light. They maintained prominent positions in the international art world, because they were popular with collectors who cared little for more realistic images of rural, masculine labor or for impressionist landscapes with their dappled light and broken brushwork. However, the critic Clarence Cook began to sound a note of resistance, when he concluded in discussion of *In October,* a painting of potato pickers: "Mr. Knight is clever at his grouping, and tells us plainly what he has to tell, but it must be confessed this generation is like to be somewhat overdosed with French peasants" (Cook 1888, 3:274). By the mid–twentieth century such pictures fell out of favor with collectors and museums, but recent years have seen a revival of interest in the international theme of peasant pictures.

P. H.

Inscription At lower right, *Ridgway Knight 1892 / Paris*

Provenance C. J. Glascow Company, Detroit. Acquired as a gift in 1968.

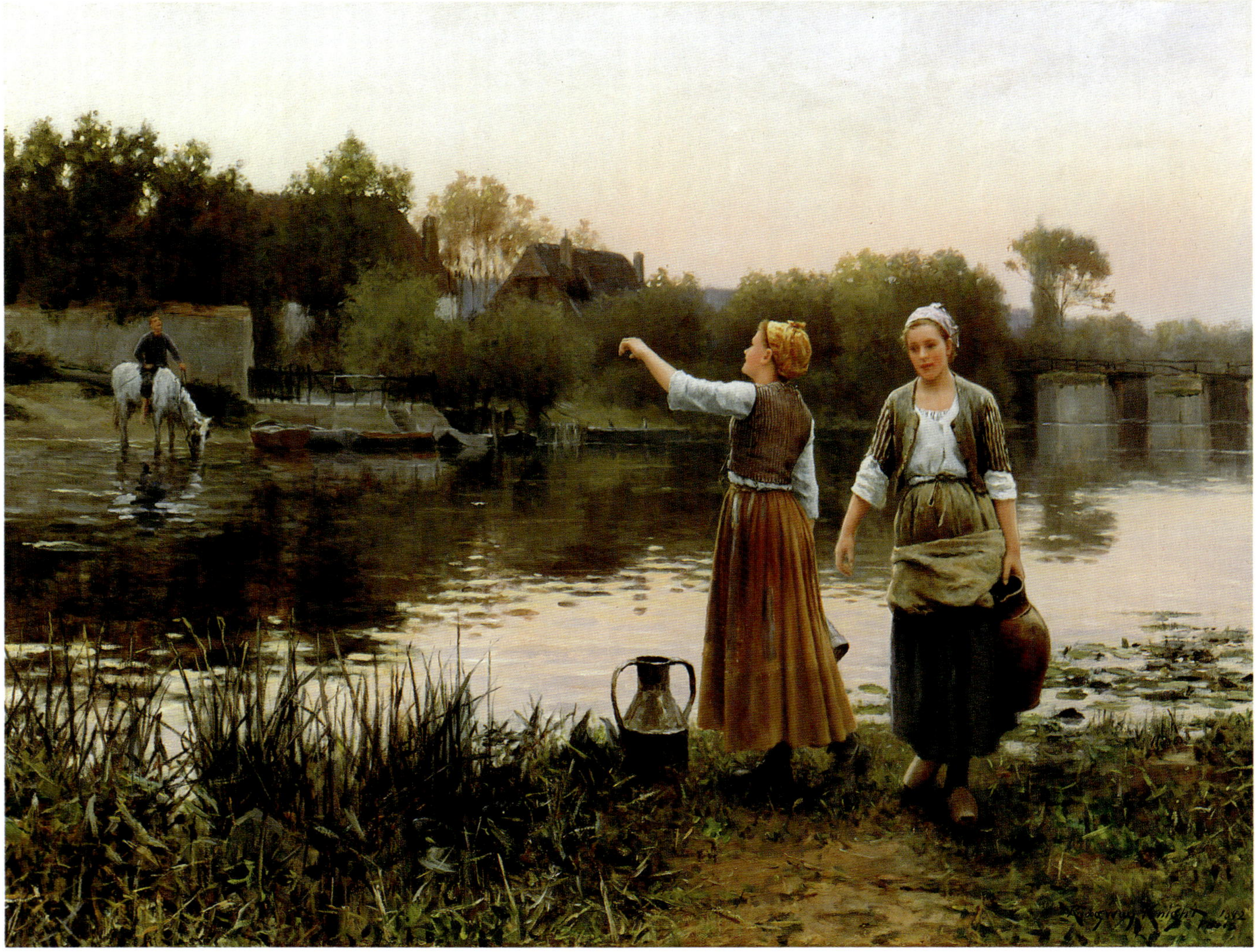

The Water Carriers

George Cochran Lambdin

1830 Pittsburgh–Philadelphia 1896

George Cochran Lambdin was the oldest of nine children born to James Read Lambdin, a prominent portrait painter, and his wife, Mary Cochran. In 1837 the family moved from Pittsburgh to Philadelphia, where James Lambdin became prominent in the art world—active in both the Artists' Fund Society and the Pennsylvania Academy of the Fine Arts and as an art teacher at the University of Pennsylvania. Thus, it is generally assumed that James taught young George the techniques of drawing and painting and helped him in his career.

Lambdin made his debut as an exhibiting artist at a Pennsylvania Academy exhibition in 1848, when he submitted three works to show off his proficiency in genre painting, portrait studies, and history painting: *Children Playing, Study of a Head,* and *Dorcas Distributing Garments to the Poor.* In the next few years he exhibited regularly at the Pennsylvania Academy as well as at the Philadelphia Art Union, where he showed crayon portraits and genre paintings, primarily of children.

In late 1854 or early 1855 he traveled to Europe and settled in Munich to study; however, he was home by late 1856 (Weidner 1986, 10). The trip polished his art, and he developed a gift for expressing sentimental themes focused on women in interiors. His major work of this period, *Our Sweetest Songs Are Those that Tell of Saddest Thought* (1857; National Academy of Design, New York), drew on Percy Bysshe Shelley's poem "To a Skylark." He sent the painting that year to the National Academy of Design in New York and in the following year to the Pennsylvania Academy and to the Royal Academy in London.

With the outbreak of the Civil War in 1861, Lambdin, Eastman Johnson (q.v.), William Hennessy, and other artists developed themes that represented the domestic trials of the conflict. Like other artists eager to help in the home effort, Lambdin submitted pictures to many of the fairs organized by the United States Sanitary Commission held in major Northern cities across the country to raise funds for hospital supplies, nurses, and doctors.

In late 1867 Lambdin moved to New York City, where he took up residence for the next two years at 51 West Tenth Street, living in a series of studios occupied by artist friends (Weidner 1986, 22). His move to New York might have been motivated by his desire to perfect his techniques and to learn from the example of the leading New York genre painters, such as John George Brown (q.v.) and Seymour Guy, who both had studios at Tenth Street, and Eastman Johnson and Winslow Homer (q.v.). (At the time critics admired the sentiment of Lambdin's pictures, but they faulted his technical abilities; see Tuckerman 1867, 450.) Like the New York painters, he specialized in genre pictures of children and women in gardens in the late 1860s and early 1870s. Previously an associate, he was elected a full academician by the National Academy of Design in 1868.

After a brief trip to Europe in 1870 with his brother Harry, he returned to the family home in the Germantown area of Philadelphia. In the next few years Lambdin turned from pictures of comely women in garden settings toward floral still lifes. He became involved in hybridizing roses, was a founder and the first secretary of the Germantown Horticultural Society during 1873–74, and increasingly believed that flowers held the key to color relationships (Weidner 1986, 47). Aside from a few portraits, his works of the late 1870s and 1880s are almost exclusively floral still lifes of different types: roses painted in their garden settings, in simple arrangements in vases, or set against black lacquered backgrounds—a type he seems to have innovated (Tulsa et al. 1981, 96). In the late 1880s Lambdin had health problems that prohibited him from carrying on his work; he died in Germantown in 1896.

P. H.

Bibliography Tuckerman 1867, 450–451. Tulsa et al. 1981, 123–125. Weidner 1986.

60

At the Front, 1866

Oil on canvas

46.4 × 61 cm (18¼ × 24 in.)

Founders Society Purchase, Director's Discretionary Fund (59.314)

Although George Lambdin seems not to have participated directly in the Civil War, like many other artists of the time, he sought out human-interest subjects that would evoke the mood of the war. His choice to focus on genre scenes of young officers was no doubt inspired by his twenty-two-year-old artist brother James Harrison "Harry" Lambdin, who in 1862 enlisted in the 121st Regiment, Army of the Potomac, and by 1865 had risen to the rank of colonel (Weidner 1986, 18).

At the Front seems to fall within a narrative grouping of four scenes representing a young Union officer departing from home and in camp at the war front. *In a Beech Wood* (1864; art market, as of 1986), shown at the Pennsylvania Academy in April 1864, precedes the other three scenes in narrative sequence. In this painting, what appears to be a youthful recruit carves his initials into a tree trunk as his sweetheart turns to watch from the log on which she is seated. Thematically close is Homer's *Initials* (1864; private collection), which depicts a young woman, leaning against a tree on which are carved the initials of her absent lover and the crossed swords of his cavalry insignia. Lambdin's *Consecration, 1861* (1865; Indianapolis Museum of Art) depicts a young woman and a young officer (slightly older than the recruit in *In a Beech Wood)* in the library of a well-appointed home. She raises his sword to her lips and kisses it, while he looks at her as he touches a rose to his own lips.

There are three versions to the third scene of the series. *Weary, Tiresome Winter Quarters—Culpeper Co., Virginia* (1864; private collection, Wilmington, Del.) depicts the same officer, seated on a folding chair in a rustic cabin with a canvas ceiling, staring into the fireplace. (The two other almost identical versions are in a private collection and the West Point Museum, N.Y.) In this scene the soldier has dropped a letter to the floor. Like the soldier in Winslow Homer's *Home, Sweet Home* (1863; art market, 1997), Lambdin's officer seems to yearn for the time to pass, when he can finish his duties as a soldier and return to his loved ones.

Detroit's *At the Front* shows a fourth scene, with the same officer seated outside his tent with his arms limply resting on his knees and his fingers lightly holding the chin strap of his hat. Behind him his saddle rests on a makeshift stand. He stares fixedly in the direction of a small fire that flickers in a pile of firewood. A sentry stands guard in the middle distance; several tents and a couple of figures articulate the hazy distant background. A viewer might imagine that this cavalry officer, fully dressed with his saddle ready to be strapped on his horse, is having a quiet moment at dawn to collect his thoughts before the next assault begins.

On the verso of *At the Front* Lambdin titled the painting and wrote, "from studies made on the Rapidan, 1864–65." The Rapidan River, in northern Virginia, runs from the Blue Ridge Mountains into the Rappahannock River. In March 1864 President Lincoln appointed General Ulysses S. Grant as commander in chief of all the Union armies. In the early morning hours of May 4, 1864, Grant led more than one hundred thousand troops from their winter quarters in Culpeper, Virginia, to the east, where they crossed the Rapidan at Germanna Ford. They were on their way to attack the eastern flank of General Robert E. Lee's Confederate troops stationed on the other side of the Rapidan. The Battle of the Wilderness began the following day, May 5, and lasted through the early morning of May 7. When the battle ended there were 15,000 Union soldiers killed, wounded, and missing; the Confederates lost about 11,400 (Cullen 1985, 15). It is known that Lambdin visited the battle site at least twice—in early 1864 and a few months after the war in 1865.

Lambdin exhibited *At the Front* at the National Academy of Design in 1866 and offered it for sale. A reviewer for the *Round Table* commented extensively on the painting, after having praised Homer's *Prisoners from the Front* (Metropolitan Museum of Art, New York) "for its downright force of hand and uncommon talent to delineate men." Turning to Lambdin, the reviewer began his remarks:

> If it is not too late for George Lambdin to learn, he might be taught a few truths by Mr. Homer's mode of study and unsentimental treatment of masculine themes. Mr. Lambdin's pictures, by their story connected with the war, are the most unmanly, the most unheroic, the most unsatisfactory examples of art and feeling that have ever come from the easel of a painter whose works have won our respect, sometimes our love.

After discussing Lambdin's other entries on exhibition that year (*Tired* and *Compensation,* one of which also included a Union soldier), the reviewer turns to discuss *At the Front:*

> The other picture, a soldier in a reverie before his campfire, is what is called "a made-up affair;" it does not tell us any truth of color or effect of out-of-door life, and it is too neat and trim in execution for the subject; it would do as an illustration for a Christmas gift-book, but it cannot be accepted as a rendering of the poetic side of camp-life. Yet this picture, unsatisfactory and almost feminine in its artistic traits, shows that Mr. Lambdin is not without some proof of the talent which in times gone by gave us so much pleasure. The conception of the situation, the pose of the figure, and the drawing—these are noteworthy and admirable.

The reviewer continued with covert advice for Lambdin:

> It seems to us that Mr. Lambdin must change the influences that are about him, that he must get into a more bracing medium, that he must not be afraid of the rude and homely and virile. If he shrinks from these, he shall go on refining his manner of painting, but become more and more purposeless, and finally be lost to the young painters who have so often greeted his works and appreciated his spirit. (*Round Table* 1866)

The *Round Table* reviewer was not the only critic at the time both to praise Lambdin and to admonish him for his deficiencies.

Lambdin must have been chastened by such comments and resolved to correct his shortcomings by moving to New York, which occurred a year later. But as times changed, taste did also, and fewer and fewer critics singled out sentimental genre paintings for notice. Thus, his transition to floral painting in the mid-1870s was a shrewd move. He gave up subject paintings meant to evoke human sympathies of sentiment and nostalgia and chose instead to paint floral arrangements that might elicit aesthetic sentiments—abstract memories of the fragile beauty and fleeting scents of roses.

P. H.

Inscription On verso, *AT THE FRONT / from studies made on the Rapidan, 1864–65 / Geo. C Lambdin / Philad. 1866*

Provenance Clarence S. Congdon, Detroit. Mrs. Janet Ehnes. Acquired in 1959.

Exhibitions Brooklyn 1960, no. 198. Bloomfield Hills 1973, no. 14.

References *Round Table* 1866. Weidner 1986, 18–19.

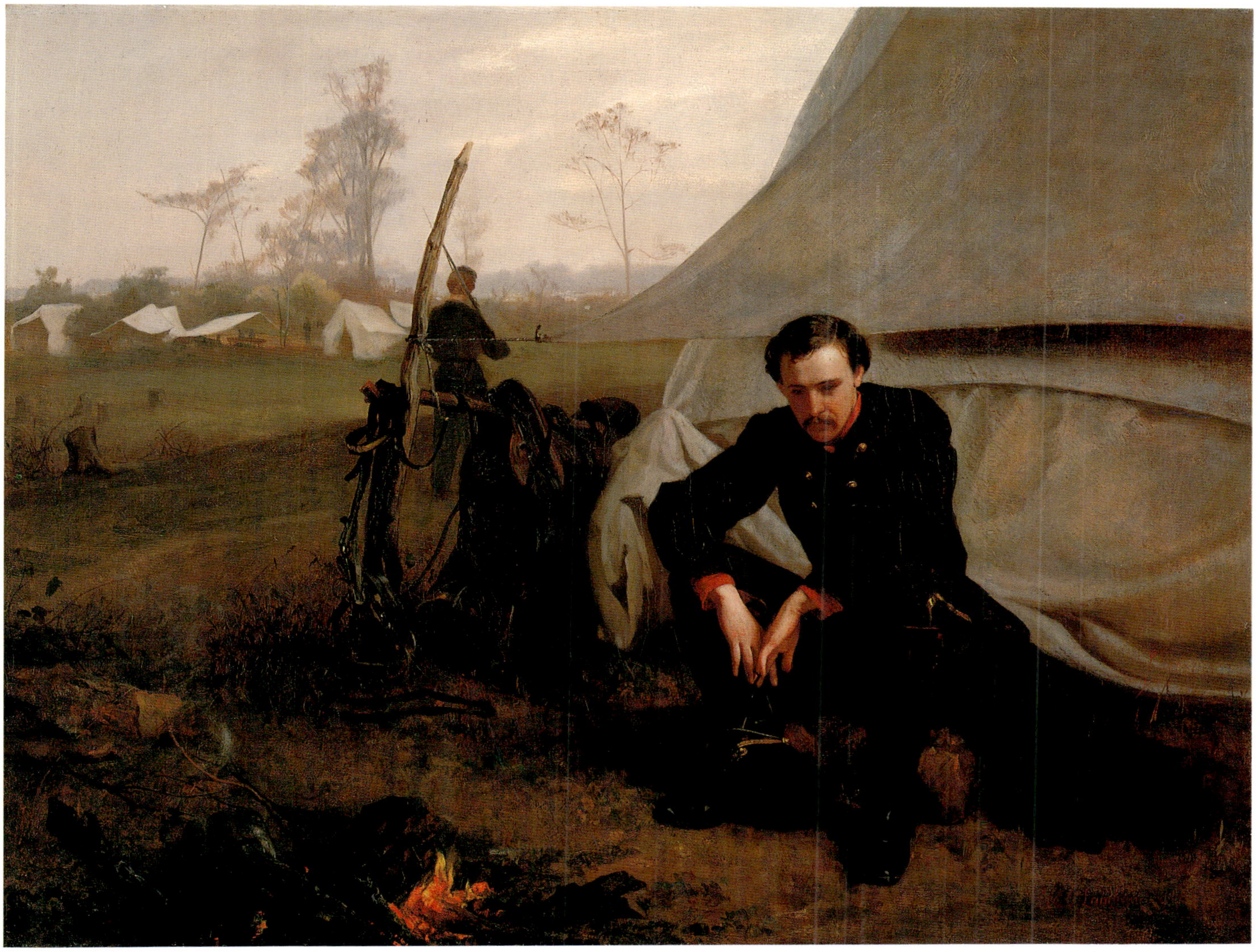

At the Front

Jervis McEntee

1828 Rondout, New York 1891

Jervis McEntee is today the least studied of major second-generation Hudson River school painters. Several factors contribute to this state of affairs, among them the artist's retiring personality and innate doleful temperament, his leisurely artistic development, his considerable but sporadic productivity, and his tendencies to repeat titles of and motifs in his compositions. Yet on closer examination his paintings hold up well, as does his historic consequence as a capable interlocutor among colleagues at the National Academy of Design. After his death he was eulogized as "one of the most thoughtful and skilled painters who rescued the Hudson River school from the commonplace" (*New York Times*, March 27, 1892).

He was a native of Rondout, Ulster County, New York, a "place . . . situated picturesquely on the west bank of the Hudson River, just within the shadows of the Catskill Mountains" (Sheldon 1879, 53) near the town of Kingston, and he lived there all his life. Years afterward he told the writer T. B. Aldrich that while he was a youth, his family had taken in the minor poet and bibliophile Henry Pickering (Aldrich 1866, 624; cited by Diane Strazdes in New York 1987, 280). From Pickering's fondness for children, cultured friends, and library of books, McEntee recalled, sprang his own love of art and literature. During the winter of 1850–51 McEntee became the second pupil of Frederic Edwin Church (q.v.), who was just two years his senior, in New York City. Little is recorded about the encounter, but from it student and teacher formed a lifelong bond. Concerning a career in the visual arts, however, McEntee was initially doubtful, so he returned to Rondout for approximately four years. During that interval, according to a report in the *New York Daily Tribune* (February 11, 1861), he tried his hand at serious poetry, some of which was printed in early volumes of *Putnam's Monthly Magazine*, first published in January 1853. The report is accurate. Attribution of most writings in *Putnam's* is now chancy since none is signed, but a few poems published by the magazine are specified by place of origin, including one entitled "The Old Mill" and dated Rondout, June 1853 (*Putnam's Monthly* 2 [August 1853]: 145–146). Other candidates in *Putnam's* for McEntee's authorship are poems entitled "November" and "December" (1 [April 1853]: 402), "Hidden Light" (1 [May 1853]: 581), and "The Rain" (7 [April 1856]: 317). In 1854 McEntee married Gertrude Sawyer, a daughter of the New York Universalist minister Thomas Jefferson Sawyer, and the following year he took a studio in New York City, advertising his services alongside colleagues in the newly founded periodical *The Crayon*.

Real recognition came his way in 1860 with his showing at the National Academy of Design of *Melancholy Days* (1860; formerly James A. Suydam collection, National Academy of Design, New York; unlocated), a sizable canvas inspired by William Cullen Bryant's poem "The Death of Flowers," from which McEntee appended a quotation in the academy catalogue. On the strength of that performance he was made associate academician, and the next year, boosted by his painting *Indian Summer* (NAD 1861; cat. no. 61), he attained full membership. From 1860 onward he was a loyal presence in New York art circles, regularly taking part in studio receptions, joining the Century Association, assisting with academy administrative matters, and saving most of his best works for academy displays. He was especially close to the writer Bayard Taylor, the actor Edwin Booth, and the painters Sanford R. Gifford (q.v.), Eastman Johnson (q.v.), and Worthington Whittredge (q.v.). Through the 1860s and 1870s McEntee gradually gained an international reputation as well, sending paintings to three world's fairs—those held in Paris in 1867 and in 1878 (where French, British, and American commentators alike praised him), and that held in Philadelphia in 1876—and to the Royal Academy and the Dudley Gallery in London. He traveled with his wife through Europe between 1868 and 1869, residing for several months in Rome, where he rented a studio next to Church's and sketched in the Campagna with Gifford. His work was noticed by London critics during the seventies, and by 1884 two of his pictures were owned by a collector resident in the vicinity of Liverpool (Liverpool 1884, nos. 24 and 71).

Yet McEntee never rose higher than a middle level of success. Less celebrated than was his teacher, Church, or Church's rivals such as Albert Bierstadt (q.v.) and William Bradford, or for that matter his friend Gifford, McEntee was also less controversial than they. By and large he kept consciously, one might say uncompromisingly, to that track. Although he often expressed disappointment at what he regarded as the inability or unwillingness of viewers to understand his art, and frequently grumbled about poor sales of his pictures, he gravitated toward unspectacular, small- to medium-size scenes infused with muted melancholic sentiment. His specialties were late fall and winter landscapes of sober tints, executed with a delicate, fairly transparent technique somewhat allied to Barbizon painting. Occasionally he varied his output, essaying large canvases such as Detroit's *Indian Summer* or strong compositions, for instance *The Danger Signal* (NAD 1871; private collection), a winter night scene of a train halted by a man carrying a lantern, and in the mid-1870s he experimented with figure pieces. During the 1880s he traveled twice to the far West and once—in 1889 with Church—to Mexico in search of new subject matter. But because he generally adhered to his established predilections, his work appealed to select audiences. A New York auction of seventy-five oil paintings by him in March 1888 fetched prices much below expectations, and the posthumous sale of 172 works by him four years later, in March 1892, fared no better. McEntee could have consoled himself with endorsements such as that offered by a writer for *Appleton's Journal*, possibly Thomas Gold Appleton, in the March 28, 1874, issue of that periodical:

> The influence on the mind of Mr. McEntee's pictures appears to us of the best kind; his color is harmonious, and its subdued richness, too pure ever to touch the senses, but showing the aesthetic feeling of the artist, is a fit woof in which he weaves good healthy sentiment, love of Nature, and sincere effort to depict her various forms and moods. McEntee's pictures, we believe, really make men better, and we hope no *ignis fatuus* will ever turn him aside from the path he has so many years trodden with profit to every one so fortunate as to come under the influence of his art.

G. C.

Bibliography Sheldon 1879, 51–56. "McEntee Diary."

61
Indian Summer, 1860–61

Oil on canvas
101.3 × 172.7 cm (39⅞ × 68 in.)
Founders Society Purchase, Gibbs-Williams Fund and Dexter M. Ferry, Jr., Fund (75.11)

The present canvas is here identified as the one McEntee painted for the annual exhibition of the National Academy of Design in 1861. Informally entitled "Morning in Autumn" and "Indian Summer among the Catskills" while he was working on it, that picture was shown at the academy between March 20 and April 20, 1861, under the title *Indian Summer* (no. 551). In the exhibition catalogue it was listed "for sale" and was accompanied by an excerpt of poetry by John Howard Bryant, brother of William Cullen Bryant:

> That soft Autumnal time
> is come, which sheds upon the
> naked scene
> Charms only known in this our
> Northern clime
> Bright seasons far between.
>
> The sunny noon is thine
> Soft, golden, noiseless as the dead
> of night
> And hues that in the flushed hori-
> zon shine
> At eve and early light.

The same painting reappeared "for sale" in exhibitions held at the Young Men's Association in Buffalo, New York, late in 1861, and at the Troy, New York, branch of the same organization early in 1862, the listings in the respective catalogues augmented with the poetry selection by John Bryant. McEntee's initial asking price for his *Indian Summer* of 1861 is not known, but by December of that year, according to the catalogue (copy, AAA) of the art exhibition held at the Buffalo Young Men's Association, he hoped to realize one thousand dollars for it. He was, however, willing to settle for considerably less. In a letter from New York on January 21, 1862, to Tallmadge Ewers, secretary to the Y.M.A. of Buffalo, the artist allowed that he could "let it [the painting] go" for seven hundred dollars, including the frame valued at seventy dollars,

> much less than my original price.... I will say further that if your association will buy it as the nucleus of a permanent Gallery (as has been done in Troy) I will take $600 for it. I should be willing to sacrifice something for the sake of having it go into some public gallery because the subject [i.e., Indian summer] is a favorite one with me, it is peculiarly American and I believe that particular phase of American Landscape has been treated by no one before. (AAA, roll DDU 1, frames 376–377)

Perhaps during 1862 and certainly by no later than 1866, the painting was acquired by James W. Pinchot (1831–1908), an entrepreneur, forestry expert, supporter of civic endeavors, and art patron who during the 1860s bought works by Frederic Edwin Church (q.v.), Sanford R. Gifford (q.v.), Worthington Whittredge (q.v.), and the sculptor Launt Thompson, as well as several by McEntee.

When it was purchased by the Detroit Institute of Arts in 1975 through Hirschl & Adler Galleries, New York, the present canvas was thought to be the painting called *Indian Summer* that McEntee sent to the National Academy of Design in 1882 (no. 103). That supposition is incorrect, however. The work shown under that title in 1882, as is affirmed by a contemporary wood engraving (Kurtz 1882, 31), was an upright scene three feet high, the composition of which differed from that of the Detroit picture. The 1882 painting, to which McEntee alluded in his diary (AAA) covering the 1870s and 1880s, but which—excepting the just-mentioned source—was not discussed in publications about the academy display of that year, is now unlocated.

Three questions pertaining to the Detroit picture must therefore be addressed immediately. The first concerns the Pinchot family provenance, which, it turns out, is secure. During the mid-1970s Hirschl & Adler handled three McEntee paintings, one of them the present work, that came directly from the Pinchot family; another one, a four-and-one-half-foot horizontal scene signed and dated 1867 and now called *Landscape, Autumn* (Manoogian Collection), loosely resembles the Detroit canvas. The second question has to do with the title *Indian Summer,* which McEntee bestowed on at least three different paintings, one of them reliably stated by Henry T. Tuckerman to have been owned by James W. Pinchot (Tuckerman 1867, 545). A propos the Detroit work, the title *Indian Summer* is inscribed with the artist's name on a plaque affixed to the front of the frame descended with the canvas; hence that designation has been for a long time intrinsic to the painting and to Pinchot family tradition. The third question concerns anomalies in the inscription: the lack of a date, an omission uncharacteristic of extant McEntee paintings of moderate to large size; and the signature itself, in which the curving capital *E* of the last name is distinct from the straight uppercase *E*'s McEntee generally used. Recent technical examination of that area of the Detroit work has proved inconclusive, although there is a substantial tear—carefully mended at an unknown date—above and to the left of the signature, and the entire canvas has been relined. The scarcity of early (ca. 1862 and before) painted images by McEntee accessible today inhibits a firm resolution to either part of the last query.

Uncertainties such as these typify current awareness of McEntee's life and oeuvre. As it happens, McEntee's three documented paintings entitled *Indian Summer,* when taken together, offer a convenient means of access to his career as a whole.

The earliest was one of six works he submitted to the National Academy of Design exhibition of 1855. After entrusting just two paintings to the academy display of 1853 and none to that of 1854, he decided to commit himself as a professional artist. The six-work showing of 1855 therefore amounted to a pivotal gesture for him. In this he was not then alone. Concurrently his former teacher, Church, exhibited at the academy four canvases of South American scenery, the first fruits of his (Church's) new expertise with equatorial subjects, which signaled both a reinvigoration and a shift of emphasis in Church's own art. Church's latest works were widely noticed in the press, while McEntee's generated little or no discussion. Probably the latter's painting of 1855 called *Indian Summer* (NAD, no. 40; unlocated), unmentioned in known academy exhibition reviews, was of moderate size and ambition.

Not quite six years later, in early 1861, having just gained associate membership in the academy, McEntee was poised to advance himself further. Toward the end of 1860 he had sketched in "the neighborhood of Kingston" *(Crayon* 1860, 353)—that is, near the southern tip of the eastern range of the Catskills. His activities of January 1861 were best summarized by the art critic of the *New York Commercial Advertiser,* who called on McEntee during a tour of local artists' studios. The journalist began that part of his published report by commending McEntee's painting of the previous year, *Melancholy Days* (NAD 1860; unlocated), which "was very much admired [at the academy exhibition] . . . for its feeling and original treatment of a subject which had almost become common place" (February 2, 1861). The writer then turned to "a large picture of a Morning in Autumn" underway on McEntee's easel. The former's description, so far as it goes, coincides with the Detroit painting:

> It is not completed, but it is far enough advanced to show that it is to be one of his most successful pictures. On the right hand side of the composition we behold a large and fantastic pine stretching out its long branches toward the centre of the painting. It is a difficult thing to paint with success. But Mr. McEntee seems to have thoroughly mastered his subject. The tree is as admirable in its drawing as it is in the texture of its leafage. It is not a conventional pine, but the natural pine, with some marks of individuality about it. Then there is the high bank, with its rock, and stones, and old decaying stuff lying rotting on the ground,—all this is painted with more than usual strength, and shows all those rich browns and greys of earth, and leaf and bark, that marked it as being the very inspiration of nature.

Soon afterward the art correspondent of the *New York Daily Tribune* noted that McEntee "is at present engaged upon a larger picture than he has exhibited to the public, representing Indian Summer among the Catskills" (February 11, 1861). In early March a writer for the *New York Herald* added: "McEntee has on his easel an 'Indian Summer,' rich in promise; it will be one of his most elaborate works" (March 2, 1861).

Through the winter of 1860–61, several New York landscape painters, including McEntee, all of whom were cognizant of each other's current productions, were occupied with ambitious works. Church was completing his mammoth *Icebergs* (1861; Dallas Museum of Art), which he exhibited as a "Great Picture" in April 1861, while Gifford was finishing a large *Twilight in the Catskills* (unlocated), shown "for sale" at the academy in 1861 (no. 225); the *Commercial Advertiser*'s reporter lauded both paintings before they were finished (January 21, 1861; March 9, 1861). Contemporaneously, Régis François Gignoux, the French-born New York landscapist and sometime rival of Church, had just completed a "grand and imposing" canvas that he called *Indian Summer* (unlocated). After unveiling it at the Brooklyn Art Association in February 1861, he repainted it, retitled it *Indian Summer in Virginia* as an emblem of Union nostalgia during the Civil War, and eventually sent it on tour as a "Great Picture." And George Loring Brown, who occasionally ventured to compete with Church, had recently finished a ten-foot canvas. That painting, a scene of autumn in the White Mountains that Brown entitled *The Crown of New England* (1861; Her Majesty the Queen, Sandringham House, England), was displayed first at the Athenaeum Gallery and then the Crayon Gallery in New York before it was sold to the Prince of Wales.

The field of comparison could be broadened to include Martin Johnson Heade (q.v.), whose *Seascape: Sunset* (1861;

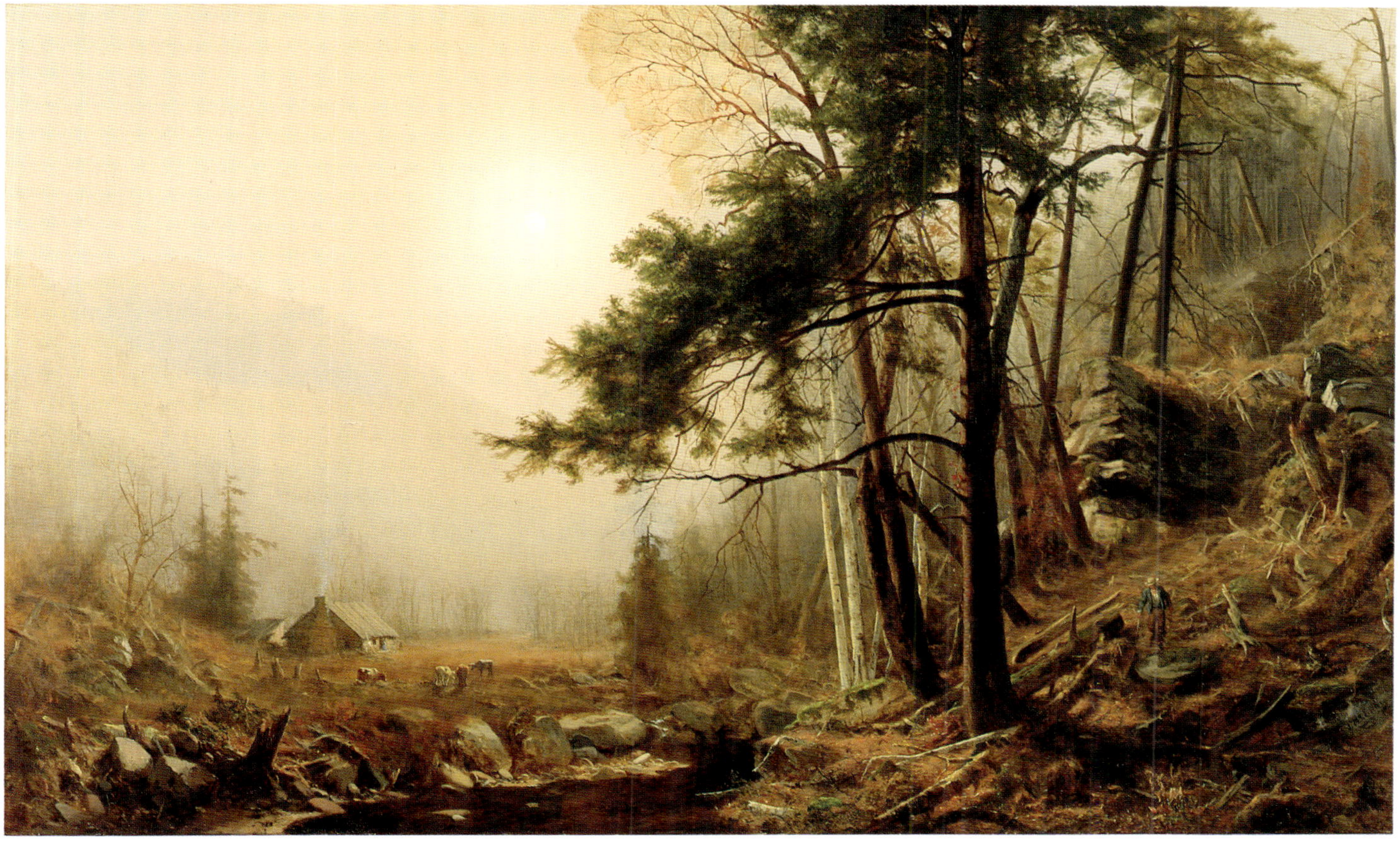

Indian Summer

cat. no. 34) was extensively discussed during its display at the academy in 1861; William Bradford, whose *Shipwreck off Nantucket (Wreck off Nantucket, after a Storm)* (NAD 1861; Metropolitan Museum of Art, New York) was likewise the subject of newspaper discourse both before and during its showing at the academy; John F. Kensett (q.v.), who produced his own *Indian Summer* (NAD 1862; unlocated) the following year; and back to Sanford Gifford, aspects of whose luminous *Kauterskill Clove* (1862; Metropolitan Museum of Art, New York), although not exhibited at that time, may well owe something to the present work by McEntee.

McEntee sent three paintings to the academy exhibition of 1861, where they were complemented by Edward Bowers's portrait of him (no. 394; National Academy of Design, New York). *Indian Summer*, the largest of the group, gained its share of notice. The *Commercial Advertiser*'s correspondent, slightly disappointed with the completed canvas, declared that there was "yet . . . much fine painting in the work and it carries out the spirit of the scene. Grey November it is, rather than that rich time when opulent nature clothes her forests in Venetian hues" (April 5, 1861). Other metropolitan writers voiced preponderantly favorable opinions, which when taken together fit well with the Detroit picture. As had the critics for the *Commercial Advertiser* and the *Tribune*, several journalists described *Indian Summer* as "large"; one referred to "some well painted trees and some good atmospheric effects" *(New York Herald*, March 31, 1861); and at least three writers, using similar phrases, complimented the "very good effect of sunlight through the mist" (Norton 1861, 17). The fullest descriptive assessments were published in the morning and evening editions of the *New York Express* (April 12, 1861) and *New York Albion* (April 20, 1861). According to the former,

> the "Indian Summer in the Catskills" is the largest, and probably the most elaborate [of McEntee's works then on view]. It succeeds in presenting very naturally the effects to be witnessed in our mountain landscapes when the brilliancy of the foliage has waned, but some delicious warm days return to remind us of the summer that is gone. The haziness of the atmosphere is capitally rendered; and the peculiar skill with which the trees in the foreground are depicted, nearly stripped of their foliage, which lies piled up and rotting beneath them, is also admirable.

For the latter,

> In [this work] indeed we are not sorry to take refuge in the misty haze, through which the sun is struggling to force his way, from the uneasiness and dismemberment that prevail where light is permitted to enlighten us as to the subject. Hewn fragments of wood and jagged rocks present an uncomfortable series of angular lines and fragmentary details, that do not quite accord, in our mind, with the sentiment at which the artist seems to have aimed. But Indian Summer has a pleasant sound; and there is something attractive in a good place on the walls, and a happy quotation in the Catalogue from the verses of John Bryant. The picture evidently has many admirers.

For late-twentieth-century viewers, the principal components of the Detroit painting, besides the group of foreground trees, are the wooden cabin in the left middle distance, its chimney exhaling thin smoke, and the accompanying two human figures and four cows. That none of these elements was mentioned by reviewers in 1861 somewhat perturbs the identification proposed here. Yet the rugged woodland area at right and, especially, the inhabited pioneer cabin in a clearing were—were still—ingredients apposite to American landscape painting of the early 1860s. The trees and rocks remind us of Asher B. Durand's compositions throughout the 1850s; Durand was still a commanding presence in American art as the decade of the 1860s opened. Thomas Cole effectively had introduced the pioneer-cabin theme to American art during the mid-1820s, bringing it to achievement twenty years later with his paintings *The Hunter's Return* (1845; Amon Carter Museum, Fort Worth, Tex.) and *Home in the Woods* (1847; Reynolda House, Winston-Salem, N.C.). In turn, Cole's former pupil, Church, extended it with his *Home by the Lake* (NAD 1852; Jo Ann and Julian Ganz collection), as did Durand with his paintings *Progress* (NAD 1853; Warner Collection of the Gulf States Paper Corporation, Tuscaloosa, Ala.) and *First Harvest* (1855; Brooklyn Museum), and Jasper Cropsey (q.v.) with his *Backwoods of America* (1858; Manoogian Collection), to cite but four examples. Church's *Home by the Lake* was reshown at the Y.M.A. in Troy, New York, in 1860, where McEntee could have seen it; one of the latter's works was included in that display.

As the palpable moodiness of the Detroit painting intimates, by the early 1860s such imagery was of fading relevance for American artists. Indeed, one of the other works McEntee prepared for the academy in 1861 (no. 266; unlocated) he called *Deserted Homestead*. That picture, a small, solemn winter scene, was enthusiastically received by contemporary journalists. Through the 1860s McEntee occasionally depicted pioneer cabins, as did his friend Sanford R. Gifford, for instance in the aforementioned *Kauterskill Clove* (1862), and especially in *Hunter Mountain, Twilight* (1867; Terra Museum of American Art, Chicago), which was purchased by James W. Pinchot.

McEntee completed the last of the three paintings he entitled *Indian Summer* in mid-March 1882, sending it and a smaller canvas commenced in January 1882, a view of the Humboldt Valley in

Nevada where he had traveled the previous year, to the academy exhibition. It is tempting to equate the despondency evident in his diary writings of the period with the former picture. Throughout 1881 and into 1882 he often referred in his journal to pervasive feelings of sadness that at times left him unable to paint. On November 30, 1881, while supervising the construction of a barn on his farm at Rondout, he noted: "It has been a lovely Indian summer day." The next day (December 1, 1881) he visited the nearby cemetery where his lamented wife, Gertrude, who had died in 1878, was buried, and he "had the satisfaction of seeing our lot entirely completed and the sodding of the border all done." On Christmas Day 1881, despite a congenial ambience of family and friends, he willingly succumbed to emotional doldrums:

> I read my diary and recalled the past Christmases when dear Gertrude was with me and the bitterness of her absence was as fresh and sharp as the day she left me. I read over her letters and the letters of Mrs. Wheeler [?] and [Sanford] Gifford and Eastman Johnson written to me when she died and gave myself up to the luxury of a sorrow which time does not efface. I thought I should never try to celebrate the holidays again for every thing about them reminds me of my loss and recalls the days that are no more.

Yet on balance, the image and remarks apropos *Indian Summer* published in 1882 (Kurtz 1882, 30–31), schematic though they are, convey little effect of psychological oppression. One might try instead to see them through the lens of the artist's enduring attachment to the natural surroundings amid which he resided all his life.

G. C.

Inscription At lower right, *J. McEntee*

Provenance James W. Pinchot, New York and Washington, D.C., ca. 1862–66 until 1908. Governor Gifford Pinchot. Mr. Gifford Pinchot, until 1975. Hirschl & Adler Galleries, New York. Acquired in 1975.

Exhibitions New York, National Academy of Design Annual, 1861, no. 551. Buffalo 1861, no. 144. Troy 1862, no. 87.

Reference Hood et al. 1977, 91–92.

Homer Dodge Martin

1836 Albany, New York–Saint Paul, Minnesota 1897

Homer Martin was neither the last of the Hudson River school artists nor the first of the American impressionists, as he has been described. Instead, he was—like George Inness (q.v.), Alexander H. Wyant (q.v.), R. Swain Gifford, and Dwight W. Tryon—an artist who assimilated aspects of progressive trends in the last third of the nineteenth century with a strong subjective bias. His largest debts were to the French Barbizon painters—especially Camille Corot, Théodore Rousseau, and Charles-François Daubigny—and to the American expatriate James McNeill Whistler (q.v.).

Martin quit school at thirteen to work in his father's carpentry shop in Albany, New York, but his passion for drawing landed him in the studio of the local sculptor Erastus Dow Palmer in the early 1850s. Palmer was supportive, introducing Martin to patrons and artists who shared a belief in nature as a source of revelation, including the Reverend Elias L. Magoon and the New York landscapists Asher B. Durand, John F. Kensett (q.v.), Sanford R. Gifford (q.v.), and Frederic Edwin Church (q.v.)—the core, that is, of the Hudson River school. Martin studied with James M. Hart for two weeks, the sum of his professional training: the obstinate meagerness of his formal education was cause for both amazement and apology: "if there ever was a self-taught painter, it was Homer Martin" (Meyer 1908, 255); there was "a certain stumbling in the artist's work, the result of Martin's lack of training in the art schools" (*New York Daily Tribune,* March 19, 1910). Martin made his debut at the National Academy of Design in 1857 with views of natural attractions in the Berkshire region.

Productive years followed. In 1861 he tried to enlist in the Union army but was rejected because of a "congenital inability to see perpendicular lines distinctly" (E. Martin 1904, 8). Shortly after, he married Elizabeth Gilbert Davis, an Albany woman of high learning and saintly sensibility who became a much-published author of fiction and literary criticism. She read poetry to him, especially the work of Keats, and provided an income. They moved to New York, where they resided until 1881 and where Martin achieved celebrity as a picturesque raconteur and a hale-fellow-well-met among the literati; his most influential and unswerving backers were the critics Montgomery Schuyler and William C. Brownell, later editor of *Scribner's,* and the artists John La Farge and Elihu Vedder (q.v.). Known at first for the fidelity of his views in the Catskills and Adirondacks, Martin was commissioned to join railway surveys to the west in 1871 and to Cumberland Gap in 1872. In 1876 he traveled to France, where he worked at Saint-Cloud, and to England, where he worked in Whistler's studio.

In the late 1870s Martin faced tremendous hardships as his eyesight degenerated and he slouched into poverty and alcoholism. He journeyed along the Saint Lawrence River in 1879 and in 1881 went to London; the following year he settled in Normandy, where he remained until 1886, making occasional trips to Paris. He returned to France in 1893, but by that time he was a wreck, "very broken and almost blind" (Mather 1912, 56). Elizabeth Martin, recovering from a nervous breakdown, moved to Saint Paul, Minnesota, and Martin joined her there. In 1895, in a bolt of inspiration and activity that startled even himself, he painted three large, expressionistic landscapes, including *View of the Seine: Harp of the Winds* (Metropolitan Museum of Art, New York), which friendly critics identified as emanations of genius. Soon after, he died of throat cancer; his wife, left with ten dollars, entered a convent.

Both supporters and detractors exaggerated Martin's position. Sadakichi Hartmann, proponent of artists who were "insensible to mercenary temptations ... in this very era of commercialism," heroized Martin and Dwight Tryon as those "who brought American landscape to its highest pinnacle of perfection" (Hartmann 1902, 2:101, 280–281), and Charles Caffin ranked Martin "highest of all the poet-painters of American landscape" (Caffin 1913, 126). Conversely, the artist John F. Weir confided: "I knew Martin very well, but never saw in him the intellectual attraction that some others seemed to find. A laconic, ejaculatory expression, followed by long silences summed it up. As to his art I think he was greatly overrated" (Mandel 1973, 81). The artist Worthington Whittredge (q.v.) dimly recalled "poor Martin, who died before anybody discovered that he was a painter" (Whittredge 1942, 61). Perhaps Frank Jewett Mather hit closer to the mark: "he seems to me a singularly appealing type of the minor artist" (Mather 1912, 75).

W. T. O.

Bibliography E. Martin 1904. Mather 1912. Mandel 1973.

62

Autumn, ca. 1865

Oil on canvas

44.5 × 80 cm (17½ × 31½ in.)

Gift of the Associates of the American Wing in memory of James A. Beresford (77.94)

The span between the Civil War and the Centennial was the most productive and secure period of work in Martin's career. He developed a distinctive style, became known for lake and mountain landscapes of the Adirondacks, Catskills, and White Mountains, and built relationships with patrons, critics, and artists in New York. Probably in the winter of 1864–65 he acquired the small skylighted studio on the top floor of the Tenth Street Studio Building that he maintained until his second trip abroad in 1881.

In New York in the 1860s Martin identified with two quite different groups of painters: on the one hand, older, well-

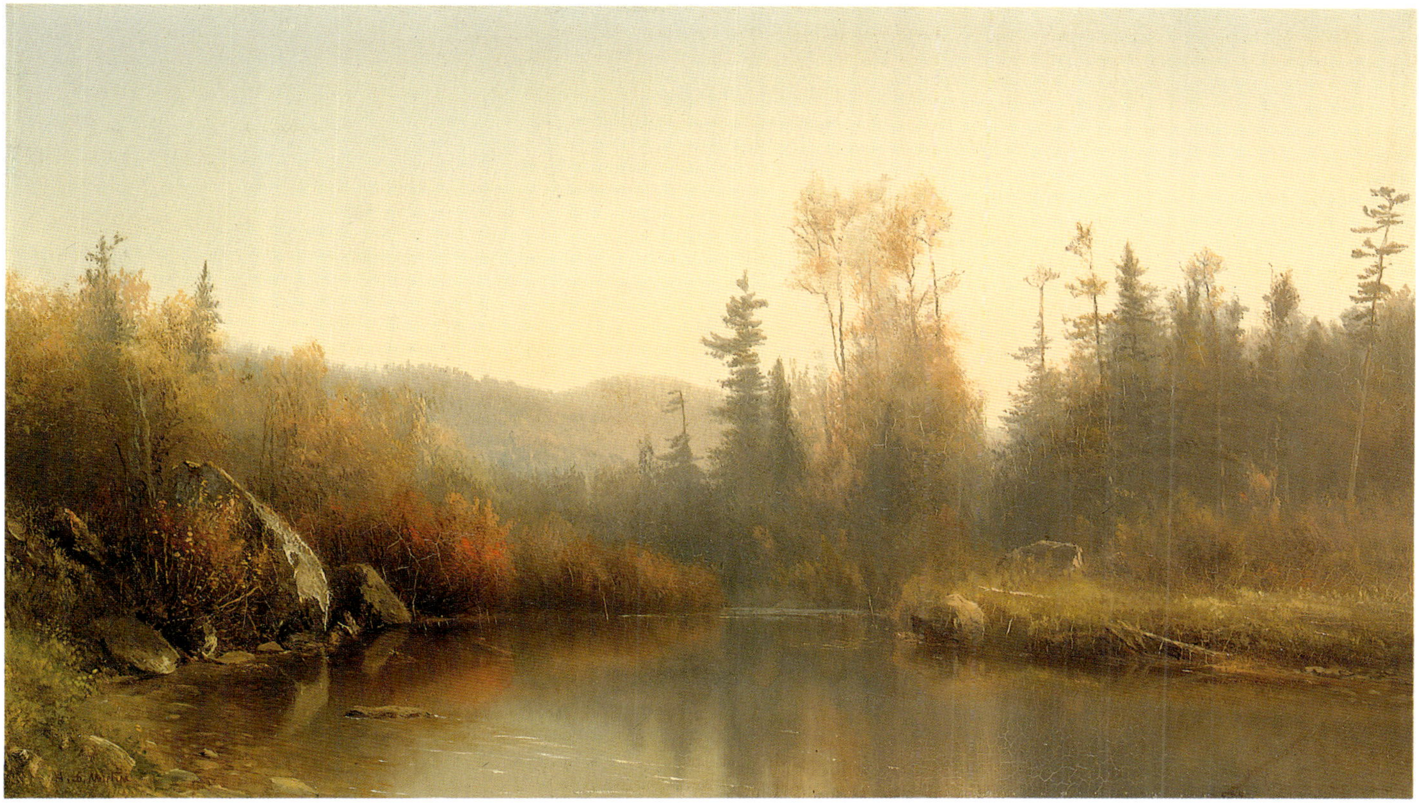

established landscape artists familiar to him from Albany, especially John F. Kensett (q.v.) and Sanford R. Gifford (q.v.); on the other hand, his contemporaries, the progressive painters Winslow Homer (q.v.), John La Farge, and Elihu Vedder (q.v.). The first group upheld the closely worked, detailed naturalism of Asher B. Durand, the widely respected exponent of the English Pre-Raphaelite movement. The second group was in the circle of Boston artist William Morris Hunt (q.v.), champion of French Barbizon painting, who emphasized freedom of brushwork, large massings of forms, expressive color, and freedom from classical compositional formulas. Martin interacted with both groups, but his friends were the younger men. Vedder, who moved to Europe in 1865, recalled the "cozy studio and tavern times I . . . had with Homer Martin. He was a Bohemian if you will" (Vedder 1910, 1:240). La Farge was equally close, even counseling Elizabeth Martin in Catholicism, and perhaps, along with Hunt and Vedder, inspiring Martin's later sand-dune and Newport, Rhode Island, paintings. Martin had much in common with Winslow Homer, especially in the realm of subject matter, as both artists painted extensively in the White Mountains and Adirondacks from the late 1860s to the mid-1870s.

Martin first worked in the Adirondacks in 1864, and he continued to visit the region in the summer and autumn until 1875. He was attracted to the Keene Valley and the wild area west of Mount Marcy, where as early as 1866 he made accurate views from the Beede Farm, Homer's later base. Martin's interest was not in guides, tourists, trappers, hunters, or hikers, but in the kind of isolated mountain lake characterized in *Autumn.* He treated the subject in a substantial series that usually focused on a small body of water enframed by rocks—some of them large boulders—a section of bog, and dense undergrowth. He individualized a screen of scrawny and weather-beaten trees at middle distance; loggers had taken the large trees years before, long enough ago, at least, that new growth had filled in the clearings and covered the stumps.

Despite such intimations of human activity, *Autumn,* like most of the paintings in the series, imparts a powerful quality of remoteness and inaccessibility, as if the viewer accidentally had bushwhacked into the scene. The scene itself is unremarkable, without central focus or dominant motif, and the composition likewise seems haphazard or happened upon by the artist, with the water pushed to the lower edge of the frame and the

Autumn

distant mountain not brought into full view. Yet, despite its asymmetry and lack of central focus, the composition is well balanced, as the mass of the boulder at left, for example, offsets the woods at right; further, the color scheme is harmonious in its tonal unity and the interplay among the complementaries. The paintings in the series share the long, low, horizontal format that imparts panoramic scope, but the dimensions are intimate and scaled to the midcentury parlor: about 18 by 32 inches, or a variation resulting in a similar ratio of height to width.

Autumn and other Adirondack lake paintings from the mid-1860s place Martin in the company of second-generation Hudson River school artists rather than the Barbizon group forming around Hunt. Commentators noted Martin's indebtedness to Kensett, whose immense popularity at the time made him a safe role model. The foreground detail, particularly the rendering of the water and boulder, is wholly in Kensett's manner; so, too, are the format, scale, and pervasive light. Martin also borrowed from Gifford, specifically in his use of backlighting (whereby the sun is screened behind the trees and mountainside) and his investigation of quietude through the medium of early evening in autumn. As the critic Charles De Kay observed, Martin "was content with the beauty of tranquil nature, almost equaling in this natural selection of quiet moods the way of Sanford Gifford, a painter essentially a lover of quiet" (De Kay 1910, 588).

Even by 1867, however, Martin inflected his style toward a Barbizon mode, gradually adopting looser brush handling, more generalized forms, and more active, if lowery, conditions of weather and light. He probably responded to the recent large shows of Barbizon paintings in New York. Thus, in 1867 Martin came to the attention of Henry T. Tuckerman, who noted that his lake scenes "have decided and progressive merit and character" (Tuckerman 1867, 566). Tuckerman perhaps referred to such a painting as *A North Woods Lake* (1867; National Museum of American Art, Washington, D.C.), exhibited at the National Academy of Design, which departs from *Autumn* in denoting elements of the new style.

If Martin attracted notice because he diverged from the prevailing style, he also had succeeded in gaining entrée to elite, supportive social circles. In 1866 he was elected to the Century Association, whose membership included artists (Durand, Kensett, Gifford, Homer, Inness), intellectuals (Henry James), critics such as Tuckerman, businessmen, and Martin's patrons; the club purchased one of Martin's best paintings, *Lake Sanford in the Adirondacks* (1870) in 1873. One patron from the club was William E. Dodge, Jr., who owned *A North Woods Lake* and was, as of 1864, partner in Phelps-Dodge and Company, his father's mining firm that was tied to extensive railroad and real-estate interests; Dodge was also president of the Young Men's Christian Association and the Evangelical Alliance. Certainly not all of Martin's patrons at the time were Christian clubmen, but many of his paintings pertained to mining and most were commissioned. Some were explicit in the reference, such as *In the Housatonic Valley* (Cleveland Museum of Art) and *Iron Mine, Port Henry, New York* (National Museum of American Art), but most, like *Autumn*, were scenes of lakes in the Adirondack mining region where businessmen from New York City, many of them mine owners, went to rough it, fish, and hunt in the summer and autumn. This was the outing-club clientele that later appreciated Winslow Homer's Adirondack watercolors and oils, and to the end of his career Martin catered to their enthusiasm and his own in recollected landscapes. As late as 1895 he explained to his dealer, Thomas B. Clarke, about "the town of Newcomb, well known to those who go up to the old Adirondack Iron Works or to Preston Ponds and you must know several members of the [Century] Club that own these ponds" (Mandel 1973a, 6).

Autumn represents, if not Martin the mature artist, at least Martin the successful artist: "we were fairly prosperous in those early years," his wife recalled (E. Martin 1904, 15). He was named a full member of the National Academy in 1874, belonged to the Tile Club, and helped found the Society of American Artists. His recognition came from relatively modest *souvenirs* of tranquil, remote Adirondack lakes.

W. T. O.

Inscription At lower left, *H. D. Martin*

Provenance John List Crawford, Bryn Mawr, Pa., 1946. Sale, Parke-Bernet Galleries, New York, February 20–21, 1946, lot 144. Dr. R. Emmet H. Conn, Los Angeles, 1946–77. Sale, Stalker and Boos, Auctioneers, Birmingham, Mich., 1977, as *Misty Landscape*. Acquired in 1977.

Reference *BDIA* 1978a, 309.

63
Landscape, ca. 1865–75

Oil on canvas
16.5 × 25.1 cm (6½ × 9⅞ in.)
Gift of Ethel and Bertha Lloyd (24.7)

In composition this little oil sketch belongs to classical conventions that Hudson River school artists sustained well into the 1870s, while the luminosity and the expansive horizontality of the design suggest a date in the 1860s. One is reminded of war-era paintings by Kensett and Gifford in the way the immediate foreground is left unencumbered, elements are organized around the body of water, and the gaze zigzags from right foreground to left middle ground to light-suffused background planes, all rendered in heavy-handed aerial perspective. The subject matter is similarly conventional, with small-scale figures rowing toward the house and stable at right;

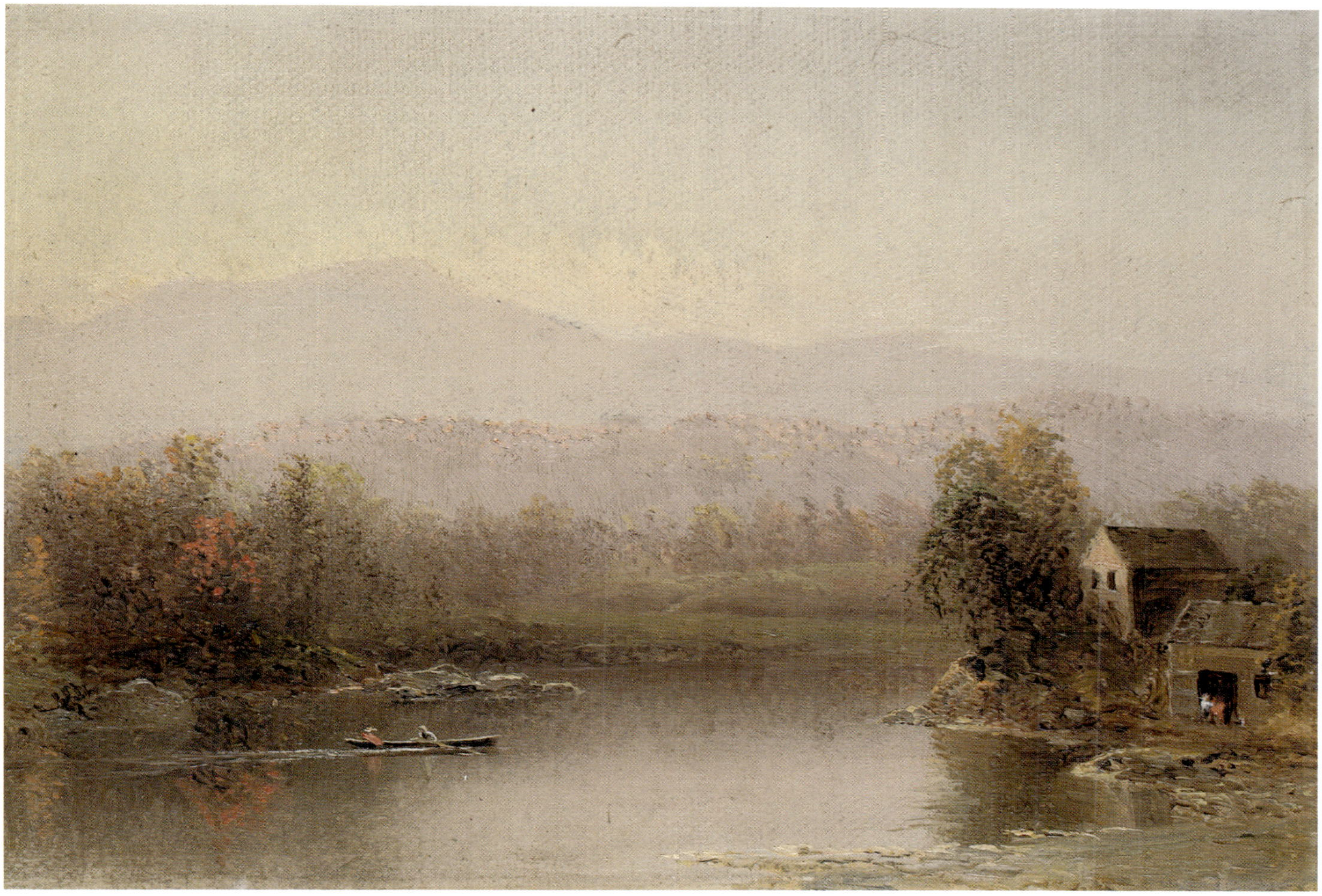

these buildings on the very edge of the water are to be understood as a hostelry or camp, since nothing alludes to a farm. If the painting thus belongs to Hudson River school stock, it is unusual in handling, even for a sketch. The exposed coarse nap of the canvas, the large brushstrokes, and, especially, the use of the palette knife and thick, creamy structures of paint in the rocks document Martin's early experiments with individualistic, expressive technique.

In the body of Martin's work, this painting relates most closely to a tiny pen-and-ink drawing that he included in a letter to his Albany friend, Thomas S. Lloyd, written on October 17, 1859, during a "ramble" through the Catskills (Mandel 1973, 288). The basic composition of the drawing is the same, in reverse, and (farm) buildings attract focus to the (left) margin in counterpoint to distant hills obliquely opposite. Lloyd, who was only slightly older than Martin, was a musician of national repute, famed as an educator and composer of hymns, church music, and ballads; he was also an accomplished draftsman in the Hudson River school fold. Lloyd married Emily B. Pulling of Detroit in 1861, and upon his death in Albany in 1883 his family moved to Detroit, where later that year Martin's landscape was hung in the Detroit Art Loan Exhibition, precursor of the Detroit Institute of Arts.

The painting, like most of Martin's work, probably is based on recollections, in this case of late summer and fall outings in the mountains, as it addresses the masculine camaraderie and sportsman's appreciation of nature that Martin's circle shared. He was so immersed in male society that he was alien and unfathomable to women. Vedder recalled that "women . . . did not exist for him, not even his wife" (Mandel 1973a, 5), and Elizabeth Martin began her biography of her husband by confessing that he "was so intensely masculine, so preeminently a man's man, that he must necessarily have escaped thorough comprehension by any woman" (E. Martin 1904, vii). To be sure, such activities as fishing, hunting, and even hiking were largely male pursuits at the time, but comments about Martin's masculinity implied something further. One critic observed, in language applicable as well to the art of Winslow Homer, that Martin's landscapes evince "the quality of an extra large-souled man. . . . [T]he quality is essentially a masculine one, and rare even among men, particularly in art, so large a portion of which is feminine in significance" (Caffin 1913, 118). The allusion may be to the epic remoteness and intangibility within Martin's paintings, which recede and dissemble upon intimate approach; Martin called this quality "a sense of the deadly loneliness I live in" (Mandel 1973a, 6).

W. T. O.

Provenance Probably Thomas S. Lloyd. His wife, Emily B. Lloyd. Her daughters, Ethel and Bertha Lloyd. Acquired in 1924.

Exhibition Detroit 1883, 45, no. 457.

64

In the Adirondacks, 1881

Oil on canvas
30.8 × 48.6 cm (12⅛ × 19⅛ in.)
Gift of Raymond C. Smith (67.253)

From 1881 to 1886 Martin resided abroad, first in London and then for five years near Villerville in Normandy. Elizabeth Martin remembered how contented they were in those years, snugly lodged in the fold of an amiable community of artists, but Martin was miserable, groping his way through midlife trials. He painted fitfully, sent little work to New York for exhibition and no work to the National Academy, and entrusted responsibility for providing a livelihood to his talented wife, who completed piecework translation jobs steered her way by William C. Brownell (Martin himself never learned French). Unnerved by the onset of cataracts and lack of general appreciation for his paintings, Martin was adrift. Edmund Gosse, who knew him in England in 1882, recalled that he "had a look of the most pathetic destitution. He dressed in very shabby black clothes . . . fit only for the dust heap," his "face was distressingly disfigured by drink—all red and pimpled," and he "had no force or courage left" (Mandel 1973, 108).

A change in technique and approach paralleled the anguished alteration in Martin's person. Since his first visit to England and France in 1876, he had developed a loose, impressionistic style that accommodated both his early interest in Barbizon landscape and his subsequent fascination with Whistler's paintings, especially the nocturnes. He also began to paint watercolors and to express affinity for Japanese art, so that by the later 1870s he was identified no longer with Kensett but with progressive artists in New York such as Inness, with whom he shared several patrons and defenders in the press. Brownell, John Van Dyke, Russell Sturgis, William M. Laffan, Charles De Kay, and Samuel G. W. Benjamin were among the coterie of "avowed Martinites" (Mather 1912, 63–64) who pushed his work upon a determinedly not-buying public.

In the Adirondacks, painted in 1881, typifies the new direction that Martin took. It is a recollected landscape of a favorite subject, envisioned after extended reflection, that imparts the look of the region in autumn, its distinguishing season; the painting's larger function, however, is to generate psychological response to vastness, process, and a specific condition of color in nature. Forms are generalized, appearing frayed and partly deconstructed, and the handling, often varied with the palette knife, is loose and suggestive. The same elements characterize *On the Hudson* and *Coast Meadows, St. Sauveur* (both unlocated), two other paintings from 1881 that are even further dematerialized, lacking foreground detail altogether (Carroll 1913, 92, 98).

Friendly critics seized on these elements in praising Martin's new style, which became more bold and experimental following the residence in Normandy. Writing in 1912, his biographer Frank Jewett Mather argued that Martin "had already mastered" the modernist-seeming "art of elimination" by the time he painted *In the Adirondacks.* "Witness a fine canvas called 'Morning' dated 1881 and exhibited that year in the Society of American Artists. Specific form is reduced to the merest indication, it seems as if nothing were left but glorious color and vast space" (Mather 1912, 49). Annie Meyer described Martin's goal as "the subordination of the things that *are not* for the things that *are.* . . . [T]he art of Homer Martin may be summed up by the word elimination. He possessed . . . the power to wrest from the scene before him its very heart, to seize the essential—the elemental" (Meyer 1908, 255). A reviewer in the *New York Evening Sun* (February 7, 1889) developed the same theme: "Homer Martin occupies a place apart in American landscape art. There is no man who can get so much out of so little. He can take the simplest, baldest theme and invest it with an interest that is almost romantic by his exhaustive and suggestive study, his investigations of its color subtleties, and his deep knowledge of what poets call the 'heart of things.'" Benjamin offered further insight: "Homer Martin . . . views nature for the sentiment it suggests, while he is impressed chiefly by color and light; for form he seems to have less feeling. But he is a lyrist with the brush . . . in all his works there is absolute freedom, freshness, and originality; his scheme of color is altogether his own, full of luminousness and purity; but he is weak in technique" (Benjamin 1880, 106). Similarly, George W. Sheldon observed that "Mr. Martin is that rarest of artists, a colorist," and "neither the subjects nor the sentiments of his pictures are commonplace" (Sheldon 1880, 106).

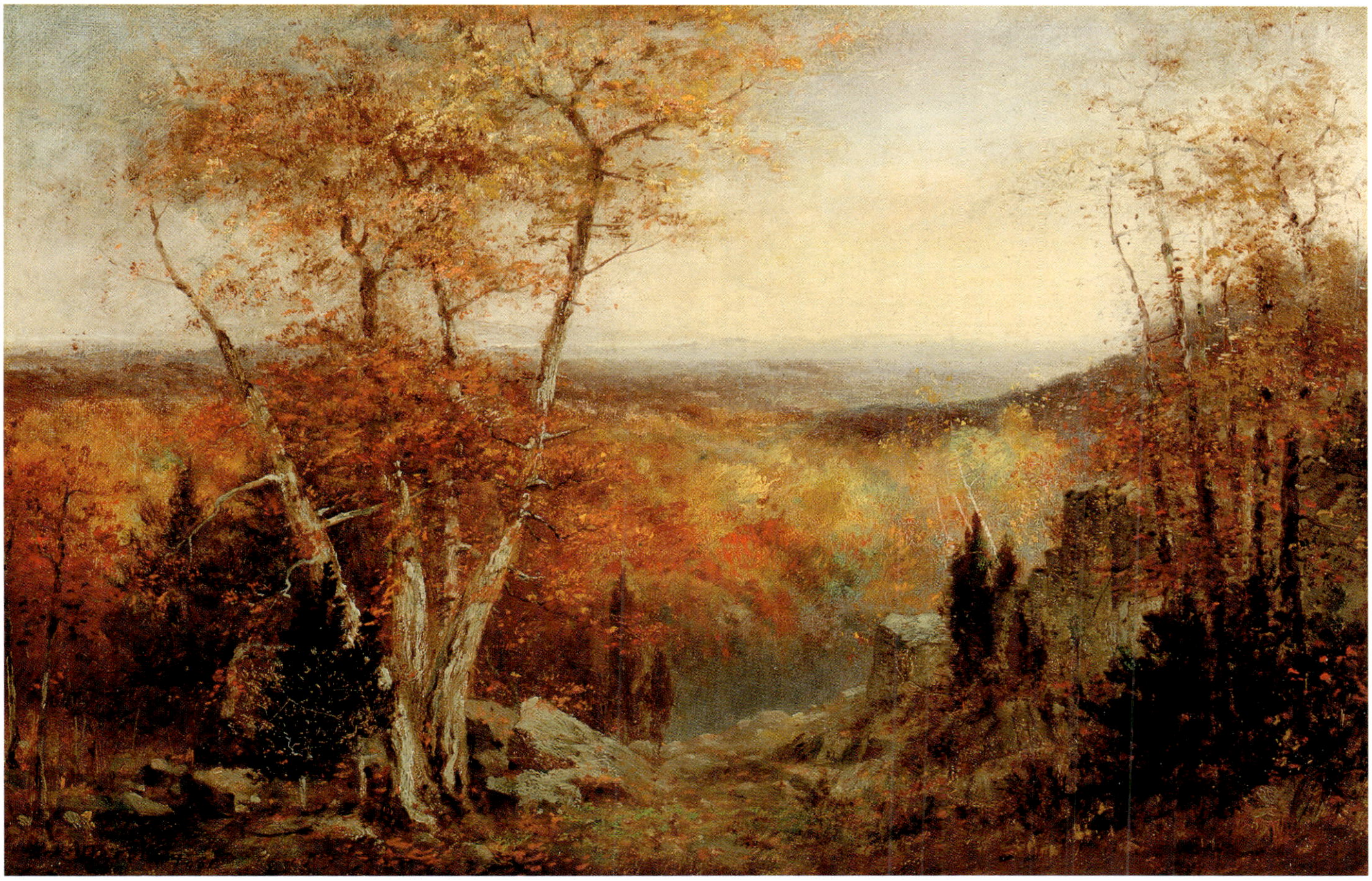

Elizabeth Martin almost despaired of writing her husband's biography after his death, urging that those who wanted to understand him should study "the landscapes into which he has put as much of his best self as any man could part with and live," and it was she who most clearly identified the landscapes as self-portrayals. In a passage that applies well to *In the Adirondacks* she wrote: "I remember the late John Richard Dennett saying of them: 'Martin's landscapes look as if no one but God and himself had ever seen the places.' There is an austerity, a remoteness, a certain savagery in even the sunniest and most peaceful of them, which were also in him, and an instinctive perception of which had made me say to him . . . that he reminded me of Ishmael" (E. Martin 1904, ix). Martin's work was often called "poetic," and he was known to have "detested what he called literary pictures—pictures, that is, that told or tried to tell a story" (E. Martin 1904, 20). While he included architecture and figures in some paintings, in most he interpreted isolated expanses of woods, lakes, rivers, or sand dunes as constituting mysteries beyond comprehension. Samuel Isham identified a "deep, grave melancholy, sobering but not saddening," as the "keynote" of Martin's landscapes (Isham 1905, 265). Martin himself left only a singular allusion to what he saw when he painted, writing of "the unknowable free, outside of man, which seems to be the charm of the more serious aspects of landscape" (1874, in Mandel 1973, 19). Perhaps the statement hints at a lingering transcendentalism, but Martin was an agnostic (Mather 1912, 24), fundamentally removed from, say, the Christian crusaders of the Hudson River school, his friend Inness, and his devoutly Catholic wife. Mather called him a Stoic: "what he seeks in nature is solace, suspension of the will, expansion of the contemplative self" (Mather 1912, 71); and his friend John Van Dyke concluded that Martin captured the "great serenity" of nature, whose "normal condition is repose—that immobility which we associate with the realms of space" (Van Dyke 1919, 85). W. T. O.

Inscription At lower left, *H. D. Martin 1881*

Provenance Raymond C. Smith. Acquired in 1967.

Reference *BDIA* 1977, 99–100.

In the Adirondacks

Louis Rémy Mignot

1831 Charleston, South Carolina–
Brighton, England 1870

"Mignot is Southern not only in color and subjects, but in sympathy" (Tuckerman 1867, 564). With those words Henry T. Tuckerman summarized his appraisal of the successful, though short-lived, landscape painter. Mignot possessed an extraordinary sense of color and light, effectively creating a brilliant or subdued scene according to the expression required. His Southern origins contributed much to his distinctive art: Charleston's blazing sun, resplendent gardens, ocean waters, and ever-changing, moisture-laden atmosphere certainly sensitized Mignot to varying climatic effects. He was at home in the humidity of tropical lagoons and forests. Winter environments fascinated him. Mignot's "remarkable facility of catching the expression, often the vague, but, therefore, more interesting, expression of a scene" stemmed from a romanticism nurtured in the South, a region in which folktales and appearances reign (Tuckerman 1867, 563).

Born to Rémy and Theonie Mignot of Charleston, Louis was raised in an environment that upheld the values of the Southern gentleman class. His father, a French Roman Catholic, owned substantial property including slaves; he died in 1848. Two years later Theonie married Adolphus John Ruljes, a confectioner from New York. Now free to pursue his early interest in art, Mignot departed for The Hague, in the Netherlands, where he studied for five years in the studio of Andreas Schelfhout, a romantic Dutch landscape painter. Mignot returned to America in 1855, settling into New York City's art world, and exhibiting at the important academies in New York, Philadelphia, and Boston. He sketched the varied terrain of upstate New York, Virginia, Maryland, and the Susquehanna River region.

In 1857, however, Frederic Edwin Church (q.v.) offered Mignot an opportunity that would alter his landscape career forever: to join the prominent painter on a four-month journey to Ecuador. Mignot recorded and remembered this diverse scenery; many years afterward it reappeared transformed into his brilliantly colored South American scenes. Back in New York, Mignot's travels and newly inspired paintings eventually enhanced his artistic and social standing. He was elected to such prestigious organizations as the Century Association (1858) and the National Academy of Design (associate in 1858; academician in 1859). On January 11, 1860, he married Zairah C. Harris of Baltimore.

Yet Mignot the Southerner remained an outsider. With the outbreak of the Civil War, this secessionist at heart could no longer remain in New York. In 1862 he left the country for England, never to return. He quickly established himself in the London art world, exhibiting tropical landscapes, British scenery, and images inspired by romantic poetry. His *Sources of the Susquehanna* (1857; National Academy of Design, New York) appeared at the Exposition Universelle of 1867 in Paris. Mignot visited Switzerland in 1868 and 1869; in 1870, caught in Paris during the outbreak of the Franco-Prussian War, he fled with his family to Brighton. There Mignot died from smallpox.

J. S.

Bibliography Tuckerman 1867, 563–564. Manthorne 1989, 133–157. Manthorne 1993. Raleigh and New York, 1996.

65
Morning in the Andes, 1863
(formerly *Lagoon of the Guayaquil River, Ecuador*)
Oil on canvas
61.5 × 96.5 cm (24¼ × 38 in.)
Founders Society Purchase, Beatrice W. Rogers Bequest Fund and contributions from Robert H. Tannahill and Al Borman (68.345)

One can easily imagine Henry T. Tuckerman having this painting in mind when he praised Mignot as "the efficient delineator of tropical atmosphere and vegetation" (Tuckerman 1867, 563). Strident green foliage, brilliant pink and red flowers, and pale purple mountains cloaked in a pinkish yellow haze effectively transport the viewer to Latin America. The sun casts a soft glow over the Cordillera mountain range, progressively revealing through the mist its geological structure. A closer look reveals how adroitly Mignot achieved this luminous view: quick, loose brushstrokes rather than painstaking details convincingly present the tropics to the viewer. Rocky cliffs and tufts of greenery are equally soft. Both seem to melt into the water, creating a sensuous, soupy mixture of green, yellow, pink, blue, white, and orange rather than the defined, mirror-like reflections identified with works of the Hudson River school. The one exception are the three palm trees. Mignot meticulously delineated their every frond against the backdrop of hazy sky and misty terrain. Their brilliant ascendancy over the indistinct mountainous landscape proclaims that we are indeed in the tropical garden of the first Creation.

Mignot painted this view based on memories of his journey to Ecuador with Church in 1857; it is a condensation of experiences, not one particular view.

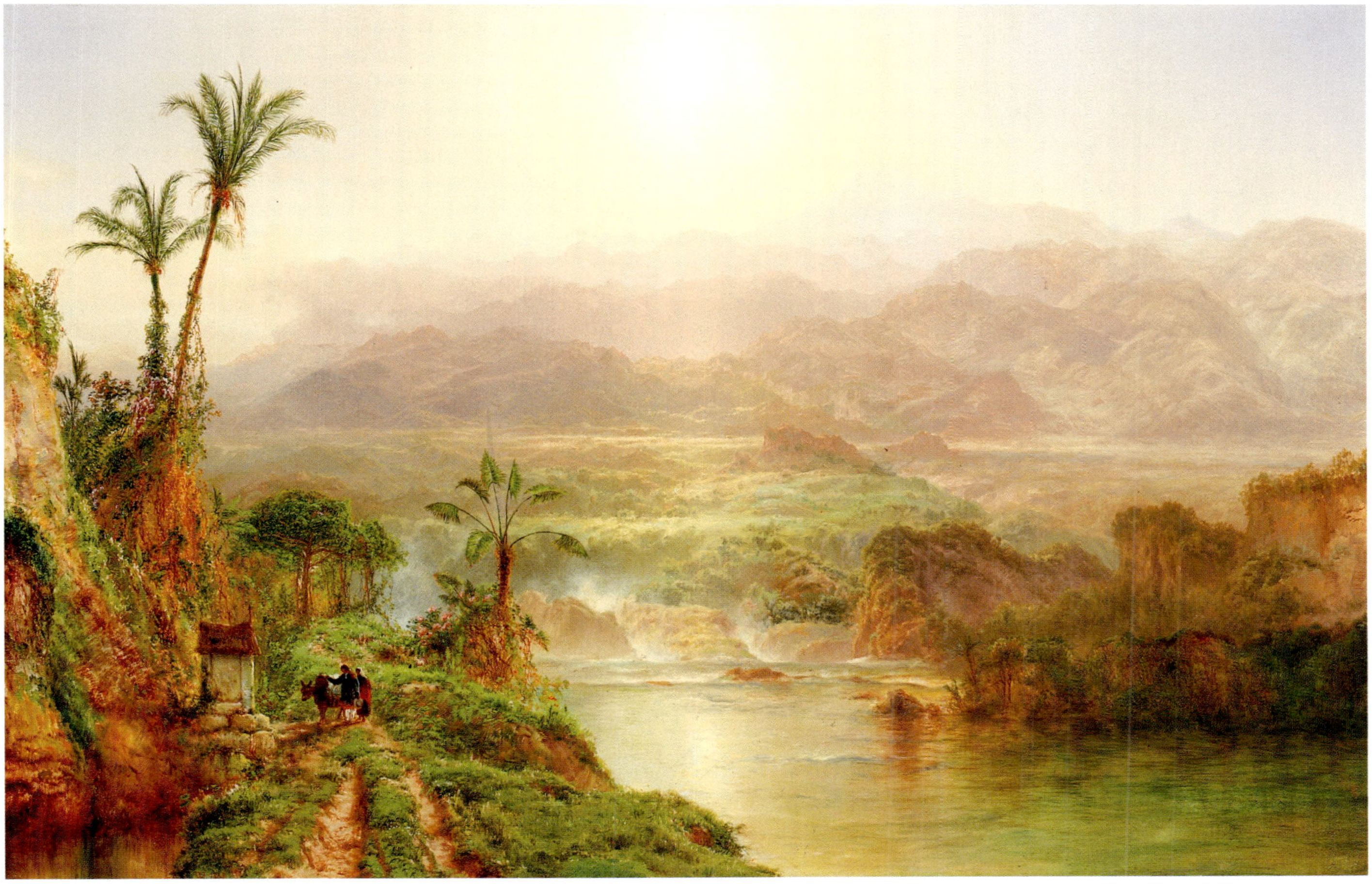

Morning in the Andes

Their four-month adventure led them through the heart of that geological and botanical Eden featured in the naturalist Alexander von Humboldt's magisterial *Cosmos*. They traversed an extraordinary diversity of terrain: they crossed the isthmus of Panama, took a steamer to Ecuador, and proceeded from the low-lying port city of Guayaquil to over ten thousand feet above sea level, across the eastern Cordillera, past Cotopaxi, Chimborazo, and Cayambe, to their ultimate goal of the active volcano Sangay. Although Mignot the Southerner favored the coastal lowlands and lagoons of Ecuador, frequently painting the marshlands along the Guayas River in twilight, he rendered as well the central highlands and the extraordinary Cordillera chain that extends from Quito to Riobamba. It is that spectacular area of the Andes that Mignot presents here, not the lowlands of the Guayas River or of the city Guayaquil.

Recently, a frame with an opening of 24 by 38 inches was found at the Metropolitan Museum of Art in New York with the label "Morning in the Andes. / Louis R. Mignot, N.A." This frame most likely belongs to the Detroit picture, which, although produced in London, may have been included in the collection Mignot sent to be auctioned in 1868 at Leeds and Miner, New York.

In 1859 Mignot painted a similar view of the Andean wilderness, *Landscape in Ecuador* (North Carolina Museum of Art, Raleigh), a distinctly less civilized environment than his various scenes of Guayaquil, Riobamba, and the Guayas River region created in the same year. As Katherine Manthorne has observed, Detroit's painting is an imaginative reworking of this earlier, more Church-like rendition of the Andean mountains. In both, the sun casts morning light over an extensive mountain range and onto still water, prominent palms frame the left side, and travelers make their way on a path that extends into the viewer's space. Detroit's picture, however, resonates with those Southern sympathies that distinguish Mignot from Church. The audacious palette and fluid paint application enhance the painting's poetic expression. The absence of relatively complex architectural structures such as the aqueduct and walled village visible in *Landscape in Ecuador* makes Detroit's Andean scene appear all the more remote and alien. A native couple pause in their journey to pray before a lone, primitive Christian shrine; this religious detail accentuates the uncivilized, Edenic nature of the landscape. A subtle cross of yellow-white light blesses the center of the Andean landscape. Mignot borrowed this detail from his friend Church, specifically from *The Andes of Ecuador* of 1855 (Reynolda House, Winston-Salem, N.C.). Church, however, rarely indulged in such freedom of color and stroke; Mignot has transformed Church's subject—the Andes—irrevocably into his own.

London imposed a beneficial artistic distance between Mignot and Church. During 1862–63 Mignot codified his distinctive interpretation of the tropics, producing some of his most chromatically energetic paintings. Mignot's firsthand exposure to the paintings of J. M. W. Turner contributed to the airy, atmospheric, fluid, and frankly romantic effect of Detroit's Andean scene. Turner, as well as the English Pre-Raphaelite and French schools, liberated Mignot's innate coloristic and expressive proclivities. Away from America, away from the South, away from the Tenth Street Studios, Mignot discovered himself.

Part of that self-discovery was Mignot's repeated inclusion of the soaring palm tree and religious shrine. The palm frequently appeared in paintings and illustrations of Latin America and, significantly, in scenes of biblical Eden by the likes of Thomas Cole. Mignot made it his signature emblem just as Martin Johnson Heade (q.v.) adopted the orchid. No matter the type of South American landscape—mountain, river, lagoon, or city scene—Mignot consistently positioned the palm tree as a dominant element of the picture; it often rises far above the earth. Its exaggerated placement, frequently contrary to botanical fact, affirms its iconographic significance. A long literary tradition associated the palm tree with the Tree of Life in the Garden of Eden. So too, the myth that the Garden of Paradise survived the Flood found renewed currency in the nineteenth century, spurring believers' expectations that vestiges could be discovered in the New World. With the expanded exploration of Latin America and publication of travel accounts by the naturalists Humboldt and James Orton, the coconut palm became the emblem of the tropics as Paradise Found. Mignot's Ecuadoran scene of 1863 celebrates the "fresher verdure," the increased "luxuriance and succulence" of tropical vegetation. Two tall, graceful palms seemingly stretch toward the centralized sun; below, marking a third of the way across the picture, a shorter palm proudly spreads out its leaves like an exotic fan. Pink flowers exuberantly decorate its base. The picture testifies to Orton's assertion that "the most conspicuous trees are the palms, to which the prize of beauty has been given by the concurrent voice of all ages. The earliest civilization of mankind belonged to countries bordering on the region of palms. South America, the continent of mingled heat and moisture, excels the rest of the world in the number and perfection of her palms" (Orton 1876, 219). Ecuador is an especially appropriate setting for extolling the paradisal significance of tropical palms: located on the equator at zero degrees latitude, Ecuador divides north from south, balances day and night, maintains a constancy of season and vegetation, and thus symbolizes for many the perfect meeting of heaven and earth.

The simple shrine and native pilgrims reinforce a sacred equilibrium. As the only signs of human presence, they indicate an environment altered little by civilization. Christianity has clearly made its mark, but the primitive cross capping the thatched roof denotes unassuming moments of worship at the wayside. Unlike the grand, though frequently decayed, Spanish baroque ecclesiastical monuments that appear in Mignot's other South American scenes, this structure was not created to compete with the sublime grandeur of nature. Intended for plain devotion, it evokes the dawning of faith rather than the arrogance of belief. One can only speculate how Mignot the Roman Catholic in an age of anti-papism reacted to the various displays of Catholicism in Latin America. One can certainly imagine, however, Mignot the Southerner, displaced in London, finding solace (as well as success) in painting a remembrance of the tropics—especially one as sensuous and unsullied as Paradise itself.

J. S.

Inscription At lower right, *L M 1863* (LM in monogram)

Provenance Van Loan family, Athens, N.Y. Hirschl & Adler Galleries, New York. Acquired in 1968.

Exhibitions San José 1978, 21, color ill., 35, no. 5, ill. New York 1987, 298–301, 299, color ill. Raleigh and New York 1996, 136–137, 140, color ill., 139–140, 199, ill., no. 78.

References *BDIA* 1977, 94–95, ill. Manthorne 1989, 81, ill., 133, 147. Minks 1989, 108–109, ill. Manthorne 1993, 23–25, 23, ill.

Francis Davis Millet

1846 Mattapoisett, Massachusetts–
down with the *Titanic* 1912

Francis Davis Millet was a true American Renaissance man. The breadth of his talents and accomplishments ranged from easel painting, mural design, interior decoration, and illustration to journalistic writing and arts administration. Fluent in many languages, Millet was conspicuous in the art world both at home and abroad. He served as an officer in enterprises as diverse as the Tile Club and the American Academy in Rome and exercised organizational skills in positions with various international exhibitions, from the 1873 Vienna Exposition to the 1893 World's Columbian Exposition. Millet was also an adviser on national and international artistic affairs to presidents Theodore Roosevelt and William Howard Taft. When he went down with the *Titanic* in 1912, the high esteem in which he was held by America's cultural and political leaders was expressed through myriad accolades (Weinberg 1977, 2).

Born in Mattapoisett, Massachusetts, to Dr. Asa and Huldah Byram Millet, Francis Davis was their second child and first son. Educated at Harvard, where he earned a master's degree in modern languages and literature in 1869, Millet went into the newspaper business, working as a writer and reporter for Boston papers. After graduation his artistic interests become more concerted. His parents encouraged him and arranged for his first substantial training at Antwerp's Royal Academy in 1871. Millet studied there for two years, winning every prize the academy offered.

In 1873 Millet was made secretary to Charles Francis Adams, Jr., Massachusetts commissioner to the Vienna Exposition. In Vienna Millet was exposed to the practice and politics of major international expositions. For the next few years he traveled throughout Europe and earned his living writing for Boston papers.

Millet continued to balance his career as an artist, journalist, and arts administrator in the 1870s on both sides of the Atlantic, sending paintings to the National Academy of Design, the Philadelphia Centennial, and the 1878 Exposition Universelle in Paris. In 1879, shortly after his marriage to Elizabeth Greeley Merrill, Millet made his first showing at the Royal Academy in London. The Millets settled in Boston in 1879, and Millet became active in the art life of that city. He was a founding member of the St. Botolph Club and of its Committee on Art and Library, he lectured on costumes at the School of the Museum of Fine Arts, and he exhibited at the Boston Art Club. He also built an elaborate studio on the grounds of the family home in East Bridgewater that included an accurately reconstructed colonial kitchen. Here he produced carefully studied paintings that portrayed women in old-fashioned costumes engaged in simple tasks. These detailed historical compositions characterized his work for the next decade.

Millet began to produce classically inspired paintings that emphasized careful research and archaeological detail, work that was influenced by that of the English aesthetic artists Sir Lawrence Alma-Tadema and Albert Moore. By 1885 the Millets were spending half the year in the Worcestershire village of Broadway in the English Cotswolds. The Millet family's presence brought a wide circle of artists and writers to the village. Soon known as the Broadway Group, this gathering eventually included Edwin Austin Abbey, John Singer Sargent, Alfred Parsons, Alma-Tadema, Henry James, and Edmund Gosse.

Mural decoration occupied much of Millet's artistic energies during the later years of his career; he created murals for both public and private buildings in Pittsburgh; New Bedford, Massachusetts; Baltimore; Newark, New Jersey; Cleveland; and others. He continued to work as a journalist; during the Spanish-American War in 1898 he was in the Philippines as a newspaper correspondent.

Few areas of the art world escaped his attention. He was a trustee of the Metropolitan Museum of Art, a member of the Copyright League, the founding secretary of the American Federation of Arts, and a charter member of the American Academy in Rome. In 1911 he accepted the directorship of the American Academy, and it was while fulfilling responsibilities for this position that he found himself on the *Titanic* in April 1912.

T. T.

Bibliography American Federation of Arts 1912. Dayton et al. 1976, 114–115. Weinberg 1977. Sharpey-Shafer 1984. Simpson 1990. Washington 1993, 288–290. Kreiner 1995, 14–15.

66

Reading the Story of Oenone, ca. 1883

Oil on canvas

76.2 × 147 cm (30 × 57⅞ in.)

Detroit Museum of Art Purchase, Art Loan Fund and Popular Subscription Fund (83.1)

In the early 1880s Millet expanded his interest in historical genre scenes to include Greek and Roman subjects. One of his earliest efforts, *Reading the Story of Oenone,* an ambitious pictorial translation of his study of classical costume, also successfully rendered the reading of a Greek tale made popular in the mid–nineteenth century through the poetry of Alfred Lord Tennyson. Millet's depiction further presents the self-conscious and nostalgic attitudes of Victorian men and women regarding their position in history and their relationship with the notable civilizations of the past (Weinberg 1977, 7; Detroit 1983, 123).

In Greek mythology Oenone was a nymph who fell in love with and married the young shepherd Paris, who subsequently abandoned her for Helen of

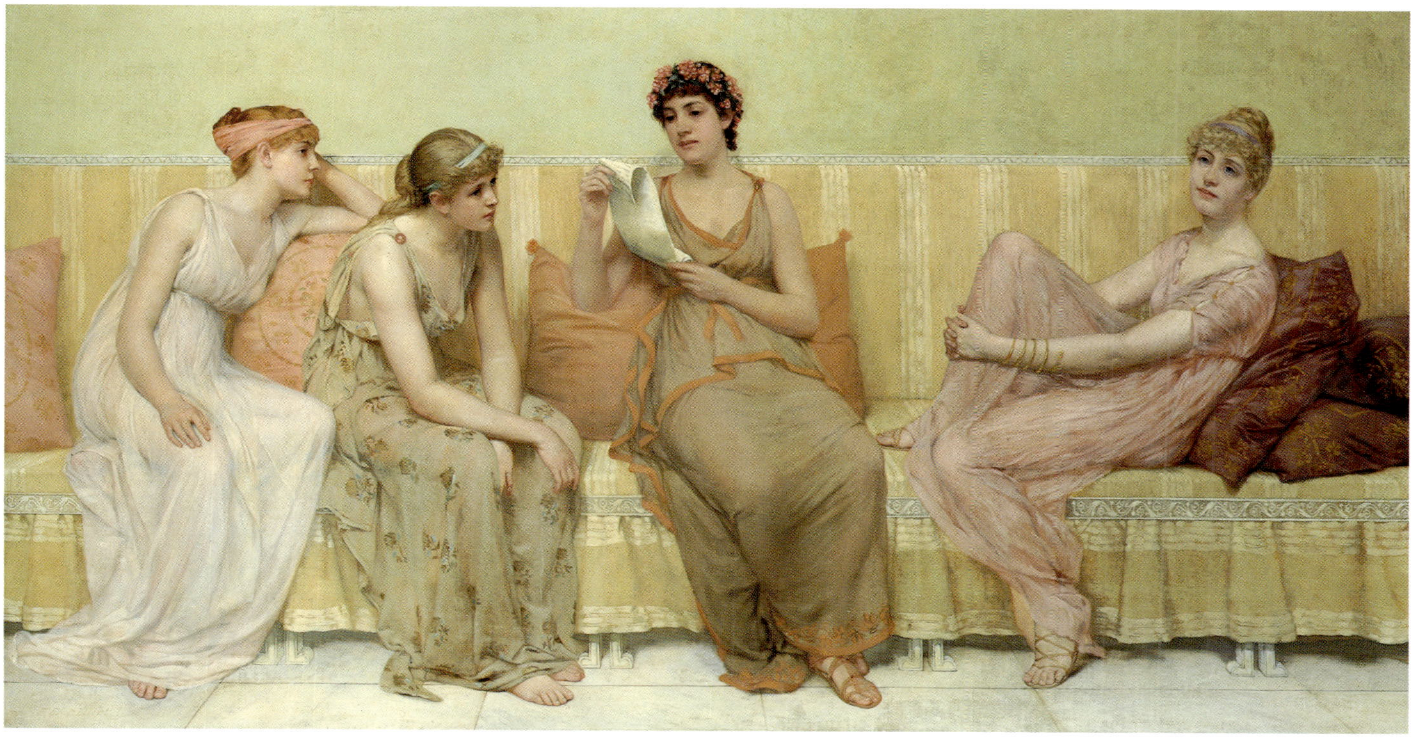

Reading the Story of Oenone

Troy. When Paris was wounded during the Trojan War, he asked Oenone to forgive him and to help heal his wounds. Oenone initially refused, and by the time she put aside her pride, Paris had already died. Grief-stricken, Oenone killed herself.

Millet constructed a friezelike image of four young women dressed in gauzy classical garments seated on a fawn-colored striped divan set against a plain gray background on a white marble tiled floor. The young beauty seated in the center reads the story of Oenone from a sheet of parchment. Her three friends listen to the story with rapt attention. Millet's interpretation suggests many cultural and artistic influences.

In 1882, shortly before he painted *Reading the Story of Oenone*, Millet delivered a series of lectures on Roman costume at the Museum of Fine Arts in Boston and at the National Academy of Design and the Union League Theatre in New York. In these talks Millet emphasized the importance of examining antique statuary to understand the function and arrangement of particular garments and to appreciate their relationship to antique manners. Millet's particular concern for archaeological exactitude was just one of the manifestations of the renewed interest in classical art and culture that occurred in the wake of nineteenth-century archaeological excavations of Greek and Roman artifacts, events the artist may have witnessed during his period of study in Rome in 1874. Millet undoubtedly took his own advice when painting *Reading the Story of Oenone*, as the four young women are both meticulously draped and carefully posed.

A taste for the delicate and restrained forms evident in Greek and Roman art was one source of inspiration for the mid–nineteenth century's aesthetic movement, and many of the artists who painted in this style often concentrated on classical themes. One such artist was the English painter Lawrence Alma-Tadema, whose work displayed an enthusiasm for the Parthenon sculptures in the British Museum. Millet greatly respected the work of Alma-Tadema and in 1882 wrote the artist's agent, "I could so easily become an imitator of him so much do I admire his things and so much do they impress me" (Weinberg 1977, 7).

Millet's *Reading the Story of Oenone* is similar to Alma-Tadema's *Reading from Homer* (1885; Philadelphia Museum of Art), a horizontal arrangement featuring Greek men and women pursuing literary interests. Yet, unlike Alma-Tadema's often sentimental and detailed narratives, Millet's classical paintings focused on predominantly pictorial concerns. Millet's lack of narrative detail, coupled with the tonality of the canvas, accomplished through his manipulation of pale harmonies and diffused light, places *Reading the Story of Oenone* closer to the compositions of James McNeill Whistler (q.v.) and Albert Moore than to the sentimental work of Alma-Tadema. While *Reading the Story of Oenone* does not approach the pure aestheticism seen in the work of Whistler and Moore, it does reveal a dominance of formal order over anecdotal concerns.

Reading the Story of Oenone was painted in New York, or possibly London, and was first exhibited in 1883 in the spring exhibition at the National Academy of Design in New York. Later that year it was shown in the first exhibition of the Detroit Art Loan Association, where its popularity was such that it became the first acquisition in the Detroit Museum's permanent collection (Detroit 1983, 123). The following year the association loaned the painting to the Southern Exposition in Louisville, Kentucky (Louisville 1884, no. 171).

Millet's success with *Reading the Story of Oenone* encouraged him to produce a series of idealized young women draped in classical robes, including *Lacing the Sandal* (1883; private collection; Kreiner 1995, fig. 8), which was shown at the World's Columbian Exposition in Chicago in 1893, as well as *Poppies* (1884; private collection) and *A Handmaiden* (1886; private collection; Kreiner 1995, fig. 10), which was exhibited at the Exposition Universelle in Paris in 1889 (Philadelphia et al. 1989, 187–189).
T. T.

Inscription At lower left, *F. D. Millet*

Provenance Acquired in 1883.

Exhibitions New York, National Academy of Design Annual, 1883, no. 462. Detroit 1883, 48, no. 498. Louisville 1884, 37–38, no. 171. Los Angeles 1974, 166, no. 78. Detroit 1983, 121–123, no. 53.

References *Harper's Weekly* 1883. *BDMA* 1904, 3. *BDMA* 1904a, 2. American Federation of Arts 1912, 58. Baxter et al. 1912. *Art Digest* 1933. Weinberg 1977, 6–7. Rivard 1978, 1050. Detroit 1985, 11. Kreiner 1995.

Thomas Moran

1837 Bolton, Lancashire, England–
Santa Barbara, California 1926

Born in England, Thomas Moran came to the United States with his family at the age of seven. Several other members of his family also entered artistic professions: two brothers became artists and one a photographer. In 1853 Moran was apprenticed to an engraver in Philadelphia, and three years later he took up painting. While Moran supported himself by magazine and book illustration, the artist James Hamilton encouraged his painting and sparked his early enthusiasm for the work of J. M. W. Turner.

In 1861 Moran made the first of several European trips, including travels to Venice in 1886 and 1890. In 1871 he turned west, accompanying the United States Geological and Geographical Survey of the Territories led by Dr. Ferdinand Hayden to Yellowstone, and began to focus on the geological wonders of the American West. Hayden used Moran's sketches of the area to argue for congressional approval of Yellowstone as a national park. In 1872 Congress purchased Moran's massive painting, *The Grand Cañon of the Yellowstone* (1872; National Museum of American Art, Washington, D.C., on loan from the Department of the Interior, Office of the Secretary), for the United States Capitol.

In 1873 Moran accompanied Major John Wesley Powell's expedition to the Grand Canyon and painted a companion to the Yellowstone painting, *The Chasm of the Colorado* (1873–74; National Museum of American Art, Washington, D.C., on loan from the Department of the Interior, Office of the Secretary), for the Capitol. In addition to a trip to Mexico and Cuba in 1883, he made several more trips west to find subjects for landscapes that he completed in his studio in oil and watercolor.

Moran moved to Newark, New Jersey, and in 1884 built a studio in East Hampton, Long Island. In 1922 he moved to Santa Barbara, California, where he died four years later.

S. M. S.

Bibliography Wilkins 1966. Kinsey 1992.

67
The Fisherman's Wedding Party, Venice, 1892

Oil on canvas
61 × 83.8 cm (24 × 33 in.)
Bequest of Alfred J. Fisher (67.118)

According to Margaretta M. Lovell, Moran painted, in watercolor and oils, more views of Venice than any other subject (San Francisco and Cleveland 1984, 66–67). He visited the city twice, in 1886 and 1890, and the sketches made then provided him with material for a large etching (*The Gate of Venice,* 1888) and for approximately one hundred paintings. Between 1887 and 1900 most of the paintings he submitted to the annual exhibitions of the National Academy of Design were Venetian subjects. They sold well after taste for western scenes diminished.

Lovell writes that Moran "repeatedly returned to the subject of Venice but never, in fact, made a portrait of its topographical or architectural facts. His intention was to allude, infer, and dramatize, not to record or analyze" (San Francisco and Cleveland 1984, 66). *The Fisherman's Wedding Party,* however, like many of his other Venetian paintings, includes the architectural skyline of the city and the distinctive Venetian fishing boats and gondolas. He employed a vantage point similar to that in his *View of Venice* (National Museum of American Art, Washington, D.C.) painted a year earlier: westward toward the mouth of the Grand Canal, what Moran called the "main artery of the city" (letter, to C. Klackner, May 1888, published in Southampton 1984, 39)—probably from the island of San Giorgio Maggiore. In the left background, framed by the masts of the foreground boats, are the domes of Santa Maria della Salute. On the right, echoing the verticality of the masts, are the domes of San Marco and the Campanile above the Doge's Palace.

Unlike his other Venetian works, here Moran focuses on a special celebration of the fisherfolk, a wedding, and not on the everyday activities of the fishermen. In the foreground, at the left, fishing boats and a gondola are filled with the wedding party. In the shallow water, several figures are wading, although, according to Lovell, no sandbar or tidal spit exists in this section of the lagoon (San Francisco and Cleveland 1984, 67). It is difficult to pick out members of the crowd in the boats; the bride could be either of the two figures in white gowns, one of whom stands out against the backdrop of a colorful sail, the other, against a mast. The elaborate costumes, rich colors of flags, tapestries, and sails, which were "gaily decorated in a variety of devices and patterns by their owners" (Moran to Klackner, as above), elevate and ennoble these humble people; Moran's subject makes clear that such brilliance was not the exclusive domain of the city's wealthy citizens.

Erica Hirshler describes Moran's painting technique in *Fisherman's Wedding Party:* "[He] used a light palette of blue, green, and pink to render the shifting surfaces of sky and water, painting thinly over a rosy ground in some areas while building up a thick impasto in others" (Boston et al. 1992, 420). Most of the canvas is taken up by shimmering expanses of sky and water. In subject, composition, jewel-like color, and fascination with light on water, Moran's Venetian paintings show the continuing influence of Turner.

The origin of the title of this painting is unknown. No work with a similar title was exhibited at the National Academy

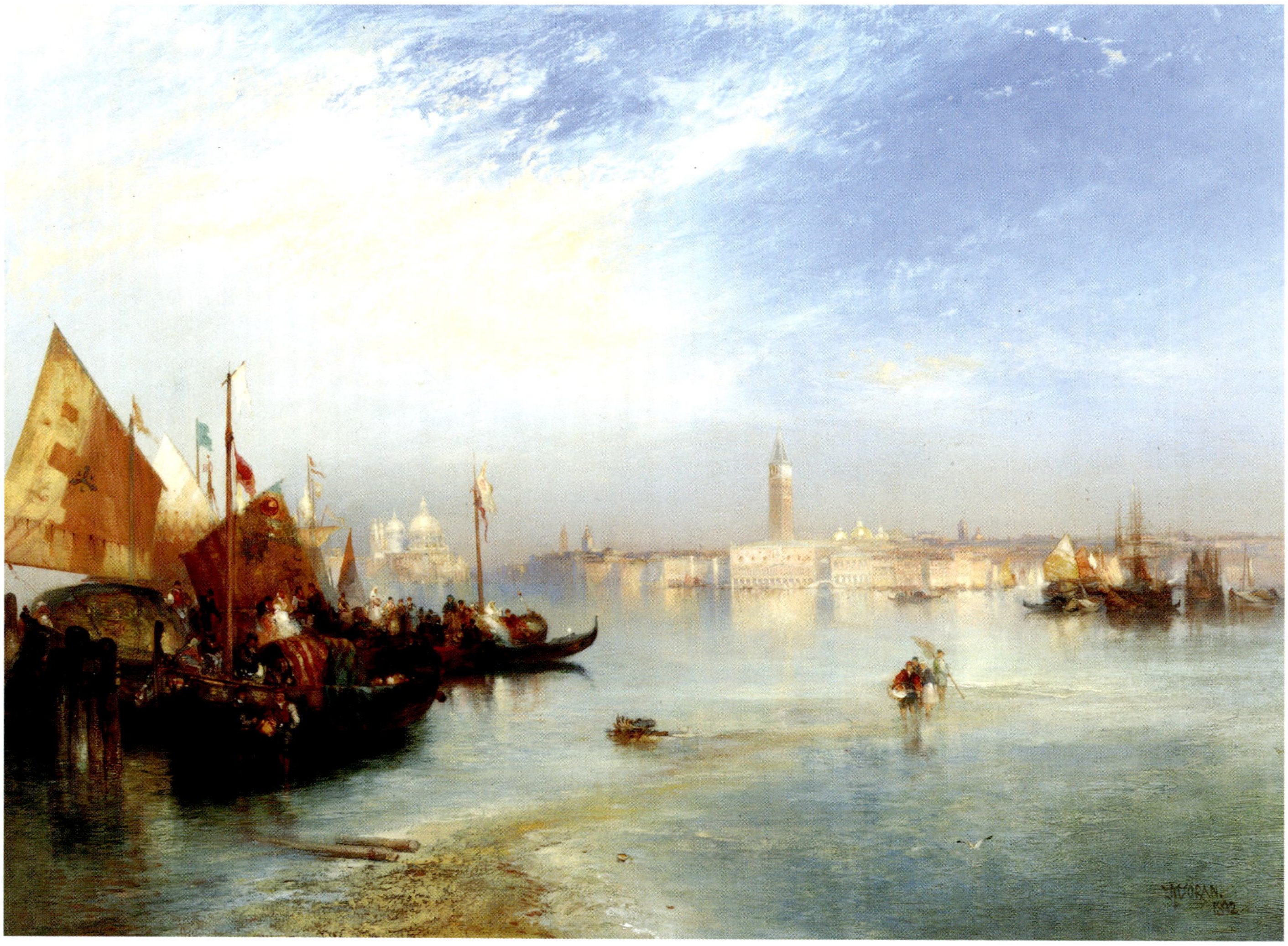

of Design. The titles of Moran's Venetian paintings are usually generalized, such as *View of Venice,* although some refer to the time of day or the architectural setting.
S. M. S.

Inscription At lower, right: *TMoran. 1892* (TM in monogram)

Provenance Howard Young Gallery, New York, ca. 1927–28. Alfred J. Fisher. Acquired in 1967.

Exhibitions San Francisco and Cleveland 1984, 68–69, no. 26. Boston et al. 1992, 419–421, no. 123.

References Hood et al. 1977, 101–102, no. 18. Lovell 1985, 862–863, ill.

The Fisherman's Wedding Party

Milne Ramsey

1846 Philadelphia 1915

One of eight children, Milne Ramsey was born to Alexander and Anna Eliza Milne Ramsey in Philadelphia on September 16, 1846. His father was a prosperous cotton merchant who had a reversal of fortune due to the Civil War. Ramsey served in the Pennsylvania Militia during the Civil War, prior to his enrollment in the Pennsylvania Academy of the Fine Arts in 1863. He began to exhibit pictures at the academy in 1865, and by 1867 he had established his own studio at 524 Walnut Street.

In mid-1867 Ramsey moved to Paris to study with Léon Bonnat, with whom he worked for five years. It was in Bonnat's studio that he met his lifelong friend, the American muralist Edward Blashfield. During his years of study in Paris Ramsey became interested in costume genre pictures. In 1869 he exhibited a still life at the Salon and continued with that theme and costume paintings through the late 1870s. He shared a studio with Blashfield at 75, boulevard de Clichy, where he remained until 1880, when he moved to 2, rue Tourlaque.

In the 1870s Ramsey traveled extensively throughout Europe while maintaining his residence in Paris and a very strong presence in Philadelphia. In 1874 he served on the advisory committee for the selection of artworks for the Centennial Exposition in Philadelphia. It was during this period that he married Annie Ruff, with whom he had two children, one, the artist Charles Frederic Ramsey; this marriage would end in divorce in the following decade. Ramsey was active in art circles on both sides of the Atlantic, exhibiting widely in Paris, New York, and Philadelphia.

In early 1882 he moved back to Philadelphia and established a studio in the Love Building. Upon his return, he exhibited ninety-two paintings at the Pennsylvania Academy, most of them landscapes, although there were also still lifes and costume pieces. Once back in the United States, he turned his complete attention to still-life painting. In 1889 he was a member of the Hanging Committee of the Pennsylvania Academy. That same year he moved his studio to the Haseltine Building. The studio has been compared to William Merritt Chase's, filled with interesting furniture, costumes, and decorative arts. Despite his success, Ramsey was not happy in Philadelphia and traveled to Europe in 1891. Although he established a studio in Europe, he returned to Philadelphia and his studio in the Haseltine Building almost within the year.

He did not remain in Philadelphia long, soon taking rooms at the Shelburne Hotel in Atlantic City, New Jersey, which was owned by the family of his former student and future wife, Rebekha Roberts. The two were married in July 1892. A year later he again gave up his studio in Philadelphia and moved to New York, where he and his new wife had five children. Before the turn of the century Ramsey had a house built in Lawrence Park, in Bronxville, New York, and the family split their time between the new home and the Shelburne. It was about this time that he turned to landscape painting, using the area around the hotel as subject matter.

The hotel was sold in the early 1900s and the family returned to Philadelphia. Ramsey established a studio in the Baker Building, where his son Charles also maintained one. Toward the end of his life Ramsey gradually withdrew from Philadelphia artistic life, his work becoming somewhat forgotten and outdated by newer interests in painting.

J. W. T.

Bibliography New York 1974.

68

Still Life with Lobster, 1898

Oil on canvas

66 × 99.1 cm (26 × 39 in.)

Founders Society Purchase, Beatrice W. Rogers Fund (74.54)

Still Life with Lobster is one of Ramsey's largest and relatively late still-life paintings. It was painted at Lawrence Park in Bronxville, New York, in May 1898 (see Inscription), when Ramsey was beginning to turn his attention to landscape painting. The canvas was probably completed just before the family went to the Shelburne Hotel in Atlantic City, New Jersey, for the summer. A lobster first appeared in his work with his 1882 entry at the National Academy of Design and recurred over the next two decades. Apparently, this was a subject newly in vogue in the late nineteenth century.

Ramsey, who in the late 1890s was at the height of his talents, created an elaborate table setting. The starched white tablecloth serves as a base for the glass, porcelain, and silver containers, which contain a variety of foods and beverages. Several bottles cluster around the central plate holding the focal point of the canvas, the lobster. To the right is an elaborate porcelain bowl, which contains the ingredients for a salad. On the lower right side, in a subtle tonal contrast, two eggs lie on the white cloth.

Ramsey has demonstrated his skill by the repeated placement of white objects on the cloth. In addition to the eggs, he has provided us with a clear glass saltcellar filled with salt and the white platter holding the lobster. All are against the white background of the cloth. While not executing a trompe-l'oeil canvas, Ramsey has delivered all the necessary illusionistic tricks, which so enamored his late-nineteenth-century audience. His palette

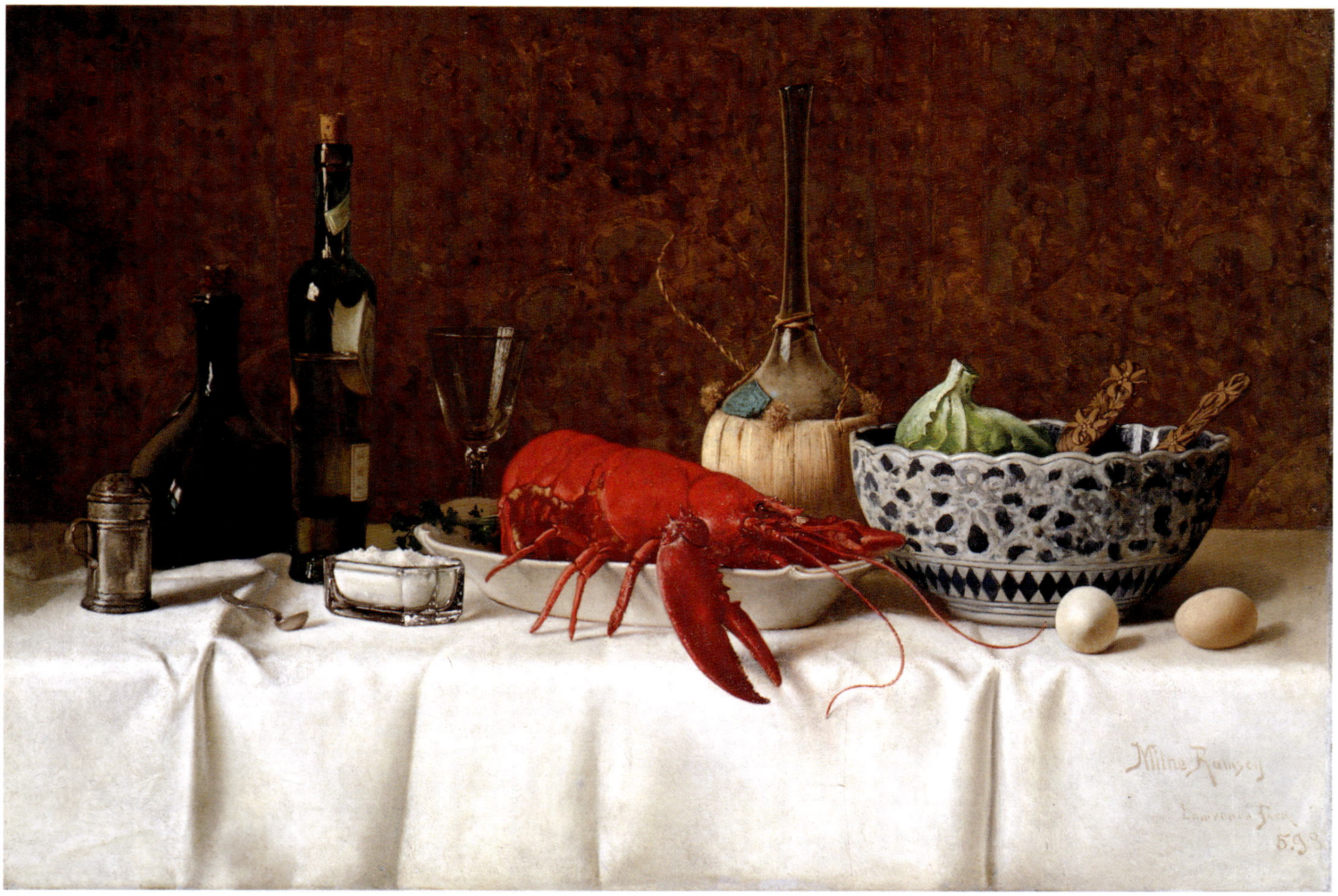

is subdued, the colors of the bottles and vegetables working in concert with the patterned wallpaper; the wicker, porcelain, eggs, and salt harmonize with the tablecloth; and then there is the great contrast of the vibrant red lobster. Ramsey has painted the boiled crustacean so as to grab the viewer visually.

J. W. T.

Inscription At lower right, *Milne Ramsey Lawrence Park 5.98*

Exhibitions New York 1974, 32–34, no. 3. Loaned to the United States Embassy, Lisbon, Portugal, 1982.

Reference *BDIA* 1974.

Still Life with Lobster

Thomas Buchanan Read

1822 Chester County, Pennsylvania–New York 1872

Born on the family farm in Pennsylvania, T. Buchanan Read was apprenticed to a tailor as a boy. But he left home at a young age, and by 1839 settled in Cincinnati, where he became an assistant to the portrait sculptor Shobal Vail Clevenger. In 1841 Read moved to Boston, where his artistic talents were encouraged by Washington Allston. He had also begun to write poetry, publishing his first volume of poems in 1846. After moving to Philadelphia, he traveled to Europe in 1850, where he became friends with the Pre-Raphaelites in London. For much of the final two decades of his life, he lived in Florence and Rome, making a living selling paintings to Americans traveling in Italy or commissioned by patrons in America.

Read maintained ties with both artistic and literary circles. In Italy, he was friendly with a group of expatriate American sculptors and painters and with British writers, including Elizabeth and Robert Browning. Although Henry T. Tuckerman, in *Book of the Artists* (1867), wrote that Read was better known for his poetry than his paintings, Read's mother-in-law noted in a letter of 1870 that his Roman studio "has offered one of the greatest attractions to strangers here and I note down as Fact—that since the 1st of January . . . up to this date, he has sold $21,000 worth of pictures!!" (quoted in Denison Laws Burton, "T. B. Read in Rome," in Highley 1972, n.p.).

In addition to portraits, his career in Italy allowed him to paint ideal subjects—literary, religious, and imaginary scenes that often featured female figures in diaphanous veils. Nathaniel Hawthorne probably described Read in his novel *The Marble Faun* (1860) as an American artist in Rome, a "poet-painter, whose song has the vividness of picture and whose canvas is peopled with angels, fairies, and water-sprites, done to the ethereal life, because he saw them face to face in his poetic mood."

During the Civil War, Read returned to the United States to work for the Union cause; he wrote a patriotic poem, "Sheridan's Ride" (1864). Read followed his poem with a series of paintings of the Union General Philip Henry Sheridan. He hoped to show that he could paint subjects other than the delicate ones for which he had become known. He proudly reported in a letter dated August 28, 1869, to James L. Claghorn, one of his collectors, that, in the estimation of the sculptor Harriet Hosmer, his painting of Sheridan "silences all the assertions made here to you that I could not paint a strong picture only light ethereal subjects" (Read family papers, AAA, roll 1478). However, contemporary taste remained strongest for his romantic Victorian pictures.
S. M. S.

Bibliography Highley 1972.

69
A Painter's Dream, 1869

Oil on canvas
75.6 × 97.8 cm (29¾ × 38½ in.)
Gift of Charles E. Feinberg in honor of Mrs. Benjamin L. Lambert's 90th birthday (59.7)

During the late 1860s in Rome, Read painted a number of imaginary and mythological subjects that included seminude female figures. In this one, a woman appears in the dream of a sleeping artist, who is dressed in a classical tunic. Illuminated by a torch, floating above him on a diaphanous robe carried by five cupids, she wears a tiara, her nudity partly covered by a thin veil. Paul L. Grigaut described her as "Venus with her retinue of cupids, resplendent in the darkness and ready to bring the Byronic hero inspiration and love" (Grigaut 1958–59, 91).

Although the painting has been known as *A Poet's Dream (Art Quarterly* 1959; correspondence, curatorial files, DIA), the blank canvas on an easel at the right clearly identifies the sleeper's occupation. Read also wrote several poems on the subject of dreams, including "Fragments from the Realm of Dreams," "Endymion," and "The Reaper's Dream" (Read 1883), which may have contributed to the misidentification of the male figure.

Read often included female figures in scanty drapery in his paintings at this time, such as Aphrodite in *Flight of the Arrow* (1868; Pennsylvania Academy of the Fine Arts, Philadelphia), and his contemporaries saw his nudes as models of restraint. Albert Bierstadt (q.v.) wrote to Read from Rome on April 5, 1868: "I have been trying to remember among the ancient and Modern artists those who have not always painted the nude without betraying something to disturb your feelings of propriety. I can recall none who have painted with that absolute delicacy and refinement that you do" (Read family papers, AAA, roll 1478).

The painting follows a tradition of visual representations of men dreaming of women. It also is one of a series of dream paintings by American artists during the mid–nineteenth century, beginning with Washington Allston's *Jacob's Dream* (1817; National Trust, England) and continued by Thomas Cole in *The Architect's Dream* (1846; Toledo Museum of Art). Paintings of artists dreaming were exhibited by George Comegys (at the Pennsylvania Academy of the Fine Arts in 1840), Daniel Dickinson (also at the Pennsylvania Academy in 1843), and Luther Terry (at the National Academy of Design in 1854) (for all, Gerdts 1979, 177). Close in conception is Emanuel Leutze's *Poet's Dream* (by 1840; Pennsylvania Academy of the Fine Arts), in which a woman—possibly Erato, the muse of lyric poetry—clothed in a filmy robe, stands over a poet asleep in a graveyard. In the early 1850s Read visited Leutze in Düsseldorf, where he painted Leutze's portrait (Craven in Highley

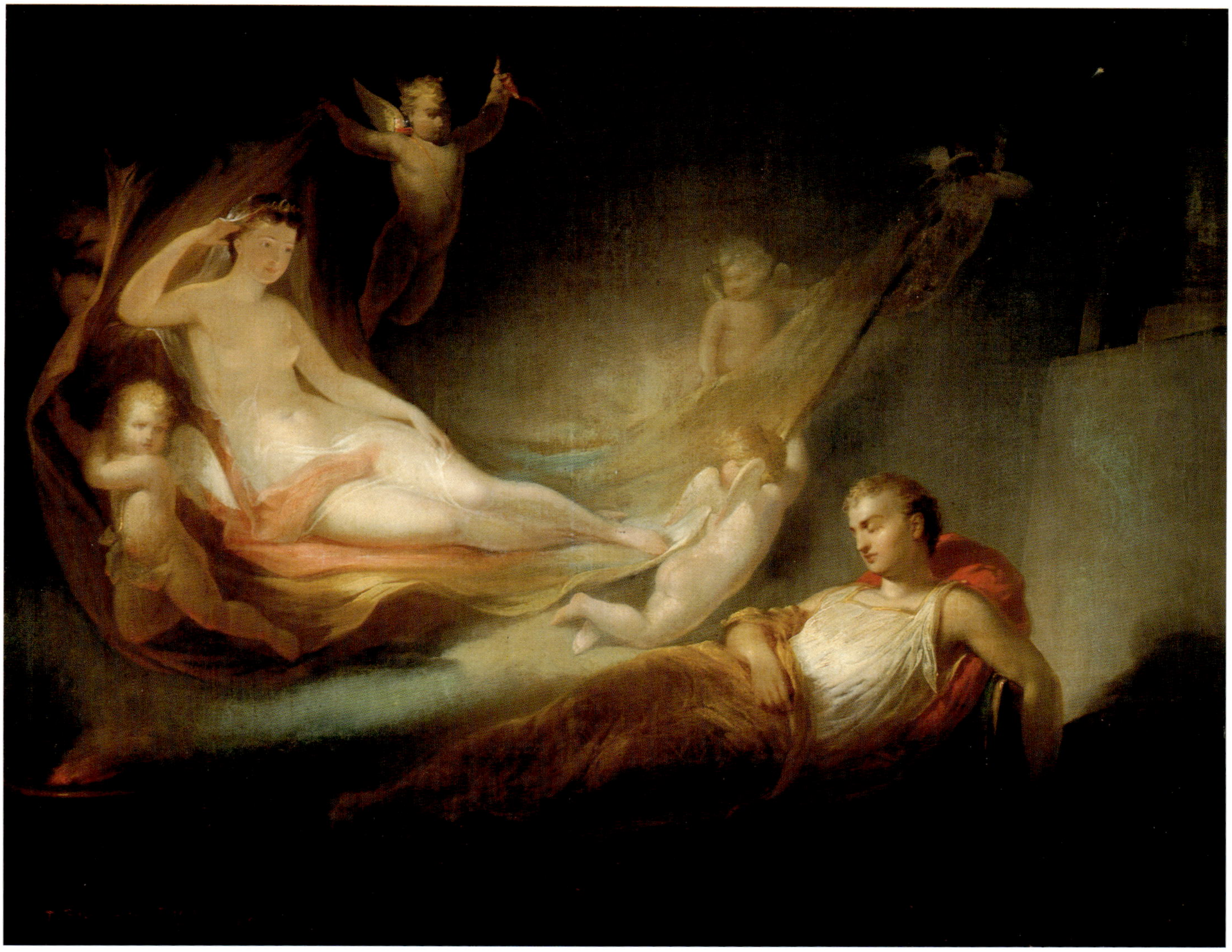

1972, n.p.) and may have become familiar with the *Poet's Dream.*

Read's second wife, Harriet Denison Butler Read, whom he married in 1856, may have been the inspiration for the subject as well as the model for the female figure. Wayne Craven notes that "we know that Mrs. Read made a practice of going to her husband's studio [at 53 Via Margutta, Rome] where she would sit at his side while he worked at his easel, and read to him from books of poetry and literature" (Craven in Highley 1972, n.p.). She apparently was the model for angelic figures in several of his paintings, such as *Star of Bethlehem* (Chester County Historical Society, West Chester, Pa.).
S. M. S.

Inscription At lower left: *T. Buchanan Read / Rome 1869*

Provenance Borneman Collection, Philadelphia. Acquired in 1959.

Exhibition Newark et al. 1974, 27–28, 106–107, no. 32.

References Grigaut 1958–59, 89–91, ill., as *The Painter's Dream. Art Quarterly* 1959, 178, ill., as *A Poet's Dream.* Craven, "The Art of Thomas Buchanan Read," in Highley 1972, n.p. Gerdts 1979, 178, 179, fig. 6.

A Painter's Dream

William Trost Richards

1833 Philadelphia–Newport, Rhode Island 1905

At an early age, William Trost Richards began sketching the landscape near his home in Philadelphia. Like William Stanley Haseltine (q.v.), he studied with the German landscape painter Paul Weber. He also worked as a designer of ornamental metalwork. In 1854 a meeting with the Hudson River school artists Frederic Edwin Church (q.v.) and John Frederick Kensett (q.v.) strengthened his commitment to landscape painting. Soon after, he made the first of many trips to Europe, where he created a stock of sketches of the scenery.

His study in Düsseldorf of "the mechanical of Art" was the foundation for his developing style of minute exactness. Other influences on his work probably included a reading of the first volumes of John Ruskin's *Modern Painters* and the viewing of the Pre-Raphaelite paintings at an exhibition of English art shown at the Pennsylvania Academy of the Fine Arts in 1858. That year he began to paint out-of-doors, in a Pre-Raphaelite manner, rendering detailed forms directly from nature. In 1863 he was elected a member of the newly founded Association for the Advancement of Truth in Art, an organization devoted to promoting Ruskin and the principles of the Pre-Raphaelite Brotherhood in America, and he became the best-known American Pre-Raphaelite artist.

Although he had painted primarily woodland views early in his career, he concentrated on marines after 1868, when he began to spend summers with his family along the eastern seaboard. In the 1870s he turned frequently to the medium of watercolor. By the end of the decade, in response to the growing popularity of painterly suggestiveness in landscape, his own precise handling broadened. Yet he never let go of the facts of a landscape, even in his many drawings, watercolors, and oil studies.

S. M. S.

Bibliography Brooklyn and Philadelphia 1973. Ferber 1980. Brooklyn and Boston 1985, 214–228.

70

Woodland Brook, 1861

Oil on canvas

92.7 × 127 cm (36½ × 50 in.)

Founders Society Purchase, Beatrice W. Rogers Fund (75.60)

When this painting was acquired by the museum, it was entitled *Woodland Brook in Vermont,* based on the family tradition of an earlier collector (correspondence, curatorial files, DIA). Linda Ferber, however, has found no evidence that Richards ever visited Vermont. She points out that he spent the summer and fall of 1861, the year this was painted, in and around Bethlehem, Pennsylvania, and speculates that this may be a view on the Wissahickon Creek, which flows through Philadelphia (Ferber 1980, 1:101).

The painting is noteworthy as being one of the largest of Richards's early landscapes and the first of a series of wooded banks and a stream that he was to paint in the 1860s and 1870s (Ferber 1980, 1:103). Richards was practicing plein-air painting by this time and may have painted this outdoors, on the spot. In the foreground, rocks and a low bank carpeted with foliage act as a viewing platform. A quiet brook meanders through a lush, wooded landscape. In the distance, two figures in a boat pole their way toward a small clearing in the center of the painting. At the left, a rocky path leads up a bank to a closed wooden gate, and at the top of the hill, the roof of a cabin hidden in the woods is visible. A bright, clear light falls on the water and rocks and contrasts with the shady areas.

Infrared photography reveals the pentimenti of a bridge with semicircular arches above and to the right of the boat and of a second cabin just above the wooden fence at center left. Richards painted over the house and the bridge, replacing them with foliage and the small boat with figures and open water. Ferber notes that "the removal of two major man-made structures for largely uninterrupted landscape served to enhance the quiet sylvan solitude of the work" (Ferber 1980, 1:102). The painting in its original state appears in a photograph taken in the artist's studio (frontispiece, Brooklyn and Philadelphia 1973). Richards is seated, holding a palette and mahlstick, in front of the painting on an easel.

The precise detail apparent in the rocks and foliage is evidence of Richards's interest in Pre-Raphaelite principles during this period. The hint of aerial perspective in the distance, however, distinguishes the painting from his more obsessively detailed, smaller paintings, such as *In the Woods* (1860; Bowdoin College Museum of Arts, Brunswick, Maine) or *Woodland Interior* (1861; private collection), in which foliage blocks out any feeling of depth. In this painting the background is more open, allowing some spatial recession, and there is a human presence not seen in the other works.

S. M. S.

Inscription At lower left, *Wm. T. Richards / Phila 1861*

Provenance "A Greater Boston Collection." Vose Galleries, Boston. Acquired in 1975, as *Woodland Brook in Vermont.*

References Rivard 1976, 8, 31, fig. 22, as *Woodland Brook in Vermont.* Hood et al. 1977, 96–97, ill. Ferber 1980, 1:101–103, 2: fig. 75.

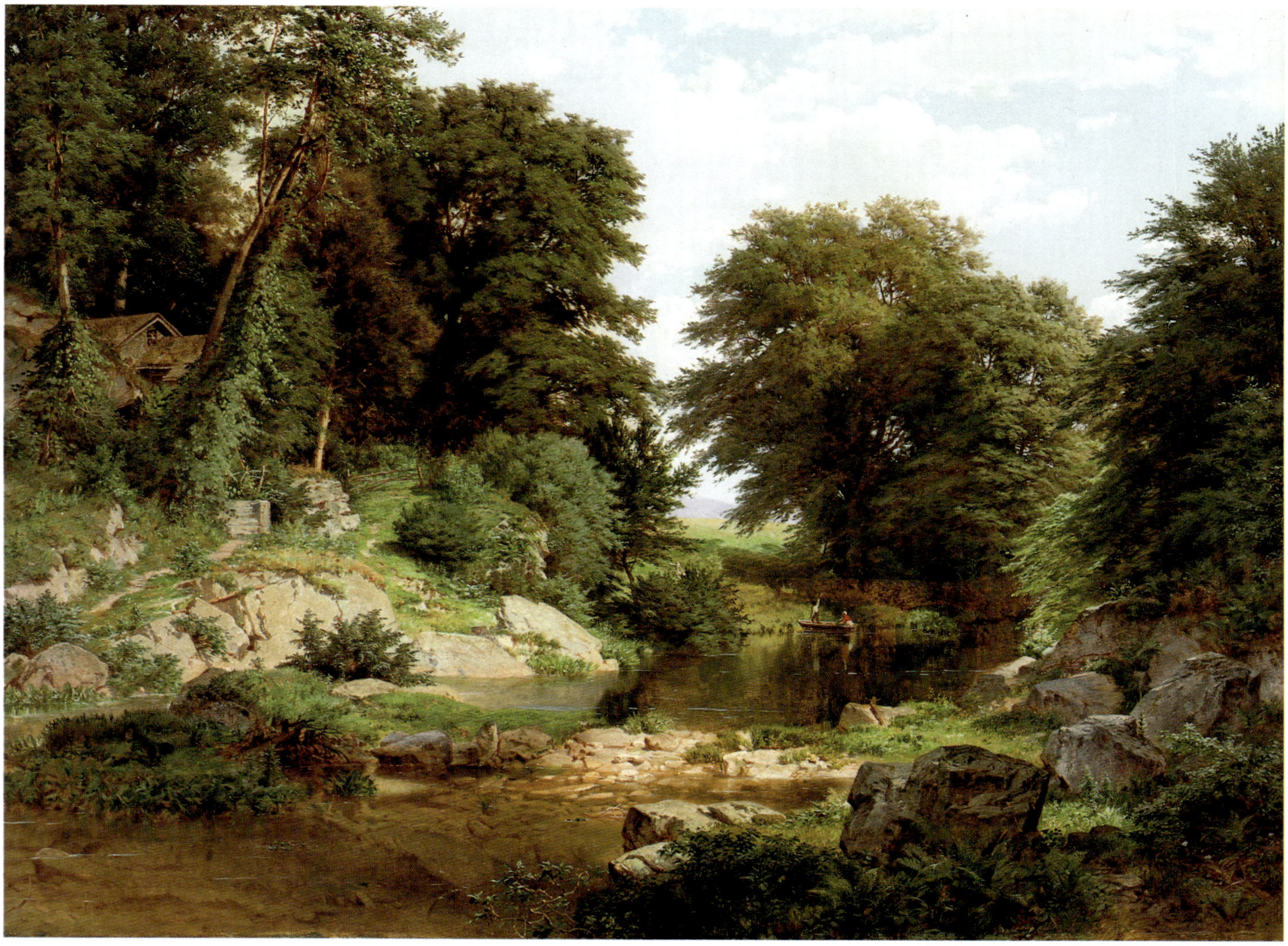

Woodland Brook

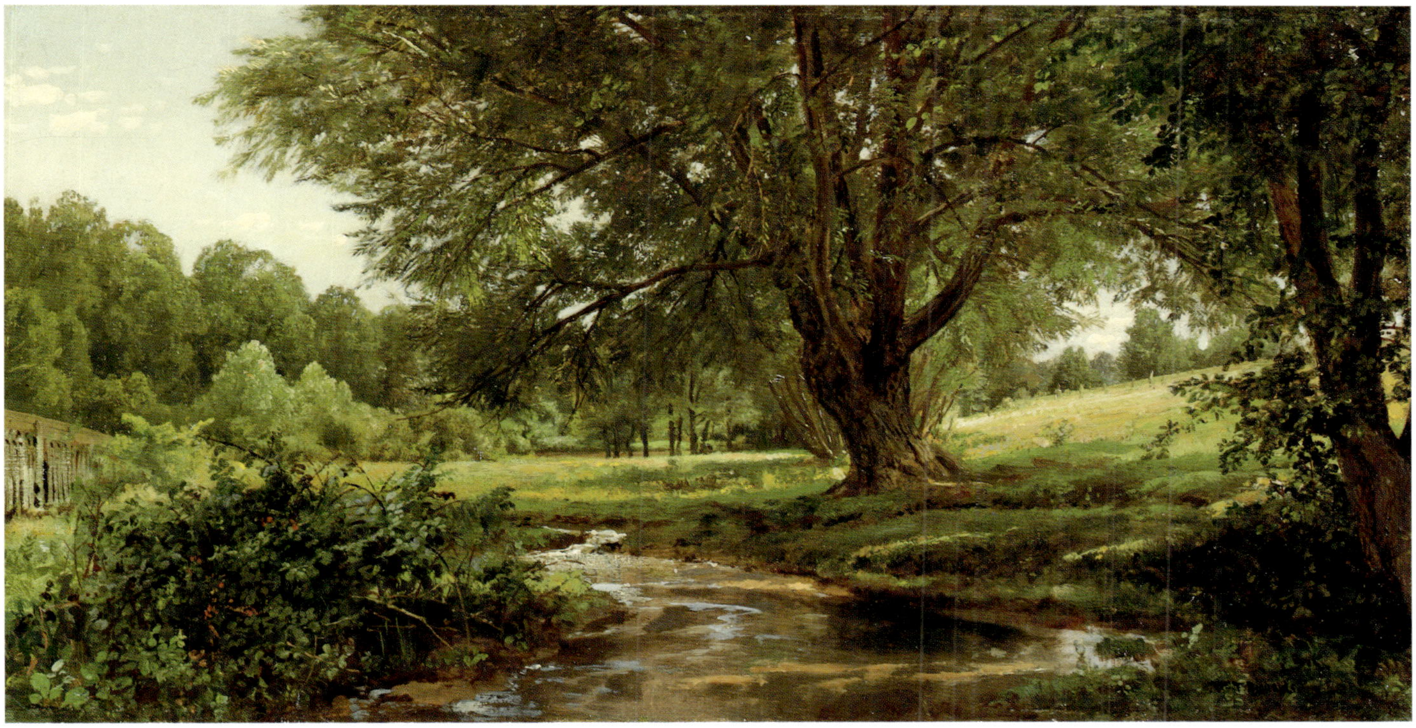

71

Glade at Oldmixon, Chester County, Pennsylvania, ca. 1881–90

Oil on Masonite
25.4 × 50.8 cm (10 × 20 in.)
Gift of the National Academy of Design, Mrs. William T. Brewster Bequest (53.379)

THIS OIL SKETCH was included in the bequest of Anna Richards (Mrs. William T.) Brewster, daughter of the artist, to the National Academy of Design. The bequest of more than five hundred works by her father included sketchbooks, watercolors, and oil paintings (New York 1980, 51–52). In 1953 the National Academy of Design distributed many of these among American museums; the Detroit Institute of Arts received six watercolors in addition to this painting.

Only about 10 percent of the works in the Brewster bequest are signed or dated by the artist. Brewster and her husband dated and identified the subjects of many of the drawings and paintings by relying on style, type of paper used, size of sketchbook, and knowledge of Richards's places of residence and travel itinerary.

The Brewsters dated this oil sketch to about 1881–90 based on their identification of it as a view of the farm Oldmixon, which Richards owned in Chester County, Pennsylvania. Linda Ferber confirms that he owned the farm from 1884, when he exchanged his house in Germantown for it, until 1891, and that his daughter Nelly and her family lived there (Brooklyn and Philadelphia 1973, 92, 102).

Richards painted a number of small landscapes of the farm, like this one, which are broad in handling rather than minutely described. Individual leaves in the shaded foreground foliage are picked out, while detail is erased in the areas in sunlight.

S. M. S.

Inscription At lower right, *W(L?). T. Richards*

Provenance Artist's estate, 1905. Anna Richards (Mrs. William T.) Brewster, daughter of the artist. National Academy of Design, 1952. Acquired in 1953.

William Rimmer

1816 Liverpool, England–
South Milford, Massachusetts 1879

William Rimmer is one of the most intriguing and singular figures in American art. His father, Thomas Simon Rimmer—born in France and raised in England—believed himself to be the younger son of Louis XVI and rightful heir to the throne of France after the death of his older brother in 1789. This supposed royal heritage provided the source for the recurring themes and motifs in William Rimmer's sculptures, drawings, prints, paintings, poetry, and other writings of exile, thwarted ambition, pursuit, confrontation, Promethean hubris, gladiators, soldiers, and ancient and biblical history and myth.

Rimmer was brought to America in 1818 and never returned to Europe. Raised in poverty, he spent most of his life eking out a meager living for himself and his large family and was virtually unknown as an artist until he was forty-five. Partially educated by his father and partially self-taught, Rimmer's diverse activities and talents extended beyond those of sculptor, painter, draftsman, printmaker, and teacher to include physician, musician and composer, inventor, poet, and philosopher. A learned anatomist, Rimmer practiced medicine in the Boston area from the late 1840s to the early 1860s and, through his study of art anatomy, fashioned a personal grammar of form in which the male nude became a metaphor for themes of heroic struggle.

In addition to lecturing on art anatomy in Boston, Providence, New Haven, New York, and other East Coast cities during the 1860s and 1870s, Rimmer served as director of the School of Design for Women at Cooper Union in New York from 1866 to 1870. He published two profusely illustrated and highly important books—*Elements of Design* (1864) and *Art Anatomy* (1877)—and taught several of the next generation's artists, notably Anne Whitney, John La Farge, and Daniel Chester French.

Rimmer was eminently familiar with Europe's artistic traditions, with his own work, for example, showing the influence of Michelangelo, William Blake, Antonio Canova, Antoine-Louis Barye, Gustave Doré, and Jean-Léon Gérôme. Rimmer's art and writings—particularly the annotated *Art Anatomy* drawings—also demonstrate his awareness of contemporary scientific and pseudoscientific areas of investigation, including photography, physiognomy, phrenology, typology, comparative anatomy, and Darwinian thought. His books and teaching produced many admirers, three of the most enthusiastic having been Gutzon Borglum, French, and Leonard Baskin.

Only about two-thirds of Rimmer's approximately six hundred works have been traced, and the quality of most of those that survive is high. Although Rimmer was especially well known in the Boston area after 1860, fewer than one-quarter of his works were commissions. He was not well paid even for works such as his only surviving public monument, the 1865 granite statue of Alexander Hamilton on Commonwealth Avenue, Boston, and the eighty-one drawings from 1876 (Museum of Fine Arts, Boston) for *Art Anatomy*. His gypsum statuette *Seated Man* (1831; Museum of Fine Arts, Boston) was the first nude sculpture in America. With *Head of a Woman* (ca. 1859; Corcoran Gallery of Art, Washington, D.C.) and bust of Saint Stephen (1860; Art Institute of Chicago), Rimmer was probably the first American sculptor to create granite carvings for other than utilitarian purposes.

The primary emphasis on and exploration of dynamic composition, powerfully expressive anatomy, and animated surfaces in Rimmer's finest sculptures—*Seated Man*, *Saint Stephen*, *Falling Gladiator* (1861; National Museum of American Art, Washington, D.C.), *Dying Centaur* (1869; Museum of Fine Arts, Boston), *Fighting Lions* (ca. 1871; unlocated), and *Torso* (1877; Museum of Fine Arts, Boston)—foreshadow the work of Auguste Rodin and are a fitting embodiment of Rimmer's repeated statement that "anatomy is the only subject."

Rimmer's paintings reflect the influence of English artists such as Charles Robert Leslie and American artists such as William Morris Hunt (q.v.), both iconographically and formally. Similarly, his well-known *Flight and Pursuit* (1872; Museum of Fine Arts, Boston) and *Sunset/Contemplation* (1876; Manoogian Collection) are comparable to the works of Washington Allston and Albert Pinkham Ryder (q.v.).

Rimmer was once seen as a predominantly enigmatic and isolated artist, but scholars are increasingly placing him within the context of his own times, while still recognizing his special achievements. Although an amateur in many respects, Rimmer is now regarded as one of the most gifted sculptors of his generation in America, a painter of compelling and evocative images, a powerful and imaginative draftsman, and an inspiring teacher.
J. W.

Bibliography Bartlett 1882. Kirstein 1946. New York 1946. Weidman 1982. Weidman 1983. Brockton et al. 1985. Greenthal et al. 1986. Weidman 1989.

72
Civil War Scene, ca. 1870–71

Oil on canvas
51.4 × 69.2 cm (20¼ × 27¼ in.)
Gift of Dr. and Mrs. Sheldon Stern (73.103)

73
Victory, 1870/ca. 1875–78

Oil on canvas
50.8 × 68.6 cm (20 × 27 in.)
Dexter M. Ferry, Jr., Fund (69.293)

As with so many of Rimmer's works, in all media, *Victory* and *Civil War Scene* are sterling examples of the artist's tendency to layer symbolic meanings within a matrix of historical, mythic, and personal associations. By vividly contrasting formal, stylistic, and iconographic elements, which embrace the pathetic and ironic themes of death amid victory, Rimmer created two of his most complex and challenging works.

Since Rimmer dated only about 10 percent of his more than six hundred known works, placing any of his paintings within his oeuvre presents a difficult task. *Civil War Scene* is easier than *Victory* to date. The reclining male is so similar, if in reverse, to figures in several of Rimmer's works from 1869 (and probably from the fall of that year) through February 1870 that *Civil War Scene* may be dated within that time span. The key work is the dated 1869 drawing *Morning/Venus and Cupid* (Fogg Art Museum, Harvard University Art Museums, Cambridge, Mass.). In addition, two dated paintings provide stylistic evidence that strongly suggests the date for *Civil War Scene* of about 1871: *Interior/Before the Picture* (1872; Richard L. Feigen) and, more convincingly, *English Hunting Scene* (1871; Museum of Fine Arts, Boston). The latter painting is suffused with coloristic qualities and formal handling of the trees, sky, and grass so reminiscent of *Civil War Scene* that it seems clear that they were painted around the same time.

A comparable stylistic analysis yields a later date for *Victory*, but physical evidence complicates the issue. *Victory* was examined by James L. Greaves in the DIA's Conservation Services Laboratory in 1970. By comparing X radiographs of *Victory* and *Civil War Scene* it was discovered that the two canvases were identical in weave and thread count and that they both had the same "grayish preprimed ground." In addition, the X radiograph of *Victory* revealed a "major change in the subject and composition of this painting. [There is a complete] landscape beneath [, which] has trees and meadow with low horizon reminiscent of the large painting in Boston [i.e., *English Hunting Scene*] and of the DIA's *[Civil War Scene]*" (Greaves report, 1970, DIA; Hood et al. 1977, 87). Greaves also discovered that *Victory*'s stretcher "appears to be original and again, it is identical to the stretcher" of *Civil War Scene*. Also noted was that the "painting was signed twice on the front: once clearly in the lower right corner and again, vaguely... with the date 1870" and the "reverse of the lower stretcher bar also bares [*sic*] the inscription (partially scratched in with a pen nib): Victory ar subject / painted by W. Rimmer." The presence of this finished landscape painting underneath *Victory* is the only known case of Rimmer's reusing a canvas. It seems clear that the landscape was initially meant as a companion to *Civil War Scene*, and the 1870 date should be associated with the underlying image, rather than with *Victory*.

Victory is stylistically much closer to paintings by Rimmer from the mid- to late 1870s than to those from the late 1860s and early 1870s. This is particularly notable in terms of color, brushwork, light, and equine form, with the closest overall parallels being Rimmer's *To the Charge (Sketch)* and *The Battlefield* (1874; Fogg Art Museum). The significant element here is that the horse in *Victory* is more reminiscent of those in these two paintings than it is of the horse in *Civil War Scene* or in other, earlier paintings. The treatment of the sky and horse in *Victory* is also quite close to the sky and the male's body in Rimmer's 1877 *Shepherd* (Boston Medical Library, Francis A. Countway Library of Medicine). Finally, the form of Rimmer's signature on *Victory*, without the date, and the treatment of the horse's mane are so similar to the signature and child's hair in Rimmer's undated, though late, painting *Sleeping* (ca. 1878; Currier Gallery of Art, Manchester, N.H.) as to suggest a comparable date for *Victory*. That *Victory* is a late painting is also suggested by its sharing with *Sleeping* the theme of death, couched within ambivalent and paradoxical forms.

The stylistic evidence that strongly suggests a date for *Victory* of about 1875 to about 1878 may or may not be reinforced by the inscription on its stretcher bar. The key word, as recorded by Greaves, is *ar*. The spaces before and after it suggest that a letter or letters may be missing. As it happens, Mary Rotan, of the Frick Art Reference Library in New York, made notes on the painting on November 25, 1946, when it was in a Rimmer exhibition at the Whitney Museum of American Art (New York 1946). Besides providing a color description, Rotan indicated: "inscribed in ink on stretcher, *Victory*, last subject painted by W. Rimmer" (Rotan 1946). There is no reason to doubt the accuracy of her observations. Nevertheless, the inscription is not in Rimmer's hand, nor is it the handwriting of Caroline Hunt Rimmer, his youngest daughter who was primarily responsible for preserving so many of his works (Weidman 1982, passim and 1310–1366: Appendix H: History of William Rimmer's Works). The *ar* most likely should be read as *as*, for *last*.

Victory and *Civil War Scene* are distinguished in Rimmer's oeuvre in that there are related drawings for each painting. If the undated drawings add nothing toward arriving at definite dates for the paintings, they do, however, provide significant information about changes Rimmer made from his initial thoughts to those embodied in the final paintings. Formally related to the painting *Victory*, the drawing *Victory* (Museum of Fine Arts, Boston) although small in size (9.5 × 13.2 cm [3¾ × 5³⁄₁₆ in.]), is monumental in impact and is essentially a fully realized work. The drawing, which includes the inscription *Victory* over the rider's head, is much less sinister in effect than is the painting. There, the lurid color, tumul-

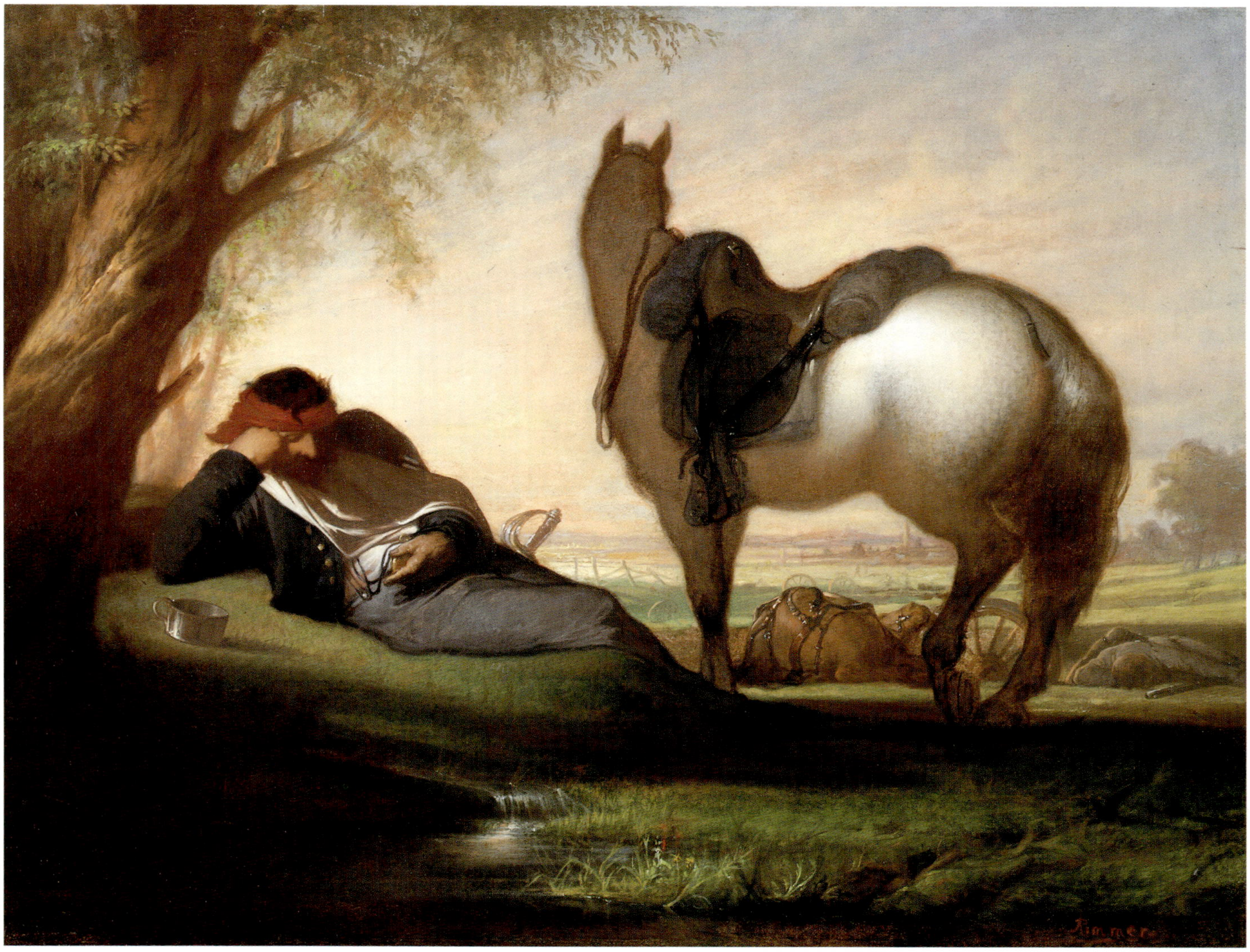

Civil War Scene

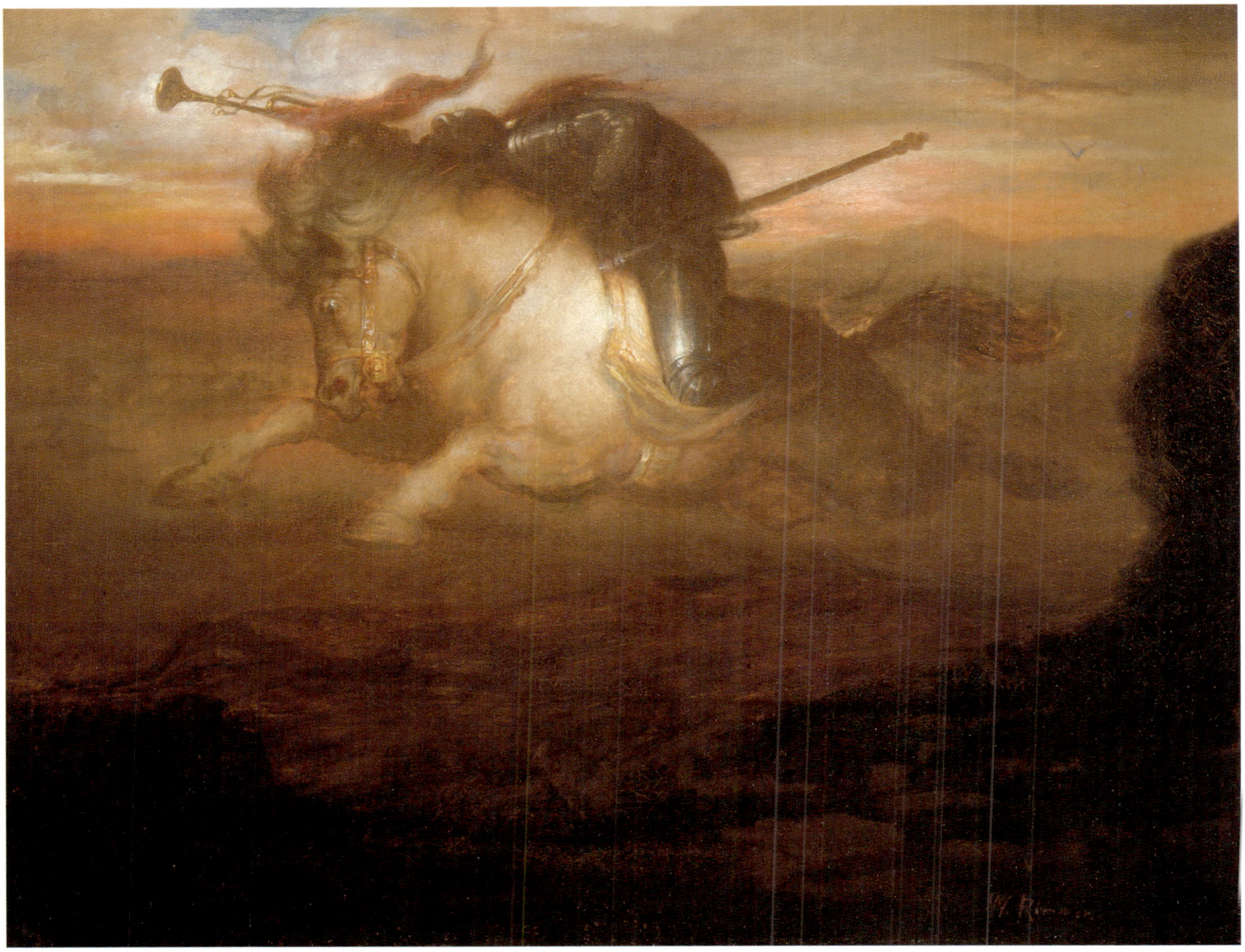

Victory

tuous sky, ominous birds, claustrophobic space, and spotlight effect, which is accentuated by the darkening of the bitumen, have transformed the drawing into a demonic and frightful image.

The drawing related to *Civil War Scene* is unique in Rimmer's oeuvre in being the only surviving preparatory drawing in the true sense for an extant painting. *Soldier and Horse under a Tree* (ca. 1871; Fogg Art Museum) has the singular feature of a sketchily drawn, yet clearly delineated, rectangular picture frame around the bottom and right-hand side, articulating the drawing's intimate association with the painting. This drawing (14 × 19.1 cm [5½ × 7½ in.]) is inscribed, at the bottom, *To [or "for"] My Mother at Home.* On a piece of paper attached to the drawing, Caroline Hunt Rimmer wrote: "Drawing for / picture — a painting / which I have in / Storage with other works / —." Also inscribed at the bottom of the verso of the drawing is: "Drawn by Dr. W. Rimmer design for painting / On the reverse side design for painting *Stored in Chelsea* —." These inscriptions make the relationship between drawing and painting certain.

The painting is more elaborate in subtle details than the drawing. The emphasis on the foreground man and horse has been retained in the painting, but the figure is now set in front of an open space, rather than in front of trees, as in the drawing. Also, the church at the far right in the drawing has been eliminated and replaced in the painting by the dead Confederate soldier. The painting's additional details, such as the brook, the empty cup, the differently colored bedrolls on the horse, and the dead horse and soldier, all increase the melancholic atmosphere and ambivalent mood of the painting. For example, the military affiliation of the soldiers is indicated by the color of their uniforms, but to which side the horse belongs is unclear. As a gray bedroll is seen at the back of the saddle, the horse may have belonged to the dead Confederate soldier, but a blue bedroll lying across the horse's neck suggests ownership by the reclining Union soldier, who may or may not have killed the Confederate soldier and his horse. Furthermore, in a scene that is painted with flowing and rhythmic forms, with lush and restful colors, suggesting peace and early morning, and with a low horizon and a broad, open-ended sky, in short, within a scene that is suffused with hope, details of a battle's aftermath and death abound. Rimmer adds elements that suggest the contrast of victory and defeat: the wounded man who finds temporary solace in the memories elicited by the image he holds in his hand touchingly embodies, generalizes, and thus universalizes the inscription on the drawing, the flowing water and the empty cups, the sunlit landscape and the destruction within it. Rimmer transformed the drawing's relatively journalistic image of a soldier in a reflective moment into a commentary on the futility of war and the suffering that must be borne by both sides.

The powerfully symbolic quality of *Civil War Scene* is representative of Rimmer's Civil War–related works created a number of years after the end of the conflict, such as the 1872 *Flight and Pursuit* (Museum of Fine Arts, Boston), the 1869 sculpture *Dying Centaur* (Museum of Fine Arts, Boston), and a series of drawings from 1867, which include *A Dead Soldier* (Museum of Fine Arts, Boston), *Philip Preparing the Funeral of Pompey the Great* (Fogg Art Museum), and *Achilles* (Museum of Fine Arts, Boston). Most of these works allude to the Civil War by portraying war-related classical subjects. The symbolic nature of these works invests them with universal meanings, principles, and ideals of nobility, heroism, and self-sacrifice.

Rimmer often extended mythic material to embrace historical content, and these symbolic and universal qualities also inform Rimmer's painting of *Victory* as well as its related drawing. Although Truman Bartlett did not include the *Victory* drawing in the group of Civil War drawings he described in his biography of Rimmer (Bartlett 1882, 125), and despite the fact that the riders in both the drawing and the painting are dressed in very non–Civil War medieval armor, it is appropriate to include the two versions of *Victory* within the group of Rimmer's post–Civil War–related works. Rimmer's creative and symbolic response to the temporal particularities of a devastating national conflict was to transform the temporal and the specific into the everlasting and the universal.

Rimmer may have turned to Scripture when looking for universalizing themes, where he would have found, in Revelation 6:7–8, the image of Death on a Pale Horse, an allusion that could easily encompass the tragedy of the Civil War. Rimmer's *Victory* can also be seen as falling securely within the tradition characterized by Morton D. Paley as the "apocalyptic sublime," established in England by John Mortimer's *Death on a Pale Horse* and continued in works by Benjamin West (Detroit Institute of Arts), Phillippe-Jacques de Loutherbourg, William Blake, J. M. W. Turner, and John Martin (Paley 1986) as well as on this side of the Atlantic by, to name but two, Washington Allston and Thomas Cole. The emphasis Rimmer gives to Victory's clarion call, as embodied in the figure's pose and in the large trumpet with its animated banner, suggests another New Testament allusion, I Corinthians 15:52 and 54: "for the trumpet shall sound, and the dead shall be raised incorruptible, and we shall be changed," and "Death is swallowed up in victory."

It is also possible to interpret *Victory* in terms of the artist's acute poor health during the last six months of his life. Rimmer may have been reading the poetry of Edgar Allan Poe, who, along with Shakespeare, Dante, Homer, and Robert Burns, was one of his five favorite poets (Bartlett 1882, 95). One of Poe's poems, "To One in Paradise," has already been singled out by Henri Dorra as evocative of Rimmer's *Victory* (Washington 1959, 15; Dorra 1961, 97): "A voice from out the Future cries, / 'On! on!'—but o'er the Past / (Dim gulf!) my spirit hovering lies / Mute, motionless, aghast!" While those lines offer the closest literary parallel to *Victory*, these from the second and third stanzas are also appropriate: "Ah, dream too bright to last! / Ah, starry Hope! that didst arise / But to be overcast!" and "For, alas! alas! with me / The light of Life is o'er! / No more—no more—no more— / (Such language holds the solemn sea / To the sands upon the shore) / Shall bloom the thunder-blasted tree, / Or the stricken eagle soar!" (Poe 1969, 214–215).

That Rimmer viewed his own life within a universal context is apparent not only from his works of visual art but also from his philosophical writings, most particularly the manuscript "Stephen and Phillip" (Rimmer ca. 1855–79). His daughter indicated on the frontispiece that it was "the volume which father read & reread even during his last days on Earth." During the final months of Rimmer's life, his reflections on his earthly existence may have included not only the lines from Poe's "To One in Paradise" but also a passage from the end of "Stephen and Phillip," a passage that is particularly poignant in terms of his late work:

> there is but one real difference in men, and it is this. All those who follow the flesh and live in its gratification, whether from weakness of conscience or the tyranny of passion are beasts, be they learned or unlearned, high or low, rich or poor. All those who master the body and believe in the soul and the conscience (striving thusly) are men, be they who or what they may.

J. W.

Civil War Scene

Inscription At lower right, *im* (underlined), *Rimmer-*

Provenance Caroline Hunt Rimmer. Unidentified male operator of horse-rental establishment near South Station, Boston, who lived in Lexington, Mass. Miss Florence M. Young and unidentified older sister, 1920s. Miss Florence M. Young, West Roxbury, Mass. Mrs. Kingsbury, Medfield, Mass., ca. 1961–mid-1970. Vose Galleries, Boston. Dr. and Mrs. Sheldon Stern, Franklin, Mich. Acquired in 1973.

Exhibition Brockton et al. 1985, 65, no. 26.

References Hood et al. 1977, 84–85, 87. Weidman 1982, 557–570.

Victory

Inscriptions At lower right, *W. Rimmer;* below outstretched rear legs of horse, *W. Rimmer* (name underlined) *1870;* on lower stretcher bar, in faded ink, *Victory ar* (or *as;* before this appears to be the faded remnants of an *L* or an *l* and after the *as* or *ar* appears to be the top or middle cross bar of a *t) subject / painted by W. Rimmer;* label on back, *Museum of Fine Arts / W. J. Gardner / 498 Boylston / no frame 35;* another label on back, *1818* (this is the shipping label for the Boston venue for New York 1946); another label on back, *Paul L. Grigaut, Detroit*

Provenance W. J. Gardner, Boston. Mr. and Mrs. William J. Gunn, Newtonville, Mass. Castano Galleries, Boston. Paul L. Grigaut, 1946. Estate of Paul L. Grigaut. Acquired in 1969.

Exhibitions New York 1946, not in cat. Washington 1959, 15, no. 67. Ann Arbor 1969, no. 52. Brockton et al. 1985, 64–65, no. 26.

References Rotan 1946. Hood et al. 1977, 84–87. Weidman 1982, 560–570.

74

Scene from "Macbeth," ca. 1850

Oil on canvas

91.4 × 66 cm (36 × 26 in.)

Gift of Sally Feldman (1994.36)

75

Scene from "The Tempest," ca. 1850

Oil on canvas

91.4 × 66 cm (36 × 26 in.)

Gift of Sally Feldman (1994.37)

Unsigned, undated, and unknown to the art world until the mid-1960s, these two Shakespearean scenes by Rimmer were soon recognized, in the words of the Rimmer scholar and collector Lincoln Kirstein, as "probably... by Rimmer" (notes, Kennedy Galleries files; Gaston 1966). There has been no lingering doubt since. Their style and subject matter clearly indicate that these two paintings are by William Rimmer.

The canvas seller's stencil on the back of each painting provides external evidence to suggest the dates of about 1850. The Boston directories for 1848–49 and 1849–50 are the only two that list a Charles A. Morris, whose business at 17 Exchange Street was selling artists' materials. Since Rimmer was poor, it is likely that he would have used canvas soon after purchasing it. It is, however, not only because of this supposition and the information provided by the stencils (Muller 1987, 452, 454) that a date of about 1850 has been assigned.

Rimmer occasionally used members of his own family as models. His sister, Jane (b. 1826), could have been the model for Miranda in *Scene from "The Tempest."* Although her own hair was dark, her features, as clearly seen in Rimmer's portrait of her from the first half of the 1850s (Indianapolis Museum of Art), are significantly similar to Miranda's to suggest a familial inspiration. Prospero's

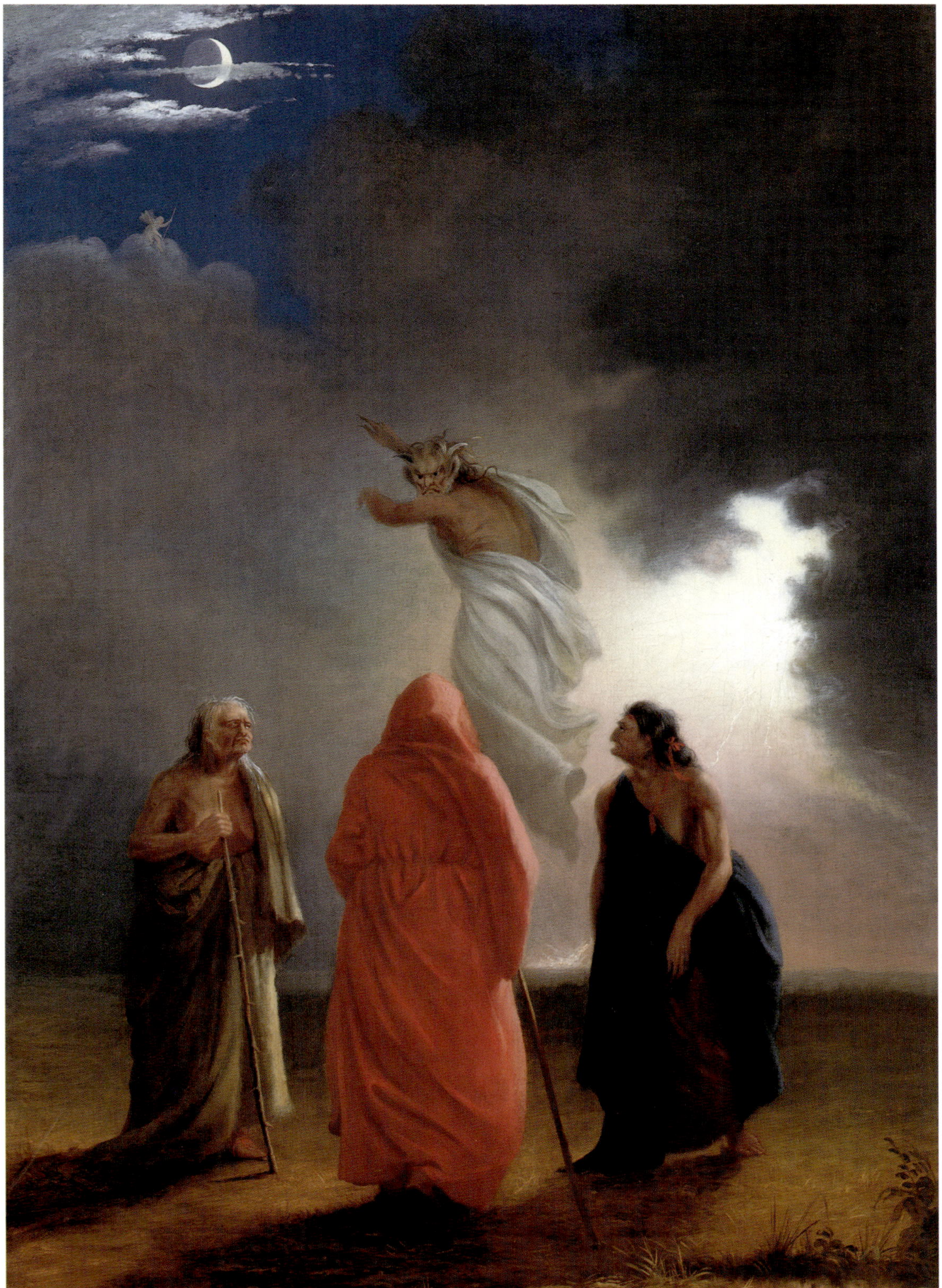

Scene from "Macbeth"

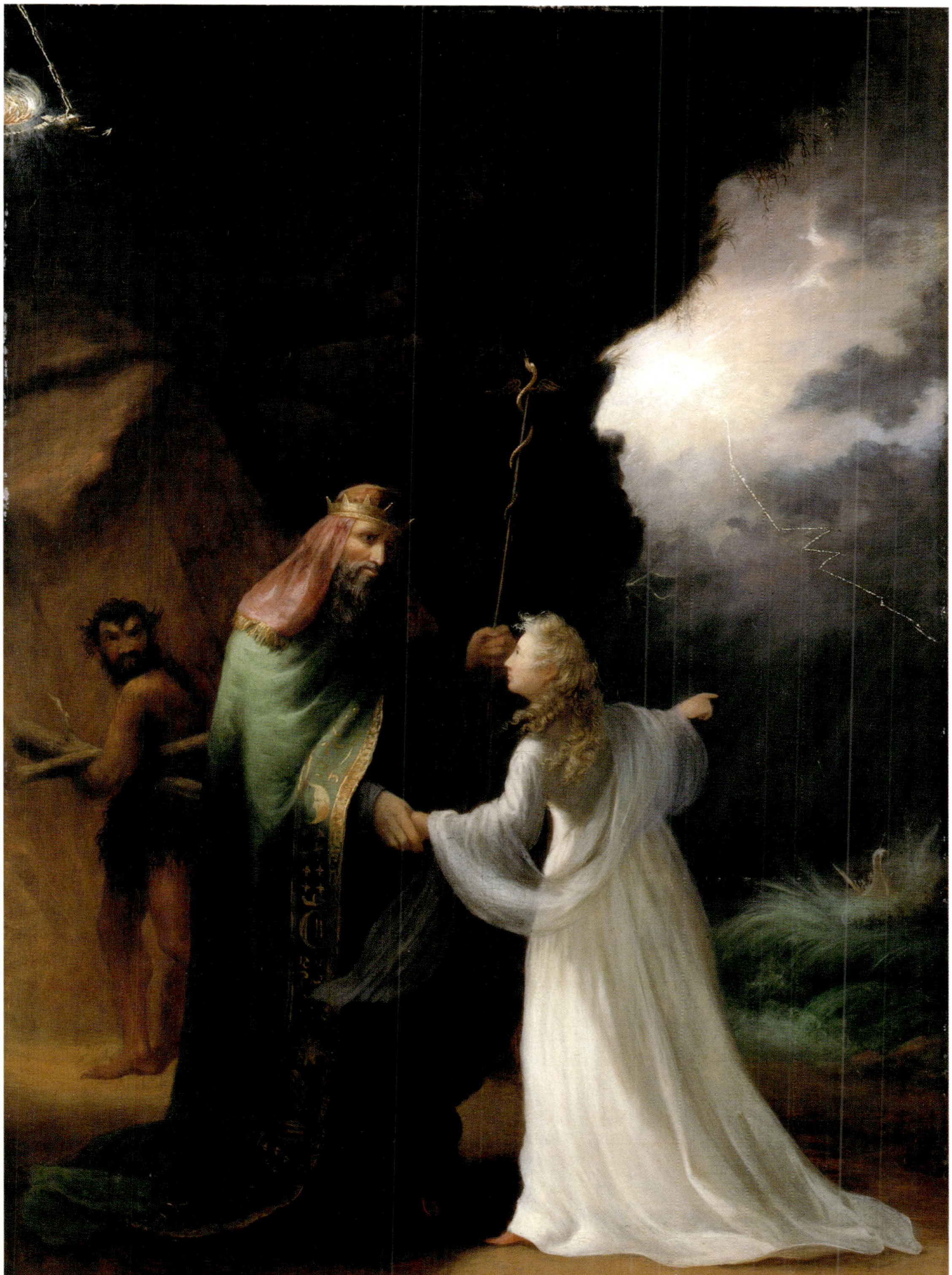

Scene from "The Tempest"

physiognomy also suggests a Rimmer family origin, most likely the conflation of the thirty-five-year-old artist and his sixty-five-year-old father (Weidman 1982, 1256–1259: Rimmer Genealogy), as suggested by an unlocated drawing of his father (ca. 1846; Bartlett 1882, pl. II; Weidman 1982, 751–752). Although it is impossible to discern any Rimmer family physiognomic input for the figures in *Scene from "Macbeth,"* a drawing from around 1850, *Head of an Old Person* (Fogg Art Museum, Harvard University Art Museums, Cambridge, Mass.), provides the strongest stylistic affinity to the witch at the far right and thus helps to date the painting.

The paintings' color schemes, the isolation and style of the figures, and their theatrical compositions and Shakespearean iconography all bear striking similarities to other paintings by Rimmer, such as *Henry VIII and Anne Boleyn* (ca. 1848; Brigham Young University Art Museum Collection, Provo, Utah), *Juliet and the Nurse* (1857; Addison Gallery of American Art, Phillips Academy, Andover, Mass.), and *Scene from "Romeo and Juliet"* (1867–68; The University of Michigan Museum of Art, Ann Arbor). The theatrical quality of these paintings, as well as of many drawings by Rimmer, including his only known watercolor, *Man in Elizabethan Costume* (ca. 1872; Fogg Art Museum), amply suggests that the theater offered him compositional and thematic material and, moreover, that Shakespeare's plays provided the most specific, pervasive, and significant of these influences. In fact, Truman H. Bartlett, Rimmer's biographer, listed Shakespeare as the first of the artist's five favorite poets and *The Tempest* as his favorite play (Bartlett 1882, 95).

These two paintings by Rimmer are iconographically unprecedented. The popular and extensive collection of prints by British artists after Shakespeare's plays, published by John Boydell first in the early part of the nineteenth century in England and available in an American edition by midcentury, contains nothing similar (Boydell and Boydell 1803[5] and Boydell 1852). Robert Edge Pine exhibited a painting in Philadelphia during 1784 that was inspired by the same act and scene as was Rimmer's painting (act 1, scene 2), but its catalogue entry, which includes lines 108–418 from the play, indicates that Pine's work depicts action later in the scene, namely the discovery of Ferdinand by Prospero and Miranda, with Ariel and Caliban present (Yarnall and Gerdts 1986, 1:39 and 4:2795).

Although well-known images of Macbeth and the witches were painted by artists on both sides of the Atlantic (e.g., Fuseli, West, and Sully), these include Macbeth and are set within or near the witches' cave (Altick 1985, passim; Pressly 1992, passim; Studing 1993, passim). Rimmer depicted act 3, scene 5, and it is possible that he received some inspiration for the faces of his witches as well as for the deformed foot of the right-hand witch from the illustrations of these figures from other scenes in the play in the well-known and popular drawings by Moritz Retzsch, perhaps either in the German edition of his illustrations to Shakespeare's plays published in Leipzig and London in 1838 or in the American edition published in New York in 1849 (Retzsch 1838; Retzsch 1849).

Scene from "The Tempest" and *Scene from "Macbeth"* convey several levels of symbolic import, esoteric and personal as well as political and universal. A theme common to both plays is that of usurped rulership and the interweavings of manipulated birthrights in the midst of complex destinies. As Prospero's legitimate ducal title was taken from him by intrigue and as Macbeth treasonably overthrew the rightful king, so did Rimmer believe, as did his entire family, that their rightful birthright had been denied them when their father's legitimate destiny as the Dauphin was usurped by his uncle, Louis XVIII. At a time when Thomas Rimmer (d. 1852) was in very poor health, William, as the firstborn male heir, was beginning to assume the full burdens and responsibilities of the Dauphin myth and his own self-definition. *Scene from "The Tempest"* and *Scene from "Macbeth"* are the earliest known companion paintings in an oeuvre replete with works that provocatively display the conflation of similar political and personal import, two of the most mature being the 1861 plaster *Falling Gladiator* (National Museum of American Art, Washington, D.C.) and the 1872 painting *Flight and Pursuit* (Museum of Fine Arts, Boston).

Rimmer's symbolic identification with Prospero offers further insights into his beliefs. Rimmer has presented Prospero in the manner in which Shakespeare portrayed him, as a magus, a good magician of noble bearing and intentions, calm and peaceful in his tranquil form and physiognomy. His regal bearing is suggested by his crown and cloak, the border of which is decorated with pseudoastronomical signs, suggesting his powers and responsibilities to maintain the balance of nature. Prospero holds in his left hand a staff, around which is entwined a winged snake. This divine accoutrement is undoubtedly the staff of Asklepios, emblematic of the god/man of medicine and of Greek physicians. Considering Prospero's role as magus, we should expect him to be holding a caduceus, identified by two intertwined snakes. That it is, rather, the staff of Asklepios is significant, for it is an attribute of Rimmer in his guise as medical doctor, symbolizing the physician's role of sacred healer.

As the wings of the snakes on the staff are often referred to by physicians as the *medica caduceus,* in *Scene from "The Tempest"* they may symbolize Hermes (Mercury), thus transforming Prospero's staff into a kind of magic wand and alluding to his traditional place within the lineage established by the archmagus, Hermes Trismegistus, the legendary founder of the

Hermetic tradition and of its branches, such as alchemy and Freemasonry. Rimmer's interest in and association with Freemasonry has been well documented in both primary and secondary sources (Bartlett 1882 and *Star of Bethlehem* 1868, 28). Cards in the secretary's office of the Grand Lodge of Masons in Massachusetts, Boston, indicate that Rimmer was initiated on September 20, 1865, that on November 14, 1865, he was both passed and raised (i.e., became a second-degree and then a third-degree Mason), and that on December 20, 1870, his membership was canceled. Rimmer's interest in esoteric subject matter, and specifically Freemasonry, is also well documented by several works from this time: a now-lost sculpture of hawk-headed Osiris (1865; Bartlett 1882, 48–49; Weidman 1982, 263–276, 304–307) and two paintings, *The Sentinel* (1866; Museum of Fine Arts, Boston), with its enigmatic Hebrew inscription ("a man of Citium") and related marks derivative of a Phoenician inscription, and *The Master Builder* (ca. 1871; Leonard and Corrine Lemberg, Southfield, Mich.).

The lanternlike object at the upper left in *Scene from "The Tempest"* suggests Rimmer's interest in alchemy. Its position indicates that it is meant to represent some kind of lantern or torch, but close examination reveals a ball of fire or light, colored gray at the edges, which is bounded at the right and intersected at the bottom by a linked chain, ending in a curved hook. This most unusual form may be an allusion to the *aurea catena* (golden chain) of alchemy, which is the series of wise men beginning with Hermes Trismegistus. Rimmer's exposure to this specialized material may have been through his close and frequent association with Bronson Alcott and his family as well as with Ralph Waldo Emerson during 1848–52. This contact would also have expanded his earlier interest in and practice of spiritualism and exposed him to Platonic and Neoplatonic material, to alchemical material, and, of course, to transcendentalism (Weidman 1982, 18–21, 77–84; Brockton et al. 1985, 5). Mary Atwood's well-known publication on alchemy may have been another source (Atwood 1850).

This pair of paintings contrasts Prospero, the enlightened, white magician, who has learned to harness and subdue his own unruly and destructive nature, symbolized in the figure of Caliban, with the witches as black magicians, who unleash their unruly and unnatural evil for destructive purposes. Their haggard faces and contorted bodies suggest deformed and twisted thoughts and inner natures, and Hecate's hideous physiognomy may be Rimmer's imaginative fusion of her often-represented triple heads of horse, dog, and lion. Conversely, Prospero and Miranda are composed and noble figures. They stand solidly on the earth, nestled and protected by the cliff overhang and the opening of the large cave, with their hands joined, creating a tranquil, secure, and closed form. The turbulent sky and sea are the only open areas of the otherwise enclosed and self-contained composition, which mirrors the central figures' inner natures. In contrast, the witches are isolated on a vast grassy plain and stand in an open semicircle. Standing apart from the natural order, these vulnerable figures are not joined in any manner, either to each other or to their environment. The deadened and heavy nature of the sky and the figures in *Scene from "Macbeth"* is absent from *Scene from "The Tempest."*

J. W.

Scene from "Macbeth"

Inscriptions On back, stamped or stenciled, except for the number, which is handwritten, PREPARED BY / MORRIS / NO 17 / Exchange St. / BOSTON; label on stretcher, now covered by relining, BRUNDIDGE

Provenance Private collection, house on Mission Hill, Milton, Mass. Mrs. Brundidge of Milton, Mass., or of Hyde Park, close to Milton, ca. 1916. Adelson Gallery, Boston. Ira Spanierman, New York. Drawing Shop-Galerie, now Shepherd Gallery, New York, 1966. On consignment at Kennedy Galleries, New York. Richard Manoogian, Detroit. Kennedy Galleries, New York. Shepherd Gallery, New York, 1984. Private collector, 1984. Joseph Feldman, Mich., 1984. His wife, Sally Feldman. Acquired in 1993.

Exhibitions Montreal 1967, no. 212, as *Scene from "The Tempest."* Brockton et al. 1985, 55, no. 17.

References *Kennedy Quarterly* 1967, 38–39, 24, as *Scene from "The Tempest."* Flexner 1970, 202, as *Scene from "The Tempest (Macbeth)."* Weidman 1982, 466–476. Studing 1993, 19, 114, 115, no. 650.

Scene from "The Tempest"

Inscriptions On back, stamped or stenciled, except for the number, which is handwritten, PREPARED BY / MORRIS / NO 17 / Exchange St. / BOSTON; label on stretcher, now covered by relining, BRUNDIDGE

Provenance Private collection, house on Mission Hill, Milton, Mass. Mrs. Brundidge of Milton, Mass., or of Hyde Park, close to Milton, ca. 1916. Adelson Gallery, Boston. Ira Spanierman, New York. Drawing Shop-Galerie, now Shepherd Gallery, New York, 1966. On consignment at Kennedy Galleries, New York. Richard Manoogian, Detroit. Kennedy Galleries, New York. Shepherd Gallery, New York, 1984. Private collector, 1984 Joseph Feldman, Mich., 1984. His wife, Sally Feldman. Acquired in 1993.

Exhibitions New York 1967, no. 95. Montreal 1967, no. 211. Cincinnati 1968, no. 2. Brockton et al. 1985, 54, no. 16. New York 1989, no. 3.

References *Kennedy Quarterly* 1967, 38–39, 43. Stratford 1978, 4. Weidman 1982, 465–476. Studing 1993, 19, 115, no. 653.

Albert Pinkham Ryder

1847 New Bedford, Massachusetts–
Elmhurst, Long Island 1917

As America's "old master in the modern movement," Albert Pinkham Ryder was given an exhibition room alongside Paul Cézanne, Vincent van Gogh, and Paul Gauguin at the famous 1913 Armory Show in New York (Charles Caffin, in *New York American,* March 10, 1913, 8). His ceaseless search for new means of expression through color and technique was celebrated by the avant-garde, while his romantic literary themes endeared him to traditionalists.

Raised in New Bedford, Massachusetts, Ryder moved to New York City between 1868 and 1870. He studied under the portrait painter William E. Marshall before being accepted as a student at the National Academy of Design in 1871. Ryder's early work consists of small, poetic landscapes, genre scenes of horse and stable, and decorative projects. His dealer, Daniel Cottier, introduced him to the paintings of Jean-François Millet and Camille Corot, whose pastoral style Ryder emulated. Through Cottier, Ryder was drawn into the decorative-arts environment and produced gilded-leather panels and folding screens. Cottier also arranged two of Ryder's four trips to Europe, where he was exposed to a variety of artistic styles.

Ryder's most celebrated paintings date from the last two decades of the nineteenth century. They include his moonlit marines and subjects derived from pastoral poetry, romantic legend, and Shakespearean drama. For Ryder, literature provided not just picturesque narrative but symbols for expressing his inner world.

Romantic love dominated many Ryder paintings and must have preoccupied the bachelor artist's thoughts. Betrayed innocence and love between people of different social classes are recurring themes. Solitary boats in tempestuous moonlit waters become symbols for the lonely voyage through life and the inability to control fate.

Ryder worked and reworked his canvases for up to ten years and more. He rarely produced initial studies or sketches. Instead, he worked out his compositions directly on the canvas, building up multiple paint layers as he refined his design. The top layers sometimes dried at a faster rate than those underneath, and, as a result, deep cracks often developed over time. In some works, the underlying paint layers were so thick that the images sagged with gravity toward the bottom of the frame.

Ryder experimented with unorthodox materials to attain his unusual translucent color effects and enamel-like surface quality. To emulate the patina of age that he revered in old-master works, he covered his surfaces with thick varnish. Such materials have caused his paintings to yellow or sometimes darken to tarlike blackness. Ryder himself was not concerned with this deterioration. He maintained that when a thing has the elements of beauty from the beginning it cannot be destroyed. "Take for instance Greek sculpture—the Venus de Milo I might say—ages & men have ravaged it—its arms & nose have been knocked off but still it remains a thing of beauty because beauty was with it from the beginning" (Sherman 1920, 43).

Toward the end of his life, Ryder lived in isolation, his studio filled with refuse, for by the mid-1890s he ceased throwing anything away. He died in New York in 1917 under the care of Louise Fitzpatrick, who, along with many others, is thought to have forged Ryder's work. Ryder's concern for the process of painting as a means of personal expression was championed by generations of American artists, especially the abstract expressionists, who followed.

L. C. AND E. B.

Bibliography Broun 1989. Homer and Goodrich 1989.

76
The Tempest, ca. 1892–1911

Oil on canvas
70.5 × 88.9 cm (27¾ × 35 in.)
Gift of Dexter M. Ferry, Jr. (50.19)

The Tempest contains within its paint layers testimony to Ryder's mastery of dramatic composition, with circular rhythms creating a mood of great emotive power. The painting also gives evidence of Ryder's obsessive and often destructive painting practices and bespeaks the dubious restoration executed by a well-intentioned friend after Ryder's death. The visual and written documents pertaining to this painting detail the height and decline of Ryder's creative conception.

With the nineteenth century's new interest in the Renaissance, a Shakespeare cult emerged in the arts, and Ryder painted at least seven works based on his plays, including the magical drama, *The Tempest.* In the play, Prospero, exiled duke of Milan, and his beautiful daughter, Miranda, have been abandoned on an enchanted island. Prospero uses his white magic to create a fierce tempest, which strands his betrayers on the same isle. With the help of Ariel, a spirit of the air, he orchestrates punishment and matchmaking through music, charmed sleep, and illusory pageants. Prospero marries his daughter to a prince, thwarts murder plots, and forgives repentant enemies before abdicating his magic to resume his ducal duties.

This play embodies Ryder's favored themes of love and dreams, repentance and forgiveness. In Ryder's portrayal, Miranda fearfully clings to her commanding father. As in act 1, scene 2 of the play, Miranda, a traditional romantic heroine, mourns the suffering of those aboard the wrecked ship and implores her father to calm the wild waters. Ryder conflates several narrative elements, for Miranda can

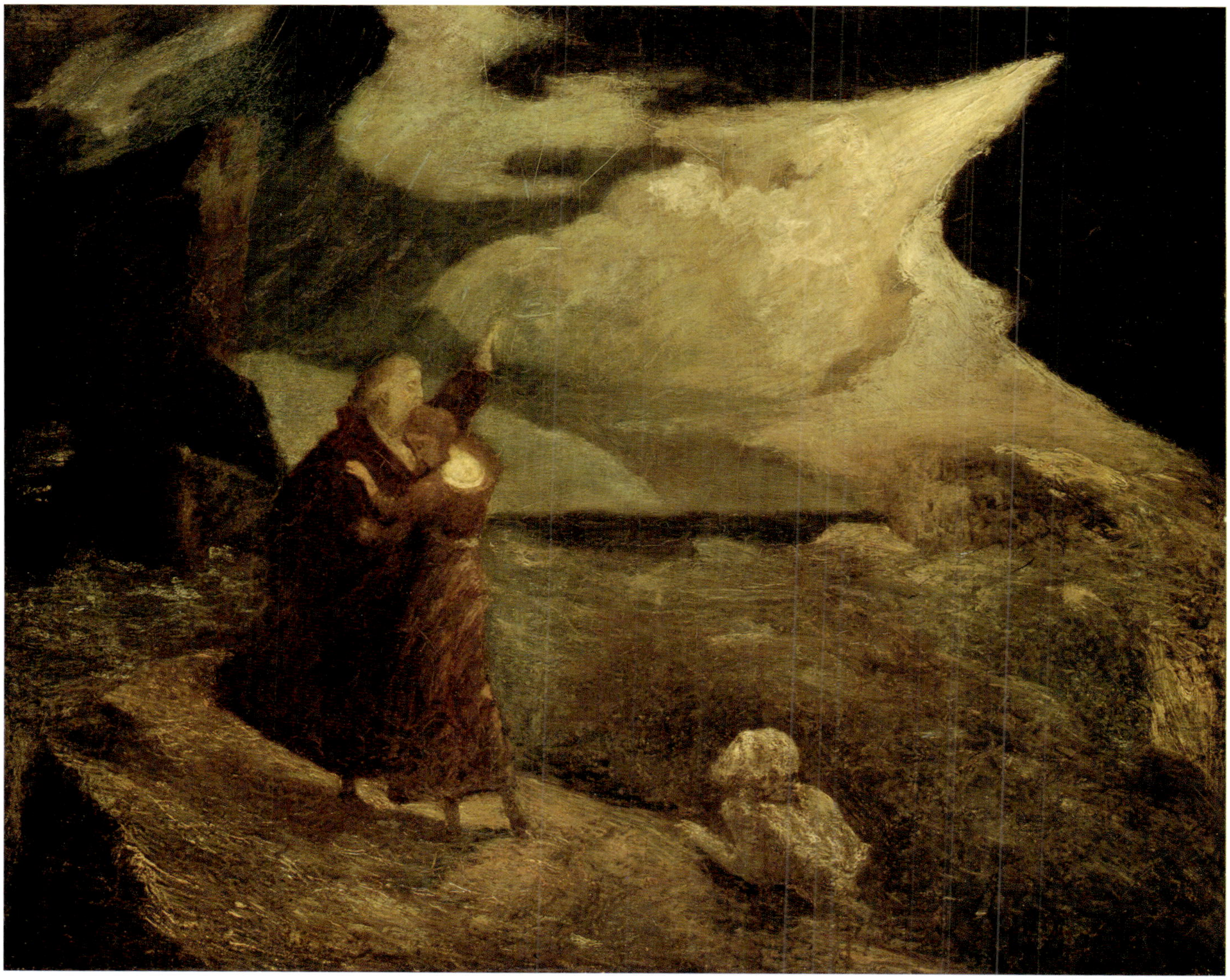

The Tempest

be understood as seeking fatherly protection both from the ravages of the storm and from Caliban, the crawling savage at her feet.

An autoradiograph of the painting, made at the Smithsonian's Conservation Analytical Laboratory, under the direction of Jacqueline Olin and Ingrid Alexander, reveals additional features and a more elaborate composition than what appears on the paint surface today. Autoradiography records on film where the organic and inorganic elements found in pigments are distributed throughout the paint layers. The cloud forms in the autoradiograph show thick outlines similar in style to other Ryder works, such as *Lord Ullin's Daughter* (National Museum of American Art, Washington, D.C.), *Landscape* (Metropolitan Museum of Art, New York), and *Macbeth and the Witches* (Phillips Collection, Washington, D.C.). The autoradiographic image also shows Ariel, foreshortened and gliding to the right of Prospero's raised arm, and vestiges of the wrecked ship on the far right. Neither Ariel nor the ship is discernible on the surface image today.

As revealed by the autoradiograph, a dynamic tension and balance of forces are created as the lines of Prospero's and Ariel's outstretched arms counter the opposing diagonals of Caliban and the ship's masts. Our eyes follow a circular path starting from the foreground figure of Caliban, to Prospero and Miranda, across Prospero's outstretched arm toward Ariel, and then back down the line of the wrecked masts to the seething waters. Opposing elements—of earth and air, rock and water, good and evil, life and death—polarize within this dynamic circle.

The autoradiographic evidence enables us better to appreciate a 1918 statement that *The Tempest* had once been "one of the greatest of his canvases, equal to the 'Jonah'" (Wood 1918). In *Jonah* (National Museum of American Art, Washington, D.C.), Ryder rendered dynamic visual echoes and tensions between four essential narrative elements of the Old Testament story: God and Jonah, ship and whale. We now see that Ryder at one point had proposed similar oppositions and contrasts for *The Tempest.*

An X radiograph of *The Tempest* also reveals an image different from that seen on the surface today. This X radiograph reveals Ryder's capable handling of anatomy and interest in detail no longer visible in the vague, generalized figures as they have been repainted by another hand. As evidenced in the X radiograph, Ryder had once articulated such nuances as Miranda's shoulder blades, the detailing of her sleeve, and the strong angle formed by her back and waist. Her windswept skirt, now hanging limply, once whipped across Prospero's form and served to unite the two visually.

The radiographic evidence visually confirms the written accounts of the painting's history. Begun in the late 1880s and first exhibited in New York in 1892, the canvas was obsessively reworked by Ryder until his death more than twenty years later. The Portland, Oregon, collector C. E. S. Wood, who had paid for the work around 1896, recalled, "I tried several times to get the picture . . . and [J. Alden] Weir tried for me and Mrs. [Louise] Fitzpatrick [a friend and self-proclaimed pupil of Ryder], but we all found if we could get it at all, which was doubtful, it would only be by tearing out his heart, and on my later visits to New York he would never even let me see it, telling me to wait until next time" (Wood 1918).

A 1906 letter from Ryder to Wood states, "The Tempest seems to want but little; but oh, how much that little may be; however I really believe if anything happened to me, if the blue of the sky in upper left hand corner was matched it would be about as valuable as finished. Judging from the work of Millet and others, it is so nice in color and other good things" (Ryder to Wood, February 9, 1906, Love papers, AAA).

Critics and friends also praised the color in *The Tempest;* Wood remembered that the color had once been "as vivid as a Monticelli but more gemlike" (Wood to Lloyd Goodrich, quoted in Homer and Goodrich 1989, 220). In a 1918 letter he recalls "the clearing away of the storm sky with the creamy rifts of light, and the majestic sea beating over the rocks and the wreck of the vessel, and against these masses of subtle transparent greens, blues, and green of clouds, sky and sea, Prospero and Miranda glowed like jewels in the foreground, his amethyst-colored robe and her emerald-green dress, with Caliban a dull orange green hidden in the cleft at their feet, Ariel floating in the clouds" (Wood 1918).

Harold W. Bromhead, a friend and dealer, also waxed eloquent, saying, "Generally using his instrument at half swell, R[yder] has here pulled out all the stops, and we have the thunder of his diapason. The result is tremendous . . . Prospero and Miranda, Caliban, Ariel, the wrecked vessel, the heaving and yeasty sea. And then the colour! The last vivid flash of the lightning in which Prospero holds up his hand to tell Caliban [*sic*] to end the storm. . . . The power of it, the grasp, the sympathetic insight into Shakespeare" (quoted in Homer and Goodrich 1989, 220).

The paint surface today shows nothing of the glowing color once described by these friends. Wood wrote that "through twenty years I saw it become lower in tone and more subtle[,] more imaginative" (Wood 1918). One can only speculate the extent to which the shifting of tonalities resulted from Ryder's changing color sense or the ravages wrought by time as a result of his unorthodox working methods and materials, or the restoration of the painting after his death. Marsden Hartley, in his rhapsodic reminiscences of Ryder, recalled "axing and fatal abrasions in matters of technique, for Ryder had run a hot poker through the thickest part of the sky, and these jags were filled with new paint whitish of course of which he was to build eventually by tonal processes the sense of jags of lightning as it cuts through the dark densities of cloud bodies in a summer storm. The rest of the surface of this picture was all scum. . . . These scums that were added by dust and abuse, were doubtless part of the process, as if he had reasoned that nature herself must have a hand in it too" (Hartley 1982, 264). Toward the end of Ryder's life, visitors to his studio reported that the canvas was nearly black.

L. C. AND E. B.

Provenance Paid for by C. E. S. Wood, ca. 1896/1903, delivered to Wood, 1918. Macbeth Gallery, New York, from *John List Crawford and Other Collections Sale,* Parke-Bernet, New York, February 20–21, 1946, lot 58. Dr. Chester J. Robertson, Pelham Manor, N.Y. Consigned by Robertston to Macbeth Gallery, New York, September 9, 1948. Acquired in 1950.

Exhibitions San Francisco, San Francisco Art Association, n.d. San Francisco, California Palace of the Legion of Honor, 1926, no. 159. New York 1947, no. 46. Washington 1961, no. 52. Mason City 1966, 14. Baltimore et al. 1976, no. 30. Broun 1989, no. 66.

References Wood 1918. Price 1932, no. 182. G. Brown 1979–80, 44, ill. Homer and Goodrich 1989, 133–134, 168–169, plate 13.

Walter Shirlaw

1838 Paisley, Scotland–Madrid, Spain 1909

An organizer of the Society of American Artists and its first president, Walter Shirlaw was an extremely active and important member of the New York artistic community. He taught at the Art Students League, where he instructed Robert Reid in addition to countless other artists.

Shirlaw's family immigrated to the United States when he was three years old. At an extremely early age he demonstrated a strong fascination with drawing. When he was twelve he left school and took a position as an office boy at Tirrel and Valentine, real-estate speculators in New York. Although his parents bitterly opposed this, he found it a rewarding experience, because he was given the opportunity to execute maps, plans, and other real-estate drawings. Shirlaw soon discovered that he was not receiving the type of training he desired and in 1852 took a position with the American Bank Note Company in addition to enrolling in a night school with classes in drawing and painting.

By his twentieth year he had established a studio at 444 Broadway. From there he was able to submit paintings to the National Academy of Design, his first, in 1861, being *Eager for the Fray* (unlocated). It was received favorably, "hung on line," and eventually sold. A year later he accepted a position with the Western Bank Note Company of Chicago, where he worked for more than three years before taking a six-month sojourn to the Rocky Mountains. He returned to Chicago in 1865, established a studio, and began taking classes.

Eventually, Shirlaw decided he needed to expand his artistic influences, and study in Europe seemed appropriate. In 1870 he sailed for Paris. However, the ongoing Franco-Prussian War altered his plans and he settled in Munich. There he studied with some of the leading artists of the period and was provided with a studio and models by the German government. In the summers he would make trips to the countryside around Munich, although he also spent time in other regions.

Shirlaw submitted *Toning of the Bell* (Art Institute of Chicago) to the Centennial Exposition in Philadelphia, where it won a medal. A year later, in 1877, he returned to New York with one of his most important works, *Sheep-Shearing in the Bavarian Highlands* (St. Louis Art Museum). It was immediately exhibited at the National Academy of Design. That same year he established a studio at 3 North Washington Square. Florence Manchester and Shirlaw were married in 1880 and spent most of the following year in England.

Upon his return to New York he became increasingly interested in painting murals, leaving many sketches and drawings for proposed projects. Shirlaw also turned his attention to painting outdoors, especially during his summers in Vermont. He was elected a full member of the National Academy in 1888. The federal government sent him to the Crow and Cheyenne reservations in 1889 to document Indian life.

J. W. T.

Bibliography Chicago 1911. Brooklyn 1929.

77
Wheat Fields, Vermont, ca. 1880–90

Oil on canvas

38.7 × 76.2 cm (15¼ × 30 in.)

Gift of Mrs. Walter Shirlaw (13.2)

Within a few years of Walter Shirlaw's death in 1909, his widow, Florence, began to contact museums and schools to determine their interest in her late husband's work. Many unsold canvases, watercolors, drawings, and etchings remained in her possession. It was her belief that these works should be in institutions, and to that end she offered the material to those who were interested in them. In a letter to the director of the Detroit Museum of Art, Armond Griffith, she wrote, "I have a large and very varied collection, and, if you wished you could indicate the medium you preferred. Whether light or dark tone and if, you would pay for packing and expenses as the others do?" In Griffith's response he indicated that the museum would be pleased to have any of her husband's works and then went on, "I think however, that we had better leave the sole matter to you as to selection of such as you are willing to send to us. When you have them ready, if you will kindly notify W. S. Budworth & Son . . . they will relieve you of all trouble in the matter of packing and shipping." With her concerns answered, she sent the museum seven works, including *Wheat Fields, Vermont.*

The canvas was painted in Vermont during one of Shirlaw's summer retreats from New York. In a letter to Griffith, the artist's wife indicated that the painting was a sketch from nature. Whether this was a model for a later canvas or an exercise in plein-air painting is not known. However, it does begin to capture ideas that more progressive artists of the period were practicing. There is a sense of spontaneity to the overall scene with very little attention paid to the three figures. It would appear that in this instance Shirlaw gave up his genre and allegorical paintings in favor of a realist's approach.

J. W. T.

Inscription At lower right, *W. Shirlaw*

Provenance The artist to his wife, Florence M. Shirlaw, 1901. Acquired in 1913.

References Letters between Mrs. Shirlaw and Armond Griffith, curatorial files, DIA. *BDMA* 1913.

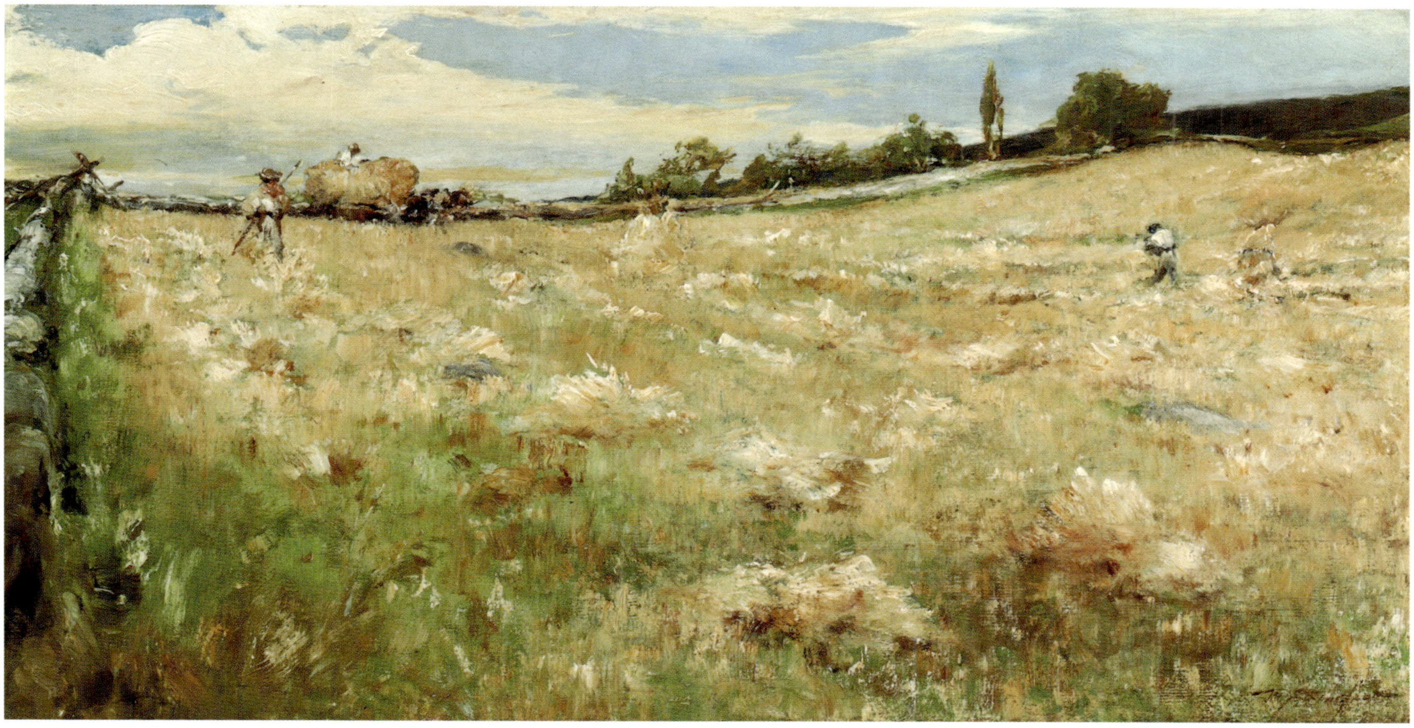

Wheat Fields, Vermont

Mortimer Smith

1840 Busti, New York–Detroit 1896

Mortimer Smith was born in Busti, New York. His parents, Sheldon and Amelia, moved the family sometime between 1840 and 1848 to Oberlin, Ohio, where by 1850 his father had established himself as an architect and had opened a drawing or design school. In 1853 the family moved to Sandusky, Ohio. It was there that Smith's early interest in art was fostered at the Cosmopolitan Art Association gallery. Sheldon Smith decided to relocate his family yet again, possibly because the railroad had bypassed Sandusky for Chicago; they moved to Detroit in 1855. Smith received architectural training in his father's office and joined the firm as a draftsman in 1857. Two years later he married Nellie Fowler of Rockford, Illinois. At twenty-one he became a principal in his father's firm, and its name was changed to Sheldon Smith and Son, Architects.

During the 1860s Smith began to turn his attention to painting. *Home Late* (1866; unlocated) was his first documented painting. A year later, he exhibited *The Frontier Home* (private collection) at the Michigan State Fair, where it was extremely well received. In 1868 he offered the painting in an art lottery. Smith painted sixty small pictures and framed each, selling them for ten dollars apiece and a chance to win *The Frontier Home*. It was not a successful venture, and the prize was not awarded. The large painting was exhibited again, along with others, at the 1869 state fair.

After the death of Smith's father in 1870, the name of the firm was changed to Mortimer L. Smith, Architect. During this decade the firm grew and the office became a training ground for young architects. His eldest son, Fred, joined the firm as a draftsman in 1879.

With the early 1880s Mortimer's interest in architecture began to decline and he spent more time painting. This is documented by a letter to his son written in 1881 discussing his decision to begin to charge eastern prices for his work, which would then allow him more time to paint (Holleman and Gallagher 1978, 54). Smith exhibited locally through the 1870s and 1880s and was represented at the Detroit Art Loan Association exhibition of 1883. In that same year his son Fred returned to Detroit after a two-year absence and became a partner in the firm.

Smith continued to pursue architectural commissions, granting additional responsibility to his son, which in turn provided more time for him to paint and travel to distant sites such as Alaska. He died unexpectedly in 1896 at the age of fifty-six. The cause of death was reported as brain trouble.

J. W. T.

Bibliography Holleman and Gallagher 1978.

78

Winter Landscape, 1878

Oil on canvas

76.2 × 127.6 cm (30 × 50¼ in.)

Gift of James L. Edison (05.411)

Mortimer Smith was one of Detroit's most prominent architects, responsible for buildings ranging from a seed warehouse to the city's opera house. His father was an architect, as was his son; however, this form of artistic expression was his vocation. Smith's avocation and true love was painting, to which he devoted many of his off-hours. In 1881, having achieved an acceptable level of success, his firm well in order, he began to withdraw from active practice and devote more time to painting. *Winter Landscape* was painted shortly before his move to semiretirement.

Smith was a great outdoorsman, often traveling to the pristine wilderness to hunt and paint. This canvas was a response to one such outing, representing an anonymous scene from Michigan's Upper Peninsula, probably the northwest region. Quite mountainous and once rich with ore deposits, the area nurtured many wealthy mining towns, which could provide the most fashionable and up-to-date lodgings. It was the perfect setting for the gentleman hunter. Smith could, with relative ease, go on countless sketching trips while still enjoying the finest in nineteenth-century comforts. The panoramic splendor that northern Michigan offered was similar to those majestic natural effects that intoxicated the painters of the Hudson River school, dominating their canvases. However, for Smith, who did not have the luxury of time, this area proved to be a close answer for like source material.

Smith was certainly aware of and influenced by the Hudson River school artists. Their work was represented in Detroit collections and he would certainly have seen it on one of his many trips to the East Coast. Although Smith did not achieve the success of Frederic Edwin Church (q.v.) or Martin Johnson Heade (q.v.), he did embrace their ideas of light and atmospheric quality. *Winter Landscape,* typical of Smith's winter scenes from the late 1870s through the 1880s, attempts to capture the shimmering light and translucent clouds for which his eastern counterparts were so noted. Smith provided a canvas replete with all the required landscape elements—the fallen trees in the foreground, unfettered wildlife, classically balanced groups of white pine trees, and imposing mountains, a bit obscured by a hazy mist. It has been suggested that Smith's organization of the canvas provides overt religious symbolism, which would have been apparent to his generation (Muskegon and Detroit 1987, 69). While there is validity in his debt to Thomas Cole and his followers, it might be considered that in Smith's case he may

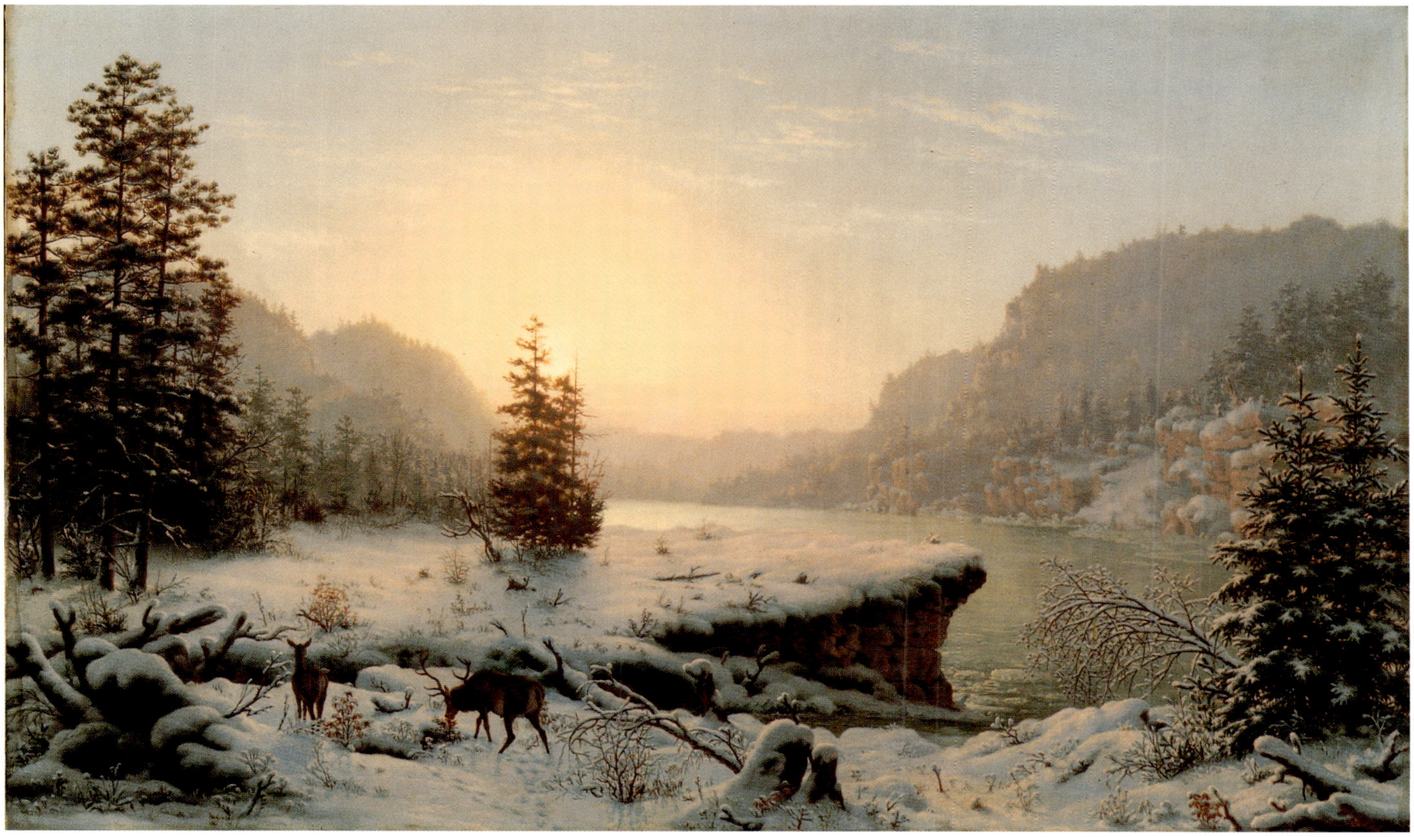

just have been recording aspects of the landscape that were typical of Michigan, and not mythical. His winter scenes, which were a dominant aspect of his oeuvre, often received the greatest praise from the local press. He exhibited locally and did not venture far beyond. This in itself, coupled with his somewhat conservative style, relegated him to the level of a regional artist, never achieving true national recognition.

J. W. T.

Inscription At lower left, *Mortimer L. Smith*

Exhibitions Muskegon and Detroit 1987, 47, 68–71. Greenville 1990.

Reference Ferry 1986, 87.

Winter Landscape

William Louis Sonntag

1822 East Liberty, Pennsylvania–New York 1900

As an infant, William L. Sonntag moved with his family from his birthplace to Cincinnati, where he spent his youth and his formative years as an artist. In about 1840 he was apprenticed to a carpenter but remained only three days. The youth possessed a greater interest in art and later was apprenticed to an architect to learn the rudiments of drawing. Around 1845, when the Sonntag family returned to the East, William remained behind to pursue his artistic ambitions. During the third quarter of the nineteenth century he was an established artist and an active member of the circle of Hudson River school painters.

At midcentury Cincinnati was the commercial and cultural center of the western United States. The city had founded an art academy, art fairs, and the Western Art Union, institutions that created a burgeoning cultural community. The introduction of Hudson River school landscapes at the Western Art Union exhibitions inspired Sonntag and his contemporaries Worthington Whittredge (q.v.) and Robert S. Duncanson (q.v.) to pursue landscape painting. Together they formed a group of Ohio River valley landscape painters who painted the regional scenery. In 1847 Sonntag painted an ambitious cycle of four landscapes, *Progress of Civilization* (unlocated). This series was inspired by Cole's *Voyage of Life* (1846; National Gallery of Art, Washington, D.C.) and reinforced Sonntag's stature as a serious landscape painter.

After Whittredge departed for Düsseldorf in 1849, it was proclaimed that in Cincinnati, "the most eminent in landscape is Sonntag" (Heilbron 1932). His reputation was based on his stylized rendering of Ohio River valley scenery in paintings such as *Scene on the Little Miami River* (1853; Cincinnati Art Museum). By 1853 his ambitions outgrew the frontier city and he departed for his first tour of Europe with his colleague Duncanson and his student, John R. Tait. The artists spent most of their trip in Florence, living in the American artistic community centered on the sculptor and fellow Cincinnatian Hiram Powers. Sonntag was overwhelmed with the culture and landscape of Italy and longed to establish residence there. Although he did return in 1855–56, 1858, 1861, and 1862, he did not become an expatriate.

On his return to the United States in 1854, he settled in New York, where, during the next twenty years, he reached the pinnacle of his artistic career. There, the landscape painter created a sensation with his compositions based on his sketches of Italy such as the *Landscape with Classical Ruins* (1858; Hood Museum of Art, Dartmouth College, Hanover, N.H.). In December 1858 the *Cosmopolitan Art Journal* ran an extended article on the artist that announced, "we see no reason why his hand shall not produce works which shall . . . give his name to immortal mention in the category of truly great artists" (28).

During the Civil War he began to paint in upstate New York and New England; these subjects came to dominate his art. In the mid-1870s Sonntag's style began to change from the tightly delineated, panoramic landscapes of the Hudson River school toward canvases with a more painterly handling and intimate mood. During his summer sketching tours in Vermont and New Hampshire, he began to experiment with watercolors to achieve the fluid light-and-dark contrasts that he was attempting in his work. In 1881 he began to exhibit his watercolors at the American Watercolor Society. By this time his work was falling from popular favor. After 1890 the cool public reception to his work and his fragile health forced him to withdraw from the art scene. A decade later he died in his home from an "affection of the lungs" (Los Angeles 1980, 34). J. K.

Bibliography Los Angeles 1980.

79
October Morning in New Hampshire, 1881

Oil on canvas
40.6 × 61 cm (16 × 24 in.)
Bequest of Mary M. Stevens (10.16)

This small painting was probably begun as a sketch of an autumnal scene near Sonntag's summer home in Shelbourne, New Hampshire, and completed back in his New York studio with details of the fishermen and foreground. The scene of a forested riverbank is indicative of the artist's late style with passages of broad paint handling that emphasize light-and-dark contrasts and convey an intimate, atmospheric quality.

Throughout his career Sonntag painted only the scenery that he knew well from his sketching tours. In the late 1840s and early 1850s, when he was developing his early style, the artist concentrated on the Ohio River valley regions: Kentucky, Pennsylvania, and West Virginia. At that time he utilized standard Hudson River school compositions, motifs, and landscape aesthetics for his canvases. His personal style was characterized by a very linear and mannered treatment of natural forms that created a stiff and arid quality in works such as *Mountain Landscape* (1854; Muskegon Museum of Art, Muskegon, Mich.). After the artist returned from Italy in 1854 and settled in New York, he focused on views of Italian scenery that were painted in a similar manner.

Sonntag continued to return to the Ohio River valley regions for his summer tours in search of landscape subjects until the outbreak of the Civil War. Seeking safer sketching grounds, the artist began to tour the North, particularly upstate New York and New England. These regions came to dominate the subjects of his paintings for the remainder of his artistic career. Beginning in 1870 Sonntag

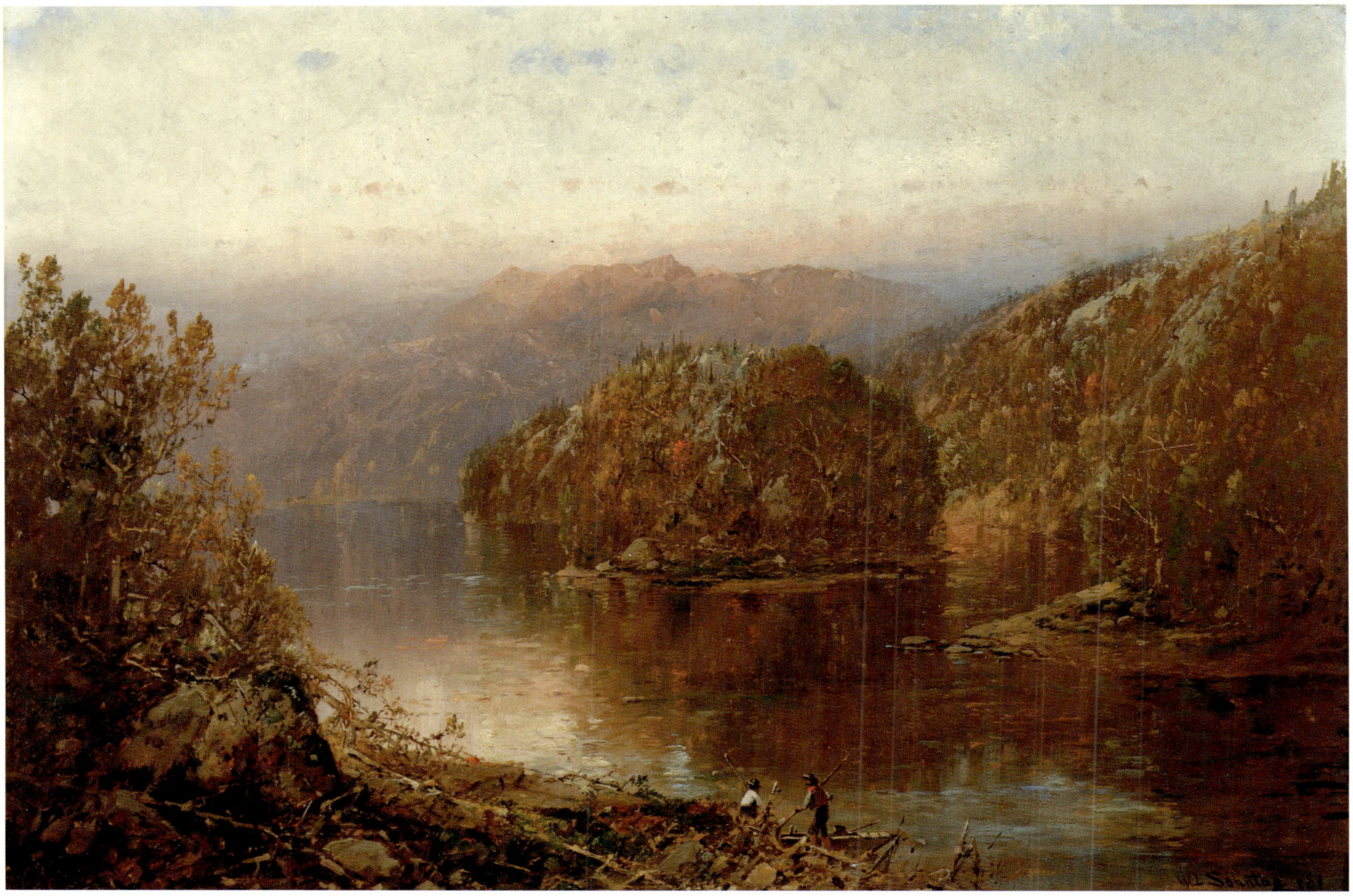

spent his summers in Shelbourne, from where he could sketch his favorite landscapes in Vermont, New Hampshire, and Maine. At the same time he came under the influence of the French Barbizon landscapes that were being introduced to the United States by William Morris Hunt (q.v.) and the Vose Gallery in Boston. Sonntag was swept up into the enthusiam for the Barbizon style, as were a number of other Hudson River school artists, including George Inness (q.v.) and Alexander H. Wyant (q.v.). The French Barbizon paintings dramatically altered Sonntag's style toward broader paint handling with a more fluid mix of pigments and a more intimate scale. His new interests led him to experiment with watercolors in the mid-1870s.

October Morning in New Hampshire is emblematic of this stylistic change in Sonntag's work. The river flowing past the forested banks is rendered with broad strokes of paint that play the bright highlights off the darker river for a shimmering effect. The artist painted the autumnal foliage with rich, dark tones that he applied with a dappled touch, creating a thick texture. The stylistic transformation is most evident in the atmospheric effect of the background and the sky. The darker areas of shadow are contrasted to whipped whites of the clouds to capture effectively the rapidly changing weather conditions of autumn. The only indication of his earlier, linear style is found in the drawing of the fallen trees and fishermen in the foreground. Although the specific location of this scene is not known, around this time the artist was painting numerous views of the Pennegewasset River in nearby Plymouth, New Hampshire, which may be the subject. This painting is similar to other works from this era, such as *Mountain Scene with Stream* (1881; Fruitlands Museum, Harvard, Mass.) and *Landscape* (1883; New Britain Museum of American Art, New Britain, Conn.). However, *October Morning in New Hampshire* is larger in scale, suggesting that it may be a more ambitious summa-

October Morning

tion of the artist's work during this period.

J. K.

Inscription At lower right, *W. L. Sonntag 81*

Provenance Mary M. Stevens, until 1910. Acquired in 1910.

Exhibitions Columbus et al. 1953, no. 32. Los Angeles 1980, no. 192.

80

View in the White Mountains, 1888

Oil on canvas
50.8 × 91.4 cm (20 × 36 in.)
Gift of Dr. Charles Hitchcock (22.139)

ALTHOUGH *View in the White Mountains* is later than *October Morning in New Hampshire* (cat. no. 79), it is executed in a tight, linear style that is more typical of Sonntag's earlier work. This painting was previously known as *A Lake in the Mountains* until examination by a conservator revealed a penciled inscription on the stretcher, *88 View in the White Mts,* which appears to be in the artist's hand. The contrast between the style and the date causes some difficulty in understanding the artist's stylistic development. The problem is resolved only with a close examination of his work during the 1880s.

In the 1870s Sonntag came under the spell of the French Barbizon landscape painters and began to develop a broader style with an intimacy of scale and mood that contrasted with his earlier Hudson River school–style canvases. This evolution was fully realized by the 1880s in such works as *October Morning in New Hampshire,* where a loose application of pigments, liberally mixed with oil, creates an atmospheric effect based on the contrast of light and shadow. Throughout the remainder of his active career, this style dominated Sonntag's production. This is true of the artist's major paintings such as *Ingalls Brook* (1886; Evansville Museum of Arts and Science, Evansville, Ind.), which was painted for the National Academy of Design and later exhibited at the World's Columbian Exposition at Chicago in 1893.

View in the White Mountains is atypical of this development in Sonntag's art. The painting depicts a calm river that cascades down a mountainous background past some fishermen boating in the foreground. The shoreline is strewn with rocks and tree stumps, while the forest recedes up the hillsides. The compositional format is very similar to *October Morning in New Hampshire,* particularly in the conception and treatment of the fallen trees and fishermen in the foreground. (Throughout Sonntag's career these were stock motifs.) Yet the differences in handling between these two works are marked, in that the later painting is much more controlled and tightly rendered in the details and underpainting. These traits may relate to the artist's commissioned work. In 1882 and 1883 Sonntag replaced James M. Hart on landscape projects with Arthur F. Tait. Tait was a very popular animal painter who often had his landscape backgrounds executed by other artists. For two years Sonntag was commissioned to paint Adirondack landscapes for five or six works finished with animal subjects and jointly signed by Tait. None of these canvases is extant. However, if one may judge by Tait's other works of this era, it is reasonable to assume that Sonntag's landscape backgrounds were painted in a similar manner, with well-defined and detailed natural forms. Such a linear manner is also evident in Sonntag's largest known painting, *View of the Grand Canyon* (1886; formerly Knoedler Gallery, New York). This was probably painted after Thomas Moran's famous prints of the subject. Sonntag was not known to have traveled west and had not done any similar subjects, suggesting that this may have been painted on commission. The subject is entirely different from *View in the White Mountains,* but the linear definition of the rocks in *View of the Grand Canyon,* from only two years earlier, is very similar. Sonntag's ability to work in both a broad, Barbizon style and a more detailed, linear style indicates the artist's versatility. *View in the White Mountains* must have been commissioned for a particular patron or purpose that remains unknown.

J. K.

Inscriptions At lower left *W. L. Sonntag;* on stretcher, *88 View in the White Mts*

Provenance Dr. Charles Hitchcock, until 1922. Acquired in 1922.

Exhibition Los Angeles 1980, no. 291.

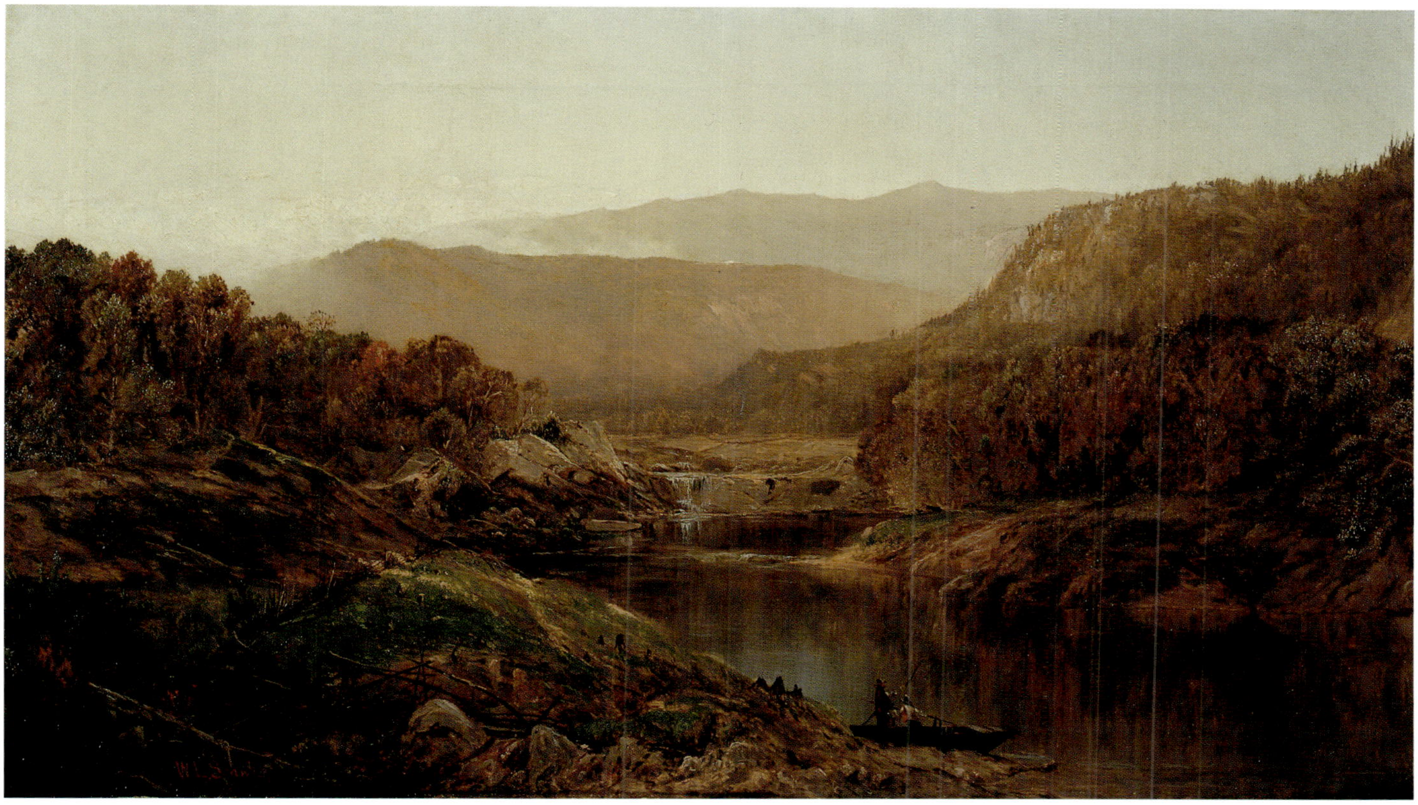

View in the White Mountains

Lilly Martin Spencer

1822 Exeter, England–New York 1902

Lilly Martin Spencer's parents, Giles and Angélique Martin, were French nationals living and teaching at Exeter, England, when Spencer (baptized Angélique Marie Martin) was born. In 1830 the family immigrated to New York; three years later they moved on to Marietta, Ohio. They had originally hoped to organize a communal society, along the lines advocated by the French socialist Charles Fourier. Instead, they settled on a farm, and Spencer's father taught at Marietta Collegiate Institute and Western Teacher's Seminary.

Spencer drew as a teenager, receiving encouragement from local artists, some of whom had been trained at the Pennsylvania Academy of the Fine Arts in Philadelphia. In 1841 she showed her work in an exhibition at the rectory of a Marietta church; admission was charged to benefit her further education. The exhibition prompted the Cincinnati patron Nicholas Longworth to offer her five hundred dollars to cover costs of a trip to the East to meet John Trumbull and Washington Allston (Freivogel 1972, 9–10). Although the Spencers turned down Longworth's generosity, his encouragement motivated the artist's father to take her to Cincinnati, then a bustling city with a developing cultural component. She had another exhibition of her work in Cincinnati, and the two of them settled in, her father earning money by tutoring in French.

In 1844 the artist married the cloth merchant Benjamin Rush Spencer, and the next year the first of their thirteen children was born. (Only seven reached adulthood.) Her sympathetic husband encouraged her to continue her career, and as the years passed and her work continued to sell, he took over the household responsibilities.

During seven years in Cincinnati, with the support of the city's senior artists, including James Beard, her career as a portrait and genre painter blossomed. When the Western Art Union held its first exhibition in 1847, Spencer showed eight paintings and sold four. The Western Art Union continued to buy her work, and in 1849 it engraved and distributed *Life's Happy Hour* to its members.

These early successes spurred her ambitions to become a nationally known artist. In 1848 she moved her growing family to New York, the art center of the country, where she had already exhibited at the American Art-Union and the National Academy of Design. For the next ten years she negotiated commissions and hoped to advance herself, although finances were always difficult. William Schaus, the American agent for the French firm Goupil, Vibert & Co., commissioned works that proved to be popular in lithographic form but which did not bring financial reward. She also sold paintings to the Cosmopolitan Art Association, a commercial art organization that rose to prominence after the demise of the American Art-Union, and she sent paintings to exhibitions in Cincinnati and other cities outside New York.

In 1858 she moved to Newark, New Jersey, to a house rented from her patron Marcus L. Ward. Although she continued to exhibit, her career did not prosper as it had in New York; therefore in 1867 she attempted a comeback by renting a studio in lower Manhattan. To accommodate her ever-growing family, she made several moves to larger living quarters, eventually settling in Highland, New York, in 1879. She never stopped painting her genre pictures, although public interest waned. When she auctioned paintings in New York in 1890, the highest price she received was ten dollars. Ten years following her husband's death in 1890, she moved back to New York, still with hopes of resurrecting her faltering career. She died on the Upper West Side on May 22, 1902, after having spent the early part of the day at her easel.

P. H.

Bibliography Hadry 1851. Freivogel 1972. Washington 1973. Johns 1991, 160–175. Lubin 1994, 158–203.

81

Domestic Happiness, 1849

Oil on canvas

141 × 114.9 cm (55½ × 45¼ in.)

Bequest of Dr. and Mrs. James Cleland, Jr. (34.274)

In 1849, when Lilly Martin Spencer painted *Domestic Happiness,* the artist had recently moved to New York. She had hit her stride with popular paintings, especially ones with mothers and children. She sent *Domestic Happiness* to the National Academy of Design in 1849 and then sent it on to the American Art-Union with a price of $500. The managers of the Art-Union seem not to have accepted the painting, although they did purchase for distribution that year her *Thoughts on a Flower,* depicting a woman resting on a bank and looking at a flower, for which she was asking $150, and *Youth and Age,* showing a grandfather surrounded by three children, for which she was asking $300 (*Bulletin of the American Art-Union,* December 1849, nos. 91 and 228).

Two years later Spencer exhibited *Domestic Happiness,* with the subtitle *"Hush, Don't Wake Them,"* at the galleries of the Philadelphia Art Union with the considerably lower sale price of $200. Henriette A. Hadry, writing for *Sartain's Union Magazine* in August 1851, called the painting *Domestic Felicity,* described its subject for her readers, and praised it at length:

> The scene represented in this composition . . . consists of a mother and father, their faces beaming with affection, bending over the couch where repose their two children, in all the happy unconsciousness of peaceful slumber.

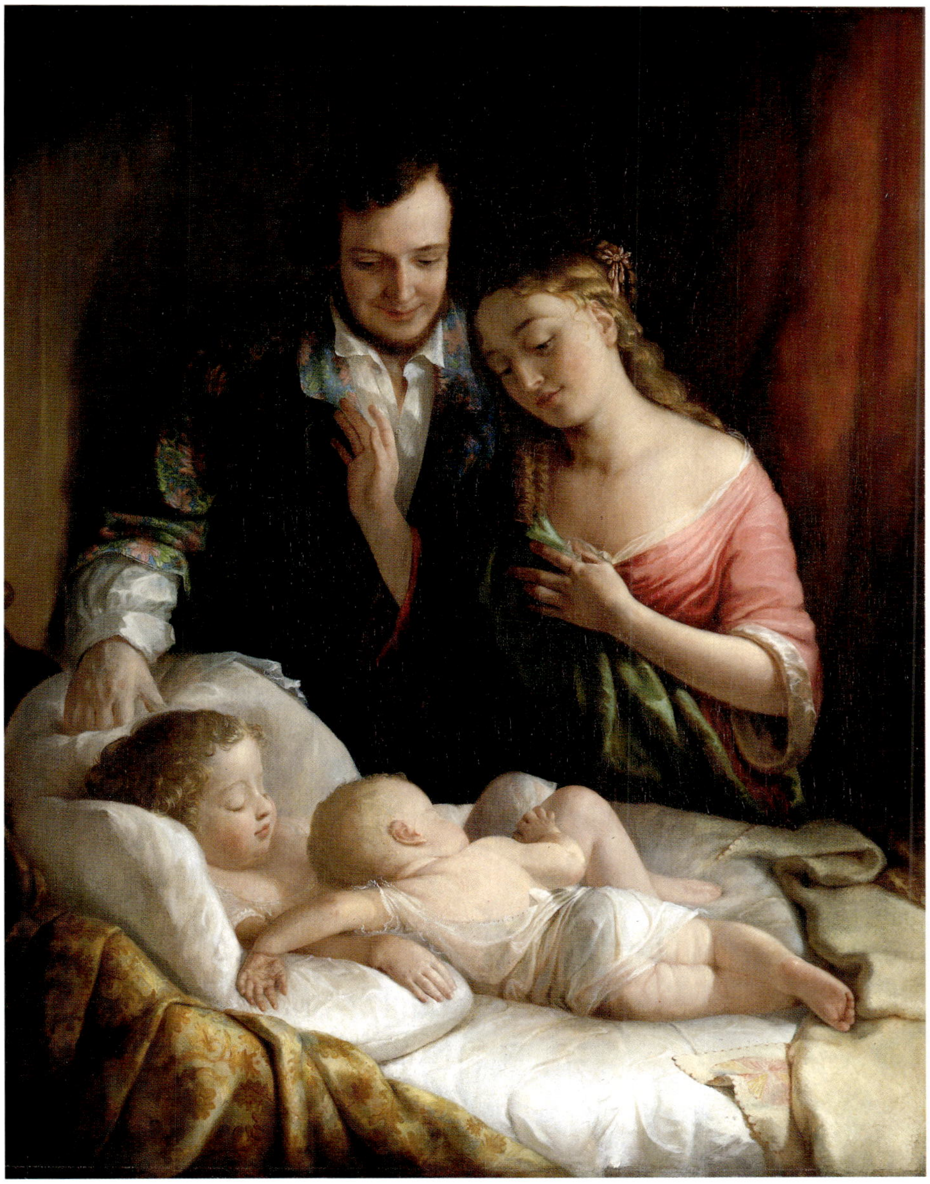

> This painting of Mrs. Spencer's is well deserving of the attention so generally accorded to it, and which, I think, has exceeded that given to any other single production that has appeared on the walls of the Gallery since it was first opened. Not from the novelty of its being the work of a female artist, do I so estimate it, but from its intrinsic merits as a work of art. It is highly wrought, yet without the usual result observable from elaboration, tameness and insipidity: its vigour and freshness being as remarkable as the colouring is rich and harmonious, while the drawing and general arrangement are in all particulars admirable. I don't know where I have seen a hand, in any picture, better drawn and painted than the right hand of the mother, and I have heard eminent members of the profession remark on difficult parts of this composition, that they could not name the male artist who was able to surpass them. (Hadry 1851, 153)

Throughout her essay, Hadry explained the difficulties for women pursuing an art career but noted that Spencer's supportive parents had always given the somewhat impetuous young girl free rein to develop her talents. The painting was subsequently sold to the Western Art Union of Cincinnati, which distributed it by lottery to a Captain Waterman.

With this image Spencer reveals her personal circumstances in 1848 and 1849 vis-à-vis her children—specifically her concerns about their welfare and her responsibility for watching over them. And she paints these concerns with an imagery that connects to the literary and visual culture of her own middle-class, urban milieu—a culture fascinated by and nostalgically yearning for representations of innocent, sleeping, entwined children.

Spencer did several drawings of mothers and their children, such as *Mother Holding a Child in Her Arms* (1846–48; Washington 1973, ill. 107), representing a mother tenderly gazing into the eyes of her child. In *The Baby's Dream* (Washington 1973, ill. 124), a mother clasps to her chin a chain with a cross while she leans on her arms and stares at her sleeping child. Beneath the drawing is inscribed: *The Baby's dream / Or the / Angels Whisper.* Such drawings would seem to come naturally from the pencil of a mother who has to tend to her babies while finding time for her art.

Spencer was painfully aware that babies were also creatures who might at any minute be snatched away by death, as indeed some of her own were. Childhood diseases were epidemic at midcentury. Spencer's first daughter, Angelica, died in infancy in either 1846 or 1847, while the family still lived in Cincinnati. Spencer drew the dead child staring upward with her arms laid across her chest and inscribed the drawing, *My poor sweet little Angelica,* followed by a poem: "She took the cup of life to sip / but bitter t'was to drain / She meekly put it from her lip / and went to sleep again" (Washington 1973, 108). The recognition of the correspondence between the sleep of innocent children and their premature death permeates the literature of mourning for children in the early nineteenth century and produced heartrending images as tomb monuments. Indeed, those states of being and nonbeing merge in the phrase "the sleep of death."

In England, Thomas Banks carved an effigy of a recumbent, sleeping child when he executed the tomb for six-year-old Penelope Boothby in 1793 (Penny 1977, 115). Other English sculptors followed suit with marble images of sleeping children recumbent upon their tombs. The most famous of these was Francis Chantrey's *Sleeping Children,* shown at the Royal Academy in 1817 and subsequently installed in Lichfield cathedral as a monument to the deceased daughters of the Reverend W. Robinson. Chantrey's sculpture was admired on both sides of the Atlantic, through engravings made after the image and small ceramic replicas (Penny 1977, 119), as well as through written commentary in the literature of the period. For example, the American gift annual *The Offering* of 1829 published an extended commentary on Chantry's sculpture:

> It is while lying in the helplessness of innocent sleep, that infancy and childhood are viewed with the most touching interest; and this, and the loveliness of the children, the uncertainty of the expression at first view, the dim shadowing forth of that sleep from which they cannot be awakened, their hovering, as it were, upon the confines of life, as if they might still be recalled, all conspire to render the last feeling, that death is indeed before us, most deeply affecting. (Parkman 1829, 243)

The essay continues with seven stanzas of poetry, which described the "gentle forms, entwined / Like tendrils." The popularity of Chantrey's image influenced the American sculptor Thomas Crawford, who carved a similar image, *Babes in the Woods* (Metropolitan Museum of Art, New York), in 1851. Chantrey's effigy, Crawford's sculpture, the words of solace in *The Offering,* and Spencer's painting all share the Rousseauian ideal of the beauty of the innocence of children.

Spencer's children in *Domestic Happiness,* however, at the moment are not dead, but alive, for which Spencer would have been most grateful. The larger child would be modeled on her son Benjamin, born in 1845; the other, Angelo Paul, was born in March 1848—both ages would be about right for this picture. Benjamin was named after her husband and Angelo Paul after her first deceased daughter, who in turn had been named after her mother, Angélique. Happy indeed the home with healthy, sleeping children over whom an indulgent father and responsible mother can watch. But as one little mourning book reminded midcentury parents, "While they [children] yet live, we bend over them with a breathless solicitude. We watch each varying symptom with feverish anxiety" (Parkman 1854, 25).

Spencer did a drawing, inscribed *Don't Wake Them* (Washington 1973, ill. 34), which is clearly a study for *Domestic Happiness* but differs from the painting in a few of its details. The infant's head is twisted toward his sibling in the drawing, whereas the pose is more relaxed in the finished painting. Also, in the drawing the mother splays out her fingers and presses her hand against her husband's chest as if to stay him. In the finished painting her hand merely brushes against his smoking jacket and it is posed in the gesture of "hush." The mother controls the situation in both drawing and painting, just as Spencer controls the picture because she is constructing it. Painted mother and painter mother thus merge. If the former exhibits "breathless solicitude" toward the children, Spencer analogously held a similar anxiety toward the fortunes of the painting, the chef d'oeuvre of her career. Nevertheless, Spencer could be assured of an empathetic response from those middle-class people who sought out pictures of domestic happiness and understood the very fragility on which such happiness rested—health, loving affection, the security of a cozy home as well as a steady source of income.

P. H.

Inscription On verso, *Lilly M. Spencer / Painter 1849*

Provenance Philadelphia Art Union. Western Art Union, Cincinnati. Captain Waterman. Mrs. E. M. Brady. Dr. and Mrs. James Cleland, Jr. Acquired in 1934.

Exhibitions New York, National Academy of Design Annual, 1849. Philadelphia Art Union, 1851. Detroit 1883, as "Father Returns." Washington 1973, no. 133.

References Hadry 1851. Lubin 1994, 162–169.

Elihu Vedder

1836 New York–Rome, Italy 1923

Elihu Vedder was one of the more original yet eclectic American artists of the nineteenth century. His mature work, like much late-nineteenth-century symbolist art, can be understood as an intuitive amalgam of varied influences, including Greco-Roman and Renaissance sculpture, Early Christian and Byzantine mosaics, Gothic stained-glass windows and tile work, Italian quattrocento and mannerist paintings, the prints of William Blake, Nazarene and Pre-Raphaelite paintings, Japanese woodcuts, astrology, and Oriental mysticism, all founded on a personal propensity toward fantastical, sometimes erotic, sometimes morbid, dreams and visions.

Born in New York City, Vedder grew up shuttling between three places he called home: his father's principal residence in Cuba; his parents' house in New York City; and his grandfather's farm in upstate New York near Schenectady. Doubtless those varied topographies steered the incipient artist toward landscape painting and poetry. But to judge by his oeuvre rather than by a remark in his autobiography (Vedder 1910, 139), he was primarily interested in the human figure.

To that end, Vedder studied briefly in 1854 with Tompkins Harrison Matteson, a historical, genre, and portrait painter from Sherburne, New York, and then in early 1856 he went to Europe hoping to secure in-depth training. At first he enrolled in the Paris atelier of the aged academician François-Edouard Picot, himself a former student of François-André Vincent, a contemporary of Jacques-Louis David. But within months—the boisterous milieu of Picot's pupils notwithstanding—Vedder became restive, and he set his sights on Italy. After an entranced exploration of several Italian cities, among them Genoa, Rome, and Venice, he settled in Florence, where he soon associated with a group of young, nonconformist Italian artists who by the early 1860s were calling themselves Macchiaioli. In addition, during his Florentine sojourn Vedder met several English and American expatriates, notably the critic and collector James Jackson Jarves, with whom Vedder developed close personal ties. A blend of radicalism and a corollary wariness of academic environments on the one hand and what might be called a probing traditionalism on the other hand remained at the heart of Vedder's creativity for the rest of his life.

He spent most of that long life in Italy. First, however, late in 1860, following his father's wishes, Vedder returned to the United States via Spain and Cuba, arriving just as the Civil War started. He stayed in New York and Boston for the next five years, between 1861 and 1866. Over that interval he gained recognition among colleagues and art critics, especially for his paintings *The Sphinx,* or *The Questioner of the Sphinx* (1864; Museum of Fine Arts, Boston), *Lair of the Sea Serpent* (1864; Museum of Fine Arts, Boston), and *A Lost Mind* (1865; Metropolitan Museum of Art, New York), all of which he showed at the National Academy of Design; that organization accepted him for associate membership in 1864 and full membership one year later. While in New York he acquired a string of literary and artistic friends, among them Herman Melville, and in Boston he kept company with two artists, William Morris Hunt (q.v.) and John La Farge, whose sensibilities had much in common with his. On balance, though, he found himself in reduced circumstances, devoid of the fundamental inspiration he craved. Hence, he went back to Italy via France in 1866, settling this time in Rome, where he maintained a domicile until his death. Except for periodic return visits to the United States and sojourns in London in 1870 and 1876, Vedder became a devoted Italophile. During one of his trips to the United States, in 1869, he married Elizabeth Caroline Rosencrans, of Glens Falls, New York, with whom he had become acquainted in Paris during 1866. From this time on she handled many of his business affairs.

During the 1870s and early 1880s Vedder produced designs for decorative arts and dabbled in illustrations of poetry. The fifty-five illustrations of the *Rubáiyát of Omar Khayyáam* that were published in 1884 gained him international success lasting into the new century. He carried out several cycles of murals in the United States during the 1890s, and his late work in general has affinities with international Art Nouveau.

Vedder's career could be divided into several phases, but even during periods of high repute his art was controversial. In reply, his defenders usually stressed his individuality. "If it be the mission of an original talent to bring into the world, not peace, but a sword, Vedder has had the compliment of creating this kind of a disturbance. There began to be Vedderites and Anti-Vedderites very early in his career, and moderation in the expression of their opinions has never been the most marked trait of either," declared William H. Bishop in the first of two articles favorable to Vedder written for the *American Art Review* in 1880 (Bishop 1880, 325). Notwithstanding their occasional virulence—of which the commentaries pertaining to his painting *The Cumaean Sibyl* (cat. no. 83) comprise illustrative examples—reviewers also voiced astute opinions about him, comparing him to Edgar Allan Poe, Nathaniel Hawthorne, Gustave Doré, and Blake, calling him "a Burne Jones, Delacroix, and Leighton rolled into one" *(Athenaeum* 1883) and citing his oeuvre as "a rare instance of the perfect sympathy that may exist between poet and painter" *(Atlantic Monthly* 1885). A discerning critic, possibly Thomas Gold Appleton *(Appleton's Journal* 1874), responding to a canvas entitled *Fête Champêtre* (1870–72; unlocated; Bishop 1880a, ill. 369), one of just four submissions by Vedder to the National Academy of Design after 1867, likened

the work at once to Pre-Raphaelitism, "Japanese art," and "painting on a tile, or the decoration on a porcelain cup." Eighteen months later, the same magazine *(Appleton's Journal* 1875), in discussing two of Vedder's pictures on view at Doll & Richards's gallery in Boston, stated that "Vedder's position as an artist is a difficult one to define," adding: "Whether he is spiritual, sensual, or intellectual, we cannot define, nor whether his pictures are elevating or demoralizing. We are inclined to think the latter." Yet the writer was transfixed, asserting that despite perceived thinness of draftsmanship and modeling, Vedder's "people live in the memory longer than men and women whose hands are moulded to look like flesh and blood, or whose forms appear like veritable bone and muscle."
G. C.

Bibliography Vedder 1910. Soria 1970. Washington and Brooklyn 1979.

82
Fiesole, 1859

Oil on canvas
38.1 × 74.3 cm (15 × 29¼ in.)
Gift of Mr. and Mrs. James S. Whitcomb (56.19)

PAINTED EARLY in Vedder's first Italian sojourn, this cabinet-sized canvas is a characteristic example of what might be called his reductive-classicist/reductive-realist landscapes. Regina Soria has identified the site as the Mugnone Torrent, a tributary of the Arno, a short distance west of Fiesole (Soria 1970, 28–29, 280; Soria 1989, 169). The locale was a favorite of Vedder's. As he later recalled:

> Walking past Porta San Gallo . . . on the high banks of this stream you finally reached the spot where it passes under a bridge at the foot of the long ascent which leads [northeast] to Fiesole. Here I painted two of my best studies and also a little picture I always thought highly of. (Vedder 1910, 164; quoted by Soria 1989, 169, 175)

Soria further convincingly equates the painting itself to that which Vedder entitled *Landscape near Florence* in a letter to his father of March 13, 1860 (AAA; Soria 1989, 169), in turn probably the "little picture" to which he referred in 1910.

Vedder produced and exhibited landscapes, principally of Italian subjects, throughout his career. Certain works by contemporary American landscapists, among them George Inness (q.v.), who traveled in Italy for about a year between 1851 and 1852, and Sanford R. Gifford (q.v.), who spent approximately a year in Italy between 1856 and 1857, are close analogies to Vedder's Italian landscapes. Recently Soria (Soria 1989; see also K. Quinn, in Boston et al. 1992, 364) has persuasively expanded on her thesis of 1970 (Soria 1970, 27–30; see also Grigaut 1955–56), paralleling Vedder's Florentine landscapes to those of the Macchiaioli, contemporary young Italian painters with whom Vedder associated while he lived in Florence.

To these observations may be added two more. One of them, expressed by Vedder's contemporaries, held that his landscape creativity was both attached and subservient to his efforts with the human figure. For example, one English critic *(Examiner and London Review* 1870), confronted with Vedder's *View from the Porta Romana [Bordighiera], Cornice Road* (unlocated) at Ernest Gambart's French Gallery, London, in 1870, categorized the picture among the exhibit's figure subjects because "the figures form an important part of the work, and because the landscape is treated in a way which shows it at once to be the work of a figure painter." The writer's words are creditable if comprehended within the international context of the French Gallery, where they bring to mind works by selected contemporary French figure specialists, particularly Pierre Puvis de Chavannes, and through them the heritage of French classicist landscape and figure artists extending from Camille Corot back through Nicolas Poussin.

An equally apt analogy to contemporaneous British watercolors was made by another London reviewer *(Athenaeum* 1870), presumably Vedder's friend William Davies, when he discussed Vedder's *Dead Abel* (1869; Fine Arts Museums of San Francisco), then on view at the Dudley Gallery. The *Abel*, Davies opined,

> suggest[ed] in many respects studies in a vein similar to that of J. Moore's landscapes from the Tiber and the Arno. A mode of treating local colour and form, and light and shade, which is best styled "monumental," obtains in both artists' productions: generalization carried to an extreme, and abnegation of what may be called individuality of all the elements of their paintings, profound pathos, and a solemnity which is inexpressively mournful, are obvious in the picture here, as well as in the landscapes we have [just] named. A northern land would not supply, unless in exceptional cases, elements of pathetic expression which are at once so sad and sweet, so dignified and so severe, as those of Mr. Vedder's *Dead Abel* (no. 34).

Davies, who knew Vedder well, was referring to John Collingham Moore, a brother of British painter Albert Moore. Primarily a painter of portraits and genre scenes, John C. Moore traveled to Italy in 1858 and subsequently exhibited watercolor views of the Roman Campagna and other Italian locations at the Dudley Gallery (founded in 1865) and elsewhere in London. We might add that during the 1850s and 1860s other British artists —notably Frederic Leighton—who traveled in Italy and elsewhere in the Mediterranean responded similarly to the varied topographies they encountered.

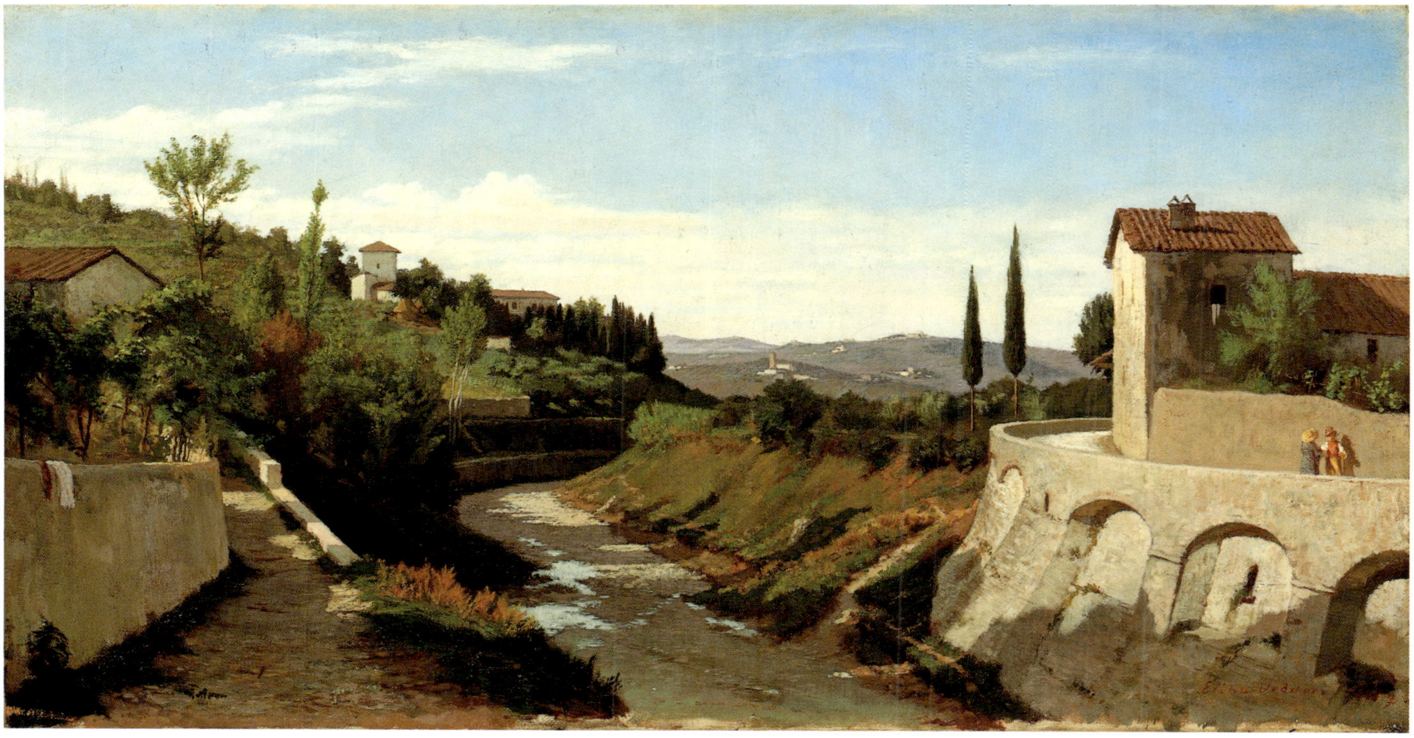

Fiesole

Covering most of the panoramic canvas and respectfully deferential to the recumbent figure like a scenic backdrop, the desolate twilight landscape of Vedder's *Dead Abel* is a composed scene appropriately imbued with a mournful sentiment tinged with tragedy. The mood of his oblong, topographically explicit *Fiesole* is nostalgic but not cheerless. The scene blends generalized natural features and simplified, time-worn human artifacts with specifics that bespeak an informality of the everyday; that is, classicism with realism.

By the time he painted the present work, Vedder doubtless had read about Fiesole and its history stretching from ancient Etruria and Rome through the Renaissance. Yet no renowned buildings or identifiable ruins are visible here, nor is there evidence of urban Fiesole, itself a hilltop outpost of the much larger city of Florence during the Renaissance. Instead, the artist has depicted a domesticated Tuscan landscape that focuses on a feature at once natural and artificial. The time of day is late afternoon; amber sunlight enters at a low angle from the left, casting long but fairly transparent shadows toward the right. The viewer's eye is led easily into deep space by the spacious, curving Mugnone sluice, parched in summer like a dirt road, at lower middle. At the near right, substantial foundations reinforced by blind arches provide a platform for a brightly lit, two-segment cubic structure with tile roofs and a curving walkway on which two figures stand. The walkway is protected on its near edge by a low parapet and on the other side by a high wall. Additional simplified structures are stationed at the left, their walls mostly in shadow, while a towered edifice, evidently a monastery or convent church, is the foremost among several buildings in the far distance. Trees of various shapes and densities and clumps of low vegetation are disposed throughout the scene. Geology, vegetation, and human artifact appear to meld or, better yet, to have arisen from allied generative processes.

The snakelike sluice seems to offer access to the distant church, yet Vedder places the viewer above the bed on a cobble path that rises toward the left. Bordered by a wall at the near left (over which are draped two pieces of laundry), reinforced on the right edge by a low parapet, and partially overhung by trees, the shadowed footway offers a human-scale but roughened alternative to the expansive, comparatively serene streambed below, and to the crystal-clear promenade at the right. The three divergent thoroughfares therefore present a modest conundrum that the painter savors: should the spectator follow the artificial and natural one, or one of the two lesser, differing artificial ones?

G. C.

Inscriptions At lower right, *Elihu Vedder / 1859;* on the verso, *Elihu Vedder / Florence 1859*

Provenance George Riddle, Cambridge, Mass. Arunah S. A. Brady, Baltimore. Mr. and Mrs. James S. Whitcomb, Baltimore. P. Gilbert Broculette, Staten Island, N.Y. Mr. and Mrs. James S. Whitcomb, Grosse Pointe, Mich. Acquired in 1956.

Exhibitions Detroit and San Francisco 1957, no. 149. Buffalo et al. 1976, no. 15. Washington and Brooklyn 1979, 40–42, no. 6. West Palm Beach et al. 1984.

References Grigaut 1955–56. Soria 1970, 28–29, 289. Soria 1989, 168–169.

83
The Cumaean Sibyl, 1875–76

Oil on canvas
96.5 × 149.9 cm (38 × 59 in.)
Founders Society Purchase, Merrill Fund (57.235)

PAINTED IN ROME between 1875 and early 1876 as an exhibition piece, *The Cumaean Sibyl* ranks among Vedder's largest and self-consciously most important works. The unusual subject, in which the gloomily moralistic narrative is (one may say) conveyed figurally, naturally, and literarily, and the work's heterogeneous stylistic character (see below) doubtless were the artist's principal concerns. Yet Vedder had difficulty obtaining display situations for the picture and in dealing with the problematic responses it generated. Those circumstances, frustrating though they were to the artist, typified the disparate public perception of his work in general and the inclement relations on both sides of the Atlantic among artists, art organizations, and art critics at the time.

The sibyls, mythic female personifications of prophecy described by several Greco-Roman authors and, in turn, by Christian theologians and by compilers of classical dictionaries that Vedder could have read, were unusual though not unprecedented subjects in American art. Vedder's depiction of the Cumaean Sibyl, one of two prophetesses who were supposed to have resided in Italy and the single most famous sibyl, in this, the concluding event of her long life, separates his representation from all prior American ones.

The Cumaean Sibyl lived to an extreme age. According to some ancient accounts, she was so beautiful in her youth that the god Apollo became enamored of her and offered to grant her any wish. She asked for a life lasting as many years as the grains of sand she then held in her hand but neglected to request good health and/or youthful vigor. In consequence, she lived for centuries in decrepit physical condition. Near the end, she encountered Tarquin II (also called Tarquin Superbus), the last king of Rome, who eventually was banished from the city after a tyrannical reign. As a warning, the sibyl offered to sell to him, at an extravagant price, her nine books of prophecy. When he refused, she

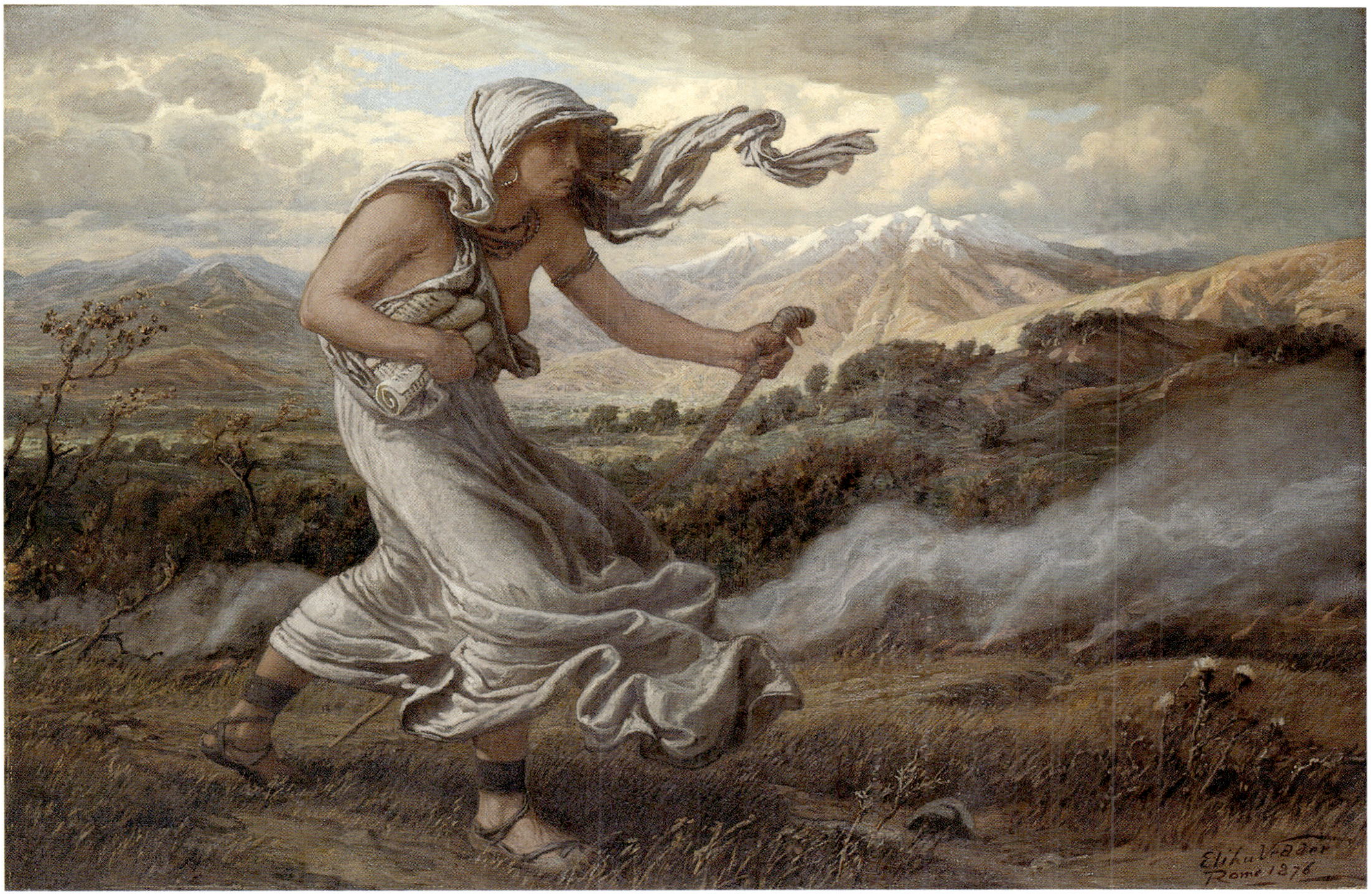

The Cumaean Sibyl

retreated into the countryside, burned three of the volumes, and returned with the remaining six, demanding the price she had for the original nine. When he turned her down again, she burned three further books, then reoffered him the three that were left at the same price. This time, though, having consulted his advisers, the apprehensive Tarquin relented. Afterward the Cumaean Sibyl disappeared and was not heard of again. Meanwhile the Sibylline Verses (as they were known) were tended by a designated priesthood who consulted them during momentous periods, although some sources say that the writings were never deciphered. Eventually the manuscripts were either destroyed when the Capitol was burned under Sulla or were carried off by barbarians.

As he discussed in his autobiography (Vedder 1910, 236–239) and in surviving documents (summarized by Soria 1960; Soria 1970; J. Dillenberger in Washington and Brooklyn 1979, 125–126; K. Quinn in Boston et al. 1992, 366), Vedder was initially inspired to depict the Cumaean Sibyl by an aged former slave, Jane Jackson, who sold peanuts on a street corner near his New York studio during the early 1860s. "Her meekly bowed head and a look of patient endurance and resignation touched my heart," he recalled. They became friends, whereupon he had her pose for him and had a photograph taken of her; from his portrait drawing (1863; private collection) he developed a tondo oil painting (1865), which he held in sufficient regard to submit as his reception piece to the National Academy of Design, where it remains. The strong impression she made remained with him, and eventually "Jane Jackson became the Cumaean Sibyl" (his words).

During his second Italian sojourn, Vedder translated those memories into two drawings (unlocated), an oil sketch (private collection), an oil painting (private collection), all done in 1869, and a medium-size watercolor (1872; Brooklyn Museum). The finished oil, painted for Vedder's friend David Gray of Buffalo, New York, was exhibited at the Fine Arts Academy there in 1871 under the title *Sibyl Burning Her Books* (Yarnall and Gerdts 1986, 5:3690). In the watercolor of 1872, the ample barefoot figure, grasping a long walking stick in her left hand and holding three scrolls under her right arm, strides powerfully from left to right through the bleak Campagna, a strong wind at her back billowing her draperies before her; a small fire, doubtless consuming one of the manuscripts, burns in the grass behind her at near left. Hence the artist had developed the basic thematic and compositional premises by 1869, and he adhered closely to them through the 1870s.

Vedder began the Detroit picture, "the largest I have as yet painted" (Vedder to his father, Rome, December 12, 1875; quoted in Soria 1960, 75; Soria 1970, 103), during the fall of 1875, thinking he would "send it to the Academy Exhibition in London next spring" (Carrie Vedder to Henry Sampson, Rome, November 24, 1875, AAA, roll 517, frame 578; quoted in Soria 1960, 75), that is, the annual exhibition of the British Royal Academy. Before applying brush to canvas he sketched the composition full size in sepia (unlocated). He was encouraged by the London dealer Thomas Agnew, who visited Vedder's studio and complimented the works he saw there, and by friends in Rome. The winter of 1875–76 was an interval of personal crisis for the artist and his family, but he was able to finish the picture by early spring.

In the present painting, the figure is proportionately close to those in the 1869 oil and 1872 watercolor, but her stride has been slightly amplified and the number of fires in the grasses behind her increased. Various details also have been introduced, notably the sandals, necklace, armlet, and large earrings and the knotted strands of hair stirred by the wind. Although her left breast is now bare, her draperies are weightier and enlivened with linear folds, and the top of her walking stick is either carved or wrapped with a tightly twisted covering, the grooves resembling the segments of an insect or the skin of a reptile. The landscape is both more mountainous and more fertile, and the chiaroscuro of the scene is stronger than before, as well.

The sibyl's pose and flowing draperies recall diverse prior works of art, among them sculptures such as the Niobid group (Uffizi, Florence; Vatican collections) and Randolph Rogers's *Nydia, the Blind Flower Girl of Pompeii* (first version 1855), and Jean-François Millet's painting *The Sower* (first version ca. 1846–47). Vedder would have seen the Niobid statues and Rogers's *Nydia* during his Italian sojourns, and he surely was well aware of Millet's famed work, the foremost rendition of which (1850; Museum of Fine Arts, Boston) Vedder's close friend, the Boston artist William Morris Hunt (q.v.), had owned since the early 1850s. The scenic iconography of Vedder's composition, in which a single figure commands a space by moving through it with right leg forward and both arms raised, resonates with those of Rogers's and Millet's compositions; likewise, Rogers's *Nydia* walks through fire and smoke. Further, Vedder's *Sibyl* and his oeuvre in general have affinities with the productions of certain Pre-Raphaelite and Victorian classicist painters—Edward Burne-Jones, Frederic Leighton, Albert Moore, Edward James Poynter, George Frederick Watts, and the Dutch-born Lawrence Alma-Tadema—with which Vedder was familiar.

The thick weave of the canvas that Vedder used for the *Sibyl* was queried by contemporaries, but to twentieth-century eyes it helps evoke—in tandem with the predominantly transparent paint handling, linear drapery rhythms, and narrow color range—effects analogous at once to charcoal drawing, "tapestry" (a word used pejoratively by French artists who saw the picture in 1878), fresco, and oil techniques as practiced in Venice during the Renaissance. While working on the canvas, he read "old Italian works on the Venetian painters and their methods (Boschini and other authors)" (Carrie Vedder to Rose Sanford, Rome, January 8, 1876; quoted in Soria 1960, 75; Soria 1970, 104). The appearance of the painting in early 1876 is now difficult to judge, however, because he retouched it after it was returned to his studio by the end of that year.

The inferred presence of a spiteful Apollo is intriguing, the more so since Vedder has the sibyl herself behaving in a determined and malevolent manner. He portrays her as a swarthy, virile being whose face seems only moderately aged, unlike, for example, Michelangelo's Cumaean Sibyl from the Sistine Chapel ceiling, whose body is heroic but whose head is haggard, and unlike Vedder's own late depictions of the Cumaean Sibyl (Vedder 1910, ill. 239; Soria 1960, 85; Washington and Brooklyn 1979, 127), whose weathered countenances strongly recall Jane Jackson's. In 1878 Vedder completed what amounted to a pendant to the Detroit picture, *The Young Marsyas* (unlocated; presumed destroyed), a slightly smaller canvas in which the diminutive half-man, half-goat, seated beneath a tall tree in winter, played a pair of pipes to a gathering of hares. Marsyas, too, was a fated victim of Apollo's wrath, but Vedder gave the satyr playful if temporary sovereignty over his domain. Symbolizing two of the four classic Ages of Man and contrasting in their temperaments, *The Cumaean Sibyl* and *The Young Marsyas* were joined by their subjects' presumptuous and inopportune associations with a god who, in another of his many guises, personified the fine arts, and in yet another one—the serpent slayer, which Vedder also painted—was a destroyer of evil.

The manuscripts carried by the sibyl are the pivot of Vedder's parable, and the prominent script itself (although illegible) keys its meaning. For Vedder, whose alternate creative outlet was literature, the process of image making was one that wedded the visual and the verbal through handicraft. In that regard, he was kin to William Blake, whose work he deeply admired when he visited London in 1876. The American's pendant paintings are larger in both size and visual impact than most of Blake's, and *The Cumaean Sibyl* and *Young Marsyas* could also be considered painted parallels to tragedy and comedy in classical literature.

Soria (Soria 1960, 75) has proposed that the deaths in 1871 and 1875 of two of Vedder's infant sons underlay the theme of the Detroit painting, but Karen E. Quinn (in Boston et al. 1992, 366 n. 6) aptly notes that he had conceived the composition before either of those events had occurred. That the sibyl stares intently forward, "full of indignation at this want of appreciation" (Carrie Vedder to her mother, Rome, March 31, 1878; quoted in Soria 1960, 71), toward the distant city of Rome, suggests that the theme had pertinence for the artist on a more practical level. As he wrote much later (Vedder 1910, 239), not wholly in jest: "In plain English it [the story] meant: If you don't buy my pictures now when they are cheap, you will have to pay dearer for them later on."

Back in 1870 Vedder and his family had resided in London for several months, and between late 1870 and late 1871 he had shown at least seven sets of pictures there, three at successive displays at the Dudley Gallery, three more at the Society of Artists exhibition of 1870–71, and another at Ernest Gambart's French Gallery, for all of which he received good notices in the metropolitan press. By late 1875 he was planning another London sojourn, evidently believing that he could reenter the art ambiance there, reestablish personal connections, and gain access to the Royal Academy without trouble. Instead, the academy authorities, who in previous years had resorted to mass rejections to stem the tide of submissions, refused *The Cumaean Sibyl,* by which time it was also too late to send it to the United States Centennial Exposition in Philadelphia. The rebuff, of which Vedder was apprised in Rome, did not cancel the English journey, during which he and his friends in the British capital sought alternate venues for the *Sibyl.* They succeeded in placing it briefly but unadvantageously at Colnaghi's gallery in June 1876. His initial asking price for the work was £500 (about $2,500).

Then, probably with help from William John Hennessy, the expatriate American painter, the canvas was sent to the sixth annual autumn exhibition of modern paintings sponsored by the Corporation of Liverpool, held at the Public Library and Museum. Hennessy, Frederick Arthur Bridgman (q.v.), and Eastman Johnson (q.v.) also participated in the corporation display of that year, which ran from early September to early December. The bustling port city's art scene was lively at that period: the recently founded Liverpool Art Club generated a slate of exhibitions of its own, and Thomas Agnew also hosted a yearly presentation of modern paintings at the Exchange Gallery, most of them previously shown at London's Royal Academy but as yet unsold. The corporation exhibition, which one commentator *(Manchester Guardian,* September 11, 1876) gently chided for its resemblance to that of the Royal Academy, likewise comprised works for sale; Vedder asked £250 (about $1,250) for the *Sibyl,* half his London price. No buyer came forward, but the painting—entitled *The Cumoean* [sic] *Sybil returning with the last of the Sybilline Books to Tarquin*—did garner two notices, one favorable and the other unfavorable, in the local press. The former *(Liverpool Daily Courier,* September 27, 1876) is perceptive:

> [It] is a picture of more than ordinary importance. Apart from the landscape (to some extent imaginary, of course), which is rendered

so cleverly as to form an appropriate basis for the picture, the figure of the hag-like Sibyl is remarkably forcible and dramatic. Anatomically this figure is very fine. With her loose garments blown close to her shrinking form, and clutching under her arm the mystic volumes, she speeds eagerly along a dreary heath. Immediately to the left, and almost at the feet of the hurrying Sibyl, is a fagot fire, the dark blue smoke from which blows low over the heath and lends additional weirdness to the scene beyond. It is a picture that appeals intelligently and effectually to the imagination, and with its technical execution there is no fault to find.

The latter *(Liverpool Mercury,* September 15, 1876) is dismissive: "A specimen of locomotion we do not like. The head and face are particularly forbidding to look at. Why artists paint this kind of pictures [*sic*] we cannot say." The variances in Vedder's asking prices and in the two Liverpool reviews presage later developments on both counts.

In early 1878 Vedder partially repainted the canvas, intending to submit it and the newer *Young Marsyas* to the American section of the Exposition Universelle in Paris. His *Old Madonna* (unlocated) was accepted by the United States–based jury, but the two Roman pictures were entered at a later date through the Paris branch of the committee, whose members were also responsible for hanging the exhibition. They favored Vedder by placing his two largest works "on the line." Critics did not necessarily return the compliment, however. French reviewers tended either to give them short shrift or to overlook them, the few English reporters who cited them were generally pleased, and American writers ran the gamut of opinion. Most disappointed among the Americans was a Paris correspondent of the *New York Times* ("American Genre Painters," August 25, 1878). Janus-like, he retold the story of the sibyl and Tarquin at length and complimented Vedder for "transparent and wonderfully luminous," "most admirable," and "masterly" technique, but he censured the conception on the whole as "grotesque and ludicrous" and "a miserable failure":

> [T]here is a certain ... indignation in the one eye [of the figure], which the profile allows us to see, which is impressive.... But this, in the midst of so much that is laughter-inspiring, is too much like Robson, the comedian, when he played in the burlesque of "Medea." He kept every one in roars of laughter until a certain scene, when he exhibited such ferocity of hate and passion, by a single gesture and glance, that the audience forgot to laugh, and were very thoroughly frightened.... Vedder evidently is all abroad as to the Cumaean Sibyl, and has made a sort of compromise between a full-fed Witch of Endor and a Sibyl, and as no man can paint what he does not know, he has made a disastrous blunder and has wrecked his picture.

The writer expressed much the same reservation about *The Young Marsyas*—despite "wonderfully good" technique, "the picture is also a complete failure."

The *New York Times* critique may have furnished ammunition for the editors of *L'Art,* the large-format, illustrated periodical recently founded in Paris. In August 1878 they contacted Vedder in Rome and asked permission to engrave *The Cumaean Sibyl* for a forthcoming issue. He consented, but three months later he was chagrined to find that his two largest paintings were the leading targets of *L'Art*'s preponderantly negative overview (December 1, 1878, 197–214) of American art at the Paris exposition. The writer, Charles Tardieu, after introducing his commentary by several discursive paragraphs, commenced his item-by-item survey with Vedder's *Sibyl* and *Marsyas* (both of which were reproduced), declaring: "Of these two pictures, one would be embarrassed to say which is the more bizarre." Tardieu's tone did not relent throughout his dissection of Vedder, and he added insult to injury by asserting that the engraver for *L'Art,* Charles Kreutzberger, had improved the painter's originals; the print of *The Cumaean Sibyl* exaggerates the size of the sibyl's right eye and the grimness of her facial expression.

Incensed, Vedder quickly penned a protest, sending copies to *L'Art* and to numerous colleagues and several publications in Britain and the United States. In it he carefully avoided the substance of Tardieu's critique, focusing instead on the "trap" (his word) of "assist[ing] at his own execution" (the words of a sympathizer) into which he felt he had been lured.

Fellow artists rallied around him, but a mere handful of journals aired his complaint and fewer still were drawn into the matter of it. Probably the Anglo-American press was both unsympathetic and skittish. On the one hand, journalistic criticism of modern works of art was by then an established mode of discourse in North America as well as in Europe, especially during the 1870s, which witnessed multiple acts of dissension by individual artists and the foundings of breakaway artists' groups on both sides of the Atlantic. Of three major New York newspapers that reviewed the December 1, 1878, issue of *L'Art,* two did not allude to the condemnation of Vedder, while the third, the *New York Herald* (December 23, 1878), noted merely that he had been among those American artists "honored" with reproductions and that he had been advised by Tardieu "to leave Rome and go home to paint." Moreover, most Anglo-American journalists regarded the high-profile lawsuit of 1877–78 brought by James McNeill Whistler (q.v.) against John Ruskin, in which a prominent artist contested a prominent critic but not a publishing house, as both trivial and overblown. Reverberations from the

Whistler-Ruskin episode continued into 1879. When the editors of Appleton's Americanized *Art Journal* ([March 1879]: 96) coupled "the Vedder and the Whistler cases" in a two-paragraph discussion, they tilted more toward critics than toward artists.

On the other hand, the *New York Times,* which had already reviewed the paintings in question (and would do so again in 1880), lost a libel suit in January 1879. Although the legal wrangle had nothing to do with art, the normally competitive New York press was well aware of the *Times*'s predicament. In the event, Vedder's argument was disseminated principally through two New York papers, the *Evening Post* and *Nation,* of which only the latter sided unconditionally with him. The editors of *L'Art* printed a lengthy rebuttal of their own on March 23, 1879 (297–298), declaring, in essence, that they could say whatever they pleased and that for some artists adverse publicity was better than none. At that juncture, the *New York Times* (April 9, 1879) and the *New York Herald* (April 8, 1879) finally weighed in, the former concurring with *L'Art,* the latter dismissing Vedder's objection as an "effusion" and the entire matter as "insignificant." He did, however, belatedly benefit from a spirited appraisal of the beaux-arts displays at the Paris exposition written for *Scribner's* ([June 1879]: 161–182) by his friend Russell Sturgis.

Vedder brought *The Cumaean Sibyl* and *The Young Marsyas* among other paintings with him when he returned to New York in November 1879. As Soria (Soria 1970, 136–141) recounts, once settled he industriously lobbied artists, potential patrons, social clubs, and journalists, renting a studio on Union Square and displaying his works there four days per week *(American Art Review* 1880). Before he formally opened his rooms to public view on February 3, 1880, the *New York Herald* (January 19, 1880) gave his paintings, especially the *Sibyl* and the *Marsyas,* generally commendatory notice, briefly referring—as did subsequent commentators—to the dispute with *L'Art.* He also managed to show most of the works, including the *Sibyl* and the *Marsyas,* at a one-evening reception held at the Art Students League on March 2, 1880, this time prompting a laudatory response from the *New York Times* (March 3, 1880). At that juncture, the *Evening Post* (March 6, 1880) ventured that the *Sibyl* was worthy of the Corcoran Gallery or the newly opened Metropolitan Museum of Art, a sentiment later echoed by the *New York Evening Mail* (March 29, 1880). Yet while in New York Vedder was able to dispose of only a few paintings, and several daily and weekly papers disregarded his presence. The periodical press, by contrast, was aroused: by November 1880 the *American Art Review, Art Amateur, Art Interchange, Atlantic Monthly,* and *Scribner's* had all published articles praising him and *The Cumaean Sibyl; Art Amateur* and *Scribner's* adapted Kreutzberger's engraving of the *Sibyl* for their essays.

Early in his New York sojourn, Vedder arranged with the Boston dealers Williams & Everett for a two-week display and sale of his works during late March and early April 1880. His adoptive hometown welcomed him when the time came, and most of the remaining paintings, among them *The Young Marsyas,* sold quickly. Despite attracting considerable attention, *The Cumaean Sibyl* took a while longer. Several weeks after the exhibition closed, the canvas was purchased for Wellesley College. According to his own records (see Soria 1970, 148–149), Vedder accepted $1,250 for it because he thought it looked "so well placed" in the college art gallery. It remained at Wellesley until 1957.

G. C.

Inscription At lower right, *Elihu Vedder / Rome 1876*

Provenance Elihu Vedder, to 1880. Welleseley College, Wellesley, Mass., 1880, gift of Elisha S. Converse. Hirschl & Adler Galleries, New York. Acquired in 1957.

Exhibitions London, Colnaghi's Gallery, June–ca. August 1876. Liverpool, *Autumn Exhibition of Modern Pictures,* 1876, no. 163. Rome, Vedder's studio, March 1878. Paris, Exposition Universelle, 1878, no. 101. New York, Vedder's studio, February 1880. New York, Art Students League, March 2, 1880. Boston 1880a, no. 1. American tour, 1900–1901: Washington 1901, no. 5, and Chicago 1901, no. 12. New York 1937, no. 90. United States Information Agency, Greece and Israel tour, 1958. Washington et al. 1966a, no. 42. Dayton et al. 1976, no. 51. Washington and Brooklyn 1979, no. 153. Boston et al. 1992, 366–367, no. 95.

References *Liverpool Daily Courier,* September 27, 1876, 5. *Liverpool Mercury,* September 15, 1876, 6. *New York Evening Post,* May 1, 1878, 1. *Athenaeum* 1878. *Illustrated London News,* June 29, 1878, 612. "American Genre Painters," *New York Times,* August 25, 1878, 10. Stillman 1878. *Aldine* 9 (1878): 249. *New York Evening Post,* January 8, 1879, 1. *Nation,* January 16, 1879, 51. *New York Evening Post,* January 24, 25, 27, 1879, 1. *Nation,* February 13, 119–120, and March 6, 1879, 163. *New York Evening Post,* April 7, 1879, 4. *Nation,* April 17, 1879, 267. *New York Herald,* January 19, 1880, 5. *New York Evening Post,* March 6, 1880, 4. *Art Interchange* 1880. *New York Evening Mail,* March 29, 1880, 1. *Boston Daily Advertiser,* April 1, 1880, 1. "Elihu Vedder," *Art Amateur* 1880. *Atlantic Monthly* 1880. Bishop 1880a, 369–370. De Kay 1880, 112, 117. Story 1880, 113. Montgomery 1889, 1:170–171. Boston 1910. Soria 1960, fig. 1. Soria 1970, 32, 87–88, 103, 104, 106, 112, 118–119, 122–124, 134, 148–149, 313–314. Washington and Brooklyn 1979, 100–102, 125–127.

84

Samson, 1886

Oil on cradled wood panel
45.1 × 69.9 cm (17¾ × 27½ in.)
Gift of Dr. and Mrs. Joseph Chazan, Arthur and Joyce Hurvitz, and Irwin and Gloria Sparr, in honor of Mr. and Mrs. Richard A. Manoogian (1994.123)

85

Delilah, 1886

Oil on cradled wood panel
45.1 × 69.9 cm (17¾ × 27½ in.)
Gift of Dr. and Mrs. Joseph Chazan, Arthur and Joyce Hurvitz, and Irwin and Gloria Sparr, in honor of Mr. and Mrs. Richard A. Manoogian (1994.124)

VEDDER BEGAN PAINTING biblical subjects in the 1860s, depicting both Old and New Testament stories dealing with such topics as treachery and heroism, death and mourning, the Crucifixion, and the Resurrection. The themes of treachery and heroism are illustrated in Vedder's various studies of the Old Testament story of Samson. A drawing of the head of Samson first appeared in *Harper's Christmas Supplement* of 1882. At that time Vedder wrote his wife, Carrie: "They have made a regular poster of it, and one sees it in every railroad station and in the elevated trains" (Soria 1970, 157; New York 1989a, 12).

In 1886 Vedder again turned to the subject. *Samson and Delilah* (1886; National Academy of Design, New York), a small painting rich in color and monumental in conception, more fully explores the themes of sexual deceit and predatory treachery, while at the same time conveying a sense of intrigue and hushed drama. Elaborating on the biblical account, Vedder portrayed the nude Delilah, open scissors in hand, arising from the couch of the sleeping Samson, whose shorn locks she leaves scattered around him. The stilled moment, just before Delilah's Philistine lords enter the bedroom and claim their hapless victim, features the approaching dagger and the nude form of the seductress—both symbolic representations of her ultimate betrayal. This small oil study may have been a preparation for a bigger composition (New York 1979, 83; Washington and Brooklyn 1979, 151).

While Vedder's larger work was apparently never completed, that same year he again turned to the subject of Samson and Delilah, approaching the story from an entirely different perspective. In two striking pendant pictures of the heads of Samson and Delilah, Vedder contrasted the strength of his hero with the seductive charms of his beguiler. Displayed in handsome gold frames designed by Vedder and made in Italy by the Roman frame maker Giuseppe Berardi, the pair are identified by the inscriptions of their names in Hebrew and by the carved symbols that associate the paintings with the story of Samson. Featured on the frames are the head of the young lion Samson killed with his bare hands, three bees representing the swarm that produced honey in the lion's carcass, the jawbone of the ass with which he killed one thousand Philistines, the ropes that he facetiously told Delilah would bind him, the scissors used to shear his seven locks of hair, the silver coins Delilah was paid by her Philistine masters for her betrayal, the millstone with which Samson ground grain when, sightless, he worked in the Philistines' prison, and the two cracked pillars of the house that he tore down, annihilating both himself and his enemies (Washington and Brooklyn 1979, 151; New York 1989, 12).

Instead of depicting a precise moment in the story of Samson and Delilah, as he did in his other composition, Vedder chose to create images of idealized heads that accentuate the predominant characteristics of the two adversaries and that juxtapose them in a timeless and passionate encounter. Samson, according to Judges 13:5, was a "Nazarite unto God from the womb," and his divinely given strength, which came from his uncut hair, was to be used to "deliver Israel out of the hand of the Philistines." Vedder represented Samson at his full and unbridled power, constructing a heroic image that suggests a godly force that is scarcely to be contained within the constricting picture frame. The ropes that bind his sturdy neck, his cascading cinnamon-colored hair, flowing beyond the boundaries of the picture, and his clear-sighted gaze and resolute expression indicate that he has not yet divulged the secret of his strength to his charming and insistent consort, who is, according to the biblical account, the embodiment of his one moral deficiency.

Delilah, as recorded in Judges 16:4, was a woman from "the valley of Sorek," whom Samson foolishly loved. Blinded by her dynamic sensuality, he failed to see her magnetism as the camouflage for her treachery and deceit. For eleven hundred pieces of silver the Philistines had been able to persuade her to entice Samson into revealing the source of his strength, which she accomplished through erotic seduction and daily verbal torment. Vedder's image of Delilah, redolent with expectant sexuality, displays her shadowed face peering intently beyond the drapery she has pushed aside and set in motion. Her provocatively exposed shoulders, her ornamental headdress and coral-colored jewelry, and her smoldering downward gaze and lowered eyelids suggest a temptress about to approach her prey. Samson's appetite for this alluring woman gave Delilah just the power she needed to succeed in weakening him.

In 1887, shortly after the paintings were completed, Vedder included them in exhibitions in Boston and New York. They were also among the nine paintings that he sent in 1893 to the World's Columbian Exposition in Chicago. Five years later, in 1898, he executed a replica of *Samson* for an Italian client that had slight variations in the treatment of the head, as well as the frame, including the substitution of the Italian *Sansone* for the Hebrew lettering. There were also variations in the placement of the signature and the date, as well as the additional inscription *Rome* on the frame at the lower right (Soria 1970, ill. 40; New York 1989a, 10; Washington 1993, 337).
T. T.

Inscriptions Both, on gold coin on frame designed by the artist and in lower left corner, *18 V.86*

Provenance Colonel J. G. Moore, New York. Private collections. Graham Williford, New York. Jordan-Volpe Gallery, New York. Acquired in 1994.

Exhibitions Boston, Doll & Richards, 1887. New York, H. Wunderlich and Co., 1887. Chicago, World's Columbian Exposition, 1893, nos. 1035–1036. Dayton et al. 1976, 140–141, nos. 53–54. Washington and Brooklyn 1979, 150–151, nos. 185–186. New York 1989a, 10–13. Washington 1993, 337, nos. 1006–1007.

References *Critic* 1887. New York 1887, nos. 9–10. Goodyear 1894, frontispiece, 303. Clement 1895, 138–139. Lusk 1903. Vedder 1910, 485. Soria 1970, 331–332, nos. 431–432. New York 1979, 83.

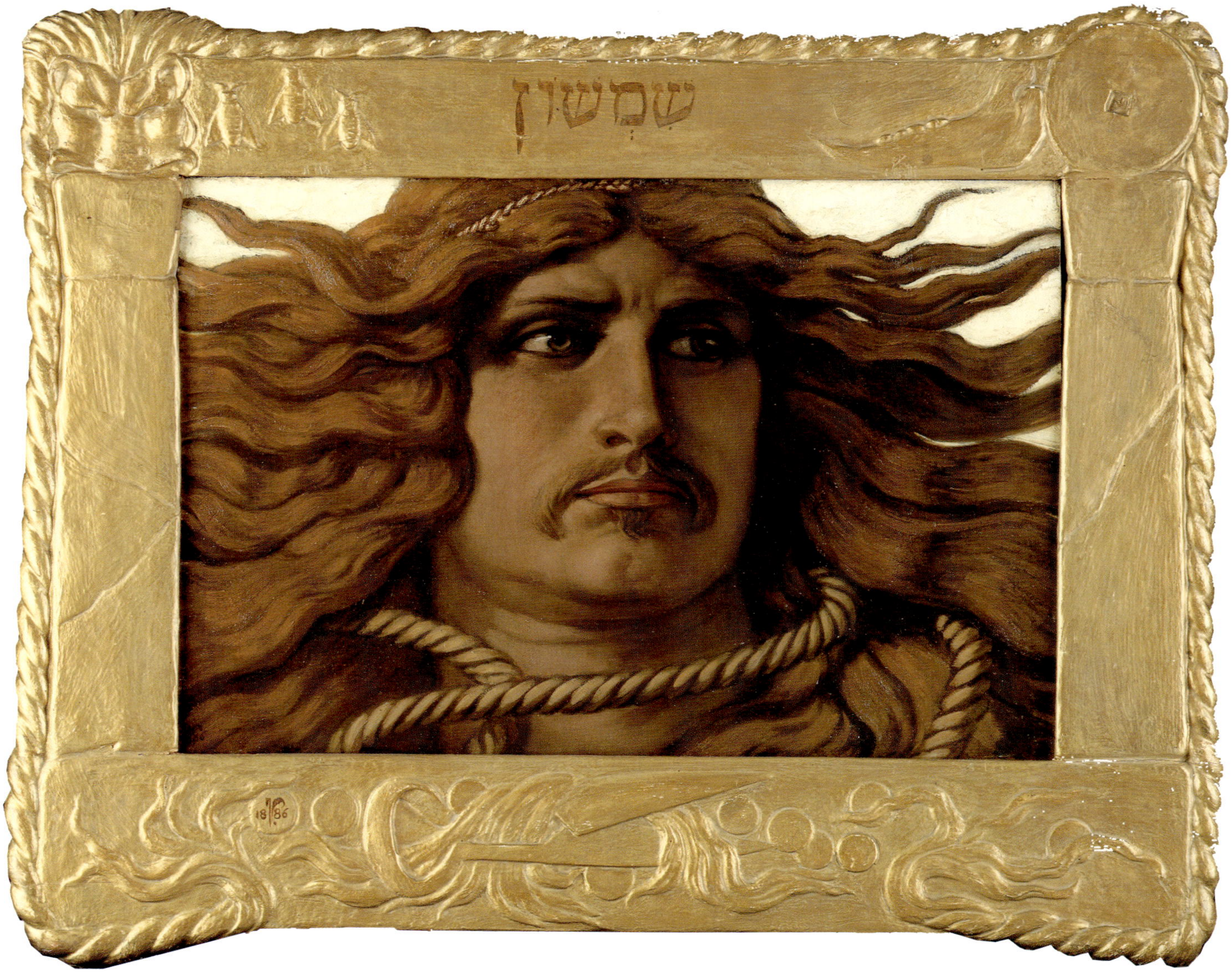

Samson

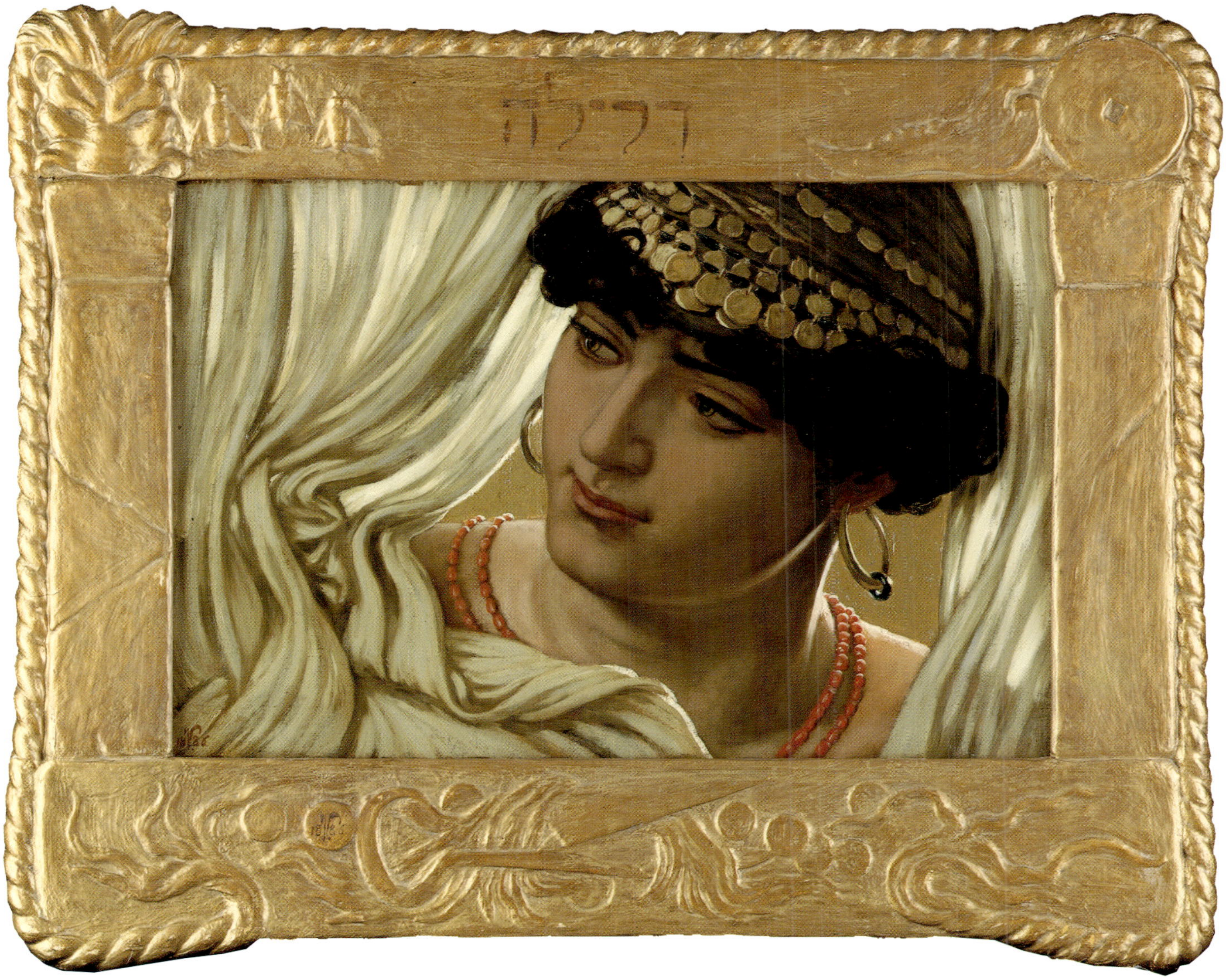

Delilah

James McNeill Whistler

1834 Lowell, Massachusetts–London 1903

A New Englander by birth, Whistler was taken to St. Petersburg, Russia, in 1843, where his father worked as a railroad engineer for Czar Nicolas I. Whistler returned to the United States in 1849, entering West Point two years later, but he proved himself ill-suited to a career in the military; he was expelled for failing his chemistry exam. Thereafter he worked several months for the Coast and Geodetic Survey in Washington, D.C.; during this time he received invaluable training in etching, an area in which his subsequent contribution was enormous. By 1856, having decided to pursue an artistic career, Whistler was enrolled in the Paris academic studio of Charles Gleyre. Far more important to his artistic formation than Gleyre's instruction was the time he spent studying the collections in the Louvre and pursuing friendships with younger French artists. Through Henri Fantin-Latour he was drawn into the circle of Gustave Courbet, whose realist practice, along with seventeenth-century Dutch and Spanish painting, was an invigorating new force in French art. Rembrandt and Velázquez remained significant sources for Whistler long after his youthful informal relationship with Courbet.

Although Whistler maintained his French contacts, painting with Courbet at Trouville on the coast of France as late as 1865, he had established himself in London by 1863, drawn there by what he felt was the greater openness of England to young artists. This sentiment was not to last, and Whistler found himself professionally at odds with the Royal Academy and the art establishment throughout much of his career. During the 1860s he produced a series of languorous figural compositions incorporating Japanese and Grecian motifs. Only later, however, did Whistler fully assimilate the underlying aesthetic of Japanese art into his painting, flattening his backgrounds and developing a delicate sense of silhouette.

In 1866 Whistler traveled to Chile, ostensibly to assist that country's war with Spain. This was the only time he ever returned to the New World. Beginning in 1870–71, he became preoccupied with the landscape of the Thames River near his Chelsea residence, painting a series of nocturnes, studies of twilight in muted color harmonies. These works—etchings as well as oils—distilled, in the words of Baudelaire, "the profound and complex poetry of a vast city." During these same years, Whistler's art assumed its most characteristic features. In 1872 he had begun to give musical titles to his works (Harmonies, Symphonies, and Arrangements), rechristening older works and finding a new and consistent rationale for his interest in a nonliterary painting free of extra-artistic measures of meaning, be they moral, religious, or natural. His growing dedication to subjective experience and to the synaesthetic mood-evoking qualities of color linked Whistler to a symbolist sensibility and distinguished him from the impressionists, whose devotion to the modern city he shared. Whistler's dependence on a finely tuned and reduced visual memory (aided only by schematic color notations) likewise freed him from reliance on external frames of reference. Instead, he wove delicate variations on themes sounded by the personal experience of nature. His aesthetic credo was briefly set forth in his "Ten O'Clock" lecture (1885), which was translated into French by no less a symbolist than Stéphane Mallarmé. Whistler was by no means indifferent to subject matter. His final loyalty, however, was to the independent order of art, rather than to a nature he felt was arbitrary and chaotic. "[T]he artist is born to pick, and choose, and group with science . . . elements [of nature], that the result may be beautiful—as the musician gathers his notes, and forms his chords, until he brings forth from chaos glorious harmony" ("Ten O'Clock" lecture). Form and content were for him inextricably bound. Among his finest work are portraits of friends, family, and patrons in which Whistler's precise and disciplined sense of color harmony and design, and his preoccupation with a reduction and simplification of forms, reached their fullest expression. Out of these materials Whistler conjured the identities of his sitters.

Whistler's highly serious approach to art was often overshadowed in the eyes of contemporaries by his flamboyant dandyism and by cultivated eccentricities with which he rejected the confining moral posture of the Victorian artist as well as the banalities of English bourgeois life. An irascible temper brought him notoriety and periods of artistic isolation. His campaign against art critics was fueled by his famous libel suit against John Ruskin. In the wake of the resulting financial debacle, he was forced to give up his Chelsea White House designed by the English reform architect E. W. Godwin in 1877 and inhabited by Whistler all too briefly. Soon after, Whistler spent a year in Venice executing a suite of twelve etchings of the city for the London Fine Arts Society.

The 1880s found Whistler alienated from patrons and critics, though he had by this time acquired a following of younger artists. By 1892, the date of a major London retrospective of the artist's work at the Goupil Gallery, appreciation for his achievements in etching and painting had grown in both France and England; that same year he was made an officer of the Légion d'Honneur. Although interest in Whistler grew markedly in England following the Goupil exhibition, he moved to Paris in 1892 with his wife of four years, Beatrix Godwin. After she died in 1896 the artist wandered restlessly between Paris and London. By the time of his death in 1903, his career tirelessly recorded by numerous admirers and biographers, he had attained the status of a modern old master.

A. M.

Bibliography Young et al. 1980. London et al. 1994.

86

Arrangement in Gray: Portrait of the Painter, ca. 1872

Oil on canvas
74.9 × 53.3 cm (29½ × 21 in.)
Bequest of Henry Glover Stevens in memory of Ellen P. Stevens and Mary M. Stevens (34.27)

OVER THE COURSE OF HIS CAREER, Whistler produced numerous self-portraits in oil, along with sketches and pastels. (Andrew McLaren Young [in Young et al. 1980] records eleven oils between 1857 and 1896, two of which are unlocated.) Of these, the half-length *Portrait of the Painter* of about 1872, described by Whistler years later in 1892 as "a fine portrait of me by myself, life sketch" (Young et al. 1980, 1:74), is generally considered the finest. *Arrangement in Gray* balances the artist's public and professional identity with elements of his private personality. Shown in studio dress—black beret, black tie, and light gray painting coat—Whistler gazes out at the spectator, his head turned left in three-quarter profile. In his right hand he grasps two (possibly three) upright brushes, tokens of the artist's métier. Whistler's pyramidal form is placed off-center and close to the picture plane. On the flat, neutral background, at the juncture of the dark dado with the wall plane, Whistler has included his butterfly signature inscribed in a circle, the only decorative note in an austere and sober portrait. The signature, of the type common to the early 1870s, is repeated at nearly the same point on the frame, also decorated by Whistler. The reeded and lightly gilded frame is concurrent with the painting, employing a basket-weave design derived from oriental matting of a kind Whistler favored in the early 1870s (Ira H. Horowitz, correspondence, curatorial files, DIA).

There is more than a hint of professional pride in the confidence with which Whistler meets our gaze, echoed in the firm grasp with which he wields the implements of his art, and in the spare economy of his signature. The paint texture itself belies the appearance of rapid execution indicated by the slashed strokes of the artist's torso and by the thinness of the paint surface. The modeling of the face and hand—the two most important areas for the artist—is deliberate, thoughtful, self-analyzing. This tentative, apparently unresolved quality provoked criticism of the kind Whistler received frequently during these years. Discussing the portrait in 1872, the critic of the *London Times* complained that "[t]his is the laying in of a head, excellent in modelling and relation of tone and colour, as far as it goes, but only the beginning and suggestion of something which the painter lacks either power or patience to carry out" (Young et al. 1980, 1:74). Critics who employed the standard academic criterion of finish were unprepared to understand Whistler's effort to evolve a new artistic language for portraiture, free from the demands of literal likeness. As Whistler wrote in *The Gentle Art of Making Enemies,* "The imitator is a poor kind of creature. If the man who paints only the tree, or flower, or other surface he sees before him were an artist, the king of artists would be the photographer. It is for the artist to do something beyond this: in portrait painting to put on canvas something more than the face the model wears for that one day; to paint the man, in short, as well as his features; in arrangement of colours to treat a flower as his key, not his model" (Whistler 1892, 128).

It is less the inner man that Whistler reveals in this painting, however, than a carefully posed portrait of himself in his professional identity as artist. Unlike the more direct encounter of subject with spectator in his earlier Courbet-like *Portrait of Whistler with Hat* (1857–58; Freer Gallery of Art, Washington, D.C.), the 1872 self-portrait is impersonal and gravely concerned with public presentation. The self-portrait was exhibited widely. It was first shown in the 1872 Society of French Artists in London, and subsequently in Durand-Ruel's 1873 Paris exhibition, as well as in Whistler's 1892 retrospective at the Goupil Gallery and in his 1905 memorial exhibition in London. It also served as the frontispiece to the 1874 Liverpool Art Club's *Catalogue of the Etchings and Drypoints of J. A. M. Whistler.*

By the 1870s Whistler had begun to evolve a personal iconography, evident in his white forelock and his characteristic butterfly signature. Pennell and Pennell (1908, 1:137) write that the present work was the first in which the white forelock appears. (They mistakenly identified the present portrait with another completed sometime before 1867 and described by William Michael Rossetti in 1903 [see Young et al. 1980, 1:74].) Yet alongside such strongly personal signatures, Whistler also identified himself with a wider artistic tradition in which he had struggled to gain a foothold since 1855. By 1872 Whistler had succeeded in securing both patronage and critical esteem from a small if loyal following. Having passed through a period of artistic apprenticeship and self-discovery, first to the French realism of Courbet, and then to Japanese, Greek, and contemporary English influences, Whistler had begun by the 1870s to explore a style that was both original and highly schooled, one that harmonized his various sources into an art that his more perceptive contemporaries acknowledged to have achieved a certain classical repose, synthesis, and simplification.

Portrait of the Painter is a very self-conscious work of art, claiming for Whistler a place in the artistic fraternity of Titian, Rembrandt, and Velázquez. Whistler's pose and his artist's beret refer

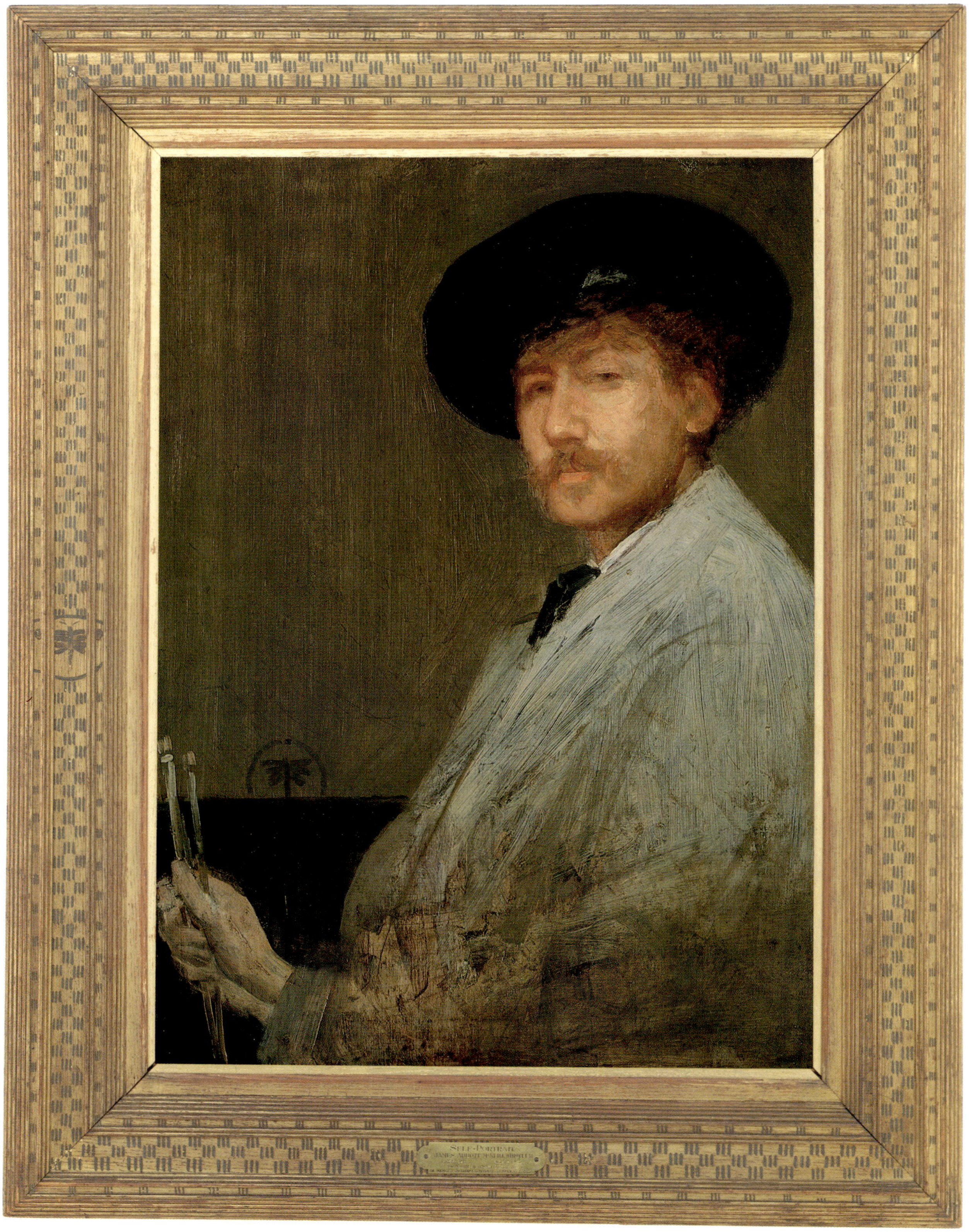

Portrait of the Painter

back to a series of self-portraits painted by Rembrandt wearing a similar beret, and done in the 1630s when the artist had reached a point in his career parallel to Whistler's. Another later example easily known by Whistler is Rembrandt's *Self-Portrait* of 1659 (National Gallery of Art, Washington, D.C., but in Europe in Whistler's lifetime). Likewise, the device of the clasped paintbrushes derives from several later self-portraits by the Dutch artist, such as the undated *Self-Portrait* in Kenwood House, London. The shallow space of *Arrangement in Gray* and the attention to silhouette reveal the impact of Japanese woodcut prints, from which Whistler had drawn important lessons in the 1860s. Yet this Asian influence is mediated by Whistler's deepening knowledge of Velázquez, one of his sustaining inspirations. The Spanish artist's close and subdued color harmonics and concern with figure-ground relationships left a lasting impression on Whistler. Velázquez's influence is most evident in Whistler's harmonized palette of black, gray, brown, and ocher. Whistler also admired Velázquez's approach to composition—the placement of the figure within the frame of the painting. In *Portrait of the Painter,* "the swinging energy of the line of the head" is accentuated by the tense boundaries of the frame; the form of the subject activates the neutral background space, dividing it into compressed angular forms on the right and an expansive field of subdued color on the left (R. A. Stevenson, *Art Journal* [October 1897], quoted in Way and Dennis 1903, 38–39). With apparently limited means, Whistler achieved a portrait of considerable authority and presence, which reveals in its public language the artist's ambition to become a legitimate heir to the great painters of the ages.

On a rather different level, however, the *Portrait of the Painter* bears a striking similarity to the somewhat looser portrait Whistler painted of his brother, the surgeon Dr. William McNeill Whistler, who had moved to London in 1865 (1871–73; Art Institute of Chicago). Way and Dennis confidently stated in 1903 that the work was a companion picture to the self-portrait (p. 40). Though their sizes differ, the two paintings form a roughly symmetrical pair of bookends; the brothers are dressed alike and placed on the canvas in such a way as to suggest a resemblance. This, added to the fact that the self-portrait was painted during the same period as Whistler's famous portrait of his mother *(Arrangement in Gray and Black,* 1871; Musée du Louvre, Paris), suggests that during these years of growing professional confidence, Whistler was also reflecting on his own most lasting emotional bonds. The three paintings together form a loose family trilogy, formalizing and fusing Whistler's aesthetic and personal loyalties.

A. M.

Inscriptions Signed on the verso, according to the 1905 memorial exhibition catalogue; frame decorated by Whistler; butterfly signature on left

Provenance Alexander Ionides. Alecco Ionides. George McCulloch, London, 1895. To his widow, Mrs. Coutts Michie, 1907. Henry Glover Stevens, Detroit, 1909. Acquired in 1934.

Exhibitions London 1872, no. 130. Paris, Durand-Ruel, 1873. Paris 1883, no. 2. London 1892, no. 30. London 1895, no. 10. London 1905, no. 30. London 1909, no. 299. Detroit 1921, no. 134. New York 1947b, no. 20. New London 1949, no. 14. Birmingham 1951. Utica 1953, no. 4. Chicago and New York 1954. London and New York 1960, no. 29. New York 1963, no. 67. Brooklyn et al. 1967, no. 7. Berlin 1969. Buffalo et al. 1976. Detroit 1976, no. 245. Ann Arbor 1978.

References *Art Journal* 1897, 290, ill. Way and Dennis 1903, 38–39, ill. Pennell and Pennell 1908, 1:80, 137. Gallatin 1913, no. 4. Gallatin 1913a, 154. Richardson 1934, ill. Richardson 1954, 21, ill. Sutton 1966, 190, pl. 59. Spenser 1972, 94, ill. McMullen 1973, 246, 274, pl. 7. Young et al. 1980, 1:74–75, no. 122. Spencer 1989, 108, pl. 44. Washington 1995, 59, fig. 2:10.

87
Nocturne in Black and Gold: The Falling Rocket, ca. 1874

Oil on oak panel
60.3 × 46.7 cm (23¾ × 18⅜ in.)
Gift of Dexter M. Ferry, Jr. (46.309)

Nocturne in Black and Gold: The Falling Rocket is among Whistler's best-known paintings, a key work in his artistic and personal biography. Sparks from a fireworks explosion in London's Cremorne Gardens cascade down in vivid pinpricks of paint, forming the painting's central motif. The fireworks dramatically offset without overcoming the insistent darkness of the night, evoked in diaphanous veils of closely keyed dark blue-green that approaches black. In the left center background are the twin towers of the fireworks platform, encircled by lights. (These towers are more fully depicted in Whistler's *Nocturne: Black and Gold—The Fire Wheel* [1872/77; Tate Gallery, London].) The left side of the composition is framed by a dark clump of trees, suggested by a denser coloration. In the left foreground ghostly shadows of paint intimate a group of spectators gazing toward the fireworks. The darker markings in the painting's lower right remain unidentified.

In the nocturnes of the 1870s, Whistler applied oil paint mixed with copal, mastic, and turpentine (his "sauce") to an absorbent canvas, creating fields of muted color (Pennell and Pennell 1908, 1:164). In *Falling Rocket,* the vertical striations left by the track of the paintbrush accent the pattern of sparks drifting down through the night sky. The closely graded tones of the painting are coloristically activated by a wide range of hues—flecks of salmon pink, lemon yellow, blue-green, and beige—that belie the monochromatic appearance of *Falling Rocket.* Traces of the red ground Whistler occasionally used for his nocturnes add warmth to the cool dark blues of the lower right-hand passages. Despite the title, there is little actual black in the painting, a fact Whistler acknowledged years later when he wrote to his wife in 1892 that the painting "ought not to have been called *Black* & Gold—but Blue" (Young et al. 1980, 1:99).

Falling Rocket is one of a series of oils inspired by Cremorne Gardens—all of them nocturnes—that Whistler painted between 1872 and 1877. Cremorne was the last of London's great pleasure gardens. Like its predecessors Vauxhall and Ranelagh, it was located in Chelsea near the Thames River. Pyrotechnic displays were an established feature of the gardens' entertainments by 1836 (Washington 1984, 76) and one of the nighttime attractions that drew Whistler there on frequent visits following his move to Chelsea in 1863. The Cremorne Gardens series resembles related subjects of modern life among Whistler's French colleagues. Whistler's treatment, like that of Manet and Monet, emphasizes the anonymous character of public life in the modern city. Although inspired by a visual experience, *Falling Rocket* represents a remembered event, shaped not by a quest for optical truth but by an independent aesthetic order based on an experienced mood evoked through color.

Two previous paintings by Whistler featured fireworks: his *Nocturne: Black and Gold—The Fire Wheel* and *Nocturne in Blue and Gold: Old Battersea Bridge* (ca. 1872/73; Tate Gallery, London). The subject furnished the artist with a dramatic variation on the nocturnal themes that preoccupied him beginning in the late 1860s and throughout the 1870s. The sudden burst of color caused by the exploding rockets was a moment whose intense ephemerality brought into relief the brooding darkness of the night. A popular spectacle geared to the Cockney crowds who flocked to Cremorne Gardens, fireworks also exercised Whistler's faith in the power of art to transform the sordid realities of nineteenth-century urban life into moments of evanescent beauty.

Whistler may have been alerted to the pictorial possibilities of fireworks through the medium of Japanese prints such as Shuntosai's *Fireworks over Bridge,* an 1857 woodcut he owned (Washington 1984, 85), or Hiroshige's *Fireworks at Ryogoku,* number ninety-eight of the artist's *One Hundred Famous Views of Edo.* Whistler may also have been drawn to the contrast between the fireworks, long associated with court display and with war, and the poetic reticence of the night. But it also presented him with a challenge suited to his own brand of color theory: the chromatically intense rocket bursts bring out the delicate tones of the neutral background, "fill[ing] the gray atmosphere with the colour of the night" (Cary 1907, 64).

A victim of London's urban expansion, Cremorne Gardens was closed in 1877. *Falling Rocket* was first exhibited at the Dudley Gallery in 1875. Two years later it was among eight paintings Whistler sent to Sir Coutts Lindsey's Grosvenor Gallery. There it was seen by John Ruskin, for a quarter of a century the undisputed arbiter of art values in the Anglo-American world. In a famous denunciation published as Letter 79 (July 2, 1877) in *Fors Clavigera,* a series of letters addressed to British workingmen, Ruskin attacked Whistler's supreme arrogance in offering for public sale a work that appeared to Ruskin's eyes confused and carelessly painted. Whistler was compared unfavorably to Edward Burne-Jones, whose work, also included in the Grosvenor exhibition, was "wrought with utmost conscience of care." Condemning the eccentricities of the modern school, Ruskin then named the object of his famous attack: "For Mr. Whistler's own sake, no less than for the protection of the purchaser, Sir Coutts Lindsey ought not to have admitted works into the gallery in which the ill-educated conceit of the artist so nearly approached the aspect of wilful imposture. I have seen, and heard, much of cockney impudence before now; but I never expected to hear a coxcomb ask two hundred guineas for flinging a pot of paint in the public's face" (Ruskin 1903–12, 29:160).

Whistler sued Ruskin for libel. The artist was accustomed to critical misunderstanding; coming from such an eminence, however, the threat to Whistler's standing was very real. Ruskin's charge of Cockneyism and imposture willfully misread the artist's carefully cultivated technique and his aristocratic pose. The ensuing trial on November 25 and 26, 1878, brought to the stand some of the most prominent figures of the London art world. What was really on trial was Whistler's belief in a nonliterary painting in which artistic worth was measured not by the criterion of external truth but by consistency with its own internal rules. Whistler explained his use of the term *nocturne* in the title: "I have perhaps meant rather to indicate an artistic interest alone in the work, divesting the picture from any outside sort of interest which might have been otherwise attached to it. It is an arrangement of line, form and color first, and I make use of any incident which shall bring about a symmetrical result. . . . I have chosen the word 'nocturne' because it generalizes and simplifies the whole set of them." Awarded one farthing in damages, Whistler won a Pyrrhic victory. The libel trial broke him financially, leaving him embittered toward the public and ostracized by key sectors of the London art world. Not until the 1890s did he succeed in securing the critical recognition for his work for which he had tirelessly campaigned. Years later Whistler announced to the artist Sidney Starr that *Falling Rocket* was

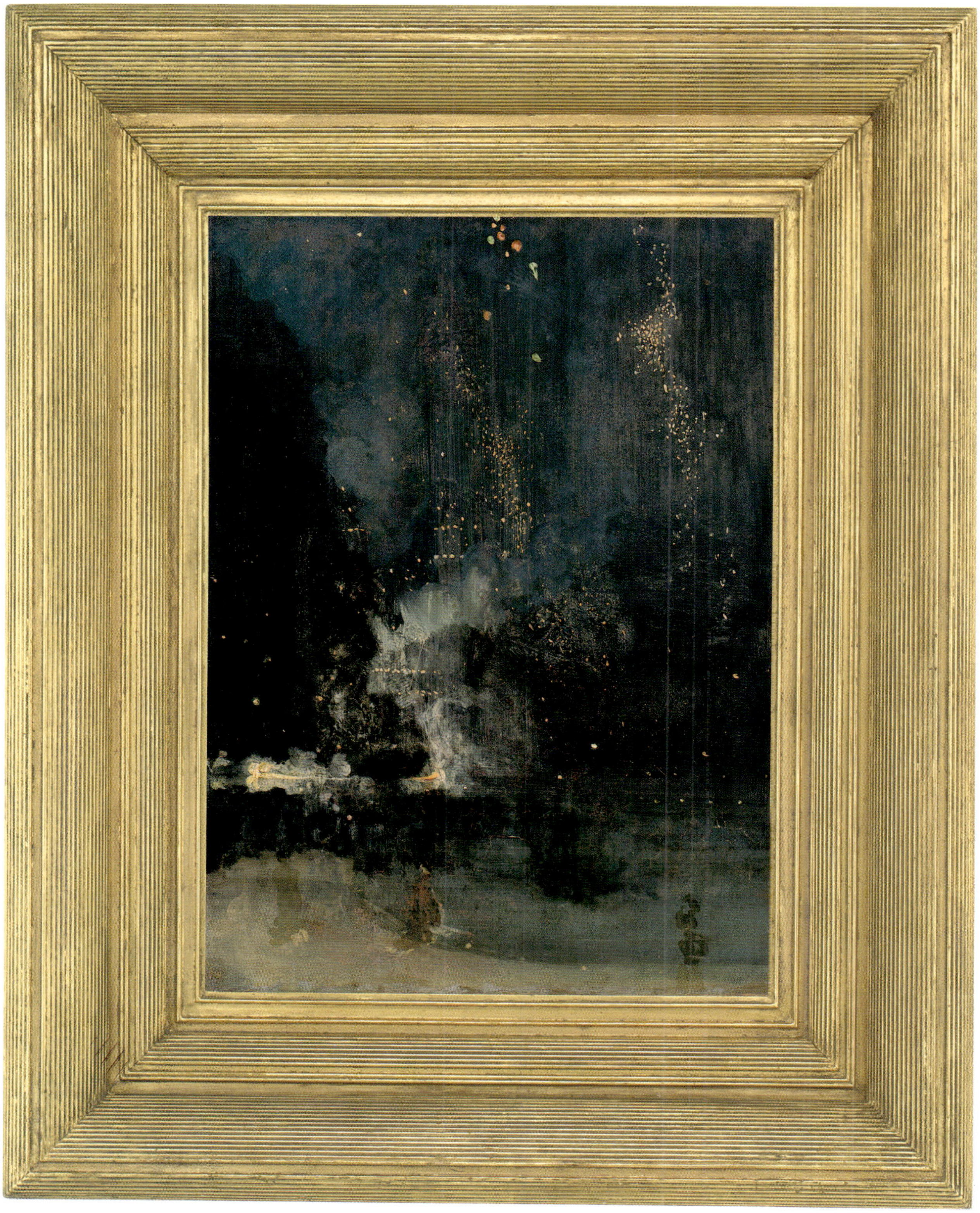

The Falling Rocket

"the finest thing that ever was done. Critics pitch into it. But bring tots, idiots, imbeciles, blind men, children, anything but Englishmen, or Ruskin, here, and of course they know" (Pennell and Pennell 1908, 2:4). The trial was a pivotal event in Whistler's life, furnishing the seed of his wittily acerbic attack on critics, *The Gentle Art of Making Enemies* (1890).

In 1892 Whistler held a retrospective of his work at the Goupil Gallery in London; the event regained for him some of the public respect he had lost as a result of Ruskin's attack. It was at this exhibition that Samuel Untermeyer of New York purchased the work for eight hundred guineas, a price that, Whistler exulted, was worth in Ruskin's terms, "four pots of paint" (Pennell and Pennell 1908, 2:127). Whistler asked Untermeyer for permission to exhibit the painting at the Columbian Exposition of 1893 in Chicago, but for unknown reasons the painting was never sent. The Untermeyer collection was auctioned in 1940, and in 1946 *Falling Rocket* was purchased and donated to the Detroit Institute of Arts by Dexter M. Ferry, Jr.

A. M.

Provenance Artist sold to Samuel Untermeyer, New York, 1892; family's sale, Parke-Bernet, New York, May 10, 1940, lot 29. Charles Sessler. Knoedler, New York. Scott & Fowles, New York, 1946. Acquired in 1946.

Exhibitions London 1875, no. 170. London 1877, no. 4. Paris 1883, no. 8. New York 1883 [not numbered in cat.]. London 1892, no. 10. Philadelphia 1900, no. 30. New York 1902, no. 241. Pittsburgh 1902, no. 150. Boston 1904, no. 64. London 1905, no. 5. Paris 1905, no. 66. New York 1912, no. 12. New Britain 1943. Toronto 1944, no. 89. New York 1947b, no. 16. New London 1949, no. 15. New York 1953, no. 53. Chicago and New York 1954, no. 105. Columbus 1956. London and New York 1960, no. 33. Brooklyn et al. 1967, no. 87. Ann Arbor 1978. Detroit 1983, no. 159. Phoenix and Indianapolis 1993, 116, fig. 83. London et al. 1994, no. 58.

References Rossetti 1875. Stephans 1875, 581. Ruskin 1877, 124. Wilde 1877, 124. Lostalot 1883, 80. Huysmans 1889, 67. Whistler 1892, 3–15, 304–305. MacColl 1893, 90. Alexandre 1903, 22, 25, ill. Duret 1904, 65. Bénédite 1905, pl. 38. Ruskin 1903–12, 29:xxii-xxiv, xxix, 160, 580–587. Starr 1908, 536. Cary 1907, 64, ill. Pennell and Pennell 1908, passim. Parry 1921. Pennell and Pennell 1921, 4–6, 316–327. Ludovici 1926, 90–91. Richardson 1947. Richardson 1954, 20–23. Sutton 1966, 191, pl. 70. Holden 1969, 38, pl. 9. McMullen 1973, 23, ill. Young et al. 1980, 1:97–99, no. 170. Washington 1984, 70, ill. Shaw 1986, 528, fig. 4. Spencer 1989, passim., ill. Merrill 1992. Siewert 1995, fig. 1.

88
Robert Barr, ca. 1894–95

Oil on canvas
39.4 × 32.4 cm (15½ × 12¾ in.)
Gift of the Witenagemote Club (20.42)

Robert Barr is a frontal bust portrait of Whistler's friend, a Scottish journalist and writer. Barr, tightly framed against a shallow background, gazes out at the viewer, his right eye shadowed by the sweeping S-shaped brim of the black hat he wears. He is dressed for the outdoors, in a dark overcoat and highlighted blue-gray cravat.

Whistler's portrait of Barr has the character of a thinly painted sketch, which may have been rubbed down between portrait sittings and repainted (Young et al. 1980, 1:190). The weave of the canvas shows through the surface, particularly in the lower area of Barr's coat. The informal, sketchlike nature of the portrait is consistent with the circumstances of its execution. Barr and Whistler most likely met in the winter of 1894 in London. The artist, having taken up Parisian residence in 1892, had returned to London in search of specialized medical care for his wife, Beatrix Godwin, whom Whistler had married in 1888. During this troubled period, ending with her death in 1896, Barr became an intimate of Whistler's, visiting him frequently to buoy up his spirits in the studio of Walter Sickert, where Whistler worked during his stay in London.

A native of Glasgow, Barr was a peripatetic journalist and writer who had studied in Toronto, worked as a young man for the *Detroit Free Press*, and then settled in 1881 in London, where he cofounded a literary journal entitled *The Idler* in 1892. While in Detroit he joined the Witenagemote Club, a gathering of fellow literary men who subsequently purchased the Whistler portrait of their associate and colleague in 1920 and gave it to the Detroit Institute of Arts that year. Barr appears in Whistler's portrait as a professionally established man of the world, direct, terse, and unsentimental.

Barr sat frequently for Whistler, who appears to have painted him in a somewhat desultory fashion. Bringing his charming young daughter with him one day to the studio, Barr furnished Whistler a fresh subject on which he eagerly seized (Young et al. 1980, 1:190). The resulting portrait is unlocated (Young et al. 1980, 1: no. 249).

A pentimento of Barr's hat is visible just above the current outline. Such adjustments in an otherwise quickly painted portrait show the importance that silhouette held for Whistler, who made minor changes in the relationship of the figure to the background in order to move the top of the hat away from the upper border of the canvas. A single serpentine line connects Barr's shoulder with his head and the outline of his hat, loose and flowing on the right side of the portrait, more taut and angular on the left side.

Along with his attention to outline and to the balanced geometry of inverted triangular cravat, ovoid face, and cone-shaped hat, Whistler employed an array of pink flesh tones, gray-greens, browns and charcoals, warm and cool colors, in an attractive if apparently casual portrait. The brownish red background is harmonized in the salmon pink flesh tones of Barr's face. Whistler's treatment of Barr, who appears detached and impersonal, is informed less by a preoccupation with the character of the sitter than with a by-now instinctive sense of composition, placement, and color harmonies.

Though he completed a number of finished full-length portraits in the last decade of his career, Whistler's portrait of Robert Barr is one of a smaller group of uncommissioned sketchlike portraits. A close parallel is the contemporaneous *Head of Mrs. Beaumont* (1894–95; Charles and Emma Frye Art Museum, Seattle), like *Robert Barr,* a frontal bust portrait also painted in Sickert's studio.

A. M.

Provenance Robert Barr. Barr's widow. Kennedy Gallery, New York, through a London dealer who acquired it from Mrs. Barr. Witenagemote Club, Detroit, 1920. Acquired in 1920.

Exhibitions London 1905, no. 30. Detroit 1920a, no. 167. Grand Rapids 1955. Kalamazoo 1966, 10.

Reference *BDIA* 1920, 13, ill. Young et al. 1980, 1:190, no. 428.

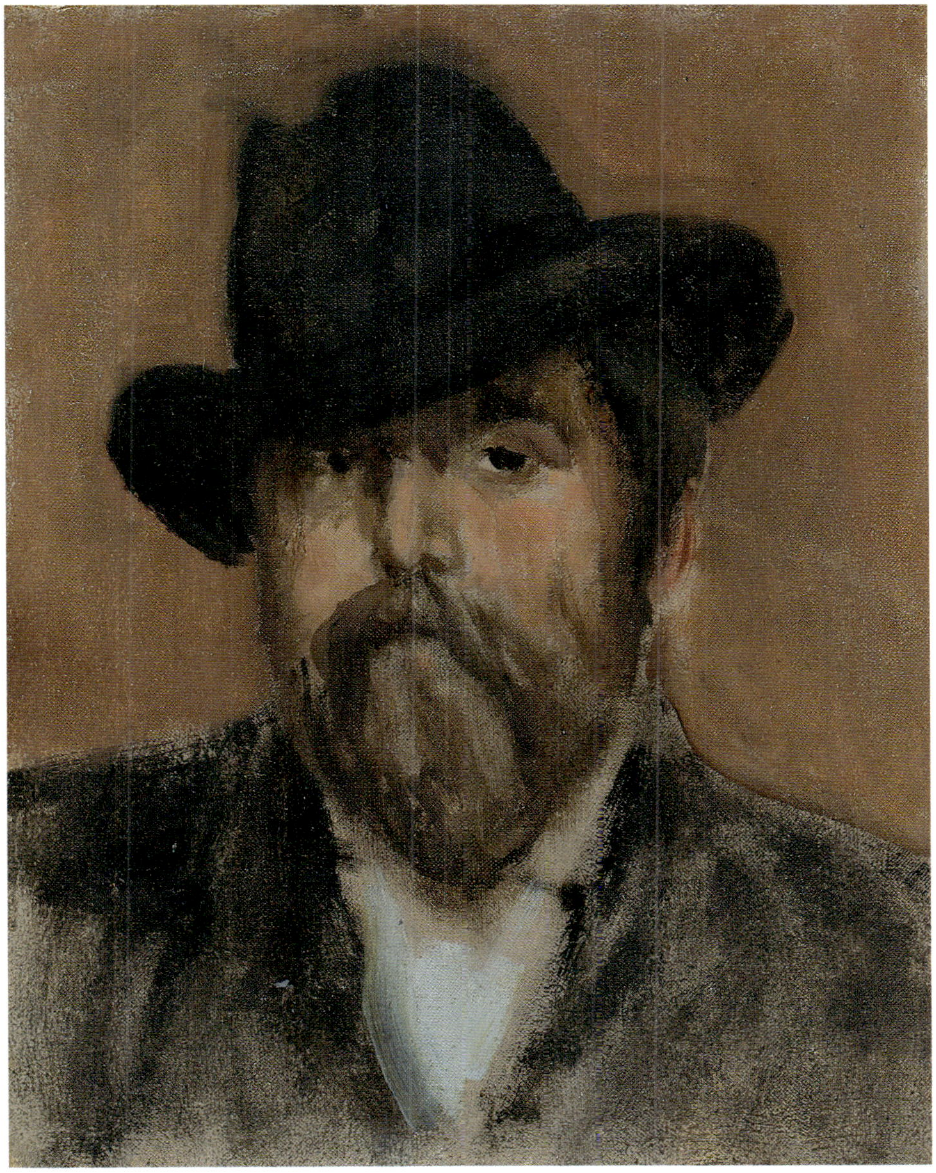

Robert Barr

[Thomas] Worthington Whittredge

1820 Springfield, Ohio–Summit, New Jersey 1910

At the height of his career, from 1860 until 1876, Worthington Whittredge was one of the leading American landscape painters, being an active member of the Tenth Street Studio Building, the Century Association, and the National Academy of Design. He professed that his interest in art and nature began in his youth as a farmboy outside Springfield, Ohio: "My ardent love of nature which dominated my whole being from my earliest recollections is the only thing I can look to as finally leading to . . . art" (Whittredge papers, AAA, roll D28, frame 13). Desiring to further his education, he moved to Cincinnati around 1837 to live with a sister, whose husband apprenticed Whittredge in his house- and sign-painting trade. After several unsuccessful attempts to establish businesses in daguerreotypes, portraiture, and landscape painting in Cincinnati, Indianapolis, and West Virginia, Whittredge returned to Cincinnati around 1844.

In the 1840s Cincinnati was the cultural center of the western United States with a vital arts community that was cultivated by the local art academy, art fairs, and the Western Art Union. Inspired by the beauty of Ohio River valley scenery, Whittredge began to specialize in landscape painting in the mid-1840s. His trips to West Virginia and the Kanawha River valley provided much of the material for his first mature landscapes such as *Scene near the Hawk's Nest* (1845; Cincinnati Art Museum). At this time he also came under the influence of Thomas Cole's paintings from his colleague Benjamin McConkey (a former pupil of Cole) and the Western Art Union. Cole's example helped coalesce Whittredge's vision of the landscape in works such as *Crow's Nest* (cat. no. 89), which stands as a hallmark of the Ohio River valley group of Hudson River school–style paintings.

By 1849 Whittredge felt the need to travel to Europe to complete his art education. In May he departed with McConkey for London on a ten-year tour. He landed in London, visited Paris, and moved on to Düsseldorf, the center for American artists in Europe from 1840 to 1860. Here, Whittredge enjoyed the artistic community and the liberal teaching of Wilhelm von Schadow, which included a substantial landscape school under Johann Schirmer. The artist worked in the home of Andreas Achenbach and was markedly influenced by his landscapes. Although he professed to be interested in the work of Carl F. Lessing, his paintings such as *Landscape in the Harz Mountains* (cat. no. 90) demonstrate greater affinity with Schirmer and Achenbach. In fact, after the departures of Achenbach and Schirmer in 1853 and 1854, Whittredge lost interest in Düsseldorf and in the summer of 1856 moved on to Italy, where he remained until returning to the United States in 1859.

Upon his return Whittredge settled in New York's Tenth Street Studio Building and entered the mainstream of American painting at that time. In 1860 he submitted four entries to the National Academy of Design including *Aqueducts of the Campagna* (1859; Cincinnati Art Museum), which earned him associate status. He was subsequently nominated to full membership in 1862. During this period the artist spent several summers immersing himself in the Catskill wilderness. Whittredge's style evolved through his study of nature and the influence of his colleagues at the National Academy of Design, the Studio Building, and the Century Association. Several trips to the West in 1866, 1870, and 1877 broadened the scope of the artist's subjects. And, by the mid-1870s, his work began to demonstrate the use of light as the vehicle for mood and compositional unity. The climax of his career was his appointment as president of the National Academy of Design from 1874 to 1876. Following this period Whittredge lived out the remainder of his life pursuing his aesthetic interests while a younger generation of American artists established new artistic directions in post–Reconstruction America.

J. K.

Bibliography Janson 1989.

89

Crow's Nest, 1848

Oil on canvas

101 × 142.2 cm (39¾ × 56 in.)

Gift of Mr. and Mrs. William D. Biggers (41.12)

Crow's Nest is the most ambitious and accomplished painting from Whittredge's early period in Cincinnati. The painting constitutes a summation of his art from his first attempts at landscape painting up to his departure for Europe in 1849. One can read in this work the influence of the Hudson River school artists, especially Thomas Cole and Thomas Doughty, as well as the traits of the regional landscape painting school.

The economic success and population explosion of the 1830s created a fertile environment for the development of culture in Cincinnati in the 1840s and 1850s, when it aspired to become the "Athens of the West" (Janson 1982). The local historian Charles Cist wrote that "Cincinnati must be regarded as one of the points where art in these latter times is one day to rear proud trophies and speak with a new power to the sense of the beautiful, the divine in man" (Cist 1841, 139). Whittredge was at the forefront of the arts in Cincinnati, particularly as the fulcrum of a triumvirate of artists who matured in the 1840s and were the foundation of the Ohio River valley landscape tradition. Since 1838, when he began in the painting business, Whittredge painted landscapes. Around 1842, when he exhibited five landscapes at the Society for the Promotion of Useful Knowledge, Whittredge began to concentrate his

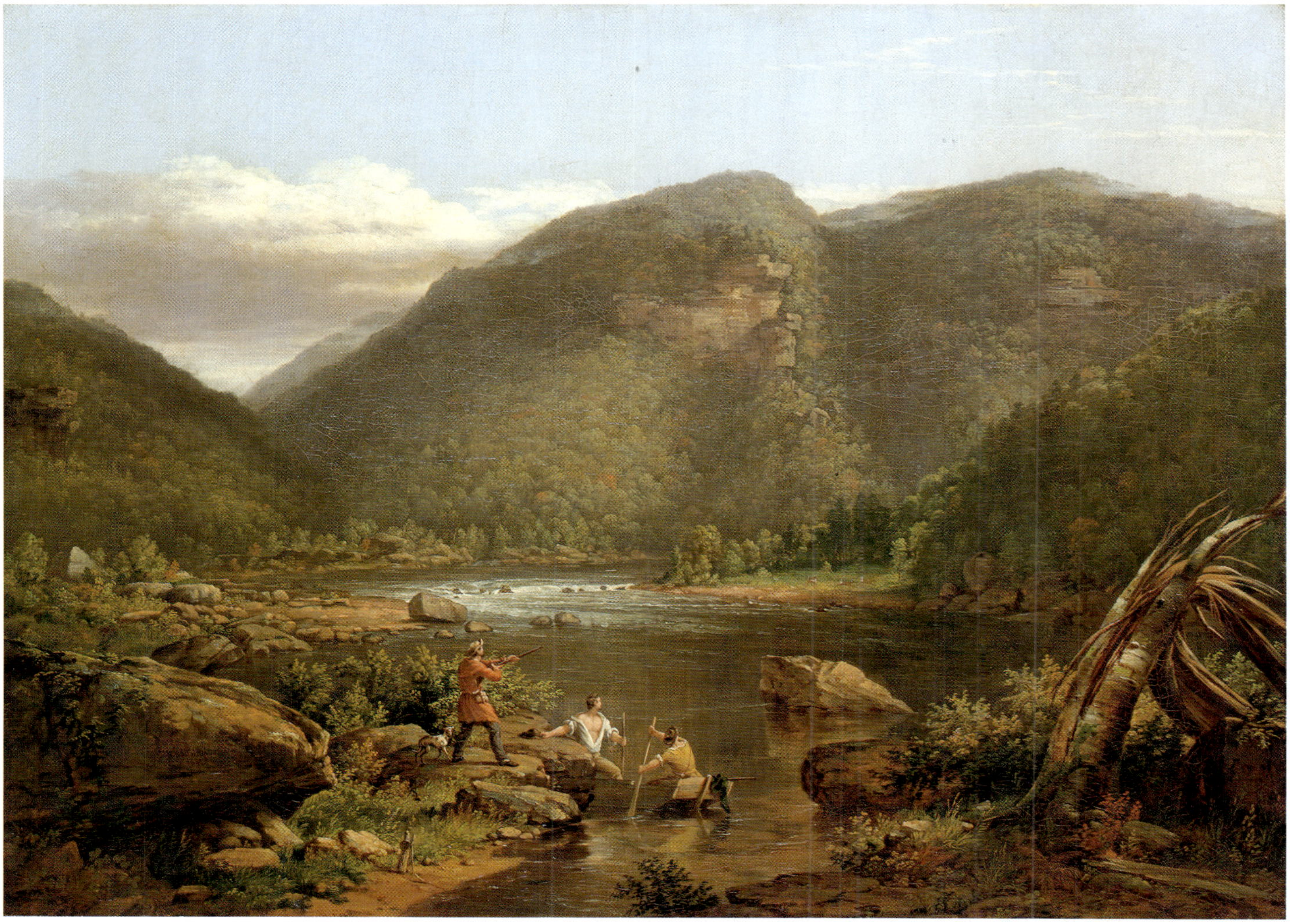

efforts on that genre. By 1845 he was working exclusively in this mode and was creating respectable paintings. He submitted seven landscapes to the local Firemen's Fair in 1845, which attracted considerable attention and patronage. He was rewarded for his work in 1846 and 1847 with entries at the National Academy of Design, which won praise from President Asher B. Durand, and at the American Art-Union. When the Western Art Union opened in Cincinnati in 1847 he became a regular exhibitor, even after his departure for Europe in 1849. Whittredge's early works were inspired by his travels up the Ohio River to the Kanawha Valley in West Virginia. His first datable paintings are *Scene near the Hawk's Nest* (Cincinnati Art Museum) and *View in West Virginia* (private collection, Cincinnati), both dated *May 1845*. These works are competently painted picturesque views reminiscent of Doughty's landscapes, which Whittredge could have seen in local collections. During the following year Whittredge's style was transformed through exposure to the works of Cole, which Whittredge certainly knew from popular periodicals and engraved prints of Cole's paintings that circulated across the United States. In 1847 he had the opportunity to see Cole's work firsthand at the Western Art Union, where Cole's series *Voyage of Life* (1846; National Gallery of Art, Washington, D.C.), acquired by a local patron, was exhibited.

Whittredge progressed rapidly and in 1848 created his largest and most significant Ohio River valley painting, *Crow's Nest*. The composition is a refined variation on the formula he had used in *View of the Hawk's Nest* (1847; formerly Hirschl & Adler Galleries, New York). In *Crow's Nest* the artist has skillfully orchestrated the scene to control the movement diagonally through the picture. A stream flowing into the spectator's space leads the eye past a storm-blasted tree trunk toward

Crow's Nest

a group of rustic woodsmen disembarking from a crude boat to shoot at deer fleeing from the opposite bank. The dramatically twisted and torn tree trunk and the intersecting wedges of the winding stream and hillsides used to create spatial recession are standard motifs and compositions in the Hudson River school tradition. Unlike Whittredge's previous paintings, the details are painstakingly drawn, and the foliated hillsides are created with dappled touches of rich colors that recall Cole's landscapes of the late 1820s and 1830s such as *The Clove, Catskills* (1827; New Britain Museum of American Art, New Britain, Conn.) and *Schroon Mountain* (1838; Cleveland Museum of Art).

In addition to the formal elements that Whittredge had borrowed from Cole, the young artist has captured the general trend toward depicting a more domesticated landscape, evident in such works by Cole as *Home in the Woods* (1847; Reynolda House, Winston-Salem, N.C.). Common in American paintings of the 1840s was an optimistic attitude concerning a benevolent relationship between man and nature. Painters who sketched the lands east of the Mississippi River in the 1840s did not find the vast, sublime wilderness that many early Hudson River school artists had discovered. By this time the eastern states had largely become settled with farms, villages, and towns. This affected the aesthetic response of landscape painters, who began to capture the presence of man, shaping a picturesque nature and reaping its bounty. Such an approach is reflected in Whittredge's *Crow's Nest,* where the woodsmen are hunting deer in a rustic setting.

The title, *Crow's Nest,* was given by the owners when they donated the painting to the museum. Oral history has suggested that this was a site in Kentucky, Virginia, or the Catskills, but this has not been substantiated by geographical evidence (curatorial files, DIA). The title is apparently a misnomer, probably assigned by a dealer who confused the scene with very similar views of Hawk's Nest, the painter's favorite sketching spot in the Kanawha Valley. Contemporary accounts do not clarify the problem. Despite the fact that this was Whittredge's most ambitious undertaking of the 1840s, the records and reviews of the American Art-Union and the Western Art Union in 1848 and 1849 do not provide any clues. If it was exhibited, *Crow's Nest* could be any of the five landscapes that he submitted to the Western Art Union in 1848. In the reviews of that year's lottery none of these works received special mention. The scale and quality of *Crow's Nest,* however, suggest that it may have been one of the works at the Art Union.

The distinctive linear quality of this painting is highly refined, with each leaf and twist of bark painstakingly rendered. This trait is particularly pronounced among the Ohio River valley landscapists of this period. Perhaps it is related to the habit of copying prints, from which the local artists learned the fundamentals of drawing and composition. The primary landscape painter in the region during Whittredge's formative years was Godfrey Frankenstein, a founder of the short-lived Cincinnati Academy of Fine Arts and a leading figure in local cultural circles. His works, such as the views of Niagara Falls (Cincinnati Art Museum) exhibited at the Firemen's Fair in 1845, have a stiff, linear quality that seems to have influenced the group of painters maturing at that time: Whittredge, William L. Sonntag (q.v.), and Robert S. Duncanson (q.v.). In works around midcentury each of these artists demonstrated tendencies toward a mannered, linear stylization of details, which became the distinguishing trademark of the Ohio River valley group of Hudson River school–style paintings.
J. K.

Inscription At lower left, *T. Whittridge 1848*

Provenance Mr. and Mrs. William D. Biggers, until 1941. Acquired in 1941.

Exhibitions Macbeth Gallery, New York, 1943 or 1944. Brooklyn 1960, no. 213. Trenton 1965.

References Richardson 1942. Janson 1977. Janson 1982, 14.

90

Landscape in the Harz Mountains, 1854

Oil on canvas
68.6 × 90.8 cm (27 × 35¾ in.)
Founders Society Purchase, Dexter M. Ferry, Jr., Fund (45.468)

THIS CANVAS IS A COPY of one of Whittredge's most successful Düsseldorf-period images, demonstrating his command of Düsseldorf academy landscape painting techniques. According to his account book, *Landscape in the Harz Mountains* duplicates a "composition from studies made in the Harz Mountains, motive near Langenfeld," which is now in the West Foundation Collection of the High Museum of Art in Atlanta. Apparently after seeing the original canvas in the collection of Whittredge's Cincinnati patron John Groesbeck, who commissioned the work, Thomas B. Read (q.v.), a Cincinnati artist, commissioned the copy on September 20, 1853, on behalf of a Philadelphia collector, James B. Claghorn (Whittredge papers, AAA, roll D28, frame 481).

Sometime after completing his Ohio River valley masterwork, *Crow's Nest* (cat. no. 89), Whittredge began to plan his tour of Europe to further his art education. In the company of his colleague Benjamin McConkey, he departed from New York in May 1849. After a month at sea, the painters arrived in London, but Whittredge stayed only briefly. He accepted an invitation to travel to Belgium, then toured the Rhine, and settled in

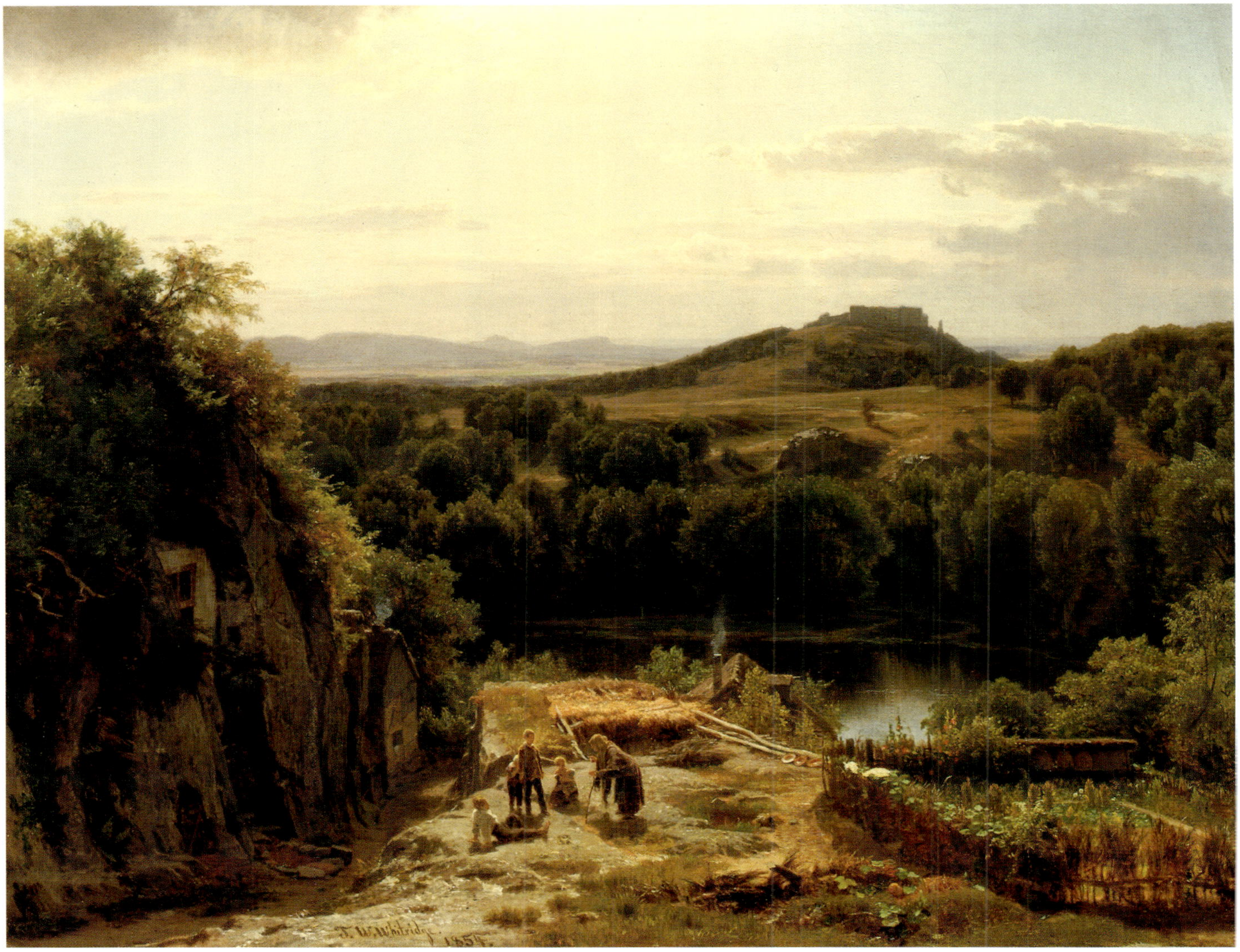

Paris by September. Whittredge was not inspired by what he saw and decided to move to Düsseldorf. Düsseldorf was the mecca for American artists studying in Europe from 1840 to 1860, due to the presence of the German-American artist Emanuel Leutze and the liberal atmosphere for teaching art in the academy there, particularly for landscape painting. Whittredge, like most Americans who traveled to Düsseldorf, did not enroll in the academy but worked in the independent ateliers associated with it. In addition, he participated in the active artistic community that focused on the Mahlkasten (Paintbox), the artists' social club. The American contingent, centered on Leutze, constituted a significant faction in the Düsseldorf artistic community.

Shortly after his arrival, Whittredge convinced the wife of Andreas Achenbach to rent him the attic space in their home for his studio. In this manner he hoped to work under the famous landscapist, who, unfortunately for Whittredge, did not like to teach. Achenbach rarely spent time criticizing the student's works and preferred the forum of the Mahlkasten for expressing his opinions on landscape aesthetics. Instead, the American painter was befriended by Carl F. Lessing, who was primarily a history painter at the academy but who was also recognized for his landscapes. Lessing and Whittredge periodically went on sketching trips together and developed a close personal relationship.

Although Whittredge professed to aspire to the style of Lessing, his works do not support such a claim. Whittredge's earliest Düsseldorf paintings, such as *Battle before the Castle* (1849; private collec-

Landscape in the Harz Mountains

tion), do resemble Lessing's historical painting style in subject and composition, particularly evident in a comparison with *Siege* (1848; Kunstmuseum Düsseldorf). However, Whittredge's subsequent work bears little relationship to Lessing's manner. Lessing's landscape sketches are marked by tightly controlled paint handling with cool blue-gray skies and whitened tan grounds that are decidedly different from the warm and verdant scenes by Whittredge. Perhaps what the American painter learned from Lessing was a sense of drawing and compositional design. In his autobiography the painter noted that the Düsseldorf works were "colorless and with nothing to recommend them except their design."

The practice of sketching from nature was strongly encouraged by the Düsseldorf landscape painters. Whittredge had developed the habit of taking sketching trips through the Ohio River valley. He remarked that while in Germany, "my summers went spent in Westphalia, in the Harz mountains or in the more immediate neighborhoods of Düsseldorf" (Whittredge 1942, 56). In the spring of 1852 the American accompanied Lessing on a sketching tour through the Harz Mountains. Three compositional sketches from this trip appear in his account book dated April 21, 1852, and led to three of his most important Düsseldorf-period paintings: *View of Kallenfels (Summer Pastorale)* (1854; Indianapolis Museum of Art), *From the Harz Mountains* (1854; formerly Berry-Hill Galleries, New York), and *Landscape in the Harz Mountains* (1854; West Foundation Collection, High Museum of Art, Atlanta). The Detroit version of the latter painting was commissioned in the next year. Previous scholars believed that this work was executed in 1853, despite being dated 1854 (Janson 1977, 205, 208). The artist's "Account Book of Completed Commissions and Other Pictures" dates the commission to September 20, 1853, and the completion of the painting to June 10, 1854.

This canvas is nearly an exact duplicate of the larger version in the High Museum, which was developed from sketches taken near the village of Langenfeld, just down the Rhine from Düsseldorf. In the foreground an old peasant woman is talking to children who sun themselves before their huts along a tributary of the Rhine, perhaps the Nahe River. Across the river a castle dominates a hill with the distinctive profiles of the Siebengebirge on the horizon. The artist has carefully controlled the progression into the distance by utilizing diagonal landscape wedges that intersect and alternate between warm and cool hues.

The paint handling and palette in this work characterize the changes in Whittredge's style that came about under the influence of the Düsseldorf painters Schirmer and Achenbach. The treatment of the foliage and foreground is not as stilted and linear as in *Crow's Nest* but is more generalized, in the manner of the Düsseldorf painters. This is evident in a comparison with Schirmer's *Wetterhorn* (1838; Kunstmuseum Düsseldorf). In addition, the idyllic mood of peasant life in the tame European landscape impresses a pastoral sentiment that is comparable to Achenbach's *Erfmühle* (1866; Kunstmuseum Düsseldorf). *Landscape in the Harz Mountains* successfully integrates what Whittredge learned about design, composition, and paint handling into his landscape painting style, making this work one of the first distinctive works in his Düsseldorf period.

J. K.

Inscription At lower left, *T. W. Whittridge 1854*

Provenance Commissioned by Thomas B. Read, Cincinnati, 1853. James L. Claghorn, Philadelphia, 1854–ca. 1857. Paul Weber, Philadelphia, from ca. 1857. Brigadier General Cornelius Vanderbilt. William M. Vanderbilt. Acquired in 1945.

Exhibitions Utica and Albany 1969, 29, no. 6. New York and Washington 1975.

References Whittredge's account book, 1849–59, AAA, roll D28, frame 481. Janson 1977.

91

The Baptism, 1868

Oil on canvas

48.3 × 68.6 cm (19 × 27 in.)

Purchase (1994.88)

The Baptism is perhaps Whittredge's most profoundly personal expression of his philosophy of art and life. Painted in 1868 shortly after his marriage to Euphemia Foote and during his ascendance to critical and commercial success as an artist, *The Baptism* conveys Whittredge's joie de vivre, his elation over his recent marriage, and his love of nature as expressed through Christian symbolism.

Following the end of the Civil War, Whittredge was summoned to join the federal government expedition under General John Pope to survey the western territories in 1866. His experience of the West irrevocably altered his conception of nature. For an artist accustomed to the landscape of Europe and the eastern woodlands, Whittredge was overwhelmed by the grandeur and expanse of the western territories, especially the Great Plains: "I had never seen the plains or anything like them. They impressed me deeply" (quoted in Whittredge 1942, 45). At every opportunity he avidly sketched the new scenery. The resulting paintings that he created in his New York studio capture the panoramic horizontality and the dry tan and ocher tones that he had discovered in the West.

In the midst of Whittredge's exciting adventure absorbing the landscape, navigating hostile Indian territory, and meeting legendary frontiersmen such as Kit

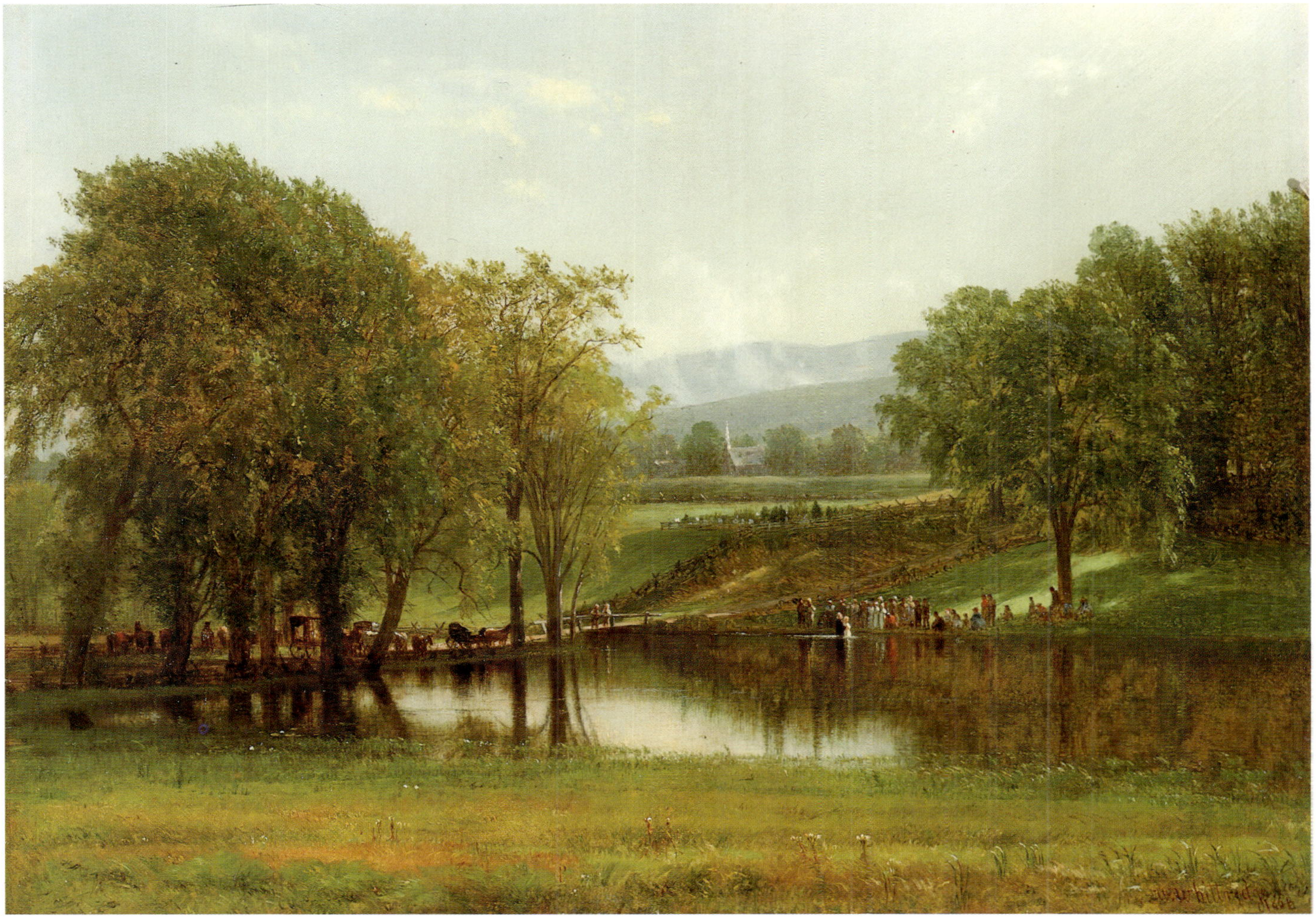

Carson, he found time to strike up a lengthy correspondence with a woman he had known for many years, Euphemia Foote of Geneva, New York. Their correspondence evolved and, on his return from the West, culminated in their marriage on October 16, 1867. The few lines that Whittredge devoted in his autobiography to his marriage and family life belie the great significance his family held for him. Whittredge's ideas concerning life and nature were deeply influenced by Emerson, Thoreau, and transcendentalist philosophy. He believed in the integral spiritual relationship between God, man, and nature. He viewed his family as the foundation of his life and a microcosmic reflection of God's larger order in nature. When writing, he regularly mixed his metaphors of nature and family, revealing his belief in the intimate interrelationship between the two. Whittredge often described nature as a landscape painter's "home." He wrote that a "great love of home" must be the inspirational source for a landscape painter (Whittredge papers, AAA, roll D28, frame 53). If in this quotation Whittredge discussed "home" as the artist's native land, on a more personal level he also associated it with his homestead and family. He claimed that it was his "love" for nature and his family that compelled him to leave the urban bustle of New York City to live in the rural New Jersey countryside (Whittredge papers, AAA, roll D28, frame 167). It is this deeply personal sentiment that is symbolically represented in *The Baptism.*

The bright rays of a spring morning sun fall on the scene of a river baptism in the foreground. In the middle ground the artist silhouetted a sparkling church spire against the distant hills and crowned it with a morning mist rising into the sky. The baptism is thus anointed with a divine circle of light, which symbolizes the providential blessing on the sacra-

The Baptism

ment of baptism and draws parallels with the renewal of nature in the spring. The cemetery on the hillock above reminds us of our eventual demise, yet the heaven-directed church spire offers to devout Christians the opportunity for spiritual salvation and rebirth in the afterlife.

The Baptism is distinctive among Whittredge's works of this period for its symbolic, almost allegorical, portrayal of the artist's philosophy of life founded in the spiritual relationship among God, nature, and man. Late in life Whittredge summed up his convictions, remarking that he was

> not always observing the Sabbath in the strict manners of my fore-fathers, but, after church in the mornings, and while my children were small, devoting my Sunday afternoons to walks with them, spring, summer, and autumn—walks on which we picked many chrysalis and brought it home and hung it up, and watched for the butterfly to escape as the warm days of Spring gave it life. (Whittredge papers, AAA, roll D28, frame 167)

Whittredge's nostalgic account reveals his pantheistic beliefs and perception of a spiritual relationship among the butterfly, spring, the youth of his children, and God's renewal of nature.

Seven years later Whittredge returned to this composition to create *The Morning Stage* (1875; private collection), an ambitious canvas that he exhibited at the National Academy of Design in 1875. The composition is virtually identical to that of *The Baptism,* yet some significant changes in subject alter the metaphorical content of the painting and reflect the complex changes in Whittredge's life and career. Instead of a baptismal scene, Whittredge focused on the coach that has driven farther down the path to approach the dark, wooded entrance to a cemetery. In the years since he painted *The Baptism* Whittredge had reached a pinnacle of critical and commercial success, and personal happiness. His colleagues elected him to the prestigious post of president of the National Academy in 1874, a post he would hold for two years. In addition, he witnessed the births of two daughters, Euphemia and Olive, in 1874 and 1875. His dear friend Sanford R. Gifford (q.v.) observed that at this time, "Whittredge was well and happy because his income last season was sufficient to relieve him of anxiety about ways and means, and his baby is a source of perpetual pleasure" (Janson 1989, 154).

Nonetheless, these were troubled years for Whittredge. The national economic crash of 1873 launched a period of tremendous economic difficulty. Facing imminent bankruptcy, the National Academy brought in Whittredge, a highly respected member of the institution, to sustain it through this difficult phase. His tremendous commercial success of the previous decade had waned considerably and painting sales were few. Most significant, Whittredge was distraught over the death in 1873 of his first child, Jeannie.

Whittredge's emotions of joy over the birth of his children and his appointment to the presidency of the academy mixed with his depression resulting from his fiscal problems and the death of his first daughter shape the mood and content of *The Morning Stage.* The painting still portrays the nostalgic charm of an Arcadian rural scene with a stagecoach carrying its passengers through the stages of life. The emphasis of *The Morning Stage* has shifted from the renewal of life in *The Baptism* to the close of life, emphasized by the triumvirate of the coach, cemetery, and church in the center of the painting. Indeed, one author has suggested that the man carrying his daughter on his back symbolizes the artist's sorrow over the first daughter's death and joy over the birth of two daughters in the following years (Janson 1989, 135). Whittredge retains the key motif of salvation in the sparkling church spire and the clouds ascending from the hills into the heavens. These certainly represent his hopes for his deceased daughter and his aspirations for his two young ones. Whittredge copied an unidentified poem into his account book that reflects his attitude toward death and rebirth through spiritual salvation:

> O ye! who talk of Death, and mourn for Death,
> Why do you muse a phantom of your weakness,
> And then shriek loud to see what ye have made?
> There is no Death, to those who know of Life,—
> No time to those who see Eternity.
> (Whittredge papers, AAA, roll D28, frame 166)

The fact that Whittredge chose to copy in his personal papers this poem reveals his convictions concerning spiritual rebirth through God and nature which is symbolized in *The Baptism.*

J. K.

Provenance The artist to Emil Rothengatter, New York. By family descent to his great-granddaughter. Adelson Gallery, New York, 1994. Acquired in 1994.

Thomas Waterman Wood

1823 Montpelier, Vermont–New York 1903

Born in Montpelier, Vermont, Thomas Waterman Wood was educated in the local schools, then worked for a time in his father's cabinetmaking shop, designing and constructing furniture. An itinerant portrait painter visiting Montpelier inspired his interest in art, and Wood may have received some training with Chester Harding in 1846–47, but he was essentially self-taught, learning to draw by copying from instruction books. His earliest known works—a series of pencil sketches of the Vermont countryside—were made in the mid-1840s. In the late 1840s and early 1850s Wood earned a living in a variety of ways that included playing the guitar at the local agricultural fair, tuning pianos, designing "Gothic" nightstands and bedsteads, and painting signs for the Vermont Central Railroad. In 1850 Wood married Minerva Robinson of Waterbury and built Athenwood, a summer home and studio in Montpelier.

From 1852 to 1858 Wood painted portraits in New York, Quebec, Washington, D.C., and Baltimore. During this period he developed an interest in genre painting, and before leaving for Europe in 1858 he submitted a genre study, *Moses, the Baltimore News Vendor,* to the National Academy of Design. Prior to sailing, Wood arranged to sell *Moses* and a companion piece entitled *Market Woman* (also known as *Negress)* (both Fine Arts Museums of San Francisco) to his principal patron in Baltimore, J. C. Brune, who had previously commissioned portraits of himself and his family. Once in Paris, Wood established a studio and painted pictures "to order" for his American patrons. He also made copies after the old masters in the Louvre.

Wood returned to America late in 1859 to find the abolition of slavery an immediate and pressing domestic issue. During the next seven years, in spite of the Civil War, he managed to maintain a steady income as a portrait painter in Nashville, Tennessee, and Louisville, Kentucky. His interest in the ethnic and regional diversity of American life is revealed in a series of genre pictures that served to establish his reputation in New York. Painted in 1866 in Louisville, *A Bit of War History: The Contraband, The Recruit,* and *The Veteran* (Metropolitan Museum of Art, New York) are said to have been inspired by a black soldier injured in the Civil War.

In the autumn of 1866 Wood moved to New York and took a room in the Tenth Street Studio Building, which housed almost every important artist of the time. His models added to the traffic up- and downstairs of street urchins, charwomen, and derelicts who came to pose for John George Brown (q.v.). Friends and neighbors in Montpelier, where he was a frequent visitor, posed for his scenes of country life. Wood's images of a hardworking, egalitarian society mirrored the perception that the American middle class had of itself, and he became a favorite with the public. He also earned the respect of his colleagues, who elected him vice president of the National Academy of Design in 1879, and president in 1891, an office he held for eight years. In 1878 Wood helped found the New York Etching Club, and in the same year he began the first of nine consecutive terms as president of the American Watercolor Society.

Though Wood's official posts left him less time in which to construct elaborate scenes, he continued to produce genre pictures during the 1880s. In the 1890s he returned to portraiture, producing strong, impressive likenesses of such important Americans as the steel magnate Andrew Carnegie, the longtime Vermont senator Justin Smith Morrill, and the artist William Beard. In 1895, with the financial support of John W. Burgess, Wood founded the Wood Art Gallery in Montpelier and gave his remaining works to it. During the final years of his life, the artist devoted much of his time to acquiring works by his contemporaries and to copying the old masters for the gallery that bore his name.
N. R. S.

Bibliography Benjamin 1879, 43–47. Wood correspondence and papers, AAA, roll N2810, frame 1587. This information comes from Wood's diary and account book, Monday, February 3, 1890. Montpelier 1972.

92
Sherry Sir? 1890

Oil on canvas
61.6 × 46.4 cm (24¼ × 18¼ in.)
Gift of Mr. and Mrs. James O. Keene
(72.257)

According to a label affixed to the back of the canvas, this painting was added to the Detroit venue of Alfred Frankenstein's 1970 exhibition *The Reality of Appearance: The Trompe l'Oeil Tradition in American Painting,* though it was not included in the catalogue. The descriptive title it bore in the exhibition, *Serving Maid with Decanter and Glasses,* was shortened to *Serving Maid* when the picture was accessioned in 1972.

Paul Worman, who is preparing a catalogue raisonné on Wood's oeuvre, has recently identified the picture as *Sherry Sir?,* a work exhibited by Wood at the Century Club in New York in 1890 (correspondence, curatorial files, DIA). The artist recorded the picture in his diary on February 1, 1890. A second notation, on February 3, indicates that the painting was sold to the well-known financier and Civil War veteran General Brayton Ives through Thomas B. Clarke for four hundred dollars (AAA, roll N2810, frame 1587). Ives, a former president of the New York Stock Exchange and of the Northern Pacific Railroad, as well as many other large corporations, was an avid collector. At one time he had a library of more than six thousand volumes, including two hundred rare books relating to the settlement of this country. He also collected ceramic art and engravings.

Sherry Sir? belongs to a series of paintings the artist produced in the 1890s on the theme of the domestic servant of a wealthy family. In most of these, such as *Gossip* (1890; Wood Art Gallery, Montpelier, Vt.), *The Faithful Nurse* (1893; Wood Art Gallery), and *Orchid* (1890s; unlocated), the subject is a black woman. In *Coffee Sir?* (1896; Wood Art Gallery), a painting similar in composition to the Detroit work, the serving maid is white. William Lipke and others have aptly characterized these late works as more sentimental, trivial, and urban in subject than the fresh realism the artist had displayed in the decade and a half after the Civil War. By this date, Wood's official posts, and the portrait commissions that inevitably followed, left him little time to work out the exacting details required for more elaborate genre themes. Nonetheless, as Lipke observes, these paintings "have a charm to them" and reflect the ease with which Wood could paint images that appealed to both rural and urban audiences (Montpelier 1972, 54). According to Worman, the model for *Sherry Sir?, Gossip,* and possibly the unlocated *Orchid* was a Mrs. Soto. Her young son also posed for the artist.

Although it was painted thirty-two years later, *Sherry Sir?* is similar to *Market Woman* (Fine Arts Museums of San Francisco), Wood's earliest essay in genre painting. A comparison of the two illustrates the direction of the artist's development. Both canvases reveal a careful attention to surface detail; there is the same dramatic lighting and brilliant coloring in costume. But in the mature work the subject is presented much closer to the picture plane and is rendered with a minimum of brushstrokes in a decidedly less formal manner. Wood's respect for the properties of weight and volume and his insistence on the importance of each individual object here result in a moment captured and hermetically sealed in time.
N. R. S.

Inscriptions On hem of apron, lower left, *T. W. Wood / 1890;* label affixed to verso, *"Reality of Appearance," 1970. / Serving Maid with Decanter and Glasses*

Provenance General Brayton Ives, New York, from 1890. Mr. and Mrs. John Droska, Detroit, 1957–59. Mr. and Mrs. William Kahlich, Detroit, 1959–66. Mr. and Mrs. James O. Keene, Birmingham, Mich., 1966–72. Acquired in 1972.

Exhibitions Century Club, New York, 1890. Added to Detroit venue of Berkeley et al. 1970 (not in catalogue).

Reference Rivard et al. 1977, 89–91, ill.

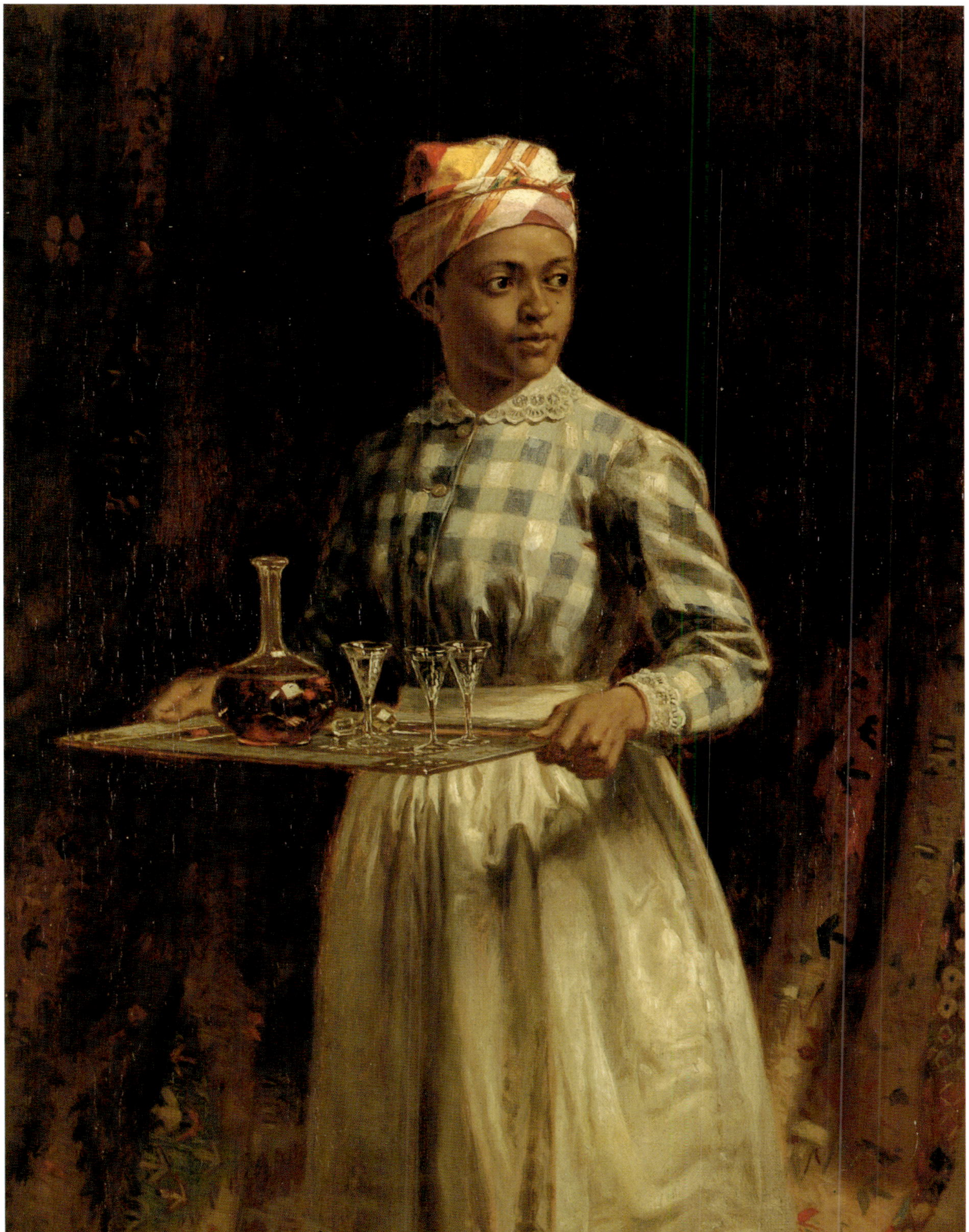

Sherry Sir?

Richard Caton Woodville

1825 BALTIMORE–LONDON 1855

RICHARD CATON WOODVILLE could be called the Masaccio of American genre painting. His early death cut short a promising career that, under more favorable circumstances, might have rivaled those of the top British and Continental European genre specialists of his day.

Born in Baltimore to parents of "good English stock" (*New York Daily Tribune*, January 22, 1867, 2), Woodville evidenced precocious artistic talent in his early teens. Initially he had to contend with parental skepticism about a vocation in the visual arts, but by the spring of 1845 his father relented, and in May of that year, the recently married neophyte painter, not yet twenty years old, embarked for Europe with his wife and a female attendant. Their goal was Italy, but after an interval in Paris they went instead to Düsseldorf. There Woodville remained for five years, from 1846 to 1851, returning home in 1851 and possibly again in 1854. A search of U.S. passport data by Merl M. Moore, Jr., has revealed that the artist's father, William Woodville V, who already had traveled to Europe in 1844, did so twice more during the early 1850s, presumably to visit and consult with his son. With his son's help, the father amassed a consequential collection—eventually sold in New York on May 31 and June 1, 1864—of contemporary German art and old masters, interspersed with works from elsewhere in Europe and at least two paintings by his son's American colleagues, William Sidney Mount and Albert Bierstadt (q.v.); Bierstadt studied in Düsseldorf after Woodville had left there.

The younger Woodville, meanwhile, painted all but one of his best-known pictures abroad, sending them to the United States through his father; then through the American Art-Union, where they were exhibited and in some cases were engraved; and then again through his father. He resettled in Paris for a time in 1851. After remarrying, he moved to the British capital with his second wife later in 1851, where he died from "poisonous effects of an overdose of morphia, medicinally taken," according to his death certificate (quoted by Francis Grubar in Washington et al. 1967, n.p.), on August 13, 1855, aged thirty. His own son, also named Richard Caton Woodville, born in London after his father's death, became a well-known Victorian illustrator and painter of battle scenes.

As a schoolboy Woodville won honors for drawing and penmanship at St. Mary's Seminary in Baltimore. In that regard, his artistic beginnings were not unlike those of his contemporary, Frederic Edwin Church (q.v). A handful of Woodville's paintings and a larger number of drawings from before his departure for Europe, most of them descended through his heirs, are extant. They demonstrate a predilection for genre, specimens of which from both the European seventeenth and American nineteenth centuries were accessible to him in the Baltimore collection of Robert Gilmor; for characters and costumes from chivalric times; and to a lesser extent for portraiture and battle scenes. Woodville's training in Germany is not readily pinpointed, but it is known that he studied at the Düsseldorf Academy of Art for about a year, after which he became a private pupil of Carl Ferdinand Sohn, a Düsseldorf history painter, portraitist, and art teacher of repute whose portraits have something in common with those of his American protégé. Works by several contemporary Düsseldorf genre artists, notably Rudolf Jordan, Johann Peter Hasenclever, Adolf Schroedter, and August Friedrich Seigert, are generally comparable to Woodville's, but his for the most part exceed theirs in delineation of individual human characters and social strata, deft use of accessories, and fastidiousness of technique. In this last respect, his art looks forward to American trompe-l'oeil painting, much of it rooted in contemporary German art, of the third and fourth quarters of the nineteenth century. A well-informed New York commentator of 1867 (*New York Daily Tribune*, January 22, 1867) favorably likened two of the deceased artist's last pictures, *Waiting for the Stage* (1851; Corcoran Gallery of Art, Washington, D.C.) and a version of *The Sailor's Wedding* (ca. 1852; unlocated), to works by Ernest Meissonier.

Precious little documentation survives for whole segments of Woodville's brief life. One may suppose that he moved to London in 1851 to reinstate himself privately and to affiliate himself professionally with the flourishing ambiance of British mid-nineteenth-century genre painting, exemplified by such established practitioners as Charles Robert Leslie, William Mulready, Richard Redgrave, and Thomas Webster. In 1852 Woodville submitted a four-year-old work, *Politics in an Oyster House* (1848; Walters Art Gallery, Baltimore), to the annual exhibition of London's Royal Academy, where it was successfully shown under the title *A New York Communist Advancing an Argument* (*Illustrated London News*, July 31, 1852, 84). Yet of the two paintings—the version of *The Sailor's Wedding* (1852) now in the Walters Art Gallery, Baltimore, and *The Italian Boy with Hurdy Gurdy* (1852; private collection)—securely datable to his English period, the first was begun in Paris and completed in London, while the second also could have been commenced before 1852. For reasons that are now unclear, Woodville seems to have virtually ceased painting for about three years prior to his demise. A depiction unusual and perversely prophetic for him, a "Burial at Sea," said in 1867 to have been unfinished on his easel at his death (*New York Daily Tribune*, January 22, 1867), may coincide with a "Burial of an Emigrant at Sea" already described in progress by late 1849 (*Bulletin of the American Art-Union*, December 1849, 21; *New York Daily Tribune*, April 9, 1850).

One may wonder, as well, about his preferred subject matter. He came artistically of age at midcentury, while wars of

various kinds raged in Europe and North America. Although a methodical worker in his studio and evidently a contented European resident, he focused on topical American themes with military or political overtones. For models he turned occasionally to family and Baltimore acquaintances, working out the accessories through data supplied by correspondence from home, discourse with compatriot colleagues in Düsseldorf, and contact with American newspapers. Indeed, one of his best-known paintings, *War News from Mexico* (1848; National Academy of Design, New York), concentrates—as Woodville himself must often have done—on journalistic immediacy and the urgency of communication with far-flung places in stressful times.
G. C.

Bibliography Cowdrey 1944. Grubar 1966. Grubar 1967. Washington et al. 1967.

93
The Card Players, 1846

Oil on canvas
47 × 63.5 cm (18½ × 25 in.)
Gift of Dexter M. Ferry, Jr. (55.175)

The Card Players was Woodville's first major artistic success. Shortly after completing it in Düsseldorf, where he had recently settled, he sent the picture home to his father, William Woodville V, who, in turn, negotiated exhibition venues for it in Baltimore, Philadelphia, and perhaps Boston, before overseeing its acquisition by the American Art-Union by November 1847. Through exposures at the regular Art-Union displays of 1847 and 1849 in New York, and especially by means of an engraving issued by the Art-Union in 1850, the work became nationally renowned. Over the next quarter century the painting itself resurfaced at several exhibitions held in northeastern cities.

As its title suggests, the scene focuses on a game of chance, specifically an episode of cheating at cards involving three principals, an onlooker, and numerous accessories. The theme and cast of characters bring to mind works by Caravaggio and his followers during the early seventeenth century, while the detailed interior setting and modest size of *The Card Players* recall cabinet paintings of various subjects by Flemish and Dutch genre specialists of the seventeenth century. Further, the compositional arrangement and physiognomies of Woodville's figures resonate with Renaissance and baroque depictions of certain biblical scenes, especially the Supper at Emmaus, of which the one by Caravaggio (ca. 1602), acquired in 1839 by the National Gallery in London, is a pertinent parallel. That historical antecedents were important for the fledgling American artist—and for contemporary Düsseldorf artists—at that moment is affirmed by his next major picture, *The Cavalier's Return* (1847; New-York Historical Society), a demure family gathering with military overtones set in the Elizabethan period.

The Card Players takes place inside an 1840s Baltimore pub or inn of modest but not dissolute rank. Two men, one of them middle-aged at the left, and the other a youth at the right, sit facing each other in profile across a small wooden table with folding leaves. A second young man, frontal to the viewer and dressed differently from his contemporary, stands between the seated figures on the far side of the table. In the left background, separated from the others, a black man with graying hair sits against the back wall. Facing the viewer, he warms himself at the stove at far left as he glances toward the viewer's right.

The balding, middle-aged man is the "mark." Bareheaded, wearing a stiff high white collar, velvet-trimmned jacket, and large soiled boots, he occupies an armchair with a wicker seat, the most elaborate piece of furniture in the room, over the back of which he has thrown a heavy coat. His top hat and tall umbrella, the former upside down and the latter propped handle-up against the table, are on the floor to his right near his feet. The curved umbrella handle almost touches a glass of amber liquid on the table; the glass is about one-fifth full. A thin stack of cards rests on the table immediately in front of him. Looking up with an expression of determined discontent toward the standing youth, he clutches four cards close to his chest in his right hand while he places his left hand on the table, jabbing with the index figure at a card lying face up on the table.

The young man seated opposite is the "con." Wearing dashing garb and a cap that partially shadows his face, and smoking a slender cigar, he occupies an armless, cushioned chair, which he has turned nearly back-to-front toward the table. His arms rest atop the back of the chair. While several of his cards lie separated on the table, he awaits his opponent's next move with bent left arm and extended right arm, holding his left hand—in which he grasps four more cards—beneath his left ear, while his right hand slowly stirs with a spoon the amber liquid in a glass; his glass is two-thirds full. He sits on a nearly concealed card, while in his left pants pocket, mostly covered by the pocket flap and the edge of his jacket, is a metal object, perhaps a weapon. His slender build, pliant pose, dour expression, rakish clothing (including spats), disciplined drinking habits, and maneuverable lightweight chair connote a flexibility that the older man does not possess. The extra card all but assures a winning hand for him, while the cloaked object intimates a threat of violence.

The pose of the standing youth is also pliant, the S-curve—although not so much the crossed legs—reminiscent of classical sculpture. Lightly bearded with a thin mustache, he looks down toward the table surface, leaning casually on his extended right arm and hand. He wears a knit sweater and over it a vest from which dangle a chain and key above his waist, and a fezlike cap. There is a prominent ring on the index finger of his right hand. He holds in his left hand a long pipe, the painted ceramic stem resting on his left shoulder and the end curving behind his left ear. Ostensibly he is an interlocutor. Yet his flexed left arm gives way to the seated young man, while his straight right arm divides the two sides of the table with a barrier that, it seems, the older man cannot penetrate.

The black man is subservient to the others, but he is also preoccupied with keeping warm. He may be a slave, although many free blacks did live in Baltimore during the 1840s (see Clayton 1987), in which case he is probably a servant. Hands folded, wearing dark clothing and (evidently) boots, he is screened from the other figures and partially from the viewer by his background location and by the middle-aged participant's coat and chair. A striped blanket rests across the lower part of his left leg. With a bemused expression, he turns his eyes and slightly rotates his head toward the center of the room.

The various accessories amplify the narrative, enhance the effect of one-point perspective, and demonstrate the artist's skills as a painter of still life. On the right are a basin, water jug, towel, brushes, and mirror, with which a male customer may primp himself. Broadsides posted on and hung from the half-open door next to the mirror advertise a stagecoach service, a sale, and the Baltimore Lock Hospital, which, as Francis Grubar has noted (Grubar 1966, 57), was dedicated to charlatan remedies for afflictions supposedly induced by masturbation. Bunched theatrical advertisements, all of them for the Front Street Theatre in Baltimore, are unfurled on the wall in the exact center. One of them specifies a "Battle," perhaps the "Battle of New Orleans," a patriotic diversion performed at the Front Street Theatre for a few days in early July 1845, shortly after Woodville's departure for Europe. An equestrian conflict is also the theme of a framed print partially covered by the theater bills. On the wall above the older man's chair, a clock with a pulley mechanism shows the time, seven past four. An ashtray on the floor at right, and various objects toward the left—among them tongs, a broken (corncob?) pipe, a rolled-up newspaper or broadside, a wicker basket containing a corked bottle, and a metal pan atop the stove—add careful clutter as well as multiple shapes and textures to the ensemble. Besides the aforementioned cards and drinking glasses, several coins and pieces of paper money are scattered across the table surface; one of the bills droops over the near edge of the table.

Two aspects of the scene need clarification. The first is the character of the locale itself. Elizabeth Johns (Johns 1991, 179) recently has identified it as a waiting room, but two American commentators of 1847, one of whom was a Baltimore resident, called it either a bar or an inn.

Woodville's *Scene in a Bar-room* (unlocated), a depiction of "two bar-room loafers sitting over a stove" *(New York Daily Tribune,* January 22, 1867) painted the previous year and exhibited at the National Academy of Design in 1845, tends to confirm the reviewers' identifications of 1847. At the same time, one must acknowledge that genre artists of the mid–nineteenth century did not make hard-and-fast distinctions among bars, inns, and waiting rooms. Between legible words visible in the painting itself and an explanation he wrote to his patron, Robert Gilmor of Baltimore, William Sidney Mount referred to all three identities apropos his *Long Story* (1837; Corcoran Gallery of Art, Washington, D.C.), a painting that Woodville knew, in which seated and standing figures occupy a spare interior. Woodville's own painting of six years later, *Waiting for the Stage* (1851; Corcoran Gallery of Art), an interior scene of cardplaying comprising three figures and anchored by a folding-leaf table, could be interpreted as a reconsidered, reconfigured *Card Players.*

The second concerns the standing youth. Given his proximity and gestural deference to the con, one might assume that the two young men are cohorts in a scam. Again, however, the situation may not be what it appears. A reviewer for the *Baltimore American & Commercial Daily Advertiser* (May 25, 1847) said that "the third person is a German, evidently a newly arrived emigrant [*sic*], who is called upon to judge in the matter, and who is somewhat perplexed by the difficulty of the case," an ethnic interpretation echoed by a New York critic six months later and by a Philadelphia reviewer in 1876 *(Evening Bulletin,* June 24, 1876). Now, the Baltimore writer surely exaggerated the figure's simplicity (the latter is not *that* upright), but his and the other journalists' recognition of German-style facial hair, costume, and the ceramic pipe displaying a painted portrait of a bearded male, rings true. Hence it is likely that Woodville intended the standing youth to represent the living German heritage of mid-nineteenth-century Maryland. Further, the figure could be construed autobiographically, as a stand-in for the artist, signifying both the melting-pot atmosphere of the port of Baltimore, where he was born, and the cultural dynamism of Düsseldorf-on-the-Rhine, where he painted the picture.

While still in Baltimore Woodville had sketched a seventeenth-century Flemish interior scene of cardplaying (William Woodville VIII, Washington, D.C.; Düsseldorf 1976, ill. no. 194). An extant preparatory drawing for the present picture (ca. 1845–46; private collection; Atlanta 1972, ill. no. 143; Düsseldorf 1976, ill. no. 195) done in Düsseldorf is considerably more sophisticated, although as yet lacking the finesse of the finished composition. Of the numerous differences between that drawing and

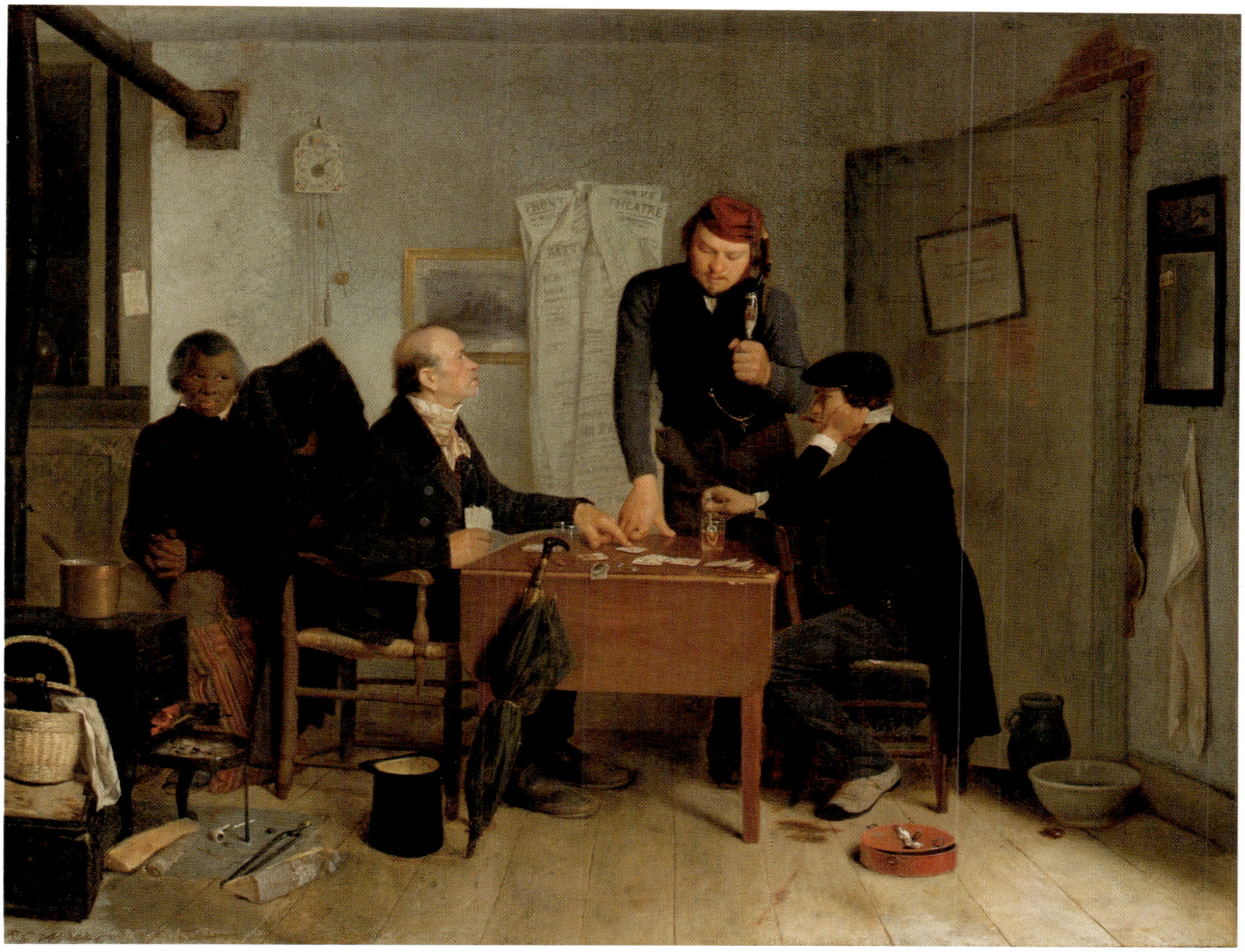

the painting, those having to do with the back wall of the room, the design of the table, and the three principal figures are the most important. In the drawing, the man seated at left looks relatively young and wide-eyed, while the standing man has a wan (tobacco-induced?) expression and the seated youth a grimacing one, and both youths are dressed in similar garb. In the painting, the mien of the older man is strengthened, while the two young men are at once brought closer together through countenance and separated through costume. The cavalry print behind the former's head vivifies the left-to-right thrust of his inquiry-accusation.

The Baltimore reviewer of *The Card Players* invoked the name of David Wilkie, the Scottish painter. Woodville had not stopped in Britain on his way to Europe, and during 1846 he was immersing himself in the practices and precedents of Düsseldorf art. Even so, the analogy to Wilkie, the foremost European genre specialist of the early nineteenth century, whose work Woodville must already have known through prints and whose posthumous biography by Allan Cunningham, published in 1843, Woodville could have read by 1846, is appropriate. Wilkie had painted several indoor scenes of card-players. In the major version (1808; Lord Denham; Raleigh 1987, ill. no. 9), engraved in 1838 to favorable response (*Art-Union* [London], February 1, 1839), an elderly but vigorous man seated at the left dominates a boisterous company, while in a smaller "sketch, with variations" (unlocated), cited by Cunningham (see Raleigh 1987, 138), "a black man is introduced as a looker-on, [which] adds much merit to the work." Worth mention, as

The Card Players

well, is that one of Wilkie's best-known works set outdoors, *Chelsea Pensioners Reading the Waterloo Dispatch* (1822; Apsley House, London), engraved in 1831, revolves around a table placed parallel to the front edge of the scene, its near side largely unobstructed.

The Card Players was well received when it was unveiled at Samson Cariss's looking-glass and frame shop in Baltimore during May 1847. The aforementioned writer for the *American & Commercial Daily Advertiser,* a morning paper, rendered a solid verdict of approval:

> It is only necessary to refer persons of taste and judgment to the picture itself, which bespeaks its own quality and the genius of the artist. The scene is in Baltimore—a barroom, with three figures prominent, and a negro at the side, sitting by a stove. The observer sees as plainly as though he were present on the occasion, a game at cards, between two, one of whom has slipped a card, and is charged with it by the other....
>
> Without pretending to any especial connoisseurship in reference to performances of this kind, we are inclined to believe that WILKIE's earlier paintings gave not such indications of genius as this. It has won upon our admiration very much; and we hope that persons of better judgment in these things than we can lay claim to, will not only examine this painting, but also express their opinions concerning it. We may give here utterance also to another wish—which is that this work of art may be secured for Baltimore, since it is local in its design and is the first work of an artist of Baltimore, who is likely to reflect credit upon his native city as well as upon the art to which he is devoted.

The editors of the *Baltimore Republican & Argus* (May 25, 1847), an evening paper, quickly seconded the *American*'s sentiments, declaring that "the picture evinces talents of the highest order," and adding their "hope that it will not be allowed to leave the city."

A prospective Baltimore buyer did approach William Woodville (see Grubar 1966, 53–54), but the latter, intent on furthering his son's reputation, sent the painting on to the Pennsylvania Academy of the Fine Arts, where it was accepted for the annual exhibition already under-way. Given a late arrival number, "11½," in the second edition of the academy catalogue and entitled *Card Party,* it apparently generated no notice from local critics. From there William Woodville tried to add the work to the annual display of the Boston Athenaeum, also in progress. Athenaeum administrators were favorably impressed (see Grubar 1966, 53), although no known catalogue or press review refers to the painting there.

In late October 1847 William Woodville offered the work to the American Art-Union for two hundred dollars, a price equaling the bid he had received in Baltimore but higher than most accepted by the Art-Union that year. At first, Art-Union officials deferred action (Committee of Management Minutes, November 1, 1847, 77; New-York Historical Society), but nine days later they agreed (Executive Committee Minutes, November 10, 1847; New-York Historical Society), to William Woodville's delight. Laconically entitled *Interior, with Figures* in the Art-Union catalogue, the painting was discussed in a two-paragraph review in the *New York Evening Express* (November 17, 1847), which mixed complimentary and puritanically critical observations, with emphasis on the latter. On the one hand the reporter extolled the work as "worth every dollar which it cost" and "full of merit," while on the other hand he lashed out, declaring, "To paint such subjects as this is to forget the true mission of art, and prostitute the pencil":

> If there was a single feature in the picture which merely intimated that the vices of gambling and intemperance never go unpunished, we should be satisfied; or if it contained a single laughable idea, we should not object, but remember it as a painted joke. We seldom look upon well-executed paintings of this class without a feeling of regret,—it pains us to see the hand of genius lending itself to perpetuate what is low and unworthy of a man. As we have frequently remarked, the true province of art is to instruct the mind and heart, and please the fancy. If this be true, how preposterous it is, therefore, for the artist to portray objects or incidents which are loathsome, not only in themselves but in their associations!

The writer found further fault with the perspective of the room, and with "the giant feet of the old man sitting at the table." His concluding remarks evidence an unfamiliarity with the ethnic diversity of contemporary Baltimore: "Another feature in the picture which we must censure is, the want of nationality in the subject, and its management. It is composed of a queer mixture of German and Yankee countenances, and at the first glance it would be difficult to say what sphere of life it was intended to illustrate."

Doubtless the critic's moral stance toward Woodville's painting was fueled by the mood of searching assessment that surrounded the display of Hiram Powers's *Greek Slave* in New York beginning in September 1847. In any case, Woodville soon modified his art while adhering to his predilection for genre. His *Game of Chess* (1850; unlocated), a decorous Tudor scene which was engraved by 1856 (see Cowdrey 1944, 14), and the aforementioned *Waiting for the Stage,* engraved by the American Art-Union in 1851, were comparatively upscale and reserved human dramas.
G. C.

Inscription At lower left, *R C W 1846 / Dusseldorf*

Provenance Thomas Foster, Utica, N.Y., 1847–49. William J. Hoppin, from 1849. The Hoppin family. Argosy Gallery, New York. Dexter M. Ferry, Jr., Grosse Pointe, Mich. Acquired in 1955.

Exhibitions Baltimore, Cariss's Store, May 1847. Philadelphia, Pennsylvania Academy of the Fine Arts Annual, 1847, no. 11½. Boston Athenaeum Annual, 1847 (?). New York, American Art-Union Annual, 1847, no. 180. New York, American Art-Union Annual, 1849, no. 1366. New York 1853, no. 87. Providence 1854, no. 170. New York, Artists' Fund Society Annual, 1860, no. 77. Philadelphia, Centennial Exposition, 1876, no. 81. Raleigh 1960, no. 15. Washington et al. 1967, no. 7. Buffalo et al. 1976, no. 18.

References William Woodville V, to Charles Folsom, July 22, 1847, and October 3, 1847, Library of the Boston Athenaeum. William Woodville V to American Art-Union, October 26, 1847, and November 14, 1847, New-York Historical Society. "Fine Arts. Playing at Cards in an Inn—By R. C. Woodville," *New York Evening Express,* November 27, 1847, 1. *Literary World,* September 27, 1851, 251. *Crayon* 1861. *Philadelphia Evening Bulletin,* June 24, 1876, 1–2. Cowdrey 1944. Payne 1955–56. Green 1966, 274. Grubar 1966, 52–59, 222–228. Grubar 1967. Johns 1991, 179.

Alexander Helwig Wyant

1836 Evans Creek, Ohio–New York 1892

A popular landscape painter after the Civil War, Alexander Wyant was known for his quiet views of eastern scenery. The son of an itinerant farmer and carpenter, Wyant grew up in Defiance, Ohio, where he was apprenticed to a harness maker and worked as a sign painter. He decided to become an artist following a visit to an art exhibition in Cincinnati, where he was struck by landscapes by George Inness (q.v.), who later became a friend. Little is known about his early artistic training. In 1859 Wyant visited New York to meet Inness; four years later he settled there. The landscapes that he began exhibiting revealed the influence of the Hudson River school in composition and in their crisp details.

In 1863 a second exhibition impressed him, that of paintings by Düsseldorf artists, whose linear, tightly painted style Wyant soon emulated. This time he traveled to Karlsruhe, Germany, to study with Hans Fredrik Gude, a Norwegian artist who had been trained in Düsseldorf. While there, Wyant continued to paint with realistic clarity, as in *Tennessee* (previously titled *Mohawk Valley;* 1866; Metropolitan Museum of Art, New York). He was drawn, however, to the landscapes of John Constable that he saw in England, and on his return to America his own work gradually became more atmospheric and broader in brushstroke.

Back in New York, he became an active member of the New York art community. His paintings were increasingly popular among New York collectors, such as Thomas B. Clarke and George A. Hearn, who each owned more than fourteen. In 1873, while on a government expedition to Arizona and New Mexico, Wyant suffered a stroke, after which he lost the use of his right arm. He developed his left hand for painting and drawing and as a result began painting smaller and more intimate scenes. He spent summers in the Adirondacks before buying a house in Arkville, New York, in 1889.

His late landscapes, such as *An October Day* (ca. 1888; Rhode Island School of Design, Museum of Art, Providence), owe much to the paintings of Inness and the French Barbizon painters. They are subdued in color, introspective and melancholy in mood, and free in technique. While he painted out-of-doors up to the last decade of his life, after that he worked mainly from memory in his studio, and simplified his compositions into large masses of forms.

S. M. S.

Bibliography Salt Lake City 1968. Olpin 1978.

94

Sunset in the Hills, New York, 1869

Oil on canvas

38.1 × 68 cm (15 × 26¾ in.)

Founders Society Purchase, Dexter M. Ferry, Jr., Fund (35.113)

Sunset in the Hills, New York was painted three years after Wyant's return from study in Europe and the year he was elected an academician of the National Academy of Design. During this transitional period, Wyant painted fewer topographically accurate landscapes in favor of more generalized views. In addition, his earlier tight and precise drawing gave way to broader, softer brushstrokes.

Wyant painted the same favorite views many times. A painting similar to this one, titled *Landscape: Sunset* (unlocated), was sold by M. Knoedler and Co., New York, in 1958 (letter from Melissa De Madeiros, librarian, M. Knoedler, and photograph in curatorial files, DIA). When the painting was acquired by Knoedler, it was titled *Potomac River at Hancock, Maryland;* it is unclear why the title was changed. Since, like many of his contemporaries, Wyant rarely titled his paintings with more than a slight indication of the site depicted, and since his works have frequently been retitled over their history, it is almost impossible to identify the specific location portrayed in these two landscapes. In 1919 John C. Van Dyke wrote, "Any one at all familiar with the Adirondacks or the Catskills will recognize in Wyant's landscapes not their topography, perhaps, but their characteristics" (Van Dyke 1919, 57).

The foreground foliage and cows of the undated *Landscape: Sunset* are depicted in greater detail than in the Detroit work, suggesting it was painted earlier. In *Sunset in the Hills* Wyant moved toward the indistinct forms and quiet tonality evident in his late work while retaining an interest in light effects that he had acquired during his study in Europe. E. P. Richardson described that interest as central to the painting: "The sureness with which Wyant records the characteristic light and color of central New York and the use of rose madder and violet tones in the shadows shows that he, like [Winslow] Homer, followed his own road toward an exploration of light, independent of the course of French impressionism" (Richardson 1944, 50).

S. M. S.

Inscription At lower right, *A. H. Wyant / 1869*

Provenance Thomson Galleries, Detroit, 1935, as *Along the Hudson.* Acquired in 1935.

Exhibitions Saginaw 1948. Columbus et al. 1953. Wilmington 1962, 20, 83, no. 90. Salt Lake City 1968, 6, 12, 18, no. 27.

References *Art Digest* 1936. C. Burroughs 1936, 88. Detroit 1944, 147, no. 801, as *Sunset in the Hills.* Richardson 1944, 50. *Index of Twentieth-Century Artists* 1970, 627, 633. Olpin 1978, 274–275, no. 38.

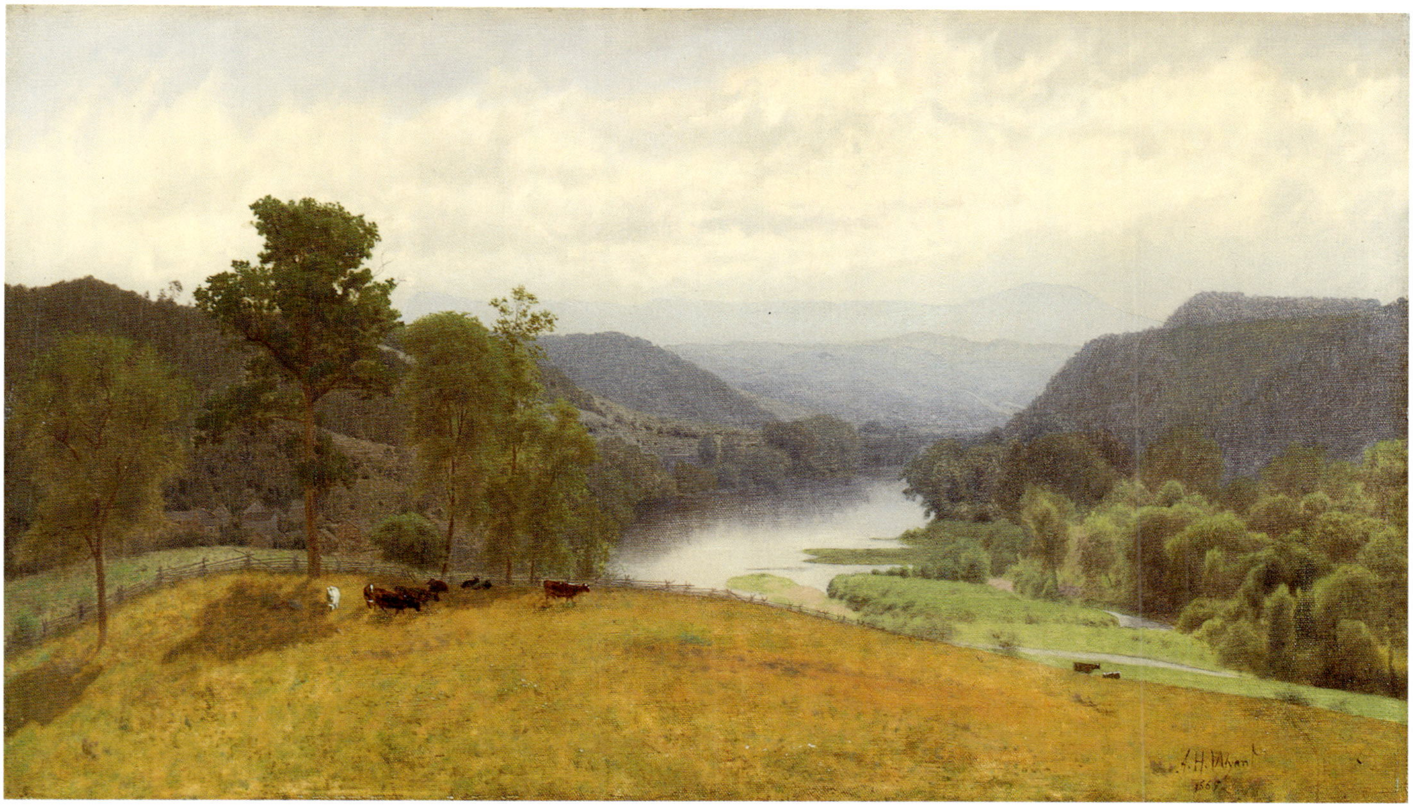

95

View of Whiteface Mountain, ca. 1883

Oil on canvas

43.2 × 36.8 cm (17 × 14½ in.)

Bequest of Mrs. Almeda H. Pickering (17.4)

WHITEFACE MOUNTAIN is near Wilmington, New York, in the Adirondack Mountains. Beginning in the 1870s, Wyant spent much time in the Adirondacks. He owned a house in Keene Valley until 1889, when he moved to Arkville, New York, near the Delaware River.

John C. Van Dyke wrote that while an occasional cottage, road, or bridge could be found in a landscape by Wyant, "I cannot remember any picture by him that shows man, woman, or child. . . . He believed that nature was sufficient unto itself and needed no association with mankind to make it beautiful or interesting" (Van Dyke 1919, 61). However, uncharacteristically, a small figure appears in this vertical view. As in many of his works, the time of day appears to be dusk, when the mountains in the distance turn pale blue and shadows fall across the quiet stream.

S. M. S.

Inscription At lower left, *A. H. Wyant*

Provenance Almeda H. Pickering, Los Angeles. Acquired in 1917.

Exhibition Regina 1971, 25, 44, no. 80.

References *BDMA* 1917. *BDMA* 1917a. Detroit 1930, no. 411. Detroit 1944, 147, no. 411. Salt Lake City 1968, 18. *Index of Twentieth-Century Artists* 1970, 627, 633. Olpin 1978, 336–337, no. 148.

96

Summer Landscape, ca. 1889

Oil on canvas

50.8 × 74.9 cm (20 × 29½ in.)

City of Detroit Purchase (29.259)

THE NEW YORK ART COLLECTOR George A. Hearn bought this painting after Wyant's death. In the catalogue of Hearn's collection published in 1908, this painting was titled *Summer Morning.* However, in the auction catalogue of the collection in 1918, it appeared as *Summer Landscape* and has retained that title.

Wyant included a season in the title of many of his paintings; two others by Wyant in the Hearn collection were titled *Summer* and *Summer Landscape.* He also titled works with reference to the time of day or weather conditions depicted, or

Sunset in the Hills

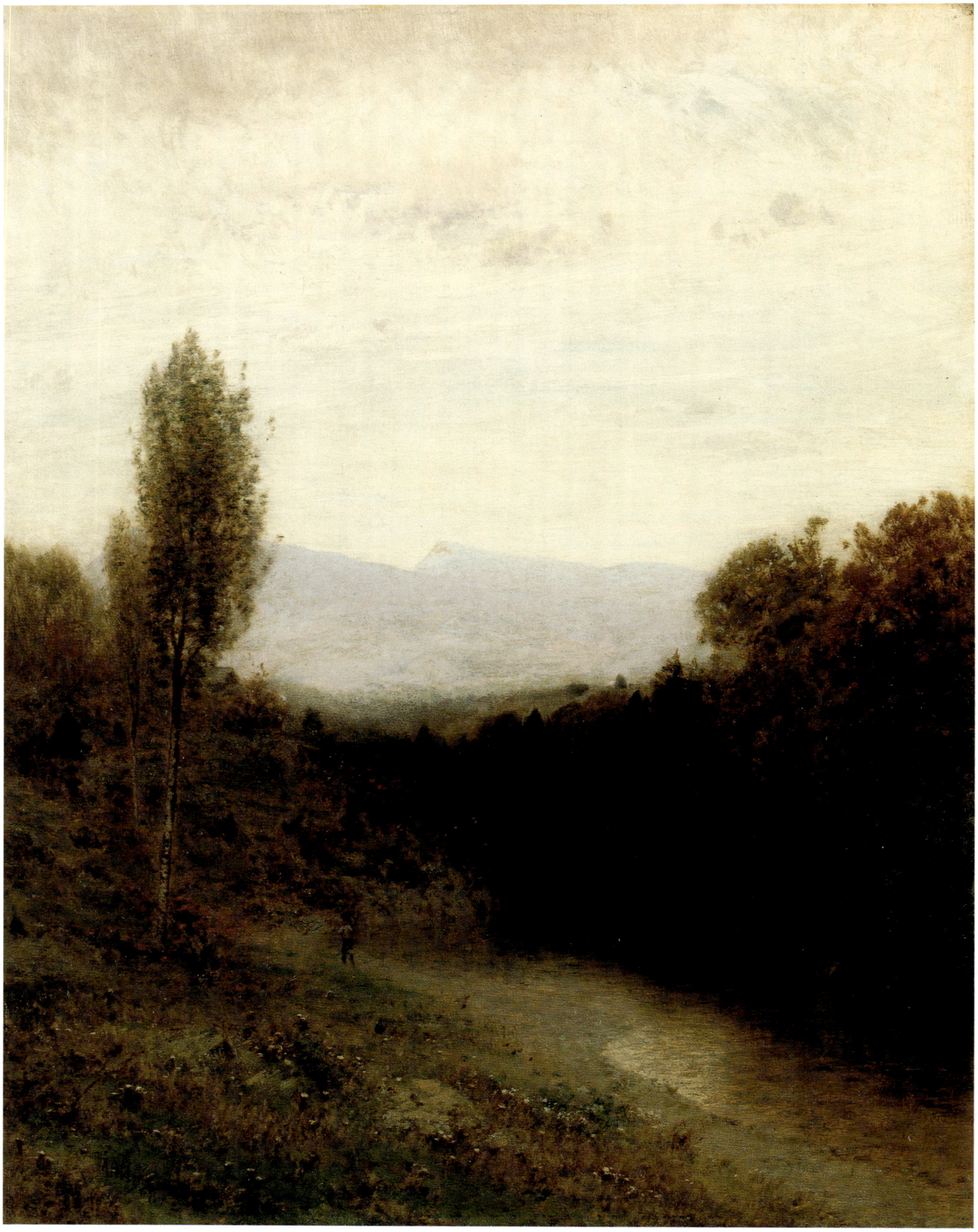

View of Whiteface Mountain

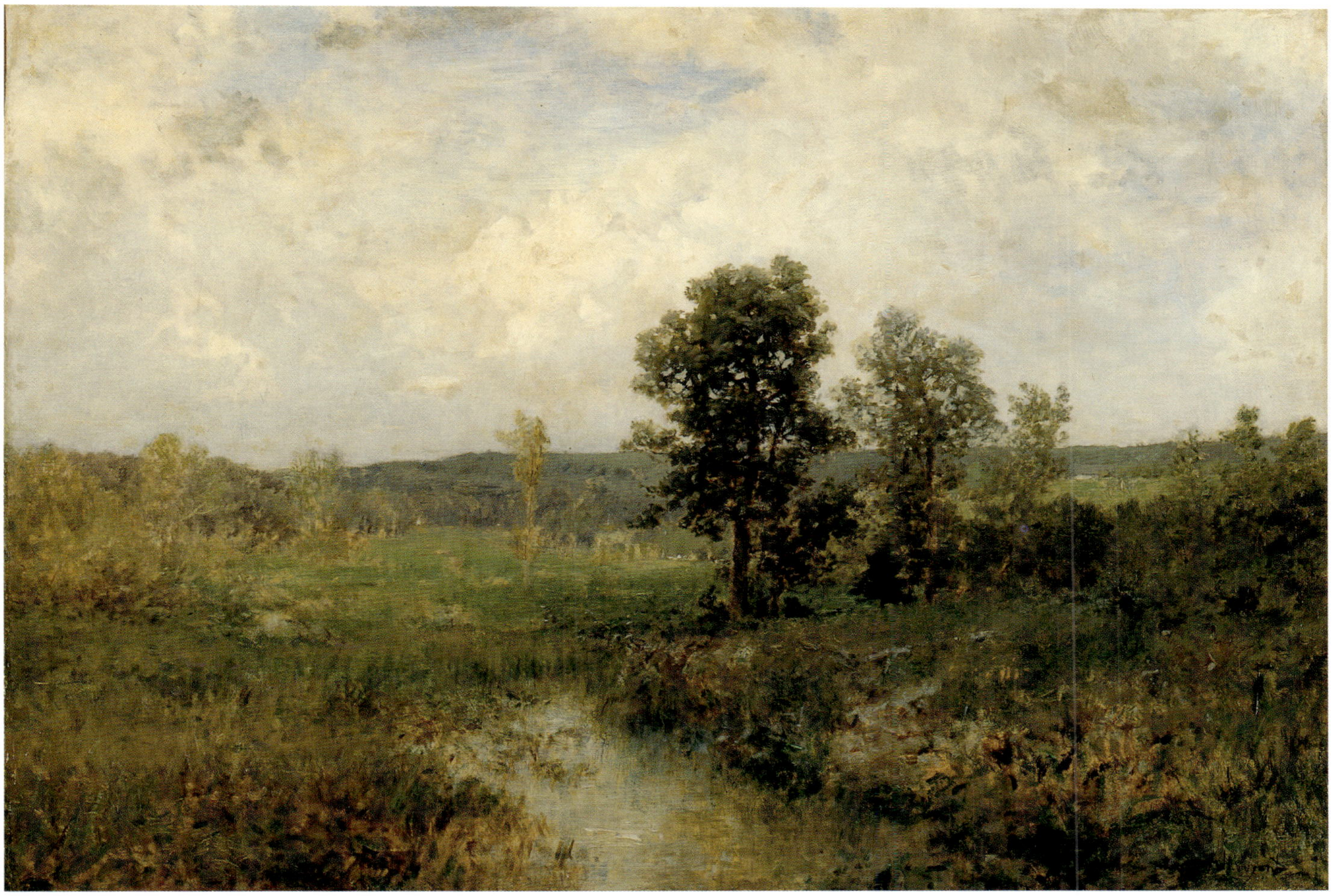

with a general rather than specific indication of place, such as the Catskills or the Adirondacks.

Summer Landscape is described in the Hearn sale catalogue: "Green pastures, on the left, and a slope with trees, on the right, border a little stream which winds its way into the foreground. In the distance appear the edge of a wood, at the left, and a line of hills. The fine atmospheric sky is composed of masses of gray and white clouds with some spaces of blue" (Hearn 1908, no. 115). The composition and style of the painting are characteristic of Wyant's work in the 1880s, revealing the influence of Barbizon landscapes. As in his *Landscape in the Adirondacks* (ca. 1885–86; Metropolitan Museum of Art, New York), short brushstrokes define the foreground foliage and the water in the center. A dark clump of trees interrupts the horizon, which bisects the painting. The heat, haze, and stillness of a summer day are evoked.
S. M. S.

Inscription At lower right, *A. H. Wyant*

Provenance Ortgies and Co., New York, 1894. George A. Hearn, New York; his sale, American Art Association, New York, February 25–March 4, 1918, no. 115. Reinhardt Galleries, New York, 1919. Acquired in 1929.

Exhibitions Saginaw 1948. Columbus et al. 1953, no. 42. Wilmington 1962, no. 90. Big Rapids 1964. Salt Lake City 1968, 18, no. 27.

References Hearn 1908, 181, no. 228, as *Summer Morning*. Brewster 1919, 198. Detroit 1930, no. 412. C. Burroughs 1936, 88–89. Detroit 1944, 147, no. 412. *Index of Twentieth-Century Artists* 1970, 627, 633. Olpin 1978, 380, no. 217.

Summer Landscape

Appendix

UNKNOWN ARTIST (FORMERLY ATTRIBUTED TO RALPH BLAKELOCK)

1A

Indian Encampment

Oil on canvas

49.5 × 80.6 cm (19½ × 31¾ in.)

Gift of Mrs. Helen L. De Roy (72.840)

THE THEMES IDENTIFIED with Blakelock that are most frequently imitated are the Indian encampments and the moonlight landscapes. Of the two, the encampments are the more complicated in that they contain a wider range of specific elements within the setting of a wooded landscape, such as tepees, sitting or standing figures, horses, canoes, campfires, and frequently the peculiar outline of a travois. These elements are usually used with discretion as accents in the middle ground of the picture. They are embedded in the sheltered areas of darkness under the trees, only dimly or partially seen. The human presence is fused with the natural envelope of sky and trees, of light and dark. When examined closely, the specific forms are delineated with a minimal touch of the brush, mere dabs of color placed with an uncanny skill to establish the three-dimensional form in the space it occupies.

In this example, which contains an excess of all the requisite parts, there is none of the richness of pigment or the subtlety of color one expects. The handling is thin and cursory. The trees are conspicuously uniform in shape. The spatial recession is abrupt and emphatic and the color of the sky is harsh and devoid of any suggestion of atmosphere.

The presence of a full-length female figure, revealed by X radiograph, on the verso of this canvas does not add any stylistic data that would suggest the work of Blakelock, whose figure subjects are rare and of an entirely different character.

N. G.

Inscription At lower left, *R. A. Blakelock*

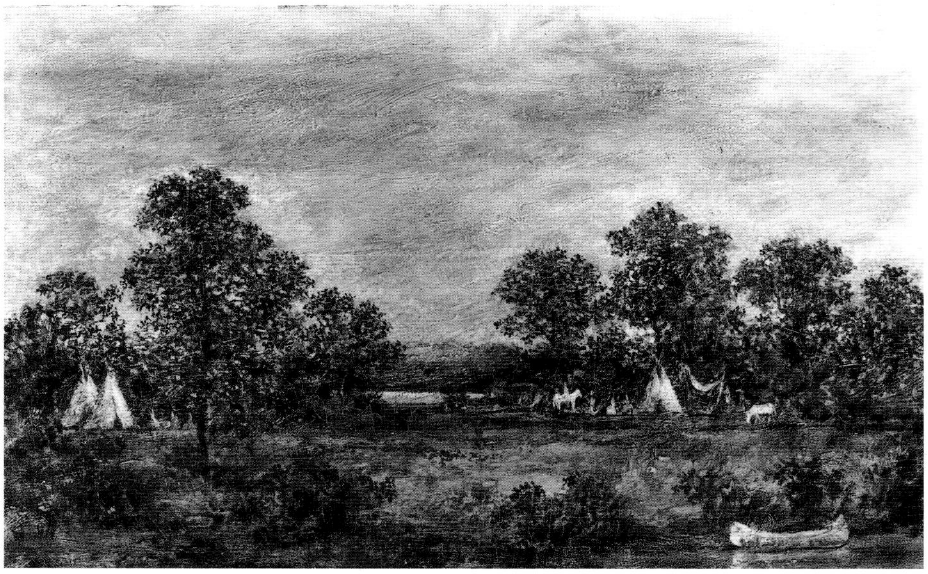

Indian Encampment

Provenance Mrs. Helen L. DeRoy, Detroit. Acquired in 1972.

Reference Nebraska Blakelock Inv. no. NB1–578-IV.

UNKNOWN ARTIST (FORMERLY ATTRIBUTED TO RALPH BLAKELOCK)

2A

Landscape

Oil on canvas

30.8 × 36.2 cm (12⅛ × 14¼ in.)

Gift of Raymond C. Smith (67.271)

PAINTINGS OF WOODED LANDSCAPES, not at all uncommon in Blakelock's work, show characteristics that are consonant with his work as a whole. First of all, their spatial structure is marked by a gradual recession into the depths of the image, frequently with a patch of bright sky in the distance. The enframing trees and shrubs are clearly discernible in their outline and texture. In many of these paintings the focus of the composition is a human figure, usually moving away from the observer. The figure is frequently that of a woman, an Indian, or sometimes an animal.

In the present example the spatial structure is vague and undefined. The trees and the foreground are rendered with loose and unrelated touches of pigment over a generalized dark ground. The tree trunks are heavily painted without any of the linear highlighting that is usually present. The white cloud that all but fills the sky is an opaque mass that, in effect, overhangs the entire image. It is notable but, surprisingly, not noticeable that there is a stag standing in the middle ground. Ordinarily such a form would be emphasized, dark against light or the reverse. Although it is rendered with considerably more skill than is seen in the rest of the picture, this actual center of interest is all but invisible.

It would seem that this painting is more probably a demonstration of Blakelock's influence on an aspiring admirer rather than an attempt to create an image that would pass muster as the real thing. The presence of a not very convincing signature in the lower left corner suggests the further possibility that the hand that signed the painting was not the hand that painted it.

N. G.

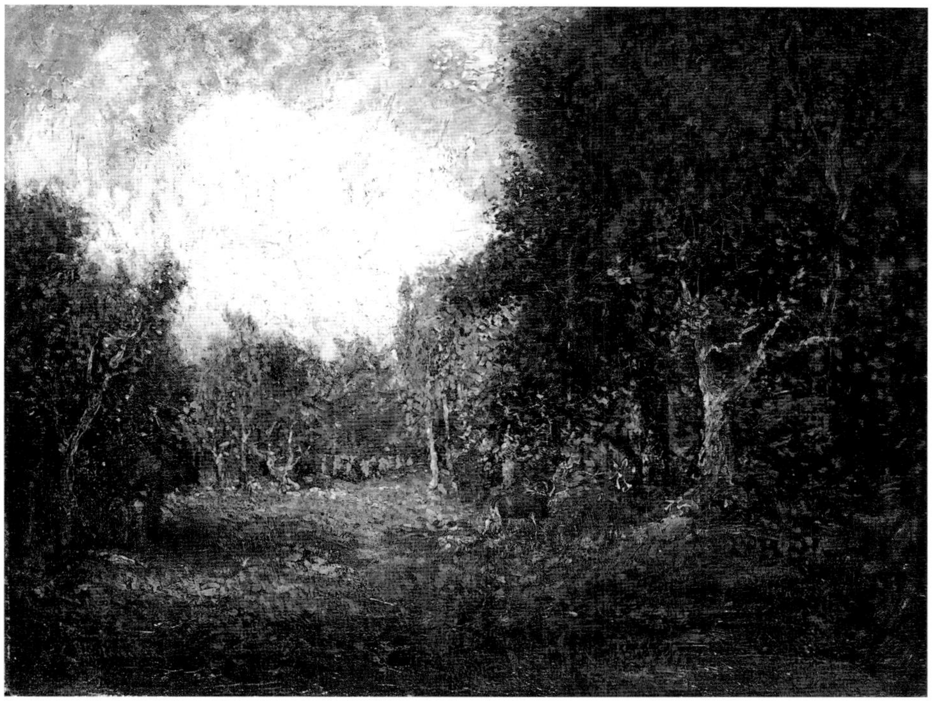

Landscape

Inscription At lower left, *R. A. Blakelock*

Provenance Conrad H. Smith, Grosse Pointe Farms, Mich. By descent, Raymond Smith, Grosse Pointe Farms, Mich. Acquired in 1967.

Exhibition Minneapolis 1973, no. 159.

Reference Nebraska Blakelock Inv. no. NB1–579-IV.

UNKNOWN ARTIST AFTER THOMAS EAKINS

3A

Arthur B. Frost, ca. 1886

Oil on canvas
68 × 55.9 cm ($26\frac{3}{4}$ × 22 in.)
Gift of Dexter M. Ferry, Jr. (37.68)

THE BOOK ILLUSTRATOR Arthur Burdett Frost (1851–1928) was a student of Thomas Eakins at the Philadelphia Sketch Club in 1874–76 and at the Pennsylvania Academy of the Fine Arts, where he was enrolled after spending a year in London (Siegl 1978, 113–114). By this time he was working as an illustrator for *Harper's Weekly.* When Frost married Emily Louise Phillips in October 1883 and moved to Long Island, he gave up the studio that he had rented at 1330 Chestnut Street. Eakins used this studio until the turn of the century (Siegl 1978, 114; Goodrich 1982, 1:200, 332 n. 5). Frost became a very successful illustrator of more than ninety books, including Joel Chandler Harris's *Uncle Remus* stories (Siegl 1978, 114) and works by Theodore Roosevelt and Mark Twain. He was also well known for *Shooting Pictures,* a portfolio of lithographs of sporting scenes published by Charles Scribner's Sons (New York, 1895).

This portrait is a copy of Thomas Eakins's portrait of Frost in the Philadelphia Museum of Art. The original shows Frost, with his reddish beard and mustache and brown hair, against a dark background, his face almost in shadow. Frost's dark coat is buttoned, the collar folded open. The painting measures $27\frac{7}{16}$ by $21\frac{15}{16}$ inches, is signed *T. E.* on the reverse, and bears a label written by Mrs. Eakins, giving the date of the portrait as about 1884 (Siegl 1978, 114). Eakins recorded a payment of $150 from Frost's wife for a portrait of Frost on July 19, 1887: "to Frost's portrait 150—Emily Frosts check for portrait of husband painted in 1886" (Eakins 1883–88, 119). Although this is generally described as the payment for the so-called sketch of Frost also at Detroit (Hendricks 1974, 162; Siegl 1978, 114; Goodrich 1982, 2:166), it is undoubtedly for the portrait at the Philadelphia Museum, which Mrs. Eakins insisted was the only one that her husband painted of Frost. (For the so-called sketch, which is here identified as a copy, see cat. no. 4A.)

The Detroit painting is identical in composition and very similar in size and coloring to the original, but it has a generally lighter tonality and a notably lighter background. It is flatter in technique, with little impasto, and is more precisely painted, the brushstrokes well blended. X radiography reveals no changes. In 1934, when Mrs. Eakins and Charles Bregler saw it in a Chestnut Street, Philadelphia, bookstore, in a display advertising Henry Lanier's biography of Frost, they protested that it was not by Eakins. Henri Marceau of the Philadelphia Museum of Art saw the painting and agreed. When it was acquired three years later by the Detroit Institute of Arts, considerable debate ensued over its authorship. Although it is now accepted as a copy, an attribution is difficult. The provenance in the Frost family suggests that it is the work of one of the four members of that family, all of whom were painters. In 1977 the museum reattributed it to A. B. Frost's younger son John Frost (1890–1936; see Hendricks 1974, 163), probably based on earlier suggestions by others, including George Barker of Pacific Palisades,

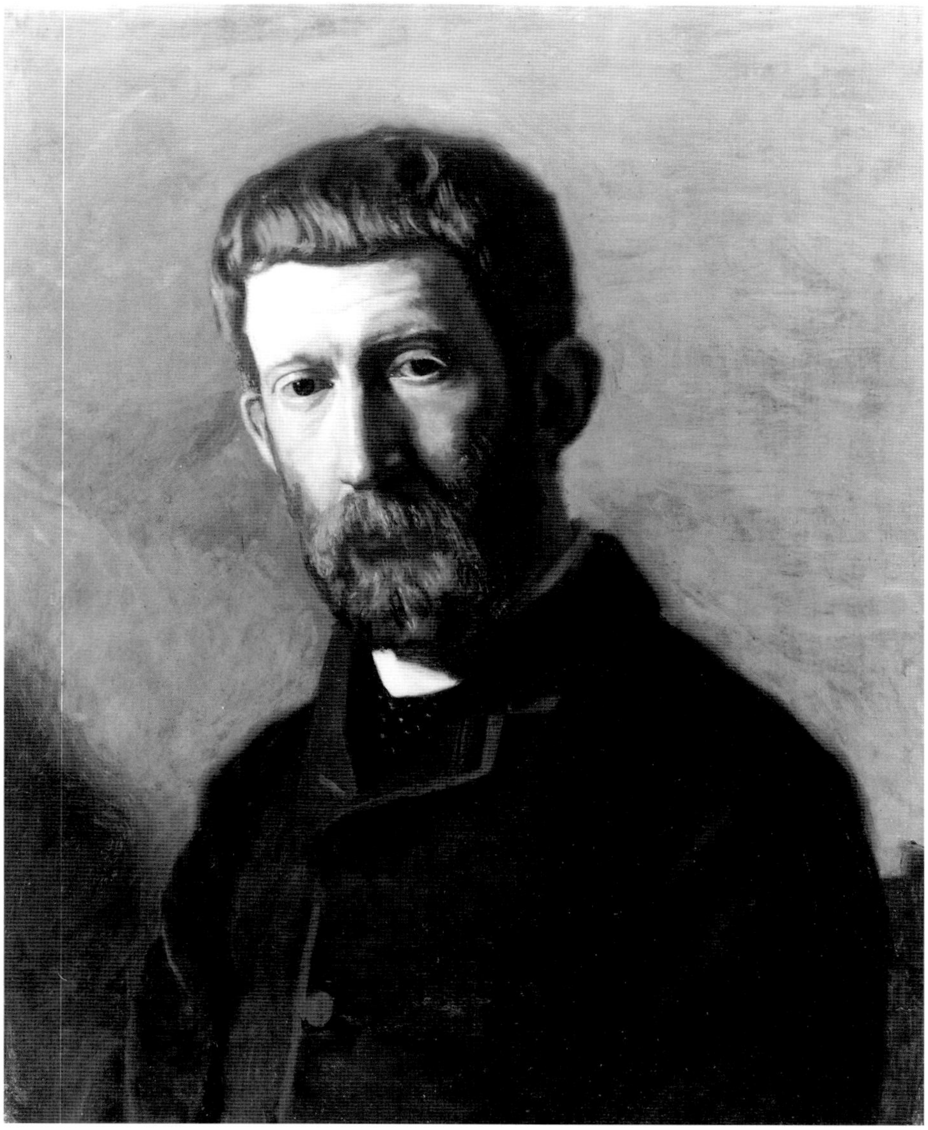

Arthur B. Frost (3A)

California, who wrote in 1941 that he remembered Frost's saying that one of his sons had made a copy of Eakins's portrait (correspondence, curatorial files, DIA). Barker was a student of Eakins's pupil J. Laurie Wallace, who also remembered the portrait and thought it was by John Frost (correspondence, curatorial files, DIA). However, a letter from Frost to his father's friend Augustus S. Daggy indicates that this is not possible. He wrote Daggy on September 29, 1934, after both of his parents had died, asking him to document the "Aikins [*sic*] portrait of Dad . . . to substantiate its authenticity, in case something may happen to me" (Reed 1993, 38). He would not have written this if he had painted the portrait himself.

The copy could be the work of A. B. Frost's wife, Emily (1851–1929), who with her husband was a student of Eakins's at the Pennsylvania Academy. It is similar in technique to her portrait of Frost, also a head and shoulders (Lanier 1933, ill. opp. 25). Perhaps Mrs. Frost made the copy before returning the original to Eakins for some correction or adjustment. She would not have been the first of Eakins's friends to return a portrait; Horatio Wood did the same at about this time (see cat. no. 24).

E. G. M.

Provenance The A. B. Frost family. Sold from the collection of Henry Wysham Lanier at the American Art Association, Anderson Galleries, New York, February 11, 1937, lot 101. Purchased by Dr. Karl Lilienfeld, Lilienfeld Galleries, New York, for the Detroit Institute of Arts. Acquired in 1937.

Exhibitions Detroit 1937, no. 11. Grand Rapids 1958, n.p. Montclair 1983, no. 43, as attributed to John Frost.

References Lanier 1933, 29. Richardson 1937, 131–134. Hendricks 1974, 162–163. Siegl 1978, 114. Goodrich 1982, 2:166. Reed 1993, 34–38.

UNKNOWN ARTIST AFTER THOMAS EAKINS

4A

Arthur B. Frost, ca. 1886

Oil on canvas
63.5 × 43.2 cm (25 × 17 in.)
Gift of Dexter M. Ferry, Jr. (37.69)

THIS PAINTING WAS ACQUIRED as the sketch for a portrait of Frost (cat. no. 3A) believed at the time to be by Eakins. The painting is in a thick impasto applied with quick, broad strokes. The right side of Frost's face is in dark shadow, while the left is strongly lighted. There is a deep red-brown shadow to the right of his nose, and a gray triangle for the tie. Frost's hair is light to medium brown. The background is a yellow-khaki brown. This painting instead is a copy of Eakins's portrait of Frost (Philadelphia Museum of Art). A comparison shows that the

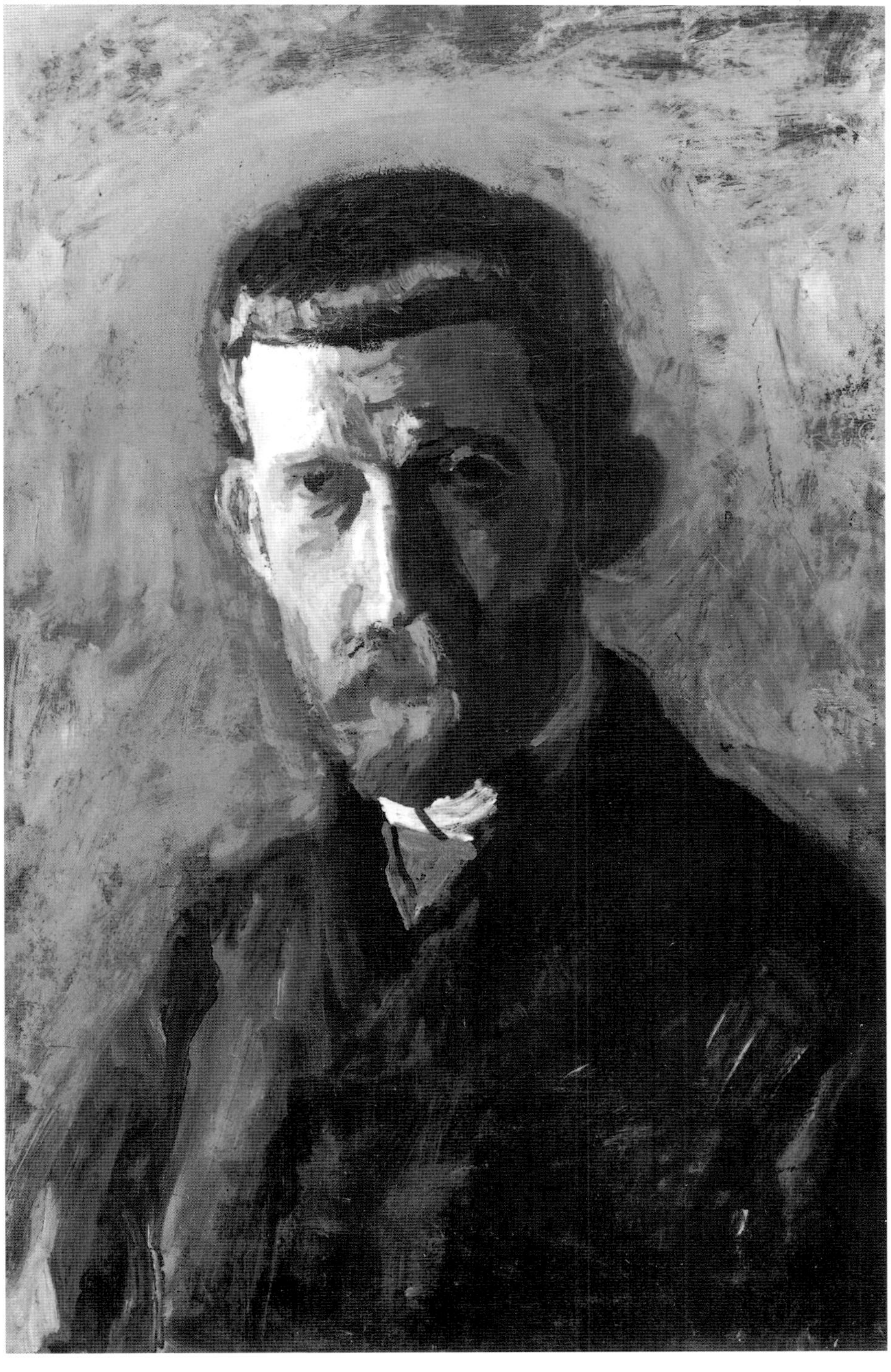

Arthur B. Frost (4A)

sketch is a study of darks and lights painted in reference to the details of the Philadelphia painting. The ears are awkwardly positioned, the shadows of the nose askew in relationship to the mustache. In addition, underneath, in an inverted position, is an oil study of a seated man and woman, engaged in conversation, which can be identified as a study for Susan Macdowell Eakins's prize-winning painting *The Old Clock on the Stairs,* now unlocated. The painting is known from Frederick Gutekunst's phototype (Charles Bregler's Thomas Eakins Collection, Pennsylvania Academy of the Fine Arts, Philadelphia). The painting was commissioned by Fairman Rogers and exhibited at the Pennsylvania Academy in 1882 (Foster and Leibold 1989, 261, fig. 41). The presence of the figures underneath may explain the light background of the copy of Frost's portrait; the thicker light paint may have been needed to cover the two figures.

Since an artist rarely covers the work of another, the copy may be by Susan Eakins, who made a number of copies on commission in the 1880s. At the same time, the painting is similar in technique to a portrait of Frost painted in January 1884 by his close friend Augustus S. Daggy (Reed 1967, frontispiece).

E. G. M.

Provenance The A. B. Frost family. Sold from the collection of Henry Wysham Lanier, American Art Association, Anderson Galleries, New York, February 11, 1937, lot 102. Purchased by Dr. Karl Lilienfeld, Lilienfeld Galleries, New York, for the Detroit Institute of Arts. Acquired in 1937.

Exhibitions Detroit 1937, no. 10. Montclair 1983, no. 56.

References Richardson 1937. Hendricks 1974, 162–163. Goodrich 1982, 2:166. Reed 1993, 34–38.

UNKNOWN ARTIST (FORMERLY ATTRIBUTED TO THOMAS EAKINS)

5A

Reclining Nude, late nineteenth century

Oil on canvas

30.8 × 53.3 cm (12⅛ × 21 in.)

Bequest of Robert H. Tannahill (70.147)

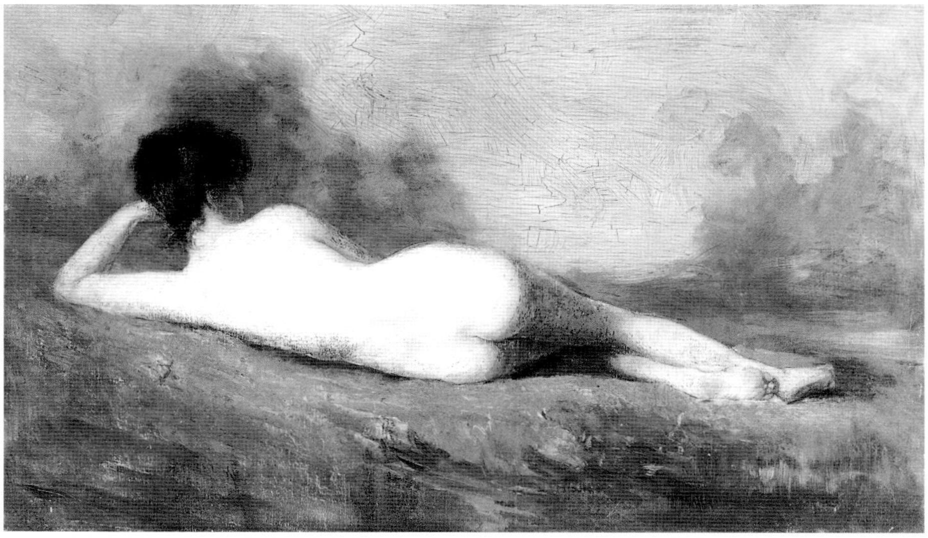

Reclining Nude

THIS PAINTING WAS ACQUIRED with an attribution to Thomas Eakins that has never been accepted by scholars. The delicate, somewhat timid handling and the relationship of the figure to the landscape are not at all typical of his figure studies, which focus on highlighting and shadow, and on the figure and not its setting (see, for example, *Figure Study: Nude Woman, Seated, with Arms Raised,* oil on cardboard, ca. 1875–85; Pennsylvania Academy of the Fine Arts, Philadelphia, Charles Bregler's Thomas Eakins Collection). The painting is not listed in catalogues or studies of Eakins's work, and the signature is not typical. However, the painting is similar to nudes of an Arcadian theme that Eakins and his students painted in the early and mid-1880s. These include Eakins's *Arcadian* (ca. 1883; Spanierman Gallery and Alexander Gallery, New York) and its study (Hirshhorn Museum and Sculpture Garden, Washington, D.C.; for ills., see Hendricks 1974, 154, fig. 131, and 321, no. 62). The type and pose of the figure are similar to a photograph attributed to Eakins (ca. 1883; Metropolitan Museum of Art, New York; see Hendricks 1974, 212, fig. 224).

The subject and manner of the painting suggest interesting associations with Eakins's pupil Susan Macdowell (1851–1938), who became the artist's wife in 1884. The model is similar to the one that Macdowell is sketching in Alice Barker's *Female Life Class* at the Pennsylvania Academy (1879; Pennsylvania Academy of the Fine Arts; see Hendricks 1974, 126, fig. 102). She is also similar to two photographs of Mrs. Eakins that are in Charles Bregler's Thomas Eakins Collection at the Pennsylvania Academy of the Fine Arts. One, an albumen print, shows Mrs. Eakins in almost the same pose. Perhaps Susan Eakins was the painter of the Detroit nude. According to Jeannette Toohey, who has closely studied the material in the Bregler Collection at the Pennsylvania Academy, the *Nude* resembles some figure studies that Susan Eakins painted in the 1930s, which in turn resemble her work of the 1880s.

Whatever the attribution, the painting is not considered the work of Thomas Eakins.

E. G. M.

Inscription At lower right, in red, *EAKINS*

Provenance Acquired by the donor from the dealer J. P. Hartert, New York, who said it was from the collection of Mrs. J. Butler of New York and Cottekill, Ulster County, N.Y., whose father was a well-known shoe manufacturer in Philadelphia and purchased the painting from Eakins in 1904; this has not been confirmed.

UNKNOWN ARTIST (FORMERLY ATTRIBUTED TO HOMER DODGE MARTIN)

6A

Autumn Landscape, ca. 1866

Oil on canvas

15.9 × 25.4 cm (6½ × 10 in.)

Gift of the Archives of American Art (57.109)

ALMOST IMMEDIATELY after his death in 1897, Martin's landscapes soared in value. The sudden demand for the limited supply of his art was glaringly at odds with his narrow reputation during his lifetime. It was a market fabrication, trumped up to vindicate the artist and his patrons and to enrich dealers. Martin's case was analogous to Ralph A. Blakelock's and typical of the avaricious age, as speculators reaped huge profits trading his paintings, while Elizabeth Martin and her two sons received little of the proceeds. She could barely bring herself to utter the name of Thomas B. Clarke, who had been Martin's dealer in fair weather but had dumped him in 1896. With the artist gone, Clarke sold his paintings for fabulous sums; the most flagrant exchange occurred in 1899,

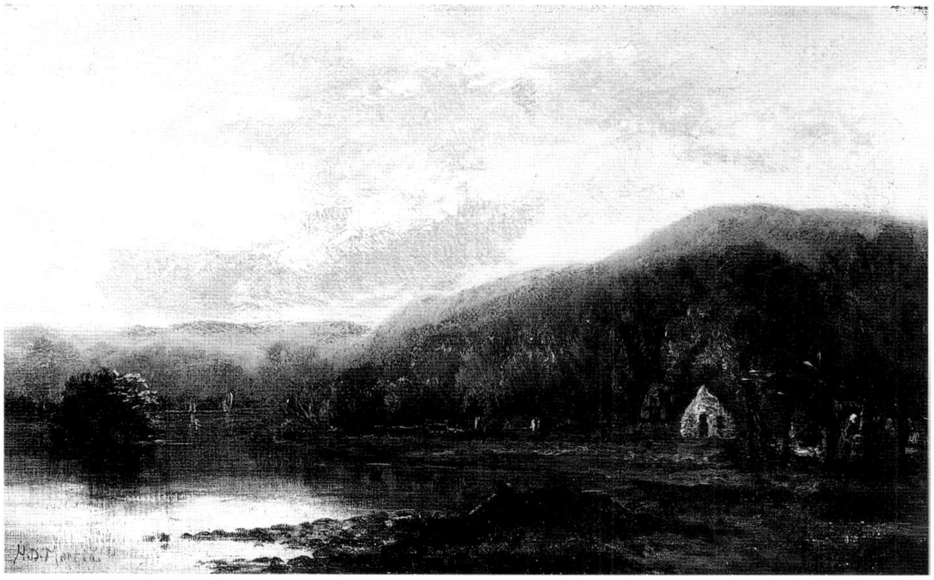

Autumn Landscape

when *Adirondack Scenery* (1895; private collection), which Clarke had bought for an "extremely small" amount, fetched $5,500 at auction (Mandel 1973a, 5). Similarly, the collector William T. Evans bought *Westchester Hills* (ca. 1887; private collection) for $1,000 in 1899 and sold it within a year for $4,750 (Mandel 1973a, 3–4).

The market success of Martin following his death engendered fakes. "His pictures soon received the flattery of imitation," Frank Jewett Mather wryly observed. "From 1903 or so there was a steady production of rather specious false Martins which found a ready sale at prices to which he himself had never aspired. At a club exhibition given in honor of his memory about this time, a third of the entries were spurious" (Mather 1912, 62). The "scandal of the studios" was "ventilated" in 1908, when Evans sued the art dealer William Clausen for selling forged Martins, Innesses, and Wyants *(New York Sun,* May 15, 1908).

Autumn Landscape is a convincing forgery in many respects. Martin used small canvases for sketches, he was known for such broad handling and generalization of forms in the landscape, and he treated the subject of a lakeside encampment. This particular subject, however, was not in his repertoire, as two sailboats skirt the far shore and a woman and children—so ill-rendered that they are practically illegible—apparently prepare a meal under a crude lean-to structure that shelters a large pot suspended over a fire. Thomas Cole had established this kind of cabin-in-the-wilderness formula in, for example, his *Home in the Woods* (1847; Reynolda House, Winston-Salem, N.C.). The brushwork and color scheme lack Martin's characteristic finesse and complexity, and, finally, the signature at lower left is not in his hand. Even by 1901 forgeries were so numerous that Elizabeth Martin assisted the dealer William Macbeth in authenticating paintings: "His customary signature, as of course you know, was H. D. Martin and he liked to make it in a tint very close to that of the part of the picture on which he painted it" (Mandel 1973, 226). That much the artist of *Autumn Landscape* knew, but Martin initialed most of his sketches and signed most of his paintings at lower right, where, in this instance, a partially effaced inscription has emerged owing to oxidation over time. The ruse served its purpose: the painting was owned by no less an authority than the art patron and editor Frederic Fairchild Sherman, who underwrote publication of Mather's 1912 biography of Homer Martin.

W. T. O.

Inscriptions At lower left, *H. D. Martin;* at lower right, *E Ch [indecipherable]er / 66*

Provenance Howard W. Lipman. Frederic Fairchild Sherman. Archives of American Art. Acquired in 1957.

Exhibition Regina 1971.

UNKNOWN ARTIST (FORMERLY ATTRIBUTED TO ALBERT PINKHAM RYDER)

7A

Early Morning

Oil on panel
28.3 × 40.3 cm (11⅛ × 15⅞ in.)
Gift of Dexter M. Ferry, Jr. (34.9)

Early Morning is paradigmatic of the forgeries inspired by Albert Pinkham Ryder's well-known marine paintings. Ryder's success at the 1913 Armory Show had sealed his reputation as an important "old master in the modern movement" (Charles Caffin, *New York American,* March 10, 1913). The few paintings he had produced during his lifetime could not meet market demands after his death in 1917, and as his style was superficially easy to imitate, he became one of the most widely forged painters. Forgers could simulate Ryder's simple abstract patterning, limited palette, small size, and dark varnished surfaces. Less easy to replicate were the unusual color effects and elemental compositions. In *Early Morning* the forger has rendered several elements that are staples in Ryder's marine paintings: the dark silhouette of a lone boat slanting upward into cresting waves, a full moon overhead, and abstract cloud patterns serving as a backdrop.

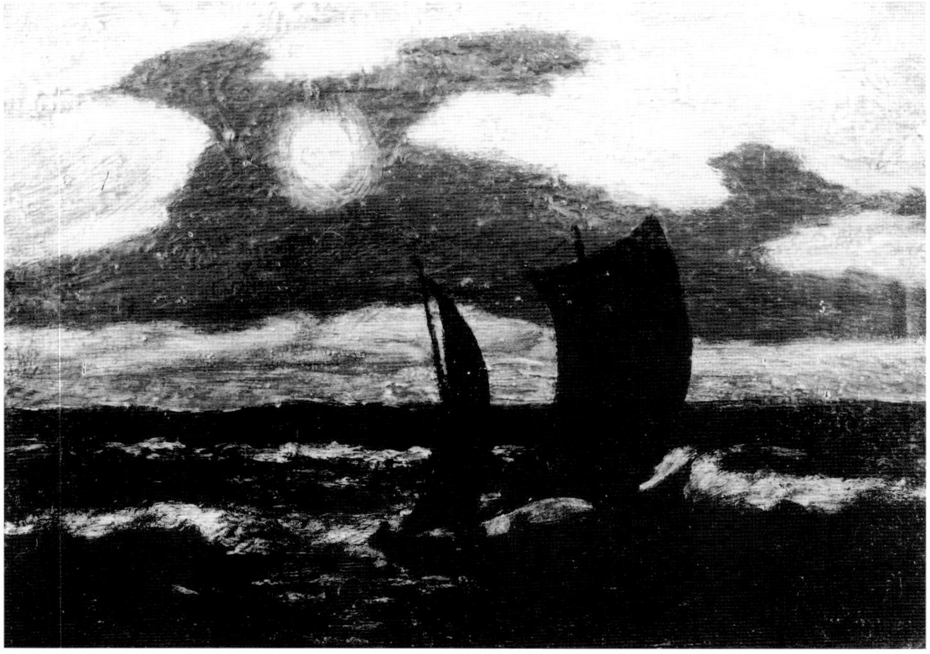

Early Morning

The composition of *Early Morning* lacks the dynamic tension and interplay between moon and ship that are indicative of Ryder's greatest marines. In his *Toilers of the Sea* (Metropolitan Museum of Art, New York) the boat surges in the direction of the moon, as if drawn toward a symbolic beacon of hope. The gently curving boat in *With Sloping Mast and Dipping Prow* (National Museum of American Art, Washington, D.C.) moves in tandem with a crashing wave that once arched inward on the left, sensed to visually encircle the central moon. Such compositional dialogue between moon and boat is comparatively absent in *Early Morning*.

Lloyd Goodrich, the first scholar systematically to sort authentic Ryder paintings from forged ones, commented that *Early Morning*'s "relatively weak, flat forms of the clouds . . . show none of Ryder's observation of the effect of moonlight on clouds." The razor-sharp contours of the boat, thinly painted on top of the sky, were also noted as uncharacteristic of Ryder's hand (correspondence, curatorial files, DIA).

Goodrich, working with the Brooklyn Museum's conservator Sheldon Keck, discovered that the X radiographs of authentic Ryders differ significantly from those of forgeries. Because Ryder built his works with multiple, thick layers of paint, the image is visible on the X radiograph, with strong highlights showing white on the film. With the forgeries, on the other hand, the image typically cannot be distinguished on the film as the paint layers are relatively thin. Such is the case with the X radiograph of *Early Morning*, which, according to Goodrich, reveals nothing of the surface image.

The film does show, however, "a tree trunk with branches, running up the long way of the picture." This indicates that the forger painted the marine on top of an already painted panel. This was not uncommon practice for artists concerned with economy, and Ryder himself is known to have worked on used canvases. Forgers, however, had an additional incentive for painting on used panels or canvases, for the exposed backs of these older supports serve to convince buyers of the authenticity of the work.

Other elaborate documentation was often forged to persuade purchasers concerned about authenticity. The back of *Early Morning* bears the stamp, *Cottier & Company, New York & London 88.* Alfred Henri Peiffer had purportedly purchased the work directly from Cottier, a life-long dealer and supporter of Ryder's art. However, several other forgeries bear comparable stamps, and Peiffer was a notorious collector of fakes.

Likewise, the signature, *A. P. Ryder,* in the lower right of *Early Morning,* cannot be used as proof of authenticity. Ryder stated in 1915, "I rarely sign my pictures, having always felt that they spoke for themselves" (Ryder to Alexander Morten, November 1915, AAA).

Once spurious pictures began to appear on the market, friends had him sign his works, but forged signatures on forged works proliferated. In the final analysis, only those paintings that have a sound provenance and that pass the tests of connoisseurship and laboratory analysis can be considered true works by Ryder.

L. C. AND E. B.

Inscription At lower right, *A. P. RYDER;* on the back the stamp, *Cottier & Co., New York & London 88.*

Provenance Alfred Henri Peiffer. Acquired in 1934.

Exhibition East Lansing 1966.

Reference C. Burroughs 1934, 9, ill.

UNKNOWN ARTIST (FORMERLY ATTRIBUTED TO ALBERT PINKHAM RYDER)

8A

Summer Night, Moonlight

Oil on canvas
35.6 × 50.8 cm (14 × 20 in.)
City Purchase (25.22)

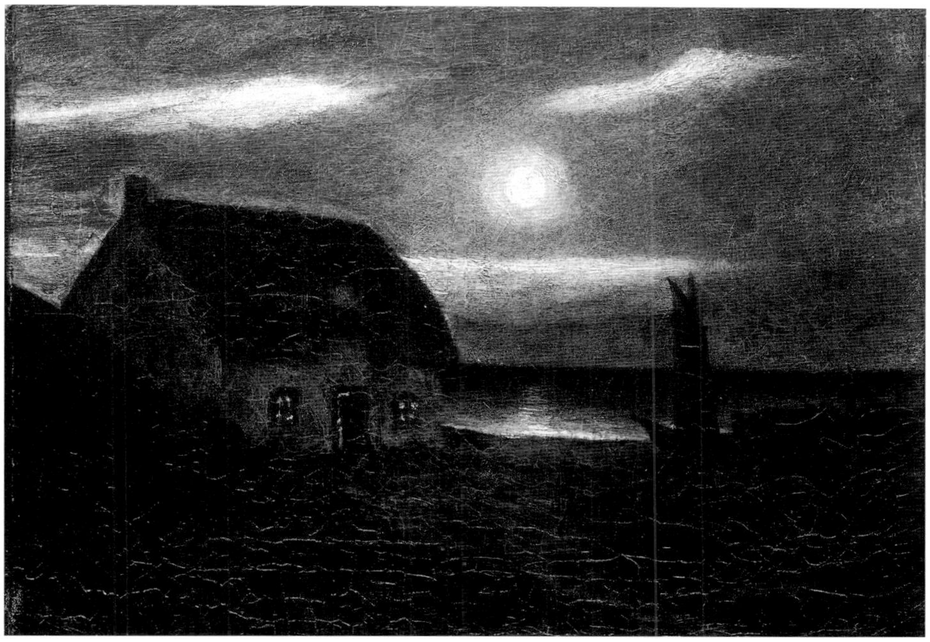

Summer Night, Moonlight

Summer Night, Moonlight, formerly attributed to Albert Pinkham Ryder, is a pastiche of Ryder's marine and farmyard themes. This forgery portrays a thatch-roofed cottage, vaguely reminiscent of Ryder's building in *The Barnyard* (Munson-Williams-Proctor Institute, Utica, N.Y.), and a sailboat moored beyond a rail fence. In the background, a full moon highlights thin cloud forms and calm waters below. The forger has attempted to combine the sentimental, pastoral qualities of Ryder's earlier work with the abstract, romantic elements of his later marine paintings. As a result, the work lacks the compositional unity that is standard in Ryder's paintings.

Lloyd Goodrich identified this work as a forgery based on stylistic analysis amid dubious provenance. He has noted the "inept design, the lack of Ryder's characteristic rhythmic pattern, the undistinguished color and the sentimentality of the lighted windows" as atypical of Ryder's style. The "stiff brushwork" and lack of paint build-up and glazes also suggest a hand other than Ryder's (correspondence, curatorial files, DIA). The X radiograph records the lead white areas in the moon, clouds, and water highlights, yet it lacks the density of image indicative of X radiographs of authentic Ryder works.

The first record of this painting is a photograph dated by Frederic Fairchild Sherman, *1st May 1924*. Sherman claimed to have purchased the work in 1923, six years after Ryder's death, from an unnamed "private source in New York City" (correspondence, curatorial files, DIA). He sold the painting to the Detroit Institute of Arts in 1925.

Sherman, an author and cofounder of the journal *Art in America,* wrote the first book-length study of Ryder's art in 1920. Relying on the opinions of three artists, Alexander Shilling, Albert Groll, and Elliott Daingerfield, Sherman created a list of 130 authentic Ryder paintings. No evidence, other than these artists' own accounts, proves that they were close to Ryder, and Sherman did not solicit the opinions of other artists known to have been Ryder's friends. By 1921 Sherman had become a professional art dealer, regularly "discovering" lost Ryder paintings and selling them to museums across the country. Many of the paintings that Sherman authenticated are known forgeries today.

Only the paintings that are stylistically analogous to known Ryder works, that follow a familiar pattern in laboratory analysis, and that have an indubitable provenance can be considered authentic. The numerous forgeries of Ryder's paintings give testimony to the aesthetic qualities valued in the market of Ryder works, and thus are of educational value today.
L. C. AND E. B.

Inscriptions At lower left, *A. P. RYDER;* on the verso a stenciled stamp, *Robert Fullerton, Art Dealer*

Provenance Frederic Fairchild Sherman, 1923. Acquired in 1925.

Exhibitions Chicago 1946, no. 13. East Lansing 1966.

Reference *BDIA* 1924–25, 85, ill.

Short References

References to newspapers, annual exhibitions (such as the National Academy of Design annuals in New York and the Salons in Paris), and international expositions are given in full in the text of the entries and not abbreviated here. Standard sources such as the *Dictionary of American Biography* and the Archives of American Art are abbreviated as follows.

AAA: Archives of American Art, Smithsonian Institution

DAB: Dictionary of American Biography. 20 vols. New York, 1927–36. With supplements. New York, 1944–95. 1974 ed. 2 pts. in 1 vol.

NCAB: The National Cyclopaedia of American Biography. New York, 1898–1984 (publication stopped with vol. 63, N; changed to *The National Cyclopedia* with vol. 53)

Adams 1990
Adams, Henry. "The Identity of Winslow Homer's 'Mystery Woman.'" *Burlington Magazine* 132 (April 1990): 244–252.

Albuquerque 1965
Albuquerque, New Mex., University Art Gallery. *Impressionism in America.* Exh. cat. 1965.

Aldrich 1866
Aldrich, Thomas B. "Among the Studios. No. V." *Our Young Folks* 2 (October 1866): 622–625.

Alexandre 1903
Alexandre, Argè. "J. McNeill Whistler." *Les Arts* 21 (September 1903): 22–32.

Altick 1985
Altick, Richard D. *Paintings from Books: Art and Literature in Britain, 1760–1900.* Columbus, Ohio, 1985.

***American Art Annual* 1907–8**
American Art Annual. Vol. 6. New York, 1907–8.

***American Art Annual* 1914**
American Art Annual. Vol. 11. New York, 1914.

***American Art Review* 1880**
"Exhibitions and Sales." *American Art Review* 1, no. 1 (1880): 225.

American Federation of Arts 1912
American Federation of Arts. *Francis Davis Millet Memorial Meeting.* Washington, 1912.

Anderson 1980
Anderson, Nancy K. "Cowboys in the Badlands and the Role of Avondale." In Newark, University of Delaware, and Chadds Ford, Pa., Brandywine River Museum. *Eakins at Avondale and Thomas Eakins: A Personal Collection.* Exh. cat. edited by William Innes Homer. 1980.

Ann Arbor 1961
Ann Arbor, University of Michigan Museum of Art. "Michigan and the Civil War." [No cat.] 1961.

Ann Arbor 1969
Ann Arbor, University of Michigan Museum of Art. *A Connoisseur's Choice: From the Collection of Paul L. Grigaut.* Exh. checklist. 1969.

Ann Arbor 1978
Ann Arbor, University of Michigan Museum of Art. *Whistler: The Later Years.* Exh. cat. 1978.

***Antiques* 1965**
"Paintings: The People and Places of the Old Northwest Territory." *Antiques* 87 (March 1965): 302–309.

***Apollo* 1972**
"Art across the U.S.A." *Apollo* 95, no. 124 (June 1972): 501–502, fig. 2.

***Appleton's Journal* 1874**
"Art. Composition Pictures at the Academy." *Appleton's Journal* 11 (May 16, 1874): 636.

***Appleton's Journal* 1875**
"The Arts." *Appleton's Journal* 14 (October 9, 1875): 471.

Armstrong 1920
Armstrong, D. Maitland. *Day before Yesterday: Reminiscences of a Varied Life.* New York, 1920.

***Art Amateur* 1880**
"Charles C. Coleman." *Art Amateur* 2 (February 1880): 45–46.

***Art Amateur* 1880a**
"Elihu Vedder." *Art Amateur* 2 (April 1880): 89–90.

***Art Amateur* 1883**
"Pictures by American Women in the Paris Salon." *Art Amateur* 9 (August 1883): 46.

***Art Digest* 1933**
"Detroit Took up Art Just Fifty Years Ago." *Art Digest* 8, no. 2 (October 15, 1933): 32.

***Art Digest* 1936**
"Titian, Poussin, Caravaggio, Cranach, Wyant Acquired by Detroit." *Art Digest* 10 (August 1, 1936): 10–11.

***Art Interchange* 1880**
"Studio Notes." *Art Interchange* 4 (March 17, 1880): 47.

***Art Interchange* 1900**
"Editorial Comment." *Art Interchange* 45 (July 1900): 12.

***Art Journal* 1865**
"Minor Topics of the Month." *Art Journal* (London), n.s., 4 (July 1, 1865): 227.

***Art Journal* 1865a**
"Minor Topics of the Month: By Mr. F. E. Church." *Art Journal* (London), n.s., 4 (August 1, 1865): 257–258.

***Art Journal* 1897**
"Some Early Pictures by Mr. Whistler." *Art Journal* (London), 49 (October 1897): 289–291.

***Art Quarterly* 1959**
"Accessions of American and Canadian Museums: January–March, 1959." *Art Quarterly* 22, no. 2 (Summer 1959): 178, 187.

***Athenaeum* 1870**
"Winter Exhibition at the Dudley Gallery." *Athenaeum* (London), no. 2245 (November 5, 1870): 598.

***Athenaeum* 1878**
"The International Exhibition. (Second Notice)." *Athenaeum* (London), no. 2638 (May 18, 1878): 640.

***Athenaeum* 1883**
"Fine Arts. Review of *The History of Wood Engraving in America,* by W. J. Linton." *Athenaeum* (London), no. 2884 (February 3, 1883): 160.

Atlanta 1972
Atlanta, Ga., High Museum of Art. *The Düsseldorf Academy and the Americans: An Exhibition of Drawings and Watercolors.* Exh. cat. by Wend von Kalnein and Donelson F. Hoopes. 1972.

***Atlantic Monthly* 1885**
"Vedder's Drawings for Omar Khayyám's Rubaáiyát." *Atlantic Monthly* 55 (January 1885): 111.

Atwood 1850
Atwood, Mary Anne. *A Suggestive Inquiry into the Hermetic Mystery with a Dissertation on the More Celebrated of the Alchemical Philosophers: Being an Attempt towards the Recovery of the Ancient Experiment with Nature.* London, 1850.

Austin et al. 1970
Austin, University of Texas Art Museum; Albany, N.Y., Albany Institute of History and Art; and New York, Hirschl & Adler Galleries. *Sanford Robinson Gifford (1823–1880).* Exh. cat. by Nicolai Cikovsky, Jr. 1970.

Bacon 1883
Bacon, Henry. *Parisian Art and Artists.* Boston, 1883.

Baltimore 1882
Baltimore, Academy of Music. *Art Loan Exhibition for the Benefit of the Nursery and Child's Hospital.* Exh. cat. 1882.

Baltimore 1949
"Peabody Institute List." Baltimore, 1949.

Baltimore et al. 1976
Baltimore Museum of Art; Bonn, Rheinisches Museum; Belgrade, Museum of Modern Art; Rome, Gallery of Modern and Contemporary Art; and Warsaw, National Museum of Poland. *Two Hundred Years of American Painting.* 1976.

Bartlett 1882
Bartlett, Truman H. *The Art and Life of William Rimmer: Sculptor, Painter, and Physician.* Boston, 1882. Reprint. New York, 1970.

Battle Creek et al. 1977
Battle Creek, Mich., Battle Creek Civic Art Center; Alpena, Mich., Jesse Besser Museum; Midland, Mich., Midland Art Center. *American Black Art: The Known and the New.* Exh. cat. 1977.

Baur 1957–58
Baur, John I. H. "From Apples to Goddesses: The Paul Magriel Collection." *Art in America* 45 (Winter 1957–58): 14–21.

Baxter et al. 1912
Baxter, Sylvester, William A. Coffin, Edwin Howland Blashfield, Carroll Beckwith, and George W. Maynard. "Francis Davis Millet Memorial Number." *Art and Progress* 3, no. 9 (July 1912): 635–655.

Bayley 1865
[Bayley, W. P.]. "Mr. Church's Pictures. Cotopaxi, Chimborazo, and the Aurora Borealis. Considered also with Reference to English Art." *Art Journal* (London) (September 1865): 265.

***BDIA* 1920**
B., C. H. "Whistler's Portrait of Robert Barr." *Bulletin of the Detroit Institute of Arts* 2, no. 2, 13–14.

***BDIA* 1923**
P., R. "Memorial Gift of Innes Landscape." *Bulletin of the Detroit Institute of Arts* 5, no. 2 (November 1923): 11–12.

***BDIA* 1924**
P., R. "An Inness Given by the Detroit Museum of Art Founders Society." *Bulletin of the Detroit Institute of Arts* 5, no. 6 (March 1924): 44–45.

***BDIA* 1924–25**
"Two Paintings by American Artists." *Bulletin of the Detroit Institute of Arts* 6, no. 8 (May 1925): 84–87.

***BDIA* 1928**
B., C. H. "A Landscape by Kensett." *Bulletin of the Detroit Institute of Arts* 9, no. 1 (January 1928): 43–44.

***BDIA* 1934**
"American Portrait Painting from the Seventeenth to the Late Nineteenth Century." *Bulletin of the Detroit Institute of Arts* 14, no. 1 (October 1934): 11–14.

***BDIA* 1938**
"Alger House Exhibition of Portraits of Prominent Detroiters." *Bulletin of the Detroit Institute of Arts* 17, no. 6 (March 1938): 55–56.

***BDIA* 1957–58**
Bulletin of the Detroit Institute of Arts 37, no. 2 (1957–58): 31.

***BDIA* 1960–61**
P., E. H. "A Bequest from Dexter M. Ferry, Jr." *Bulletin of the Detroit Institute of Arts* 40, no. 1 (1960–61): 16–17.

***BDIA* 1960–61a**
Bulletin of the Detroit Institute of Arts 40, nos. 3–4 (1960–61): 52–53.

***BDIA* 1974**
"Curatorial Reports." *Bulletin of the Detroit Institute of Arts* 53, no. 2 (1974): 57–58, ill.

***BDIA* 1977**
"American Paintings Acquired during the Last Decade." *Bulletin of the Detroit Institute of Arts* 55 (1977): 69–108.

***BDIA* 1978**
"Curatorial Reports." *Bulletin of the Detroit Institute of Arts* 56, no. 5 (1978): 267–289.

***BDIA* 1978a**
"Associates of the American Wing." *Bulletin of the Detroit Institute of Arts* 56, no. 5 (1978): 309–310, fig. 30.

***BDIA* 1988**
"Notes on Recent Acquisitions." *Bulletin of the Detroit Institute of Arts* 64, no. 1 (1988): 56.

***BDMA* 1904**
"Museum Notes." *Bulletin of the Detroit Museum of Art* 1, no. 2 (April 1904): 3.

***BDMA* 1904a**
"Modern Pictures." *Bulletin of the Detroit Museum of Art* 1, no. 4 (October 1904): 2.

***BDMA* 1907**
"Charles Caryl Coleman Exhibition." *Bulletin of the Detroit Museum of Art* 1, no. 14 (July 1907): 4.

***BDMA* 1909**
"Two Notable Gifts." *Bulletin of the Detroit Museum of Art* 3, no. 1 (January 1909): 1–2.

***BDMA* 1909a**
"Gift of a 'Hopkin.'" *Bulletin of the Detroit Museum of Art* 3, no. 2 (April 1909): 14.

***BDMA* 1910**
"Important Gifts." *Bulletin of the Detroit Museum of Art* 4, no. 2 (April 1910): 15.

***BDMA* 1910a**
"Important Acquisitions." *Bulletin of the Detroit Museum of Art* 4, no. 4 (October 1910): 43, 50–51.

***BDMA* 1911**
"A Painting Added to the Permanent Collection." *Bulletin of the Detroit Museum of Art* 5, no. 2 (April 1911): 13.

***BDMA* 1913**
"Examples of the Work of Walter Shirlaw, N.A." *Bulletin of the Detroit Museum of Art* 7, no. 2 (April 1913): 21–22.

***BDMA* 1917**
"Accessions." *Bulletin of the Detroit Museum of Art* 11, no. 5 (February 1917): 43.

***BDMA* 1917a**
"Painting by Wyant Bequeathed." *Bulletin of the Detroit Museum of Art* 11, no. 6 (March 1917): 49, 52–53.

Beam 1966
Beam, Philip C. *Winslow Homer at Prout's Neck.* Boston, 1966.

Bearden and Henderson 1972
Bearden, Romare, and Harry Henderson. *Six Black Masters of American Art.* New York, 1972.

Beecher 1862
Beecher, Henry Ward. *Eyes and Ears.* Boston, 1862. Reprint. Boston, 1864.

Bénédite 1905
Bénédite, Léonce. *L'oeuvre de James McNeill Whistler.* Paris, 1905.

Benjamin 1879
Benjamin, Samuel G. W. *Our American Artists.* Boston, 1879.

Benjamin 1880
Benjamin, Samuel G. W. *Art in America.* New York, 1880.

Benjamin 1882
Benjamin, Samuel G. W. "A Painter of the Streets." *Magazine of Art,* ser. 1, 5 (1882): 265–270.

Berkeley et al. 1970
Berkeley, Calif., University of Caliornia, University Art Museum, and San Francisco, California Palace of the Legion of Honor; Washington, D.C., National Gallery of Art; New York, Whitney Museum of American Art; and Detroit Institute of Arts. *The Reality of Appearance: The Trompe L'Oeil Tradition in American Painting.* Exh. cat. by Alfred Frankinstein. 1970.

Berlin 1969
Berlin, Nationalgalerie. *James McNeill Whistler.* Exh. cat. 1969.

Big Rapids 1964
Big Rapids, Mich., Ferris State College. "Sixth Annual Festival of the Arts." [No cat.] 1964.

Birmingham 1951
Birmingham, Ala., Museum of Art. *Opening Exhibition.* Exh. cat. 1951.

Bishop 1880
Bishop, W. H. "Elihu Vedder. First Article." *American Art Review* 1 (May 1880): 325–329.

Bishop 1880a
Bishop, W. H. "Elihu Vedder. Second and Concluding Article." *American Art Review* 1 (June 1880): 369–373.

Bloomfield Hills 1973
Bloomfield Hills, Mich., Cranbrook Academy of Art Museum. *Genre, Portrait, and Still-Life Painting in America: The Victorian Era.* Exh. cat. by E. Gaidos. 1973.

Boime 1971
Boime, Albert. *The Academy and French Painting in the Nineteenth Century.* London, 1971.

Bolton 1932
Bolton, Theodore. "The Art of Winslow Homer." *Fine Arts* (February 1932): 29.

Boston 1874
Boston, Museum of Fine Arts. *Pictures Exhibited by the Athenaeum: Pictures and Engravings Bequested to the Museum of Fine Arts by the Hon. Charles Sumner.* Exh. cat. 1874.

Boston 1880
Boston, No. 1 Park Square. *Exhibition Catalogue of the Paintings and Drawings of the Late William Morris Hunt at His Studio.* Exh. cat. introduction by T. H. Bartlett. 1880.

Boston 1880a
Boston, Williams & Everett's Gallery. *Pictures, Sketches of Pictures and Studies, by Elihu Vedder.* Exh. cat. 1880.

Boston 1884
Boston, Museum of Fine Arts. *Memorial Exhibition of the Works of George Fuller.* Exh. cat. essay by M. G. Van Rensselaer. 1884.

Boston 1886
Boston, Art Club. *Thirty-third Exhibition of the Boston Art Club.* Exh. cat. 1886.

Boston 1904
Boston, Copley Society, Copley Hall. *Oil Paintings, Water Colors, Pastels, and Drawings: Memorial Exhibition of the Works of Mr. J. McNeill Whistler.* Exh. cat. 1904.

Boston 1910
Boston, Curtis & Cameron. "Vedder Subjects in the Copley Prints." Boston, 1910.

Boston 1963
Boston, Vose Galleries. *Mark Fisher 1841–1923: The Impressionist.* Exh. cat. by M. L. d'Otrange Mastai. 1963.

Boston 1972
Boston, Museum of Fine Arts, and National Center of Afro-American Artists. *Nineteenth-Century Afro-American Artists: Duncanson and Bannister.* Exh. cat. 1972.

Boston 1979
Boston, Museum of Fine Arts. *William Morris Hunt: A Memorial Exhibition.* Exh. cat. by Martha J. Hoppin, essays by Martha J. Hoppin and Henry Adams. 1979.

Boston et al. 1969
Boston, Museum of Fine Arts; College Park, University of Maryland Gallery; and New York, Whitney Museum of American Art. *Martin Johnson Heade.* Exh. cat. 1969.

Boston et al. 1978
Boston, Museum of Fine Arts; University of Pittsburgh Art Gallery; Wichita (Kansas) State University, Ulrich Museum of Art; Ann Arbor, University of Michigan Museum of Art; Madison, University of Wisconsin, Elvehjem Museum of Art; Washington, D.C., Corcoran Gallery of Art; Ames, Iowa State University, Brunnier Gallery; Kansas City, Nelson Gallery–Atkins Museum; Montclair, N.J., Art Museum; and New York, Cooper-Hewitt Museum. *Close Observation: Selected Oil Sketches by Frederic Edwin Church.* Exh. cat. by Theodore E. Stebbins, Jr. 1978.

Boston et al. 1983
Boston, Museum of Fine Arts; Washington, D.C., Corcoran Gallery of Art; and Paris, Grand Palais. *A New World: Masterpieces of American Painting, 1760–1910.* Exh. cat. by Theodore E. Stebbins, Jr., Carol Troyen, and Trevor J. Fairbrother, with essays by Pierre Rosenberg and H. Barbara Weinberg. 1983.

Boston et al. 1992
Boston, Museum of Fine Arts; Cleveland Museum of Art; and Houston, Museum of Fine Arts. *The Lure of Italy: American Artists and the Italian Experience, 1760–1914.* Exh. cat. by Theodore E. Stebbins, Jr., William H. Gerdts, Erica E. Hirschler, Fred S. Licht, William L. Vance, et al. 1992.

Botkin 1960
Botkin, B. A., ed. *A Civil War Treasury of Tales, Legends, and Folklore.* New York, 1960.

Boydell 1852
Boydell, John. *The American Edition of Boydell's Illustrations of the Dramatic Works of Shakespeare, by the Most Eminent Artists of Great Britain.* 2 vols. New York, 1852.

Boydell and Boydell 1803[5]
Boydell, John, and Josiah Boydell. *Collection of Prints, from Pictures Painted for the Purpose of Illustrating the Dramatic Works of Shakespeare by the Artists of Great Britain.* London, 1803. Preface dated 1805. Reprint. New York, 1979.

Breeskin 1970
Breeskin, Adelyn Dohme. *Mary Cassatt: A Catalogue Raisonné of the Oils, Pastels, Watercolors, and Drawings.* Washington, D.C., 1970.

Bregler 1989
"Charles Bregler's Thomas Eakins Collection." Pennsylvania Academy of the Fine Arts, Philadelphia. Microfiche edition. 1989.

Brewster 1919
Brewster, Eugene V. "Wyant—The Nature-Painter." *Arts and Decoration* 10, no. 4 (February 1919): 197–200, 234.

Brockton et al. 1985
Brockton, Mass., Art Museum/Fuller Memorial; Cleveland Museum of Art; and Brooklyn Museum. *William Rimmer: A Yankee Michelangelo.* Exh. cat. entries by Jeffrey Weidman. Essays by Jeffrey Weidman, Neil Harris, and Philip Cash. 1985.

Brooklyn 1929
Brooklyn Museum. *Exhibition of Paintings and Drawings by the Late Walter Shirlaw and a Group of His Pupils.* Exh. cat. by Katherine S. Dreier. 1929.

Brooklyn 1940
Brooklyn Museum. *An American Genre Painter: Eastman Johnson, 1824–1906.* Exh. cat. essay by John I. H. Baur. 1940.

Brooklyn 1960
Brooklyn Museum. *Victoriana.* Exh. cat. 1960.

Brooklyn 1987
Brooklyn, Museum of the Borough of Brooklyn at Brooklyn College. *The Grand Game of Baseball . . . and the Brooklyn Dodgers.* Exh. cat. 1987.

Brooklyn and Boston 1985
Brooklyn Museum, and Boston, Museum of Fine Arts. *The New Path: Ruskin and the American Pre-Raphaelites.* Exh. cat. by Linda S. Ferber and William H. Gerdts. 1985.

Brooklyn and Philadelphia 1973
Brooklyn Museum, and Philadelphia, Pennsylvania Academy of the Fine Arts. *William Trost Richards: American Landscape and Marine Painter, 1883–1905.* Exh. cat. by Linda S. Ferber. 1973.

Brooklyn et al. 1967
Brooklyn Museum; Richmond, Virginia Museum of Fine Arts; and San Francisco, California Palace of the Legion of Honor. *Triumph of Realism.* Exh. cat. 1967.

Brooklyn et al. 1991
Brooklyn Museum; Fine Arts Museums of San Francisco; and Washington, D.C., National Gallery of Art. *Albert Bierstadt: Art & Enterprise.* Exh. cat. by Nancy K. Anderson and Linda S. Ferber, with Helena E. Wright. 1991.

Broun 1989
Broun, Elizabeth. *Albert Pinkham Ryder.* Washington, D.C., 1989.

G. Brown 1979–80
Brown, Gaye L. "Albert Pinkham Ryder's *Joan of Arc:* The Damsel in Distress." *Worcester Art Museum Journal* 3 (1979–80): 37–51.

M. Brown 1977
Brown, Milton W. *American Art to 1900: Painting, Sculpture, Architecture.* New York, 1977.

M. Brown 1988
Brown, Milton W. *The Story of the Armory Show.* New York, 1988.

Brunswick 1964
Brunswick, Maine, Bowdoin College Museum of Art. *The Portrayal of the Negro in American Painting.* Exh. cat. 1964.

Buffalo n.d.
"Miss Baker's Pictures." Unidentified newspaper article in the collection of the Albright-Knox Art Gallery Library, Buffalo, N.Y.

Buffalo 1861
Buffalo, N.Y., Young Men's Association. *Catalogue of the First Exhibition of Painting and Statuary, at the American Hall, Main Street, Buffalo.* Exh. cat. 1861.

Buffalo 1891(?)
Buffalo, N.Y., Hoddick and Company. *Catalogue: An Exhibition of Original Oil Paintings, by Miss Ellen K. Baker, of Paris.* Exh. cat. 1891(?).

Buffalo 1924
Buffalo, N.Y., Fine Arts Academy, Albright Art Gallery. *Centennial Exhibition of Paintings by William Morris Hunt.* Exh. cat. introduction by Cornelia B. Sage Quinton. 1924.

Buffalo 1925
Buffalo, N.Y., Fine Arts Academy, Albright Art Gallery. *George Inness Centennial Exhibition, 1825–1925.* Exh. cat. 1925.

Buffalo et al. 1976
Buffalo, N.Y., Albright-Knox Art Gallery; Detroit Institute of Arts; Toledo Museum of Art; and Cleveland Museum of Art. *Heritage and Horizon: American Paintings, 1776–1976.* Exh. cat. by L. Curry with an essay by Nancy Rivard. 1976.

Burns 1979
Burns, Sarah Lea. "The Poetic Mode in American Painting: George Fuller and Thomas Dewing." Ph.D. diss. University of Illinois at Urbana–Champaign, 1979.

Burns 1981
Burns, Sarah. "A Study of the Life and Poetic Vision of George Fuller (1822–1884)." *American Art Journal* 13, no. 4 (Autumn 1981): 11–37.

Burns 1989
Burns, Sarah. *Pastoral Inventions: Rural Life in Nineteenth-Century American Art and Culture.* Philadelphia, 1989.

A. Burroughs 1924
Burroughs, Alan. "Catalogue of Works by Thomas Eakins (1869–1916)." *Arts* 5, no. 6 (June 1924): 328–333.

C. Burroughs 1922
Burroughs, Clyde H. "Painting by Mary Cassatt Presented." *Bulletin of the Detroit Institute of Arts* 3 (April 1922): 66–67.

C. Burroughs 1930
Burroughs, Clyde H. "A Portrait by Thomas Eakins." *Bulletin of the Detroit Institute of Arts* 12, no. 2 (November 1930): 21–23.

C. Burroughs 1934
Burroughs, Clyde H. "Paintings by Homer and Ryder." *Bulletin of the Detroit Institute of Arts* 14, no. 1 (October 1934): 8–10.

C. Burroughs 1935
Burroughs, Clyde H. "A Painting by Thomas Eakins." *Bulletin of the Detroit Institute of Arts* 14, no. 7 (April 1935): 86–88.

C. Burroughs 1936
Burroughs, Clyde H. "Early American Landscape Paintings." *Bulletin of the Detroit Institute of Arts* 15, no. 6 (March 1936): 86–89.

C. Burroughs 1936a
Burroughs, Clyde H. "Painting and Sculpture in Michigan." *Michigan History Magazine* 20 (1936): 395–409.

C. Burroughs 1937
Burroughs, Clyde H. "Painting and Sculpture in Michigan." *Michigan History Magazine* 21 (1937): 39–54.

C. Burroughs 1940
Burroughs, Clyde H. "Three Paintings by American Artists." *Bulletin of the Detroit Institute of Arts* 20, no. 1 (October 1940): 2–7.

Burton 1922
Burton, Clarence M., ed. *The City of Detroit, Michigan, 1701–1922.* 5 vols. Chicago, 1922.

Caffin 1913
Caffin, Charles H. *American Masters of Painting.* Garden City, N.Y., 1913.

***California Art Research* 1937**
"Thomas Hill, 1829–1908: Biography and Works." *California Art Research* (WPA, San Francisco), 2, 1st ser. (1937): 67–97A. Microfiche ed. La Jolla, Calif., 1987.

Cambridge 1939
Cambridge, Mass., Harvard University, Fogg Art Museum. *Art in New England: New England Genre.* Exh. cat. 1939.

Canaday 1969
Canaday, John. *Lives of the Painters.* Vol. 4. London, 1969.

Carr 1980
Carr, Gerald L. *Frederic Edwin Church: The Icebergs.* Dallas, 1980.

Carr 1992
Carr, Gerald L. "Frederic Edwin Church and Italy." In *The Italian Presence in American Art, 1860–1920.* Edited by Irma B. Jaffe. New York and Rome, 1992.

Carr 1994
Carr, Gerald L. *Frederic Edwin Church: Catalogue Raisonné of Works of Art at Olana State Historic Site.* 2 vols. New York and Cambridge, 1994.

Carroll 1913
Carroll, Dana H. *Fifty-eight Paintings by Homer D. Martin.* New York, 1913.

Cary 1907
Cary, Elisabeth Luther. *The Works of James McNeill Whistler.* New York, 1907.

Cavallo 1950–51
Cavallo, A. S. "Uncle Tom and Little Eva: A Painting by Robert S. Duncanson." *Bulletin of the Detroit Institute of Arts* 30, no. 1 (1950–51): 21–25.

Cerio 1929
Cerio, Edwin. *That Capri Air.* London and New York, 1929.

Cerio 1957
Cerio, Edwin. *The Masque of Capri.* London, 1957.

Chadbourne, Gabosh, and Vogel 1991
Chadbourne, Janice H., Karl Gabosh, and Charles O. Vogel. *The Boston Art Club: Exhibition Record, 1873–1909.* Madison, Conn., 1991.

Champney 1885
Champney, Lizzie W. "The Summer Haunts of American Artists." *Century Magazine* 30 (October 1885): 845–860.

Champney 1900
Champney, Benjamin: *Sixty Years' Memories of Art and Artists.* Woburn, Mass., 1900. Reprint. New York and London, 1977.

Chicago 1881
Chicago, Inter-State Industrial Exposition. *Illustrated Catalogue of the Art Hall.* Exh. cat. 1881.

Chicago 1901
Art Institute of Chicago. *Exhibition of Works by Elihu Vedder.* Exh. cat. 1901.

Chicago 1911
Art Institute of Chicago. *A Memorial Collection of Works by Walter Shirlaw, N.A.* Exh. cat. 1911.

Chicago 1943
Arts Club of Chicago. *American Primitive Painting of Four Centuries.* Exh. cat. introduction by Sidney Janis. 1943.

Chicago 1946
Arts Club of Chicago. "Albert Pinkham Ryder and Arthur Bowen Davies." [No cat.] 1946.

Chicago 1990
Chicago, Terra Museum of American Art. *Winslow Homer in Gloucester.* Exh. cat. essays by D. Scott Atkinson and Jochen Wierich. 1990.

Chicago and New York 1954
Art Institute of Chicago, and New York, Metropolitan Museum of Art. *Sargent, Whistler, and Cassatt.* Exh. cat. 1954.

Child 1885
Child, Theodore. "Daniel Ridgway Knight." *Art Amateur* 7 (April 1885): 101–106.

Child 1889
Child, Theodore. "American Artists at the Paris Exhibition." *Harpers's New Monthly Magazine* 79 (September 1889): 489–521.

Chotner 1992
Chotner, Deborah, ed. *American Naive Paintings.* Washington, D.C., 1992.

Cikovsky 1971
Cikovsky, Nicolai, Jr. *George Inness.* New York, 1971.

Cikovsky 1977
Cikovsky, Nicolai, Jr. *The Life and Work of George Inness.* New York, 1977.

Cikovsky 1978
Cikovsky, Nicolai, Jr. "Winslow Homer's *Prisoners from the Front.*" *Metropolitan Museum of Art Journal* 12 (1978): 163–164.

Cikovsky 1990
Cikovsky, Nicolai, Jr. *Winslow Homer.* New York, 1990.

Cincinnati 1955
Cincinnati Art Museum. *Rediscoveries in American Paintings.* Exh. cat. by Edward H. Dwight. 1955.

Cincinnati 1968
Cincinnati Art Museum. *American Paintings on the Market Today.* Exh. cat. 1968.

Cincinnati 1972
Cincinnati Art Museum. *Robert S. Duncanson: A Centennial Exhibition.* Exh. cat. by Guy McElroy. 1972.

Cist 1841
Cist, Charles. *Cincinnati in 1841: Its Early Annals and Future Prospects.* Cincinnati, 1841.

Clark 1854
Clark, Lewis Gaylord. "Editor's Table." *Knickerbocker* 43 (May 1854): 539.

Clayton 1987
Clayton, Ralph. *Black Baltimore, 1820–1870.* Baltimore, 1987.

Clayton 1990
Clayton, Virginia Tuttle. "Reminiscence and Revival: The Old-Fashioned Garden, 1890–1910." *Antiques* 137, no. 1 (April 1990): 892–905.

Clement 1895
Clement, Clara Erskine. "Later Religious Painting in America." *New England Magazine* n.s., 12, no. 2 (April 1895): 138–139.

Cobb 1963
Cobb, Stanwood. "Reminiscences of George Inness by Darius Cobb." *Art Quarterly* 26 (Summer 1963): 234–242.

Cody 1990
Cody, Wyo., Buffalo Bill Historical Center. *Rendezvous to Roundup: The First One Hundred Years of Art in Wyoming.* Exh. cat. by Sarah E. Boehme. 1990.

College Park 1968
College Park, University of Maryland Art Gallery. *Jasper F. Cropsey, 1823–1900: A Retrospective View of America's Painter of Autumn.* Exh. cat. by Peter Bermingham. 1968.

College Park and Albany 1976
College Park, University of Maryland Art Gallery, and Albany, N.Y., Albany Institute of History and Art. *The Late Landscapes of William Morris Hunt.* Exh. cat. by Marshal E. Landgren and Sherman Wallace McGurn. 1976.

Columbus 1937
Columbus, Ohio, Columbus Gallery of Fine Arts. "Winslow Homer Exhibition." Exh. checklist in *Columbus Gallery of Fine Arts Monthly Bulletin* 7, no. 6 (March). 1937.

Columbus 1948
Columbus, Ohio, Columbus Gallery of Fine Arts. "Romantic America." [No cat.] 1948.

Columbus 1956
Columbus, Ohio, Columbus Gallery of Fine Arts. *International Masterpieces.* Exh. cat. 1956.

Columbus et al. 1953
Columbus, Ohio, Gallery of Fine Arts; Dayton, Ohio, Dayton Art Institute; Akron, Akron Institute; and Toledo Museum of Art. *Painters of Ohio's Past.* Exh. cat. 1953.

***Columbus Gallery of Fine Arts Bulletin* 1948**
"Collection of Paintings and Sculpture in the Exhibition 'Romantic America.'" *Columbus Gallery of the Fine Arts Bulletin* 19, no. 1 (1948): 5.

Cook 1888
Clarence Cook. *Art and Artists of Our Time.* Vol. 3. New York, 1888.

Cooperstown et al. 1958
Cooperstown, N.Y., State Historical Society; Rochester, N.Y., Memorial Art Gallery; Albany, N.Y., Albany Institute of History and Art; Utica, N.Y., Munson-Williams-Proctor Institute; Syracuse, N.Y., Everson Museum of Art; and New-York Historical Society. *Rediscovered Folk Painters of Upstate New York.* Exh. cat. by Agnes Halsey Jones. 1958.

Coral Gables 1974
Coral Gables, Fla., University of Miami. *Nineteenth-Century Topographic Painters.* Exh. cat. 1974.

Cowdrey 1943
Cowdrey, Bartlett. *National Academy of Design Exhibition Record, 1826–1860.* 2 vols. New York, 1943.

Cowdrey 1944
Cowdrey, Bartlett. "Richard Caton Woodville, an American Genre Painter." *American Collector* 13 (April 1944): 6–7, 14, 20.

Cowdrey 1953
Cowdrey, Bartlett. *American Academy of Fine Arts and American Art-Union.* New York, 1953.

Coxe 1908
Coxe, Reginald Cleveland. "George Inness." *Scribner's Magazine* 44 (November 1908): 509–512.

Cragsmoor et al. 1981
Cragsmoor, N.Y., Henry Home; Albany, New York State Museum; Utica, N.Y., Munson-Williams-Proctor Institute; Binghamton, N.Y., Roberson Center for the Arts and Sciences; East Hampton, N.Y., Guild Hall; and Newark, N.J., Newark Museum. *E. L. Henry's Country Life: An Exhibition.* Exh. cat. introduction by Maureen Radl and Jan Christman. 1981.

Crayon 1860
"Sketchings." *The Crayon* 7 (December 1860): 353.

Crayon 1861
"Sketchings." *The Crayon* 8 (January 1861): 21.

Critic 1887
"Art Notes." *Critic: A Weekly Review of Literature and the Arts* 10, n.s., 7, no. 127 (April 23, 1887): 210.

Cropsey 1855
Cropsey, Jasper F. "Up among the Clouds." *Crayon* 2 (August 8, 1855): 79–80.

Crosby 1944
Crosby, Everett. *Eastman Johnson at Nantucket: His Paintings and Sketches of Nantucket People and Scenes.* 1944.

Cullen 1985
Cullen, Joseph P. "Battle of the Wilderness." *Wilderness and Spotsylvania.* New York, 1985.

Cummings and Elam 1971
Cummings, Frederick J., and Charles H. Elam, eds. *The Detroit Institute of Arts Illustrated Handbook.* Detroit, 1971.

Daingerfield 1911
Daingerfield, Elliott. *George Inness: The Man and His Art.* New York, 1911.

Daingerfield 1917
Daingerfield, Elliott. "George Inness." *Century Magazine* (November 1917): 69–77.

Dallas 1971
Dallas Museum of Fine Arts. *The Romantic Vision in America.* Exh. cat. by John Lunsford. 1971.

Davidson 1987
Davidson, Abraham. "The Wretched Life and Death of an 'American Van Gogh.'" *Smithsonian,* December 1987, 80–91.

Davidson 1996
Davidson, Abraham. *Ralph Albert Blakelock.* University Park, Pa., 1996.

Davis 1983
Davis, William C., ed. *Fighting for Time.* Vol. 4 of *The Image of War, 1861–1865.* Garden City, N.Y., 1983.

Davis 1987
Davis, John Harlan. "Frederic Church's *Sacred Geography.*" *Smithsonian Studies in American Art* 1 (Spring 1987): 78–96.

Davis 1991
Davis, John Harlan. "Picturing Palestine: The Holy Land in Nineteenth-Century American Art and Culture." Ph.D. diss., Columbia University, 1991.

Davis 1996
Davis, John Harlan. *The Landscape of Belief: Encountering the Holy Land in Nineteenth-Century American Art and Culture.* Princeton, N.J., 1996.

Dayton et al. 1976
Dayton, Ohio, Dayton Art Institute; Philadelphia, Pennsylvania Academy of the Fine Arts; and Los Angeles County Museum of Art. *American Expatriate Painters of the Late Nineteenth Century.* Exh. cat. by Michael Quick. 1976.

Dearborn 1964
Dearborn, Mich., Henry Ford Museum. "Arts and Crafts of the Old Northwest Territory." [No cat.] 1964.

De Kay 1880
De Kay, Charles [Henry Eckford, pseud.]. "Elihu Vedder." *Scribner's Monthly* 21 (November 1880): 111–124.

De Kay 1882
De Kay, Charles [Henry Eckford, pseud.]. "George Inness." *Century Magazine* 24 (May 1882): 57–64.

De Kay 1902
De Kay, Charles. "A Villa in Capri." *Architectural Record* 12 (May 1902): 71–92.

De Kay 1910
De Kay, Charles. "The Art of Homer Martin." *Century Illustrated Monthly Magazine* 79 (February 1910): 587–588.

Denver 1953
Denver Art Museum. "Art Tells the Story." [No cat.] 1953.

Detroit 1852
Detroit, Firemen's Hall. *Catalogue of Articles on Exhibition, at the Gallery of Fine Arts, Firemen's Hall, February, 1852.* Exh. cat. 1852.

Detroit 1853
Detroit, Firemen's Hall. *Catalogue of Articles on Exhibition, at the Gallery of Fine Arts, in the Firemen's Hall, February, 1853.* Exh. cat. 1853.

Detroit 1877
Detroit, Angell's Art Gallery. *Fall Exhibition: Detroit Artists.* Exh. cat. 1877.

Detroit 1883
Detroit Art Loan Association. *Catalogue of Art Works Exhibited.* Exh. cat. 1883.

Detroit 1888
Detroit Museum of Art. *Catalogue of Paintings and Sculpture: Opening Exhibition.* Exh. cat. 1888.

Detroit 1889
Detroit Museum of Art. *Catalogue of Paintings, Water Colors, Drawings, Etchings, and Collection of Corean Antiquities: Second Exhibition.* Exh. cat. 1889.

Detroit 1896
Detroit Museum of Art. *A Memorial Exhibition of Paintings and Drawings Made by the Late L. T. Ives.* Exh. cat. 1896.

Detroit 1901
Detroit Museum of Art. *Mr. Robert Hopkin's Collection of Paintings.* Exh. cat. 1901.

Detroit 1903
Detroit Museum of Art. *Catalogue of Paintings Exhibited during the Summer.* Exh. cat. 1903.

Detroit 1907
Detroit Museum of Art. *Special Exhibition of Paintings by Charles Caryl Coleman.* Exh. cat. 1907.

Detroit 1907a
Detroit Museum of Art. *Supplement to the Handbook of Paintings Belonging to the Detroit Museum of Art.* Detroit, 1907.

Detroit 1910
Detroit Museum of Art. *Handbook of Modern Paintings Belonging to the Detroit Museum of Art.* Detroit, 1910.

Detroit 1920
Detroit Institute of Arts. *Catalogue of the Paintings, Sculpture, and Contemporary Arts and Crafts.* Exh. cat. 1920.

Detroit 1920a
Detroit Institute of Arts. *Sixth Annual Exhibition of American Artists.* Exh. cat. 1920.

Detroit 1921
Detroit Institute of Arts. *Seventh Annual Exhibition of American Artists.* Exh. cat. 1921.

Detroit 1922
Detroit Institute of Arts. *Eighth Annual Exhibition of American Artists.* Exh. cat. 1922.

Detroit 1930
Detroit Institute of Arts. *Catalogue of Paintings in the Permanent Collection of the Detroit Institute of Arts.* Detroit, 1930.

Detroit 1930a
Detroit Institute of Arts. *A Guide to the Collections of the Detroit Institute of Arts of the City of Detroit.* Detroit, 1930.

Detroit 1932
Detroit Society of Arts and Crafts. *American Folk Art, Painting and Sculpture.* Exh. cat. 1932.

Detroit 1934
Detroit Institute of Arts. "American Portrait Painting." [No cat.] 1934.

Detroit 1937
Detroit Institute of Arts. *Eighteenth Annual Exhibition of American Artists.* Exh. cat. 1937.

Detroit 1938
Detroit, Alger House. "Portraits of Prominent Detroiters." [No cat.] 1938.

Detroit 1944
Detroit Institute of Arts. *Detroit Institute of Arts Catalogue of Paintings.* Detroit, 1944.

Detroit 1944a
Detroit Institute of Arts. *The World of the Romantic Artist; A Survey of American Culture from 1800 to 1875.* Exh. cat. by E. P. Richardson. 1944.

Detroit 1949
Detroit Institute of Arts. "An Exhibition of the Work of Painters in Detroit before 1900." Typewritten exh. list. 1949.

Detroit 1952
Detroit Historical Museum. "Negro Culture Exhibition." [No cat.] 1952.

Detroit 1952a
Detroit Institute of Arts. "Michigan Painters before 1900." Typewritten exh. list. 1952.

Detroit 1952b
Detroit Public Library. *Centenary Exhibition of "Uncle Tom's Cabin."* Exh. cat. 1952.

Detroit 1962
Detroit Historical Museum. [No cat.] 1962.

Detroit 1964
Detroit Institute of Arts. *The Institute Collects.* Exh. cat. 1964.

Detroit 1969
Detroit, Scarab Club. "Robert Hopkin Retrospective." [No cat.] 1969.

Detroit 1976
Detroit Institute of Arts. *Arts and Crafts in Detroit, 1906–1976: The Movement, the Society, the School.* Exh. cat. essays by Sheila K. Tabakoff and Thomas Holleman. 1976.

Detroit 1980
Detroit Historical Museum. *Historical Roots: The Black Artist in Michigan.* Exh. cat. 1980.

Detroit 1983
Detroit Institute of Arts. *The Quest for Unity: American Art between World's Fairs, 1876–1893.* Exh. cat. edited by Nancy Rivard Shaw with essays by various authors. 1983.

Detroit 1985
Detroit Institute of Arts. *One Hundred Masterworks from the Detroit Institute of Arts.* New York, 1985.

Detroit and San Francisco 1957
Detroit Institute of Arts and San Francisco, M. H. de Young Memorial Museum. *Painting in America: The Story of 450 Years.* Exh. cat. 1957.

Dewing 1915
Dewing, Maria Oakey. "Flower Painters and What the Flower Offers to Art." *Art and Progress* 6, no. 8 (June 1915): 255–262.

Didymus 1891
Didymus [Martin Johnson Heade]. "Florida Hummingbirds." *Forest and Stream* 36 (June 25, 1891): 455.

Didymus 1892
Didymus [Martin Johnson Heade]. "Taming Hummingbirds." *Forest and Stream* 37 (April 14, 1892): 348.

Didymus 1892a
Didymus [Martin Johnson Heade]. "Hummingbirds." *Forest and Stream* 38 (August 25, 1892): 158.

Didymus 1904
Didymus [Martin Johnson Heade]. "Hummingbirds." *Forest and Stream* 53 (August 6, 1904): 111.

Dover 1960
Dover, Cedric. *American Negro Art.* Greenwich, Conn., 1960.

Downes 1911
Downes, William Howe. *The Life and Works of Winslow Homer.* Boston, 1911.

Downes 1922
Downes, William Howe. "George Fuller's Pictures." *International Studio* 75, no. 302 (July 1922): 264–273.

Drepperd 1942
Drepperd, Carl W. *American Pioneer Arts and Artists.* Springfield, Mass., 1942.

Duret 1904
Duret, Théodore. *Histoire de J. McN. Whistler et de son oeuvre.* Paris, 1904.

Durham 1984
Durham, North Carolina Central University, Museum of Art. *Duncanson: A British-American Connection.* Exh. cat. 1984.

Durham et al. 1980
Durham, University of New Hampshire, University Art Galleries; New-York Historical Society; and Hanover, N.H., Dartmouth College Museum and Galleries. *The White Mountains: Places and Perceptions.* Exh. cat. by Catherine H. Campbell with essays by Donald D. Keyes, Robert L. McGrath, and R. Stuart Wallace. 1980.

Düsseldorf 1976
Düsseldorf, Germany, Kunstmuseum Düsseldorf. *The Hudson and the Rhine. Die amerikanische Malerkolonie in Düsseldorf im 19. Jahrhundert.* Exh. cat. 1976.

Dwight 1953
Dwight, Edward H. "Art in Early Cincinnati." *Cincinnati Art Museum Bulletin,* n.s., 3, no. 4 (August 1953): 3–11.

Dwight 1954
Dwight, Edward H. "Robert S. Duncanson." *Museum Echoes* 27, no. 6 (June 1954): 43–45.

Eakins 1883–88
Eakins, Thomas. "Journal of Thomas Eakins, January 1, 1883–July 7, 1888." Transcript in the collection of the Philadelphia Museum of Art, Department of American Art (original in the collection of Mr. and Mrs. Daniel W. Dietrich II). 1883–88.

Earle 1924
Earle, Helen L. *Biographical Sketches of American Artists.* 5th ed. Lansing, Mich., 1924.

East Lansing 1966
East Lansing, Michigan State University, Kresge Art Center Gallery. *American Nineteenth-Century Painting.* Exh. cat. 1966.

East Lansing et al. 1986
East Lansing, Michigan State University, Kresge Art Center Gallery; Grand Rapids, Mich., Art Museum; Midland, Mich., Center for the Arts; and Kalamazoo, Mich., Institute of Arts. *The Michigan Experience.* Exh. cat. by Sadayoshi Omoto and Eldon Van Liere. 1986.

Edwards 1987
Edwards, Lee M. "Noble Domesticity: The Paintings of Thomas Hovenden." *American Art Journal* 19, no. 1 (1987): 4–38.

***Examiner and London Review* 1870**
"French Gallery. Winter Exhibition." *Examiner and London Review,* no. 3277 (November 19, 1870): 598.

Falk 1985
Falk, Peter Hastings, ed. *Who Was Who in American Art.* Madison, Conn., 1985.

Falk 1988
Falk, Peter Hastings, ed. *The Annual Exhibition Record of the Pennsylvania Academy of the Fine Arts, 1807–1870.* Madison, Conn., 1988.

Falk 1989
Falk, Peter Hastings, ed. *The Annual Exhibition Record of the Pennsylvania Academy of the Fine Arts, 1876–1913.* Madison, Conn., 1989.

Falk 1990
Falk, Peter Hastings, ed. *The Annual Exhibition Record of the Art Institute of Chicago, 1888–1950.* Madison, Conn., 1990.

Farmer 1884
Farmer, Silas. *The History of Detroit and Michigan.* Detroit, 1884.

Farmer 1890
Farmer, Silas. *History of Detroit and Wayne County and Early Michigan.* 3d ed. Detroit, 1890. Reprint. Detroit, 1969.

Ferber 1980
Ferber, Linda S. *William Trost Richards (1833–1905): American Landscape and Marine Painter.* 2 vols. New York, 1980.

Ferry 1986
Ferry, W. Hawkins. *The Buildings of Detroit.* Detroit, 1986.

Fine 1973
Fine, Elsa Honig. *The Afro-American Artist: A Search for Identity.* New York, 1973.

Fink 1990
Fink, Lois Marie. *American Art at the Nineteenth-Century Paris Salons.* Cambridge, 1990.

Flexner 1970
Flexner, James Thomas. *Nineteenth-Century American Painting.* New York, 1970.

Flint 1961
Flint, Mich., Institute of Arts. *Michigan Museums Exhibition.* Exh. cat. 1961.

Flint 1963
Flint, Mich., Institute of Arts. *Michigan Art: Yesterday and Today.* Exh. cat. 1963.

Forbes 1894
Forbes, Edwin. *The Army Sketchbook: An Artist's Story of the Great War.* 20 vols. New York, 1894.

***Forest and Stream* 1904**
"Martin Johnson Heade." *Forest and Stream* 53 (September 17, 1904): 233.

Fort 1990
Fort, Ilene Susan. "Frederick Arthur Bridgman and the American Fascination with the Exotic Near East." Ph.D. diss., City University of New York, 1990.

Fort Worth 1972
Fort Worth, Amon Carter Museum. *A Bierstadt.* Exh. cat. by Gordon Hendricks. 1972.

Fort Worth 1994
Fort Worth, Amon Carter Museum. *Ominous Hush: The Thunderstorm Paintings of Martin Johnson Heade.* Exh. cat. by Sarah Cash. 1994.

Foshay 1979
Foshay, Ella Milbank. "Nineteenth-Century American Flower Painting and the Botanical Sciences." Ph.D. diss., Columbia University, 1979.

Foshay 1990
Foshay, Ella M. *Art in Bloom.* New York, 1990.

Foster and Leibold 1989
Foster, Kathleen A., and Cheryl Leibold. *Writing about Eakins: The Manuscripts in Charles Bregler's Thomas Eakins Collection.* Philadelphia, 1989.

Freivogel 1972
Freivogel, Elsie F. "Lilly Martin Spencer." *Archives of American Art Journal* 12, no. 4 (1972): 9–14.

***Galaxy* 1868**
"Mr. Bierstadt's New Picture." *Galaxy* 6 (December 1868): 858–859.

Gallatin 1913
Gallatin, A. E. *The Portraits and Caricatures of James McNeill Whistler: An Iconography.* London, 1913.

Gallatin 1913a
Gallatin, A. E. "Whistler—the Self-Portraits in Oil." *Art in America* 1 (July 1913): 151–158.

Gaston 1966
Gaston, Godfrey O. Notation in Kennedy Galleries folder by the librarian, Godfrey O. Gaston. December 15, 1966.

Gerdts 1979
Gerdts, William H. "Daniel Huntington's *Mercy's Dream:* A Pilgrimage through Bunyanesque Imagery." *Winterthur Portfolio* 14, no. 2 (Summer 1979): 171–194.

Gerdts 1990
Gerdts, William H. *Art across America: Two Centuries of Regional Painting, 1710–1920.* 3 vols. New York, 1990.

Geske 1976
Geske, Norman A. "Ralph Blakelock in the West." *American Art Review* (January–February 1976): 123–135.

Gibbs 1899
Gibbs, Frederick S. *The Private Collection of Frederick S. Gibbs, 421 W. 22nd Street, New York.* New York, 1899.

Gibson 1962
Gibson, Arthur Hopkin. *Robert Hopkin: Master Marine and Landscape Painter.* Ann Arbor, Mich., 1962.

Gibson 1975
Gibson, Arthur Hopkin. *Artists of Early Michigan: A Biographical Dictionary of Artists Native to or Active in Michigan, 1701–1900.* Detroit, 1975.

Giese 1990
Giese, Lucretia. "Winslow Homer: 'Best Chronicler of the War.'" In *Winslow Homer: A Symposium.* Edited by Nicolai Cikovsky, Jr. Washington, D.C., 1990.

Goldstein 1989
Goldstein, Warren. *Playing for Keeps: A History of Early Baseball.* Ithaca, N.Y., and London, 1989.

Goodrich 1929
Goodrich, Lloyd. "Thomas Eakins, Realist." *Arts* 16, no. 2 (October 1929): 72–83.

Goodrich 1933
Goodrich, Lloyd. *Thomas Eakins: His Life and Work.* New York, 1933.

Goodrich 1944
Goodrich, Lloyd. *Winslow Homer.* New York, 1944.

Goodrich 1982
Goodrich, Lloyd. *Thomas Eakins.* 2 vols. Cambridge, Mass., and London, 1982.

Goodyear 1894
Goodyear, William H. *Renaissance and Modern Art.* New York, 1894.

Gowans 1966
Gowans, Alan. *The Restless Art: A History of Painters and Painting, 1760–1960.* Philadelphia, 1966.

Grand Rapids 1955
Grand Rapids, Mich., Art Gallery. *Sargent, Whistler and Cassatt.* Exh. cat. 1955.

Grand Rapids 1958
Grand Rapids, Mich., Art Gallery. *The Art of Seeing: Painting in America from the Eighteenth Century to 1958.* Exh. brochure. 1958.

Grand Rapids 1974
Grand Rapids, Mich., Art Museum. *Mary Cassatt.* Exh. cat. 1974.

Grand Rapids 1977
Grand Rapids, Mich., Art Museum. *Themes in American Painting.* Exh. cat. by J. Gray Sweeney. 1977.

Green 1966
Green, Samuel M. *American Painting: A Historical Survey.* New York, 1966.

Greenhouse 1987
Greenhouse, Wendy. "The Daniel Huntington Sketchbook Collection in the National Academy of Design: Catalogue and Indexes." MS in the collection of the National Academy of Design. New York, 1987.

Greenhouse 1989
Greenhouse, Wendy. "The American Portrayal of Tudor and Stuart History, 1835–1865." Ph.D. diss., Yale University, 1989.

Greenthal et al. 1986
Greenthal, Kathryn, Paula M. Kozol, and Jan Seidler Ramirez. *American Figurative Sculpture in the Museum of Fine Arts, Boston.* Boston, 1986.

Greenville 1990
Greenvile, S.C., Greenville County Museum of Art. *Regional American Painting to 1920.* Exh. cat. 1990.

Grigaut 1947
Grigaut, Paul. "Two Paintings by Martin Johnson Heade." *Bulletin of the Detroit Institute of Arts* 27 (1947): 16–18.

Grigaut 1955–56
Grigaut, Paul L. "A Tuscan Hillside by Elihu Vedder." *Bulletin of the Detroit Institute of Arts* 35 (1955–56): 90–92.

Grigaut 1958–59
Grigaut, Paul L. "An American Painter's Dream." *Bulletin of the Detroit Institute of Arts* 38, no. 4 (1958–59): 89–91.

Groce and Wallace 1957
Groce, George C., and David H. Wallace. *The New-York Historical Society's Dictionary of Artists in America, 1564–1860.* New Haven and London, 1957.

Grosse Pointe 1978
Grosse Pointe, Mich., War Memorial. "Robert H. Tannahill Memorial Exhibition." [No cat.] 1978.

Grossman 1974
Grossman, Julian. *Echo of a Distant Drum: Winslow Homer and the Civil War.* New York, 1974.

Grubar 1966
Grubar, Francis S. "Richard Caton Woodville: An American Artist, 1825 to 1855." Ph.D. diss., Johns Hopkins University, 1966.

Grubar 1967
Grubar, Francis S. "Gentlemanly Genre." *Art News* 66 (May 1967): 32–35, 76–77.

Hadry 1851
Hadry, Henriette A. "Mrs. Lilly M. Spencer." *Sartain's Union Magazine* 9 (August 1851): 152–154.

Hale 1975
Hale, Nancy. *Mary Cassatt: A Biography of the Great American Painter.* Garden City, N.Y., 1975.

Hamilton 1961
Hamilton, Ontario, Art Gallery of Hamilton. *American Realists.* Exh. cat. 1961.

***Harper's Weekly* 1867**
"American Artists." *Harper's Weekly* 11 (July 13, 1867): 433–434.

***Harper's Weekly* 1880**
"John G. Brown." *Harper's Weekly* 24 (June 12, 1880): 373.

***Harper's Weekly* 1883**
"Sketches from the New York National Academy of Design." *Harper's Weekly* (April 14, 1883): 229.

Hartley 1982
Hartley, Marsden. "Albert Pinkham Ryder: The Spangle of Existence" (1936). In *Marsden Hartley: On Art.* Edited by Gail R. Scott. New York, 1982.

Hartmann 1902
Hartmann, Sadakichi. *A History of American Art* 2 vols. Boston, 1902.

Hearn 1908
Hearn, George A. *Catalogue of the Collection of Foreign and American Paintings Owned by Mr. George A. Hearn.* New York, 1908.

Heilbron 1932
Heilbron, Bertha, ed. *With Pen and Pencil on the Frontier in 1851.* St. Paul, 1932.

Heineman 1907
Heineman, David E. "The Portraits of Governor Mason." *Historical Collections: Collections and Researches Made by the Michigan Pioneer and Historical Society* 35 (1907): 238–243.

Hemans 1920
Hemans, Lawton T. *Life and Times of Stevens Thomson Mason, the Boy Governor of Michigan.* Lansing, Mich., 1920.

Hendricks 1964
Hendricks, Gordon. "The First Three Western Journeys of Albert Bierstadt." *Art Bulletin* 46 (September 1964): 333–365.

Hendricks 1973
Hendricks, Gordon. *Albert Bierstadt: Painter of the American West.* New York, 1973.

Hendricks 1974
Hendricks, Gordon. *The Life and Work of Thomas Eakins.* New York, 1974.

Hendricks 1979
Hendricks, Gordon. *The Life and Work of Winslow Homer.* New York, 1979.

Henry 1901
Henry, Kirk D. "An American Patron of American Art." *Brush and Pencil* 8 (July 1901): 207–222.

Heslip 1978
Heslip, Michael. "Conservation Notes on *Cotopaxi.*" *Bulletin of the Detroit Institute of Arts* 56 (1978): 196–198.

Highley 1972
Highley, George Norman, ed. *T. Buchanan Read: Artist, Poet, Sculptor, March 12, 1822–May 11, 1872, on the Occasion March 12, 1972, of the Sesquicentennial of His Birth.* Glen Loch, Pa., 1972.

A. Hill 1922
Hill, Arthur Turnbull. "Early Recollections of George Inness and George Waldo Hill." *New Salmagundi Papers. Series of 1922.* New York, 1922.

M. Hill 1992
Hill, May Brawley. "Grandmother's Garden." *Antiques* 142, no. 5 (November 1992): 726–735.

Hills 1972
Hills, Patricia. *Eastman Johnson.* New York, 1972.

Hills 1977
Hills, Patricia. *The Genre Painting of Eastman Johnson: The Sources and Development of His Style and Themes.* New York, 1977.

Hobbs 1985
Hobbs, Susan. "Thomas Dewing in Cornish, 1885–1905." *American Art Journal* 17, no. 2 (Spring 1985): 2–32.

Holbrook 1955
Holbrook, Stewart. "Ah Winter!" *American Heritage* 7 (December 1955): 14–19.

Holden 1969
Holden, Donald. *Whistler Landscapes and Seascapes.* New York, 1969.

Holleman and Gallagher 1978
Holleman, Thomas J., and James P. Gallagher. *Smith, Hinchman & Grylls: 125 Years of Architecture and Engineering, 1853–1978.* Detroit, 1978.

Homer and Goodrich 1989
Homer, William Innes, and Lloyd Goodrich. *Albert Pinkham Ryder: Painter of Dreams.* New York, 1989.

Homer and Robb 1961
Homer, William I., and David M. Robb, Jr. "Paintings by George Fuller in American Museums and Public Collections." *Art Quarterly* 24, no. 3 (Autumn 1961): 286–294.

Hood et al. 1977
Hood, Graham, Kathleen Pyne, and Nancy Rivard. "American Paintings Acquired during the Last Decade." *Bulletin of the Detroit Institute of Arts* 55, no. 2 (1977): 69–108.

Hoppin 1974
Hoppin, Martha J. "William Morris Hunt: Aspects of His Work." Ph.D. diss., Harvard University, 1974.

Hoppin 1981
Hoppin, Martha J. "Women Artists in Boston, 1870–1900: The Pupils of William Morris Hunt." *American Art Journal* 13, no. 1 (Winter 1981): 17–46.

Houston 1976
Houston, Meredith Long and Company. "Tradition and Innovation: American Painting of the 1860s." [No cat.] 1976.

Houston et al. 1988
Houston, Menil Collection; Richmond, Virginia Museum of Fine Arts; and Raleigh, North Carolina Museum of Art. *Winslow Homer's Images of Blacks: The Civil War and Reconstruction Years.* Exh. cat. introduction by Richard J. Powell with essays by Peter H. Wood and Karen C. C. Dalton. 1988.

Huntington 1872
Huntington, Daniel, et al. *Proceedings at a Meeting of the Century Association Held in Memory of John F. Kensett.* New York, 1872.

Huntington 1960
Huntington, David C. "Frederic Edwin Church, 1826–1900: Painter of the Adamic New World Myth." Ph.D. diss., Yale University, 1960.

Huntington 1966
Huntington, David C. *The Landscapes of Frederic Edwin Church.* New York, 1966.

Huysmans 1889
Huysmans, J. K. *Certains.* Paris, 1889.

***Index of Twentieth-Century Artists* 1970**
The Index of Twentieth-Century Artists, 1933–1937. New York, 1970.

Indianapolis 1961
Indianapolis, John Herron Art Museum. *Romantic America.* Exh. cat. 1961.

Indianapolis et al. 1991
Indianapolis, National Art Museum of Sport; Phoenix Art Museum; Washington, D.C., Corocoran Gallery of Art; and New York, IBM Gallery of Science and Art. *Sport in Art from American Museums: Inaugural Exhibition of the National Art Museum of Sport.* Exh. cat. foreword by George A. Plimpton, intro. by J. Carter Brown. 1991.

Inness 1878
Inness, George. "A Painter on Painting." *Harper's New Monthly Magazine* 56 (February 1878): 458–461.

Inness 1879
Inness, George. "Mr. Inness on Art-Matters." *Art Journal,* n.s., 5 (1879): 374–377.

Inness 1879a
Inness, George. "Strong Talk on Art." *New York Evening Post,* June 3, 1879.

Inness 1884
Inness, George. "A Letter from George Inness to Ripley Hitchcock, March 23, 1884." New York, 1928.

Inness 1917
Inness, George, Jr. *Life, Art, and Letters of George Inness.* New York, 1917. Reprint. New York, 1969.

Inventory of American Painting
Washington, D.C., National Museum of American Art, Smithsonian Institution, Inventory of American Painting.

Ireland 1965
Ireland, LeRoy. *The Works of George Inness: An Illustrated Catalogue Raisonné.* Austin, Tex., and London, 1965.

Isham 1905
Isham, Samuel. *The History of American Painting.* New York, 1905. Reprinted with chapters by Royal Cortissoz. New York, 1927. New York, 1943.

Ishmael 1891
Ishmael [pseud.]. "Through the New York Studios. By Ishmael: V. Albert Bierstadt." *Illustrated American* 6 (March 21, 1891): 245–247.

Ishmael 1891a
Ishmael [pseud.]. "Through the New York Studios: By Ishmael." *Illustrated American* 6 (May 16, 1891): 622.

Ithaca 1989
Ithaca, N.Y., Cornell University, Herbert F. Johnson Museum of Art. *A Pastoral Legacy: Paintings and Drawings by the American Artists Ridgway Knight and Aston Knight.* Exh. cat. essay by Ridgway B. Knight. 1989.

Jacksonville and Palm Beach 1981
Jacksonville, Fla., Cummer Gallery of Art, and Palm Beach, Fla., Flagler Museum. *Martin Johnson Heade.* Exh. cat. 1981.

Jacobs 1985
Jacobs, Michael. *The Good and Simple Life: Artist Colonies in Europe and America.* Oxford, 1985.

James 1875
James, Henry, Jr. "On Some Pictures Lately Exhibited." *Galaxy* (July 1875): 89–97.

Janson 1977
Janson, Anthony F. "Worthington Whittredge: Two Early Landscapes." *Bulletin of the Detroit Institute of Arts* 55, no. 4 (1977): 199–208.

Janson 1982
Janson, Anthony F. "The Cincinnati Landscape Tradition." In *Celebrate Cincinnati Art,* 11–27. Cincinnati, 1982.

Janson 1989
Janson, Anthony F. *Worthington Whittredge.* Cambridge and New York, 1989.

Janson and Fraser 1981
Janson, Anthony F., and Ian A. Fraser. *Handbook of European and American Paintings to 1945: Indianapolis Museum of Art.* Indianapolis, 1981.

Jarves 1869
Jarves, James Jackson. *Art Thoughts.* New York, 1869.

Jerome 1902
Jerome, Thomas Spencer [Rusticus, pseud.]. "A Letter to Pliny the Younger, Relating to the Villa Castello, on Capri." *House and Garden* 2 (August 1902): 342–354.

Jewett 1896
Jewett, Sarah Orne. *The Country of the Pointed Firs and Other Stories.* Boston and New York, 1896. Reprint. New York, 1989.

Johns 1983
Johns, Elizabeth. *Thomas Eakins: The Heroism of Modern Life.* Princeton, N.J., 1983.

Johns 1991
Johns, Elizabeth. *American Genre Painting: The Politics of Everyday Life.* New Haven and London, 1991.

Kalamazoo 1964
Kalamazoo, Mich., Art Center. "American Artists and Nature, 1860–1940." [No cat.] 1964.

Kalamazoo 1966
Kalamazoo, Mich., Art Center. *Paintings by American Masters.* Exh. cat. 1966.

Keck 1942
Keck, Sheldon. "The Technical Examination of Paintings, Its Uses and Limitations in Art Criticism." *Brooklyn Museum Journal* (1942): 71–82.

Kelly 1988
Kelly, Franklin W. *Frederic Edwin Church and the National Landscape.* Washington, D.C., and London, 1988.

Kelly and Carr 1987
Kelly, Franklin W., and Gerald L. Carr. *The Early Landscapes of Frederic Edwin Church, 1845–1854.* Fort Worth, Tex., 1987.

Kennedy Quarterly 1967
"An American Survey: Paintings from Two Centuries." *Kennedy Quarterly* 7, no. 1 (March 1967): 2–76.

Kenny 1965
Kenny, Sister M. Kilian. "A History of Painting in Michigan, 1850 to World War II." Ph.D. diss., Wayne State University, 1965.

Ketner 1983
Ketner, Joseph D. "Robert S. Duncanson (1821–1872): The Late Literary Landscape Paintings." *American Art Journal* 15, no. 1 (Winter 1983): 35–47.

Ketner 1987
Ketner, Joseph D. "Robert S. Duncanson (1821–1872)." In *Artists of Michigan from the Nineteenth Century.* Edited by J. Gray Sweeney. Muskegon, Mich., 1987.

Ketner 1988
Ketner, Joseph D. "The Belmont Murals in the Taft Museum." *Queen City Heritage* (Cincinnati Historical Society) 46, no. 1 (Spring 1988): 51–63.

Ketner 1993
Ketner, Joseph D. *Robert S. Duncanson: The Emergence of the African-American Artist.* Columbia, Mo., 1993.

Kinsey 1992
Kinsey, Joni Louise. *Thomas Moran and the Surveying of the American West.* Washington, D.C., and London, 1992.

Kirstein 1946
Kirstein, Lincoln. "Who Was Dr. Rimmer?" *Town & Country* (July 1946): 72–73, 118, 132–133.

Klackner 1906
Klackner, C. *Reproductions of the Work of E. L. Henry.* New York, 1906.

Knickerbocker 1852
"Editor's Table." *Knickerbocker* 39 (June 1852): 567.

Knowlton 1899
Knowlton, Helen M. *Art-Life of William Morris Hunt.* Boston, 1899.

Kreiner 1995
Kreiner, Mary Beth. "Francis Davis Millet's *Reading the Story of Oenone.*" *Bulletin of the Detroit Institute of Arts* 69, nos. 1–2 (1995): 14–25.

Kurtz 1882
Kurtz, Charles. *Illustrated Art Notes upon the Fifty-seventh Annual Exhibition of Design, New York.* New York, 1882.

Lanier 1933
Lanier, Henry Wysham. *A. B. Frost, the American Sportsman's Artist.* New York, 1933.

Lansing 1985
Lansing, Mich., Historical Museum. "From Territory to Statehood." [No cat.] 1985.

La Roche sur Von 1993
La Roche sur Von, France, Conservation Départementale des Musées de Vendée, Château de la Chabotterie. *Les Guerres de Vendée.* Exh. cat. 1993.

Lathrop 1893
Lathrop, George P. "The Progress of Art in New York." *Harper's Monthly* 86 (1893): 86.

Lawrence 1961
Lawrence, University of Kansas Museum of Art. *Kansiensana.* Exh. cat. 1961.

Leibold 1988
Leibold, Cheryl. "Thomas Eakins in the Badlands." *Archives of American Art Journal* 28, no. 2 (1988): 2–15.

Leningrad et al. 1976
Leningrad, Hermitage Museum; Moscow, Pushkin Museum of Fine Arts; Kiev, State Museum of Ukrainian Art; and Minsk, State Museum of Belorussian SSR. *Exhibition of Pictures from Museums of the United States of America.* Exh. cat. in Russian. 1976.

Life History 1963
The Life History of the United States. Vol. 6. Chicago, 1963.

Lincoln and Trenton 1975
Lincoln, Neb., Sheldon Memorial Art Gallery, and Trenton, New Jersey State Museum. *Ralph Albert Blakelock 1847–1919.* Exh. cat. by Norman Geske. 1975.

Lindquist-Cock 1970
Lindquist-Cock, Elizabeth. "Stereoscopic Photography and the Western Paintings of Albert Bierstadt." *Art Quarterly* 33, no. 4 (1970): 360–378.

Literary World 1850
"Fine Arts: The American Art-Union." *Literary World* 7 (November 30, 1850): 432.

Liverpool 1884
Liverpool, Eng., Art Club. *Catalogue of a Loan Exhibition of Modern Oil Paintings by Foreign Artists.* Exh. cat. 1884.

London 1872
London, Society of French Artists. *Fifth Exhibition.* Exh. cat. 1872.

London 1875
London, Dudley Gallery. *Ninth Winter Exhibition.* Exh. cat. 1875.

London 1877
London, Grosvenor Gallery. *I Summer Exhibition.* Exh. cat. 1877.

London 1892
London, Goupil Gallery. *Nocturnes, Marines, and Chevalet Piece.* Exh. cat. 1892.

London 1895
London, Goupil Gallery. *A Connoisseur's Collection.* Exh. cat. 1895.

London 1905
London, New Gallery, *Memorial Exhibition of the Works of the Late James McNeill Whistler, First President of the International Society of Sculptors, Painters, and Gravers.* Exh. cat. by John Lavery, Albert Ludovici, and Joseph Pennell. 1905.

London 1909
London, Royal Academy of Arts. *Exhibition of Modern Works in Painting and Sculpture Forming the Collection of the Late George M. McCulloch, Esq., Winter Exhibition Fortieth Year.* Exh. cat. 1909.

London 1993
London, National Portrait Gallery. *Thomas Eakins.* Exh. cat. by John Wilmerding et al. 1993.

London and New York 1960
London, Arts Council of Great Britain, and New York, Knoedler Galleries. *James McNeill Whistler.* Exh. cat. by A. McLaren Young. 1960.

London et al. 1994
London, Tate Gallery; Paris, Musée d'Orsay; and Washington, D.C., National Gallery of Art. *Whistler.* Exh. cat. by Richard Dorment and Margaret F. MacDonald with contributions by Nicolai Cikovsky, Jr., Ruth Fine, and Geneviève Lacambre. 1994.

London Review 1865
"Fine Arts. American Landscapes." *London Review* 10 (June 1865): 662–663.

Los Angeles 1974
Los Angeles County Museum of Art. *American Narrative Painting.* Exh. cat. essay by Donelson F. Hoopes, and notes by Nancy Wall Moure. 1974.

Los Angeles 1980
Los Angeles, Goldfield Galleries. *William Louis Sonntag: Artist of the Ideal, 1822–1900.* Exh. cat. by Nancy Wall Moure. 1980.

Los Angeles 1987
Los Angeles, California Afro-American Museum. *The Portrayal of the Black Musician in American Art.* Exh. cat. 1987.

Los Angeles et al. 1976
Los Angeles County Museum of Art; Atlanta, High Museum of Art; Dallas Museum of Fine Arts; and Brooklyn Museum. *Two Centuries of*

Black American Art. Exh. cat. by David C. Driskell with notes by Leonard Simon. 1976.

Los Angeles et al. 1985
Los Angeles County Museum of Art; New York, Metropolitan Museum of Art; Cleveland Museum of Art; Minneapolis Institute of Arts; and Washington, D.C., National Gallery of Art. *George Inness*. Exh. cat. essays by Nicolai Cikovsky, Jr., and Michael Quick. 1985.

Lostalot 1883
Lostalot, Alfred de. "Exposition internationale de peinture. Galerie Georges Petit." *Gazette des Beaux-Arts* 28 (July 1883): 77–80.

Lott 1993
Lott, Eric. *Love and Theft: Blackface Minstrelsy and the American Working Class*. New York, 1993.

Louisville 1884
Louisville, Southern Exposition. *Illustrated Catalogue of the Art Gallery of the Southern Exposition*. Exh. cat. 1884.

Lovell 1985
Lovell, Margaretta M. "American Artists in Venice, 1860–1920." *Antiques* 127 (April 1985): 862–869.

Lovell 1989
Lovell, Margaretta M. *A Visitable Past: Views of Venice by American Artists, 1860–1915*. Chicago and London, 1989.

Lubin 1994
Lubin, David M. *Picturing a Nation: Art and Social Change in Nineteenth-Century America*. New Haven, 1994.

Ludlow 1870
Ludlow, Fitz Hugh. *The Heart of the Continent: A Record of Travel across the Plains and in Oregon*. New York, 1870.

Ludovici 1926
Ludovici, Albert. *An Artist's Life in London and Paris, 1870–1925*. London, 1926.

Lusk 1903
Lusk, Lewis. "The Later Work of Elihu Vedder." *Art Journal* 55 (1903): 142–146.

McCausland 1945
McCausland, Elizabeth. *The Life and Work of Edward Lamson Henry N.A. (1841–1919)*. Albany, N.Y., 1945.

McCausland 1955
McCausland, Elizabeth. "American Still-Life Paintings in the Collection of Paul Magriel." *Antiques* 67 (April 1955): 324–327.

McClinton 1979
McClinton, Katharine M. "John George Brown: Sentimental Painter of the American Scene." *Connoisseur* 200 (April 1979): 242–247.

MacColl 1893
MacColl, Dugald S. "Mr. Whistler's Paintings in Oil." *Art Journal* (March 1893): 88–93.

"McEntee Diary"
"The Jervis McEntee Diary." *Archives of American Art Journal* 8 (July–October 1968): 1–29.

McMullen 1973
McMullen, Roy. *Victorian Outsider: A Biography of J. A. M. Whistler*. New York, 1973.

McPherson 1988
McPherson, James K. *Battle Cry of Freedom: The Civil War Era*. New York, 1988.

Mandel 1973
Mandel, Patricia C. F. "Homer Dodge Martin: American Landscape Painter, 1836–1897." Ph.D. diss., New York University, 1973.

Mandel 1973a
Mandel, Patricia C. F. "The Stories behind Three Important Late Homer D. Martin Paintings." *Archives of American Art Journal* 13, no. 3 (1973): 2–8.

Mangravite 1935
Mangravite, Peppino. "The American Painter and His Environment." *American Magazine of Art* (April 1935): 199.

Mansfield 1991
Mansfield, Ohio, Mansfield Art Center. *The American Garden*. Exh. cat. 1991.

Manthorne 1989
Manthorne, Katherine Emma. *Tropical Renaissance: North American Artists Exploring Latin America, 1839–1879*. Washington, D.C., and London, 1989.

Manthorne 1993
Manthorne, Katherine Emma. "On the Road: Louis Rémy Mignot's Landscape in Ecuador." *North Carolina Museum of Art Bulletin* 16 (1993): 13–30.

Marceau 1930
Marceau, Henri G. "Catalogue of the Works of Thomas Eakins." *Pennsylvania Museum Bulletin* 25 (March 1930): 17–33.

Marlor 1970
Marlor, Clark S. *A History of the Brooklyn Art Association with an Index of Exhibitions*. New York, 1970.

E. Martin 1904
Martin, Elizabeth Gilbert. *Homer Martin: A Reminiscence*. New York, 1904.

J. Martin 1976
Martin, Jennifer A. "The Rediscovery of Maria Oakey Dewing." *Feminist Art Journal* 5, no. 2 (Summer 1976): 24–27, 44.

J. Martin 1977
Martin, Jennifer A. "Portraits of Flowers: The Out-of-Door Still-Life Paintings of Maria Oakey Dewing." *American Art Review* 4 (December 1977): 48–55, 114–118.

Mason City 1966
Mason City, Iowa, Charles MacNider Museum. *A Look at American Landscapes*. Exh. cat. 1966.

***Masters in Art* 1908**
Inness. Masters in Art 9 (June 1908): 22–42.

Mather 1912
Mather, Frank Jewett, Jr. *Homer Martin: Poet in Landscape*. New York, 1912.

Mather 1930
Mather, Frank Jewett, Jr. "Thomas Eakins Art in Retrospect." *International Studio* 95 (January 1930): 44–49, 90–91.

Mathews 1984
Mathews, Nancy Mowll, ed. *Cassatt and Her Circle: Selected Letters*. New York, 1984.

Mathews 1987
Mathews, Nancy Mowll. *Mary Cassatt*. New York, 1987.

Mathews 1994
Mathews, Nancy Mowll. *Mary Cassatt: A Life*. New York, 1994.

Memphis 1945
Memphis, Tenn., Brooks Memorial Art Gallery. *A Loan Exhibition of American Paintings: Portraits, Landscapes, and Genre of the Eighteenth and Nineteenth Century*. Exh. cat. 1945.

Merrill 1992
Merrill, Linda. *A Pot of Paint: Aesthetics on Trial in "Whistler v Ruskin."* Washington, D.C., 1992.

Meyer 1908
Meyer, A. Nathan. "Homer Martin: American Landscape Painter." *International Studio* 35 (October 1908): 255–262.

Michigan Writers' Program 1941
Michigan Writers' Program. *Michigan, a Guide to the Wolverine State*. 1941. Reprint. St. Clair Shores, Mich., 1973.

Millet 1886
Millet, Josiah B., ed. *George Fuller: His Life and Works*. Boston and New York, 1886.

Milwaukee 1960
Milwaukee Art Center. *At Work*. Exh. cat. 1960.

Minks 1989
Minks, Louise. *The Hudson River School*. New York, 1989.

Minneapolis 1973
Minneapolis Institute of Arts. *Fakes and Forgeries*. Exh. cat. 1973.

Money 1986
Money, James. *Capri: Island of Pleasure.* London, 1986.

Montclair 1964
Montclair, N.J., Art Museum. *George Inness of Montclair.* Exh. cat. 1964.

Montclair 1983
Montclair, N.J., Art Museum. *The World of A. B. Frost: His Family and Their Inner Circle.* Exh. cat. 1983.

Montgomery 1889
Montgomery, Walter, ed. *American Art and American Art Collections: Essays on Artistic Subjects by the Best Art Writers, Fully Illustrated with Etchings, Photo-Etchings, Photogravures, Phototypes, and Engravings on Steel and Wood by the Most Celebrated Artists.* 2 vols. Boston, 1889. Reprint. New York, 1978.

Montpelier 1972
Montpelier, Vt., Wood Art Gallery. *Thomas Waterman Wood.* Exh. cat. by William C. Lipke. 1972.

Montreal 1967
Montreal Museum of Fine Arts, Québec. *The Painter and the New World: A Survey of Painting from 1564 to 1867, Marking the Founding of the Canadian Federation.* Exh. cat. 1967.

Moore 1893
Moore, George. *Modern Painting.* New York, 1893.

Moscow et al. 1987
Moscow, Pushkin Museum of Art; Leningrad, Hermitage Museum; and Tbilisi (Georgia) Museum of Art. *New Horizons: American Painting, 1840–1910.* Exh. cat. 1987.

Muller 1976
Muller, N. C. *Paintings and Drawings at the Shelburne Museum, Shelburne, Vermont.* Shelburne, Vt., 1976.

Muller 1987
Muller, Norman E. "Checklist of Boston Retailers in Artist's Materials: 1823–1887." In *American Artists' Materials Suppliers Directory Nineteenth Century: New York, 1810–1899, Boston 1823–1887,* by Alexander W. Katlan. Park Ridge, N.J., 1987.

Muskegon and Detroit 1987
Muskegon, Mich., Museum of Art, and Detroit Historical Museum. *Artists of Michigan: From the Nineteenth Century.* Exh. cat. edited by Andrea P. A. Belloli and Michael P. DeMarsche. 1987.

Nagoya 1983
Nagoya, Japan, Musée Prefectoral d'Aichi. *Six Femmes Peintres.* Exh. cat. 1983.

Naylor 1973
Naylor, Maria. *The National Academy of Design Exhibition Record, 1861–1900.* 2 vols. New York, 1973.

Nebraska Blakelock Inventory
The Nebraska Blakelock Inventory, University of Nebraska, Lincoln, Library, Special Collections.

Newark et al. 1974
Newark, N.J, Museum; Mobile, Ala., Museum; Columbus, Ohio, Gallery of Fine Arts; Athens, Georgia Museum of Art; and Sacramento, Calif., E. B. Crocker Art Gallery. *Revealed Masters: Nineteenth-Century American Art.* Exh. cat. essay by William H. Gerdts. 1974.

New Britain 1943
New Britain, Conn., Art Museum of New Britain. *Nineteenth-Century and Contemporary Watercolors.* Exh. cat. 1943.

New London 1949
New London, Conn., Lyman Allen Museum. *Exhibition of James McNeill Whistler.* Exh. cat. 1949.

New Orleans 1884
New Orleans. *Catalogue of the Art Collection of the World's Industrial and Cotton Centennial Exposition.* Exh. cat. 1884.

New York 1853
New York, American Art-Union. *The Washington Exhibition, in Aid of the New-York Gallery of the Fine Arts, at the American Art-Union Gallery, 497 Broadway.* Exh. cat. 1853.

New York 1873
New York, Century Association. Exh. cat., transcribed by Louis Lang. See Yarnall and Gerdts 1986, 1:32.

New York 1881
New York, Metropolitan Museum of Art. *A Memorial Catalogue of the Paintings of Sanford Robinson Gifford, N.A.* Essay by John F. Weir. New York, 1881. Reprint. New York, 1974.

New York 1883
New York, H. Wunderlich and Co. *Fifty Etchings and Drypoints (Venice Second Series).* Exh. cat. 1883.

New York 1887
Catalogue of Vedder's Phototypes. Exh. cat. New York, 1887.

New York 1893
New York, Art House. Thomas B. Clarke collection sale catalogue. June 1893.

New York 1894
New York, American Fine Arts Society. *Exhibition of the Works of George Inness.* Exh. cat. 1894.

New York 1898
New York, Manhattan Club. *Loan Exhibition.* Exh. cat. 1898.

New York 1902
New York, Society of American Artists. *Twenty-fourth Annual Exhibition.* Exh. cat. 1902.

New York 1912
New York, Metropolitan Museum of Art. *Paintings in Oil and Pastels by J. A. M. Whistler.* Exh. cat. 1912.

New York 1917
New York, Metropolitan Museum of Art. *Loan Exhibition of the Works of Thomas Eakins.* Exh. cat. 1917.

New York 1923
New York, Joseph Brummer Galleries. *Exhibition of Paintings and Water Colors by Thomas Eakins.* Exh. cat. 1923.

New York 1929
New York, Babcock Art Galleries. *Paintings by Thomas Eakins.* Exh. cat. 1929.

New York 1935
New York, Whitney Museum of American Art. *American Genre: The Social Scene in Paintings and Prints (1800–1935).* Exh. cat. by Lloyd Goodrich. 1935.

New York 1936
New York, Whitney Museum of American Art. *Winslow Homer Centenary.* Exh. cat. 1936.

New York 1937
New York, American Academy of Arts and Letters. *Exhibition of the Works of Elihu Vedder.* Exh. cat. 1937.

New York 1942
New York, Century Association. "Oils and Watercolors by Edward Lamson Henry." [No cat.] 1942.

New York 1943
New York, Museum of Modern Art. *Romantic Painting in America.* Exh. cat. 1943.

New York 1946
New York, Whitney Museum of American Art. *William Rimmer, 1816–1879.* Exh. cat. entries and essay by Lincoln Kirstein. 1946.

New York 1947
New York, Whitney Museum of American Art. *Albert P. Ryder Centenary Exhibition.* Exh. cat. by Lloyd Goodrich. 1947.

New York 1947a
New York, Whitney Museum of American Art. *Ralph Albert Blakelock Centenary Exhibition.* Exh. cat. by Lloyd Goodrich. 1947.

New York 1947b
New York, Macbeth Gallery. *Whistler Loan Exhibition.* Exh. cat. 1947.

New York 1952
New York, Museum of the City of New York. [No cat.] 1952.

New York 1953
New York, Wildenstein & Co. *Landmarks in American Art, 1670–1950.* Exh. cat. 1953.

New York 1961
New York, Bramhall House. *Winslow Homer, American Artist: His World and His Work.* Exh. cat. by Albert Ten Eyck Gardner. 1961.

New York 1962
New York, IBM Gallery, for the National Art Museum of Sport. "Fine Art in Sports." [No cat.] 1962.

New York 1963
New York, Wildenstein & Co. *The Birth of Impressionism.* Exh. cat. 1963.

New York 1964
New York, Gallery of Better Living Center, New York World's Fair. *Four Centuries of American Masterpieces.* Exh. cat. 1964.

New York 1966
New York, Knoedler & Co. *Mary Cassatt.* Exh. cat. 1966.

New York 1966a
New York, Museum of Modern Art. *Turner: Imagination and Reality.* Exh. cat. essay by Lawrence Gowing. 1966.

New York 1967
New York, Marlborough-Gerson Gallery. *The New York Painter: A Century of Teaching, Morse to Hofmann.* Exh. cat. 1967.

New York 1968
New York, American Federation of Arts. *John Frederick Kensett, 1816–1872.* Exh. cat. essay by John K. Howat. 1968.

New York 1968a
New York, National Art Museum of Sport. "The Ball in Sports." [No cat.] 1968.

New York 1969
New York, Hirschl & Adler Galleries. *The American Scene: A Survey of the Life and Landscape of the Nineteenth Century.* Exh. cat. 1969.

New York 1970
New York, Metropolitan Museum of Art. *Nineteenth-Century American Paintings and Sculpture: Centennial Exhibition of the Metropolitan Museum of Art.* Exh. cat. by John K. Howat, John Wilmerding, Natalie Spassky, et al. 1970.

New York 1970a
New York, Whitney Museum of American Art. *Thomas Eakins Retrospective Exhibition.* Exh. cat. 1970.

New York 1974
New York, Chapellier Gallery. *The Art of Milne Ramsey.* Exh. cat. by William H. Gerdts. 1974.

New York 1976
New York, Museum of Modern Art. *The Natural Paradise: Painting in America, 1800–1950.* Exh. cat. edited by Kynaston McShine, with essays by Barbara Novak, Robert Rosenblum, and John Wilmerding, and a chronicle by Mary Davis. 1976.

New York 1976a
New York, Metropolitan Museum of Art. *Selections of Nineteenth-Century Afro-American Art.* Exh. cat. by R. A. Perry. 1976.

New York 1977
New York, Hirschl & Adler Galleries. *A Gallery Collects.* Exh. cat. 1977.

New York 1978
New York, ACA Galleries. *American Flower Painting, 1850–1950.* Exh. cat. 1978.

New York 1979
New York, National Academy of Design. *From All Walks of Life: Paintings of the Figure from the National Academy of Design.* Exh. cat. introduction by John H. Dobkin, text by William H. Gerdts. 1979.

New York 1980
New York, National Academy of Design. *Next to Nature: Landscape Paintings from the National Academy of Design.* Exh. cat. edited by Barbara Novak and Annette Blaugrund, introduction by Barbara Novak. 1980.

New York 1983
New York, Davis and Langdale Company, with Ben Ali Haggin. *William Stanley Haseltine (1835–1900): Drawings of a Painter.* Exh. cat. essay by John Wilmerding. 1983.

New York 1984
New York, Whitney Museum of American Art. *Reflections of Nature: Flowers in American Art.* Exh. cat. by Ella M. Foshay. 1984.

New York 1987
New York, Metropolitan Museum of Art. *American Paradise: The World of the Hudson River School.* Exh. cat. by John K. Howat, Kevin J. Avery, Doreen Bolger Burke, Catherine Hoover Voorsanger, et al. 1987.

New York 1987a
New York, Alexander Gallery. *The Hudson River School: Congenial Observations.* Exh. cat. 1987.

New York 1987b
New York, Salander-O'Reilly Galleries. *Ralph Albert Blakelock (1847–1919).* Exh. cat. essay by Norman Geske. 1987.

New York 1988
New York, Berry-Hill Galleries. *American Paintings V.* Exh. cat. 1988.

New York 1989
New York, Babcock Galleries. *Traditions: Babcock Galleries and American Art.* Exh. cat. 1989.

New York 1989a
New York, Jordan-Volpe Gallery. *Nineteenth- and Twentieth-Century Paintings.* Exh. cat. text by Mary Lublin. 1989.

New York and Washington 1975
New York, National Academy of Design, and Washington, D.C., National Collection of Fine Arts. *150th Anniversary of the National Academy of Design.* Exh. cat. 1975.

New York et al. 1972
New York, Whitney Museum of American Art; Cincinnati Art Museum; and Milwaukee Art Center. *Eastman Johnson.* Exh. cat. by Patricia Hills. 1972.

New York et al. 1973
New York, Whitney Museum of American Art; Los Angeles County Museum of Art; and Art Institute of Chicago. *Winslow Homer.* Exh. cat. by Lloyd Goodrich. 1973.

New York et al. 1993
New York, Fraunces Tavern Museum; New York, IBM Gallery of Science and Art; Washington, D.C., Corcoran Gallery of Art; Dallas Museum of Art; Miami, Center for Fine Arts; and Phoenix Art Museum. *Picturing History: American Painting, 1770–1930.* Exh. cat. edited by William Ayres. 1993.

Northampton 1951
Northampton, Mass., Smith College Museum of Art. *Winslow Homer: Illustrator.* Exh. cat. 1951.

Northampton 1964
Northampton, Mass., Smith College Museum of Art. "Loan Exhibition." [No cat.] 1964.

Northfield 1967
Northfield, Minn., Carleton College. "Centennial Anniversary Exhibition." [No. cat.] 1967.

Norton 1861
Norton, Frank H. *A Few Notes on the Thirty-sixth Annual Exhibition of the National Academy of Design.* New York, 1861.

Novak 1969
Novak, Barbara. *American Painting of the Nineteenth Century.* New York, 1969.

NYPL 1989
New York Public Library, the Artists File. Microfiche ed. Alexandria, Va., 1989.

Oakland 1980
Oakland, Calif., Museum Art Department. *Thomas Hill: The Grand View.* Exh. cat. essay by Marjorie Dakin Arkelian. 1980.

Oakland and Santa Barbara 1978
Oakland, Calif., Museum Art Department, and Santa Barbara, Calif., Santa Barbara Museum of Art. *George Inness Landscapes: His Signature Years, 1884–1894.* Exh. cat. by Marjorie Dakin Arkelian and George W. Neubert. 1978.

Oberlin 1946
Oberlin, Ohio, Oberlin College, Allen Memorial Art Gallery. *American Artists Discover America.* Exh. cat. 1946.

Olpin 1978
Olpin, Robert Spencer. *Alexander Helwig Wyant (1836–1892) American Landscape Painter: An Investigation of His Life and Fame and a Critical Analysis of His Work with a Catalogue Raisonné of Wyant Paintings.* Ph.D. diss., Boston University, 1971. Microfilm ed. Ann Arbor, Mich., 1978.

Orton 1876
Orton, James. *The Andes and the Amazon; or, Across the Continent of South America.* 3d ed. New York, 1876.

Oshkosh 1962
Oshkosh, Wisc., Paine Art Center. *A Retrospective Exhibition of Paintings by George Inness.* Exh. cat. 1962.

Oxford 1959
Oxford, Ohio, Miami University. "150 Years of American Art." [No cat.] 1959.

Paley 1986
Paley, Morton D. *The Apocalyptic Sublime.* New Haven and London, 1986.

[Palgrave] 1865
[Palgrave, F. T.] "English Pictures in 1865." *Fortnightly Review* (London) 1 (August 1, 1865): 666.

Palmer 1906
Palmer, Friend. *Early Days in Detroit.* Detroit, 1906.

Paris 1883
Paris, Galerie Georges Petit. *Exposition Internationale.* Exh. cat. 1883.

Paris 1905
Paris, Palais de l'École des Beaux-Arts. *Oeuvres de James McNeill Whistler.* Exh. cat. by L. Bénédite. 1905.

Paris 1976
Paris, Musée Marmottan. *Chefs-d'oeuvre de Musées des États-Unis de Giorgione à Picasso.* Exh. cat. 1976.

Parkman 1829
Parkman, Reverend Francis. *The Offering for 1829.* Cambridge, Mass., 1829.

Parkman 1854
Parkman, Reverend Francis. *An Offering of Sympathy to the Afflicted: Especially to Bereaved Parents.* Boston and Cambridge, Mass., 1854.

Parks 1980
Parks, James D. *Robert S. Duncanson: Nineteenth-Century Black Romantic Painter.* Washington, D.C., 1980.

Parry 1921
Parry, His Honor Judge. "Whistler versus Ruskin." *Cornhill Magazine* 50 n.s. (January 1921): 21–33.

Parsons 1856
Parsons, Samuel B. *The Rose: Its History, Poetry, Culture, and Classification.* 1847. New York, 1856.

Pasadena 1917
Pasadena, Calif. *Catalogue of the David Hewes Collection of Valuable and Historical Paintings by the Late Thomas Hill.* Auction cat. 1917.

Passport Applications
Washington, D.C., National Archives. Records of the Department of State, Passport applications, record group 59.

Pattison 1911
Pattison, James William. "The Detroit Museum of Art." *Fine Arts Journal* 25, no. 2 (August 1911): 67–76.

Payne 1955–56
Payne, Elizabeth. "America at Leisure in the 1840s." *Bulletin of the Detroit Institute of Arts* 35, no. 1 (1955–56): 12–14.

Pennell and Pennell 1908
Pennell, E. R., and J. Pennell. *The Life of James McNeill Whistler.* 2 vols. Philadelphia, 1908.

Pennell and Pennell 1921
Pennell, E. R., and J. Pennell. *The Whistler Journal.* Philadelphia, 1921.

Penny 1977
Penny, Nicholas. *Church Monuments in Romantic England.* New Haven and London, 1977.

Peoria 1968
Peoria, Ill., Lakeview Center for the Arts and Sciences. *Westward the Artist.* Exh. cat. 1968.

Perkins and Gavin 1980
Perkins, Robert F., Jr., and William J. Gavin III. *The Boston Athenaeum Art Exhibition Index, 1827–1874.* Boston, 1980.

Petteys 1985
Petteys, Chris. *Dictionary of Women Artists: An International Dictionary of Women Artists Born before 1900.* Boston, 1985.

Philadelphia 1900
Philadelphia, Pennsylvania Academy of the Fine Arts. *Sixty-ninth Annual Exhibition.* Exh. cat. 1900.

Philadelphia 1917
Philadelphia, Pennsylvania Academy of the Fine Arts. *Memorial Exhibition of the Works of the Late Thomas Eakins.* Exh. cat. 1917.

Philadelphia 1931
Philadelphia, McClees Gallery. *Mary Cassatt.* Exh. cat. 1931.

Philadelphia 1965
Philadelphia Museum of Art. *The Art of Philadelphia Medicine.* Exh. cat. edited by Kneelan McNulty. 1965.

Philadelphia 1969
School District of Philadelphia. *Afro-American Artists, 1800–1969.* Exh. cat. 1969.

Philadelphia 1985
Philadelphia Museum of Art. *Mary Cassatt and Philadelphia.* Exh. cat. by Suzanne G. Lindsay. 1985.

Philadelphia et al. 1982
Philadelphia, Pennsylvania Academy of the Fine Arts; Fort Worth, Amon Carter Museum; Phoenix Art Museum; and Washington, D.C., National Museum of American Art. *Americans in Brittany and Normandy, 1860–1910.* Exh. cat. essay by David Sellin. 1982.

Philadelphia et al. 1989
Philadelphia, Pennsylvania Academy of the Fine Arts; Norfolk, Va., Chrysler Museum; Memphis, Brooks Museum of Art; and New-York Historical Society. *Paris 1889: American Artists at the Universal Exposition.* Exh. cat. essays by Annette Blaugrund, Albert Boime, D. Dodge Thompson, H. Barbara Weinberg, and Richard Guy Wilson. 1989.

Phoenix and Indianapolis 1993
Phoenix Art Museum and Indianapolis Museum of Art. *John Ruskin and the Victorian Eye.* Exh. cat. with essays by Susan P. Casteras et al. 1993.

Pittsburgh 1902
Pittsburgh, Carnegie Institute. *Seventh Annual Exhibition.* Exh. cat. 1902.

Pittsburgh 1936
Pittsburgh, Carnegie Institute. *Exhibition of American Genre Paintings*. Exh. cat. 1936.

Pittsburgh 1945
Pittsburgh, Carnegie Institute. *Thomas Eakins Centennial Exhibition (1844–1944)*. Exh. cat. 1945.

Pittsburgh 1976
Pittsburgh, Carnegie-Mellon University. *Nineteenth-Century American Flower and Fruit Painting and Graphics*. Exh. cat. 1976.

Plowden 1947
Plowden, Helen Haseltine. *William Stanley Haseltine: Sea and Landscape Painter (1835–1900)*. London, 1947.

Poe 1969
Poe, Edgar Allan. *Collected Works of Edgar Allan Poe*. Vol. 1. *Poems*. Edited by Thomas Ollive Mabbott. Cambridge, Mass., 1969.

Pollock 1980
Pollock, Griselda. *Mary Cassatt*. New York, 1980.

F. Porter 1959
Porter, Fairfield. *Thomas Eakins*. New York, 1959.

J. Porter 1943
Porter, James A. *Modern Negro Art*. New York, 1943.

J. Porter 1951
Porter, James A. "Robert S. Duncanson: Midwestern Romantic-Realist." *Art in America* 39, no. 3 (October 1951): 99–154.

Pressly 1992
Pressly, William L. *A Catalogue of Paintings in the Folger Shakespeare Library: "As Imagination Bodies Forth."* New Haven and London, 1992.

Price 1932
Price, Frederic Newlin. *Ryder: A Story of Appreciation*. New York, 1932.

Pringle 1985
Pringle, Allan. "Robert S. Duncanson in Montreal, 1863–1865." *American Art Journal* 17, no. 4 (Autumn 1985): 28–50.

Providence 1854
Providence, R.I., Rhode Island Art Association. *Catalogue of the First Exhibition of Paintings, Statuary and Other Works of Art*. Exh. cat. 1854.

Quimby 1967
Quimby, Ian M. G. "Mark Fisher: An American Impressionist." *Antiques* 91, no. 6 (June 1967): 780–783.

Raleigh 1960
Raleigh, North Carolina Museum of Art. *Tobacco and Smoking in Art*. Exh. cat. 1960.

Raleigh 1987
Raleigh, North Carolina Museum of Art. *Sir David Wilkie of Scotland (1785–1841)*. Exh. cat. by William J. Chiego, H. A. D. Miles, David Blaney Brown, Sir Ivor Batchelor, Lindsey Errington, and Arthur S. Marks. 1987.

Raleigh and New York 1996
Raleigh, North Carolina Museum of Art, and New York, National Academy of Design. *The Landscapes of Louis Rémy Mignot: A Southern Painter Abroad*. Exh. cat. by Katherine E. Manthorne with John W. Coffee. 1996.

Read 1883
Read, T. Buchanan. *The Poetical Works of T. Buchanan Read*. Philadelphia, 1883.

***Reader* 1865**
"Art. Church's New Pictures of Chimborazo and Cotopaxi." *Reader* (London) 6 (July 2, 1865): 18–19.

Reed 1967
Reed, Henry M. *The A. B. Frost Book*. Rutland, Vt., 1967.

Reed 1993
Reed, Henry M. *The A. B. Frost Book*. Rev. ed. Charleston, S.C., 1993.

Regina 1971
Regina, Saskatchewan, Norman Mackenzie Art Gallery. *In Search of America: Nineteenth-Century Painters and Writers*. Exh. cat. essays by Nancy E. Dillow and Robert C. Cosbey. 1971.

Retzsch 1838
Retzsch, Moritz. *Gallerie zu Shakespeare's Dramatischen Werken Macbeth*. Leipzig and London, 1838.

Retzsch 1849
Retzsch, Moritz. *Gallery to Shakespeare's Dramatic Works in Outlines Invented and Engraved by Moritz Retzsch: Complete in One Volume with Explanations*. New York, 1849.

Richardson 1934
Richardson, Edgar P. "A Self-Portrait by Whistler." *Bulletin of the Detroit Institute of Arts* 14, no. 2 (Nov. 1934): 20–23.

Richardson 1937
Richardson, Edgar P. "Two Portraits by Thomas Eakins." *Bulletin of the Detroit Institute of Arts* 16, no. 8 (May 1937): 131–134.

Richardson 1942
Richardson, E. P. "*The Crow's Nest* by Worthington Whittredge." *Bulletin of the Detroit Institute of Arts* 22, no. 3 (1942): 22–23.

Richardson 1944
Richardson, Edgar P. *American Romantic Painting*. New York, 1944.

Richardson 1947
Richardson, Edgar P. "*Nocturne in Black and Gold: The Falling Rocket*." *Art Quarterly* 10, no. 1 (Winter 1947): 3–10.

Richardson 1948
Richardson, Edgar P. "'The Dinner Horn' by Winslow Homer." *Art Quarterly* 11 (Spring 1948): 153–157.

Richardson 1951–52
Richardson, E. P. "Three Early Works by Winslow Homer." *Bulletin of the Detroit Institute of Arts* 31, no. 1 (1951–52): 6.

Richardson 1954
Richardson, Edgar P. "Sophisticates and Innocents Abroad." *Art News* 53 (April 1954): 20–23, 61–62.

Richardson 1956
Richardson, Edgar P. *Painting in America: The Story of 450 Years*. New York, 1956.

Richardson 1965
Richardson, E. P. *Painting in America from 1502 to the Present*. 2d ed. New York, 1965.

Richmond 1947
Richmond, Virginia Museum of Fine Arts. *Nineteenth-Century Virginia Genre*. Exh. cat. 1947.

Rimmer ca. 1855–79
Rimmer, William. "Stephen and Philip." Holograph, ca. 1855–79. Collections of the Francis A. Countway Library of Medicine, Boston Medical Library.

Rivard 1976
Rivard, Nancy J. "Curatorial Reports: American Art." *Bulletin of the Detroit Institute of Arts* 55, no. 1 (1976): 7–8.

Rivard 1978
Rivard, Nancy J. "American Paintings at the Detroit Institute of Arts." *Antiques* 114 (November 1978): 1044–1055.

Rivard 1978a
Rivard, Nancy J. "Notes on the Collection: *Cotopaxi*." *Bulletin of the Detroit Institute of Arts* 56 (1978): 193–196.

Roberts 1884
Roberts, Robert Ellis. *Sketches and Reminiscences of the City of the Straits and Its Vicinity*. Detroit, 1884.

Robinson 1953
Robinson, Francis W., to David H. Wallace, November 27, 1953. Registrar's files, DIA.

Rome 1993
Rome, Palazzo delle Esposizioni. "The American West/L'Arte della Frontiera Americana." [No cat.] 1993.

Ross 1894
Ross, Robert Budd. "Detroit in 1837, V: Fine Arts." *Detroit Sunday News Tribune,* September 9, 1894, 17.

Rossetti 1875
Rossetti, William M. "The Dudley Gallery." *Academy* 8 (October 30, 1875): 462.

Rotan 1946
Rotan, Mary. Frick Art Reference Library, New York. Folder on Rimmer's painting *Victory.* Notations from viewing the painting on November 25, 1946.

***Round Table* 1866**
"About 'Figure Pictures' at the Academy." *Round Table* (May 12, 1866): 295.

Ruskin 1877
Ruskin, John. "Letter the Seventy-ninth." *Fors Clavigera* 2 (July 1877), 181–213.

Ruskin 1903–12
Ruskin, John. *The Works of John Ruskin.* Edited by E. T. Cook and Alexander Wedderburn. 39 vols. London, 1903–12.

Saginaw 1948
Saginaw, Mich., Museum of Art. "Exhibition of American Painting from Colonial Times until Today." [No cat.] 1948.

St. Louis 1977
St. Louis Art Museum. *Currents of Expansion: Painting in the Midwest, 1820–1940.* Exh. cat. by Judy A. Barter and L. E. Springer. 1977.

St. Louis et al. 1995
St. Louis, Washington University Gallery of Art; Cincinnati, Taft Museum; Fort Worth, Amon Carter Museum; Atlanta, Clark-Atlanta University Art Gallery. "Lifting the Veil: Robert S. Duncanson and the Emergence of the African-American Artist." [No cat.] 1995.

Salt Lake City 1968
Salt Lake City, University of Utah, Museum of Fine Arts. *Alexander Helwig Wyant, 1836–1892.* Exh. cat. by Robert S. Olpin. 1968.

Salt Lake City 1976
Salt Lake City, University of Utah, Museum of Fine Arts. *American Painting 1950.* Exh. cat. 1976.

San Diego 1970
San Diego, University of California Museum of Art. *Dimensions of Black.* Exh. cat. edited by Jehanne Teilhet. 1970.

San Diego 1986
San Diego, Timken Art Gallery. *Albert Bierstadt: "Cho-looke, the Yosemite Fall."* Exh. cat. by Nancy K. Anderson. 1986.

San Diego et al. 1990
San Diego, Timken Art Gallery; Fine Arts Museums of San Francisco; New Haven, Conn., Yale University Art Gallery; and New York, National Academy of Design. *Eastman Johnson: "The Cranberry Harvest, Island of Nantucket."* Exh. cat. essays by Marc Simpson, Sally Mills, and Patricia Hills. 1990.

Sandwich 1985
Sandwich, Mass., Heritage Plantation of Sandwich. *Young America: Children and Art.* Exh. cat. 1985.

San Francisco 1916
San Francisco. *Catalogue of the David Hewes Collection of Valuable and Historical Paintings by the Late Thomas Hill.* Auction cat. 1916.

San Francisco and Chadds Ford 1992
San Francisco, Fine Arts Museums, and Chadds Ford, Pa., Brandywine River Museum. *Expressions of Place: The Art of William Stanley Haseltine.* Exh. cat. by Marc Simpson, Andrea Henderson, and Sally Mills. 1992.

San Francisco and Cleveland 1984
San Francisco, Fine Arts Museums, and Cleveland Museum of Art. *Venice: The American View, 1860–1920.* Exh. cat. by Margaretta M. Lovell. 1984.

San Francisco et al. 1988
San Francisco, Fine Arts Museums; Portland, Maine, Art Museum; and Fort Worth, Amon Carter Museum. *Winslow Homer: Paintings of the Civil War.* Exh. cat. essay by Marc Simpson with contributions by Nicolai Cikovsky, Jr., Lucretia Hoover Giese, Kristin Hoermann, Sally Mills, and Christopher Kent Wilson. 1988.

San José 1978
San José, Costa Rica, Museo de Jade. *Cinco Siglos de Obras Maestras.* Exh. cat. 1978.

Santa Barbara et al. 1969
University of California, Santa Barbara, Art Galleries; San Francisco, California Palace of the Legion of Honor; Phoenix Art Museum; and Huntington, N.Y., Heckscher Museum. *The Enigma of Ralph Blakelock.* Exh. cat. essays by David Gebhard and Phyllis Stuurman. 1969.

Schendler 1967
Schendler, Sylvan. *Eakins.* Boston and Toronto, 1967.

Scott 1851
Scott, Sir Walter. *The Lady of the Lake.* Philadelphia, 1851.

Scripps 1895
Scripps, James E. *Handbook of the Paintings Ancient and Modern, Belonging to the Detroit Museum of Art.* Detroit, 1895.

Sharpey-Schafer 1984
Sharpey-Schafer, J. A. *Soldier of Fortune: F. D. Millet, 1846–1912.* Utica, N.Y., 1984.

Shaw 1936
Shaw, Virginia W. V. "O, Call Back Yesterday." Detroit, 1936.

Shaw 1986
Shaw, Nancy Rivard. "Rebellion, Defiance, and Beauty: Two Centuries of American Painting." *Apollo* 124, no. 298 (December 1986): 527–533.

Sheldon 1877
Sheldon, George W. "How One Landscape-Painter Paints." *Art Journal* 3 (1877): 284–285.

Sheldon 1879
Sheldon, George W. *American Painters: With Eighty-three Examples of Their Work Engraved on Wood.* New York, 1879.

Sheldon 1880
Sheldon, George W. *American Painters: With One Hundred and Four Examples of Their Work Engraved on Wood.* 1878. Enl. ed. New York, 1880.

Sheldon 1881
Sheldon, George W. *American Painters.* 1878. Enl. ed. New York, 1881. Reprint. New York, 1972.

Sheldon 1882
Sheldon, George W. *Hours with Art and Artists.* New York, 1882.

Sheldon 1882a
Sheldon, George W. "George Inness." *Harper's Weekly* 26 (April 22, 1882): 244–246.

Sheldon 1890
Sheldon, George W. *Recent Ideals of American Art.* New York and London, 1890.

Sheldon 1895
Sheldon, George W. "Characteristics of George Inness." *Century* 49 (February 1895): 530–533.

Sherman 1920
Sherman, Frederic Fairchild. *Albert Pinkham Ryder.* New York, 1920.

Sherwood 1900
Sherwood, M. E. W. "Frederick [*sic*] E. Church. Studio Gatherings from Thirty Years Ago—New York's Former Bohemia." *New York Times,* April 21, 1900, 260.

Shreveport 1973
Shreveport, La., R. W. Norton Art Gallery. *The Hudson River School: American Landscape Paintings from 1821 to 1907.* Exh. cat. 1973.

Siegl 1978
Siegl, Theodor. *The Thomas Eakins Collection.* Philadelphia, 1978.

Siewert 1995
Siewert, John. "Suspended Spectacle: Whistler's *Falling Rocket* and the Nocturnal Subject." *Bulletin of the Detroit Institute of Arts* 69, nos. 1–2 (1995): 36–48.

Simon 1993
Simon, Janice. "Sanford Gifford's *Kaaterskill Falls*." *Bulletin of the Detroit Institute of Arts* 67, no. 4 (1993): 4–13.

Simpson 1990
Simpson, Marc. "Windows on the Past: Edwin Austin Abbey and Francis Davis Millet in England." *American Art Journal* 22, no. 3 (1990): 64–89.

***Smith College* 1964**
Smith College Museum of Art Bulletin 46, no. 3 (December 1964): 333–365.

Soria 1960
Soria, Regina. "Some Background Notes for Elihu Vedder's *Cumaean Sibyl* and *Young Marsyas*." *Art Quarterly* 23 (Spring 1960): 71–87.

Soria 1970
Soria, Regina. *Elihu Vedder: American Visionary Artist in Rome (1836–1923)*. Rutherford, N.J., 1970.

Soria 1982
Soria, Regina. *Dictionary of Nineteenth-Century Artists in Italy, 1760–1914*. Rutherford, N.J., London, and Toronto. 1982.

Soria 1989
Soria, Regina. "An American Macchiaiolo: New Insights into Elihu Vedder's Florentine Experience, 1857–1860." In *The Italian Presence in American Art, 1760–1860*. Edited by Irma B. Jaffe. New York and Rome, 1989.

Southampton 1984
Southampton, N.Y., Parrish Art Museum. *The American Painter-Etcher Movement*. Exh. cat. by Maureen C. O'Brien and Patricia C. F. Mandel. 1984.

Spassky 1985
Spassky, Natalie, with Linda Bantel, Doreen Bolger Burke, Meg Perlman, and Amy L. Walsh. *American Paintings in the Metropolitan Museum of Art, Vol. II: A Catalogue of Works by Artists Born between 1816 and 1845*. Edited by Kathleen Luhrs. New York, 1985.

Spencer 1972
Spencer, Robin. *The Aesthetic Movement*. London and New York, 1972.

Spencer 1989
Spencer, Robin, ed. *Whistler: A Retrospective*. New York, 1989.

Springfield et al. 1946
Springfield, Mass., George Walter Vincent Smith Art Museum; Brooklyn Museum; and Montclair, N.J., Art Museum. *George Inness: An American Landscape Painter, 1825–1894*. Exh. cat. essay by Elizabeth McCausland. 1946.

Springfield et al. 1989
Springfield, Mass., George Walter Vincent Smith Art Museum; New York, National Academy of Design; and Omaha, Joslyn Art Museum. *Country Paths and City Sidewalks: The Art of J. G. Brown*. Exh. cat. edited by Martha J. Hoppin. 1989.

***Star of Bethlehem* 1868**
Chelsea, Mass., *Star of Bethlehem Lodge. By-Laws of Star of Bethlehem Lodge, Chelsea*. Boston, 1868.

Starr 1908
Starr, Sidney. "Personal Recollections of Whistler." *Atlantic Monthly* 101 (April 1908): 528–537.

Stebbins 1975
Stebbins, Theodore E., Jr. *The Life and Works of Martin Johnson Heade*. New Haven and London, 1975.

Stein 1985
Stein, Roger B. "Packaging the Great Plains: The Role of the Visual Arts." *Great Plains Quarterly* 5 (Winter 1985): 5–23.

Stephans 1875
[Stephans, Frederick G.] "The Winter Exhibition, Dudley Gallery." *Athenaeum* no. 2505 (October 1875): 580–581.

Stillman 1878
Stillman, William, J. "The Paris Exposition.—IX. American Paintings." *Nation*, October 3, 1878, 210–211.

Stockholm and Gothenburg 1986
Stockholm, Nationalmuseum, and Gothenburg, Museum of Art. "American Nineteenth-Century Landscape Painting." [No cat.] 1986.

Story 1880
Story, William Wetmore. "Fine Arts." In vol. 2 of *Reports of the United States Commissioners to the Paris Universal Exposition*. Washington, D.C., 1880, 3–179.

Stowe 1852
Stowe, Harriet Beecher. *Uncle Tom's Cabin*. 2 vols. Boston, 1852.

Stratford 1978
Stratford, Ontario, The Gallery. *Fantastic Shakespeare*. Exh. cat. by Brian Arnott and Richard D. Studing. 1978.

Studing 1993
Studing, Richard. *Shakespeare in American Painting: A Catalogue from the Late Eighteenth Century to the Present*. Rutherford, N.J., London, and Toronto, 1993.

Suffolk County 1979
Suffolk County Archaeological Association. *The History and Archaeology of the Montauk Indians*. Vol. 3 of *Readings in Long Island Archaeology and Ethnohistory*. Lexington, Mass., 1979.

Sutton 1966
Sutton, Denys. *James McNeill Whistler: Paintings, Etchings, Pastels, and Watercolours*. London, 1966.

Sweet 1966
Sweet, Frederick. *Miss Mary Cassatt, Impressionist from Philadelphia*. Norman, Okla., 1966.

Talbot 1972
Talbot, William S. "Jasper F. Cropsey, 1823–1900." 3 vols. Ph.D. diss., Institute of Fine Arts, New York University, 1972.

Talbot 1980
Talbot, William S. "*Indian Summer* by Jasper F. Cropsey." *Bulletin of the Detroit Institute of Arts* 58 (1980): 150–161.

Tatham 1970
Tatham, David. *A Note about David Claypoole Johnston with a Check List of His Book Illustrations*. Syracuse, N.Y., 1970.

Terhune 1983
Terhune, Anne Gregory. "Thomas Hovenden (1840–1895) and Late-Nineteenth-Century American Genre Painting." Ph.D. diss., City University of New York, 1983.

Thompson 1889
Thompson, Slason. *The Humbler Poets: A Collection of Newspaper and Periodical Verse*. 4th ed. Chicago, 1889.

Thornton 1983
Thornton, Lynne. *The Orientalists: Painter-Travellers, 1828–1908*. Paris, 1983.

Tokyo 1989
Tokyo, Bunkamura Museum of Art. *Masterworks from the Detroit Institute of Arts*. Exh. cat. 1989.

Toledo 1912
Toledo Museum of Art. *Catalogue of the Inaugural Exhibition*. Exh. cat. 1912.

Topeka 1985
Topeka, Kansas Museum of History. *Prairie Visions: Art of the American West*. Exh. cat. by James H. Nottage. 1985.

Toronto 1944
Toronto Art Gallery. *Loan Exhibition of Great Paintings, in Aid of Allied Merchant Seamen*. Exh. cat. 1944.

Tracy 1868
Tracy, C. M. "The Orchids." *American Naturalist* 2 (September 1868): 349.

Traubel 1953
Traubel, Horace. *With Walt Whitman in Camden, January 21–April 7, 1889*. Philadelphia, 1953.

Trenton 1965
Trenton, New Jersey State Museum. *New Jersey and the Artist.* Exh. cat. 1965.

Troy 1862
Troy, N.Y., Young Men's Association. *Catalogue of the Fifth Annual Art Exhibition of the Young Men's Association at Their Gallery in the Athenaeum, Troy, N.Y., 1862.* Exh. cat. 1862.

Tuckerman 1867
Tuckerman, Henry T. *Book of the Artists: American Artist Life.* New York, 1867. Reprint. New York, 1967.

Tucson 1963
Tucson, University of Arizona Art Gallery. *Yankee Painter: A Retrospective Exhibition of Oils, Watercolors, and Graphics by Winslow Homer.* Exh. cat. 1963.

Tucson 1964
Tucson, University of Arizona. "The Bird in Art." [No cat.] 1964.

Tulsa et al. 1981
Tulsa, Okla., Philbrook Art Center; Oakland, Calif., Museum; Baltimore Museum of Art; and New York, National Academy of Design. *Painters of the Humble Truth: Masterpieces of American Still Life, 1801–1929.* Exh. cat. by William H. Gerdts. 1981.

U.S. Department of Commerce 1975
U.S. Department of Commerce. *Historical Statistics of the United States: Colonial Times to 1970.* Bicentennial ed., part 1. Washington, D.C., 1975.

Utica 1953
Utica, N.Y., Munson-Williams-Proctor Institute. *Expatriates: Whistler, Cassatt, Sargent.* Exh. cat. 1953.

Utica and Albany 1969
Utica, N.Y., Munson-Williams-Proctor Institute, and Albany, N.Y., Albany Institute of History and Art. *Worthington Whittredge (1820–1910): A Retrospective Exhibition of an American Artist.* Exh. cat. 1969.

Valentiner and C. Burroughs 1927
Valentiner, W. R., and Clyde H. Burroughs. *A Guide to the Collections of the Detroit Institute of Arts.* Detroit, 1927.

Vancouver 1955
Vancouver, British Columbia, Art Gallery. *Two Hundred Years of American Painting.* Exh. cat. 1955.

Van Dyke 1919
Van Dyke, John C. *American Painting and Its Tradition.* New York, 1919.

Vedder 1910
Vedder, Elihu. *The Digressions of V.* 2 vols. Boston and New York, 1910.

Wallace 1953
Wallace, David H. "Notes on Thomas Mickell Burnham, from the American Art-Union letter books," 1953. New-York Historical Society. National Portrait Gallery library, vertical files, Smithsonian Institution, Washington, D.C.

Wallach 1976
Wallach, Alan. "Trouble in Paradise." *Artforum* 15 (January 1976): 28–35.

Walton 1906
Walton, William. "Eastman Johnson, Painter." *Scribner's Magazine* 40 (1906): 263–274.

Walton 1911
Walton, William. "The Field of Art: The Galleries of Paintings of the New York Public Library." *Scribner's* 50 (November 1911): 637–640.

Warner 1959
Warner, Ezra J. *Generals in Blue: Lives of the Union Commanders.* Baton Rouge, 1959.

Washington 1901
Washington, D.C., Fischer Galleries. *Exhibition of Works by Elihu Vedder.* Exh. cat. 1901.

Washington 1944
Washington, D.C., National Gallery of Art. *American Battle Painting, 1776–1918.* Exh. cat. 1944.

Washington 1950
Washington, D.C., Corcoran Gallery of Art. *American Processional, 1492–1900.* Exh. cat. 1950.

Washington 1955
Washington, D.C., Corcoran Gallery of Art. *American Still-Life Paintings from the Paul Magriel Collection.* Exh. cat. 1955.

Washington 1959
Washington, D.C., Corcoran Gallery of Art. *The American Muse: Parallel Trends in Literature and Art.* Exh. cat. by Henri Dorra. 1959.

Washington 1961
Washington, D.C., Corcoran Gallery of Art. *Albert Pinkham Ryder.* Exh. cat. by Henri Dorra and Lloyd Goodrich. 1961.

Washington 1967
Washington, D.C., Howard University Gallery of Art. *Ten Afro-American Artists of the Nineteenth Century.* Exh. cat. by James Ames Porter. 1967.

Washington 1973
Washington, D.C., National Collection of American Art. *Lilly Martin Spencer (1822–1902): The Joys of Sentiment.* Exh. cat. essays by Robin Bolton-Smith and William H. Truettner. 1973.

Washington 1975
Washington, D.C., National Collection of Fine Arts. *American Art in the Barbizon Mood.* Exh. cat. by Peter Bermingham. 1975.

Washington 1984
Washington, D.C., Freer Gallery of Art. *James McNeill Whistler at the Freer Gallery of Art.* Exh. cat. by David Park Curry. 1984.

Washington 1985
Washington, D.C., National Museum of American Art. *Creation and Renewal: Views of Cotopaxi by Frederic Edwin Church.* Exh. cat. by Katherine Manthorne. 1985.

Washington 1985a
Washington, D.C., National Museum of American Art. *Sharing Traditions: Five Black Artists in Nineteenth-Century America.* Exh. cat. by Lynda Roscoe Hartigan. 1985.

Washington 1989
Washington, D.C., National Gallery of Art. *Frederic Edwin Church.* Exh. cat. essays by Franklin Kelly, James Anthony Ryan, and Stephen J. Gould. 1989.

Washington 1993
Washington, D.C., National Museum of American Art and National Portrait Gallery. *Revisiting the White City: American Art at the 1893 World's Fair.* Exh. cat. essays by Robert W. Rydell and Carolyn Kinder Carr, catalogue of works by Brandon Brame Fortune and Michelle Mead. 1993.

Washington 1995
Washington, D.C., National Portrait Gallery. *In Pursuit of the Butterfly: Portraits of James McNeill Whistler.* Exh. cat. by Eric Denker. 1995.

Washington and Boston 1961
Washington, D.C., Corcoran Gallery of Art, and Boston, Museum of Fine Arts. *The Civil War: The Artists' Record.* Exh. cat. 1961.

Washington and Brooklyn 1979
Washington, D.C., National Collection of Fine Arts, and Brooklyn Museum. *Perceptions and Evocations: The Art of Elihu Vedder.* Exh. cat. by Regina Soria, Joshua C. Taylor, Jane Dillenberger, and Richard Murray. 1979.

Washington and Brooklyn 1990
Washington, D.C., Corcoran Gallery of Art, and Brooklyn Museum. *Facing History: The Black Image in American Art, 1710–1940.* Exh. cat. by Guy C. McElroy. 1990.

Washington et al. 1958
Washington, D.C., National Gallery of Art; Boston, Museum of Fine Arts; and New York, Metropolitan Museum of Art. *Winslow Homer.* Exh. cat. 1958.

Washington et al. 1961
Washington, D.C., National Gallery of Art; Art Institute of Chicago; and Philadelphia Museum of Art. *Thomas Eakins: A Retrospective Exhibition.* Exh. cat. 1961.

Washington et al. 1966
Washington, D.C., National Collection of Fine Arts; New York, Knoedler & Company; and Albany, N.Y., Albany Institute of History and Art. *Frederic Edwin Church*. Exh. cat. by David C. Huntington and Richard Wunder. 1966.

Washington et al. 1966a
Washington, D.C., National Collection of Fine Arts; Jacksonville, Fla., Cummer Gallery of Art; and ten other locations. *Paintings and Drawings by Elihu Vedder*. Exh. cat. introduction by Regina Soria, 1966.

Washington et al. 1967
Washington, D.C., Corcoran Gallery of Art; Baltimore, Walters Art Gallery; Utica, N.Y., Munson-Williams-Proctor Institute; Atlanta, High Museum; and Brooklyn Museum. *Richard Caton Woodville: An Early American Genre Painter*. Exh. cat. by Francis S. Grubar. 1967.

Washington et al. 1970
Washington, D.C., National Collection of Fine Arts; Cleveland Museum of Art;, and Utica, N.Y., Munson-Williams-Proctor Institute. *Jasper F. Cropsey, 1823–1900*. Exh. cat. by William S. Talbot. 1970.

Washington et al. 1986
Washington, D.C., National Gallery of Art; Fort Worth, Amon Carter Museum of Art; and New Haven, Conn., Yale University Art Gallery. *Winslow Homer Watercolors*. Exh. cat. by Helen A. Cooper. 1986.

Washington et al. 1995
Washington, D.C., National Gallery of Art; Boston, Museum of Fine Arts; and New York, Metropolitan Museum of Art. *Winslow Homer*. Exh. cat. by Nicolai Cikovsky, Jr., and Franklyn W. Kelly. 1995.

Watson 1942
Watson, F. *Winslow Homer*. New York, 1942.

Way and Dennis 1903
Way, Thomas R., and George R. Dennis. *The Art of James McNeill Whistler*. London, 1903.

Webster 1991
Webster, Sally. *William Morris Hunt, 1824–1879*. Cambridge, 1991.

Weidman 1982
Weidman, Jeffrey. *William Rimmer: Critical Catalogue Raisonné*. Microfilm. Ann Arbor, Mich., 1982.

Weidman 1983
Weidman, Jeffrey. "William Rimmer: Creative Imagination and Daemonic Power." In *Art Institute of Chicago Centennial Lectures. Museum Studies 10*. Chicago, 1983, 146–163.

Weidman 1989
Weidman, Jeffrey. "William Rimmer's *Arab Guarding a Tomb*, c. 1872." Authentication essay written for Hirschl & Adler Galleries, New York, November 1, 1989, 1–16.

Weidner 1986
Weidner, Ruth Irwin. *George Cochran Lambdin, 1830–1896*. Chadds Ford, Pa., 1986.

Weinberg 1976
Weinberg, H. Barbara. "Thomas B. Clarke: Foremost Patron of American Art from 1872 to 1899." *American Art Journal* 8, no. 1 (May 1976): 52–83.

Weinberg 1977
Weinberg, H. Barbara. "The Career of Francis Davis Millet." *Archives of American Art Journal* 17, no. 1 (1977): 2–18.

Weinberg 1991
Weinberg, H. Barbara. *The Lure of Paris: Nineteenth-Century American Painters and Their French Teachers*. New York, 1991.

Weiss 1977
Weiss, Ila. *Sanford Robinson Gifford*. New York, 1977.

Weiss 1987
Weiss, Ila. *Poetic Landscape: The Art and Experience of Sanford R. Gifford*. Newark, Del., 1987.

West Palm Beach 1953
West Palm Beach, Fla., Norton Gallery. *French Painting*. Exh. cat. 1953.

West Palm Beach et al. 1984
West Palm Beach, Fla., Norton Gallery and School of Art; New York, National Academy of Design; Tulsa, Okla., Philbrook Art Center; and St. Petersburg, Fla., Museum of Fine Art. *Artists in Arcadia: The International Inspiration of Italy, 1760–1915*. Exh. cat. 1984.

Whistler 1892
Whistler, James McNeill. *The Gentle Art of Making Enemies*. 2nd ed. London, 1892. Reprint. New York 1967.

Whittredge 1942
Whittredge, Worthington. *The Autobiography of Worthington Whittredge, 1820–1910*. Edited by John I. H. Baur. New York, 1942. Reprint. New York, 1969.

***Who Was Who in America* 1966**
Who Was Who in America. Chicago, 1966.

***Who Was Who in American Art* 1985**
Falk, Peter Hastings, ed. *Who Was Who in American Art*. Madison, Conn., 1985.

Wilde 1877
Wilde, Oscar. "The Grosvenor Gallery." *Dublin University Magazine* 90 (July 1877): 118–126.

Wilkins 1966
Wilkins, Thurman. *Thomas Moran: Artist of the Mountains*. Norman, Okla., 1966.

Williams 1973
Williams, Hermann Warner, Jr. *Mirror to the American Past: A Survey of American Genre Painting, 1750–1900*. Greenwich, Conn., 1973.

Wilmerding 1972
Wilmerding, John. *Winslow Homer*. New York, 1972.

Wilmington 1962
Wilmington, University of Delaware, and the Wilmington Society of Fine Arts, Delaware Art Center. *American Painting, 1857–1869*. Exh. cat. by Wayne Craven. 1962.

Wirt 1855
Wirt, E. W. *Flora's Dictionary*. Baltimore, 1855.

Wood 1918
Wood, Charles Erskine Scott, to Robert C. Vose, August 9, 1918. Wood papers, The Huntington Library, San Marino, Calif.

Woodford and Woodford 1969
Woodford, F. B., and A. M. Woodford. *All Our Yesterdays*. Detroit, 1969.

Worcester et al. 1985
Worcester, Mass., Art Museum; Los Angeles County Museum of Art; and New York, Metropolitan Museum of Art. *John Frederick Kensett: An American Master*. Exh. cat. edited by Susan E. Strickler, essays by John Paul Driscoll, John K. Howat, Oswaldo Rodriguez Roque, and Dianne Dwyer. 1985.

Yarnall and Gerdts 1986
Yarnall, James L., and William H. Gerdts. *The National Museum of American Art's Index to American Art Exhibition Catalogues from the Beginning through the 1876 Centennial Year*. Boston, 1986.

Yonkers et al. 1988
Yonkers, N.Y., Hudson River Museum; Rochester, N.Y., Margaret Woodbury Strong Museum; Albany, N.Y., Albany Institute of History and Art; and Syracuse, N.Y., Everson Museum of Art. *The Catskills: Painters, Writers, and Tourists in the Mountains, 1820–1895*. Exh. cat. essay by Kenneth Myers. 1988.

Young 1878
Young, Jennie J. "Seawanhaka, the Island of Shells." *Lippincott's Magazine* 22 (November 1878): 521–540.

Young et al. 1980
Young, Andrew McLaren, Margaret McDonald, and Robin Spencer. *The Paintings of James McNeill Whistler*. 2 vols. New Haven, 1980.

Index of Works by Accession Number

Numbers in *italics* refer to pages upon which illustrations appear.

Index

Page numbers in *italics* refer to illustrations.